Career Counseling

Applied Concepts of Life Planning

Career Counseling
Applied Concepts of Life Planning

6th Edition

Vernon G. Zunker

BROOKS/COLE
TM
THOMSON LEARNING

Australia ■ Canada ■ Mexico ■ Singapore ■ Spain ■ United Kingdom ■ United States

Sponsoring Editor: *Julie Martinez*
Editorial Assistant: *Cat Broz*
Marketing: *Caroline Concilla/Megan Hansen*
Assistant Editor: *Jennifer Wilkinson*
Project Editor: *Kim Svetich-Will*
Production Service: *Forbes Mill Press*
Manuscript Editor: *Robin Gold*

Permissions Editor: *Lillian Campobasso*
Interior Design: *Robin Gold*
Cover Design: *Irene Morris*
Print Buyer: *Vena Dyer*
Compositor: *Thompson Type*
Cover Printing: *R.R. Donnelley*
Printing and Binding: *R.R. Donnelley*

Printed in the United States of America

10   9   8   7   6   5   4   3   2   1

Library of Congress Cataloging-in-Publication Data

Zunker, Vernon G.
    Career counseling : applied concepts of life planning / Vernon G. Zunker.—6th ed.
        p. cm.
    Includes bibliographical references and index.
    ISBN 0-534-36723-2
        1. Vocational guidance. I. Title

HF5381 .Z86 2001
371.4'25—dc21   2001025891

Contents

Part One

FOUNDATIONS AND RESOURCES   2

3 Theories of Career Development II 84

4 Career Counseling Models 107

Part Two

Part Three

CAREER COUNSELING IN EDUCATIONAL SETTINGS 424

Preface

ONCE AGAIN, AND FOR THE SIXTH TIME, SIGNIFICANT CHANGES HAVE BEEN MADE IN this book to keep abreast with an ever-changing society in an emerging techno-logical revolution that will significantly change the way we work and fulfill our life roles. Each preceding edition also contained new materials and procedures that evolved from changing individual needs and a growing data base of research that provided the backdrop and direction for developing career counseling models. The ongoing process of change is expected to intensify and escalate in the future.

The detailed descriptions of models and their procedures found in this book are not meant to be prescriptions that should be rigidly followed. More appro-priately, techniques described should be considered as examples from which counselors can build a repertoire of career counseling skills. As special needs of special populations emerge in the future, it seems reasonable to suggest that new and different procedures and techniques can be built from the framework of cur-rent career development theories and counseling models. Thus, the major pur-pose of this edition is to familiarize readers with different counseling techniques, their origins, and how they may be applied to individualized needs.

This sixth edition contains three new chapters. Chapter 4 contains detailed descriptions of five career counseling models with case illustrations. Another new chapter (8) focuses on assisting individuals to self-assess by using nontradi-tional methods of self-estimates. Chapter 8 also contains a model for using assess-ment results. Chapter 15 identifies the needs of gay, lesbian, and bisexual persons and offers counseling suggestions for these clients. In addition, every chapter has been revised or updated with recent research and current programs. A greater emphasis has been given to diversity issues including the special needs of multi-cultural groups.

Career Counseling is divided into four parts. Part One, "Foundations and Resources," covers career counseling today, historical developments, career development theories, career counseling models, intake interview techniques, use of assessment results, and computer programs including the Internet. The first chapter provides a perspective of developing challenges to the career counseling profession and its historical development. Chapters 2 and 3 provide career counselors with a philosophical frame of reference. The fourth chapter covers five career counseling models and case illustrations. Chapters 5 and 6 are devoted to intake interview techniques with case examples. Chapter 7 covers the use of standardized tests. Nonstandardized methods of using assessment results are reviewed in Chapter 8, which includes a model for using assessment results. Chapter 9 focuses on interactive and information-oriented computer programs designed to enhance the career counseling process, including the appropriate use of Internet resources.

Part Two, "Career Counseling for Special Populations," includes a discussion of innovative counseling models and career counseling programs for special populations. Chapter 10, focusing on multicultural groups, has been completely revised to emphasize how counselors can apply culturally appropriate techniques and procedures. The special needs of women are identified and discussed in Chapter 11. Chapter 12 reviews the socialization process that has shaped men's lives, influencing their perspectives of appropriate masculine roles. Career counseling procedures designed to help men meet the needs of their career life roles in a changing society are also discussed. Chapter 13 covers the family's influence on career development and the issues facing dual-career marriages. Special counseling components for meeting the unique needs of persons with disabilities are discussed in Chapter 14. In Chapter 15, issues and needs of gays, lesbians, and bisexuals are discussed, followed by suggested intervention strategies.

Part Three, "Career Counseling in Educational Settings," provides innovative counseling models and programs for elementary through senior high school and for postsecondary institutions of higher learning. Chapter 16 presents implications of human development and relevant research for career guidance programs in schools. Chapter 17 explores a variety of approaches to career counseling for elementary, junior high, and senior high schools. The characteristics of individuals in college and the development of career guidance programs to help meet their varied needs are the subjects of Chapter 18.

Part Four, "Career Counseling in Work Settings and Career Transitions Throughout Life," is intended to build an understanding of adults' career development in new and developing organizations, changes in work requirements and in workplace environments, stages and transitions in adult development, and career counseling programs designed to meet their needs. Chapter 19 discusses several work-related issues. Chapter 20 covers a national survey of working America, major themes in human development, and counseling components for adults in career transition. Changing organizational structures and operational procedures plus new concepts in career development in organizations are discussed in Chapter 21.

A companion text, *Using Assessment Results in Career Development,* Sixth Edition (Zunker & Osborn, 2002), has been developed as a supplement to this book. This ancillary text illustrates how assessment results can be used to increase self-awareness and rational choices. Readers will find that *Using Assessment*

Results provides detailed information about applying knowledge of tests and measurements in counseling encounters and using assessment results in a wide variety of counseling situations.

I am indebted to many individuals who assisted and encouraged me through these six editions. I owe a special thanks to users who responded to a national survey designed to improve this edition. Without listing names for fear of leaving someone out, I wish to thank everyone, including those who read and offered suggestions and those who offered words of encouragement and understanding. I am most appreciative.

Finally, I must recognize the assistance of Bob Lyons who helped me make the best use of my computer. Also, I am most grateful to the following individuals who provided me with very special suggestions that should make this edition a most relevant one: Dr. Joan T. England, University of South Dakota; Dr. Sharon Johnson, CSU Los Angeles; Dr. Alan Davis, Montana State University; Dr. Robert Chope, San Francisco State; Dr. David Reile, University of Maryland; John Hansen, Career Counselor, Center for Career Planning & Placement, CSU Los Angeles; Dr. Marcel Soriano, CSU Los Angeles; Dr. Stewart Cooper, Valparaiso University; Dr. Larry Osborne, University of North Carolina at Greensboro; and Dr. William Salazar, Morehead State University.

I dedicate this book to my wife, Rosalie, who gave me the moral support to get it done, and who made many sacrifices in the process. We sincerely hope that this book will add something positive to your life as much as it has to ours!

Vernon G. Zunker

Career Counseling

Applied Concepts of Life Planning

1

Career Counseling Today and Its Historical Development

Chapter Highlights

- *Major issues of the career counseling profession today*
- *Key terms from throughout the text*
- *How and why the career counseling profession evolved*
- *Beginnings of the counseling profession*
- *Early contributors*
- *Early governmental programs*
- *Professional organizations development*
- *Career counseling from past and future perspectives*

CURRENT LITERATURE ON CAREER DEVELOPMENT SUGGESTS THAT WE ARE at a crossroads in the career counseling movement. Career counseling increasingly is being challenged to meet the needs of a society that is experiencing vast changes in the workplace and that is rapidly becoming more diverse. There is a call for career counseling to unite its efforts with the entire counseling profession and other mental health workers and to clarify its role for future direction. This movement is precipitated by the fact that the role and scope of career counseling has expanded to include clients' mental health concerns and to address the needs of multicultural groups. These examples represent a growing list of issues that will confront the career counseling profession well into the 21st century.

The first section of this chapter, "Career Counseling Today," addresses some current issues facing the profession. The second part of this chapter covers the historical development of career counseling.

Career Counseling Today

A colleague of mine recently asked me how we could inform interested students about how the career counseling profession has become so challenging and rewarding. We both agreed that it would be difficult to share meaningful experiences during the last 30 years in a profession that has grown to include so many different kinds of counseling encounters. As my colleague said, "You had to be there"! As we reflect on the career counseling movement today, however, we first recognized that the changes in counseling needs have perhaps occurred because work is so pervasive in our lives; work greatly influences all our life roles. But more important, career counseling has expanded its role and scope to include more than just helping someone find a job. Although finding an optimal career is of utmost importance, career counseling now includes a broad spectrum of concerns such as mental health issues that restrict career choice, changes in the workplace, meeting needs of workers in a competitive global economy, and how to restructure counseling procedures to better meet the needs of multicultural groups and other special populations. These issues and more involve the career counselor today. These and other issues are covered more in depth in several chapters that follow, but the next few paragraphs provide an overview. We invite you to become involved in an exciting arena of challenges and rewards!

The changing work force and changing workplace have created several relevant needs for our society today that will extend well into the 21st century. In the last decade the economy has been rated as stronger than ever and unemployment is comparatively low. More jobs have been created than lost, but the new jobs pay less than those they have replaced. Sadly, many workers in the United States have lost the old certainties of job security. Getting a lifetime job in our postbureacratic society is no longer probable.

The workplace will become more diverse in the 21st century. More women will find their way into the workplace, and the work force will become more culturally diverse. Working relationships are being tested in a changing work environment that will grow even more diverse in the future. Industrial organizations in the United States are competing in a global economy that has necessitated changes in strategies and operating procedures. Many organizations have significantly reduced their work forces and are retraining workers for different jobs that fit into different work environments. Changes in the workplace have changed the "American dream" of job, security, home, and family. The typical worker of tomorrow faces a different set of circumstances; for instance, the work done today may change tomorrow or be whisked off to another site, possibly overseas. "Be flexible and adaptable" is the message relayed to the worker, and most important, "use personal agency" (take responsibility for your own career development) to keep abreast with changing times. Today's worker is to be a team player; interpersonal skills are highly valued.

What we are discussing here touches practically every U.S. family because one's work or career is so pervasive in U.S. lifestyles. Our careers determine where we live, how we live, and, to a great extent, with whom we associate. Americans have long believed that their freedom to choose work is a sacred privilege, and the patterns of work—such as joining an organization that will provide security for a lifetime—were deeply embedded in our society in previous decades. In many ways, the very foundations of our society will be tested by the changes we have only briefly discussed.

A number of academic disciplines, including sociology and developmental psychology, have addressed the subject of work. We need to combine the efforts of all academic disciplines in an attempt to assist individuals who have work-related problems. Some specific work-related problems to be discussed in this text are

stress at work	fired workers
career burnout	unsatisfied workers
occupational insecurity	workers with disabilities
coping with joblessness	multicultural workers
developing work roles	depressed workers
changing workplaces	schizophrenic workers
work overload	workers with personality disorders
work commitment	how work affects other life roles
work dysfunctions or impairment	

There are more topics to add to this list, but what we have so far illustrates the pervasive nature of work and the implications of the psychological constructs that accompany it. Career counselors face problems that require a working knowledge not only of career counseling techniques but also of many different counseling strategies and interventions. An integrated approach to career counseling means that career counselors will need a wide background of counseling skills to meet their clients' needs.

Other mental health workers also will need knowledge of career-related problems and subsequent solutions. For instance, career counselors will come face-to-face with marital conflicts in dual-earner homes, and marriage counselors may need to assess some clients' work-related problems. Moreover, for the depressed client who seeks a job change, counselors will need to determine whether the work is responsible for the depression or whether the depression has caused the poor work habits.

Case 1-1: THE CASE OF THE DEPRESSED WORKER

Alma, a worker in her late thirties, told her career counselor that she wanted to change jobs. Alma was currently doing secretarial work in a large firm, a job she had held for two years. Her reasons for seeking a change were somewhat vague: she stated, "I just don't like it there any more." And she added, "I'm very depressed." Depression can come from a variety of sources, and it can be work-related, non–work-related, or both. As Lowman (1993) points out, however, depression can both lower work performance and affect nonwork factors. In Alma's case, work seems to be at the center of her problem. Many aspects of work have been found to influence depression, such as problems with supervision, overly demanding work, ambiguity of authority, lack of social support, and corporate instability (Golding, 1989; Firth & Britton, 1989, cited in Lowman, 1993). The source of Alma's depression seems to be the work climate.

The career counselor was able to determine that Alma's perception of her problems had to do with a poor relationship with her immediate supervisor. Alma also perceived that her work was demanding and that she received little feedback support. When clients present signs of depression, there are many questions to be answered. For instance: What are possible sources of stress in the workplace? in the home? Is this client predisposed to depression? How do we decrease depression or anxiety?

Such cases may follow several pathways. If the counselor determines that the client is suffering from work-related depression, the choices usually are to change the job situation or to change the individual—or both. When job change is the best choice, the client must reevaluate goals, changing values, and developed abilities. A person-environment fit suggests congruence between the individual's needs and abilities and the requirements of a work environment.

The choice to change the person could involve stress reduction exercises, drug therapy, physical activity programs, and interpersonal skills training, among others. Combinations of such programs are often used. More than likely, Alma's career counselor would suggest programs of stress reduction to accompany the process of choosing a different occupation.

In this brief review of a case study, several counseling skills were suggested and implied: for example, skills in diagnosing symptoms of depression, skills of interviewing, skills in anxiety-reduction programs, and skills in career decision-making procedures. A more integrative approach to counseling recognizes that an individual's total development includes a broad spectrum of domains; we are not just career counselors, we counsel individuals. As always, counselors must recognize their limitations and refer clients when it is in their clients' best interest.

The issue of special populations is an ongoing process of discovery. For example, more women are working full time, and many are working by choice. The special needs of women in the work force continue to be viable topics in career counseling. Growing cultural diversity has also created special needs that affect the career counseling profession. Changing career counseling procedures suggests that counselors become aware of their own cultural values and biases, develop an awareness of the client's worldview, and develop a repertoire of culturally appropriate intervention strategies. We must add that meeting the needs of multicultural groups is only in its infancy.

In the meantime, technological advances have provided counseling tools that have gone far beyond the expectations of most career counselors. Today's technology will continue to make rapid changes. The increase in number of users of computer-based tools to help with their career searches has been phenomenal; in 1994, more than 9 million individuals at 20,000 different sites used career information delivery systems (Mariani, 1995–96). The potential use of computer-based tools seems unlimited. For instance, consider the global webs of career information that are being developed. If you wish to move to Bangkok, job openings will be available on global webs right in your own living room. The "Web Generation" should increase and enhance the use of the Internet.

Other Important Current Career Counseling Programs

Career counselors do offer a large number of career-related programs. For example, in many K–12 schools, students receive comprehensive counseling programs that require written career and life plans beginning in middle school, and school-to-work programs focus on preparing students for work through experiential activities in communities. Colleges and universities have career centers that offer placement or employment services. In organizations, career planning specialists offer workers a variety of services.

A large volume of career-related background information has developed, some of which is included in most career counseling courses. For instance, theories of career development suggest how and why people chose certain career paths. What factors influence individuals in the career decision-making process are debated and have been empirically evaluated. How theories translate into practical application, however, needs much more refinement. Some established theories have a long history, whereas other theories are new and emerging. How they mesh with sociological and developmental psychological perspectives is yet to be determined, but some beginnings have been made.

The use of assessment results has had a long association with career counseling. Not only have interest inventories been refined, but new and different tests are being used with other information in the counseling process to assess important variables. The almost immediate availability of assessment results via the computer enhances their use. A model for using assessment results, in Chapter 8, has been designed to be used in several career counseling models.

As you read the following pages, become more aware of the changing roles of career counselors. The time has passed—though it never really existed—when all counselors had to do was test clients, tell them the results, find job openings, and move on "in a cloud of dust."

The Historical Development of Career Counseling

The career guidance movement is a product of our development as a nation. It is the story of human progress in a nation founded on the principle of human rights. Career guidance touches all aspects of human life, for it has involved political, economic, educational, philosophical, and social progress and change. To think of the career guidance movement as merely another educational event is a gross misinterpretation of its broader significance for social progress. In fact, this movement has had and will have a tremendous impact on the working lives of many individuals. Understanding the historical perspectives of this movement will provide a greater insight into the development of the career counselor's role in career guidance.

Many terms will be introduced and defined throughout this book. Some of the terminology that is briefly described in this chapter to clarify the theoretical concepts discussed will be explained in greater detail in succeeding chapters, within the context of the program descriptions and practical illustrations.

Career development as defined by the American Counseling Association "is the total constellation of psychological, sociological, educational, physical, economic, and chance factors that combine to influence the nature and significance of work in the total life span of any given individual" (Engels, 1994, p. 2). Specifically, the term reflects individually developed needs and goals associated with stages of life and with tasks that affect career choices and subsequent fulfillment of purpose.

The terms *vocation, occupation,* and *job* are used interchangeably to indicate activities and positions of employment. *Career* refers to the activities and positions involved in vocations, occupations, and jobs as well as to related activities associated with an individual's lifetime of work.

Career counseling includes all counseling activities associated with career choices over a life span. In the career counseling process, all aspects of individual needs (including family, work, and leisure) are recognized as integral parts of career decision making and planning. *Career guidance* encompasses all components of services and activities in educational institutions, agencies, and other organizations that offer counseling and career-related educational programs.

The Birth of the Career Guidance Movement

The career guidance movement from 1850 to 1940 encompasses the following events: (1) the Industrial Revolution, (2) the study of individual differences, (3) World War I, (4) the National Conference on Vocational Guidance, (5) the measurement movement, and (6) significant federal acts. Individuals who made significant contributions during this period include Francis Galton, Wilhelm Wundt, James Cattell, Alfred Binet, Frank Parsons, Robert Yerkes, and E. K. Strong.

The Rise of Industrialism

The rise of industrialism in the late 1800s dramatically changed work environments and living conditions. Urban areas grew at tremendous rates, largely through immigration. In addition, the rapid growth and centralization of industry attracted many from rural areas who needed work. Many people found the long hours required by industrial establishments and the harsh and crowded living conditions in tenement houses to be undesirable. Perhaps even more significant was a loss of identity many experienced in these crowded work and living environments. A spirit of reform emerged in reaction to the impersonal industrial systems and chaotic conditions of urban life in the United States and in Europe. As if in response to deteriorating social conditions, several outstanding scientists turned their attention to human behavior and to the study of individual differences.

THE STUDY OF HUMAN ABILITIES. Francis Galton of England published his first and second books devoted to the origins of human abilities in 1874 and 1883. In 1879, Wilheim Wundt established an experimental laboratory in Leipzig, Germany, to study human behavior. In France, Alfred Binet and V. Henri published an article in 1896 describing mental measurement concepts (Borow, 1964). These studies of human differences turned our attention to the conditions of life and work in a society changed by the Industrial Revolution.

In the United States, G. Stanley Hall founded a psychological laboratory in 1883 to study and measure physical and mental characteristics of children. In 1890, James Cattell published an article in which he referred to mental tests as measures of individual differences. John Dewey called for reforming the lockstep method of education to one in which more attention was given to individual motivations, interests, and development. The case for the individual was being carefully formulated.

Early Programs of Career Guidance

Early in the 20th century, public schools established isolated programs of career guidance. In San Francisco, George A. Merrill developed a plan for students to explore industrial arts courses. Brewer (1918) credits Merrill as being a forerunner of vocational guidance, but Merrill's primary interests were in vocational education (Picchioni & Bonk, 1983). Many of his innovations resemble the career education movement of the 1970s (see Chapter 17).

In Central High School in Detroit, Jesse B. Davis served as counselor for 11th-grade students from 1898 to 1907 (Brewer, 1918). His major duties involved educational and vocational counseling. Later, as principal of the school, he required all 7th-grade students to write a weekly report on occupational interests for their English class. Davis emphasized the moral value of hard work as well as the benefits of occupational information.

These guidance activities and others were indeed innovative, but a logical and straightforward conceptualization of career guidance was needed for a viable movement. In the early 1900s, Frank Parsons provided a systematic plan for career guidance that has endured, with some modifications, to the present time. According to his philosophical orientation to social reform, there was to be equality and opportunity for all. The procedures he outlined for helping individuals select an occupation were to be based primarily on people's interests and aptitudes and on occupational information.

Frank Parsons

The social reform movements and civic developments of the late 1800s captured the interest of young Frank Parsons, who had been educated as an engineer at Cornell University. He wrote several books on social reform movements and articles on such topics as women's suffrage, taxation, and education for all. Parsons taught history, math, and French in public schools, worked as a railroad engineer, and passed the state bar examination for lawyers in Massachusetts in 1881 (Picchioni & Bonk, 1983). He also taught at Boston University's law school and at Kansas State Agricultural College, and he was academic dean of the extension division of Ruskin College in Trenton, Missouri. However, his real interests appeared to lie in social reform and in helping individuals make occupational choices. These interests surfaced when Parsons returned to Boston in the early 1900s.

In 1901, the Civic Service-House had been established in Boston to provide educational programs for immigrants and young persons seeking work. In 1905, Parsons was named director of the Breadwinner's Institute, which was one of the Civic Service-House programs. Eventually, through Parsons's leadership, the Vocation Bureau of Boston was established on January 13, 1908.

On May 1, 1908, Parsons presented a lecture that had a tremendous impact on the career guidance movement. His report described systematic guidance procedures used to counsel 80 men and women who had come to the vocational bureau for help. Frank Parsons died on September 26, 1908 (Picchioni & Bonk, 1983), and his major work, *Choosing a Vocation*, was posthumously published in May 1909.

One of Parsons's important contributions to the career guidance movement was his conceptual framework for helping an individual select a career. Parsons defined his three-part formulation as follows:

First, a clear understanding of yourself, aptitudes, abilities, interests, resources, limitations, and other qualities

Second, a knowledge of the requirements and conditions of success, advantages and disadvantages, compensations, opportunities, and prospects in different lines of work

Third, true reasoning on the relations of these two groups of facts (Parsons, 1909, p. 5)

Edmund G. Williamson (1965) pointed out that, with some modification, Parsons's three-part formulation greatly influenced the procedures used in career counseling over a significant period of time. Parts of Parsons's three-part formulation are practices used in many career counseling programs today.

Moreover, Parsons's conceptual framework ignited a national interest in career guidance.

First National Conference on Vocational Guidance

In 1910, the First National Conference on Vocational Guidance was held in Boston. Several speakers, including Charles W. Elliott, president of Harvard, emphasized the need for school guidance personnel. Other speakers, including the superintendent of schools in Boston, strongly suggested that methods for determining each student's potential be an objective of future scientific investigations. Understandably, the spread of organized guidance in other cities was greatly influenced by this conference and by the second national conference in New York City in 1912. At the third national conference in Grand Rapids, Michigan, in October 1913, the National Vocational Guidance Association, Incorporated, was founded. This organization, now called the National Career Development Association (NCDA), was most instrumental in providing the leadership to advance the career guidance movement.

INDUSTRIAL PSYCHOLOGY.   An important related development that influenced the career guidance movement was the work of the German psychologist Hugo Munsterberg. He joined the Harvard faculty in 1897 and introduced several methods of determining aptitudes and characteristics of men successfully employed in certain occupations in Germany. In his 1912 book, *Psychology and Industrial Efficiency,* Munsterberg reported several studies of occupational choice and worker performance. In this publication and in others, Munsterberg pointed out the benefit of psychological testing instruments and techniques for selecting industrial employees. Munsterberg was influential in establishing industrial psychology as a relevant field of applied psychology.

The Measurement Movement, 1900–1940

The measurement and guidance movements coincided in development in many respects and shared many of the same roots. One of the early, influential individuals was Wilheim Wundt of Leipzig, Germany, who had established the first experimental laboratory in psychology. His work in measurement was confined to evaluating reaction times to certain stimuli. However, Kraepelin and Ebbinghaus, two other German psychologists who were influenced by Wundt's work, became directly involved in constructing measuring devices and were among the pioneers of the measurement movement (Ross & Stanley, 1954). Wundt also contributed directly to the measurement movement by his standardization of procedures that became models for developing standardized tests.

James M. Cattell, who studied at Wundt's laboratory in Germany, became interested in individual differences. When Cattell returned to the United States, he became active in the measurement movement and first used the term *mental test* in an article written in 1890 (in Ross & Stanley, 1954). He also studied the work of Galton, another pioneering force in the measurement movement, who had devised sensory discrimination tests as measures of judgment and intelligence.

The credit for constructing the first intelligence test is generally given to Alfred Binet and Theophile Simon of France. This test, published in 1905, is administered individually and is known as the Binet-Simon scale, or simply the 1905 scale. In 1916, under the direction of L. M. Termen of Stanford University, the revised Binet-Simon scales were published as the Stanford-Binet. The introduction of the term *intelligence quotient* contributed to the popularity of this test and of tests in general.

The need for testing the abilities of large groups became apparent at the beginning of World War I. Almost 1.5 million people needed classification and subsequent training for the armed services. Under the direction of Robert M. Yerkes, the first group intelligence tests were developed. Arthur S. Otis, who had constructed (but not published) an objective item test for group administration, contributed his work to the cause. The tests developed for the army became known as the Army Alpha and Beta Tests. Unlike the more typical verbal Alpha Test, the Beta Test contained a nonlanguage scale for illiterate and foreign recruits. After the war, these tests were made available to counselors of the general public.

The testing movement made rapid advances during the next two decades. Special aptitude tests were developed; Clark L. Hull published *Aptitude Testing* in 1928 (in Ross & Stanley, 1954). This publication was devoted to the use of aptitude-test batteries in vocational guidance and emphasized his concept of matching human traits with job requirements. The idea of forecasting job satisfaction and success from standardized measures of aptitude succinctly linked the measurement and guidance movements.

Another direct link between the measurement and guidance movements was the development of interest assessment. In 1927, Edward K. Strong, Jr., of Stanford University published the first edition of an interest inventory, *The Strong Vocational Interest Blank*. This measure of interest, constructed from the responses of individuals in certain occupations, provided career counselors with a most important tool for linking assessment results with certain occupations.

Achievement testing in public schools made rapid progress during the 1920s. Personality testing began during World War I but was much slower in development. For many career counselors, however, the testing movement also had its pitfalls. Too much reliance was placed on assessment results in the career-decision process; excessive dependence on testing provided little opportunity for considering many other aspects of human development and experience. Nevertheless, the testing tools developed during this period for measuring individual differences provided the much-needed standardized support materials for the career guidance movement.

Significant Federal Acts and Contributions from the Private Sector

The federal government has played a significant role in the career guidance movement. Relevant national legislative acts passed from 1917 to 1940 are summarized in this section, and other significant national legislation is reported in subsequent sections of this chapter.

In 1917, the Smith-Hughes Act established federal grants for support of a nationwide vocational educational program. This act was also influential in supporting the establishment of counselor-training departments at major universities. The George-Dean Act of 1936 continued the support of the vocational education movement. In response to the Great Depression, the Wagner-Peyser Act of 1933 established the U.S. Employment Service. The Civilian Conservation Corps was created in 1933, and the Works Progress Administration was established in 1935. All these legislative acts were designed to provide employment for the masses who could not find jobs during this period. In 1939, the first edition of the *Dictionary of Occupational Titles* was published by the U.S. Employment Service (U.S. Department of Labor, 1939).

In the private sector, the B'nai B'rith Vocational Service Bureau was established in 1938 to offer group vocational guidance programs in metropolitan areas. In 1939, the Jewish Occupational Council was established to conduct counseling, placement, and rehabilitation services for Jewish immigrants through the B'nai B'rith, other offices, and sheltered workshops. The Jewish Occupational Council's efforts established models for career guidance program delivery.

Growth of the Career Guidance Movement: 1940 to the Present

Significant events covered from 1940 to the present are as follows: (1) major counseling publications, (2) World War II, (3) significant federal programs, (4) the formulation of theories of career development, (5) the development of career education, (6) the professionalism movement, and (7) the advances of technology. Significant contributors to the career guidance movement during this period are E. G. Williamson, Carl Rogers, Eli Ginzberg, Ann Roe, Donald Super, John Holland, David Tiedeman, and H. B. Gelatt.

Edmund G. Williamson's Directive Counseling

During the early 1940s, E. G. Williamson's publication, *How to Counsel Students* (1939), made a tremendous impact on the career guidance movement. This comprehensive work was, in many respects, an extension of Parsons's formulations. Williamson's straightforward approach to counseling was thoroughly illustrated, however, and contained six sequential steps: analysis, synthesis, diagnosis, prognosis, counseling, and follow-up. Williamson's approach to counseling became known as *directive counseling*. Williamson was one of the members of the Minnesota Employment Stabilization Research Institute who were influential in developing vocational psychology at the University of Minnesota. This group was later identified with trait-and-factor approaches to career guidance as discussed in the next chapter.

Carl R. Rogers's Nondirective Counseling

In 1942, Carl R. Rogers's influential book, *Counseling and Psychotherapy*, was published. Although as a therapist Rogers had worked primarily with emotionally distressed clients, his method of *nondirective counseling* or *client-centered counseling* caused others to completely reexamine the early established assumptions in career counseling. The Rogerians attacked directive counseling procedures and philosophical orientation in numerous articles and debates. First, according to directive counseling opponents, the relatively straightforward concept of matching human traits with job requirements had to be revamped. The concepts of affective and motivational behavior were among other considerations to be included in the counseling process. Second, client self-acceptance and self-understanding were primary goals. Third, more attention was to be given to client-counselor interactions and to the clients' verbalization in the counseling process. In essence, the counseling relationship was to be one of mutual respect, directed toward the client's gaining an understanding of self and taking steps to control his or her destiny. The center of attention shifted to the client and to counseling techniques, with less emphasis given to testing, cumulative records, and the counselor as an authority figure.

Rogerian theory was responsible for the first major breach from Parsons's straightforward approach. Many Rogerian concepts were later endorsed and integrated into directive counseling, resulting in an approach to career guidance that included a broader perspective of human development and life experience. However, the psychotherapy movement and the growing interest in expanding the professional role of counselors had to wait until after World War II.

World War II and Federal Programs

During World War II, the armed services once again needed testing procedures to classify recruits. In response, the army created a personnel and testing division in 1939. The Army General Classification Test (AGCT) was produced in 1940, and this instrument became the principal general-ability test used by the armed services during World War II. The points of influence here were the counseling programs established by the military. These programs were designed to maximize individual potential as measured by assessment results when recruits were placed in various components of the armed services.

At the end of World War II, the armed services established separation counseling programs. These programs were to assist veterans returning to civilian life; counseling procedures introduced various options to veterans, including future educational and vocational planning suggestions. In 1944, the Veterans Administration established centers throughout the country for career guidance and other services. Many were established on college and university campuses; these counseling services became models for development of career guidance programs at many institutions of higher learning.

In recognition of the general need for more guidance services, Congress passed the George-Barden Act in 1946. This act provided funds for establishing academic counselor-training programs and provided a more liberal method of distributing funds to states for maintaining vocational guidance programs.

The Testing Movement After World War II

The growth of applied psychology after World War II contributed significantly to the growth of the measurement movement. Such branches of psychology as industrial psychology, counseling psychology, educational psychology, and school psychology were incorporated into formal training programs at many institutions of higher learning. Courses in testing principles and practices were major components of these training programs. A renewed interest in using tests in all branches of applied psychology had direct links with career guidance practices. For example, using tests in counseling individuals for various life roles, including the work role, was recognized as a viable component of applied psychology. Moreover, the increased emphasis on the applied use of assessment results created a need for instruments that could be used as counseling support tools. This applied emphasis continues to motivate the development of instruments that are designed for individuals of both sexes and all age groups, ethnic minorities, and special populations. The use of assessment results in career counseling is discussed in Chapter 7.

After World War II, there was a significant increase in enrollment at colleges and universities. This increased enrollment and subsequent need for educational planning created a wider use of the College Entrance Examination Boards and the American College Testing Program (ACT). These tests, designed to predict success at the college level, are also used as one means for helping individuals select academic majors and careers. The ACT also contains an interest inventory report that is directly related to jobs and college majors.

The passage of the National Defense Educational Act in 1958 greatly influenced the career guidance movement in general and had a special impact on the testing movement. In fact, this act endorsed the close relationship between testing and the career guidance movement. The act's primary purpose was to identify students of outstanding aptitude and ability early in their public secondary schooling and to provide them with counseling programs designed to help them best use their talents. The specific use of tests mandated by this act significantly increased the opportunity to incorporate tests in public school counseling programs through federal funds that were made available to state departments of education.

Shortly before World War II, and especially after the war, a significant number of books on testing were published. For example, the first *Mental Measurements Yearbook* was published in 1938 (Buros, 1938) and has been followed by several editions. Books by F. B. Davis (1947), D. C. Adkins (1947), L. J. Cronbach (1949), F. L. Goodenough (1949), W. Stephenson (1949), D. E. Super (1949), R. L. Thorndike (1949), H. Gulliksen (1950), and A. Anastasi (1954) are other significant publications on testing that appeared following World War II.

Two recent publications that limit their discussion of assessment instruments to career development are *A Counselor's Guide to Assessment Instruments*, 3rd edition, by J. T. Kapes, M. M. Mastie, and E. A. Whitfield (1994), and *Using Assessment Results for Career Development*, 6th edition, by V. G. Zunker and D. S. Osborn (2002).

During the rapid growth of testing after 1945, there was a move toward centralizing the publication of tests. The Educational Testing Service was formed in 1948 by combining several specialized testing programs. The American College Testing Program was founded in 1959. Other commercial publishers merged into larger companies and corporations. These mergers primarily occurred because of the financial and technical commitments necessary to develop and maintain the current variety of testing programs (Cronbach, 1984). Currently, the design, construction, and updating of tests requires sophisticated technical support systems.

The advances in technology that have led to rapid scoring procedures have made testing more attractive to career guidance personnel. Computerized printouts of scores and narrative descriptions of assessment results have increased testing use in career guidance. This immediate access to assessment results for career counselors and their counselees allows greater variety of testing instruments in the career counseling process.

The future use of assessment results in career counseling will be greatly influenced by advancements in technology. However, the use of assessment results in career counseling must be kept in perspective; assessment results should not dominate the decision-making process in career guidance. Skills developed through work and leisure experiences are other considerations that are as important as assessment results are in career decision making.

Theories of Career Development

In the early 1950s, Ginzberg, Ginsburg, Axelrad, and Herma (1951), Roe (1956), and Super (1957) published career development and occupational choice theories that have become landmarks in the career guidance movement. Understandably, these publications were instrumental in creating a greater interest in career guidance practices and support materials used by practitioners. These theories have led to numerous research projects and subsequent methods for delivering career guidance programs. (Other theorists who followed and have significantly contributed to the career development process are discussed in Chapters 2 and 3.) Theories of career development and choice have become enduring issues the counseling profession addresses in important publications and professional meetings.

Theoretical perspectives on career development have contributed a great deal to career guidance programs by providing insights into developmental stages and tasks associated with transitions between stages, identification of personality types and corresponding work environments, and decision-making techniques. In addition, these theories have delineated the effects of sex-role stereotyping, provided special insights into the career development of women, ethnic minorities, and other groups, and clarified aspects of social learning theory and its relationship to career development. For each new practitioner, theories serve as a starting point from which new ideas and practices can be generated and validated (Zunker, 1987).

The Career Guidance Movement from the 1960s

We have now covered more than 100 years during which the career guidance movement made giant strides. National and local organizations provided leadership for the counseling profession. Child labor laws prohibited the exploitation of the very young, and working conditions for most Americans generally improved. There was a growing interest in increasing and improving social services for all citizens at all age levels. At the end of the 1950s, the career guidance movement had strong, organized leadership, but the 1960s were not destined to be peaceful times for the United States.

The turbulent 1960s have been described as a period of unrest that was precipitated by an awakened social conscience and the loss of a sense of meaning among the young. Several descriptions have been used to characterize the youth of the 1960s, including rebellious, militant, restless, and hippie. A questioning of all aspects of the U.S. way of life erupted into overt acts of militant rioting in cities, protest marches on college campuses, and a general rebellion against many established social values. With these events came further challenges for the counseling profession in general and for career guidance specifically. For example, the role and meaning of work in society was seen as a major issue in the 1960s and 1970s. Other issues, such as the women's movement and guidance for older people were dominant forces in shaping the career guidance movement.

During the last 20 years, the career guidance movement has broadened its role and scope. There is greater emphasis on a humanistic, existential orientation (Picchioni & Bonk, 1983). The humanistic approach, designed to expand one's awareness of life, brings greater meaning to all aspects of lifestyle. The philosophical rationale of an existential approach provides a greater recognition of individual significance in society. In essence, the more an individual is aware of his or her potential and experience, the greater the likelihood of self-assertion and direction. These philosophical orientations have set the patterns for career guidance models now in vogue.

The federal government continued its support of programs that directly and indirectly affected career guidance. During the early 1960s, Congress passed manpower legislation designed to create new jobs through occupational training programs. In addition, funds were made available for placement counseling in a variety of settings, including agencies established in communities. Other legislation under the Economic Opportunity Act funded such projects as Head Start, Job Corps, Neighborhood Youth Corps, and Community Action Programs. Many of these programs involved special counseling services like the Job Training Partnership Act (JTPA).

The Vocational Educational Act of 1963 deserves special recognition for its influence on the career guidance movement. According to Picchioni and Bonk (1983), this act "provided individual job seekers the formal preparation through guidance and training necessary for occupational adjustment in an increasingly technical and sophisticated economy" (p. 81). Later amendments to the act provided funds for guidance services in elementary and secondary schools, public community colleges, and technical institutes.

CAREER EDUCATION. A new concept of education emerged in the early 1970s in reaction to the charge that current educational systems were not adequately preparing youth for work. In 1971, Commissioner of Education Sidney P. Marland proposed a plan that would specifically address career development, attitudes, and values in addition to traditional learning. This new educational philosophy—career education—was considered integral to the education process, from kindergarten through adulthood. The career education programs that evolved during the

1970s centered on such topics as career awareness, career exploration, value clarification, decision-making skills, career orientation, and career preparation. Understandably, career education programs have focused more attention on the career guidance movement. The concept of career education is discussed in Chapter 17, and the career counselor's role in delivering various components of career education programs is also explored.

VOCATIONAL-TECHNICAL EDUCATION CHANGES.   During the last decade, there have been significant changes in vocational education as we once knew it. The major thrust of current programs centers around the goal of teaching students employable skills needed in the changing technological workplace. Students now face new technologies and business management systems that require high-level worker skills. As the result of vast technological changes, vocational education focuses more on technology than on vocational educational perspectives. The growing interest in integrating academic and vocational education has primarily evolved from a need to encourage vocational education students to take more rigorous academic courses. In fact, "Tech-Prep" programs are designed to offer vocational education students more advanced academic courses that meet the admission requirements at some institutions of higher education. More information about the changing role of vocational education can be found in Chapter 17.

The National Occupational Information Coordinating Committee

In 1976, the National Occupational Information Coordinating Committee (NOICC) was established by Congress. This committee is supported by four federal agencies: the Bureau of Labor Statistics, the Employment and Training Administration, the Office of Vocational and Adult Education, and the National Center for Educational Statistics. NOICC has defined four basic functions: (1) to develop an occupational information system that provides information about employment and training programs at federal, state, and local levels; (2) to assist in the organization and operation of state committees, referred to as State Occupational Information Coordinating Committees (SOICCs); (3) to help all users of occupational information share information; and (4) to provide labor market information for the needs of youth (Flanders, 1980).

NOICC sponsored projects to establish national career counseling and development guidelines to encourage career guidance standards development at the state and local levels. Specifically, the guidelines were used to develop standards of client competencies, counselor competencies, and institutional capabilities at all educational levels. Likewise, standards were developed for young adult and older adult career guidance programming. The effectiveness of these programs were evaluated to encourage program improvement.

The implementation of national guidelines by states and local communities helped facilitate (1) achievement of career development competencies by all students; (2) improved career guidance and counseling programs that are comprehensive and integrated within the total guidance and counseling program; (3) clearly defined staff roles, increased teaming with teachers and other school and district staff, and improved counselor expertise; (4) greater program accountability; and (5) improved articulation of career-related programs across educational levels (NOICC, 1989, p. 30).

The steps for implementing national guidelines include developing a needs analysis, establishing local career development standards, securing the resources and staff, conducting staff development, and designing and conducting program evaluations. In 1992, NOICC established the National Career Development Training Institute to build career development training programs that states used to train personnel who helped students and adults acquire career planning skills and make career decisions. All SOICCs assisted the institute in designing and implementing the National Career Development Training agenda.

The NOICC no longer exists as a functioning committee, however, the accomplishments of this national committee continue to influence the role and scope of career guidance programs for individuals of all ages. Later in this text we will refer to National Career Guidelines that were developed by NOICC.

PROFESSIONALISM.   In the early 1970s attention shifted to standards of counselor preparation and to the general advancement of the counseling profession. In 1972, standards for entry preparation of counselors were approved by the Board of Directors of the American Personnel and Guidance Association (APGA). In 1977, APGA established guidelines for doctoral training programs in counselor education (Picchioni & Bonk, 1983). These actions were followed by the APGA's declared interest in state licensure of professionals. The APGA (now the American Counseling Association, or ACA) has enhanced public recognition of all counseling efforts and has added support to counseling as a distinct social service. In 1984, the National Career Development Association set up procedures for credentialing career counselors, referred to as the National Board of Certified Counselors (NBCC). Currently, state career registries are taking the place of national career certification, so counselors should check the requirements of their state.

A Glance into the Past and a Look into the Future

In the beginning of this discussion, we referred to events and social conditions that determined the course of the career guidance movement. The chronology of the career guidance movement reflects the continuous influence of social, political, economic, and other changes in our nation. In the political arena, the career guidance movement has found support. Federal legislation has provided funds for underwriting several career counseling programs and training programs for counselors. The federal government has played a significant role in the career guidance movement.

We cannot overlook the foresight, dedication, and pioneering efforts of many individuals. Those who came forth with conceptualizations of career guidance that have endured for many decades provided the guidelines for contemporary practices. Other individuals concentrating on basic research in human development also contributed immeasurably to the career guidance movement. The leaders in related branches of applied psychology and contributors to technological advancements all played a part in developing what has become the mainstream of this movement.

Career guidance was developed to help people choose vocations. The early, straightforward procedures used in helping individuals choose occupations have evolved into diverse strategies, incorporating career decision making and life planning. The development of career guidance programs has been largely dictated by societal changes and subsequent needs of the society, and the future will no doubt provide changes and issues that we cannot fully anticipate at this time. It should be clear that career guidance is not a drab, static profession but, on the contrary, provides vast opportunities for future leaders. The career counselors of today and tomorrow will become catalysts for expanding the guidance movement in this country.

Summary

1. The career counseling profession is increasingly being challenged to meet the needs of a society that is experiencing vast changes in the workplace.

2. The work force will become more diverse in the 21st century. More women and a more culturally diverse group of workers will enter the work force.

3. Organizations that have reduced their work forces are retraining workers to fit different work environments.

4. Work in the United States is very pervasive in our society; it determines to a great extent how we live, where we live, and with whom we associate.

5. Work-related problems will continue to be a key focus of the career counselor.

6. An integrated approach to career counseling suggests that counselors must have a wide background of skills to meet clients' needs. A more integrative approach recognizes that an individual's total development includes a broad spectrum of domains.

7. Career counselors are involved in numerous career-related programs. In schools, comprehensive counseling programs require that each student have a written plan. School-to-work programs focus on preparing students for work via cooperating workplaces in the community used as experiential sites.

8. Colleges and universities have active career centers for their students, and some offer their services to the community.

9. Theories of career development have received more attention with the aim of merging them with knowledge of career development from other academic disciplines.

10. Special issues of special populations are an ongoing process of discovery. Special needs of women, culturally diverse groups, and individuals with disabilities must continue to receive attention.

11. Technological advances have provided counseling tools that have gone far beyond the expectations of most career counselors. In 1994, 9 million individuals used computerized career information delivery systems.

12. The rise of industrialism in the late 1800s dramatically changed work environments and living conditions for many Americans. A spirit of reform emerged in reaction to the impersonal industrial systems and chaotic conditions of urban life in the United States and in Europe.

13. Several outstanding scientists turned their attention to human behavior and to the study of individual differences. Francis Galton of England, Wilheim Wundt of Germany, and Alfred Binet and V. Henri of France published studies of human abilities and human differences.

14. In the United States, G. Stanley Hall became interested in mental characteristics of children, James Cattell published an article referring to mental tests, and John Dewey called for reforms in our educational system.

15. Frank Parsons developed a vocational bureau in Boston, in which he provided systematic guidance to 80 men and women. Parsons's major work, *Choosing a Vocation*, was posthumously published in May 1909. His three-part formulation of career guidance provided the foundation for early career counseling procedures.

16. In 1910, the First National Conference on Vocational Guidance was held in Boston.

17. The measurement and guidance movements coincided in development and shared many of the same roots. In France, the first intelligence test was published in 1905. The Army Alpha and Beta Tests were made available to the public shortly after World War I. The first edition of *The Strong Vocational Interest Blank* was published in 1927.

18. The federal government played a major role in the career guidance movement by passing significant national legislation between 1917 and 1940. These acts included the Smith-Hughes Act, George-Dean Act, Wagner-Peyser Act, Civilian Conservation Corps, and Works Progress Administration. The first edition of the *Dictionary of Occupational Titles* was published in 1939.

19. The private sector, through the Jewish Occupational Council, established counseling, placement, and rehabilitation services for Jewish immigrants.

20. Two books had a dramatic impact on the career counseling movement: Williamson's book *How to Counsel Students* was published in 1939, and Rogers's influential *Counseling and Psychotherapy* was published

in 1942. Rogerian theory was responsible for the first major break from Parsons's straightforward approach to career counseling.

21. At the end of World War II, the armed services established separation counseling programs. The testing movement made rapid advances, and several significant books were published on testing.

22. In the early 1950s, career development and occupational choice theories were developed. The theories of career development and choice have become enduring issues addressed by the counseling profession, major publications, and professional meetings.

23. During the last 20 years, the career guidance movement has broadened its role and scope. The trend is toward greater emphasis on a humanistic and existential orientation.

24. Other developments that have influenced the career guidance movement are career education, the focus on professionalism, advances in technology, and NOICC.

Supplementary Learning Exercises

1. Write a summary of the relevant issues facing career counselors in the 21st century. Share it with your class.

2. What does an integrative approach to counseling suggest relative to career counseling procedures and strategies? Defend your conclusions with examples.

3. Give an example of how a career counselor and another mental health worker could work together to meet a client's needs.

4. Should the training of most counselors include a course in career counseling? Defend your conclusions.

5. Compare Parsons's three-part formulation of counseling procedures with Williamson's six sequential steps. Describe similarities and differences.

6. Describe how the development of industrial psychology has aided the career guidance movement.

7. Defend or criticize the following statement: The federal government should take an active role in supporting career guidance activities in this country.

8. Choose either directive or nondirective methods of counseling as being the most influential to the career guidance movement. Defend your choice in a debate or in writing.

9. Write to one of the National Career Training Institutes established by the NOICC and share with the class its plans for training.

10. Should a career counselor have courses in marriage counseling? Defend your conclusion with examples.

For More Information

Feller, R., & Walz, G. (1996). *Career Transitions in turbulent times: Exploring work, learning and careers.* Greensboro, NC: ERIC Counseling and Student Services Clearing House, University of North Carolina.

Neukrug, E. (1999). *The world of the counselor.* Pacific Grove, CA: Brooks/Cole.

Parsons, F. (1909). *Choosing a vocation.* Boston: Houghton Mifflin.

Picchioni, A. P., & Bonk, E. C. (1983). *A comprehensive history of guidance in the United States.* Austin: Texas Personnel and Guidance Association.

Rogers, C. R. (1942). *Counseling and psychotherapy.* Boston: Houghton Mifflin.

Williamson, E. G. (1965). *Vocational counseling: Some historical, philosophical, and theoretical perspectives.* New York: McGraw-Hill.

2

Theories of Career Development I

Chapter Highlights

- *Why have career development theories*
- *Trait-and-factor theory*
- *Person-environment-correspondence counseling*
- *Ginzberg and associates*
- *Super's life-span, life-space approach*
- *Tiedeman's decision-making approach*
- *Gottfredson's circumscription and compromise*
- *Roe's needs approach*
- *Holland's typology approach*
- *Krumboltz's learning theory of career counseling*
- *Sociological perspective of work and career development*
- *Diversity issues*
- *Implications for career guidance*
- *Table of all theories: basic assumptions, key terms, and outcomes*

IN THE BEGINNING OF ANY STUDY, SOMEONE USUALLY FORMS THE SHAPE, provides the model, establishes the pattern, and introduces the basic concepts. The theories discussed in this chapter have been most instrumental in providing the foundation for research in vocational behavior. To comprehend these theories is to understand the priorities in career counseling today. The conceptual shifts in career counseling, test format, work satisfaction studies, and classification systems of occupations have primarily evolved from theories. Understandably, the study of career counseling should begin with the theories.

We begin with a brief discussion of several established and historically significant theories that provides references for greater in-depth study of these theories. This introduces trait-and-factor theory, work adjustment and person-environment-correspondence counseling theory, several developmental theories, needs-theory approach, typology approach theory, learning theory of career choice and counseling, and sociological perspective on work and career development. The final sections include implications for career guidance and a summary of the basic assumptions, key terms, and outcomes of the theories. The renewed interest in career development theories during the last two decades has led to several evolving theories that have been added to this edition. In Chapter 3, "Theories of Career Development II," five emerging theories will be introduced. We will refer to the information contained in both Chapters 2 and 3 throughout the book.

Trait-and-Factor Theory

Among early theorists on vocational counseling, Parsons (1909) maintained that vocational guidance is accomplished first by studying the individual, second by surveying occupations, and finally by matching the individual with the occupation. This process, called trait-and-factor theory, became the foundation of many vocational counseling programs such as those of the Veterans Administration, the YMCA, the Jewish vocational services, and colleges and universities (Super, 1972).

The trait-and-factor approach has been the most durable of all career guidance theories. Simply stated, it means matching the individual's traits with requirements of a specific occupation, subsequently solving the career-search problem. The trait-and-factor theory evolved from early studies of individual differences and developed closely with the testing, or *psychometric*, movement. This theory greatly influenced the study of job descriptions and job requirements as theorists attempted to predict future job success by measuring job-related traits. The key characteristic of this theory is the assumption that individuals have unique patterns of ability or traits that can be objectively measured and correlated with the requirements of various types of jobs.

The development of assessment instruments and refinement of occupational information are closely associated with the trait-and-factor theory. The study of aptitudes in relation to job success has been an ongoing process. Occupational interests occupy a major part of the research literature on career development.

Developing individual values in the career decision-making process is also a significant factor.

Through the efforts of Parsons (1909) and Williamson (1939, 1965), components of the trait-and-factor theory were developed into step-by-step procedures designed to help clients make wise career decisions. Parsons's three-step procedures—studying the individual, surveying occupations, and finally matching the individual with an occupation—may at first glance be judged to be completely dominated by test results. But, on the contrary, Parsons's first step suggests that evaluating each individual's background is an important part of his counseling paradigm.

Williamson (1939, 1949) was a prominent advocate of trait-and-factor counseling. Williamson's counseling procedures maintained the early impetus of the trait-and-factor approach that evolved from Parson's work. Even when integrated into other theories of career guidance, the trait-and-factor approach plays a very vital role on the development of assessment techniques and the use of career information.

Brown, Brooks, and Associates (1990) argued that trait-and-factor theory has never been fully understood. They suggested that advocates of trait-and-factor approaches never approved of excessive use of testing in career counseling. For example, Williamson (1939) suggested that test results are but one means of evaluating individual differences. Other data, such as work experience and general background, are as important as test results are in the career counseling process.

Recently, Sharf (1996) summarized the advantages and disadvantages of trait-and-factor theory and suggested that it is a static theory rather than a developmental one. Furthermore, it focuses on identifying individual traits and factors but does not account for how interests, values, aptitudes, achievement, and personalities grow and change. The major point is that clients can benefit from dialogue that is directed toward continually evolving personal traits and how changes affect career decision making.

The following assumptions of the trait-and-factor approach also raise concerns about this theory: (1) there is a single career goal for everyone, and (2) career decisions are primarily based on measured abilities (Herr & Cramer, 1996). These assumptions severely restrict the range of factors that can be considered in the career development process. In essence, the trait-and-factor approach is far too narrow in scope to be considered a major theory of career development. However, we should recognize that standardized assessment and occupational analysis procedures stressed in trait-and-factor approaches are useful in career counseling.

In fact, assessment instruments designed primarily to assist in career decision making continue to be developed and refined. The same may be said about occupational information, as growing numbers of research projects have focused on optimal use of job descriptions and requirements, work environments, and job satisfaction studies. Bridging the gap between assessment scores and work environments is a huge challenge for career counselors now, as in the past (Prediger, 1995).

Of related interest is the theory of work adjustment and person-environment-correspondence counseling (Dawis, 1996), discussed more fully in the next section of this chapter. This theory involves workplace reinforcers that can lead to job satisfaction. But more relevant to our discussion here is the profound emphasis on "satisfactoriness" that is predicted from correspondence between the work environment and several variables, including the individual's *measured* abilities and values (Dawis, 1996). This theory is a good example of how trait-and-factor theory has been integrated into an evolving theory of career development.

The more generic label given to person-environment-correspondence is person-environment-fit models discussed by Chartrand (1991), who concludes that trait-and-factor approaches have evolved into contemporary career development models. These counseling procedures include acquiring and compiling information—*some by standardized testing instruments*—in a structured, systematic manner. The client's "best fit" in a work environment—that is, one that matches such human factors as ability, achievement, interests, personality, values, and other characteristics—will more than likely continue to be a major focus of career counseling objectives in the future.

Will trait-and-factor theory be revitalized for the 21st century? Prediger (1995) suggests that person-environment fit theory has indeed enhanced the potential for a closer relationship between assessment and career counseling; assessment information can provide the basis for developing career possibilities into realities. For example, assessment results along with other information can provide a pathway for growth and how that growth can be accomplished. Prediger suggested a *similarity model,* designed not to predict success or to find the "ideal career" but to provide a means of evaluating occupations that "are similar to you in important ways" (Prediger, 1995, p. 2).

Using the similarity model to provide client focus when exploring careers revitalizes the role of trait-and-factor in current career counseling models (Rounds & Tracey, 1990; Zytowski, 1994). The relevant message here is that trait-and-factor theory has an important future role in career development theory.

ⅢⅢ➡ Summary of Practical Applications

1. One of the major career counseling roles of early trait-and-factor approaches was that of diagnosis. In this context, diagnosis was the process of analyzing data collected through a variety of tests. Individual strengths and weaknesses were evaluated with the primary purpose of finding a job that matched measured abilities and achievements. Assessment data was used primarily to predict job satisfaction and success.

2. Contemporary career counseling practices are expanding the use of test data. One example is the study of the relationship between human factors and work environment variables. The results of this research are used to find congruences between individual human factors and reinforcers that exist in work environments.

3. Instead of predicting the possibility of success in a particular career on the basis of actuarial information, the counselor interprets test data and informs the client of observed similarities to current workers in a career

DIVERSITY ISSUES

African Americans. In the 1970s Sewell and Martin (1976) found differences in interests of African American and white high school students. More recently, M. T. Brown (1995) suggested that trait-and-factor theory is not relevant for African Americans primarily because their career behavior has not been fully delineated.

Asian Americans. Research on the career interests of Asian Americans is very limited. However, Chu (1975), who compared *Strong Interest Inventory* (Strong, 1983) scores of college freshmen students in this country with Chinese students, concluded that currently used inventories in the United States were not effective in identifying interests of Chinese students.

Latino(a). In a recent study Fouad (1995) found that there was no significant difference in interest patterns between Latino(a)s and whites.

Native Americans. There is a significant difference between Native Americans and whites in occupational knowledge and work requirements (Peterson & Gonzalez, 2000). Likewise, Native Americans have different work values when compared with whites (Richardson, 1981; Sharf, 1992). Lack of occupational knowledge and different work values suggests that assessment norms based on studies of white Americans are not valid for Native Americans.

Most of these research studies suggest that standardized tests must be used with caution or not used at all because assessment techniques, content, and norms are not applicable "because of an individual's gender, age, race, ethnicity, national origin, religion, sexual orientation, disability, language, or socioeconomic status" (American Psychological Association, 1992, p. 1601). Equity issues are the most important considerations in selecting and interpreting assessment data. Counselors should not accept inventories that assume the cultural homogeneity of all clients.

field. Clients use this information along with other data in the career decision process. Assessment data are considered to be *one source* of information that can be most effectively used in conjunction with other data.

Person-Environment-Correspondence Counseling

This theory has a long history, and as late as the early 1990s it was referred to as the theory of work adjustment (TWA). In 1991, it was once again revised to include descriptions of the differences between personality structure and personality style and between personality style and adjustment style. The theory at that point had become more inclusive, embracing how individuals interact in their everyday lives as well as how they interact in the work environment. The broader label of person-environment-correspondence (PEC) was added in 1991 (Lofquist & Dawis, 1991).

PEC theory has always emphasized that work is more than step-by-step task-oriented procedures. Work includes human interaction and sources of satisfaction, dissatisfaction, rewards, stress, and many other psychological variables. The basic assumption is that individuals seek to achieve and maintain a positive relationship with their work environments. According to Dawis and Lofquist, individuals bring their requirements to a work environment, and the work environment makes its requirements of individuals. To survive, the individual and the work environment must achieve some degree of congruence (correspondence).

To achieve this consonance, or agreement, the individual must successfully meet the job requirements, and the work environment must fulfill the individual's requirements. Stability on the job, which can lead to tenure, is a function of correspondence between the individual and the work environment. The process of achieving and maintaining correspondence with a work environment is referred to as *work adjustment.*

Four key points of Dawis and Lofquist's theory are summarized as follows: (1) work personality and work environment should be amenable, (2) individual needs are most important in determining an individual's fit into the work environment, (3) individual needs and the reinforcer system that characterizes the work setting are important aspects of stability and tenure, and (4) job placement is best accomplished through a match of worker traits with the requirements of a work environment.

Dawis and Lofquist (1984) have identified occupational reinforcers found in the work environment that are vital to an individual's work adjustment. They evaluated work settings to derive potential reinforcers of individual behavior. In the career counseling process, individual needs are matched with occupational reinforcers to determine an individual's fit into a work environment. Some examples of occupational reinforcers are achievement, advancement, authority, co-workers, activity, security, social service, social status, and variety.

In related research, Lofquist and Dawis (1984) found a strong relationship between job satisfaction and work adjustment. Job satisfaction was evaluated from outcomes (results or consequences) of work experience, such as tenure, job involvement, productivity, work alienation, and morale. The researchers found that satisfaction is negatively related to job turnover, withdrawal behavior (such as absenteeism and lateness), and worker alienation. On the other hand, satisfaction is positively related to job involvement, morale, and overall life situations, or nonwork satisfaction. In general, satisfaction is only minimally correlated with job performance and productivity (pp. 228–229).

The research reviewed by Lofquist and Dawis (1984) strongly suggests that job satisfaction is a significant indicator of work adjustment. For example, job satisfaction is an indicator of the individual's perception of work and the work environment and is highly related to tenure in a work situation. The theory of work adjustment has the following implications for career counselors:

1. Job satisfaction should be evaluated according to several factors, including satisfaction with co-workers and supervisors, type of work, autonomy, responsibility, and opportunities for self-expression of ability and for serving others.

2. Job satisfaction is an important career counseling concern but does not alone measure work adjustment. Work adjustment includes other variables, such as the individual's ability to perform tasks required of work.

3. Job satisfaction is an important predictor of job tenure, and the factors associated with job satisfaction should be recognized in career counseling. An individual's abilities and how they relate to work requirements are not the only career counseling components of work adjustment.

4. Individual needs and values are significant components of job satisfaction. These factors should be delineated in career counseling programs designed to enhance work adjustment.

5. Individuals differ significantly in specific reinforcers of career satisfaction. Therefore, career counseling must be individualized when exploring interests, values, and needs.

6. Career counselors should consider the reinforcers available in work environments and compare them with the individual needs of clients.

In this conceptual framework, career counselors should consider clients' job satisfaction needs to help them find amenable work environments. Job satisfaction is a significant variable in determining productivity, job involvement, and career tenure. Career counselors should use occupational information to assist clients in matching individual needs, interests, and abilities with patterns and levels of different reinforcers in the work environment. For example, the reinforcer of "achievement" is related to experiences of accomplishment in the work situation. Social service is related to the opportunities that a work situation offers for performing tasks that will help other people.

Lofquist and Dawis warned that career counselors may have difficulty identifying occupational reinforcers because of the lack of relevant research, the vast variety of jobs in the current labor force, and emerging jobs. Meanwhile, the theory of work adjustment has focused more attention on the importance of worker satisfaction. In the future, workers may have to adjust to finding satisfaction in a variety of jobs that use their individual skills, rather than in one job setting. More recently, Dawis (1996) identified *personality structure* as stable characteristics of personality that consist primarily of abilities and values. *Personality style* is seen as "typical temporal characteristics" of an individual's interaction with the environment. *Ability* dimensions are used to estimate the individual's probable levels of work skills or abilities. *Values* are viewed as work needs and are identified primarily through the *Minnesota Importance Questionnaire* (University of Minnesota, 1984). Work needs are considered to be very similar to "ordinary psychological needs," because many needs that can develop outside the work environment also apply to the work setting—recognition and need achievement, for example. Both abilities (work skills) and values (work needs) are considered to be rather stable.

Environmental structure is identified as the characteristics of abilities and values of individuals who inhabit the environment. Therefore, the matching model of PEC can be readily applied.

Work adjustment is ideal when person and environment have matching work needs and work skills, but changes in both can lead to worker dissatisfaction. A worker's attempt to improve his or her fit within the work environment is referred to as *work adjustment,* and adjustments follow one of two modes: active and reactive. In the active mode, the worker attempts to change the work environment, whereas in the reactive mode, the worker attempts to correspond better with the work environment.

Important to the career counselor here is that work adjustment is closely related to personality style, although they are considered to be distinct concepts. Adjustment behavior—that is, degrees of flexibility, activeness, reactiveness, perseverance, and personality style—can be used in career planning and, in particular, to find the best person-environment fit.

Empirical Support for the Person-Environment-Correspondence Theory

For PEC, see Holland (1992) and Spokane (1985). For prediction of satisfactoriness, see Hunter and Hunter (1984). For prediction of satisfaction, that is, worker satisfaction from need-reinforcer correspondence, see Dawis (1991). For other studies that offer information about various propositions of the theory, see Rounds (1990) and Bretz and Judge (1994).

⑈➤ Summary of Practical Applications

1. The person-environment-correspondence theory depends heavily on client assessment because its major objective is to identify groups of occupations that hold the greatest potential for a client's satisfaction in a work environment and, conversely, those that will be less likely to meet the criteria for satisfaction. Of major concern are a client's abilities (work skills) and values (work needs).

2. The U.S. Employment Service's *General Aptitude Test Battery* (U.S. Department of Labor, 1970a) is recommended for measuring abilities, whereas the *Minnesota Importance Questionnaire* (MIQ) (University of Minnesota, 1984) is used to assess values. Personality style is to be evaluated by the counselor in an interview.

3. The *Minnesota Occupational Classification System III* (Dawis, Dohm, Lofquist, Chartrand, & Due, 1987) provides an index for level and patterns of abilities and reinforcers that different occupations provide. This index is used for matching work skills to requirements of occupations and as a means of determining reinforcers available by occupation.

TABLE 2-1	STAGES OR PERIODS IN THE GINZBERG STUDY	

Period	Age	Characteristics
Fantasy	Childhood (before age 11)	Purely play orientation in the initial stage; near end of this stage, play becomes work-oriented
Tentative	Early adolescence (ages 11–17)	Transitional process marked by gradual recognition of work requirements; recognition of interests, abilities, work rewards, values, and time perspectives
Realistic	Middle adolescence (ages 17 to young adult)	Integration of capacities and interests: further development of values; specification of occupational choice; crystallization of occupational patterns

or three possibilities but is generally in a stage of ambivalence and indecisiveness. However, the career focus is much narrower in scope. During the second stage, *crystallization,* the commitment to a specific career field is made. Change of direction for some—even at this stage—is referred to as pseudo-crystallization. The final stage, *specification,* is when the individual selects a job or professional training for a specific career.

The Ginzberg group recognized individual variations in the career decision process. Individual patterns of career development that lacked conformity with age-mates were identified as deviant—that is, deviant from the highly selected sample that comprised white males from upper-middle-class, urban families. Two primary causes for individual variations in career development were suggested: (1) early, well-developed occupational skills often result in early career patterns, deviant from the normal development; and (2) timing of the realistic stage of development may be significantly delayed because of such variables as emotional instability, various personal problems, and financial affluence.

From this study emerged a distinctive, systematic process based primarily on adolescent adjustment patterns that lead individuals to occupational choice. More specifically, the occupational choice process was the gradually developed precept of occupations subjectively appraised by the individual in the sociocultural milieu from childhood to early adulthood. As one progresses through the stages outlined by this study, vocational choice is being formulated. As tentative occupational decisions are made, other potential choices are eliminated.

In the original study, Ginzberg and associates stated that the developmental process of occupational decision making was irreversible in that the individual could not return chronologically or psychologically to the point where earlier decisions could be repeated. This conclusion was later modified to refute the irreversibility of occupational decision making; however, Ginzberg (1972) continued to stress the importance of early choices in the career decision process. The work of Ginzberg and associates has greatly influenced occupational research, particularly for developmental tasks related to career development.

In a later review of his theory, Ginzberg (1984) reemphasized that occupational choice is lifelong and coextensive with a person's working life:

> Occupational choice is a lifelong process of decision making for those who seek major satisfaction from their work. This leads them to reassess repeatedly how they can improve the fit between their changing career goals and the realities of the world of work. (p. 180)

Some evidence has supported the major theoretical tenets of this theory. O'Hara and Tiedeman (1959) investigated the four stages of the tentative period (interests, capacity, value, and transition) and found that they do occur in the order theorized, but at earlier ages. Studies by Davis, Hagan, and Strouf (1962) and Hollender (1967) tend to support the concepts of vocational development postulated, although the timing and sequence of the stages have not been completely supported.

The developmental conceptualization of the process of career decision making is quite a departure from the trait-and-factor approach. Although not fully tested, the theory provides a description of a developmental process for normal and deviant patterns of vocational development. The theory is more descriptive than explanatory in that it does not provide either strategies for facilitating career development or explanations of the developmental process. It appears that the major usefulness of this theory is in providing a framework for the study of career development (Osipow, 1983).

The Life-Span, Life-Space Approach to Careers

Donald Super (1972) thought that he had often been mislabeled as a theorist. In fact, Super did not believe that he had developed a theory that could be labeled specifically at that time. On the contrary, he viewed his work as the development of segments of possible future theories. He indicated that if he is to carry a label, it should be broad, such as differential-developmental-social-phenomenological psychologist. His multiple approach to career development is reflected first in his interest in differential psychology or the trait-and-factor theory as a medium through which testing instruments and subsequent norms for assessment are developed. He thought that differential psychology is of utmost importance in the continuing attempt to furnish data on occupational differences related to personality, aptitude, and interests. This he viewed as an ongoing process as we learn more about the world of work.

Self-concept theory is a very vital part of Super's approach to vocational behavior. This approach has generated a number of research projects aimed at determining how the self-concept is implemented in vocational behavior (Anderson & Olsen, 1965; Englander, 1960; Kibrick & Tiedeman, 1961; Norrell & Grater, 1960; Schutz & Blocher, 1961). The research projects have focused more attention on the significance of self-concept in the career development process. Specifically, the research has indicated that the vocational self-concept develops through physical and mental growth, observations of work, identification with working adults, general environment, and general experiences. Ultimately, differences and similarities between self and others are assimilated. As experiences become broader in relation to awareness of the world of work, the more sophisticated vocational self-concept is formed. Although the vocational self-concept is only part of the total self-concept, it is the driving force that establishes a career pattern one will follow throughout life. Thus, individuals implement their self-concepts into careers that will provide the most efficient means of self-expression.

Another of Super's important contributions has been his formalization of vocational developmental stages. These stages are as follows:

1. *Growth* (birth to age 14 or 15), characterized by development of capacity, attitudes, interests, and needs associated with self-concepts
2. *Exploratory* (ages 15–24), characterized by a tentative phase in which choices are narrowed but not finalized
3. *Establishment* (ages 25–44), characterized by trial and stabilization through work experiences
4. *Maintenance* (ages 45–64), characterized by a continual adjustment process to improve working position and situation
5. *Decline* (ages 65+), characterized by preretirement considerations, reduced work output, and eventual retirement (Issacson, 1985, pp. 51–53)

These stages of vocational development provide the framework for vocational behavior and attitudes, which are evidenced through five activities known as vocational developmental tasks. These five developmental tasks are shown in Table 2-2, delineated by typical age ranges (tasks *can* occur at other age levels) and by their general characteristics.

TABLE 2-2 SUPER'S VOCATIONAL DEVELOPMENTAL TASKS

Vocational developmental tasks	Ages	General characteristics
Crystallization	14–18	A cognitive process period of formulating a general vocational goal through awareness of resources, contingencies, interests, values, and planning for the preferred occupation
Specification	18–21	A period of moving from tentative vocational preferences toward a specific vocational preference
Implementation	21–24	A period of completing training for vocational preference and entering employment
Stabilization	24–35	A period of confirming a preferred career by actual work experience and use of talents to demonstrate career choice as an appropriate one
Consolidation	35+	A period of establishment in a career by advancement, status, and seniority

The *crystallization* task is the forming of a preferred career plan and considering how it might be implemented. Pertinent information is studied with the goal of becoming more aware of the preferred choice and the wisdom of the preference. The *specification* task follows, in which the individual feels the need to specify the career plan through more specific resources and explicit awareness of cogent variables of the preferred choice. The *implementation* task is accomplished by the completion of training and entry into the career. The *stabilization* task is reached when the individual is firmly established in a career and develops a feeling of security in the career position. Finally, the *consolidation* task follows with advancement and seniority in a career (Super, Starishesky, Matlin, & Jordaan, 1963). More recently, Super (1990) modified developmental tasks through the life span, as shown in Table 2-3. He uses the terms *cycling* and *recycling* through developmental tasks. This formulation clarifies Super's position, which might have been misunderstood in the past; that is, he views ages and transitions as very flexible and as not occurring in a well-ordered sequence. A person can recycle through one or more stages, which he refers to as a *minicycle*. For example, an individual who experiences disestablishment in a particular job may undergo

TABLE 2-3	THE CYCLING AND RECYCLING OF DEVELOPMENTAL TASKS THROUGH THE LIFE SPAN

	Age			
Life stage	Adolescence 14–25	Early adulthood 25–45	Middle adulthood 45–65	Late adulthood over 65
Decline	Giving less time to hobbies	Reducing sports participation	Focusing on essential activities	Reducing working hours
Maintenance	Verifying current occupational choice	Making occupational position secure	Holding own against competition	Keeping up what is still enjoyed
Establishment	Getting started in a chosen field	Settling down in a permanent position	Developing new skills	Doing things one has always wanted to do
Exploration	Learning more about more opportunities	Finding opportunity to do desired work	Identifying new problems to work on	Finding a good retirement spot
Growth	Developing a a realistic self-concept	Learning to relate to others	Accepting one's limitations	Developing nonoccupational roles

SOURCE: From "A Life-Span, Life-Space Approach to Career Development," by D. E. Super. In *Career Choice and Development: Applying Contemporary Theories to Practice*, 2nd ed., by D. Brown, L. Brooks, and Associates, p. 206. © 1990 by Jossey-Bass, Inc., Publishers. Reprinted by permission.

new growth and become ready to change occupations. In this instance, the individual has reached the point of maintenance but now recycles through exploration in search of a new and different position.

The concept of career patterns was an early interest of Super (1957) and his colleagues. He was particularly interested in the determinants of career patterns revealed by the research of Davidson and Anderson (1937) and Miller and Form (1951). Super modified the six classifications used by Miller and Form in their study of career patterns for men into four classifications, which are outlined in Table 2-4. Super also classified career patterns for women into seven categories ranging from a stable homemaking career pattern to a multiple-trial career pattern. Recently, he suggested that these classifications were no longer valid for women in modern society and has applied the principles of his theory to both genders (Super, 1990).

One of Super's best-known studies, launched in 1951, followed the vocational development of ninth-grade boys in Middletown, New York (Super & Overstreet, 1960). One emphasis of this study was to identify and validate the vocational developmental tasks relevant to each stage of development. Super thought that the completion of the appropriate tasks at each level was an indication of what he termed *vocational maturity.* The findings suggest that the ninth-grade boys in this study had not reached a level of understanding of the world of work or of themselves sufficient to make adequate career decisions. Vocational maturity seemed to be related more to intelligence than to age.

Various traits of vocational maturity (such as planning, accepting responsibility, and awareness of various aspects of a preferred vocation) proved to be irregular and unstable during a three-year period in high school. However, those individuals who were seen as vocationally mature in the ninth grade (based on their knowledge of an occupation, planning, and interest) were significantly more successful as young adults. This suggests that there is a relationship between career maturity and adolescent achievement of a significant degree of self-awareness, knowledge of occupations, and developed planning capability. Thus, ninth-grade

TABLE 2-4	SUPER'S CAREER PATTERNS FOR MEN	
Classification of pattern	**Classification of typical career**	**Characteristics**
Stable career pattern	Professional, managerial, skilled workers	Early entry into career with little or no trial work period
Conventional career pattern	Managerial, skilled workers, clerical workers	Trial work periods followed by entry into a stable pattern
Unstable career pattern	Semiskilled workers, clerical and domestic workers	A number of trial jobs that may lead to temporary stable jobs, followed by further trial jobs
Multiple-trial career pattern	Domestic workers and semiskilled workers	Nonestablishment of career marked by continual change of employment

vocational behavior does have some predictive validity for the future. In other words, boys who successfully accomplish developmental tasks at periodic stages tend to achieve greater maturity later in life.

The career maturity concepts developed by Super have far-reaching implications for career education and career counseling programs. The critical phases of career maturity development provide points of reference from which the desired attitudes and competencies related to effective career growth can be identified and subsequently assessed. Moreover, the delineation of desired attitudes and competencies within each stage affords the specification of objectives for instructional and counseling projects designed to foster career maturity development. Super (1974, p. 13) identified six dimensions that he thought were relevant and appropriate for adolescents:

1. *Orientation to vocational choice,* an attitudinal dimension determining whether the individual is concerned with the eventual vocational choice to be made
2. *Information and planning,* a competence dimension concerning specificity of information individuals have concerning future career decisions and past planning accomplished
3. *Consistency of vocational preferences,* individuals' consistencies of preferences
4. *Crystallization of traits,* individual progress toward forming a self-concept
5. *Vocational independence,* independence of work experience
6. *Wisdom of vocational preferences,* dimension concerned with individual's ability to make realistic preferences consistent with personal tasks

Translating these dimensions into occupational terms provides clarity for program considerations. For example, the attitudinal dimension of orientation to vocational choice may translate for one individual to mean "I don't know what I'm going to do and haven't thought about it" and for another to mean "I really want to decide, but I don't know how to go about it." The difference in levels of career maturity development are apparent from these remarks, providing clues from which the counselor may stimulate the growth of both individuals.

The dimensions of career maturity developed by Super support the concept that education and counseling can provide the stimulus for career development. The index of career maturity can be assessed by standardized inventories, which are discussed in Chapter 7. Career maturity is concerned not only with individually accomplished developmental tasks but also with the behavior manifested in coping with the tasks of a given period of development. Individuals' readiness to enter certain career-related activities helps focus the career counseling process.

The phenomenology of decision making and career development, according to Super, is indeed the combined complexities and variables of differential psychology, self-concept theory, developmental tasks, and sociology of life stages. Primarily, Super took a multisided approach to the career development process. His theory of vocational development is considered the most comprehensive of all developmental theories (Bailey & Stadt, 1973, p. 88) and offers valid explanations of developmental concepts that have been generally supported by numerous research projects (Osipow, 1983). The theory is highly systematic and is useful for developing objectives and strategies for career counseling and career education programs. The developmental aspects of Super's theory provide explanations of the various factors that influence the career choice process. The following two major tenets of his theory give credence to developmental theories in general: (1) career development is a lifelong process occurring through defined developmental periods, and (2) the self-concept is being shaped as each phase of life exerts its influence on human behavior. More recently, Super (1984) clarified his position on self-concept theory as "essentially a matching theory in which individuals consider both their own attributes and the attributes required by an occupation" (p. 208). Super saw self-concept theory as divided into two components: (1) personal or psychological, which focuses on how individuals choose and adapt to their choices; and (2) social, which focuses on the personal assessment individuals make of their socioeconomic situations and current social structure in which they work and live. The relationship of self-concept to career development is one of the major contributions of Super's theory.

Super's concept of vocational maturity should also be considered a major contribution to career developmental theories. Conceptually, career maturity is acquired through successfully accomplishing developmental tasks within a continuous series of life stages. Career maturity on this continuum is described in attitudinal and competence dimensions. Points of reference from this continuum provide relevant information for career counseling and career education objectives and strategies.

In a more recent classification of stage transitions, Super (1990) illustrated a life-stage model by using a "life rainbow" as shown in Figure 2-1. This two-dimensional graphic schema presents a longitudinal dimension of the life span, referred to as a "maxicycle," and corresponding major life stages, labeled "minicycles." A second dimension is "life space," or the roles played by individuals as they progress through developmental stages, such as child, student, "leisurite," citizen, worker, spouse, homemaker, parent, and pensioner. People experience these roles in the following theaters: home, community, school (college and university), and workplace. This conceptual model leads to some interesting observations: (1) Because people are involved in several roles simultaneously within several theaters, success in one role facilitates success in another; and (2) all roles affect one another in the various theaters.

In the early 1990s, Super created an "archway model" to delineate the changing diversity of life roles experienced by individuals over the life span. This model is used to clarify how biographical, psychological, and socioeconomic determinants influence career development. Figure 2-2 illustrates the archway model. One base stone in the arch supports the person and his or her psychological characteristics, and the other base stone supports societal aspects such as economic resources, community, school, family, and so on. The point is that societal factors interact with the person's biological and psychological characteristics as he or she functions and grows.

The column that extends from the biological base encompasses the person's needs, intelligence, values, aptitudes, and interests—those factors that constitute

FIGURE 2-1 *The life-career rainbow: six life roles in schematic life space*

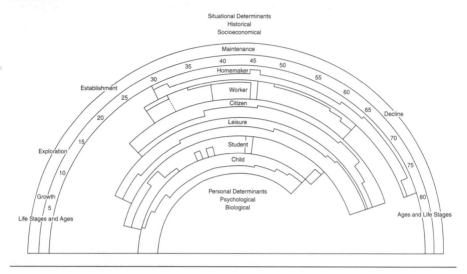

SOURCE: From "A Life-Span, Life-Space Approach to Career Development," by D. E. Super. In *Career Choice and Development, Applying Contemporary Theories to Practice,* 2nd Ed., edited by D. Brown, L. Brooks, and Associates, p. 212. © 1990 by Jossey-Bass, Inc. Reprinted by permission of Jossey-Bass, Inc., a subsidiary of John Wiley & Sons, Inc.

personality variables and lead to achievement. The column rising from the geographical base stone includes environmental influences such as family, school, peer group, and labor markets—factors that affect social policy and employment practices.

The arch joining the columns is made up of conceptual components, including developmental stages from childhood to adulthood and developed role self-concepts. The keystone of the archway is the self or person who has experienced the personal and social forces that are major determinants of self-concept formation and active life roles in society.

In essence, interactive learning is the fundamental concept that forms the keystone (self) of the archway as the individual encounters people, ideas, facts, and objects in personal development. The relationship of all the model's segments highlights the profound interactional influences in the career development process. The integration of life activities and developmental stages is a prime example of perceiving career development as a pervasive part of life. Career guidance programs that incorporate developmental concepts must address a broad range of counseling techniques and intervention strategies. This seems to be the message that Super has promoted for several decades.

Donald Super died in 1994, and in a recent publication his theory was labeled "the life-span, life-space approach to careers" (Super, Savickas, & Super, 1996). Because this theory evolved during 60 years of research, it is no wonder that it

FIGURE 2-2   *A segmental model of career development*

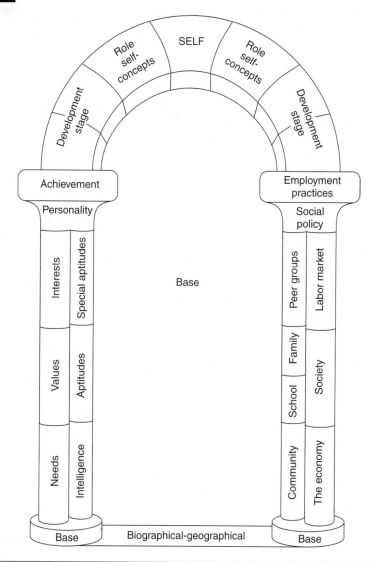

SOURCE: From "A Life-Span, Life-Space Approach to Career Development" by D. E. Super in *Career Choice and Development: Applying Contemporary Theories to Practice,* 2nd ed., by D. Brown, L. Brooks and Associates, pp. 206–208. © 1990 by Jossey-Bass, Inc., Publishers. Reprinted by permission.

stands out as one of the most comprehensive vocational development models in the career counseling profession. Over this 60-year period, Super's theory was constantly refined and updated, once being labeled "career development theory" and later "developmental self-concept theory." The recent name change reflects contemporary issues related to life-span needs and Super's most recent research of life roles. In this broad-based approach, gender and cultural differences are also addressed; the needs of cultural and ethnic minorities are considered important variables in the career counseling process.

Empirical Evaluations of Super's Theory

Recent evaluations of Super's theory have been predominantly positive, although empirical research has been difficult to accomplish because of the theory's broad scope (Brown, Brooks, & Associates, 1990). Swanson (1992) has suggested that more segments of the theory be empirically evaluated, especially the life space of adolescents and young adults and the life-span research of adults.

In a very provocative article that traces the development of Super's theory, Salomone (1996) suggested that Super has not offered testable hypotheses for various propositions of his theory. Salomone argued that Super failed to consistently define hypothetical constructs that are operational and that lend themselves to quantitative measures that support his statements. In Salomone's opinion, such constructs as work satisfaction, career maturity, and vocational development are not readily measurable, either because they are rather vague in concept or instruments at a given point in time were not available to measure them. Perhaps Salomone's criticism of Super's concepts can best be explained with the example of Super's definition of career. Salomone contended that Super expanded the concept of career (child, leisurite, and citizen) to be too inclusive for "three ingredients of good definitions—clarity, specificity, and exclusivity"; thus, when concepts are vague and nonspecific, they lose their usefulness. In this respect, Super's theory is very elusive; the relationship between theoretical propositions and empirical findings is not clearly delineated. However, despite the limitations of Super's theory as outlined in his article, Salomone did recognize that Super has had a monumental impact on career development.

Finally, Osipow and Fitzgerald (1996) and Hackett, Lent, and Greenhaus (1991) support Super's theory in general, and specifically as one that describes the process of vocational development and one that will provide the mainstream of research for developmental psychology in the future.

⟩⟩⟩ Summary of Practical Applications

When observing Super's suggestions for practical applications, we must remember that he remained dedicated to the roles of developmental stages within three major segments of his theory—life space, life span, and self-concepts. He and his colleagues developed numerous assessment instruments designed to measure developmental tasks over the life span that are currently used in the career counseling process. Following are summaries of the counseling steps.

1. *Assessment:* A career development assessment and counseling model (C-DAC) was developed to measure constructs from the basic life-span, life-space theory in four phases: (1) life structure and work-role salience;

(2) career development status and resources; (3) vocational identity with its work values, occupational interests, and vocational abilities; and (4) occupational self-concepts and life themes. The counselor begins with an intake interview, encouraging the client to express career concerns. Background information is gathered from school records and other sources. After comparing background information with the client's career concerns in the first interview, the counselor begins a four-step procedure to complete the assessment component.

a. The first step focuses on the client's life structure (social elements that constitute an individual's life) and work-role salience. If the client considers the work role to be important, further assessment will be more meaningful. If not, career orientation programs are recommended. The *Salience Inventory* (Nevill & Super, 1986) is used to determine the client's life space (participation and commitment to five life roles for school, work, family, community, and leisure). Scores for the client's life structure are also obtained from the constellation of 15 scores from the inventory, and they provide clues to the pattern of the client's activity in and hopes for five major life roles.

b. The second assessment phase measures the client's perception of the work role, referred to as the client's *career stage* (vocational developmental tasks that concern the client) and *career concerns* (the amount of concern the client has with exploration, establishment, maintenance, and disengagement). The *Adult Career Concerns Inventory* (ACCI) (Super, Thompson, & Lindeman, 1988) measures career stage and career concerns, or they can be obtained through an interview.

   In addition, assessment within this step includes a measure of the client's resources for choosing or coping with tasks when making decisions. The *Career Development Inventory* (Thompson, Lindeman, Super, Jordaan, & Myers, 1984; Savickas, 1990) is used to measure the variables of career planning, career exploration, information about work, and knowledge of occupations. Finally, an assessment is made of the client's resources of adapting through use of the *Career Mastery Inventory* (Crites & Savickas, 1995).

c. The third phase includes measures of abilities, interests, and values. Interest inventories that provide estimates of realistic, investigative, artistic, social, enterprising, and conventional (RIASEC) types as defined in Table 2-6 (Holland, 1992) are recommended. The *Differential Aptitude Test* (Bennett, Seashore, & Wesman, 1974) is recommended to measure aptitudes, and the *Values Inventory* (Nevill & Super, 1986) or the *Work Value Inventory* (Super, 1970) are recommended to measure values.

d. The fourth phase includes assessment of self-concepts and life themes by using adjective checklists, card sorts, or a repertory grid technique to assess the client's self-schema in world space.

2. *Data integration and narrative interpretation:* After assessment has been accomplished, the counselor interprets the data to the client. The

interpretation process is referred to as *integrative interpretation,* in which the client's life story unfolds.

3. *Counseling goals:* In the process of setting goals, the counselor attempts to assist the client to develop an accurate picture of his or her self and life roles. Choices are to be based on implementing the self-concept into the work world in a realistic manner.

4. *Procedures:* Career development counseling procedures pertinent to career development tasks such as exploration, establishment, maintenance, and disengagement are recommended. A variety of techniques may be used that incorporate life stages and developmental tasks.

5. *Processes:* Counseling to promote career development may use coaching, educating, mentoring, modifying, or restructuring during an interview. Super also recommends cyclical counseling, in which the counseling interviews sometimes are directive and nondirective at other times. For example, directive approaches can be used to provide confrontations with reality, whereas nondirective approaches assist the client with interpreting the meanings associated with confrontations.

Life-span, life-space theory is indeed a comprehensive framework from which career development counseling has emerged. The counseling procedures developed from this theory are designed to foster maximal development (Super, Savickas, & Super, 1996).

David Tiedeman

The key concept of Tiedeman's approach to career development is self-development in the broadest sense (Tiedeman & O'Hara, 1963). The total cognitive development of the individual and the subsequent process of decision making have been its main focus. According to Tiedeman, career development unfolds within the general process of cognitive development as one resolves ego-relevant crises. He believed the evolving ego identity is of central importance in the career development process. He referred to the evolving self-in-situation from the earliest awareness of self to the point at which the individual becomes capable of evaluating experiences, anticipating and imagining future goals, and storing experiences in memory for future reference.

Within this context, the path of career development parallels stages of development drawn from the theoretical orientation of Erikson's (1950) eight psychosocial crises, as follows: (1) trust, (2) autonomy, (3) initiative, (4) industry, (5) identity, (6) intimacy, (7) generativity, and (8) ego integrity. Self-in-situation, self-in-world, and the orientation of work evolve as one resolves the psychosocial crises of life. As the ego identity develops, career-relevant decision-making possibilities also develop; one can contemplate broad career fields and specific occupations, taking all possible situations into consideration.

Eventually in career decision making, one reaches the point that Tiedeman referred to as *differentiation and integration.* Differentiation is the process of evaluating self or self-in-world through identification and study of various aspects of occupations. The process is complex and yet unique for each individual, depending on biological potential and the social structure of the individual's milieu. Influences are both internally and externally generated. As the individual's cognitive structure develops, impetus for differentiation may be internally provided either physiologically or psychologically. Activities within the individual's environment, including formal education, provide external stimulation.

One of the major goals of differentiation is to resolve the trust-mistrust crisis (Erikson, 1950) as it relates to the world of work. Tiedeman and O'Hara (1963) postulated that society and the individual continually strive toward a common goal: to establish what meaning each has for the other. In essence, the individual is striving to integrate within society—more specifically, within a career—searching for acceptance by members of a career field yet retaining some individuality. If the uniqueness of the individual finds congruency with the uniqueness of the world of work, integration, synthesis, success, and satisfaction will follow. According to Tiedeman, theories of occupational choice and vocational development have not explored how the evolutionary process of differentiation and integration could apply to career development. He has, therefore, conceptualized a pattern or paradigm of problem solving as the mechanism of career decision making. His paradigm covers four aspects of *anticipation* or *preoccupation* (exploration, crystallization, choice, and clarification) and three aspects of *implementation* or *adjustment* (induction, reformation, and integration), which are summarized in Table 2-5.

Tiedeman viewed decision making as a continuous process in which individuals will change their courses of career action, generally by leaving a particular setting or environment. The departure from a particular setting may be caused by external forces (such as the call of the armed services, an economic crisis, the work setting itself) or by broad internal psychological drives (such as unmet needs, changing aspirations, role diffusion). A new decision unfolds and must be made according to the prescribed sequence, beginning with exploration and eventually reaching integration. If integration is not reached once again, the individual may adapt to a career environment or may simply withdraw and begin a new search for eventual integration.

The duration and timing of developmental stages is critically important in career development, according to Tiedeman. The individual's self-awareness and total combined activities make up part of the time that must be spent in career decision making. But how much of the individual's time, awareness, and activities are concerned with considering the world of work? Is there a time-occupancy framework pertinent to work per se within personal development patterns?

Tiedeman suggested that time occupancy is preempted by biological requirements (such as sleeping and eating), expectations of independence (at work, in the community, and so on), and the quest for identity (as a citizen, parent, worker, and other roles). These particular aspects of human time commitment are assigned stages of timing within the overall pattern of human development. As individuals fit their careers into life plans, the study of the time invested in this activity as well as its particular time staging may yield valuable information for the study of career development patterns and personal development patterns. Tiedeman and others

| TABLE 2-5 | ASPECTS OF ANTICIPATION, PREOCCUPATION, IMPLEMENTATION, AND ADJUSTMENT |

Aspects of anticipation or preoccupation	Characteristics
Exploration	1. Thinking is rather temporary and evanescent in nature. 2. There is consideration and reconsideration of possible courses of action. 3. Through imagination, one experiences numerous activities by relating feelings of self within certain structures or premises. 4. There is searching through projection into tentative goals. 5. There is a focus on future behavior with alternative courses of action. 6. There is reflection upon aspirations, abilities, interests, and future societal implications related to career choice.
Crystallization	1. There is a continued assessment of alternatives. 2. Fewer alternatives are under consideration. 3. There is an emergence of tentative choices. 4. Tentative choices may be reevaluated in the process of valuing and ordering. 5. Goals become more definite and formed but are not irreversible. 6. There is a definite move toward stability of thought.
Choice	1. A definite goal is chosen. 2. There is focus on the particular behavior necessary to reach the chosen goal.
Clarification	1. This period is marked by further clarification of self in the chosen position. 2. Further consideration of the anticipated position lessens the doubts of the career decision. 3. A stronger conviction about the career decision is developed. 4. This ends the anticipatory or preoccupational stage.

SOURCE: Adapted from Tiedeman and O'Hara, 1963.

(Dudley & Tiedeman, 1977; Miller-Tiedeman & Tiedeman, 1990; Peatling & Tiedeman, 1977) have recently focused on ego development as a major component for the career decision process. Their position was that each person has I-power, or potential for self-improvement. Clarifying one's current status and projecting oneself into anticipated career environments are examples of self-development. Understanding of one's belief system is a product of the decision-making process and allows one to live a decision-guided life. Moreover, in viewing life as a career, individuals should be guided to become more self-directed. As Miller-Tiedeman (1988)

Aspects of implementation or adjustment	Characteristics
Induction	1. This period begins the social interaction experience with career identification. 2. There is a further identification of self and defense of self within the career social system. 3. As acceptance is experienced within the career, part of self is merged with the accepting group. 4. There is further progression of the individualized goal but within the framework of the totality of a career concerning social purpose.
Reformation	1. The career group offers acknowledgment acceptance as a group member. 2. There is assertive action by the individual within the career group and outside the career group, spawned by the newfound conditions. 3. Assertive action takes the form of convincing others to conform to the self-view held by individual and toward greater acceptance of modified goals.
Integration	1. A compromise of intentions of goals is achieved by the individual as he or she interacts with the career group. 2. Objectivity of self and the career group is attained. 3. Identification of a working member within the total system of the career field emerges. 4. Satisfaction of a committed cause or action is at least temporarily attained.

stated, "One is essentially a scientist applying and observing the results of moving to one's own inner wisdom" (p. 34). Whereas theorists have generally focused on the decision-making process itself, Tiedeman and Miller-Tiedeman have researched individual processes in decision making. Individual experiences and understanding of the decision-making process are important outcomes for career development and selection.

In sum, Tiedeman conceptualized career development within a framework of time stages. The process is one of continuously differentiating one's ego identity, processing developmental tasks, and resolving psychosocial crises. Career decisions are reached through a systematic problem-solving pattern requiring the individual's total cognitive abilities and combining both the uniqueness of the individual and the uniqueness of the world of work.

Miller-Tiedeman and Tiedeman (1990) currently advocate a "lifecareer theory." Based on self-organizing systems, process, and decision theory, lifecareer theory views career choices as a "shift and focus to one's internal frame of reference" (p. 31). Following this logic, one searches from within to find career direction and then applies the strategies of career development for a career decision. However, to find career direction, one must view life as a learning process, recognizing that one should be flexible in using various methods to solve problems and meeting one's needs as life unfolds. In reviewing the theory, Wrenn (1988) observed, "Don't push life in *your* direction (or what you assume this direction to be), life has a direction for you to learn; learn from life, and let life teach you" (p. 340).

A major contribution of Tiedeman's and O'Hara's (1963) theory is the focus on increased self-awareness as important and necessary in the decision-making process. Attention is directed toward effecting change and growth through adjustment to the mores of existing career social systems. Adaptation to a working environment for meaningful peer group affiliation and work performance is stressed. Although this theory has had an important impact on the career decision process, it is limited by lack of empirical data. It was theoretically formulated in accord with Erikson's stages on the basis of the vocationally relevant experiences of five white males.

⫸ Summary of Practical Applications

The authors of this theory have more recently concentrated on developing a specific design of personal use of decision making (Miller-Tiedeman & Tiedeman, 1990). The major element of their model is one of self-constructionism within which the individual views career and the process of career development as a whole, particularly along with one's ego development and value level. The objective of the model is to guide clients in selecting experiences that are potentially growth promoting and that are designed to build ego development from which priorities in the value structure are defined and rearranged. This model has been used to develop a curriculum in a variety of classroom settings, ranging from classes for students with learning disabilities to humanities classes. The learning objectives are paraphrased as follows:

Learning Objective 1: Identify and define several levels of ego development.

Learning Objective 2: Identify and define nine decision-making strategies.

Learning Objective 3: Identify some examples of experience that illustrate stages of ego development and decision-making strategies.

Learning Objective 4: Compare stages of ego development with decision-making strategies.

Learning Objective 5: Point out the importance of ego development and decision making in life situations.

Learning Objective 6: Have students teach a class on the ego development model.

Learning Objective 7: Have each student help another student with a career planning unit. While helping students achieve an understanding of their own career development vis-à-vis ego development and value structure, each student is encouraged to pursue a holistical life. Ideally, students advance to a level of self-awareness that releases them to make wise decisions (Miller-Tiedeman & Tiedeman, 1990).

Circumscription and Compromise: A Developmental Theory of Occupational Aspirations

The development of occupational aspirations is the main theme of Gottfredson's (1981) theory. Incorporating a developmental approach similar to Super's developmental stages, her theory describes how people become attracted to certain occupations. Self-concept in vocational development is a key factor to career selection, according to Gottfredson, because people want jobs that are compatible with their self-images. Yet self-concept development in terms of vocational choice theory needs further definition, argued Gottfredson: key determinants of self-concept development are one's social class, level of intelligence, and experiences with sex-typing. According to Gottfredson, individual development progresses through four stages:

1. *Orientation to size and power (ages 3–5):* Thought process is concrete; children develop some sense of what it means to be an adult.

2. *Orientation to sex roles (ages 6–8):* Self-concept is influenced by gender development.

3. *Orientation to social valuation (ages 9–13):* Development of concepts of social class contributes to the awareness of self-in-situation. Preferences for level of work develop.

4. *Orientation to the internal, unique self (beginning at age 14):* Introspective thinking promotes greater self-awareness and perceptions of others. Individual achieves greater perception of vocational aspirations in the context of self, sex-role, and social class.

In this model of development, occupational preferences emerge within the complexities that accompany physical and mental growth. A major determinant of occupational preferences is the progressive circumscription of aspirations during self-concept development; that is, from the child's rather simplistic and concrete view of life to the more comprehensive, complex, abstract thinking of the adolescent and adult. For example, in stage 1, the child has a positive view of occupations based on concrete thinking. In stage 2, the child makes more critical assessments of preferences, some of which are based on sex-typing. In stage 3, the child adds more criteria to evaluate preferences. In stage 4, the adolescent develops greater awareness of self, sex-typing, and social class, all of which are used with other criteria in evaluating occupational preferences.

Gottfredson suggested that socioeconomic background and intellectual level greatly influence individuals' self-concept in the dominant society. As people project into the work world, they choose occupations that are appropriate to their "social space," intellectual level, and sex-typing. In the Gottfredson model, social class and intelligence are incorporated in the self-concept theory of vocational choice.

Another unique factor in this theory is the concept of compromise in decision making. According to Gottfredson, compromises are based primarily on generalizations formed about occupations or "cognitive maps" of occupations. Although each person develops a unique map, each uses common methods of evaluating similarities and differences, namely through sex-typing, level of work, and field of work. In this way, individuals create boundaries or tolerable limits of acceptable jobs. Gottfredson suggested that people compromise their occupational choices because of the accessibility of an occupation or even give up vocational interests to take a job that has an appropriate level of prestige and is an appropriate sex-typing. In general, individuals are less willing to compromise job level and sex-type because these factors are more closely associated with self-concept and social identity.

This theory has a strong sociological perspective. The external barriers that limit individual goals and opportunities concern Gottfredson, and her theory differs from other theories in four major ways. First, in career development, there is an attempt to implement the social self and, secondarily, the psychological self. Gottfredson places much more emphasis on the idea that individuals establish social identities through work. Second, how cognitions of self and occupations develop from early childhood is a major focus of the theory. Third, the theory's premise is that career choice is a process of eliminating options, thus narrowing one's choices. Fourth, the theory attempts to answer how individuals compromise their goals as they try to implement their aspirations. In Gottfredson's view, career choice proceeds by eliminating the negative rather than by selecting the most positive.

Although these differences make this theory distinctive, the theory also shares some fundamental assumptions with other theories. For example, career choice is a developmental process from early childhood. Second, individuals attempt to implement their self-concepts into career choice selections. Finally, satisfaction of career choice is determined largely by a "good fit" between the choice and the self-concept.

Major Concepts of Gottfredson's Theory

SELF-CONCEPT.   Following Super and associates (1963), Gottfredson defines *self-concept* as one's view of self that has many elements, such as one's appearance, abilities, personality, gender, values, and place in society.

IMAGES OF OCCUPATIONS.   Images of occupations refer to occupational stereotypes (Holland, 1992) that include personalities of people in different occupations, the work that is done, and the appropriateness of that work for different types of people.

COGNITIVE MAPS OF OCCUPATIONS.   These cognitive maps constitute how adolescents and adults distinguish occupations into major dimensions, specifically, masculinity/femininity, occupational prestige level, and field of work. A two-dimensional map of sextype (Holland's term) and prestige level has been constructed to portray certain occupations by these two dimensions, and Holland's typology is used to indicate field of work. For example, an accountant (field of work), has above-average prestige level, and sex-type is rated as more masculine than female. This map is primarily used to locate "areas" of society that different occupations offer.

Individuals use images of themselves to assess their compatibility with different occupations. Some refer to this process as congruence, or person-environment fit. If the core elements of self-concept conflict with an occupation, that occupation is rejected in Gottfredson's scheme.

SOCIAL SPACE.   This term refers to the zone of acceptable alternatives in each person's cognitive map of occupations, or each person's view of where he or she fits or would want to fit into society. Gottfredson suggests that career decision making should center around points of reference as "territories," either measured or contemplated, rather than around specific points of reference to a single occupation.

CIRCUMSCRIPTION.   Circumscription reflects the process by which an individual narrows his or her territory when making a decision about social space or acceptable alternatives. The stages of circumscription were outlined earlier.

COMPROMISE.   This is a very significant process in Gottfredson's theory. As she puts it, "Individuals often discover, when the time comes, that they will be unable to implement their most preferred choices" (Gottfredson, 1996, p. 187). Within this process, individuals will settle for a "good" choice but not the best possible one. Compromise is the process of adjusting aspirations to accommodate external reality, such as local availability of educational programs and employment, hiring practices, and family obligations. According to Gottfredson, individuals will not compromise their field of interest by prestige or sex type when there are small discrepancies. When there are moderate trade-offs within the process of compromise, people avoid abandoning prestige rather than sex-type. In major trade-offs, people will sacrifice interests rather than prestige or sex-type (Gottfredson, 1996).

Empirical Support

Lapan and Jingeleski (1992) found some agreement with the concept of social space in that individuals did assess compatibility with regard to zones of alternatives within the broad scope of the occupational world. Sastre and Mullet (1992) confirmed that gender, social class, and intelligence are related to work field and level of occupational aspirations. Leung, Conoley, and Scheel (1994) studied 149 immigrant and native-born Asian American college students to determine whether the boundaries of social space are set by age 13 (stage 3). They concluded that social space increased in size from age 8 through 17, disconfirming the theory's predictions. Although this one study should not negate Gottfredson's individual development through four stages, there remains the possibility that some students widen their range of career exploration during high school.

⥤ Summary of Practical Applications

Gottfredson directs career counselors to what she refers to as underappreciated problems and possibilities in career development. Counselors should encourage clients to be as realistic as possible when exploring potential occupational goals. She concludes that reality is either ignored, or the client fails to deal effectively with it. She recommends five developmental criteria to aid the counselee in dealing with reality.

1. *The counselee is able to name one or more occupational alternatives.* If not, then the counselor is to determine whether indecision reflects the inability to choose among high-quality alternatives or whether there is an unwillingness to attempt to choose. Some questions to be answered are the following: Is there a lack of self-confidence? Are there internal or external conflicts in goals? Is there impaired judgment?

2. *The counselee's interests and abilities are adequate for occupations chosen.* If not, is this the result of misperceptions about self? Are there external pressures from parents or other important adults?

3. *The counselee is satisfied with the alternatives he or she has identified.* If dissatisfied, does the counselee consider the selected alternatives as an unacceptable compromise of interests, sex type, prestige or family concerns, or other concerns? Attempt to determine internal or external constraints.

4. *The counselee has not unnecessarily restricted his or her alternatives.* Did the counselee consider suitable and accessible alternatives? Has there been a lack of exposure to compatible alternatives? Does the counselee have an adequate knowledge of his or her own abilities?

5. *The counselee is aware of opportunities and is not realistic about obstacles for implementing the chosen occupation.* What are the reasons the counselee has not been realistic about obstacles? Is there wishful thinking or a lack of information or planning? Information to seek during the counseling interview includes why certain options seem to be rejected and why some compromises are more acceptable than others. Use the following questions: What is the preferred self, in both sociability and personality type? Are the perceptions of boundaries in social space adequate? Who are the primary reference groups, and what family circumstances influence the counselee?

Finally, Gottfredson suggests that information that provides compatibility and accessibility are essential. One may do this through exploration of social space that includes aptitude requirements of occupations, arrays of occupational clusters, and the counselee's perceptions of sex-type and prestige. Occupational clusters depicted on a map are to be used to focus attention on compatible clusters. As the counselee selects more specific occupations, the characteristics of the occupation and the availability of training should be discussed. Eventually, as the client reaches the realm of constructive realism, a subset of best choices can be realistically made and, subsequently, one best choice with a list of alternatives.

Ann Roe: A Needs Approach

Early relations within the family and their subsequent effects on career direction have been the main focus of Ann Roe's work (1956). Her main thrust was analyzing differences in personality, aptitude, intelligence, and background as related to career choice. She studied several outstanding physical, biological, and social scientists to determine whether vocational direction was highly related to early personality development.

Roe (1956) emphasized that early childhood experiences play an important role in finding satisfaction in one's chosen field. Her research led her to investigate how parental styles affect need hierarchy and the relationships of these needs to later adult lifestyles. She drew heavily from Maslow's hierarchy of needs in developing her theory. The need structure of the individual, according to Roe, is greatly influenced by early childhood frustrations and satisfactions. For example, individuals who desire to work in contact with people are primarily drawn in this direction because of their strong needs for affection and belongingness. Those who choose the nonperson-type jobs are meeting lower-level needs for safety and security. Roe hypothesized that individuals who enjoy working with people were reared by warm and accepting parents and those who avoid contact with others were reared by cold or rejecting parents.

Roe (1956) classified occupations into two major categories: *person-oriented* and *nonperson-oriented*. Examples of person-oriented occupations are (1) service (concerned with service to other people); (2) business contact (person-to-person contact, primarily in sales); (3) managerial (management in business, industry, and government); (4) general culture (teaching, ministry, and journalism); and (5) arts and entertainment (performing in creative arts). Examples of nonperson-oriented jobs are in the arenas of (1) technology (production, maintenance, and transportation); (2) the outdoors (agriculture, forestry, mining, and so on); and (3) science (scientific theory and application).

Within each occupational classification are progressively higher levels of functioning. Roe (1956) contended that the selection of an occupational category was primarily a function of the individual's need structure but that the level of attainment within the category depended more on the individual's level of ability and

■ DIVERSITY ISSUES ■

In reviewing the research that focuses on career development of children and adolescents of color, Sharf (1992) found that African Americans, Hispanics, and Native Americans have less information about occupations than white Americans do. In addition, Sharf found that white young Americans score higher on career development than do African Americans. However, a most severe criticism of career development theory comes from Smith (1983) who suggests that career development theories were developed using a restricted population and ignore such factors as social-psychological issues and economic conditions that affect the lives of diverse populations.

In a related publication, Osipow and Littlejohn (1995) point out that we do not have an identity stage of occupational developmental for minority groups. Sue (1981) has developed a minority identity model that describes the psychological development of minority group members as discussed in Chapter 10. This model can reveal relevant information for the career counselor, but the fact remains that career development studies have not focused on diverse populations. These issues support the need for more research that addresses the career development of special populations and appropriate career counseling procedures for diverse groups.

socioeconomic background. The climate of the relationship between child and parent was the main generating force of needs, interests, and attitudes that were later reflected in vocational choice.

When thinking back on how she developed the classification system, Roe says she was greatly influenced by research on interests and the development of interest inventories (Roe & Lunneborg, 1990). Nevertheless, six studies reported by Roe and Lunneborg (1990) support the validity of the classification system in that approximately two-thirds of job changes by the individuals studied occurred within the same occupational classification group.

Roe modified her theory after several studies refuted her claim that different parent-child interactions result in different vocational choices (Green & Parker, 1965; Powell, 1957). She currently takes the position that the early orientation of an individual is related to later major decisions—particularly in occupational choice—but that other variables not accounted for in her theory are also important factors. The following statements by Roe (1972) express her own viewpoint on career development:

1. The life history of any man and many women, written in terms of or around the occupational history, can give the essence of the person more fully than can any other approach.

2. Situations relevant to this history begin with the birth of the individual into a particular family at a particular place and time and continue throughout his or her life.

3. There may be differences in the relative weights carried by different factors, but the process of vocational decision and behavior do not differ in essence from any others.

4. The extent to which vocational decisions and behaviors are under the voluntary control of the individual is variable, but it could be more than it sometimes seems to be. Deliberate consideration of the factors involved seems to be rare.

5. The occupational life affects all other aspects of the life pattern.

6. An appropriate and satisfying vocation can be a bulwark against neurotic ills or a refuge from them. An inappropriate or unsatisfying vocation can be sharply deleterious.

7. Because the goodness of life in any social group is compounded by and also determines that of its individual members, the efforts of any society to maintain stability and at the same time advance in desired ways can perhaps be most usefully directed toward developing satisfying vocational situations for its members. But unless the vocation is adequately integrated into the total life pattern, it cannot help much.

8. There is no single specific occupational slot that is a one-and-only perfect one for any individual. Conversely, there is no single person who is the only one for a particular occupational slot. Within any occupation, there is a considerable range in a number of variables specifying the requirements.

Roe's theory is usually referred to as a *needs-theory approach* to career choice (Bailey & Stadt, 1973; Zaccaria, 1970). According to Roe, combinations of early parent-child relations, environmental experiences, and genetic features determine the development of a need structure. The individual then learns to satisfy these developed needs primarily through interactions with people or through activities that do not involve people. Thus, Roe postulated that occupational choice primarily involves choosing occupations that are person-oriented, such as service occupations, or nonperson-oriented, such as scientific occupations. The intensity of needs is the major determinant that motivates the individual to the level hierarchy within an occupational structure (Zaccaria, 1970).

There have been several practical applications of Roe's classification system (Lunneborg, 1984). For example, both dimensions of the system were used to construct the *Occupational Preference Inventory* (Knapp & Knapp, 1977), the *Vocational Interest Inventory* (Lunneborg, 1981), and an interest inventory used in the fourth edition of the *Dictionary of Occupational Titles* (U.S. Department of Labor, 1977).

Roe's theory has generated considerable research but little support for her theoretical model (Osipow, 1983). Roe's postulated effect of the parent-child interactions on later vocational choices is difficult to validate. Differing parental attitudes and subsequent interactions within families present such an overwhelming number of variables that no study could be sufficiently controlled to be considered empirical. The longitudinal requirements necessary to validate the theory present another deterring factor. Notwithstanding, Roe made a great contribution to career counseling in having directed considerable attention to the developmental period of early childhood.

⫸ Summary of Practical Applications

1. Roe and Lunneborg (1990) did not present step-by-step career counseling procedures, but they did include examples of Roe's two-way occupational classification system in a variety of career-related programs that have existed in several states.

2. Roe's theory has been applied to career exploration programs and career choice measures based on the two-way occupational classification system.

3. Anyone familiar with Roe's views concerning counseling applications of her work will not be surprised that she has not constructed a counseling program per se, for as she puts it, "Osipow's (1983) major objection throughout seems to be that the theory is not specifically adapted to or drawn up for the counseling situation. I can only remark that it was not devised to be" (Roe & Lunneborg, 1990, p. 80).

4. Three examples of the use of Roe's theory have been selected to illustrate the practical application of her work in interest measurement and in career guidance programs. For example, the *Career Occupational Preference System (COPS) Interest Inventory* (Knapp & Knapp, 1984, 1985) was based on Roe's two-way classification system. The major purpose was to foster greater career awareness through a two-dimensional perspective of careers.

5. In a career development program developed by Miller (1986), clients organize vocational card sorts according to Roe's eight interest groups. One of the first decisions made is between two major groups; occupations oriented toward people or occupations oriented away from people. Discussions follow with the purpose of narrowing choices to fields of work and, if possible, to specific occupations.

6. Educational and vocations decisions are the major focus of a guidance program sponsored by colleges in Washington state. Interest feedback is given to students through Roe's two-way classification system, and a guide uses Roe's framework to project employment opportunities in Washington, Idaho, Montana, Oregon, and Alaska (Roe & Lunneborg, 1990).

John Holland: A Typology Approach

According to John Holland (1992), individuals are attracted to a given career by their particular personalities and numerous variables that constitute their back-

---

■ DIVERSITY ISSUES ■

Roe suggested that interactions within families is significantly important in the early career development of children. Although her theory was never proven by research, we have come to realize the important contribution to career development of contextual interactions and the salient messages that children receive from them in early childhood. Although Roe's theory has little support because it is difficult to validate, its historical significance may be vitally important as we delve deeper into the relevance of life histories of clients from diverse backgrounds.

---

grounds. First, career choice is an expression of, or an extension of, personality into the world of work followed by subsequent identification with specific occupational stereotypes. A comparison of self with the perception of an occupation and subsequent acceptance or rejection is a major determinant in career choice. Congruence of one's view of self with occupational preference establishes what Holland refers to as the *modal personal style*.

Modal personal orientation is a developmental process established through heredity and the individual's life history of reacting to environmental demands. Central to Holland's theory is the concept that one chooses a career to satisfy one's preferred modal personal orientation. If the individual has developed a strong dominant orientation, satisfaction is probable in a corresponding occupational environment. If, however, the orientation is one of indecision, the likelihood of satisfaction diminishes. The strength or dominance of the developed modal personal orientation as compared with career environments will be critical to the individual's selection of a preferred lifestyle. Again, the key concept behind Holland's environmental models and environmental influences is that individuals are attracted to a particular role demand of an occupational environment that meets their personal needs and provides them with satisfaction.

For example, a socially oriented individual prefers to work in an environment that provides interaction with others, such as a teaching position. On the other hand, a mechanically inclined individual would seek out an environment where trade could be quietly practiced and would avoid socializing to a great extent. Occupational homogeneity provides the best route to self-fulfillment and a consistent career pattern. Individuals out of their elements who have conflicting occupational environmental roles and goals will have inconsistent and divergent career patterns. Holland stressed the importance of self-knowledge in the search for vocational satisfaction and stability.

From this frame of reference, Holland proposed six kinds of modal occupational environments and six matching modal personal orientations. These are summarized in Table 2-6, which also offers representative examples of occupations and themes associated with each personal style.

Holland proposed that personality types can be arranged in a coded system following his modal-personal-orientation themes such as R (realistic occupation), I (investigative), A (artistic), S (social), E (enterprising), and C (conventional). In this way, personality types can be arranged according to dominant combinations. For example, a code of CRI would mean that an individual is very much like people in conventional occupations, and somewhat like those in realistic and investigative occupations. Holland's Occupational Classification (HOC) system has corresponding *Dictionary of Occupational Titles (DOT)* numbers for cross-reference purposes. The four basic assumptions underlying Holland's (1992) theory are as follows:

1. In our culture, most persons can be categorized as one of six types: realistic, investigative, artistic, social, enterprising, or conventional (p. 2).

2. There are six kinds of environments: realistic, investigative, artistic, social, enterprising, or conventional (p. 3).

3. People search for environments that will let them exercise their skills and abilities, express their attitudes and values, and take on agreeable problems and roles (p. 4).

4. A person's behavior is determined by an interaction between his personality and the characteristics of his environment (p. 4).

The relationships between Holland's personality types are illustrated in Figure 2-3. The hexagonal model provides a visual presentation of the inner relationship of personality styles and occupational environment coefficients of correlation. For example, adjacent categories on the hexagon such as realistic and investigative are most alike, but opposites such as artistic and conventional are most unlike. Those of intermediate distance such as realistic and enterprising are somewhat unlike.

According to Holland, the hexagonal model introduces five key concepts. The first, *consistency,* relates to personality as well as to environment. Some of the types have more in common than others; for instance, artistic and social types have more in common than do investigative and enterprising types. The closer the types are on the hexagon, the more consistent the individual will be. Therefore, high consistency is seen when an individual expresses a preference for adjoining codes such as ESA or RIC. Less consistency would be indicated by codes RAE or CAS.

The second concept is *differentiation.* Individuals who fit a pure personality type will express little resemblance to other types. Conversely, those individuals who fit several personality types have poorly defined personality styles and are considered undifferentiated or poorly defined.

Identity, the third concept describes those individuals who have a clear and stable picture of their goals, interests, and talents. In the case of environments, identity refers to the degree to which a workplace has clarity, stability, and integration of goals, tasks, and rewards. For example, individuals who have many occupational goals, as opposed to a few, have low identity.

The fourth concept, *congruence,* occurs when an individual's personality type matches the work environment. Social personality types, for example, prefer

TABLE 2-6	HOLLAND'S MODAL PERSONAL STYLES AND OCCUPATIONAL ENVIRONMENTS

Personal styles	Themes	Occupational environments
May lack social skills; prefers concrete vs. abstract work tasks; may seem frank, materialistic, and inflexible; usually has mechanical abilities	Realistic	Skilled trades such as plumber, electrician, and machine operator; technician skills such as airplane mechanic, photographer, draftsperson, and some service occupations
Very task-oriented; is interested in math and science; may be described as independent, analytical, and intellectual; may be reserved and defers leadership to others	Investigative	Scientific such as chemist, physicist, and mathematician; technician such as laboratory technician, computer programmer, and electronics worker
Prefers self-expression through the arts; may be described as imaginative, introspective, and independent; values aesthetics and creation of art forms	Artistic	Artistic such as sculptor, artist, and designer; musical such as music teacher, orchestra leader, and musician; literary such as editor, writer, and critic
Prefers social interaction and has good communication skills; is concerned with social problems, and is community-service-oriented; has interest in educational activities	Social	Educational such as teacher, educational administrator, and college professor; social welfare such as social worker, sociologist, rehabilitation counselor, and professional nurse
Prefers leadership roles; may be described as domineering, ambitious, and persuasive; makes use of good verbal skills	Enterprising	Managerial such as personnel, production, and sales manager; various sales positions, such as life insurance, real estate, and car salesperson
May be described as practical, well-controlled, sociable, and rather conservative; prefers structured tasks such as systematizing and manipulation of data and word processing	Conventional	Office and clerical worker such as timekeeper, file clerk, teller, accountant, keypunch operator, secretary, bookkeeper, receptionist, and credit manager

SOURCE: Adapted from Holland, 1985a, 1992.

environments that provide social interaction, concerns with social problems, and interest in educational activities. In reviewing the major studies investigating this concept, Spokane (1985) concluded that the research did support the theory that congruence is highly related to academic performance and persistence, job satisfaction, and stability of choice.

Finally, Holland's model provides a *calculus* (the fifth concept) for his theory. Holland proposed that the theoretical relationships between types of occupational environments lend themselves to empirical research techniques. Further

| FIGURE 2-3 | *Holland's model of personality types and occupational environments* |

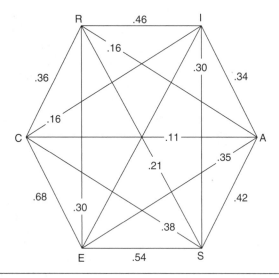

SOURCE: From *An Empirical Occupational Classification Derived from a Theory of Personality and Intended for Practice and Research,* by J. L. Holland, D. R. Whitney, N. S. Cole, and J. M. Richards, Jr., ACT Research Report No. 29, The American College Testing Program, 1969. Copyright 1969 by the American College Testing Program.

research will provide counselors and clients with a better understanding of Holland's theory.

As important as the individual's self-knowledge is occupational knowledge. Holland believed critical career judgments are partially drawn from the individual's occupational information. The importance of identification with an occupational environment underscores the significance of occupational knowledge in the process of appropriate career choice. Knowledge of both occupational environment and corresponding modal personal orientations is, according to Holland, critical to appropriate career decision making.

In the process of career decision making, Holland postulated that the level hierarchy or level of attainment in a career is determined primarily by individual self-evaluations. Intelligence is considered less important than personality and interest (Holland, 1966). Furthermore, the factor of intelligence is subsumed in the classification of personality types; for example, individuals who resemble the investigative type of modal personal orientation are generally intelligent and naturally have skills such as analytical and abstract reasoning.

According to Holland, the stability of career choice depends primarily on the dominance of personal orientation. Putting it another way, individuals are products of their environment, which greatly influence their personal orientations and eventual career choices. Personality development is a primary consideration in Holland's career-typology theory of vocational behavior.

Holland's theory is primarily descriptive, with little emphasis on explaining the causes and the timing of the development of hierarchies of the personal modal styles. He concentrated on the factors that influence career choice rather than on the developmental process that leads to career choice. Holland's early theory was developed from observations made on a population of National Merit Scholarship finalists. He later expanded the database to include a wider sample of the general population. His research has been extensive and longitudinal. Recently, Holland (1987a) compared his theories with developmental positions:

> I find experience for a learning theory perspective to be more persuasive (than developmental views). In my scheme, different types are the outcomes of different learning histories. Stability of type is a common occurrence because career (types) tend to snowball over the life course. The reciprocal interaction of person and successive jobs usually leads to a series of success and satisfaction cycles. (p. 26)

There is some evidence to suggest that Holland's theory applies to male and female nonprofessional workers (Salomone & Slaney, 1978). However, the widely used *Self-Directed Search (SDS)* and Holland's theory in general have been attacked as being gender-biased. The major criticism centers on the claim that *SDS* limits the career considerations for women and that most females tend to score in three personality types (artistic, social, and conventional) (Weinrach, 1984, p. 69). In defense of the *SDS*, Holland suggested that in our sexist society, females will display a greater interest in female-dominated occupations.

Holland's theory places emphasis on the accuracy of self-knowledge and career information necessary for career decision making. The theory has had a tremendous impact on interest assessment and career counseling procedures; a number of interest inventories present results using the Holland classification format. Its implications for counseling are apparent; a major counseling objective would be to develop strategies to enhance knowledge of self, occupational requirements, and differing occupational environments.

In sum, Holland's theory has proved to be of more practical usefulness than any of the other theories discussed in this text. In addition, most of his propositions have been clearly defined, and they lend themselves to empirical evaluations. The impact of his scholarly approach to RIASEC theory has had and will continue to exert tremendous influence on career development research and procedures.

Empirical Support for Holland's Theory

Extensive testing of Holland's theory suggests that his constructs are valid, and in fact the body of evidence is extremely large and almost overwhelming. Recent research is reviewed by Spokane (1996), whereas Osipow and Fitzgerald (1996), Holland, Fritzsche, and Powell (1994), Holland, Powell, and Fritzsche (1994), and Weinrach and Srebalus (1990) have reported more extensive reviews. Examples of other research topics include the interplay between personality and interests by Gottfredson, Jones, and Holland (1993) and Carson and Mowesian (1993); the studies of the hexagon by Rounds and Tracy (1993); and person-environment congruence and interaction by Spokane (1985) and Meir, Esformes, and Friedland (1994). The best current statements about exploring careers with a typology are by Holland (1996). The original documents should be read for more details of current research projects.

Ⅲ➡ Summary of Practical Applications

Applying Holland's theory in career counseling requires a working knowledge of several inventories and diagnostic measures. Some of these instruments will only be introduced here, as more information is given about some of them in Chapter 7.

1. The *Vocational Preference Inventory* (Holland, 1985b) has undergone eight revisions.

2. *My Vocational Situation* (Holland, Daiger, & Power, 1980) and *Vocational Identity Scale* (Holland, Johnston, & Asama, 1993) provide information about goals, interests, and talents.

3. The *Position Classification Inventory* (Gottfredson & Holland, 1991) is a job analysis measure of RIASEC environmental codes.

4. The *Career Attitudes and Strategies Inventory* (Gottfredson & Holland, 1994) measures work environment variables.

5. The *Self-Directed Search* (SDS) (Form R) (Holland, 1994a) is one of the most widely used interest inventories, has more than 20 foreign language versions, can be administered by computer, and includes computer-based reports. It has been revised four times, most recently in 1994. Accompanying the assessment booklet are several companion materials: the *The Occupations Finder* (Rosen, Holmberg, & Holland, 1994b), the *Dictionary of Educational Opportunities* (Rosen, Holmberg, & Holland, 1994a), the *You and Your Career Booklet* (Holland, 1994c), a *Leisure Activities Finder* (Holmberg, Rosen, & Holland, 1990), and a *Dictionary of Holland Occupational Codes* (Gottfredson & Holland, 1989).

Figure 2-4 presents the steps for using the SDS assessment booklet and *The Occupations Finder.*

Krumboltz's Learning Theory of Career Counseling

A social-learning theory approach to career decision making was first proposed by Krumboltz, Mitchell, and Gelatt (1975), and then several years later by

FIGURE 2-4 *Steps in using the SDS*

Step 1
Using the assessment booklet, a person:

– lists occupational aspirations
– indicates preferred activities in the six areas
– reports competencies in the six areas
– indicates occupational preferences in the six areas
– rates abilities in the six areas
– scores the responses he/she has given and calculates six summary scores
– obtains a three-letter summary code from the three highest summary scores

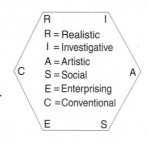

R = Realistic
I = Investigative
A = Artistic
S = Social
E = Enterprising
C = Conventional

Step 2
Using the occupations finder, a person locates among the 1,335 occupations those with codes that resemble his/her summary code.

Step 3
The person compares the code for his/her current vocational aspiration with the summary code to determine the degree of agreement.

Step 4
The person is encouraged to take "Some Next Steps" to enhance the quality of his/her career decision making.

Mitchell and Krumboltz (1990). More recently, Mitchell and Krumboltz (1996) have extended the earlier social-learning theory approach to include Krumboltz's learning theory of career counseling, and they now suggest that the entire theory be referred to as learning theory of career counseling (LTCC). In this review of the two parts of the theory, part one will explain the origins of career choice, and part two will address the important question of what career counselors can do to help solve career-related problems.

The theory is an attempt to simplify the process of career selection and is based primarily on life events that are influential in determining career selection. In LTCC, the process of career development involves four factors: (1) genetic endowments and special abilities, (2) environmental conditions and events, (3) learning experiences, and (4) task approach skills.

Genetic endowments and special abilities include inherited qualities that may set limits on the individual's career opportunities. The authors do not attempt to explain the interaction of the genetic characteristics and special abilities but emphasize that these factors should be recognized as influences in the career decision-making process.

Environmental conditions and events are factors of influence that are often beyond the individual's control. What is emphasized here is that certain events and circumstances in the individual's environment influence skills development,

■ DIVERSITY ISSUES ■

Holland's theory has been supported by research in France, Nigeria, New Zealand, and Australia (Sharf, 1992). In this country, Harrington and O'Shea (1980) conclude that Holland's typology was appropriated for four Hispanic cultures. Arbona (1989) suggests that as a result of her investigation of Holland's typology, African American and Hispanic students are exposed more to low-level jobs. More recently, Johnson, Swartz, and Martin (1995) point out that because of the general lack of occupational information and knowledge of work environments among Native Americans, care should be taken when assessing their interests.

In a similar conclusion, M. T. Brown (1995) suggests that African Americans have also experienced restricted work options. Furthermore, he supports the need for more research of congruence of African Americans with Holland's typology. Leong and Serafica (1995) also suggest that more research is needed for Asian Americans within the Holland classification system. Such factors as how parental influence, discrimination, and stereotyping reflect occupational choice among Asian Americans are important variables to investigate.

Counselors are encouraged to evaluate each individual client's unique needs for assessment and determine if an appropriate standardized instrument is available. (See Chapters 7 and 8 for information.)

activities, and career preferences. For example, government policies regulating certain occupations and the availability of certain natural resources in the individual's environment may largely determine the opportunities and experiences available. Natural disasters, such as droughts and floods, that affect economic conditions are further examples of influences beyond the control of the individuals affected.

The third factor, *learning experiences*, includes instrumental learning experiences and associative learning experiences. *Instrumental learning experiences* are those the individual learns through reactions to consequences, through direct observable results of actions, and through the reactions of others. The consequences of learning activities and their later influence on career planning and development are primarily determined by the activity's reinforcement or nonreinforcement, by the individual's genetic endowment, special abilities, and skills, and by the task itself.

Associative learning experiences include negative and positive reactions to pairs of previously neutral situations. For example, the statements "all politicians are dishonest" and "all bankers are rich" influence the individual's perceptions of these occupations. These associations can also be learned through observations, written materials, and films.

The fourth factor, *task approach skills,* includes the sets of skills the individual has developed, such as problem-solving skills, work habits, mental sets, emotional responses, and cognitive responses. These sets of developed skills largely determine the outcome of problems and tasks the individual faces.

Task approach skills are often modified as a result of desirable or undesirable experiences. For example, Sue, a high school senior, occasionally takes and studies class notes. Although she was able to make good grades in high school, she may find that this same practice in college results in failure, thus causing her to modify note-taking practices and study habits.

Krumboltz and associates stressed that each individual's unique learning experiences over the life span develop the primary influences that lead to career choice. These influences include (1) generalization of self derived from experiences and performance in relation to learned standards, (2) sets of developed skills used in coping with the environment, and (3) career-entry behavior such as applying for a job or selecting an educational or training institution.

The social-learning model emphasizes the importance of learning experiences and their effect on occupational selection. Genetic endowment is considered primarily as a factor that can limit learning experiences and subsequent career choice. Career decision making is considered to be a lifelong process and a very important skill to be taught in education and career counseling programs. In teaching decision-making skills, the identified factors that influence career choice should be stressed.

The factors that influence preferences in the social-learning model are composed of numerous cognitive processes, interactions in the environment, and inherited personal characteristics and traits. For example, educational and occupational preferences are a direct, observable result of actions (referred to as self-observation generalizations) and of learning experiences involved with career tasks. If an individual has been positively reinforced while engaging in the activities of a course of study or occupation, the individual is more likely to express a preference for the course of study or the field of work. In this way, the consequence of each learning experience, in school or on a job, increases the probability that the individual will have a similar learning experience in the future. However, an individual can become proficient in a field of work by developing skills, but even this fact does not ensure that an individual will remain in the field of work over a life span. An economic crisis or negative feedback may initiate a change of career direction.

Genetic and environmental factors are also involved in the development of preferences. For example, a basketball coach might reinforce his players for their skills, but the coach will more likely reinforce tall players than those smaller in stature.

Other positive factors influencing preferences are valued models who advocate engaging in a field of work or an educational course, or who are observed doing so. Finally, positive words and images, such as a booklet describing an occupation in glamorous terms, will lead to positive reactions to that occupation. In social-learning theory, learning takes place through observations as well as through direct experiences.

The determination of an individual's problematic beliefs and generalizations is very important in the social-learning model (Mitchell & Krumboltz, 1984). For example, identifying content from which certain beliefs and generalizations have evolved is a key ingredient for developing counseling strategies for individuals who have career decision-making problems. The counselor's role is to probe assumptions and presuppositions of expressed beliefs and to explore alternative beliefs and courses of action. Assisting individuals to understand fully the validity of their beliefs is a major component of the social-learning model. Specifically, the counselor should address the following problems (Krumboltz, 1983):

1. Persons may fail to recognize that a remediable problem exists (individuals assume that most problems are a normal part of life and cannot be altered).

2. Persons may fail to exert the effort needed to make a decision or solve a problem (individuals exert little effort to explore alternatives; they take the familiar way out).

3. Persons may eliminate a potentially satisfying alternative for inappropriate reasons (individuals overgeneralize from false assumptions and overlook potentially worthwhile alternatives).

4. Persons may choose poor alternatives for inappropriate reasons (the individuals are unable to realistically evaluate potential careers because of false beliefs and unrealistic expectations).

5. Persons may suffer anguish and anxiety over perceived inability to achieve goals (individual goals may be unrealistic or in conflict with other goals).

LTCC is both descriptive and explanatory: the process of career choice is described and examples of factors that influence choice are given. Although the authors have attempted to simplify the process of career development and career choice, the many variables introduced in this theory make the process of validation extremely complex. Meanwhile, the authors should be commended for specifying counseling objectives based on this theory and for providing strategies designed to accomplish these objectives. They also provided several observations for career counseling (Krumboltz, Mitchell, & Gelatt, 1975, pp. 11–13):

1. Career decision making is a learned skill.

2. Persons who claim to have made a career choice need help too (career choice may have been made from inaccurate information and faulty alternatives).

3. Success is measured by students' demonstrated skill in decision making (evaluations of decision-making skills are needed).

4. Clients come from a wide array of groups.

5. Clients need not feel guilty if they are not sure of a career to enter.

6. No one occupation is seen as the best for any one individual.

Empirical Support for Krumboltz's Learning Theory

The learning theory of career counseling has been developed only recently, and therefore relevant research has yet to be accomplished. The original theory, social-learning theory of career decision making, claimed validity from the development of educational and occupational preferences, the development of task approach skills and factors that cause people to take action, and from an extensive database on general social-learning theory of behavior. More information about the validity of this theory can be obtained from Mitchell and Krumboltz (1996).

⏵ Summary of Practical Applications

According to Mitchell and Krumboltz (1996), when people in modern society make career choices, they must cope with four fundamental trends. Career counselors must recognize these trends and be prepared to help.

1. *People need to expand their capabilities and interests, not base decisions on existing characteristics only.* This first trend centers around the use of interest inventories. Because many individuals have limited experiences with the vast number of activities that interest inventories measure, people may become indifferent to many activities they have not had the chance to experience personally. The point here is that career counselors should assist individuals in exploring new activities, rather than routinely directing them to career decision making based on measured interests that reflect limited past experiences.

2. *People need to prepare for changing work tasks, not assume that occupations will remain stable.* The changing role of job requirements and workplace environments in our current society suggests that career counselors must be prepared to help individuals learn new skills and attitudes so they can meet the demands of international competition. The radical restructuring of the work force and the disruptions of expectations can be very stressful. Therefore, career counselors also should be prepared to help individuals cope with stress as they learn to develop new skills on an ongoing basis.

3. *People need to be empowered to take action, not merely given a diagnosis.* Many issues about career decisions are often overlooked, including a lack of information about working per se, families' reaction to a member's taking a particular job, and how to go about getting a job. These issues and others, such as restructuring of the workplace, could cause fear of the decision-making process itself, referred to as *zeteophobia,* or cause procrastination about making a decision. Career counselors are directed to help individuals find answers to these questions and others while providing effective support during the exploration process.

4. *Career counselors need to play a major role in dealing with all career problems, not just with occupational selection.* Krumboltz (1993), Richardson (1993), and Zunker (1994), among others, have suggested that career and personal counseling should be integrated. Such issues as burnout, career change, peer affiliate relationships, obstacles to career development, and the work role and its effect on other life roles are

examples of potential problems that call for interventions by the career counselor.

Other suggestions

1. The role of career counselors and the goals of career counseling need to be reevaluated. Counselors need to continue to promote client learning, but perhaps in a different way. Counselors may have to become coaches and mentors to help individuals meet the changes in work force requirements.

2. Learning experiences should be used to increase the range of opportunities that can be considered in career exploration. Counselors should attempt to discover unlimited experiences among clients and offer proper learning solutions.

3. Assessment results can be used to create new learning experiences. For instance, aptitude test results can be used to focus on new learning. Key interests identified through interest inventories need to be developed. Assessment results can be starting points for establishing new learning experiences.

4. Intervention strategies suggested by Mitchell and Krumboltz include the use of job clubs. Individuals can offer support to each other in the job search process. A wide range of media should be made available to clients, and local employers should offer high school students structured work-based learning experiences.

5. Career counselors should become adept at using cognitive restructuring. For the youngster who is to report to work with fear of doing a poor job, the counselor can suggest another perspective. Cognitive restructuring suggests to such a client that he or she should report to the new job as a chance to impress the boss and fellow workers with enthusiasm. "Reframing" the perspective for this client should be helpful in making the first day on a job a satisfactory one.

6. Career counselors should also use behavioral counseling techniques, including role playing or trying new behaviors, desensitization when dealing with phobias, and paradoxical intention. The latter technique suggests that a client engage in the types of behavior that have created a problem (Mitchell & Krumboltz, 1996).

Sociological Perspective of Work and Career Development

This theory was built around a sociological perspective of work by Blau, Gustad, Jessor, Parnes, and Wilcox (1956) that included relationships of choice and process of selection. That is, the researchers suggested that the effects of social institutions on career choice and development emphasized the interrelationship of

> ### ▪ DIVERSITY ISSUES ▪
>
> Mitchell and Krumboltz (1996) suggest that learning theory can be applied to diverse populations with success. Although individuals do not have control over genetic predispositions and only limited control over environmental forces, they can gain control over learning experiences and task approach skills (Sharf, 1992). Discrimination and negative messages from the environment that limit career choices among ethnic minorities can be understood through social learning theory.
>
> Client and counselor can negotiate methods of removing obstructions and change a client's environment through collective action. Tailored and remedial intervention learning strategies can enhance opportunities for individuals and expand their choices for career decision making. Mitchell and Krumboltz suggest that individuals from diverse populations are to be empowered through learning to expand their capabilities and interests and shape their own career paths.

psychological, economic, and sociological determinants of occupational choice and development. Also, the authors suggested that individual characteristics that are responsible for choice are biologically determined and socially conditioned through family influences, social position and relations, and developed social-role characteristics. Eventually, the individual reaches a preference hierarchy from which choices are made.

In a more comprehensive approach to the sociological perspective of work and its relationship to career development, Hotchkiss and Borow (1996) provide a general background for the development of a model that includes recommendations for career counseling in the career decision-making process. In the sociological perspective, it must be remembered that sociologists view occupational choice as part of a broad system of social stratification, as outlined in the introductory paragraphs to this model.

The differences between the sociological perspective of work and the psychology of career development provides the counselor with key perspectives from which to better understand the sociological effects on the individual during the career decision-making process.

Work per se is viewed as much more inclusive from a sociologist's point of view than generally perceived; the status hierarchy of occupational structure, power and authority in the workplace, work socialization processes, labor unions and collective bargaining, the operation of the labor market, and sociology of professions are examples. Second, career development theories assume that individuals have at least a moderate degree of control in the process of making career decisions. In contrast, sociological theory strongly suggests that institutional and impersonal market forces constrain decision making and greatly impede satisfaction of career aspirations. Third, sociologists have done much more significantly relevant research and interest than have career development theorists on institutional factors that determine and shape workplace environments. According to sociologists, forces such as formal rules and supply and demand determine the nature and scope of work activities. Although sociologists appreciate the constellation of personal attributes that influence job performance and satisfaction, sociological research has been directed to other determinants of career development that should concern the career counselor. The following topics are used to represent sociological perspectives of work and career development.

STATUS ATTAINMENT THEORY.   The hypothesis is that parental status greatly affects the occupational level offspring attain. More fully, parental status influences attitudes concerning appropriate levels of education and the career plans (including educational level) of their children.

SOCIOLOGY OF LABOR MARKETS.   In taking this position, sociologists argue that institutional practices rather than individual career aspirations shape career outcomes. For example, in the structure of organizations, a satisfying career is not necessarily one that has been planned but is more a matter of obtaining a preferred position when the opportunity presents itself. In a much broader sense, individuals are assigned to job slots or work positions, rather than obtaining them from personal planned choices.

The structure of some business and government organizations is characterized by the institutional career ladder of promotions. Some of the ways institutional policies of management affect career development are as follows: (1) those who work in the core sector of an industry make higher wages than do those in the periphery sector; (2) level of education and experience have a greater influence on wages in the core sector than in the periphery, and (3) minorities and women have limited access to jobs in the core sector.

RACE AND GENDER EFFECTS.   Ongoing research indicates that minorities are concentrated in low-status occupations and earn less than whites do (Saunders, 1995). Some evidence suggests that there is a decline in gender segregation of jobs (Roos & Jones, 1993), but women tend to be concentrated in a narrow band of occupations that pay less than men earn (Reskin, 1993). Interestingly, men and women both earn less in jobs that are culturally defined as "women's work." One can also observe that when women enter traditionally male jobs, salaries seem to go down, but when men enter traditionally female jobs, the salaries tend to go up.

SCHOOL PROCESSES.   Ability grouping and tracking students in school have been attacked as two methods that mirror the dominant larger social system; ascribed status and adult achievement (educational, vocational, and economic achievement) influence standardized measures, which perpetuate the earlier suggestion that family status is a major determinant of educational achievement and subsequent job opportunities.

YOUTH COMPETENCE AND OUTCOMES OF YOUTH WORK. *Developed planning ability of planfulness* is a term used by Super (1990) that was also used by Clausen (1991) in a research project aimed at proving that adolescent planful competence emerges from environmental states, family status, and parental socialization processes. In addition, Clausen hypothesized that adolescent competence regarding mastery of behavior during high school years greatly influenced later educational attainment, career stability, and marital status. The results of this research suggest that adolescent competence is a very powerful predictor of adult outcomes concerning occupational attainment and marriage stability.

During the late 1980s an estimated 90% of 11th- and 12th-graders held part-time jobs during the school year. Research in the 1980s also indicated that part-time work did not provide an environment for psychological growth and development, nor did it forge links to full-time career objectives (Greenberger & Steinberg, 1986).

A more positive report was given by Marsh (1991), who indicated that summer jobs do not conflict with schoolwork and therefore are not associated with negative factors, as reported earlier. In fact, there were indications that summer employment enhanced adolescents' self-esteem.

FAMILY EFFECTS. The question here is, What role does the family play in shaping career choices and development of individuals? We have previously discussed how parental work and occupational status affects their children's future career attainment. The interest in family effects centers around how family structure and maternal work outside the home influence the choices and attitudes of youth. Because the numerically dominant family type is now a dual-work or dual-career family, research has focused on a different kind of family-work relationship. Parcel and Menaghan (1994) found no relationship between maternal employment and the child's social behavior. The most far-reaching finding indicated that a working mother's ability to transmit behavior norms to children is not diminished by her working.

WORK COMMITMENT. Sociologists view work commitment as rather transient and as being greatly affected by current social structures on the job. Research by Halaby and Weakliem (1989) proved three significant hypotheses: (1) if jobs have an intrinsically rewarding nature, the stronger the worker's attachment to the organization will be; (2) the closer the job match to the worker's abilities, the stronger the worker's commitment is to the job; and (3) workers who have greater opportunity for alternative employment have a weaker attachment to the organization. Not surprisingly, the greatest strengthening bond of the three hypotheses was the matching of job requirements and worker's abilities.

⇒ Summary of Practical Applications

1. Career counselors need to be aware of sociological research that informs them of how individuals choose and are selected for work roles. In the

career choice process, the sociologist stresses that choice is restricted by a number of variables, including status of parents, labor market demands, and structures in organizations. Thus, counseling strategies need to be developed to assist clients to cope with the social environment they encounter.

2. Career counselors should inform clients about the complexities of the work world and the difficulties they may experience when they encounter the labor market. Counselors need to develop strategies to enhance realism about the work world.

3. Career counselors need to assist clients in combating gender stereotyping, which limits career options.

4. Minority groups can be assisted in career planning by improving their chances for completing educational programs, enhancing attitudes about work, providing career information, and developing skills. Finally, clients should be offered assistance in using community resources.

5. Career counselors should provide assistance for raising educational aspirations. Counselors can display evidence of the close relationship between years of schooling and status level of parents and between years of schooling and success at work (Hotchkiss & Borow, 1996).

The table in the following section contains summaries of each theory discussed in this chapter; included are basic assumptions, key concepts, and outcomes of each theory. These summaries may serve as a handy reference or a synopsis of each theory, especially when reading the next section on implications for career guidance and the career counseling models discussed in Chapter 4.

Implications for Career Guidance

Career development theories are conceptual systems designed to delineate apparent relationships between a concomitance of events that lead to causes and effects. Although the theories described in this chapter have a variety of labels, all emphasize the relationships between the unique traits of individuals and the characteristics of society in which development occurs. The major difference among the theories is the nature of the influential factors involved in the career decision process, but all the theories have common implications for career guidance.

1. Career development takes place in stages that are somewhat related to age but are influenced by many factors in the sociocultural milieu. Because career development is a lifelong process, career guidance programs must be designed to meet the needs of individuals over their life spans.

2. The tasks associated with stages of career development involve transitions requiring individuals to cope with each stage of life. Helping individuals

■ DIVERSITY ISSUES ■

Sociological theory suggests that institutional and impersonal markets constrain decision making and thus affect career aspirations. Counselors are to be aware that career choice is restricted by status of parents, labor market demands, and certain structures in organizations. Minorities tend to be concentrated in low-status jobs, and gender segregation continues to exist although it is declining. Minority groups can be helped by raising their career aspirations through educational programs and developing marketable skills.

cope with transitions is a key concept to remember while promoting development.

3. Career maturity is acquired through successfully accomplishing developmental tasks within a continuous series of life stages. Points of reference from this continuum provide relevant information for career guidance program development.

4. Each person should be considered unique. This uniqueness is a product of many sources, including sociocultural background, genetic endowment, personal and educational experiences, family relationships, and community resources. In this context, values, interests, abilities, and behavioral tendencies are important in shaping career development.

5. Self-concept affects career decisions. Self-concept is not a static phenomenon but, rather, is an ongoing process that can gradually or abruptly change as people and situations change. Accurate self-concepts contribute to career maturity.

6. The stability of career choice depends primarily on the strength and dominance of one's personal orientation of personality characteristics, preferences, abilities, and traits. Work environments that match personal orientations provide appropriate outlets for personal and work satisfaction. Finding congruence between personality traits and work environments is a key objective of career development.

7. Individual characteristics and traits can be assessed through standardized assessment instruments. Identified traits are used to predict future outcomes of probable adjustments. Matching job requirements with personal characteristics might not dominate career-counseling strategies but remains a viable part of some programs.

8. Social learning emphasizes the importance of learning experiences and their effect on occupational selection. Learning takes place through observations as well as through direct experiences. Identifying the content

of individual beliefs and generalizations is a key ingredient in developing counseling strategies.

9. Introducing occupational information resources and developing skills for their proper use is a relevant goal for all educational institutions. Moreover, this need persists over the life span.

10. Career development involves a lifelong series of choices. Counselors help clients make appropriate choices by teaching decision-making and problem-solving skills. Understanding the individual processes involved in choices enables counselors to better assist during the decision-making process.

11. The concept of human freedom is implied in all career development theories. This concept implies that career counselors should provide avenues of freedom that allow individuals to explore options within the social, political, and economic milieu. The limits of personal freedom are often external (for example, economic conditions, discrimination, and environmental conditions), but freedom can also be constrained from such internal sources as fear, lack of confidence, faulty attitudes, poor self-concept development, and behavioral deficits. Within this context, the career counselor should be concerned not only with career development but with all facets of human development. Counseling strategies must be designed to meet a wide range of needs.

TABLE OF BASIC ASSUMPTIONS, KEY TERMS, AND OUTCOMES

Theories	Basic Assumptions
Trait-and-Factor	Individuals have unique patterns of ability or traits that can be objectively measured and correlated with requirements of occupations.
Person-Environment-Fit	Individuals bring requirements to a work environment, and the work environment makes its requirements of individuals. To survive, individuals and work environments must achieve some degree of congruence.
Ginzberg and Associates	Occupational choice is a developmental process covering 6 to 10 years beginning at age 11 and ending shortly after age 17. As tentative occupational decisions are made, other choices are eliminated.

12. The importance of cognitive development and its relationship to self-concept and subsequent occupational aspirations are receiving greater attention. This focus is concerned primarily with the role of cognitive development in terms of appropriate gender roles, occupational roles, and other generalizations that directly affect career development. This fine-tuning of relationships between human and career development implies that counselors must develop a greater sensitivity to both.

Summary

1. The trait-and-factor theory evolved from early studies of individual differences and developed closely with the psychometric movement. The key characteristic of the trait-and-factor theory is the assumption that individuals have unique patterns of ability or traits that can be objectively measured and subsequently matched with requirements of jobs.

2. The theory of work adjustment emphasizes that work is more than a step-by-step procedure; it includes human interaction, sources of satisfaction and dissatisfaction, rewards, stress, and many other psychological

Key Terms	Outcomes
Traits primarily refer to abilities and interests. Parsons's three-step model included studying the individual, surveying occupations, and matching the individual with an occupation.	The primary goal of using assessment data was to predict job satisfaction and success. Contemporary practices stress the relationships between human factors and work environments. Test data is used to observe the similarity between client and current workers in a career field.
Personality structure is a stable characteristic made up of abilities and values. *Ability dimensions* indicate levels of work skills. *Values* are considered as work needs. *Satisfactoriness* refers to clients who are more achievement oriented. *Satisfaction* refers to more self-fulfilled oriented clients. *Work adjustment* refers to a worker's attempt to improve fit in a work environment.	Client abilities (work skills) and values (work needs) are criteria used for selecting work environments. Work requirements determine reinforcers available by occupations. Knowledge of clients who are more achievement (satisfactoriness) or self-fulfilled (satisfaction) oriented enhances career choice.
Stages of career development are Fantasy, Tentative, and Realistic. In *Fantasy,* play becomes work oriented. In *Tentative,* there are recognition of work requirements and one's traits. In *Realistic,* one narrows down occupational choices.	Career choice is a developed precept of occupations subjectively appraised in sociocultural milieu from childhood to early adult. There are three stages of development from before age 11 to young adult.

TABLE OF BASIC ASSUMPTIONS, KEY TERMS, AND OUTCOMES *(continued)*

Theories	Basic Assumptions
Life-Span, Life-Space Approach	Career development is multidimensional. There are developmental tasks throughout the life-span. Vocational maturity is acquired through successfully accomplishing developmental tasks within a continuous series of life stages. Individuals implement their self-concepts into careers that will provide the most efficient means of self-expressions. Success in one life role facilitates success in another.
Tiedeman's Decision Making Model	Career development unfolds within the general process of cognitive development as one resolves ego-relevant crises. Ego identity is of central importance in career development. New decisions begin with exploration and gradually reach integration.
Circumscription and Compromise: A Developmental Theory of Occupational Aspirations	A key factor in career decision is self-concept that is determined by one's social class, level of intelligence, and experiences with sex-typing. Individual's progress through four stages and learn to compromise based on generalizations of cognitive maps of occupations. Individuals are less willing to compromise job level and sex-type.
Ann Roe: A Needs Approach	Early childhood experiences and parental style affect the needs hierarchy and the relationships of those needs to adult lifestyle. Those who choose nonperson-type jobs are meeting lower-level needs for safety and security. Those who choose to work with other people have strong needs for affection and belonging.
John Holland: A Typology Approach	Career choice is an expression of, or an extension of personality into the world of work. Individuals search for environments that will let them exercise their skills and abilities, express their attitudes and values, and take on agreeable problems and roles. There are six kinds of occupational environments and six matching personal orientations.

Key Terms	Outcomes
Stages of vocational development are Growth, Exploratory, Establishment, Maintenance, and Decline. Developmental tasks are Crystallization, Specification, Implementation, Stabilization, and Consolidation. Self-concept is the driving force that establishes a career pattern. Attitudes and competencies are related to career growth and identified as career Maturity.	Career development is a lifelong process occurring in stages. Self-concept is shaped through life experiences. Clients are involved in several life roles of child, student, leisurite, citizen, worker, spouse, homemaker, parent, and pensioner. All life roles affect one another. In development societal factors interact with biological psychological factors.
In career decision making *differentiation* is the process of evaluating self-in-world from contextual experiences. *Integration* is the process of integrating within society, yet retaining individuality. *Anticipation* in career decision making involves exploration, crystallization, choice, and clarification. *Implementation* involves induction, reformation, and integration.	Career decision making is a process involving the client's total cognitive abilities, uniqueness, and knowledge of the changing world of work. Decisional process involves differentiation (evaluating self-in-world) and integration (congruency with work).
Self-concept is one's view of self. *Cognitive maps* of occupations reflect dimensions of prestige level, masculinity/femininity, and field of work. *Social space* refers to a zone or view of where each person fits into society. *Circumscription* is the process of narrowing one's territory of social space or alternative. *Compromise* suggests individuals will settle for a good choice but not best.	Individual development consists of four stages: Orientation to size and power, orientation to sex roles, orientation to social valuation, and orientation to internal unique self. Socioeconomic background and intellectual level greatly influence self-concept. Occupational choices are determined by social space, intellectual level, and sex-typing. Career choice is a process of eliminating options through cognitive maps. Individuals compromise occupational choices because of accessibility. Circumscription of occupations occurs through self-awareness, sex-type and social class.
Examples of person-oriented occupations are service, business contact, managerial, teaching, and entertainment. Nonperson-oriented are technology, outdoors, and science.	Original position was that individuals who enjoy working with people were raised by warm accepting parents and those who avoid contact with others were reared by cold or rejecting parents. Current position is that there are other important factors that determine occupational choice not accounted for in her theory.
The six types of categories for individuals and work environment are *Realistic, Investigative, Artistic, Social, Enterprising,* and *Conventional. Consistency* refers to personality, i.e., those client's who relate strongly to one or more of the categories. *Differentiation* refers to those who have poorly defined personality styles. *Identity* refers to the degree in which one identifies with a work environment. *Congruence* is a good match between individual and work environment.	Individuals are products of their environment. Stability of career choice depends on dominance of personal orientation. Individuals who fit a pure personality type will express little resemblance to other types. Clients who have many occupational goals have low identity. Congruence occurs when client's personality type matches the corresponding work environment.

TABLE OF BASIC ASSUMPTIONS, KEY TERMS, AND OUTCOMES *(continued)*

Theories	Basic Assumptions
Krumboltz's Learning Theory Approach	Each individual's unique learning experiences over the life span develop primary influences that lead to career choice. Development involves genetic endowments and special abilities, environmental conditions and events, learning experiences, and task approach skills.
Sociological Perspective of Work and Career Development	Individual characteristics that are responsible for career choice are biologically determined and socially conditioned through family influences, social position and relations, and developed social role characteristics.

reinforcements. The basic assumption is that an individual seeks to achieve and maintain a positive relationship within his or her work environment.

3. Ginzberg, Ginsburg, Axelrad, and Herma are considered to be the first to approach a theory of occupational choice from a developmental standpoint. They suggested that occupational choice is a developmental process that generally covers a period of 6 to 10 years, beginning at around the age of 11 and ending shortly after age 17. The three periods or stages of development are called fantasy, tentative, and realistic.

4. Super has made many contributions to the study of vocational behavior, including his formalization of developmental stages: growth, exploratory, establishment, maintenance, and decline. Super considered self-concept as the vital force that establishes a career pattern one will follow throughout life. In 1951 he designed a study to follow the vocational development of ninth-grade boys in Middletown, New York. Those individuals who were seen as vocationally mature in the ninth grade (based on their knowledge of occupations, planning, and interests) were significantly more successful as young adults. His conclusions suggest that there is a relationship between career maturity and adolescent achievement of a significant degree of self-awareness, knowledge of occupations,

Key Terms	Outcomes
Genetic endowments are inherited qualities that may set limits on career choice. *Environmental conditions* are contextual interactions that influence individual choices. *Instrumental learning experiences* are those acquired through observation, consequences, and reaction of others. *Associative learning experiences* are negative and positive reactions to neutral experiences. *Task approach skills* are work habits, mental sets, emotional responses, and cognitive responses.	Learning experiences should increase the range of occupations in career counseling. Assessment is to be used to create new learning experiences. Clients need to prepare for changing work tasks. Career decision making is a learned skill. Clients need to be empowered as active participants in career search.
Status Attainment Theory suggests parental status greatly influences career choice. *Sociology of Labor Markets* refers to institutional practices that limit career aspiration such as jobs that have limited access for minorities and women. *Race and gender effects* refer to minorities being assigned to low-status jobs and women being given less status than men. Family status can limit educational aspirations.	Organizations and market forces constrain career choices. Clients are to learn to cope with social environments they encounter. Clients are to learn about the realities of the work world. Minorities are to be encouraged to complete educational programs and increase their educational aspirations.

and developed planning ability. Super's theory on the career development process takes a primarily multisided approach.

5. Tiedeman conceptualized career development as a process of continuously differentiating one's ego identity, processing developmental tasks, and resolving psychosocial crises. These ongoing activities are perceived within a framework of time stages. According to Tiedeman, career decisions are reached through a systematic problem-solving pattern that includes seven steps: (a) exploration, (b) crystallization, (c) choice, (d) clarification, (e) induction, (f) reformation, and (g) integration.

6. In Gottfredson's model, occupational preferences emerge from the complexities that accompany physical and mental growth. A major determinant of occupational preferences is the progressive circumscription of aspirations during self-concept development. Gottfredson suggested that socioeconomic background and intellectual level greatly influence self-concept development.

7. Roe's theory focuses on early relations within the family and their subsequent effects on career direction. Roe emphasized that early childhood experiences were important factors in the satisfaction of one's chosen occupation. She classified occupations into two major categories: person-oriented and nonperson-oriented.

8. Holland considered career choice as an expression or extension of personality into the world of work, followed by subsequent identification with specific occupational stereotypes. Holland considered modal personal orientation as the key to individual occupational choice. Central to Holland's theory is the concept that individuals choose careers to satisfy their developed preferred personal modal orientations. Holland developed six modal personal styles and six matching work environments: realistic, investigative, artistic, social, enterprising, and conventional.

9. Krumboltz, Mitchell, and Gelatt postulated that career selection is significantly influenced by life events. Four such factors are (a) genetic endowments and special abilities, (b) environmental conditions and events, (c) learning experiences, and (d) task approach skills. Decision making is considered to be a continuous process extending over the life span.

10. Sociologists view occupational choice as a part of a broad system of social stratification. Sociological theory suggests that institutional and impersonal market forces greatly impede satisfaction of career aspirations. Counselors need to assist clients to cope with the social environments they encounter.

Supplementary Learning Exercises

1. Why is the trait-and-factor approach considered the most durable theory? Give examples of the use of the trait-and-factor theory in current career-counseling programs.

2. Defend the statement: Career development is a continuous process.

3. Write your own definition of career development and career counseling.

4. Using the following reference, write a comprehensive report on Super's Career Pattern Study conducted in Middletown, New York. Identify the dimensions of vocational maturity used, the procedures, and the conclusions.

   Brown, D., Brooks, L., and Associates (1990). *Career choice and development* (2nd ed.). San Francisco: Jossey-Bass Publishers.

5. Compare Holland's approach to career development with Roe's. Summarize the similarities and differences.

6. Using the following reference, explain the principles behind Holland's theory of vocational choice. Defend or criticize his thesis that vocational interests are not independent of personality.

   Holland, J. L. (1992). *Making vocational choices* (2nd ed.). Odessa, FL: Psychological Assessment Resources.

7. Compare Tiedeman's aspects of anticipation and preoccupation with those he outlines for implementation and adjustment. What are the major counseling considerations for both sets of aspects?

8. Apply a career development theory to your own career development. Using Super's developmental stages, identify your current stage of development and the ages at which you accomplished other stages.

9. Outline the factor that you consider most important in the career development of an adult you know or one you interview.

10. Develop your own theory of career development. Identify the components of other theories you agree with and why you agree with them.

For More Information

Brown, D., Brooks, L., & Associates. (1990). *Career choice and development* (2nd ed.). San Francisco: Jossey-Bass.

Brown, D., Brooks, L., & Associates. (1996). *Career choice and development* (3rd ed.). San Francisco: Jossey-Bass.

Chartrand, J. M. (1991). The evolution of trait-and-factor career counseling: A person-environment fit approach. *Journal of Counseling & Development, 69,* 518–524.

Gottfredson, L. S. (1981). Circumscription and compromise: A developmental theory of occupational aspirations. *Journal of Counseling Psychology, 28* (6), 545–579.

Holland, J. L. (1992). *Making vocational choices* (2nd ed.). Odessa, FL: Psychological Assessment Resources.

Patton, W., & McMahon, M. (1999). *Career development and systems theory: A new relationship.* Pacific Grove, CA: Brooks/Cole.

Prediger, D. J. (1995). *Assessment in career counseling.* Greensboro, NC: ERIC Counseling and Student Services Clearinghouse, University of North Carolina.

Sharf, R. S. (1992). *Applying career development theory to counseling.* Pacific Grove, CA: Brooks/Cole.

Sharf, R. S. (1996). *Theories of psychotherapy and counseling: Concepts and cases.* Pacific Grove, CA: Brooks/Cole.

Super, D. E., & Overstreet, P. L. (1960). *The vocational maturity of ninth grade boys.* New York: Teachers College, Columbia University.

Super, D. E., Starishesky, R., Matlin, N., & Jordaan, J. P. (1963). *Career development: Self-concept theory.* New York: College Entrance Examination Board.

3

Theories of Career Development II

Chapter Highlights

- *Perspectives of new evolving theories*
- *Career development from a cognitive information processing perspective*
- *Social cognitive perspective*
- *Brown's values-based holistic model of career and life-role choices and satisfaction*
- *Contextual explanation of career self-efficacy theory*
- *Career guidance implications*
- *Diversity issues*
- *Table of all theories: basic assumptions, key terms, and outcomes*

THIS CHAPTER IS A CONTINUATION OF CHAPTER 2; HOWEVER, THIS CHAP-ter will introduce five evolving career development theories that have emerged in the 1990s. These theories show promise for future development, and as their constructs become more carefully defined through further research and assigned levels of importance, they will become more meaningful to the career counseling profession (Brown, Brooks, & Associates, 1996).

As you read each theory, you will find that more attention is being given increasingly to women and ethnic minorities. Some theorists also endeavor to develop practical applications for what they have theorized. There also appears to be a recognition of the necessity to carefully explain various components of each theory. As interest in career development theories continues to expand—especially to other disciplines—we should not be surprised to find other theories emerging well into the 21st century.

The five evolving theories introduced in this chapter include (1) a cognitive information processing approach to career problem solving; (2) career development from a social cognitive perspective; (3) a values-based, holistic model of career and life-role choices and satisfaction; (4) a contextual explanation of career; and (5) a summary of a self-efficacy model. Each theory is summarized in table format near the end of the chapter, highlighting basic assumptions, key terms, and outcomes. In addition, a section is devoted to how career theories may be converging. Finally, implications for career guidance are presented.

Career Development from a Cognitive Information Processing Perspective

This career development theory is based on the cognitive information processing (CIP) theory developed by Peterson, Sampson, and Reardon (1991). CIP theory is applied to career development in terms of how individuals make a career decision and use information in career problem solving and decision making. CIP is based on the ten assumptions shown in Table 3-1. Using these assumptions as a focal point, the major strategy of career intervention is to provide learning events that will develop the individual's processing abilities. In this way, clients develop capabilities as career problem solvers to meet immediate as well as future problems.

The stages of processing information begin with screening, translating, and encoding input in short-term memory; then storing it in long-term memory; and later activating, retrieving, and transforming the input into working memory to arrive at a solution. The counselor's principle function in CIP theory is to identify the client's needs and develop interventions to help the client acquire the knowledge and skills to address those needs.

Peterson, Sampson, and Reardon stress that career problem solving is primarily a cognitive process that can be improved through a sequential procedure known as CASVE, which includes the following generic processing skills: communication

TABLE 3-1	ASSUMPTIONS UNDERLYING THE COGNITIVE INFORMATION PROCESSING (CIP) PERSPECTIVE OF CAREER DEVELOPMENT

Assumption	Explanation
1. Career choice results from an interaction of cognitive and affective processes.	CIP emphasizes the cognitive domain in career decision making; but it also acknowledges the presence of an affective source of information in the process (Heppner & Krauskopf, 1987; Zajonc, 1980). Ultimately, commitment to a career goal involves an interaction between affective and cognitive processes.
2. Making career choices is a problem-solving activity.	Individuals can learn to solve career problems (that is, to choose careers) just as they can learn to solve math, physics, or chemistry problems. The major differences between career problems and math or science problems lie in the complexity and ambiguity of the stimulus and the greater uncertainty as to the correctness of the solution.
3. The capabilities of career problem solvers depend on the availability of cognitive operations as well as knowledge.	One's capability as a career problem solver depends on one's self-knowledge and on one's knowledge of occupations. It also depends on the cognitive operations one can draw on to derive relationships between these two domains.
4. Career problem solving is a high-memory-load task.	The realm of self-knowledge is complex; so is the world of work. The drawing of relationships between these two domains entails attending to both domains simultaneously. Such a task may easily overload the working memory store.
5. Motivation.	The motivation to become a better career problem solver stems from the desire to make satisfying career choices through a better understanding of oneself and the occupational world.

(receiving, encoding, and sending out queries), analysis (identifying and placing problems in a conceptual framework), synthesis (formulating courses of action), valuing (judging each action as to its likelihood of success and failure and its impact on others), and execution (implementing strategies to carry out plans). Table 3-2 describes the CASVE cycle using career information and media.

This model emphasizes the notion that career information counseling is a learning event. This is consistent with other theories that make this same assumption and present procedures for developing decision-making skills. One major difference between CIP theory and other theories discussed in this chapter, however, is the role of cognition as a mediating force that leads individuals to greater power and control in determining their own destinies. As we learn more about CIP theory, the CASVE approach will be further delineated for the counseling profession.

TABLE 3-1	ASSUMPTIONS *(continued)*

Assumption	Explanation
6. Career development involves continual growth and change in knowledge structures.	Self-knowledge and occupational knowledge consist of sets of organized memory structures called *schemata* that evolve over the person's life span. Both the occupational world and we ourselves are ever-changing. Thus, the need to develop and integrate these domains never ceases.
7. Career identity depends on self-knowledge.	In CIP terms, career identity is defined as the level of development of self-knowledge memory structures. Career identity is a function of the complexity, integration, and stability of the schemata constituting the self-knowledge domain.
8. Career maturity depends on one's ability to solve career problems.	From a CIP perspective, career maturity is defined as the ability to make independent and responsible career decisions based on the thoughtful integration of the best information available about oneself and the occupational world.
9. The ultimate goal of career counseling is achieved by facilitating the growth of information-processing skills.	From a CIP perspective, the goal of career counseling is therefore to provide the conditions of learning that facilitate the growth of memory structures and cognitive skills so as to improve the client's capacity for processing information.
10. The ultimate aim of career counseling is to enhance the client's capabilities as a career problem solver and a decision maker.	From a CIP perspective, the goal of career counseling is to enhance the client's career decision-making capabilities through the development of information processing skills.

SOURCE: *Career Development and Services: A Cognitive Approach,* by G. Peterson, J. Sampson, and R. Reardon, pp. 7–9. Copyright 1991 Brooks/Cole Publishing Company, a division of International Thomson Publishing Inc.

Empirical Support for the CIP Perspective

For a discussion of metacognitions or executive processing domain, see Helwig (1992). For information about the *Career Thoughts Inventory,* see Peterson, Sampson, and Reardon (1991) and Sampson, Peterson, Lenz, Reardon, and Saunders (1996a). Major strengths of theory are covered in Krumboltz (1992).

⟾ Summary of Practical Applications

Peterson, Sampson, Reardon, and Lenz (1996), the developers of this theory, have also proposed a seven-step sequence for career delivery service, as shown in Figure 3-1. This sequence can be used as a delivery option for both problem solving

TABLE 3-2	CAREER INFORMATION AND THE CASVE CYCLE
Phase of the CASVE cycle	**Example of career information and media**
Communication (identifying a need)	A description of the personal and family issues that women typically face in returning to work (information) in a video-taped interview of currently employed women (medium)
Analysis (interrelating problem components)	Explanations of the basic education requirements for degree programs (information) in community college catalogues (medium)
Synthesis (creating likely alternatives)	A presentation of emerging nontraditional career options for women (information) at a seminar on career development for women (medium)
Valuing (prioritizing alternatives)	An exploration of how the roles of parent, spouse, citizen, "leisurite," and homemaker would be affected by the assumption of the worker role (information) in an adult version of a computer-assisted career guidance system (medium)
Execution (forming means-ends strategies)	A description of a functional résumé emphasizing transferable skills, followed by the creation of a résumé (information) presented on a computer-assisted employability skills system (medium)

SOURCE: From *Career Development and Services: A Cognitive Approach,* by G. Peterson, J. Sampson, and R. Reardon, p. 200. Copyright 1991 Brooks/Cole Publishing Company, a division of International Thomson Publishing Inc.

and decision making, and it can be used for individual, group, self-directed, and curricular programs. Group counseling requires that the counselor do prescreening in Steps 1 and 2. In the next chapter these steps are explained in some detail in a career counseling model referred to as Cognitive Information Processing Approach. We strongly encourage you to read the original source for a more complete understanding of this theory.

Career Development from a Social Cognitive Perspective

The study of cognitive variables and processes has become a popular topic for researchers who apply what is often referred to as the "cognitive revolution" to the study of career development. This theory has indeed followed such a script by offering a social cognitive career theory (SCCT) to complement existing theories and to build connecting bridges to other theories of career development.

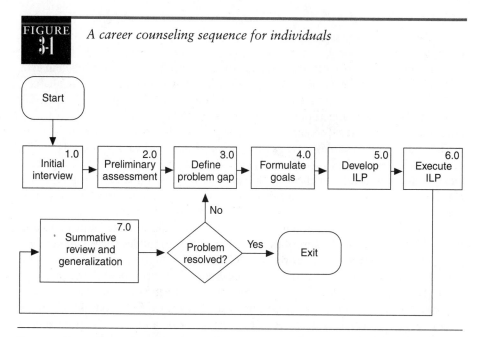

SOURCE: From *Career Development and Services: A Cognitive Approach,* by G. Peterson, J. Sampson, and R. Reardon, p. 231. Copyright 1991 Brooks/Cole Publishing Company, a division of International Thomson Publishing Inc.

According to Lent, Brown, and Hackett (1996), the theory's authors, there are three ways to translate and share knowledge with existing theories and emerging ones. The first is to agree on a common meaning for conceptually related concepts, such as self-concept and self-efficacy. Betz (1992b, p. 24) defines career self-efficacy as "the possibility that low expectations of efficacy with respect to some aspect of career behavior may serve as a detriment to optimal career choice and the development of the individual." Further delineation of this theory involves Betz's reference to career-choice content (content domains such as math, science, or writing) and career-choice process (behavioral domains that enhance career implementation). From this frame of reference, an individual might avoid areas of course work surrounding a career because of low self-efficacy. Likewise, self-efficacy deficits can lead to procrastination in or avoidance of a career decision.

Hackett and Betz (1981) suggest that social beliefs and expectations are the mechanisms through which self-efficacy deficits are developed, particularly for women. Hackett and Betz cite a restricted range of options and underutilization of abilities as important factors hindering women's career development. Using this logic, women's vocational behavior can be at least partially explained.

The second way to translate and share knowledge about existing theories and emerging ones is to fully describe and define common outcomes such as satisfaction and stability, found in a number of theories. Finally, a third way is to fully explain the relationships among such diverse constructs as interests, self-efficacy, abilities, and needs. Clearly, the plea is to find a common ground for communicating a conceptual order to the vast number of variables found in career-related literature.

The underlying assumptions and constructs of this theory are embedded in general social cognitive theory (Bandura, 1986), which blends cognitive, self-regulatory, and motivational processes into a lifelong phenomenon. More specifically, SCCT's major goals are to find methods of defining specific mediators from which learning experiences shape and subsequently influence career behavior. Furthermore, the aim is to explain how variables such as interests, abilities, and values interrelate and, most important, how all variables influence individual growth and the contextual factors (environmental influences) that lead to career outcomes. Also emphasized is the term *personal agency,* which reflects how and why individuals exert power to either achieve a solution, such as a career outcome, or adapt to career changes. To identify and conceptualize the causal influences interacting between individuals and their environment, SCCT subscribes to Bandura's (1986) model of causality known as the *triadic reciprocal.* Within this bidirectional model, there are three variables: (1) personal and physical attributes, (2) external environmental factors, and (3) overt behavior. All three interact to the point of affecting one another as causal influences of an individual's development. Using this logic, SCCT conceptualizes the interacting influences among individuals, their behavior, and their environments to describe how individuals influence situations that ultimately affect their own thoughts and behavior.

What we have here is a complex, interacting system that is bidirectional and within which behavior, as one factor, and situations in the environment, as another, act as co-determinants in shaping personal thoughts and behaviors and external environmental factors. In essence, this is a person-behavior-situation interaction.

Key Theoretical Constructs

The personal determinants of career development have been conceptualized as self-efficacy, outcome expectations, and personal goals. The "big three" are considered to be building blocks within the triadic causal system that determine the course of career development and its outcome. Self-efficacy is not viewed as a unitary or fixed trait but, rather, as a set of beliefs about a specific performance domain. Self-efficacy is developed through four types of learning experiences (Lent, Brown, & Hackett, 1996): "(1) personal performance accomplishments, (2) vicarious learning, (3) social persuasion, and (4) physiological states and reactions" (p. 380). Self-efficacy is strengthened when success is experienced within a performance domain, whereas it is weakened when there are repeated failures.

Outcome expectations are also regarded as personal beliefs about expectations or consequences of behavioral activities. Some individuals may be motivated by extrinsic reinforcement, such as receiving an award; others by self-directed activities, such as pride in oneself; and yet others by the actual process of performing an activity. Outcome expectations are shaped by learning activities similar to those of self-efficacy.

One of most important reasons for personal goals in this theory is that they are considered to be guides that sustain behavior. While processing personal goals, individuals generate *personal agency* that interacts with the three building blocks, which in effect shapes self-directed behavior.

Interest Developmental Model

Individuals develop interests through activities in which they view themselves as competent and generally expect valued outcomes. Interests fail to develop when self-efficacy is perceived as weak and negative outcomes are expected from an activity. Activities that produce valued outcomes and that have been developed as personal interests are sustained by individuals through goals that ensure their involvement in those activities. Following this logic, activity practice tends to solidify interests and reshape and reinforce self-efficacy.

Attitudes and Values

Within the framework of SCCT, values are subsumed in the concept of outcome expectation. In effect, values are preferences for particular reinforcers such as money, status, or autonomy. This theory stresses that outcome expectations are influenced by value systems that are positively reinforced when involved with a particular activity.

Gender and Race/Ethnicity

In this theory we must focus on how career development was influenced from personal reactions to the social and cultural environment. Thus, the individual's socially constructed world, not the inherited biological traits, is the focus of gender and race in the SCCT.

It is therefore not surprising that this theory focuses on the social, cultural, and economic conditions that shaped learning opportunities to which individuals were exposed, interpersonal reactions experienced for performing certain activities, and the future outcomes that have been generated. In sum, the effects of gender and ethnicity on career interests, choice, and performance are associated primarily with differential learning experiences that influenced and subsequently shaped self-efficacy and outcome expectations.

Choice Model

The choice process is divided into three components: (1) establishing a goal; (2) taking action (by enrolling in a training or school program) to implement a choice; and (3) attaining a level of performance (successes or failures) that determines the direction of future career behavior. One's personal agency is seen as a most important variable in determining the degree of progression in the choice process. The pathways to career choice in SCCT are as follows: (1) self-efficacy and outcome expectations promote career-related interests; (2) interests in turn influence goals; (3) goal-related actions lead to performance experiences; (4) the outcome determines future paths (determined by whether self-efficacy is strengthened or weakened); and (5) finally, one establishes a career decision or redirects goals.

One major hurdle in the choice model has to do with contextual or environmental influences. The rationale is based on opportunity structure experienced in the environment. For instance, individuals who experience support and other beneficial environmental conditions readily take their goals into actions more so than do those who experience the opposite from their environment.

Performance Model

The SCCT contains a performance model that appears to be a summary description of this theory. Its purpose is twofold: (1) It illustrates concern for the level and quality of an individual's accomplishments and for the personal agency involvement in career-related pursuits; and (2) it points out the interplay of ability, self-efficacy, outcome expectations, and the establishment of goals for judging performance. This model can also serve as a method of determining points of reference for implementing effective intervention strategies.

Empirical Support

Selected references on career self-efficacy include Hackett (1995), Hackett and Lent (1992), Betz and Hackett (1986), Zimmerman (1995), and Schunk (1995). For relevant findings to SCCT's major hypotheses, see Coon-Carty (1995), Multon, Brown, and Lent (1991), and Sadri and Robertson (1993).

ⅠⅠⅡ➤ Summary of Practical Applications

1. Suggestions for expanding interests and facilitating choice include educational programs in schools that concentrate on developing interests, values, and talents and also focus on the cognitive basis for linking with these variables.

2. Individuals who are experiencing great difficulty with career choice or change should be presented with an array of occupations that correspond with their abilities and values, but not necessarily with their interests. This theory's authors argue that individuals will not consider some occupations because of false impressions of their abilities and, subsequently, will respond indifferently to such occupations on interest inventories. For example, the individual who does not indicate an interest in nursing may have been told that "you will have to take a lot of science courses." Because he views his ability to pass science courses as

poor, he reacts negatively to nursing when in fact his past performance and ability scores indicate he has a better than average chance of being successful in a nursing program.

3. A strategy used to combat perceived weaknesses includes using occupational card sorts. The individual is asked to sort occupational titles into categories of "might choose," "in question," and "would not choose." The client is then asked to further sort cards from "in question" and "would not choose" into subcategories by self-efficacy beliefs ("if I had the skills I might choose"), outcome expectations ("might choose if they matched my values") and definite lack of interest ("not considered a possible choice"), and other. Clearly, the purpose of this procedure is to assist the client in fully understanding the interacting forces that determine self-appraisals in the career decision process. Individuals who have developed false notions about their abilities and values can indeed become indifferent toward certain occupations.

4. Overcoming barriers to choice and success is a significant goal for career counseling in SCCT. The rationale here is that individuals who perceive insurmountable barriers to career entry will be unwilling to pursue occupational interests in the career choice process. A decisional balance sheet is used to assist clients in evaluating perceived barriers. Each client is asked to generate a list of both positive and negative consequences for each career alternative he or she has selected. Each individual is then asked to develop strategies designed to overcome barriers that interfere with choice implementation.

5. School-to-work initiatives suggested by SCCT include designing skill programs that provide for self-efficacy enhancement, realistic outcome expectations, and goal-setting skills (Lent, Brown, & Hackett, 1996).

Brown's Values-Based, Holistic Model of Career and Life-Role Choices and Satisfaction

Brown's (1996) values-based approach to career development assumes that human functioning is greatly influenced and shaped by a person's value orientation. Certain established standards of behavior are considered important in the developmental process, are also value-based, and become the rules by which individuals judge their own actions and the actions of others. Unlike many other theories, interests play a more minor role in career decision making in this theory. For example, interests are indications of developed likes and dislikes that grow out of values, but they are not as dominant in shaping behavior as values are simply because interests do not serve as benchmarks for standards of behavior. Thus, values are most important in career decision-making processes, as they provide the direction to a desired end state and, as such, have a central role in setting goals.

Values are also seen as strong determinants in rationalizing behavior roles. For example, a strong value for social service would point an individual toward an occupation that helps others, whereas a dominant value toward independence would direct an individual toward searching for work environments that allow freedom of action with few controls. Using these assumptions, Brown has developed a values-based model for life-role decision making.

How Values Are Developed

Brown suggests that values are generally developed through the interaction of inheritance characteristics and experience. He relies on a study by Keller, Bouchard, Arvey, Segal, and Dawis (1992) that supports his position. In their conclusions, genetics accounted for 40% of variance associated with the development of work values, while the remaining 60% was environmentally influenced or was error variance. Brown further supports his assumption by observing that children are exposed to thousands of "values-laden messages" from parents, siblings, other children, many adults, and the media. He suggests that, as children assimilate values-laden messages, values are developed in "bits and pieces" and later form the core of what shapes individual cognitive, affective, and behavioral patterns.

Some values-laden information contains contradictory messages, however, and some developed values conflict with others. In this way, some values are weakened and can cause ambivalent cognitions and subsequent contradictory behavior patterns. Finally, Brown concludes that values are prioritized and crystallized at any given time in their development, but values processing can be greatly affected by an individual's cognitive clarity.

Brown makes it clear that he believes that values have the dominant role in human development. He suggests that values influence all aspects of human functioning but particularly the processing of data one experiences in daily life, although Brown concludes that some values have little effect on cognition because they are not crystallized. He explains that a value becomes crystallized when individuals are able to use that value to explain their behavior: "I am planning to be a social worker because I want to help people."

Values are prioritized by their importance as guides to behavior in one's environment. For instance, when congruence is found in the environment, such as between certain desirable actions and behaviors, values associated with these behaviors are crystallized and subsequently prioritized. However, environmental barriers can block individuals from acting on their value orientation because of their perceptions of the circumstances that discourage actions. For example, a worker desires to put forth more time, energy, and concentration to finish an assignment, but his fellow workers—the power group in this particular work environment—frown on such behavior.

The value systems of environments is an interesting concept of Brown's theory. He sees Holland's theory as a system that identifies the personality of people in an environment, but Brown reflects that this is useful only when there are well-defined boundaries. In complex environments, such as large industrial organizations, the dominant values are established by the "power elite," and their values

become the greatest single determinant in shaping the actions and reactions between individuals and the environment. Thus, complex environments require
careful scrutiny when studying individual behavioral patterns within them.

The Values-Based Model of Career Choice

The six basic propositions for this values-based model are presented here in
abridged form.

1. Individuals prioritize only a small number of values.

2. Highly prioritized values are the most important determinants of life-
   role choices if they meet the following criteria:

   a. One option must be available to satisfy the life-role value.

   b. Options to implement life-role values are clearly delineated.

   c. The difficulty level of implementing each option is the same.

3. Values are acquired through learning from values-laden information in
   the environment. This information is cognitively processed while interacting with the individual's inherited characteristics. Other factors that
   influence social interactions and opportunities are cultural background,
   gender, and socioeconomic level. According to Brown, these factors
   subsequently influence choice of careers and other life roles.

4. Life satisfaction depends on life roles that satisfy all essential values.

5. A role's salience is directly related to the degree of satisfaction of essential values within roles.

6. Success in a life role depends on many factors, some of which are learned
   skills and some of which are cognitive, affective, and physical aptitudes.

Empirical Support

For general information on values, see Rokeach (1973), Crace and Brown (1996),
Locke and Latham (1990), and Judge and Bretz (1992). For more on how values
are developed, see Stimpson, Jensen, and Neff (1992), Leong (1991), and de Vaus
and McCallister (1991).

   More on life-role satisfaction and position can be found in Super (1990), Watson and Ager (1991), and O'Driscoll, Ilgen, and Hildreth (1992). For salience of
role and satisfaction, see Brown and Crace (1995), Chusmir and Parker (1991),
Flannelly (1995), and Posner (1992).

⯈ Summary of Practical Applications

Brown suggests that all career counselors answer the following questions about
their clients: Are there mood problems that will interfere with decision making?

Are the relationships between career and life roles clear to the client? Is there evidence that values have been crystallized and prioritized?

1. In an interview, mood problems are to be carefully scrutinized. Mood problems are anxiety, depression, and other mental health problems (discussed in Chapters 5 and 6).

2. Values are to be assessed by qualitative and quantitative methods. Qualitative methods include card sorts and guided fantasies (Brown, Brooks, & Associates, 1990). Quantitative measures include value inventories and value scales (reviewed in Chapter 7).

3. The discussion of inventory results can also be considered as intervention. Individuals are to be confronted with the question of why—for instance, "Why do you believe this?" and so on. The "why" technique is designed to frustrate the client, thus raising the level of introspection that will lead to conclusions about values.

4. The counselor is to link values with careers with the *Enhanced Guide for Occupational Exploration* (JIST, 1993) and through computerized career exploration programs.

A Contextual Explanation of Career

The *Contextualism* method establishes a contextual action explanation of career research and career counseling. Contextualism is based on the philosophical position known as *constructivism* (Brown, Brooks, & Associates, 1996). According to Sharf (1996), the constructivist position suggests "that individuals construct their own way of organizing information and that truth or reality is a matter of perception" (p. 405). Understanding how clients construct personal meanings from present actions and subsequent experiences is the core of this theory.

The contextual model for human development is an ever-changing, ongoing interplay of forces. The major focus is on the relationship between person and environment because they are considered to be inseparable and are regarded as a unit. As people and the environment interact, development can proceed along many different pathways, depending on how one influences the other (Sigelman & Shaffer, 1995).

Young, Valach, and Collin (1996) propose that one way to understand a contextualist explanation of career counseling is by action theory. Action, in this sense, focuses on the whole in the context in which action is taken. For example, a career counselor, client, and a worker in the field the client is currently interested in have a discussion about the work, peer affiliates, and work environment. The total action of all three people is the context in which this particular counseling took place, and their actions form the basis for constructing personal meaning. To break the process into parts would be similar to unraveling an event into meaningless fragmentation. Thus, the wholeness of an event and the succession of changes that result from interaction with others and their contexts is the contextualist perspective. In essence, contextualists support the idea that events take shape as people engage in them, and only then is an analysis of actions and events practical.

The study of actions is the major focus of the contextual viewpoint. Actions are conceptualized as being cognitively and socially directed and as reflecting everyday experiences; actions are social processes and, as such, reflect each individual's social and cultural world. Actions are viewed from three perspectives: they manifest behavior, for example, taking notes of a lecture; they are internal processes, like feeling nervous about an examination; and they have social meaning, such as being successful in a career.

Action systems are composed of joint and individual actions and two terms referred to as *project* and *career. Joint actions* simply means that many career-related actions occur among people. According to the contextualist point of view, career values, interests, identity, and behaviors are constructed largely through language in conversation with others. Instead of evaluating the discussions individually between client and counselor, the contextualist conceptualizes joint action as a unit between client and counselor. The major focus here is on the action of the dyad.

Project refers to an agreement of actions between two or more people. For example, a single parent and adolescent child form an agreement of household responsibilities so that both may work. Because of changing work conditions and working hours, parent and child renegotiate responsibilities. In this example, individual and joint actions—including manifest actions—internal processes, and social meaning contribute to the project. The parent's and the child's behavior can be interpreted individually and jointly by this project.

The term *career,* as used in this theory, is similar to the term *project.* It can also be used to construct connections among actions and to evaluate plans, goals, emotions, and internal cognitions. The major difference between project and career is that career extends over a longer period of time and subsequently involves more actions. The actions can become complex and include greater social meaning. In this way, career approximates the idea of vocation.

The authors of this theory have developed an aspects-of-action theory to illustrate action systems, perspectives on action, and levels of action organization. Levels of action organization include elements, functional steps, and goals.

Elements refer to physical and verbal behavior, such as words, movements, and environmental structures. *Functional steps* refer to higher-level actions than elements—for example, pleading and reminding can be used to convey a desired action. *Goals,* the highest level of action, usually represent the general intention of the individual or group.

The major purpose of defining actions in this manner is to organize the interpretation of human actions. Interpretation within this script offers a systematic method of evaluating and interpreting actions and the context in which they happen—what the counselor and client are doing together.

Much more research is needed on how a person affects the environment and how the environment affects the person, particularly, an individual's career development. As we learn more about the ecology within which significant interactions occur, we may discover some dimensions that are relevant to career development.

A good description of how both individuals and the world interact is by Vondracek, Lerner, and Schulenberg (1986) who see "levels of being" as multiple dimensions of interdependent forces that are developing and changing over time. This is a very complex person-context model that will take time to delineate in research.

As we direct our attention to career choice, the effects of salient contextual interactions have some very important implications for career counseling. Our perception of the individual in context can be somewhat conceptualized when we consider individual and environment as a circular interaction in which an individual brings unique characteristics to environment, the demands of the environment suggest behavioral attributes from important others. This process influences the individual to either adjust or find fit. The relationship between an individual's unique characteristics and environment is the trigger to determining if there is a goodness of fit. Thus, the person-context, in terms of goodness of fit, provides insights into the significant influences from each event in the life span (Vondracek, Lerner, & Schulenberg, 1986). For example, one individual might be greatly influenced to limit career choice according to the mores of his environment, while another might not vocally express his lack of agreement, but will adapt his behavior to find some fit in the environment until support is given for a change of career direction.

Empirical Support

For more on action theory, see Polkinghorne (1990) and von Cranach and Harre (1982). For discussions on context and environment, see Holland (1992) and Krumboltz and Nichols (1990). For more on this theory in general, see Valach (1990), Young and Valach (1996), Shotter (1993), Richardson (1993), and Hermans (1992).

⟶ Summary of Practical Applications

1. Counselors must be aware of clients' conceptualizations, concepts, and constructs during the interview process and other discussions.
2. Counselors should help clients become aware of their constructs by offering support. Support could come by discussing identified constructs.
3. Clients should also be assisted in constructing a narrative, which could have the theme of frequently mentioned topics. Client and counselor should discuss the narrative with the goal of discovering the context of their lives (Young, Valach, & Collin, 1996).
4. Through joint action activities, client and counselor develop joint goals.

Self-Efficacy Theory

Most early career development theories were devoted to explaining the career development of men. Only recently has there been an attempt to explain gender differences. Some research has noted that women underuse abilities and talents, whereas other research has pointed out differences in the developmental processes of women and men (Betz & Fitzgerald, 1987). But currently we do not have a definitive career development theory for women.

One of the most promising theories that may lend itself to addressing gender differences is Hackett and Betz's (1981) self-efficacy theory that is based primarily on Bandura's (1977, 1986) social learning theory. The brief explanation that follows identifies only some major constructs of these theories. More information on self-efficacy theory can be found in Hackett and Betz (1981) and in this chapter's previous section on career development from a social cognitive perspective.

Bandura's social learning theory emphasizes that self-efficacy involves an individual's thoughts and images that influence psychological functioning. For example, an individual's belief in his or her ability to perform certain tasks determines whether the individual will attempt those tasks and how well he or she will perform. Self-efficacy also determines the intensity of an individual's effort, as explained by Bandura (1989):

> Those who have a high sense of efficacy visualize success scenarios that provide positive guides for performance, and they cognitively rehearse good solutions to potential problems. Those who judge themselves as inefficacious are more inclined to visualize failure scenarios and to dwell on how things will go wrong. Such inefficacious thinking weakens motivation and undermines performance. (p. 729)

Hackett and Betz (1981) suggest that women who believe they are incapable of performing certain tasks (low self-efficacy) limit their career mobility and restrict their career options. Also, women are hindered in developing self-efficacy when they find themselves in work environments that are less responsive to women than to men and that do not equally reward their accomplishments. Furthermore, self-efficacy is affected by a history of restricted options and underutilization of abilities. Thus, women who judge their efficacy to be low tend to give up, procrastinate, and avoid career decisions. This theory, as with many of the others mentioned in this chapter, will undoubtedly be further developed as guidelines for career development counseling and intervention strategies to meet the needs of clientele.

Convergence of Career Development Theories

There has been growing movement, particularly among vocational psychologists, to unify existing theories of career development. This movement has many roots, but the main driving force appears to be a recognition of an increasing interest in career development theories per se and the desire to bring vocational psychology out of isolation from other psychological disciplines—namely, developmental, social, cross-cultural, personality, and issues involving gender studies. Moreover, practitioners have long complained that career development theories have added little to their knowledge of how to produce beneficial results in clients, with the exception of Sharf (1996) and Jepsen (1986), who have demonstrated how theories have addressed counseling practice (Savickas, 1995). Savickas (1995) has also

■ DIVERSITY ISSUES ■

The authors of CIP theory contend that they have provided a framework for understanding how cultural background influences knowledge structures and thought processes. CIP theory says that culture and ethnic groups influence career choice in a variety of ways by contextual interactions. Through the CIP paradigm, displayed and discussed in Chapter 4, individuals can be assisted in identifying salient variables that influence thought processes.

Likewise, the SCCT career theory provides a mechanism of reference points for implementing intervention strategies for diverse populations. SCCT theorists suggest that a major hurdle involved in career choice has to do with contextual environmental influences. Those who have experienced less opportunity and support have difficulty in translating their goals into action.

In the values-based model of career choice, the concept of a value systems of environments is used to illustrate how dominant values are developed. Differences in cultural background, gender, and socioeconomic level greatly determine social interactions and opportunities and the priorities allocated to values. Thus, counselors should evaluate clients from the perspective of how values were developed and their influence on career choice.

A contextual explanation of career supports the position that one should attempt to learn how an individual has influenced his or her own development within contextual interactions. The conceptualization of these processes provides the individual with a fuller understanding of how a vocational role is developed. The socialization process afforded from history-bound features of environments can enlighten individuals about the sources of occupational knowledge and perceptions of career goals.

Few studies have been published on the relevance of self-efficacy theory for ethnic minority groups. Because of limited exposure of occupational information among some ethnic minority groups, occupational self-efficacy may be limited. Self-efficacy theory is most relevant to the career development of women.

pointed out two other schisms that have heated the convergence debate among researchers and practitioners. First, many psychologists continue to view career counseling as a subdiscipline of psychotherapy (Blustein, 1990). Some psychotherapists have argued that career counselors should adopt models or methods from psychotherapy. Second, prominent researchers in career development theory have not operationally defined constructs in the same way; instead, they have taken a developmental, differential, or decisional perspective pathway to explore vocational behavior. Furthermore, current approaches to career development theory use different operational definitions, which have contributed to the problems of research integration.

There seems to be some current justification for encouragement among career development theorists and researchers from other disciplines that theory convergence is moving ahead (Staats, 1981). Although the past emphasis on the uniqueness of theoretical approaches has created diversity through disparate views, Krumboltz and Nichols (1990) have proposed methods of bridging theories and reducing redundancy. For instance, they propose a cross-theoretical framework in which theories' major aspects can be examined and the contributing theorists can be free to maintain their particular interests. Thus, both convergence and individual initiative can be maintained.

In 1992, a career intervention special-interest group of the Counseling Psychology Division in the American Psychological Association met to discuss issues and merits of unifying the theories of career choice and development. According to Savickas (1995), although most researchers saw more disadvantages than advantages in a unification project, most did agree on theory "renovation" to clarify the constructs and purpose of theories. The major disadvantages of theory unification presented at the meeting were as follows (Savickas, 1995, pp. 9–10).

1. Unification could discourage counselors' creativity in forming their own theories.

2. Unification efforts might be premature because unification requires a larger empirical base than is now available.

3. Convergence and unification should be empirical questions, rather than literary projects.

4. Quick integration could lead to ambiguous constructs drawn from different theories.

5. Constructive, piecemeal theory building is better.

6. A unification project might force a political agenda on theorists.

7. Committees cannot construct theories.

8. The most that a unification project could achieve would be convergence in terminology, not in philosophy or theory.

9. Postmodern approaches to science are moving toward pluralism, not unity.

10. In emphasizing convergence, researchers might ignore interesting aspects of each theory.

Of significant concern to career counselors was the proposal that the *concept of career may not have a future* (Collin, 1994). The argument supporting the death of "career" as a concept centers around (1) the current restructuring of the work force and changing operational procedures in large organizations, and (2) the fact that large bureaucratic organizations that lend support to current concepts of career, such as career ladders, are disappearing (Hammer & Champy, 1993; Meister, 1994; Reich, 1991).

According to Collin (1994), organizations are changing to become more flexible, elastic, and adaptive. To survive, organizations must change slow-paced operating procedures to meet the needs of the 21st-century information age; organizations must be able to react more quickly than the bureaucratic organization does and must adapt to changing environments. There is a need for what is referred to as "elastic" employment contracts to respond to changing demands. For example, workers would be summoned when needed, but in the meantime they would be a reserve army of labor. The new metaphor for career will be the worker's portfolio of developed skills, rather than the individual's position on the career ladder and the passage through stages within bureaucratic organizations.

The debate about the procedures career development researchers should follow will continue. To more fully understand the components of the debate, read the references cited in this discussion. In the meantime, researchers have followed the recommendations of Walsh, Craik, and Price (1992), Walsh and Chartrand (1994), and Rychlak (1993), using the framework provided by theories of action discussed previously in this chapter.

Savickas (1995) suggests that the framework that theories of action provide should offer interpretative potential for vocational psychology and research. In sum, the theory of action addresses personal traits that might influence the career choice process. Second, research would focus on the external environment; social learning and social cognitive models of vocation behavior would be delineated. The third dimension includes person-environment transaction theories, in particular, the fit between individual and environment. Finally, research efforts would include developmental contextualism that emphasizes the person and the context as coexisting and as continually defining each other.

Implications for Career Guidance

A clearer understanding of the decision-making process is a major goal of cognitive theory. An understanding of self-knowledge, occupational knowledge, information processing skills, and metacognitions no doubt will provide the career counselor with valuable information to use in educational programs as well as for intervention strategies.

Career counselors must also consider sociological variables as important information in the counseling process. Social class, for example, has been used as an important variable that influences career choice. Environmental influences and personal agency are key concepts that act as interacting influences that shape behavior.

Values should be given a greater role in the career development process. How values are developed should be a growing concern of the career guidance profession. Values as a dominating role in influencing human development will provide clues about why and how decisions are made.

A clearer understanding of the relationship between person and environment should subsequently lead to clearer understanding of perceptions an individual has learned from his or her environment. One way to understand this process is to observe the actions of people in context. The pathways one follows to construct personal meaning from interacting with people in an environment will provide guidelines for counseling intervention.

The proposition of self-efficacy is a means of judging the nature of career development for women. Those career behaviors that limit career choice for women are significant factors for developing educational and counseling programs for both sexes.

Finally, an agreement among theorists and researchers of terms and constructs used in theory development should provide more guidelines for building practical applications of both established and evolving theories. Furthermore, other academic disciplines will have greater accessibility to contributing to the career counseling profession. As the pervasive nature of career counseling is recognized, it should rightfully be given equal status with other counseling endeavors.

Summary

1. Cognitive information theory has been applied to career development relative to how one makes a career decision. A sequential procedure has been developed to help individuals process information so they can make career decisions in their own best interests.

2. Career development from a social cognitive perspective is embedded in general social cognitive theory, which blends cognitive, self-regulatory, and motivational processes into lifelong phenomena. This theory seeks (a) to find definitions of specific mediators from which learning experiences shape career behavior; (b) to explain how interests, abilities, and values interrelate; and (c) to determine the contextual factors that lead to outcomes. Social beliefs and expectations are the mechanisms through which self-efficacy deficits are developed, particularly for women.

3. A values-based approach to career development assumes that one's functioning is greatly influenced and shaped by one's value orientation. Several other assumptions of this theory are that (a) values are most important in career decision-making processes because they provide the direction to setting goals; (b) values are strong determinants in rationalizing behavior roles; and (c) values are developed through the interaction of inherited characteristics and experiences.

4. The contextual model for human development is an ever-changing and ongoing interplay of forces. The major focus is on the relationship between person and environment, which are considered as a unit. The study of actions is the major focus of the contextual viewpoint. Actions are viewed from three perspectives: they manifest behavior, they are internal processes, and they have social meaning.

5. There is a growing movement to unify existing theories of career development. One goal of this movement is to bring vocational psychology out of isolation from other psychological disciplines. Most researchers of career development theories have resisted theory unification but have agreed to renovate theories to clarify their constructs and purpose.

TABLE OF BASIC ASSUMPTIONS, KEY TERMS, AND OUTCOMES

Theory	Basic Assumptions
Career Development from a Cognitive Information Processing Perspective	Ten basic assumptions of this theory are outlined and explained in Table 3-1. Two overarching assumptions are facilitating the growth of information-processing skills and enhancing the client's ability to solve problems and make career decisions.
Career Development from a Social Cognitive Perspective	This theory is embedded in general social cognitive theory, which blends cognitive, self, regulatory, and motivational processes into a lifelong phenomenon. Personal and physical attributes, external environmental factors, and overt behavior all interact as casual influences on individual development.
Brown's Values-Based, Holistic Model of Career and Life-Role Choices and Satisfaction	Human functioning is greatly influenced by value orientation. Standards and rules by which we judge actions are value based. Thus, values greatly influence the desired career outcome.
A Contextual Explanation of Career	As people and their environments interact, development can proceed along many different pathways, depending on how one influences the other. A developmental-contextual life span assumes that interacting with a changing environment provides a foundation for individuals to form their own development.
Self-Efficacy Theory	An individual's belief in his or her ability to perform certain tasks determines whether the individual will attempt those tasks and how well he or she will perform.

Supplementary Learning Exercises

1. Compare one evolving theory with an established one. What are your conclusions?

Key Terms	Outcomes
CASVE involves the following generic processing skills: *Communication* (identifying a need), *Analysis* (interrelating problem components), *Synthesis* (creating likely alternatives), *Valuing* (prioritizing alternatives), and *Execution* (forming means-end strategies).	Career problem solving is primarily a cognitive process. Information-processing can be improved through learning. Effective information-processing skills can empower individuals to determine their own destiny. Making career choices is a problem-solving activity.
Personal agency reflects how a person exerts power to achieve a solution. *Triadic reciprocal interactions,* as explained in the basic assumptions, are from Bandura's (1986) social learning theory.	Self-efficacy is strengthened when success is experienced in a performance domain and is weakened with repeated failures; outcome expectations are shaped by similar experiences. Personal goals and/or personal agency act to sustain behavior. Career choice is influenced by environmental factors. Overcoming barriers to choice is a significant goal of this theory.
Values are developed through interaction of inheritance and experiences. Value-laden sources of messages are parents, siblings, other children, many adults and media.	Individuals prioritize only a small number of values. Values of high priority are major determinants of life-role choices. Values are acquired through interactions in the environment. Life satisfaction is highly related to one's values. The perception of a role's importance depends on the satisfaction of essential values within the role.
Contextualism is a method of describing events or actions in an individual's life and a way in which counselors understand influences in career development from an individual's environmental interactions. *Actions* refer to the whole context in which an action is taken, how events take shape as people engage in them.	The study of actions is the major focus of the contextual viewpoint. Actions manifest behavior, they are internal processes, and they have social meaning. Environmental actions are to be observed from a "wholeness," that is, the influence of events that people engage in. Events take shape as people engage in them, and the totality of the actions and events influences participants.
Self-efficacy involves an individual's thoughts and images that influence psychological functioning. Self-efficacy determines the intensity of an individual's effort. Low self-efficacy limits career mobility and restricts career options.	Inefficacious thinking weakens motivation and undermines performance. Self-efficacy is to be viewed as a set of beliefs about a performance domain. Individuals limit career choice because of low self-efficacy.

2. List differences and agreements between a social cognitive perspective of career development and Krumboltz's learning theory of career choice and counseling (Chapter 2).

3. Are values more important than interests in career choice? State reasons for your position.

4. Follow the example for the Individual Learning Plan found in the cognitive information processing conceptual perspective and develop one for yourself. Explain the counseling interventions.

5. Develop a script for three individuals who are exchanging career information. Use a contextual explanation of career as a model to describe how actions influence the three individuals in the script.

6. Compare two theories to determine similarities and differences. What are your conclusions?

7. Should career development theories converge? Debate as teams or individually.

8. If you agree that self-efficacy influences career decisions, which sex does it affect most? Give your reasons.

9. Draw up a list of values that have greatly influenced your life. Use the results of an interest inventory to determine your interests. Can you explain how the values you listed influenced your measured interests?

10. Debate the pros and cons of the following statement: Career development theories lead to nowhere.

For More Information

Betz, N. E. (1992b). Counseling uses of career self-efficacy theory. *Career Development Quarterly, 41,* 22–26.

Brown, D., Brooks, L., & Associates. (1996). *Career choice and development* (3rd ed.). San Francisco: Jossey-Bass.

Hackett, G. (1995). Self-efficacy in career choice and development. In A. Bandura (Ed.), *Self-efficacy in changing societies* (pp. 232–258). Cambridge, U. K.: Cambridge University Press.

Peterson, G. W., Sampson, J. P., & Reardon, R. C. (1991). *Career development and services: A cognitive approach.* Pacific Grove, CA: Brooks/Cole.

Savickas, M. L. (1995). Current theoretical issues in vocational psychology: Convergence, divergence, and schism. In W. B. Walsh, & S. H. Osipow (Eds.), *Handbook of vocational psychology* (2nd ed.) (pp. 1–34). Hillsdale, NJ: Erlbaum.

Savickas, M. L., & Walsh, W. B. (Eds.). (1996). *Handbook of career counseling theory and practice.* Palo Alto, CA: Davies-Black.

Young, R. A., & Valach, L. (1996). Interpretation and action in career counseling. In M. L. Savickas & W. B. Walsh (Eds.), *Handbook of career counseling theory and practice.* Palo Alto, CA: Davies-Black.

Career Counseling Models

Chapter Highlights

- *Relevant issues and concepts emerging from model development*

- *Suggestions for career guidance from a career life planning model*

- *Trait-and-factor and person-environment-fit model*

- *Developmental model*

- *Learning theory model*

- *Cognitive information processing approach model*

- *Multicultural career counseling model for ethnic women*

- *Model summary of counseling goals, intake interview techniques, use of assessment, diagnosis, and counseling process*

THE CAREER DEVELOPMENT RESEARCH INTRODUCED IN THE TWO PRECEDing chapters has successfully produced guidelines for career counseling practice. However, the working relationship between practicing counselors and those who do career development research has been less than ideal, and researchers continue to search for more effective ways to communicate (Savickas & Walsh, 1996). An interesting assessment of the current status between researchers and practitioners was suggested by Arbona (1996) and Lucas (1996), who point out that career development theories should not be expected to completely guide practice. Arbona and Lucas conclude that research answers theoretical questions but the counselor needs answers to questions that focus on actual practice. Lucas (1996) suggests one solution to this problem: Counselors should build a file of effective mini-theories from their own experiences.

In a related publication, Harmon (1996) suggests that the gap between counseling skills and the current needs of a changing diverse society has increased, making it imperative for counselors to upgrade their training. Clearly, future career counselors should not only be familiar with career development research but also with effective techniques, procedures, and materials used in contemporary models that can be used for building new approaches for the future.

In this chapter we introduce four career counseling models that are embedded in career development theory. A fifth model has been developed for a specific ethnic/racial group. The career counseling models discussed in this chapter present suggestions for building a repertoire of practical applications that can serve as a foundation for career counseling models of the future.

First, we briefly discuss some basic issues and concepts that have emerged from model development. Next, five career counseling models are outlined and described. The final section is a table that summarizes the major parameters of the five models followed by a brief discussion of the parameters.

Other career counseling models can be found in Chapters 11, 12, 14, and 15 within the context of discussion of special groups. The next four chapters contain techniques used in career counseling models. Chapters 5 and 6 suggest techniques for intake interviewing while Chapters 7 and 8 cover the use of assessment in career counseling.

Some Issues and Concepts Emerging from Model Development

During the early development of career counseling models, the trait-and-factor approach received the most attention and has survived as a viable part of current trait-oriented models. In fact, Brown and Brooks (1991) point out that it may be the most popular theory among contemporary models. The key characteristic of this theory is the assumption that clients have unique traits that can be matched with requirements of occupations. This is often referred to as an *actuarial* method of predicting success in an occupation from the client's measured trait characteristics and is also associated with what is characterized as *objective data* (valid standardized test scores) rather than as *subjective* information or information clients reveal about themselves and perceptions of their environment, usually in an interview. The terms *actuarial, objective,* and *subjective* data are often mentioned in current career counseling models.

Diagnosis of client problems, at times referred to as appraisal or simply as problem identification, has involved some interesting criteria. Crites (1981) suggested three types of diagnosis—*differential, dynamic,* and *decisional. Differential* diagnosis is based on individual psychology, that is, how individuals differ from norms, and identifies the client's problems in such categories as undecided or indecisive. The focus is on describing the client's problems. A *dynamic* diagnosis is concerned with the reasons *why* the client has problems and may identify them as irrational beliefs, anxiety, or lack of information. A *decisional* diagnosis infers that the client's decision-making style, especially the process, should be addressed.

Three client labels that have been used extensively are *decided, undecided,* or *indecisive. Decided* clients are those who have made a career decision. These clients might profit from counseling that is designed to formulate other steps in decision making and to determine if choice was inappropriately made.

Undecided clients have not made a career decision but might not view their current status as a problem; they prefer to delay making a commitment. The prevalent developmental view of this client is an uninformed immature person who generally lacks self knowledge, information about occupations, or both. Yet, from another perspective, *undecided* clients could be described as multipotential individuals; they have the competencies to pursue several different types of careers.

The *indecisive* client is characterized as one who has a high level of anxiety accompanied by dysfunctional thinking. This client type is often labeled as not having cognitive clarity or as having irrational beliefs. For instance, the *indecisive* client could have problems embedded in a personality disorder that might be accompanied by depression. In general, clients with this label lack self confidence, tolerance for ambiguity, and a sense of identity. These clients often need psychotherapy or personal counseling before they can benefit from career counseling, although both personal and career needs can be introduced simultaneously (Meara, 1996).

The following diagnostic systems are often used as guidelines for designating client problems: an extensive diagnostic taxonomy by Campbell and Cellini (1981); diagnostic and treatment suggestions by Rounds and Tinsley (1984); categories and suggested treatment by Kinnier and Krumboltz (1984); and a classification of problems suggested by Holland, Daiger, and Power (1980). In sum, contemporary models employ a combination of diagnostic criteria for specifying tailored interventions to meet specific client needs.

Finally, Gysbers and Moore (1987) have envisioned the career counseling process as Life Career Planning in which a strategy is created to help clients embark on a career path that might involve a series of occupations. This plan is very inclusive and incorporates family and leisure roles. In this model the career counseling process has two major phases and several subphases as follows:

I. Client goal or problem identification, clarification, and specification

    A. Establishing a client-counselor relationship including client-counselor responsibilities

    B. Gathering client self and environmental information to understand the client's goal or problem

        1. Who is the client?

            a. How does the client view himself or herself, others, and his or her world?

            b. What language does the client use to represent these views?

            c. What themes does the client use to organize and direct his or her behavior based on views?

        2. What is the client's current status and environment?

            a. Client's life roles, settings, and events

            b. Relationship to client's goal or problem

    C. Understanding client self- and environmental information by sorting, analyzing, and relating such information to client's goal or problem through

        1. Career development theories

        2. Counseling theories

        3. Classification systems

    D. Drawing conclusions; making diagnosis

II. Client goal or problem resolution

    A. Taking action; interventions selected based on diagnosis. Some examples of interventions include counseling techniques, testing, personal styles analyses, career and labor market information, individual career plans, occupational card sorts, and computerized information and decision systems.

    B. Evaluating the impact of the interventions used; did interventions resolve the client's goal or problem?

        1. If goal or problem was not resolved, recycle.

        2. If goal or problem was resolved, close counseling relationship.

SOURCE: From *Career Counseling: Skills and Techniques for Practitioners*, by N. C. Gysbers & E. J. Moore, p. 172. Copyright 1987 by Prentice-Hall, Inc. Reprinted by permission.

    The impact of this conception of career counseling has not been fully appreciated; however, the very inclusive nature of this process suggests that career counseling is not simply dealing with static states of human behavior but, rather, with complex adaptive systems. Also, career counseling is not linear (choose, be trained, and be happy ever after); rather, it is multidimensional, involving interacting contextual variables and sophisticated cognitive domains that process information in an ever-changing environment. Finally, career counseling is future oriented. Career development is both a continuous and discontinuous process that requires clients to learn, adapt, make changes, and develop all life roles.

Five Career Counseling Models

Five career counseling models represent a broad spectrum of career counseling strategies that are directed toward a common goal of assisting clients make a career decision. Each of the following models is introduced with some brief comments about its origins: trait-and-factor and person-environment-fit (PEF), developmental, learning theory, cognitive information processing approach (CIP), and multicultural cultural career counseling model for ethnic women. Review Chapters 2 and 3 for background information on the career development theory for the first four models. The first model, trait-and-factor and PEF includes two different career development theories. The developmental model was primarily drawn from Super's (1957, 1980) work, the learning theory model from Mitchell and Krumboltz (1996), and the CIP approach from Peterson, Sampson, and Reardon (1991). The background information for the multicultural career counseling model is contained in Chapter 10. All the models are flexible enough to include occupational classification systems such as Holland's Classification System, assessment instruments discussed in Chapters 7 and 8, and a variety of occupational information resources, including written materials, computer generated materials, and multimedia aids.

The point here is that the career counseling models described in the following pages can use the very popular Holland Typology approach and materials, some of which were described in Chapter 2. All the models discussed endorse an individualized approach to career counseling. Individual needs, therefore, dictate the kind and type of assessment instruments used and the materials and procedures used in the counseling process.

Because occupational information is an important part of intervention strategies in the five counseling models described in this section, some suggestions for its effective use are summarized. The following recommendations for the effective acquisition of occupational information have been compiled by Spokane (1991) and are paraphrased as follows:

1. When exploring occupations, counselors should urge clients to record both negative and positive reactions to each occupation. Both disconfirming and confirming reactions can suggest personal constructs that need further evaluation.

2. Counselors should have clients complete a list of occupations that are most congruent with their interests and abilities and those occupations that are rated as acceptable. Clients should begin with a broad-based exploration and follow it with a more focused, complete study. This process is considered most effective in confirming congruency.

3.   Sources of occupational information that are close (proximal) such as parents or friends should be followed by more distal information (farthest) such as a job site. Counselors should prepare clients to focus their research efforts to more in-depth study of occupations (distal) from which more accurate information can be obtained.

4.   Career exploration involves both behavioral and cognitive processes; however; a framework for processing information, such as a form that requires clients to record relevant information, allows clients to derive the most benefits. Counselors can most effectively present sources of information when clients indicate readiness and an expressed interest in the information.

Trait-and-Factor and Person-Environment-Fit

The brief discussion of the historical development of trait-and-factor theory in Chapter 2 points out its controversial development. On the one hand, trait-and-factor theory is viewed as promoting a very simplistic counseling process that is characterized by "three interviews and a cloud of dust" (Crites, 1981, p. 49), whereas others have argued that the applied concepts of the theory represent a misinterpretation of what Parsons (1909) and later Williamson (1939) intended (Brown, Brooks, & Associates, 1990; Rounds & Tracey, 1990; Spokane, 1991, and Swanson, 1996). What appears to have been a theory that met society's needs in the 1930s, within the role and scope of counseling practices at that time, was eventually viewed as a counselor-dominated, very inflexible, simplistic, and extremely test-oriented method.

Current proponents of trait-and-factor approaches strongly suggest that Williamson advocated multiple sources of client information, including subjective domains of cognitive and affective processing. Williamson's (1939) own words about analysis, the first step in his model, supports their observation as follows: "Collecting data from many sources about attitudes, interests, family background, knowledge, educational progress, aptitudes, etc., by means of both subjective and objective techniques" (p. 215). Furthermore, the counseling processes used in trait-and-factor approaches suggest that this is a rational problem-solving approach similar to career counseling models currently in vogue (Rounds & Tracey, 1990; Swanson, 1996). In fact, the basic assumptions of trait-and-factor theory can be easily translated into practice and, with some modifications designed to meet contemporary societal needs, represent a viable philosophical basis for use *within* current career counseling models. What is needed, according to Rounds and Tracey (1990) and Swanson (1996) is to converge relevant trait-and-factor formulations within currently updated models of career development theory.

Trait-and-Factor and Person-Environment-Fit (PEF) Converge

During the last decade we have seen a gradual convergence of trait-and-factor methods and procedures with person-environment-fit constructs—also referred to as person-environment-correspondence in its early development (Rounds & Tracey, 1990). In general terms, some trait-and-factor methods have been adapted to determine person-environment-fit, but significant changes have also occurred: (1) both cognitive and affective processes are now involved; (2) clinical information and qualitative data are included in the appraisal process; and (3) the counselor's role has shifted from a directive approach to one in which counselor and client negotiate and collaborate (Swanson, 1996).

The following career counseling model has been extrapolated from several sources (Dawis, 1996; Rounds & Tracey, 1990; Swanson, 1996) and should be considered as examples of possible counseling procedures suggested by these authors and explicitly delineated in a career counseling model by Walsh (1990). The following model includes seven stages, which will be briefly described.

Stage 1. Intake Interview
- a. Establish client-counselor collaboration relationship
- b. Gather background information
- c. Assess emotional status and cognitive clarity
- d. Observe personality style

Stage 2. Identify Developmental Variables
- a. Perception of self and environment
- b. Environmental variables
- c. Contextual interactions
- d. Gender variables
- e. Minority group status

Stage 3. Assessment
- a. Ability patterns
- b. Values
- c. Reinforcer requirements
- d. Interests
- e. Information-processing skills

Stage 4. Identify and Solve Problems
- a. Affective status
- b. Self-knowledge needs
- c. Level of information-processing skills

Stage 5. Generate PEF Analysis
- a. Cognitive schema

　　b. Criteria on which to base choice

　　c. Optimal prediction system

Stage 6. Confirm, Explore, and Decide

　　a. Counselor and client confirm PEF analysis

　　b. Client explores potential work environments

　　c. Client makes a decision

Stage 7. Follow-up

　　a. Evaluate progress

　　b. Recycle if necessary

Dawis (1996) suggests that the major goal of PEF is the enhancement of self-knowledge. Clients who have developed an adequate self-identity are better equipped to self-assess potential satisfaction and congruence with work environments. Thus, self-knowledge promotes optimal career selection.

In Stage 1, the *Intake Interview* begins with the client and counselor forming a compatible working relationship. Counselors do not assume an authority-expert role; rather, they build a relationship in which they will share responsibility and negotiate options in a collaborative manner.

Background information includes a biographical history that can be obtained from a questionnaire and through discussion. Information about the client's environmental influences are a high priority. During the interview, the counselor evaluates the emotional status of the client and the client's cognitive clarity. Personality style and personality characteristics are also observed. The information obtained in the intake interview is used throughout the counseling process. For example, background variables are used to evaluate personality structure and style. Any problems that surfaced are further evaluated in the stages that follow.

In Stage 2, *Identify Developmental Variables,* the information obtained in the intake interview is reviewed to account for important elements that are involved in PEF counseling such as perception. Perception in this context refers to perception of self, such as one's identity, self-concept or self-image and, in addition, perception of environment, that is, its requirements, reinforcers, and demands. Environmental variables and contextual interactions are evaluated to determine a client's opportunities, relevant experiences, and limitations. Restrictions of developmental opportunities from environmental variables for women and minority groups are particularly important.

Assessment, in Stage 3, involves a comprehensive evaluation of the client's cognitive abilities, values, and interests. These measured traits are used with other variables to determine a client's reinforcement needs found in occupational environments. Thus, the major purpose of this information is to match client needs with occupations or groups of occupations that are predicted to result in satisfaction (self-fulfillment) and satisfactoriness (achievement).

Information-processing skills are important for clients to appropriately process information presented to them in PEF counseling. Those clients who need assistance for processing information are assigned intervention strategies designed to improve these skills before PEF counseling continues. More details about information processing skills can be found in stage 4.

In Stage 4, *Identify and Solve Problems,* information gathered in the first three stages is used to identify any affective concerns, self-knowledge needs, and the client's level of information processing. Clients who are identified as having serious emotional problems or dysfunctional thinking are referred for psychotherapy or for a complete psychological evaluation. Clients who have unrealistic or faulty beliefs about self-perceptions or perceptions of work environments or both are provided with tailored intervention strategies designed to assist them.

Career counseling, according to Rounds and Tracey (1990), must focus on information-processing skills for making optimal career decisions and especially for determining person-environment-fit. Adhering to this position, differential diagnosis of client problems and subsequent treatment decisions are major objectives of an effective career counseling model. To evaluate specificity of client information-processing problems and to develop appropriate timing of intervention strategies, Rounds and Tracey (1990) have adapted Anderson's (1985) Adaptive Control of Thought theory as a primary focus to determine types of treatment and intervention. Briefly, this theory proclaims that there are three types of knowledge bases: *working* (active, conscious thought), *declarative* (knowledge of facts), and *procedural* (processing the relationship between different pieces of knowledge). Beginners using a trial-and-error procedure tend to use declarative knowledge, whereas experts use procedural knowledge, that is, experts are able to process the relationship of different knowledge and information in decision making. This process in turn involves four steps of information processing: *encoding* (sorting out the information's meaning), *goal setting, plan development and pattern matching,* and *action.* Each step is briefly described in Box 4-1.

In Stage 5, *Generate PEF Analysis,* the counselor and client develop a cognitive schema or a conceptual framework to direct the search for PEF. In this context each client's ability patterns are used to predict satisfactoriness in different occupations. Values and personality style are used to predict satisfaction with certain occupations and also to describe the client's reinforcer requirements. An occupational classification system is used to locate occupations for abilities required and reinforcers provided. The next step is to list occupations that correspond to the client's satisfaction and satisfactoriness needs. Within this procedure, clients find congruent occupations and choose one that is the optimal fit. The prediction system is more accurate when the client's dominant orientation (satisfactoriness or satisfaction) is known. An illustration of PEF analysis is given Case 4-1.

Finally, for ethnic groups for which appropriate tests are not available, counselors obtain qualitative information from focused questions, contextual interactions, and nonstandardized exercises as demonstrated in Chapter 8.

Stage 6, *Confirm, Explore, and Decide,* begins when counselor and client review test data and the prediction analysis to determine if the client is comfortable with the results. If the client does not agree with work environments that are predicted to be congruent, recycling in the model may be recommended.

BOX 4-1 # Assessing Level of Information Processing

a. *Encoding* involves the client's perception and interpretation of information. For example, client can recognize relevant advantages and limitations of an occupation.

b. *Goal setting* is best accomplished by concrete, realistic steps in an organized sequential process. For example, recognizing procedural requirements to reach goals.

c. *Effective plan development and pattern matching* involves establishing alternative solutions, several means of reaching goals, and considering the consequences of actions taken.

d. In the *action* step, the client selects an appropriate behavior to solve problems exposed in previous steps.

Rounds and Tracey (1990) also point out that effective information processing includes active and conscious deliberation, which is referred to as central processing, rather than peripheral processing. The counselor's rapport with a client and the counselor's behavior in presenting information can negatively influence the client's motivation to process information and is referred to as peripheral processing. Thus, if clients appear not to be motivated, the counselor should focus on persuasion cues that are related to counselor behavior of projecting warmth, trustworthiness, and competence.

In sum, treatment interventions are a function of the following:

1. Level of client information processing

2. Client motivation

3. Relative progress in the counseling process" (Rounds & Tracey, 1990, p. 30).

Client levels of information processing are rated as very high, high, medium, and low. Very high levels of information processing indicate clients who have demonstrated competence in the four stages (encoding, goal setting, pattern matching, and action selection) as described earlier. Clients at this level need little treatment and consideration; computer-assisted career guidance programs and self-help procedures are recommended.

Those with high levels of information processing generally lack pattern matching knowledge but have mastered other steps. They should benefit from instructions on career decision-making skills. The focus should be on integrating information for a decision.

Clients rated as having medium-level information-processing skills usually have difficulty with encoding. They exhibit little insightful knowledge about the role and scope of an occupation or an academic major. The

Assessing Level *(continued)*

treatment should focus on encoding information and depth of insight through individual counseling or by taking a career course. In addition, a thorough analysis of coping and problem-solving skills is recommended.

Clients with low-level skills in information processing are characterized as having significant deficits in problem-solving, that is, they are only able to encode and process little information presented to them. These clients may require the counselor to assume a teaching role that directly provides needed skills in a step-by-step fashion. The counselor also assumes a very active role in guiding the client in the decision process.

Clients who do agree should be directed to explore potential work environments that are predicted to be congruent. Finally, a decision is reached.

Stage 7, *Follow-up,* involves evaluating the client's progress in the counseling process and the procedures used to assist clients in finding a work environment in which they experience satisfactoriness and satisfaction. Counselors also assist clients in their job searches.

In sum, this model emphasizes fit-of-person with an optimal career. Valid and reliable tests are used to determine the client's abilities, values, and interests. This information is used in conjunction with subjective data (cognitive clarity, emotional status, problem-solving processes) in the counseling process. Identifying information-processing skills and improving them are viewed as necessary steps in assisting clients in the career decision-making process. Intervention strategies that are matched to specific identified deficits in information-processing are a major focus of the career counseling process. However, the basic assumption of person-environment-fit is that individuals seek to achieve and maintain a positive relationship with their work environments. Thus, counselors assist clients in finding some degree of congruence between themselves and work environments in the career decision process.

Case 4-1: GENERATING A PEF ANALYSIS

Figure 4-1 represents the PEF analysis schematic that is used for optimal career choice. Following the steps from left to right, the client is administered an abilities test and a values questionnaire. In the second step, ability and value patterns of occupations are compared with the client's ability and values. This comparison is used to predict *satisfactoriness,* or the probability that the worker will satisfy the work requirements in a work environment, and whether the worker will find *satisfaction* performing the work

FIGURE
4-1

Use of the Theory of Work Adjustment in Career Choice

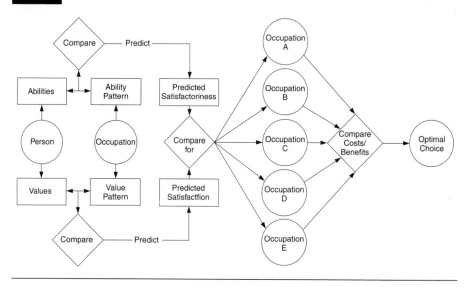

SOURCE: From "The Theory of Work Adjustment and Person-Environment-Correspondence Counseling," by R. V. Dawis. In *Career Choice and Development,* 3rd ed., by D. Brown, L. Brooks, and Associates, pp. 75–121. Copyright 1996 by Jossey-Bass, Inc. Reprinted by permission of Jossey-Bass, Inc., a subsidiary of John Wiley & Sons, Inc.

that is required. These predictions are based on comparing the individual's abilities and values with the work environment requirements and reinforcers available. Finally, the individual selects specific occupations of interest and researches each one until an optimal choice is made.

The Case for Person-Environment-Fit

A counselor's summary of the case of a 19-year-old female who was undecided about a career goal is contained in the paragraphs that follow.

Lee presented a background from a stable home environment, and there were no indications of irrational thinking or faulty beliefs. She appeared to be stable and expressed a positive self-concept. There was no evidence that she felt she must limit her career options because she is female. She felt free to explore any career of interest and was fully aware that some careers are stereotyped as male and female. Lee mentioned that her mother was a Chinese American born in this country and that her father was also American of Irish and German descent. She identified with the dominant society. She finished high school in the top 20% and was in her first semester of college. She was found to have a very high level of skills in information processing. The counselor concluded that Lee was now serious about making a career decision.

During the assessment stage, Lee and the counselor collaborated on the tests that could be helpful.

COUNSELOR: Lee, earlier I explained the idea of career counseling based on PEF. Do you have any questions at this time?

LEE: Not really, but I believe you mentioned that ability and values are used to help people like me find the right kind of job or as you said *fit* between person and work requirements.

COUNSELOR: Very good!! I'll review the procedure once more. First, we measure your abilities, and values. Second, we will both assess work environments by not only observing work requirements, but also by whether you feel a particular occupation would be satisfying for you. We will do this by matching your traits with work reinforcers found in work environments. When we find a match we refer to this as personal-environment-fit, or simply PEF.

The following tests were chosen after an introduction of the purpose and use of each test: *The General Aptitude Test Battery* (GATB) (U.S. Department of Labor, 1970b), was chosen to measure nine specific abilities as shown in Lee's score results. The *Minnesota Importance Questionnaire* (MIQ) (University of Minnesota, 1984) was chosen as a measure of needs; values represent a grouping of needs as shown in Figure 4-2.

Test score results for Lee were grouped by high, moderate, or low for nine abilities and six values as follows:

	High	Moderate	Low
GATB	Intelligence	Motor Coordination	Finger dexterity
	Numerical aptitude	Spatial aptitude	
	Verbal aptitude	Clerical perception	
	Form perception	Manual dexterity	
	Achievement	Status	
MIQ	Comfort	Altruism	
		Safety	
		Autonomy	

The counselor presented assessment results to Lee by carefully explaining the meaning of each ability and value score.

COUNSELOR: Lee do you recall the meaning of verbal aptitude from our earlier discussion?

LEE: Well, I think it has something to do with my vocabulary.

COUNSELOR: That's right! It was a vocabulary test that required you to identify words that have the same meaning or opposite meaning.

LEE: Yes, that was a tough one!

COUNSELOR: You're right—some people have a difficult time with it. But more important, how does this score link with finding a career?

LEE: I was told by one of my high school teachers that a good vocabulary is important for so many things—like meeting people, making a speech, and even studying. It also is important in work to be able to communicate with other people like a boss or a customer.

| FIGURE 4-2 | *Values, need scales, and statements from the Minnesota Importance Questionnaire* |

Value	Need Scale	Statement
Achievement	Ability utilization	I could do something that makes use of my abilities.
	Achievement	The job could give me a feeling of accomplishment.
Comfort	Activity	I could be busy all the time.
	Independence	I could work alone on the job.
	Variety	I could do something different every day.
	Compensation	My pay would compare well with that of other workers.
	Security	The job would provide for steady employment.
	Working conditions	The job would have good working conditions.
Status	Advancement	The job would provide an opportunity for advancement.
	Recognition	I could get recognition for the work I do.
	Authority	I could tell people what to do.
	Social status	I could be "somebody" in the community.
Altruism	Co-workers	My co-workers would be easy to make friends with.
	Moral values	I could do the work without feeling it is morally wrong.
	Social service	I could do things for other people.
Safety	Company policies and practices	The company would administer its policies fairly.
	Supervision-human relations	My boss would back up the workers (with top management).
	Supervision-technical	My boss would train the workers well.
Autonomy	Creativity	I could try out some of my ideas.
	Responsibility	I could make decisions on my own.

SOURCE: From *A Psychological Theory of Work Adjustment*, by R. V. Dawis and L. H. Lofquist. Copyright © 1984, University of Minnesota Press, p. 29. Reprinted by permission.

The counselor continued explaining and discussing each of the ability measures. In each case counselor and client linked score results with career choice; the focus was on the decision process. The counselor also emphasized that occupations require a combination of abilities and skills that are listed in references that describe job requirements for a variety of occupations.

After defining each value measured by the MIQ, the counselor turned to the MIQ report form as shown in Figure 4-3. The individual's responses on the MIQ that measure six values and 20 needs are compared with occupational reinforcer patterns (ORPs) for 90 representative occupations. The individual's rating of the importance of a need is represented by a C index. Thus, individual needs are matched with occupational reinforcers to determine an individual's fit into a work environment. Some examples of occupational reinforcers are achievement, advancement, authority, co-workers, activity, security, social service, social status, and variety. ORPs and occupational ability patterns are given for more than 1700 careers in the *Minnesota Occupational Classification System* (Rounds, Henly, Dawis, Lofquist, & Weiss, 1981).

COUNSELOR: On this report form a C value indicates the strength or importance of a need. For example if a C value is greater than .49 then the occupation is considered satisfying or of value to you. If the C value is between .10 and .49 there is likely to be job satisfaction but if the C value is less than .10 it is likely that there would be no job satisfaction.

LEE: That's interesting. Let me see—I have a high value in Cluster A, achievement and autonomy. What does that mean?

COUNSELOR: Good point! Let's look at the definition of each value we discussed earlier.

After reading the description of the two values, Lee was able to summarize how they could be linked to a work environment.

LEE: This means I would like to work on a job that would give me the opportunity to use my skills and be creative. But how will I know if I have the ability to be a lawyer or an architect?

COUNSELOR: Good question, Lee! After you have developed a list of occupations that interest you, we can compare your ability scores with the requirements of each occupation. As you evaluate each occupation, I will be happy to discuss what you have found and refer you to individuals who work in some of the professions.

During the course of the semester Lee was very diligent in pursuing some specific interests. She visited the university's pre-law advisor and a local attorney. She also had a conference with a representative from the School of Business and an accountant. Shortly before her sophomore year in college, Lee declared an accounting major. Her overall goal was to attend law school eventually and become a tax attorney.

In this case the client's needs and values became the central focus of discussion that led to a better understanding of how these factors affect job satisfaction and adjustment. In PEC, job satisfaction is considered a significant variable in determining job involvement and career tenure. The PEF analysis stresses the use of occupational information to assists clients in matching needs and abilities with patterns and levels of different reinforcers in the work environment. As work environments change in the future, more research will be needed to maintain the effectiveness of the MIQ.

For more information on PEF counseling and the MIQ, see Zunker and Osborn, 2002, Dawis (1996), and Sharf (1992).

FIGURE 4-3 *Correspondence report for SAMPLE REPORT   06/04/93*

The MIQ profile is compared with Occupational Reinforcer Patterns (ORPs) for 90 representative occupations. Correspondence is indicated by the C index. A prediction of *Satisfied (S)* results from C values greater than .49, *Likely Satisfied (L)* for C values between .10 and .49, and *Not Satisfied (N)* for C values less than .10. Occupations are clustered by similarity of Occupational Reinforcer Patterns.

	C Index	Pred. Sat.		C Index	Pred. Sat.
CLUSTER A (ACH-AUT-Alt)	.17	L	**CLUSTER B (ACN-Com)**	.36	L
Architect	.11	L	Bricklayer	.29	L
Dentist	.11	L	Carpenter	.44	L
Family Practitioner (M.D.)	.27	L	Cement Mason	−.03	N
Interior Designer/Decorator	.24	L	Elevator Repairer	.74	S
Lawyer	.27	L	Heavy Equipment Operator	.37	L
Minister	.11	L	Landscape Gardener	.07	N
Nurse, Occupational Health	.06	N	Lather	.11	L
Occupational Therapist	.15	L	Millwright	.29	L
Optometrist	.33	L	Painter/Paperhanger	.41	L
Psychologist, Counseling	.08	N	Patternmaker, Metal	.43	L
Recreation Leader	.02	N	Pipefitter	.58	S
Speech Pathologist	.11	L	Plasterer	.07	N
Teacher, Elementary School	.20	L	Plumber	.40	L
Teacher, Secondary School	.25	L	Roofer	.01	N
Vocational Evaluator	.06	N	Salesperson, Automobile	.51	S
CLUSTER C (ACH-Aut-Com)	.48	L	**CLUSTER D (ACH-STA-Com)**	.64	S
Alteration Tailor	.46	L	Accountant, Certified Public	.51	S
Automobile Mechanic	.43	L	Airplane Co-Pilot, Commercial	.60	S
Barber	.31	L	Cook (Hotel-Restaurant)	.57	S
Beauty Operator	.23	L	Department Head, Supermarket	.42	L
Caseworker	.31	L	Drafter, Architectural	.48	L
Claim Adjuster	.47	L	Electrician	.66	S
Commercial Artist, Illustrator	.51	S	Engineer, Civil	.35	L
Electronics Mechanic	.57	S	Engineer, Time Study	.29	L
Locksmith	.45	L	Farm-Equipment Mechanic I	.73	S
Maintenance Repairer, Factory	.49	L	Line-Installer-Repairer (Telephone)	.50	S
Mechanical-Engineering Technician	.28	L	Machinist	.67	S
Office-Machine Servicer	.69	S	Programmer (Business, Engineering Science)	.55	S
Photoengraver (Stripper)	.54	S	Sheet Metal Worker	.63	S
Sales Agent, Real Estate	.18	L	Statistical-Machine Servicer	.72	S
Salesperson, General Hardware	.35	L	Writer, Technical Publication	.55	S
CLUSTER E (COM)	.47	L	**CLUSTER F (Alt-Com)**	.33	L
Assembler, Production	.35	L	Airplane Flight Attendant	.09	N
Baker	.56	S	Clerk, General Office, Civil Service	.32	L
Bookbinder	.58	S	Dietitian	.21	L
Bookkeeper I	.55	S	Fire Fighter	.33	L
Bus Driver	.23	L	Librarian	.21	L
Key-Punch Operator	.49	L	Medical Technologist	.39	L
Meat Cutter	.49	L	Nurse, Professional	.13	L
Post Office Clerk	.43	L	Orderly	−.01	N
Production Helper (Food)	.47	L	Physical Therapist	.24	L
Punch-Press Operator	.44	L	Police Officer	.23	L
Sales, General (Department Store)	.33	L	Receptionist, Civil Service	.27	L
Sewing-Machine Operator (Automatic)	.29	L	Secretary (General Office)	.30	L
Solderer (Production Line)	.45	L	Taxi Driver	−.02	N
Telephone Operator	.42	L	Telephone Installer	.44	L
Teller (Banking)	.38	L	Waiter-Waitress	.26	L

SOURCE: *Minnesota Importance Questionnaire.* Copyright 1984 Vocational Psychology Research, Department of Psychology, University of Minnesota. Reprinted with permission.

Developmental Model

The developmental model developed from the premise that career development is a lifelong process and the career counseling needs of individuals must be met at all stages in life (Healy, 1982). The development of goals, learning strategies, and the timing of interventions in this model are guided by Super's (1957, 1990) vocational developmental tasks and stages. The overarching goals are problem identification and developing intervention strategies to overcome them. The developmental model also stresses the necessity of discovering each client's uniqueness of development. This individualized career counseling model by Healy (1982) has four stages:

Stage 1. Establishing Client Individuality

   a. Goals

   b. Obstacles

   c. Assets for Securing Goals

   d. Beliefs About Problem Resolution and Counseling

   e. Action Already Taken

   f. Feelings

   g. Learning Style

   h. Goal Impediments

Stage 2. Identifying and Selecting Strategies

Stage 3. Teaching and Aiding Implementation

Stage 4. Verifying Goal Achievement

SOURCE: From *Career Development: Counseling Through the Life Stages,* by C. C. Healy. Copyright © 1982 by Allyn & Bacon, Inc.

Stage 1   Establishing Client Individuality

To measure individuality, client and counselor collaborate on and negotiate the traits that are to be measured. Clients are given instructions about how to self-assess, and this information is used to determine further evaluations (Healy, 1990). Generally, unique traits are considered to be abilities and skills, interests, values, and personality variables. Then, the client's social network and support system are obtained through an interview or by a predetermined list of questions.

The seven diagnostic elements and goal impediments of Stage 1, as summarized in the following list, point out the importance of goal identification in this model.

   A. *Goals.* Goals are considered outcomes of counseling or what the client wants to realize, thus, evaluating the client's uniqueness is essential for the counseling process to be effective. The client's traits and background provide information for identifying and understanding obstacles that could block goal attainment. Counselors are to be aware that clients who express vague statements of outcome goals will need more specific guidelines for appropriate future actions.

B. *Obstacles.* Obstacles that are barriers to goals are classified as internal or external. Examples of internal barriers are cognitive deficiencies, emotional problems, or lack of motivation. External obstacles include unrealistic choices such as financial return of an occupation that will not meet the client's responsibilities.

C. *Assets for Securing Goals.* Counselors should be alert to make certain that each client has the potential for attaining goals that might not be apparent to the client. Assisting clients in recognizing their assets and linking them to goals is an important counseling responsibility.

D. *Beliefs About Problem Resolution and Counseling.* Healy (1982) suggests that cultural contextual experiences greatly influence each client's belief system about how to resolve problems. Thus, the counselor explores each client's background from his or her worldview perspective. The counselor's main objective here is to establish a mutually agreed upon relationship with each client. A cooperative and collaborative effort is considered most conducive to resolving problems.

E. *Action Already Taken.* Knowledge of the client's past actions to resolve problems provides clues of behavior that were ineffective in problem solutions. Correcting actions and guiding clients toward finding effective solutions reinforces a trusting relationship.

F. *Feelings.* In this context, feelings are related to how the client reacts to processes needed to realize goal attainment. For example, recognizing the rewards of goal attainment engenders motivation to offset frustrations that could distract the client. Counselors need to communicate a recognition and understanding of both positive and negative feelings that are unique to the client's pursuit of goal achievement.

G. *Learning Style.* At this point in the counseling process, counselor and client identify an individualized learning style that is primarily based on client assets and limitations as applied to problem resolution. For example, clients who are avid readers will welcome library research, but other clients might learn more effectively through observation such as job shadowing or through work experience. Still others may opt for computerized career exploratory programs or pursue a combination of learning styles. In sum, counselor and client negotiate the most effective learning situation to overcome goal impediments.

H. *Goal Impediments.* Healy (1982) has developed a list of impediments to goal establishment that usually emerge during the counseling process. Before finalizing Stage 1 of this model, he suggests that client and counselor review the following (in Healy's own words, except explanations in parenthesis):

1. The client has unrealistic or unclear goals.

2. The client has insufficient knowledge, ability, interest, training or resources, to reach goals.

3. The client does not try long or hard enough to succeed.
4. The client has misconceptions about how the system operates. (System refers to work systems and what is required in the give and take of the work place.)
5. The client's goals are thwarted by system defects or obstructions. (Clients need information about unfair employment or promotion policies.)
6. The client is unable to decide and commit to one alternative.
7. The client's problem has been formulated incompletely or inaccurately.
8. Interpersonal conflict.
9. The client's affect is inappropriate for his problem (pp. 181–185) (Counselors should assist clients in recognizing frustrating experiences associated with career decisions that often led to distress. Clients need to admit that they *are* experiencing problems, and some clients will need self-confidence building exercises that lead them to marshalling assets to overcome adversity. Yet other clients may exhibit excessive emotion that calls for the counselor to introduce methods of reducing anxiety to manageable limits.)

At this point in the model, the counselor screens clients that are likely to have problems as suggested by the seven diagnostic elements and nine goal impediments. Some clients may need to be referred for psychotherapy or further evaluation, whereas others may need prevocational training or additional educational instruction.

Stage 2 Identifying and Selecting Strategies

Stage 2 is primarily devoted to a task analysis of actions designed to overcome identified obstacles. The counseling process could include consultation and clarification of goals; for example, some clients may decide to participate in a training program for writing resumés or in interview competence training.

Stage 3 Teaching and Aiding Implementation

The counselor's major task in stage 3 is to support the client in implementing strategies developed in stage 2. The counselor may be directly involved with learning projects or secure and oversee assistance from other professionals. Examples of learning strategies include assertiveness training, discussions with employment specialists, job search training, and networking the hidden job market. See Case Example 4-2.

Stage 4 Verifying Goal Achievement

Stage 4 consists of reviewing the effectiveness of learning strategies; revising strategies is an alternative during this stage. The counselor provides support for the client's efforts for goal achievement. One major objective is to increase client confidence for developing learning strategies that can serve as examples for the future.

In sum, this model stresses client individuality, and the client's unique development is used for establishing goals and subsequent strategies to implement goals. Identifying and clarifying problems and potential problems that could hinder the success of the counseling process is very important. A list of specific impediments to goals is a unique feature of this model. Finally, evaluating the most effective learning path to goal attainment is a process that deserves consideration in all career counseling models.

Case 4-2: THE CASE OF MULTIPLE PROBLEMS

(This case presents problem identification in a developmental model. Only excerpts are used.)

Lou at age 37 needed assistance in finding an appropriate career. She had been employed in several jobs including waitress and bartender, and she is currently working in a nursing home for the elderly as an aide. While serving time in federal penitentiary for transporting illegal aliens, she enjoyed doing landscaping work. No other preferences for a future vocation were stated.

Lou came from a dysfunctional family. Her parents divorced when she was age 3, and she was placed in a foster home. She dropped out of school at age 15 when she became pregnant. She later received a GED. She has been married on two occasions and claimed incompatibility when divorcing her two husbands. She had no children from her marriages but did have a child out of wedlock when she was 16 years of age. That child, now age 21, is serving time for substance abuse. Lou is currently living alone.

Her developmental history also includes substance abuse. She began drinking alcohol at age 13 and started using drugs at age 15. Currently, she is attending a local AA group every evening and claims to have been drug and alcohol free for 26 months.

Lou was appropriately dressed and her speech was spontaneous, goal directed, and of normal rate and rhythm. She was alert, and recent and remote memory were intact. She is obviously street wise but less academically oriented.

Recent testing results revealed that Lou was functioning in the average range of intelligence. She was weak in academic subjects including the basics of reading, spelling, and arithmetic.

Lou was disappointed with herself for her past actions and for her current inability to find direction for a career. She described her current condition as constantly being tempted to drink alcohol or to use drugs. As she put it, "It's a daily fight." She feels lonely and has often considered suicide. She expresses despair for not being able to control her thoughts and find a pathway out of this "jungle" she finds herself in. As she stated, "I don't know which way to turn."

The job she now holds and has held for the past year is very stressful. Lou feels that she can do better and is searching for something more stable. When the counselor asked her to specify an interesting job she was only able to mention landscaping. This time Lou wanted to choose a job that has a future but admitted that she has given little thought to what that job may be.

From this data, the counselor was able to build a client profile using a list of impediments to goal establishment (Healy, 1982).

a. *Goals.* This client has unclear goals and has not developed any planning for finding a satisfying career. She has relatively little knowledge of work requirements and work environments.

b. *Obstacles.* A support network is needed for remaining substance abuse free. She needs to learn problem-solving and decision-making skills.

c. *Assets for Securing Goals.* She is of average intelligence but very weak academically. She appears to be currently motivated to find a career direction.

d. *Beliefs About Problem Resolution and Counseling.* Lou is unrealistic about the counseling process. She expects to be a passive participant and the counselor is magically to lead her to the optimal career. She has delayed getting help or putting a plan into action.

e. *Action Already Taken.* There is evidence of insufficient perseverance. She has not been actively involved in helping herself. This may very well be a matter of numerous personal problems, including substance abuse, that have limited her ability to plan time for career counseling.

f. *Feelings.* Her thinking tends to be very concrete. She oversimplifies solutions to problems. Currently, she is depressed and in immediate need of a support system.

g. *Learning Style.* Lou would be best equipped to learn by observing. Job shadowing is recommended. Information processing is weak.

h. *Goal Impediment.* This client has unclear goals. She has insufficient knowledge of resources to reach goals. She has misconceptions about the counseling process per se, that is, that it requires her active participation. There appears evidence of emotional instability, suicide ideation, and interpersonal conflict that is going to require psychotherapy.

The counselor decided to refer Lou for further evaluation from a clinician. He approached this referral very carefully.

COUNSELOR: Lou, you have mentioned on several occasions that you have been troubled with your personal life. Could you tell me more?

LOU: I don't know. I believe that I told you most of it. I just didn't get a good start and before I knew it I was in trouble. Then more trouble came along and I just sort of fell into a trap I couldn't get out of. I guess that I should have gotten more help along the way.

COUNSELOR: If you are really serious about wanting help, I believe I can make some recommendations that could help you.

LOU: Sure, I would like some help.

COUNSELOR: I believe you have some personal problems that could be best taken care of by a colleague of mine while I assist you with finding a career. Although you may be counseling with two different counselors, we will have the same goal of helping you establish a more stable future.

Lou appeared satisfied with the recommendation and agreed to the suggestions from the counselor. Personal counseling required Lou to focus on personal problems, which demanded considerable effort and time on her part. Lou was to continue with personal counseling as needed. She eventually continued with career counseling and was successfully placed on a job in a local factory after completing a pre-vocational training program in which she was given instructions on appropriate interactions with peer affiliates on a job, budget management, and job interview skill training. The career counselor made it clear that he was available for follow-up visits.

This example of problem identification illustrates information that can be attained from the intake interview and supplemented with assessment data. Information from an intake interview should be viewed by the counselor as material from which one can draw tentative conclusions. Such conclusions should be verified by further assessment or with a client referral to a psychologist. In the developmental model, problem identification is considered a most important stage. Armed with relevant information about the source of problems, counselor and client can negotiate intervention strategies that will assist clients in overcoming persistent crises that lead to vague goal statements and subsequent unproductive counseling.

A Learning Theory of Career Counseling (LTCC)

A most comprehensive approach to career decision making has been carefully delineated by Krumboltz, Mitchell, and Gelatt (1975), Krumboltz and Hamel (1977), Krumboltz and Nichols (1990), Mitchell and Krumboltz (1990, 1996), and Krumboltz (1996). These authors emphasize that each individual's unique learning experiences over the life span are most influential in the career choice process. Therefore, learning is a key ingredient in career counseling and career guidance, suggesting that career counselors' major task is to enhance learning opportunities for clients by using a wide array of effective methods that begin in childhood and endure throughout a lifetime.

The scope of the career counselor's role is viewed as very complex and inclusive—suggesting a number of skills, knowledge, and methods to deal with all career and personal problems that act as barriers to goal attainment. Career counselors may take the role of mentor, coach, or educator and should be prepared to solve unique beliefs that hinder personal development. As Krumboltz (1996) sees it, the counselor as educator provides the environment for clients to develop interests, skills, values, work habits, and many other personal qualities. From this learning perspective, clients can be empowered to take actions that promote the creation of satisfying lives now and in the future. For future reference, counselors help clients identify elements of a satisfying life that could change over time and especially how to adapt to changing circumstances and constantly changing work environments.

In this model, the client is viewed as one who is exploring and experimenting with possibilities and tentative decisions. A client should not be condemned for abandoning a goal in the exploratory process of learning about self, workplaces, and careers. In fact, Krumboltz (1996) strongly suggests that clients do not need to make a career decision for the sake of deciding but, rather, should be encouraged to explore, eliminate, and make tentative tryouts in a learning process that leads toward progress of accomplishing their personal goals. Within this perspective, indecision is viewed as what is expected from clients who seek assistance; indecision should not be viewed as a negative diagnosis but as an existing condition of a client who is *open* to learning and exploration.

In sum, the following practical applications for counselors are paraphrased as follows: (1) Assessment instruments are used to stimulate new learning by identifying needed new skills, cultivating new interests, and developing interpersonal competencies; (2) educational interventions should be increased to provide more opportunities of learning about one's abilities to meet career demands, the demands of the workplace, changing work habits, changing beliefs, and values; (3) success criteria should be based on learning outcomes and not solely on whether a client has made a career decision—the focus is on new behaviors, attempts to learn, and revised thoughts; and (4) counselors should integrate career and personal counseling; learning should focus on personal as well as career issues (Krumboltz, 1996).

The following career counseling model relies heavily on a decision-making model developed by Krumboltz and Sorenson (1974) and has been updated by more recent publications as noted in the beginning of this discussion and by Walsh (1990) and Savickas and Walsh (1996).

Stage 1. Interview

  a. Establish client-counselor relationship.

  b. Have client commit to time needed for counseling.

  c. Reinforce insightful and positive client responses.

  d. Focus on all career problems, family life, environmental influences, emotional instability, career beliefs and obstacles, and traditional career domains of skills, interests, values, and personality.

  e. Help clients formulate tentative goals.

Stage 2. Assessment

  a. Objective assessment instruments are used as a means of providing links to learning interventions.

  b. Subjective assessment attempts to attain the accuracy and coherence of the client's information system, identify client's core goals, and faulty or unrealistic strategies to reach goals.

  c. Beliefs and behaviors that typically cause problems are evaluated by using an inventory designed for this purpose.

Stage 3. Generate Activities

  a. Clients are directed to individualized projects such as taking another assessment instrument, reviewing audiovisual materials, computer programs, or studying occupational literature.

    b. Some clients may be directed to individualized counseling programs for personal problem solutions or lack of cognitive clarity.

Stage 4. Collect Information

    a. Intervention strategies are reviewed.

    b. Individual goals, including newly developed ones, are discussed.

    c. A format for previewing an occupation is presented.

    d. Clients commit to information gathering by job-site visit or using job-experience kits.

Stage 5. Share Information and Estimate Consequences

    a. Client and counselor discuss information gathered about occupations and together estimate the consequences of choosing each occupation.

    b. Counselor evaluates client's difficulty in processing information.

    c. Counselor evaluates client's faulty strategies in decision processing.

    d. Counselor develops remedial interventions.

    e. Clients can be directed to collect more information or recycle within the counseling model before moving to next step.

Stage 6. Reevaluate, Decide Tentatively, or Recycle

    a. Client and counselor discuss the possibilities of success in specific kinds of occupations.

    b. Counselor provides the stimulus for firming up a decision for further exploration of a career, or changing direction and going back to previous steps in making a decision.

Stage 7. Job Search Strategies

    a. Client intervention strategies can include using study materials, learning to do an interview or write a résumé, joining a job club, role playing, or doing simulation exercises designed to teach clients the consequences of making life decisions.

The following paragraphs summarize and highlight additional information to make this model more user friendly.

In Stage 1, *Interview,* client-counselor relationships are established and maintained throughout the counseling process. The client must be allotted the status of collaborator and allowed the freedom and given the encouragement to learn, explore, and experiment. A working partnership may best characterize an appropriate relationship.

Some techniques of interviewing, discussed and illustrated in the next two chapters, can be used as examples for at least partially fulfilling the requirements of an intake interview. Counselors obtain more specific information of client learning experiences and environmental conditions that have significantly influenced the development of task approach skills.

In Stage 2, *Assessment,* results are used in two ways: (1) to suggest to clients how their preferences and skills match requirements found in educational and occupational environments; and (2) to develop new learning experiences for the client (Krumboltz, 1996).

Using test results as a method of identifying what a client may want to learn for the future encourages clients to identify learning intervention strategies that are needed for occupations of interest. In this context, limited skill development is considered as a temporary state that can be improved to enhance a client's potential for career exploration. Following this logic, criterion-referenced tests that evaluate what a client can or cannot do are more desirable than are norm-referenced tests that reveal what percent of the population the client exceeds.

Assessment designed to measure interests, values, personality, and career beliefs are also used as points of reference for developing learning. In essence, using assessment results for identifying learning needs to improve career decision making suggests that (1) clients should not only base their decisions on existing capabilities and interests but expand them, and (2) occupational requirements are not expected to remain stable—thus, clients need to prepare for changing work tasks and work environments. Tailored and remedial intervention strategies designed to meet each client's unique needs are most effective (Krumboltz, 1996).

Tentative goals formulated during the intake interview are further evaluated during Stage 3, *Generate Activities*. Client and counselor determine steps necessary to reach goals. Some clients might want to confirm their goals by taking an interest inventory. Another client might want to evaluate abilities. Yet another client might best be served by personal problem counseling before making a goal commitment. Before completing this stage clients select two or more occupations to explore.

The major objectives of Stage 4, *Collect Information,* are to introduce clients to career information resources, their purpose, and use. Client and counselor also develop a format for evaluating occupations. Included in the format are opportunities for advancement, pay scales, worker associates, preparation time for certain occupations, and skills that are required. Clients are assigned individual projects involving career exploration and may be required to job shadow or use job-experience kits.

Client and counselor discuss the information gathered for each occupation evaluated in Stage 5, *Share Information and Estimate Consequences.* Counselors assist clients in estimating their chances of success in a chosen occupation. During this process, the client is directed to state tentative conclusions, reasons for conclusions, and ideas for further exploration. For example, some clients may be directed to collect more information before conclusions can be reached.

In Stage 6, *Reevaluate, Decide Tentatively, or Recycle,* client and counselor establish a firmer commitment to career direction. Some clients continue to the next step of job search while others recycle for more information or a change in direction. Counselors maintain the position that clients should not be judged harshly for changing their minds during this process of discovery. Some clients require more time and information before deciding tentatively. Counselors should support clients who make reasonable and realistic requests during this stage.

In the final stage, *Job Search Strategies,* clients become involved in the usual programs of interview training, preparing a resumé, or joining a job club. However, a unique feature of this model is the emphasis on teaching clients the consequences of making a career decision. Client and counselor reintroduce the concepts of career life planning and, specifically, how the procedures of learning to make a career decision can be used with other major decisions in life.

In an attempt to understand how clients arrive at decisions, counselors view core goals as driving forces underlying an individual's motivation toward certain activities and, as such, goals function as a fundamental sense of self. For example, one who has a core goal "to feel superior" might not be motivated to evaluate certain work environments and subsequently lacks motivation to pursue an activity agreed upon. In this case the counselor assists the client in defining core goals as underlying reasons for a lack of interest in pursuing certain activities. Some clients might be able to identify emotional highs and lows that are influenced by such core goals as an inclination "to feel free and unbound" or in another case "to feel respected." These goals may be considered potent motives for judging career-related activities as worthwhile. Counselors can assist clients in clarifying and resolving core goals, especially those that influence decision making. This step in the career counseling process is considered a key role of the career counselor (Krumboltz & Nichols, 1990).

Two major goals of this model are to build an understanding of what motivates human behavior and how thought processes and actions influence career development and subsequent career decisions. According to "The Living Systems Framework" (LSF) developed by Ford (1987) and Ford and Ford (1987) as discussed in Krumboltz and Nichols (1990, p. 175), "the primary and most direct influences on decision making are (a) one's accumulated knowledge about the world and about one's self (information processing and storage); (b) one's entire set of desired and undesired outcomes (directive cognitions); (c) evaluative thought processes that determine what one can or should try to accomplish right now (regulatory evaluations); and (d) thought processes that determine strategies for how to accomplish current objectives and coordinate action (control processes)." This explanation underscores the magnitude of extremely complex systems from cognitive science that are used as guidelines to understand what motivates human behavior and how information about self and environment is processed in decision making. See Case Example 4-3 for a case involving a reluctant decision maker.

In sum, learning is the key to enhancing self knowledge. A key focus is to develop a greater sensitivity to the advantages and limitations of environmental experiences that influence career decision making. Using learning intervention strategies to develop skills, interests, and abilities to expand a client's outcome potential is a unique feature of this model. Finally, we must recognize that cognitive functions provide clients with a model of the world and their relationship to it. As clients evaluate changing work environments, they also evaluate their skills, abilities, and other personal qualities to meet their perceptions of what is demanded. In this context, appropriate and realistic information processing is essential.

Case 4-3: CASE OF THE RELUCTANT DECISION MAKER

Joe was accompanied to a community counseling center by a friend who was also a career counseling client. Joe needed a great deal of support and encouragement before he agreed to make an appointment. He asked for help to find a better job.

Joe dropped out of high school when he was in the 10th grade to work in a fast-food establishment. He recently completed a high school equivalency course and received a diploma. Now 22, he continues to live with his parents. His father is a factory worker, his mother is a homemaker, and he has four siblings.

The counselor immediately recognized that Joe was very uncomfortable asking for help. He seemed very nervous and restless.

COUNSELOR: Joe, I am pleased to know you (shaking hands). Your buddy here has been telling me about what a nice guy you are and what a good friend you have been.

JOE: Well, ah, thank you. He is a good friend too.

COUNSELOR: It's great to have good friends. This reminds me of when a friend of mine helped me get started in college a few years ago.

The counselor continued to make small talk to help Joe feel more at ease. When it appeared that Joe was more relaxed, the counselor outlined his role as counselor and what is expected of a client during the career counseling process. Joe was receptive to suggestions and agreed to keep his appointments and complete work away from the counseling center that might be assigned during the course of counseling.

During the intake interview the counselor discovered that Joe had taken part in a career counseling while in a high school equivalency program.

JOE: Yes, I took several tests before I finished training.

COUNSELOR: Do you recall the kind of tests?

JOE: One was for interests and the other was an aptitude test.

COUNSELOR: Good! What did you decide after going over the results?

JOE: Well, I decided to think about two or three different jobs, but I didn't get anywhere.

COUNSELOR: Explain more fully.

JOE: I thought the counselor was supposed to tell me more about what I should do and what I'm qualified for.

As Joe and the counselor continued their discussion, it became apparent that Joe had some faulty beliefs about career decision making. He evidently thought that someone would decide for him or provide a recipe for choosing a job with little effort on his part. In addition, the counselor suspected that there were some underlying reasons Joe was not taking appropriate actions to solve his problems, but this would have to be confirmed by additional data and observation.

JOE: I just was not able to decide, and I really needed some help.

COUNSELOR: Could you tell me about the kind of help you needed?

JOE: I don't exactly know, but I just couldn't see myself in those jobs. I just don't know about all those jobs. My family makes fun of me when I talk about more school.

COUNSELOR: Tell me more about your family.

JOE: They all work hard. They have labor-type jobs and don't make much money. They want me to do the same kinda thing—just live from one paycheck to another and somehow get by. You know sometimes I think they are right! Maybe I'm not cut out to do any other kind of work.

After further discussion, the counselor was greatly concerned that Joe would not progress very far in the career decision-making process with faulty beliefs such as those he had expressed. The counselor jotted the following notes of a thinking pattern that could inhibit Joe's career development:

- Apparent anxiety about career planning
- Lack of flexibility in decision making
- Lack of willingness to consider a variety of occupations
- Faulty beliefs about career decision making and occupational environments
- Lack of family support
- Limited career choices from salient messages in the environment

COUNSELOR: Joe, we can help you make a career decision, but first we both should learn more about your career beliefs. Would you be interested in taking an inventory that would help us understand more about your beliefs and your assumptions about careers?

JOE: Sure, I guess so, but I don't understand how it will help me.

COUNSELOR: Let me explain how we will use the results. We can find out about some of the factors that influence your decisions, what may be necessary to make you feel happy about your future, and changes you are willing to make. Discussing these subjects should help in clarifying your role and my role in the career decision-making process.

The results of the *Career Beliefs Inventory* (CBI) (Krumboltz, 1988) described in Chapter 7, not surprisingly, indicated low scores on several scales, especially on acceptance of uncertainty and on openness. Low scores on these scales indicate that excessive anxiety can lead to viewing career decision making as overwhelming, and Joe's scores also suggested that he had fears about the reactions of others. The counselor felt more certain about his tentative conclusions from the intake interview. In the next session with Joe, and following a review of the purposes of the inventory and its scores, the following exchange took place:

COUNSELOR: Joe, could you tell me the reasons you are uncertain about your career plans?

JOE: Nobody in my family has ever had much schooling. I guess it's not in me to go for more education or training.

COUNSELOR: So you believe that you cannot be successful in higher education because your family has not?

JOE: Yes, I believe that's true.

COUNSELOR: Could you tell me why you feel this way?

JOE: They don't think I can do it.

COUNSELOR: What kind of grades did you make in the high school equivalency courses?

JOE: I made good grades—above C in every course and I got two A's.

COUNSELOR: What does this tell you about your ability to do academic work?

JOE: OK, I guess I was successful then, but that does not mean I could do the same in college.

COUNSELOR: You are absolutely right. There are no guarantees, but we have known for a long time that past academic performance is a good indicator of future performance in school.

JOE: But my brother and mom keep telling me that we aren't the kind to go to college.

COUNSELOR: If I provide you with information about your chances of making a C or better in community college, would you be willing to talk with your family about options you are considering for the future?

JOE: Well, I guess so.

Each of the scales with low scores was discussed in a similar manner, that is, faulty beliefs were identified, followed by specific plans of actions. The counselor continued to confront Joe with facts about individuals who were the first in their family to complete a college degree and stressed that he must arrive at a decision based on his own desires and potential.

The counselor and Joe agreed that he should take an achievement test to determine his academic deficiencies. Their plan was to have Joe improve his skills as a means of improving his chances of being a successful college student. In the next four months Joe spent a considerable part of his spare time in studying and being tutored to improve basic academic skills. He also gained a great deal of confidence by being involved in such a project. A follow-up test boosted Joe's confidence when he discovered that he had shown significant academic progress.

The counselor and Joe met on a regular basis to discuss his interests and to change his faulty beliefs. The counselor met with less resistance from Joe as he became more comfortable in the college environment. Finally, Joe convinced his parents to visit with the counselor about his future plans. To everyone's surprise, especially Joe's, they agreed to let Joe "give it a try for a semester."

Joe and the counselor agreed that they would delay making a firm career commitment at this time. They both felt that Joe should be open to look at several options as he progressed in college.

In this case, the CBI provided the stimulus for discussing relevant career problems that inhibited Joe from making choices in his best interests. Faulty beliefs are to be challenged in learning theory counseling. Clients are to be empowered to discover their abilities and improve them as well as to explore various options before making a firm career commitment. Learning to improve his skills gave Joe confidence in his ability to perform at a college level.

SOURCE: Adapted from Zunker and Osborn (2002).

Cognitive Information Processing Model (CIP)

Peterson, Sampson, Reardon, and Lenz (1996) have proposed a seven-step sequence for career delivery service as shown in Figure 4-4. This sequence can be used as a delivery option for both problem solving and decision making and can be used for individual, group, self-directed, and curricular programs.

**FIGURE
4-4**

Pyramid of information processing domains

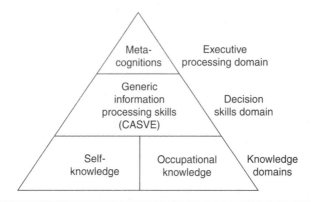

SOURCE: From *Career Development and Services: A Cognitive Approach,* by G. Peterson, J. Sampson, and E. Reardon, p. 28. Copyright 1991 by Brooks/Cole Publishing Company, a division of International Thomson Publishing, Inc.

This model is an extension of a career development theory, a cognitive information processing approach to career problem solving and decision making, developed by the same authors and introduced in Chapter 3. This unusual approach of illustrating and carefully describing how a theory can be applied to career counseling should be placed on the practitioner's list of events to celebrate.

A CIP approach to career development and its application to career counseling requires an in-depth understanding of cognitive information process theory. I strongly encourage you to read the original source for more information. This brief introduction to evaluating career information problems within a cognitive processing model should only be considered a starting point for understanding this theory's application to an individual career counseling model.

Information processing for career decision making is conceptualized within this model as an hierarchical system from a base of Knowledge Domains (self knowledge and occupational knowledge) to a Decision Skills Domain and finally to an Executive Processing Domain as shown in Figure 4-4.

In the Knowledge Domain, self-knowledge is related to one's interests, abilities, and values whereas occupational knowledge consists of an individual's view of individual occupations and structural relations between occupations.

The Decision Skills Domain consists of five stages referred to as the CASVE cycle. The acronym CASVE consists of Communication (problem perceived as a gap); Analysis (problem is reduced to components); Synthesis (problem is restructured by creating alternatives); Valuing (problem solutions are evaluated by valuing alternatives); and Execution (problem solutions are accomplished by formulating strategies).

The Executive Processing Domain consists of skills of initiating, coordinating, storing, and retrieving information. These skills are considered to be metacognitions that are used in problem solving and by self-talk, increased self-awareness, and control. Briefly, self-talk ("I think I can be a good engineer") creates expectations and reinforces behavior. Self-awareness influences decision making, in this context, by serving as a balance between individual goals and the goals of important others. Control refers to one's ability to control impulsive actions in the career decision process.

Combining this very brief introduction to cognitive information processing with the material presented in Chapter 3, a career counseling model in a seven-step sequence follows in a paraphrased format (Peterson et al., 1996, pp. 450–457):

Step 1: *Initial interview.* The major purpose of the interview is twofold. The counselor seeks information about the client's career problems and establishes a trusting relationship. More specifically, the counselor attends to both the emotional and cognitive components of the client's problems. The counselor recognizes that an effective relationship enhances client self-efficacy and fosters learning.

Step 2: *Preliminary assessment.* To determine the client's readiness for problem solving and decision making, the *Career Thoughts Inventory* (Sampson, et al., 1996a) is administered. This inventory is used both as a screening assessment and as a needs assessment; as such, it will identify clients who could experience difficulty in the career choice process as a result of dysfunctional thinking.

Step 3: *Define problem and analyze causes.* In this step, the counselor and the client agree on a preliminary understanding of the client's problem(s). For example, the problem may be defined as a "gap" between the state of the client's indecision and the ideal state of "career decidedness." A word of caution: The client's problem should be explained and stated in neutral, rather than in judgmental terms.

Step 4: *Formulate goals.* Formulating goals is a collaborative effort between counselor and client. Goals are put in writing on an individual learning plan (ILP), as shown in Figure 4-5.

Step 5: *Develop individual learning plan.* Again, the counselor and the client collaborate when developing the ILP, which provides a sequence of resources and activities that will assist the client in meeting goals established earlier. These are very evident on the written ILP. The ILP also serves as a contract between client and counselor.

Step 6: *Execute individual learning plan.* This step requires that the client take the initiative in proceeding with the agreed-on plan. The counselor encourages and directs the progress and may provide more information, clarification, or reinforcement of the client's progress and may offer planning for future experiences. With dysfunctional clients, a workbook is used as a supplement to learning about the results of the *Career Thoughts Inventory*

FIGURE 4-5	*Individual learning plan*

Individual Learning Plan

Career Resource Center
Central Community College—110 Social Science Building

Goal(s)   1. Understand personal barriers to decision making.
2. Clarify self-knowledge and occupational knowledge.
3. Improve decision-making skills.
4. _____

Goal	Priority	Activity	Purpose/Outcome
1, 2 & 3	1	Individual Counseling	Clarify issues and obtain information
1	2	modules EPØ and EP2 and cognitive exercise	Explore Self-Talk
1	3	monitor thoughts related to a real decision	monitor Self-Talk
3	4	Module IPØ	Clarify decision-making knowledge
2	5	Occ-U-Sort & Module SKØ	Self knowledge and generate options
2	6	SDS:CV	" "
2	7	written summary of self-knowledge	" "
2	8	Career Key & module OKØ	Identify resources & obtain occ. info.
2	9	CHOICES	Narrow options
2	10	Video tapes, information interviews and shadowing	" "
2	11	Print Materials	" "

Joe Williams   Marilyn Abley   3/12/90
Client   Career Counselor   Date

SOURCE: From *Career Development and Services: A Cognitive Approach,* by G. Peterson, J. Sampson, and R. Reardon, p. 231. Copyright 1991 by Brooks/Cole Publishing Company, a division of International Thomson Publishing, Inc.

administered in step 2. This workbook, entitled *Improving Your Career Thoughts: A Workbook for the Career Thoughts Inventory* (Sampson, Petersen, Lenz, Reardon, & Saunders, 1996b) is used for cognitive restructuring, within which the client uses a four-step procedure (identify, challenge, alter, and take action).

Selected strategies for enhancing career problem solving and decision making are summarized as follows: for discovering self, trace the development of your interests, write an autobiography and prepare a vocational history; for life experiences, write a description in the third person and analyze emergent themes; for linking measured interests to past experiences, take an interest inventory and relate the results to real-life events.

Step 7: *Summative review and generalization.* Progress in solving the gap that might have motivated the client to seek counseling is perceived in this last step. A determination is also made about how effective the progress has been in following through with the ILP. The focus through all steps is on the client's career decision-making status. Finally, the lessons learned within the preceding six steps are generalized as skills learned to solve future career and personal problems.

In the *Initial Interview,* the counselor's goal is to analyze the characteristics of each client's problem according to a gap, ambiguous cues, interacting courses of action, unpredictability of courses of action, and new problems. *Gap* is used to describe a career problem of dissonance between what actually exists and what the client feels should exist. For example, a low-paying job with minimal responsibilities is quite different from the client's mental image of an ideal situation of higher pay, higher status, and independence. Recognizing a gap in this manner provides viable information for problem identification and subsequent goal development.

Ambiguous cues are clues the counselor and client can use to understand sources of problems or the underlying reasons for certain behavior patterns. For instance, a client might be experiencing extreme anxiety when faced with a situation in which competing cues are difficult to resolve. A client who might be searching for a stable job that is secure could also be struggling with a desire to be in a position of risk that provides the opportunity of becoming wealthy. In such situations, personal desires and motives or internal drives that are in conflict can be sources of anxiety. Sources of anxiety can also emerge from situational conditions or external factors. Identifying sources of anxiety is a major step toward resolving conflicting ambiguous cues.

Interacting courses of action and uncertainty of outcome also affect decision making and problem solving. For instance, a client might decide to pursue a nursing career and identify requirements, but while doing so might also explore an unrelated career. In this case, this client might lack the confidence to proceed on her own and could need more information about personal traits and career information. Counselors assist clients in identifying actions and elements of actions that provide clues to solving problems. Moreover, the uncertainty of outcome is a major barrier for clients who lack self-confidence to advance on their own. Some issues might be external, such as the lack of financial means for higher education. Another client might be directed toward self-talk or be given support and reinforced by discussing unique assets. Cognitive problems that are identified as dysfunctional are directed toward interventions that replace dualistic thinking with relative thinking, methods of developing self-control strategies, and acquiring effective methods of problem-solving.

In addition to uncertainty of outcome, new problems arise during the course of decision making, and they are viewed as sets of subordinate problems. For example, should a decided client seek a low entry position or go through training for a higher level job? Another client might be searching for which university provides the best program that is affordable. The point here is that subordinate problems can tend to discourage clients who foresee insurmountable barriers to reaching their goals. The uncertainty of outcome and new problems are critical issues at critical stages in a counseling model; the counselor must be prepared to support the client and offer solutions that are discovered in a collaborative relationship between counselor and client.

The next step in the outline, *preliminary assessment,* is basically a screening and needs assessment procedure. An inventory that can be used for problem identification in the screening process is *My Vocational Situation* (Holland, Daiger, & Power, 1980). This instrument provides scores for vocational identity, need for information, and perceived barriers to occupational choice. Other instruments that measure career maturity, indecision, career beliefs, career decision making style, and occupational certainty can also be used in the preliminary assessment step.

Defining problems and analyzing causes (step 3) requires counselor and client to identify probable causes of gaps and subsequent problems. For example, a client who cannot make a decision between two plausible choices might need individual counseling to clarify life roles or other important unique issues. Collaborative interaction between client and counselor is an important relationship that fosters problem identification and, by this process, provides for client agreement and understanding of probable causes.

The formulation of goals (step 4) follows with continued collaboration for careful detailing of each goal. An active client role reduces the likelihood of misunderstandings and confusion about the sequence of the counseling process.

Client and counselor *develop an ILP* (step 5) for each counseling goal, followed by an intervention activity. Learning activities included in the ILP can also be instructional modules (see Zunker 1998) that contain objectives, self-administered diagnostic tests, alternative learning activities, and a self-administered summary assessment.

In step 6, *execute an ILP,* several practical suggestions are given in the outline, including self-talk. Self-talk comments are viewed as self-efficacy beliefs (Bandura, 1989), thus, both negative and positive statements made by clients are discussed with each client. Positive statements are used to reinforce client's actions, and negative statements are considered self-deprecating and should be fully evaluated.

Finally, step 7, *summative review and generalizations,* focuses on learned skills that can be used in problem solving and career-making decisions in the future. A review of all steps reinforces client progress and enhances learned experiences.

This model and its theory attempt to answer some important questions about problem-solving and the career decision-making process. This career counseling model is basically a learning model built around CIP theory. In applying this theory to a career counseling model, the authors have developed a sound system of steps that are clearly delineated for the practitioner. An ILP is a unique element of this model, which also has a variety of intervention modules. A career counseling case that illustrates some elements of this model is presented in Case Example 4-4.

Case 4-4: THE CASE OF A LOT OF BRAVADO

(This case was recorded by a counselor in the first person. Excerpts from the case are used as an example of one of the important stages in the Cognitive Information Processing model.)

When Pat walked in the counseling center he impressed the secretary as someone who has to be very important. Pat had a swagger to his walk that gave the impression of one who is most confident, considers himself attractive, and has got the world by the tail. He didn't ask for a counselor, he wanted to see the director or the "person who is in charge." The secretary did not question Pat's motives but meekly showed him the way to my office.

He quickly made his entry and almost cracked my knuckles while shaking hands. I am sure they could hear him clearly in the adjoining rooms as his first comments went something like this, "Howdy!! My name is Pat. I came to see you today for a little help."

As Pat and I got to know more about each other during our early conversations, he stated that he wanted help in "picking out a good job" and agreed to proceed with career counseling as it was outlined. Pat grew up on a ranch in west Texas that his father managed for a wealthy oil man. In the area where Pat grew up there were extremely large ranches, and many of them contained significant oil and gas deposits. As Pat put it, the people there were "friendly and down home." Pat felt his parents were very supportive of him and it was understood that he would attend college. He had two younger siblings. Pat was now a first semester freshman. His grades in high school were slightly above average. But he explained that he had to ride the school bus for considerable periods of time because his home was 30 miles from the school. When he got home he had to help his father, which left little time for studying.

After further discussion that was not very productive because of Pat's bravado and guarded comments, we agreed that he should write an autobiography of his life and include his perception of a career goal, his experiences at home, school, and work, and hobbies and interests.

COUNSELOR: I have learned a great deal about your background from our discussion, but I believe it would benefit both of us if you would be willing to write about some events in your life.

PAT: Yes sir, that might help to get everything down 'cause you see that I like to talk a lot and skip around.

COUNSELOR: I do enjoy hearing about your experiences on such a large ranch. We don't have a lot of students who come in here with a similar background. But we are meeting to help you, and this might be a way to get started.

Pat dropped off his autobiography at the designated time of five days. As I read the autobiography I could not help observing that this was a different Pat that I met only a few days ago. There seemed to be a private Pat that is reflected in his autobiography and a public Pat that you get when you meet him face to face. Of course I realized we all have our public and private self-concepts, but Pat's behavior appeared to be overcompensating for some reason. The Pat that wrote expressed himself as an individual who is in search of a future that was realistic. He expressed interest in jobs that he evidently observed in his environment, such as geologist, petroleum engineer, and businessman. Yet he admitted he was uncertain about a career choice. Conversely, when he spoke about possible occupations in the counseling center, he mentioned professor so he could drive a Mercedes and stockbroker so he could be rich. Beside being unrealistic about a professor's salary, his statements reflected a naïveté about occupations per se.

The gap between perceived income and actual income had to be resolved before Pat could make appropriate career decisions. In essence, Pat needed to learn more about occupations and options. But what seemed to be the most pressing matter was to discover the sources of anxiety that Pat was currently experiencing.

During the next counseling session when discussing the autobiography, Pat appeared to be very anxious. It appeared that he was experiencing ambiguous cues such as wanting a lot of money regardless of risk but also wanting a secure job that would give him "time to take care of the livestock."

COUNSELOR: I have an inventory that might help us clarify your needs and help you make some decisions. It only takes a few minutes.

PAT: That sounds good to me—let's get started.

COUNSELOR: The inventory is the *Career Thoughts Inventory* (CTI) (Sampson, Peterson, Lenz, Reardon, and Saunders, 1996a). It will give us scores about decision-making problems, anxiety, and conflicts you may have.

Pat scored high on the scale that measures commitment anxiety, and the counselor explained his score as follows:

COUNSELOR: Your high score on this scale may mean that you are having difficulty committing to a career option because you may be afraid of what might happen when you do make a decision.

PAT: I'll have to think about that but it might just be true. To tell the truth I don't really know what I want to do. I suppose that if I decide now it might be wrong and I would be wasting my time and my parents' money.

I informed Pat that many students are undecided about their future and that is understandable, but it is most important to put forth the effort to create some options during the first year in college. This was the first time I met the private Pat face to face—he was actually a down-to-earth person struggling to determine an optimal career.

COUNSELOR: Pat, I have met with many students over the years who have struggled to find a career choice. We can help you do that, and I must add that you have made a sincere effort to help yourself and that is most important!

PAT: Thank you. I can really use some help.

Pat and the counselor negotiated an ILP similar to the one displayed in Figure 4-5. Pat was to filter out barriers to decision making and to learn more about himself and about occupations. He was to improve his decision-making skills. This plan involved individual counseling and self-talk to improve his self-esteem and debunk negative thoughts. He was to identify resources for occupational information and use a computer program to narrow his career options. He would be offered training in information interviews that are designed to assist clients in learning about workplaces, and he would be able to do job shadowing to learn more about the give and take of specific occupations.

Pat continued to visit with me while reporting his progress with the ILP. We discussed options and the feasibility of choices. Pat's sophistication in career exploration improved significantly as we were able to tease out the sources of his anxiety and point out his assets. Pat's self-talk continued to be monitored to make certain that he concentrated on positive thoughts. It was noticed that he began to walk with that "peacock swagger" again, but this time it was a different Pat—he had a realistic reason for being proud of his progress in college and in the career choice process.

Pat kept in touch after he graduated from college. He married a woman from another state and moved close to the Canadian border where they also have large ranches. He once wrote that he continues to use his business major and information he learned from animal husbandry courses on a ranch that will "all be mine someday where I can take care of the livestock."

In sum, the counselor assisted Pat in closing the gap between reality and what he perceived about some professions that was incorrect. Most important, Pat learned to know more about himself and the anxiety that he had experienced from a lack of confidence that he attempted to mask and deny. A carefully thought out ILP focused on how to assist Pat make appropriate career decisions and solve personal problems.

The Multicultural Connection

A growing awareness among practitioners of demographics that predicts a more racially and ethnically diverse workforce strongly reinforces the need for modifying career counseling models. Research that addresses the career counseling needs of multicultural groups is in its infancy, although there have been significant increases in numbers of publications that focus on multicultural issues in career counseling (Arbona, 1996). What the practitioner needs is more scientifically rigorous research aimed at providing fully defined career counseling techniques, procedures, and materials for an increasing number of ethnically diverse workers. The research needs of career counseling practice already comprise an extensive list of variables, however, and with the additional dimensions of multicultural domains, we will probably experience a lengthy, time-consuming process. In the meantime, career counselors should carefully evaluate their competencies for multicultural counseling.

A Multicultural Career Counseling Model for Ethnic Women

An introduction to steps or stages in a multicultural model for ethnic women by Bingham and Ward (1996) provides a means of comparing techniques designed to identify specific needs of a special group of clients and the methods and materials used in the counseling process. This model focuses on contextual elements of influence and recognizes that salient racial factors were not a part of theoretical conceptualizations of most of the career development theories discussed in the two preceding chapters. Theories, however, cannot directly guide specific counseling processes at a micro-level that is necessary to meet the special needs of special groups; the development of mini-theories may be necessary (Herr, 1996). The potential changes in career counseling models is a clear message to counselors that a life time of learning is not only necessary for clients.

This model is presented with the recognition that background issues in multicultural counseling have not been discussed. Chapter 10 is fully devoted to multicultural counseling and should be considered as an introduction to a vast amount of published material on this subject. However, Bingham and Ward's model emphasizes contextual factors that limit career choice and stereotypes that hinder career development and introduces counselors to racial identity as a significant variable in client-counselor relationships. These unique features and others are not emphasized in the career counseling models that were developed from career development theories described in the two preceding chapters.

The following are the steps in the multicultural career counseling model for ethnic women developed by Bingham and Ward (1996):

Step 1. Establish Rapport and Culturally Appropriate Relationships

Step 2. Identify Career Issues

Step 3. Assess Impact of Cultural Variables

Step 4. Set Counseling Goals

Step 5. Make Culturally Appropriate Counseling Interventions

Step 6. Make Decision

Step 7. Implement and Follow-up

SOURCE: From "Practical applications of career counseling with ethnic minority women," by R. P. Bingham & C. M. Ward. "Modified and reproduced by special permission of the Publisher, Consulting Psychologists Press, Inc., Palo Alto, CA 94303 from **Handbook of Career Counseling Theory and Practice** by Mark L. Savickas and W. Bruce Walsh. Copyright 1996 by Davies-Black Publishing, an imprint of Consulting Psychologists Press, Inc. All rights reserved. Further reproduction is prohibited without the Publisher's written consent."

Bingham and Ward strongly suggest that counselors are to prepare for clients by using a self-administered Multicultural Career Counseling Checklist (MCCC) (Ward & Bingham, 1993) as displayed in Appendix A. The first section of this instrument assesses the counselors' preparation for counseling a culturally different client by identifying both counselor's and client's racial/ethnic backgrounds. The other sections of this instrument concern the counseling process of exploration and assessment and establishing a negotiating and working consensus.

Also in the pre-counseling phase, the client is administered a *Career Counseling Checklist* (CCC) (Ward & Tate, 1990) displayed in Appendix B. This instrument contains 42 statements that measure such factors as knowledge of the world of work, gender issues, role of family in the decision process, and client's concerns about choosing an occupation.

A *Decision Tree* (Ward & Bingham, 1993) is a schematic, as displayed in Appendix C, that provides counseling decision points and pathways. One major decision point determines if the client is to be referred for psychological or personal counseling before obtaining career counseling.

A brief explanation of each step in the career counseling model follows:

Step 1: Establish Rapport and Culturally Appropriate Relationships

Client-counselor relationships are considered to be most important in all career counseling models, but especially in this model. When clients feel free to express themselves in a counseling relationship, they can be excellent teachers as cultural informants, provided the counselor makes it clear that discussions of ethnic/racial information is welcome. Trust and collaboration are key factors in a counseling relationship, particularly when client and counselor are from different ethnic group backgrounds.

Counselors must be aware of various specific cultural cues such as nonverbal actions and reactions of the client. For example, some clients may not consider it appropriate to maintain eye contact during counseling; the counselor's reciprocal behavior will enhance the relationship. Counselors should use as much time as necessary to establish a collaborative relationship with a client who has a different worldview than that of the counselor.

Ivey and Ivey (1999) suggest that a counseling relationship should be built on trust that will usually take the entire initial counseling session to develop. Counselors should relay empathy to their clients. Listening to and observing clients is one way to determine how the counselor should respond and set the context of the working relationship. Counselors should ask clients to clarify some of their comments to demonstrate interest in their thoughts and gain a more adequate understanding of their constructs.

Step 2: Identify Career Issues

Sue and Sue (1990) suggest that a counselor's understanding of the client's worldview issues will facilitate an understanding of barriers that could impede career decision-making. Ethnic minority clients who have experienced discrimination, for example, might feel that they cannot overcome the barriers that have conditioned them to limit career choice.

Although ethnic minority clients can experience a sense of responsibility for career identification, they must also be guided to realize that past and present internal and external barriers have in some way influenced their career decisions. Quite possibly ethnic minority clients have limited experiences with other ethnic social groups and view others as being unreceptive to them. Counselors should realize that cultural groups often share a common set of experiences of oppression that can collectively limit their perspectives of future opportunities.

One major goal of this step is to assist clients in identifying those experiences that limit career choices. A good example is a client who suggests that her gender has limited her future opportunities. She could be reflecting the social mores of her ethnicity in which women are restricted from working outside the home. Yet another client who is looking for a job might be focused on taking care of immediate financial needs rather than searching for a career. This client has been forced to concentrate on short-term goals.

Salient messages received by clients from contextual interaction can cause some ethnic minority clients to circumscribe choices for what is considered an appropriate job. Some clients limit their choices without being fully aware of it. Moreover, ethnic minority groups that have developed worldviews that limit career choices present new and different challenges for career counseling.

Step 3: Assess Impact of Cultural Variables

In this step counselors identify cultural variables that have the most limiting influence on career choices. This process can also be very time consuming, yet productive, when clients recognize the importance of understanding how their family environment, religion, and cultural history, for example, have shaped their prospects for the future. Counselors need to isolate unique cultural variables that need further delineation in culturally appropriate intervention strategies.

A good example to illustrate the problems associated with this stage is the influence of family on many ethnic minorities. If you ask a Native American how her family is doing, she might respond by telling you how the entire village is attempting to solve their problems. Family for Native Americans is an extended family, which among some tribes means an entire village (Ivey & Ivey, 1999). For other ethnic groups, the extended family can include parents, siblings, grandparents, aunts and uncles, and even godfather. Thus, the influence from family among ethnic minorities, especially first generation ones, can be very extensive and inclusive. Clients are often in conflict when attempting to decide between what they want to pursue and what their families see as appropriate.

Another related issue is how decisions are made in some ethnic groups. In this country, the rugged individual takes charge of his own destiny and independently determines its course. We as a society have endorsed the individualistic mode of operation within which the individual is empowered to make decisions. In many ethnic minority groups, the opposite is true; collective decision making among family members is considered more appropriate. A friend who grew up in Puerto Rico explained that he consulted his father in all major decisions by telephone from wherever he lived, which included several countries in South America. He had been conditioned that this was the proper way to make a decision. Thus, counselors who include the family in the decision-making progress recognize client's needs.

Step 4: Set Counseling Goals

Goal setting is to be a collaborative negotiation between client and counselor. This process encourages clients to be more active in pursuing satisfactory outcomes. A collaborative counseling relationship is especially important for ethnic minority clients. Some ethnic minority clients assume that they are to be passive participants, leaving all decisions to the counselor. In this context, clients are reluctant to share their true feelings and experiences and are uncomfortable being actively involved in the entire career counseling process. Counselors should inform clients that it is proper and acceptable to negotiate activities throughout the counseling process.

Leong (1993) suggests that pragmatic goals are more appropriate for ethnic minority groups than are goals based on self-actualization. The point here seems to be that clients who are more collective oriented, that is, family before self, might be more concerned about how a career benefits the family. Also, clients might need immediate placement in a job to support their needs and plan to consider long-term goals in the future. Even though circumstances may determine goal direction, counselors and clients who confer on outcome goals within a relationship that has established trust and respect for each other have the better chance of agreeing on appropriate goals.

Step 5: Make Culturally Appropriate Interventions

Individual needs determine appropriate interventions for members of multicultural groups. For some ethnic minorities, however, family approval and involvement in developing and delivering intervention strategies are recommended. In these cases individuals turn to the family for approval before feeling free to fully involve themselves. Counselors will find that it is very productive to fully investigate which members of the family are empowered to make major decisions.

Group interventions are also considered as very productive for some cultural groups. For example, clients who are struggling to learn English may be best served by group interventions that use the client's native language. In some cases interpreters may be used to facilitate groups. Groups might be more effective when composed of same racial group, biracial group, ethnic gender group, and community members.

Bingham and Ward point out that counseling interventions may require several sessions because many ethnic minority groups take considerable time to complete an agenda. Finally, if an inventory is used during the course of an intervention strategy, it must be appropriate for the client's racial/ethnic group. (See Chapters 7 and 8).

Step 6: Make Decision

An important suggestion in this step involves continuing monitoring of the decision process to make certain that the client is free from all barriers to goals. Some barriers can be difficult to remove, and some clients will make a decision mainly to please the counselor. Clients must be invited to recycle in this model without a sense of embarrassment; in fact, a review of the model steps can suggest to the client that it is a legitimate request to continue counseling.

Step 7: Implement and Follow-up

At this point, clients are usually referred to information resources, individual contacts, or agencies for assistance. Counselors monitor clients' progress and invite them to return for counseling in the future.

The following recommendations for the multicultural career counseling process as suggested by Bingham and Ward (1996) summarize this model:

1. The counselor should be aware of a variety of world views.

2. The counselor's preparation for multicultural counseling should be directed by recommendations of Sue, Arredondo, and McDavis (1992).

3. The counselor should fully understand his or her racial identity.

4. The counselor-client relationship should be a collaborative one, that is, a negotiating and working consensus is recommended.

5. The role of the family in the decision-making and counseling process should be emphasized.

6. Worldview, history of client, local sociopolitical issues, and stereotypes should be fully discussed.

7. The influence of racial/ethnic factors that limit career choices should be discussed.

8. Nontraditional interventions such as conversing in groups in the client's native language, using interpreters, and involving community members who can offer insight and direction should be used. Encourage clients to join a biracial network.

9. Client-counselor process should be continually evaluated during counseling and after counseling is terminated.

10. An extensive follow-up should be done and counseling recycled if necessary.

Case 4-5 illustrates the use of the Multicultural Career Counseling Checklist and the Career Counseling Checklist with an Hispanic senior high school student who currently resides in a small town in Texas. Experiencing conflicts between his former culture and the dominant culture, he asks for help from a career counselor. This case illustrates a few examples of the problems faced by individuals from a different culture who want to become working American citizens.

Case 4-5:   THE CASE OF QUESTIONABLE FUTURE STATUS

Carlos wanted to go to college but was unsure of his future status as a citizen. He came from the interior of Mexico at age 8 to join his mother who had left him for one year with his grandmother while she found a place for them to live in the United States. She married a U.S. citizen and has now established a home.

For the first two years of school, Carlos was placed in a bilingual program. Once he learned the English language, he was able to make very good progress in school. He graduated from high school in the top quarter of his class and had made mainly A's and B's on most subjects. His favorite subject was pre-calculus and his least favorite was economics. He belonged to French and Spanish clubs as well as to a high school spirit club.

Carlos reported that both Spanish and English are spoken in his home. He prefers English and uses it more than his mother does. He and his family belong to the Catholic church. Carlos does not care to go to Mexico because, as he put it, "of the corruption there." The family celebrates the traditional holidays but relate more to respecting their ancestors on Halloween than is the custom here.

Carlos is now 18 years of age and is working full time at a mailing service company. He claims to identify more as an American than as a Mexican and plans to make his home permanently in this country. Carlos spoke excellent English and expressed himself very well. It was apparent that he had assimilated many of the dominant culture's social values, but he also had retained many values from his own culture.

Carlos had asked for career counseling because he was not sure about his dream career and needed more information about it and wanted to know which nearby university offered degrees in photography or in how to produce and direct films. He told the counselor that he was interested in photography and the film-making industry because he had worked on some productions at his high school. He would very much like to become a film editor or a producer. The counselor told Carlos that he could be of help but wanted to begin counseling with a Multicultural Career Counseling Checklist and a Career Counseling Checklist.

After Carlos completed the two checklists, they discussed their different worldviews and specific items on the multicultural checklist as a way of establishing rapport (Step 1). They agreed to a collaborative working relationship.

Carlos checked several items on the Career Counseling Checklist that were thoroughly discussed (Step 2. Identify Career Issues) as follows:

COUNSELOR: I noticed that you checked item 14. "My ethnicity may influence my career choice." Could you tell me more about this item?

CARLOS: What I was thinking is that people might not think I can do the kind of work I want to do.

COUNSELOR: Explain more fully.

CARLOS: Well, you know how the Mexican man is supposed to work—or not to work hard.

COUNSELOR: You feel others may judge you this way?

CARLOS: Yes! But I will work hard at any job if I am given the chance.

COUNSELOR: You are really worried about getting the opportunity to prove yourself. Is that right?

CARLOS: Yes, I believe that a lot of Americans will think I can't do it!

COUNSELOR: To an extent that is a realistic appraisal of what could happen. But on a more positive note, more and more minorities are moving into other than labor-type jobs. I would rather you think of it as a golden opportunity right now to choose the job that you are interested in and pursue it using your best abilities.

CARLOS: That is what I want to do and if I am given the chance, I can prove myself.

COUNSELOR: That is a good start, but let us try to remove the negative feelings you still have about getting an equal opportunity in the future.

Counselor and client continued their discussion and during the next session Carlos revealed that part of his worry about the future was that he must try to remain close to his mother. He was afraid that he would be required to move to another location for an education and much further away from her later to fulfill his dream of being in the film industry.

As they continued their discussion, the counselor identified several career issues including the following:

1. Fear of being stereotyped as an individual who was only capable of doing menial jobs, thus not given consideration for jobs involving creativity and responsibility.
2. Fear that family responsibilities would limit his career ambitions.
3. Fear that his immigration status would not be appropriately taken care of, or that he might have problems becoming a citizen.

The counselor concluded that Carlos had also evaluated his current situation in a fairly realistic manner. However, it was obvious that he needed more support from his family to fulfill his ambitions. For example, it was clear that his mother did not want him to move far from her, and as a result Carlos had a serious conflicts before he even launched his career journey. Even though Carlos expressed confidence, he was also doubtful about his future that included taking a calculated risk in an environment that has not always been affirmative and friendly to minorities and pursuing a career that was unknown to the family. Carlos stated that he also wanted to remain near his family for consultation on major decisions in the future.

The counselor and Carlos negotiated three goals for the time being: Carlos would (1) gather information about university programs, admission requirements, and financial aid; (2) gather information about related careers in film editing, production, and photography and probable locations of opportunities; and (3) arrange a meeting with his parents and counselor to discuss the information he had gathered.

The counselor made certain that both parents could speak and understand English. The first meeting was a difficult one. It was clear that Carlos's parents were not sure they could trust another "Gringo," but the counselor was prepared to make them as comfortable as possible by introducing a friend who was a highly respected individual in the Mexican-American community. The friend put in a good word for the counselor and made his exit. This ally tremendously helped get the first session going with some sense of trust.

Another ally was used in the second session to explain that her daughter was now attending a university in another state and she was most proud of her. Some of the conversations were in Spanish. As expected, Carlos's parents delayed a decision about his future until they could consider all the information that was discussed. Carlos was to continue working to earn money for college and was encouraged to be tutored by a volunteer from the community who had attended a university.

In this example, the counselor first made certain that he had developed a trusting relationship with Carlos. It was apparent that Carlos felt free to discuss personal and family problems with the counselor. The counselor concluded that Carlos's mother had experienced a great deal of stress in her lifetime and was very protective of her son. Carlos also recognized his mother's reluctance to agree with a plan that might require him to move to another state. There was a genuine concern that Carlos would not be given the opportunity to prove himself because of his race. Goals were set to include parents in the decision process and allies were brought in to encourage trust and an open mind about their son's future. Finally, Carlos and his family compromised by agreeing to let him apply at two universities nearby.

Major Parameters of Five Models

In this section, five career counseling models are summarized by describing each according to its counseling goals, intake interview techniques, use of assessment, diagnosis, and counseling process as shown in the following table. The process of career counseling usually begins with an intake interview, then moves to assessment, on to diagnosis and problem identification, followed by a counseling process that maintains a client-collaborative relationship, then intervention strategies, and ends with an evaluation of outcomes and future plans. Individual needs may dictate different paths for some individuals.

Counseling Goals

Counseling goals provide the reader with goals specific to the model's purpose and procedures that are described in each parameter. For example, the trait-and-factor and PEF model emphasizes optimal fit of clients with an occupation, the developmental model stresses strategies that delineate clients' individual traits to promote career development over the life span, learning theory model suggests interventions to enhance and expand the client's current status, CIP model uses a variety of individual learning plans to improve cognitive processing, and the multicultural model for ethnic women explores avenues of removing salient cultural variables that inhibit and restrict career choice. Within these frameworks, client-counselor relationships are critical. The counselor might simultaneously be a teacher, a mentor, overseer, and, in most cases, a collaborator who establishes a working consensus relationship.

Intake Interview

The intake interview has many purposes, including building the foundations from which client-counselor relationships are established, and plays a major role assessing client problems. Ivey and Ivey (1999, p. 12) make a distinction between interviewing and counseling, although they are often used interchangeably: "Interviewing may be considered the most basic process used in information gathering, problem solving, and information and advice giving," whereas "counseling is a more intensive and personal process." In the parameter descriptions that follow, the intake interview is used for information gathering, building client-counselor

TABLE OF FIVE CAREER COUNSELING MODELS

	Trait-and-Factor-PEF	Developmental
Counseling Goals	Provide information that will enhance the process of rational decision-making; foster information processing skills; determine optimal person-environment-fit.	Identify unique traits for developmental interventions; remove impediments to goals; develop learning strategies that improve current status and prepare for future.
Intake Interview	Obtain subjective criteria to evaluate personal and career problems; evaluate cognitive clarity and emotional stability; focus on career choice environmental influences.	Identify social networks, support system, unique beliefs, and outcome expectations; assess motivation and emotional problems; establish developmental approach as counseling focus.
Use of Assessment	Obtain valid and reliable information of interests, work values, and cognitive abilities; evaluate skills for information processing.	Focus on unique assets of client's abilities, interests, and relationship skills; exploit assets as important factors in career choice.
Diagnosis	Establish valid relationship between traits and occupational requirements; specify deficiencies in information processing.	Use seven diagnostic elements and nine impediments to goal achievement to specify problems.
Counseling Process	Introduce PEF process that leads to optimal career fit; use both subjective and objective information for problem identification; assist with solving information processing problems.	Focus on individual traits for career development; specify goal impediments to review; develop learning strategies to promote career development.

relationships, assessing problems, determining client's readiness for career counseling, and establishing the process of counseling.

A preliminary assessment of the client's personal and career problems are obtained through background information and observation in the trait-and-factor

Learning Theory	Cognitive Approach	Multicultural Model for Ethnic Women
Use learning strategies to foster career development; empower clients to create satisfying lives with learning opportunities that develop personal traits and qualities.	Provide five generic information processing skills for problem solving; use learning strategies for effective use of career information; develop individual learning plan; offer personal and career assistance.	Establish culturally appropriate relationships; focus on salient racial variables that inhibit choice; identify racial identity of client and counselor.
Focus on career and personal problems including career beliefs; identify learning needs; develop client-counselor collaborative relationship.	Establish trusting and collaborative relationship; attend to both career and personal problems; complete demographic information form.	Establish collaborative relationship; use structured interview to determine counseling pathway; discuss world views and racial identity.
Identify needs for skill development, and interpersonal relationships; evaluate personal beliefs.	In first stage evaluate approach to problem solving and dysfunctional thinking. In second stage measure occupation and self-knowledge, decision-making skills, and effectiveness of executive processing domains.	Use tests appropriate for client's racial/ethnic group; use test scores as an aid in career choice.
Identify career beliefs that interfere with goal achievement, and current status of skills, interests, values, work habits, and personal qualities.	Identify problems, causes of gaps, needs for cognitive restructuring, and dissonance problems.	Determine counseling path to either career or personal counseling; identify impact of cultural variables on career choice.
Provide framework for matching changing work environments with essential educational experiences; use tailored and remedial interventions; be a client mentor and coach to enhance learning.	Discuss values, interests, and cognitive abilities congruent with occupations; develop individual learning plan; resolve conflicting information; offer cognitive restructuring.	Encourage clients to discuss salient racial factors that limit career choice; use intervention strategies that meet specific needs of ethnic clients and that are culturally appropriate; be supportive and an advocate.

and PEF model. This information is used with valid test results to form a subjective and objective appraisal of the client. The client's social networks, support system, and unique beliefs are the subject of an intensive interview in the developmental model. This information is used with standardized measures to form a picture of the client's career development. In the learning theory model, the interview identifies both personal and career problems and obstacles such as career beliefs that could block optimal career decisions. The major emphasis is identifying learning opportunities for each client. Both emotional and cognitive problems are emphasized in the CIP model. Furthermore, this model considers a trusting relationship that enhances self-efficacy and fosters learning to be most important. In the multicultural model for ethnic women, culturally appropriate relationships are established. A structural interview is used to determine client needs and to discuss client world views.

Use of Assessment

In this parameter, assessment refers to both standardized and nonstandardized methods used in the five models. This broader use of assessment is found in all career models as a part of client problem identification and is used in ongoing career counseling to identify appropriate intervention strategies. Within this framework, counselors not only have to understand the technical aspects of standardized tests that determine their appropriate use but also must sharpen their skills in applying nonstandardized measures. Assessment use is determined through a consensus between client and counselor that generally leads to a client's increased self-knowledge. All models make the point that testing is not the dominant force in making career choices but, rather, is used effectively as a counseling tool.

The trait-and-factor and PEF model uses assessment to provide valid and reliable information of interests, values, and cognitive abilities. Emotional stability, cognitive clarity, and skills in information processing are also evaluated. The developmental model requires assessment of the client's uniqueness in a variety of trait characteristics. This information informs clients of their personal characteristics that are used to determine learning strategies. The learning theory model uses assessment to determine learning experiences and to determine personal beliefs. Two stages of assessment are used in the CIP model. The first stage is used to measure dysfunctional thinking and client's readiness for problem solving. The second stage is used to measure cognitive processing domains and to develop individual learning plans. The major use of assessment in the multicultural model for ethnic women is to assess salient racial factors from interview results and the results of inventories specifically designed for this purpose.

Diagnosis

Identifying client problems is a major focus of the diagnosis parameter—not only for providing a client label but, more important, as a starting point from which goals can be set to resolve client problems. The diagnostic parameter is also used to identify client mental health problems that require further psychological evaluation or treatment. In all five models, diagnosis of irrational or dysfunctional thinking is determined by appraisal systems involving subjective or objective evaluation and, in most cases, both. In sum, diagnosis primarily serves as a means of identifying the client's level of knowledge, information processing skills, readiness, and motivation to engage in intervention strategies that lead to problem solving and career decision-making.

Client deficiencies in information processing are an important function of diagnosis in the trait-and-factor and PEF model. The client's optimal person-environment-fit is determined by valid relationships. Seven diagnostic elements are used in the developmental model to determine intervention strategies. A list of goal impediments are also used to identify client problems. In the learning theory model, faulty beliefs that interfere with goal achievement are identified in the interview and with an inventory designed for this purpose. The status of client skills and their personal qualities are used to determine learning interventions. The effectiveness of cognitive processing is an important element in the CIP model. The causes of gaps between what the client desires in the future and reality provide guidelines for intervention. A decision tree schematic is used as a diagnosis procedure for determining the direction counseling may take in the multicultural model for ethnic women. In this process, clients receive career style counseling or psychological counseling. Those on the career style counseling path will be further diagnosed for the impact of cultural variables that influence career choice.

Counseling Process

The career counseling process in all five models involves a multitude of skills; although the following summary is not meant to be an all inclusive list, it does include the major focus by most models. First, the counselor must be prepared for each counseling encounter that will involve a unique individual whose uniqueness must be accurately delineated. Client and counselors need to form a bond that will endure during the entire counseling process. The counselor must be an effective interviewer. The client-counselor relationship is very inclusive as the counselor may function as a teacher, mentor, coach, advisor, confidante, and overseer, but mainly as a collaborator who involves the client in the ongoing counseling process. Counselors must be knowledgeable of a variety of standardized and nonstandardized assessment instruments. Identifying client problems is a major counseling function. Effectively using intervention strategies including occupational information is an important component of the counseling process within all models. The effective use of decision making is also a major model focus. Finally, clients need to be prepared to recycle in the future.

Counselors introduce clients to the person-environment-fit process and assist them in matching their self-knowledge with congruent work environments in the trait-and-factor and PEF model. This process may follow interventions designed to improve the client's ability to process information. Counselors discuss individual and unique traits with clients in the developmental model. After the client understands specific goal impediments, appropriate goals are established. Learning strategies are developed in collaborative client-counselor relationships. In the learning theory model, counselors assist clients in identifying career beliefs that could interfere with progress in decision making. Counselors try to motivate clients to participate in a learning process that will improve their skills and abilities to function in changing work environments. Clients are to visualize a life span of occupational decisions and learning opportunities. In a CIP model, dysfunctional thinking and cognitive processing problems are a major concern in the opening stages of counseling. Counselors clarify problems and goals and match them with intervention strategies that are developed by consensus between client and counselor. Counselors offer assistance in decision making through cognitive restructuring. The counselor must be prepared to establish and maintain a collaborative, negotiating client-counselor relationship in a multicultural model for ethnic women. An open discussion of worldviews and salient cultural variables that are unique to the client's experience is fundamental in an effective counseling process. Counselors need to respond appropriately to culturally related cues and develop culturally appropriate intervention strategies.

In sum, the parameters of five counseling models discussed in this section provide a wide range of techniques as well as a number of similar procedures. These models were developed during the last two decades of the 20th century and may serve as a foundation for building new models or mini-theories to meet clients' unique needs in the future. There seems to be a consensus among model developers that information gathering is the first step, followed by discovery of unique client needs through subjective and objective data. Standardized assessment does not dominate the counseling process. The locus of control has shifted from counselor dominant to counselor collaborator; client involvement throughout the counseling process is prevalent. The final step in all models is the client learning effective decision-making skills and the counselor extending an open invitation for future counseling.

Summary

1. Career development research has produced a solid database that answers questions about theories. Practitioners need research that focuses on effective counseling procedures and materials. Career development theory research, however, has influenced the development of counseling models.

2. Trait-and-factor is the most popular theory in practical application. Predicting success in occupations from traits measured by objective data is an actuarial method that is widely used.

3. Three types of diagnosis are differential, dynamic, and decisional. Clients can be classified as decided, undecided, or indecisive.

4. A life career planning program points out that career counseling is very inclusive, involves complex adaptive systems, is not linear, and is future oriented.

5. The five career counseling models discussed represent a broad spectrum of techniques. The trait-and-factor theory converged with the person-

environment-fit theory and emphasizes optimal fit of client with an occupation. The developmental model stresses promoting career development over the life span. The learning theory model uses learning interventions to improve each client's skills and other personal characteristics. The cognitive approach model stresses individual learning plans and cognitive restructuring. Finally, the multicultural model for ethnic women emphasizes recognizing salient cultural variables that inhibit career choice.

6. The five counseling models use a wide range of techniques but the steps in each model are very similar. A consensus of model procedures includes information gathering, assessment, diagnosis, intervention strategies, and decision making. Standardized assessment does not dominate career counseling, and the locus of control has shifted to give the client equal responsibility in counseling decisions.

Supplementary Learning Exercises

1. Design intervention strategies that you would use for each of the following clients: decided, undecided, and indecisive. Which model would you chose for each?

2. Give an example of the type of intake interview you would use to answer the question of why a client has a particular cultural problem. Explain your choice.

3. Describe the techniques you would use to discover a client's career identity and relevant environmental information about a client to help clarify the client's goal or problem. Identify models you would use.

4. Explain the influence of interacting contextual variables on career choice. What are good references for understanding more about this topic?

5. Give reasons why contemporary career counseling models employ collaborative counselor-client relationships more.

6. Debate the following: trait-and-factor counseling techniques were misinterpreted by users.

7. Which of the five models described in this chapter most often subscribes to and emphasizes the concept of learning over the life span? Give your opinion and reasons.

8. How would you characterize the use of assessment in the five models described. Which of the models are most assessment oriented?

9. Explain under what conditions racial identity of the counselor and client are most significant. Explain.

10. Give concrete examples of how salient cultural variables limit career choice of ethnic groups.

For More Information

Anderson, J. R. (1985) *Cognitive psychology and its implication* (2nd Ed.). San Francisco: Freeman.

Brown, D., & Brooks, L. (1991). *Career counseling techniques.* Boston: Allyn & Bacon.

Crites, J. O. (1981). *Career models: Models, methods, and materials.* New York: McGraw-Hill.

Gysbers, N. C., & Moore, E. J. (1987). *Career counseling, skills and techniques for practitioners.* Englewood Cliffs, NJ: Prentice-Hall.

Healy, C. C. (1982). *Career development: Counseling through life stages.* Boston: Allyn & Bacon.

Krumboltz, J. D. (1983). *Private rules in career decision making.* Columbus, OH: National Center for Research in Vocational Education.

Krumboltz, J. D. (1991). *Career beliefs inventory.* Palo Alto, CA: Consulting Psychologists Press.

Krumboltz, J. D. (1992). Thinking about careers. *Contemporary Psychology, 37,* 113.

Krumboltz, J. D. (1993). Integrating career and personal counseling. *Career Development Quarterly, 42,* 142–148.

Krumboltz, J. D. (1996). A learning theory of career counseling. In M. L. Savickas & W. B. Walsh (Eds.), *Handbook of career counseling and practice* (pp. 55–81). Palo Alto, CA: Davies-Black.

Krumboltz, J. D., & Hamel, D. A. (1977). *Guide to career decision-making skills.* New York: Educational Testing Service.

Krumboltz, J. D., Mitchell, A., & Gelatt, H. G. (1975). Applications of social learning theory of career selection. *Focus on Guidance, 8,* 1–16.

Krumboltz, J. D., & Nichols, C. (1990). Integrating the social learning theory of career decision making. In W. B. Walsh & S. H. Osipow (Eds.), *Career counseling: Contemporary topics in vocational psychology* (pp. 159–192). Hillsdale, NJ: Erlbaum.

Peterson, G. W., Sampson, J. P., Jr., Reardon, R. C., & Lenz J. G. (1996). A cognitive information processing approach to career problem solving and decision making. In D. Brown, L. Brooks, & Associates (Eds.), *Career choice and development* (3rd ed., pp. 423–467). San Francisco: Jossey-Bass.

Rounds, J. B., & Tinsley, H. E. A. (1984). Diagnosis and treatment of vocational problems. In S. D. Brown & R. W. Lent (Eds.), *Handbook of counseling psychology* (pp. 137–177). New York: Wiley.

Rounds, J. B., & Tracey, T. J. (1990). From trait-and-factor to person-environment-fit counseling: Theory and process. In W. B. Walsh & S. J. Osipow (Eds.), *Career counseling: Contemporary topics in vocational psychology* (pp. 1–44). Hillsdale, NJ: Erlbaum.

Savickas, M. L., & Walsh, W. B. (Eds.). (1996). *Handbook of career counseling theory and practice.* Palo Alto, CA: Davies-Black.

Sharf, R. S. (1992). *Applying career development theory to counseling.* Pacific Grove, CA: Brooks/Cole.

Spokane, A. R. (1991). *Career intervention.* Englewood Cliffs, NJ: Prentice-Hall.

5

Techniques for the Career Counseling Intake Interview

Chapter Highlights

- *The rationale for career counseling intake interviews*
- *Suggested sequence for an interview*
- *Interview techniques and dialogue examples*
- *How to assess the significance of life roles and potential conflicts*
- *How to discover problems that interfere with career development*
- *Informative tables: personality disorders as related to work impairments; five types of work psychopathology; a taxonomy of psychological work-related dysfunctions*

Career Counseling Intake Interview and Assessment Techniques

The preceding chapters contained examples of the growing knowledge of the foundations for career guidance, different perspectives of career development, and models for career counseling. The wide range of content in these chapters provides background information for developing techniques that assist individuals in making career decisions. Recently, more attention has been directed toward personal problems such as faulty cognitions that can adversely affect career decision making and behavioral problems that inhibit career development. For example, Brown, Brooks, and Associates (1990) suggested that deficits in cognitive clarity require intervention other than career guidance for individuals who cannot objectively assess their own strengths and weaknesses and relate them to environmental situations. Gysbers and Moore (1987) pointed out that individuals who have been found to have irrational beliefs more than likely have distorted views of self and the career decision-making process. Spokane (1991) suggested that an increasing proportion of career counseling clients have a combination of career and personal problems. Furthermore, because career problems are often an integral part of personal problems, treatment requires intervention strategies to deal with them simultaneously. In other words, one affects the other to the point that it is less productive to separate them in treatment. Finally, Krumboltz (1983) argued that certain faulty cognitions lead to serious problems in career decision making such as, "I can do anything if I work hard enough for it," or "There is only one career for me." Career counselors should make every attempt to identify problems that could impede career development or the ability to adequately process information in career decision making. One way to accomplish this goal is through an intake interview.

In this chapter the discussion of the intake interview includes a suggested sequence for an interview and interview techniques. The next section discusses the significance of life roles and potential conflicts. Finally, the supplement to the interview is designed to help counselors discover client problems that interfere with career development. In Chapter 10, interview techniques for multicultural groups are discussed and followed by some specific suggestions that should help counselors be more effective when interviewing individuals from diverse populations.

The Intake Interview

The intake interview has different meanings and purposes for mental health professionals. In counseling, the interview assists clients in developing self-understanding, forming conclusions, looking at alternative actions, and so forth; it is viewed as a "helping interview." As a key tool for establishing objectives and goals, the interview is used by social workers to build a social history. Psychiatrists and clinical psychologists use the interview as a diagnostic tool to help form treatment considerations. For career counselors, the proposed purposes of the intake interview borrow from each of these functions. As a diagnostic tool, the interview should help uncover behavioral problems that can lead to work maladjustment and faulty cognitions, which can in turn interfere with the client's ability to make career decisions. In a helping role, the interview assists clients in understanding the integral relationship of all life roles. Finally, all parts of the interview (including historical and demographic data) are used to help develop goals.

In this chapter, we focus on accomplishing the objectives of an intake interview by providing some techniques for conducting the interview, a suggested sequence for interviewing, and a brief discussion of selected life roles with suggested topics for discussion. In addition, the supplement to the interview will assist in discovering problems that interfere with career development, such as problems in living, work maladjustment, faulty cognitions, and memory and persistence. Depending on the needs of the client, the interview may take several sessions. In Chapter 6, the interview process is illustrated using case studies.

A Suggested Sequence for an Interview

The following interview sequence is designed to provide career counselors with structured guidelines for observing their clients while in dialogue with them. Most of the topics, such as demographic information and educational history, are typically found in career counseling programs; however, the discussion of selected life roles significantly increases the options for obtaining pertinent information. For example, work history and preference for a future career are discussed as part of the work role and in association with other life roles. Individual client needs will directly determine the major focus of the interview and the sequence to be followed. For instance, an interview may be terminated during the discussion of life roles if it is determined that the individual is unable to communicate effectively with a counselor because of major clinical depression. In another case, the interview might focus on only selected life roles. In yet another case, the counselor might need to evaluate memory and persistence. The flexibility suggested for the interview provides the opportunity to meet the needs of a wide range of clients. This is the suggested sequence provided by Brown, Brooks, and Associates (1990):

I. Current status information

    A. General appearance

    B. Attitude and behavior

    C. Affect and mood

    D. Demographic information

    E. Work experience

    F. Medical history

    G. Educational history

    H. Family history

  II. Discovering the significance of life roles and potential conflict

    A. Worker role

      1. Work history

    B. Homemaker

      1. Spouse

      2. Parent

    C. Leisure role

    D. Citizen role

  III. Supplement to the interview: Discovering problems that interfere with career development

    A. Problems in living

    B. Behaviors that can lead to work maladjustment

    C. Faulty cognitions

    D. Memory and persistence

  IV. Developing goals and objectives (see Chapters 6 and 14)

    A. Identifying client goals

    B. Determining the feasibility of goals

    C. Establishing subgoals

    D. Assessing commitment to goals

Interviewing Techniques

The techniques for interviewing discussed in the following paragraphs are used within a counselor-client dyadic relationship. The objectives focus on techniques and strategies that foster productive dialogue and focus on potential deficits in career decision making and other career development concerns. The major purpose for the interview, in this context, is to determine client needs and the subsequent direction that intervention strategies will take. In some instances, the following techniques are illustrated by counselor-client dialogue: (1) rapport; (2) observation; (3) self-disclosure; (4) open- and close-ended questions; (5) echoing, restatement, or paraphrasing; (6) continuation; and (7) staying on track.

Techniques for Establishing Rapport

Jan, a 28-year-old woman, was considering returning to graduate school at a local university. She asked for an appointment at the career counseling center.

On the morning Jan reported for the appointment, she was frowning notice-ably and moved around the waiting room picking up one magazine and then an-other. She constantly looked at her watch, sighing aloud as if impatient.

Ali, the counselor assigned to Jan, observed this behavior while finishing with another client. A few minutes before the time for the appointment, Ali greeted Jan with enthusiasm.

COUNSELOR: Jan, my name is Ali, and I'm here to help you.

CLIENT: Thank you, I am glad to know you.

COUNSELOR: This is Rita, our secretary, and she will help also, especially for ap-pointments, just call either one of us for anything you need.

CLIENT: (*Nodding*) Okay, nice meeting you, Rita.

COUNSELOR: Let me show you around. Here is our career library. To our left is a room used for taking interest inventories and tests. Now here is my office.

As they entered Ali's office, he made the following comments:

COUNSELOR: I'm pleased to have the opportunity to be of assistance to you and I am here to help in anyway that I can.

Thus far, Ali had responded to his client's signs of tension and continued to establish rapport. However, some clients do not exhibit signs of tension or ap-prehension as clearly as Jan did, so it is important to communicate to each client an expression of sincerity and competence. After a short period of explanation of ethical issues and confidentiality rules, Ali asked the following question.

COUNSELOR: How may we help you?

JAN: My parents want me to choose another job, so I promised them I'd come here. I'm really upset and mad about this whole idea!

COUNSELOR: You do seem upset, particularly with your parents.

By responding with empathy, the counselor continued to build rapport. Also, Ali used the client's terms for expressing an emotion rather than a psychological term. Paraphrasing responses using the client's wording communicates under-standing to the client (Othmer & Othmer, 1989). He also helped improve rap-port by expressing an interest in the anxiety that he observed through Jan's body language and verbal expressions. Ali had learned that he must be genuine and re-sist using psychological jargon, or the client might withdraw. For example, the conversation could have gone as follows:

COUNSELOR: You were apprehensive and overwrought when I met you, you must really be somewhat unstable.

JAN: Oh really! Do you honestly think you know me that well? I've heard that psychological claptrap before.

Counselors must communicate to their counselees an understanding of their emotional status and empathetically appreciate the frustrations they are experi-encing. Instead of using technical language, use clear behavioral descriptions (Hersen & Turner, 1985). The use of more technical terms may be appropriate in sessions that follow the establishment of rapport and trust.

Techniques for Observation

Mental health workers have a long history of using observation as a tool to provide insights into their client's behavior. Psychiatrists, psychologists, clinical social workers, and counselors have refined systematic procedures for observation. Then they use the information gained, along with other data, to determine intervention strategies.

Throughout the interview, the effective interviewer is alert for any clues that provide insights into the client's personality, mood, social functioning, and other characteristics. General appearance, behavior, affect, nutritional status, hygiene and dress, eye contact, psychomotor activity, speech, attitude, and other characteristics provide important information for the intake interview.

A career counseling intake interview may be conducted in a number of different types of settings, such as a high school, college or university, private practice, mental health center, rehabilitation and employment agency, or other agency. Physical appearance may then be judged from the perspective of what is considered appropriate to the environment and to the purpose for which the interview is conducted. Appropriate physical appearance in this context is relative, but in all instances, it can provide important information. The following examples illustrate this point.

> Angelo, a 17-year-old high school student, made an appointment with the school counselor for the stated purpose of "I want help in choosing a future job." He reported promptly for the interview. The counselor made the following notes: Angelo was neatly dressed in freshly pressed trousers, a clean shirt, and shined shoes. He was of average weight, clean-shaven, with combed, short hair. There were no unusual movements, and he made eye contact throughout the interview. Angelo expressed himself well and had an impressive vocabulary. There were no indications of depression.

At first glance, one could conclude that little was revealed about Angelo other than his physical appearance was unremarkable—that is, nothing negative. However, the observer could conclude that his dress was appropriate and that he was aware of social convention and had insights into how to function adequately during the interview. His appearance gave an initial impression that he was indeed serious and highly motivated to initiate a counseling relationship.

The next example takes place in a state employment agency:

> Fred was 33 and had had several different jobs during the last ten years. The reason he gave for coming for counseling was that he was out of work and looking for a job. The counselor made the following notes: Fred was a disheveled-looking man whose clothes were unpressed and soiled. He seemed to have very poor personal hygiene; he had not shaved for several days and had very strong body odor. Fred appeared to be anxious during the interview, as observed by his behavior. First, he spoke at times with a differently pitched voice, particularly when past work experiences were discussed. He also seemed to be very guarded about his reasons for leaving certain jobs. He was quite fidgety, moving around in his chair and clenching his fists. There was a strong smell of alcohol on his breath.

From just these few notes, the client's problems with getting and keeping employment are rather clear. At least two needs were obvious: personal hygiene and substance abuse. Other information obtained from Fred in the interview reinforced these conclusions.

In these two cases, the counselor jotted down first impressions. Careful scrutiny of these impressions, along with other data, may reinforce or justify modification of these impressions. Without spending more time with a client and looking beyond surface information, recommending appropriate programming might be questionable. The skilled counselor is willing to modify early conclusions when it is justified.

Other descriptions of behavior include the following:

Rapport was difficult to establish and maintain.

Appeared to be nervous.

Seemed to tire easily.

Gave up on tasks easily.

Did not appear to be well.

A speech-articulation disorder was noted.

Seldom initiated conversation.

Responded impulsively to many questions.

Talked in a loud voice.

Talked in a low voice and was hard to understand.

Was easily distracted.

Had short attention span.

Daydreamed.

Had nervous tics.

Expressed negative view of self.

Lacked interest in personal appearance.

Expressed feelings of sadness, cried readily.

Techniques for Using Self-Disclosure

At certain times during the interview, counselors may find it advantageous to convey information about themselves to their clients. This technique is known as self-disclosure and may be positive or negative in nature. Successful personal experiences, such as "I'm known as a task-oriented person and my persistence has paid off for me," convey successful positive experiences, whereas "I lacked self-confidence on my first job" conveys a negative type of experience. Both types of self-disclosure may be used effectively for establishing rapport, communicating empathy, and facilitating dialogue during the interview. Self-disclosure by counselors can also facilitate self-disclosure from clients (Cormier & Cormier, 1991; Cozby, 1973). Counselors should be very selective when using self-disclosure, however, and should use this technique only sparingly. The following example illustrates the effective use of self-disclosure:

JIN: My father has always wanted me to follow in his footsteps like owning your own business. But I have no interest in business and especially in retail—I just wish they would leave me alone.

COUNSELOR: This sounds so familiar! My parents wanted me to become an architect and applied plenty of pressure before I went to college. I thought they would never get off my back.

JIN: I can't believe it. We had similar experiences—wow! Let me tell you more about my dad. . . .

By sharing common experiences, the counselor attempts to increase the client's disclosure level and foster discussion of unresolved relationship issues. The counselor's responses to Jin's problems through self-disclosure influenced, structured, and directed the discussion topic during the interview. Immediate feedback through self-disclosure about a client's personal problems usually enhances the client's willingness to discuss them in greater depth (Cormier & Cormier, 1991; Halpern, 1977; Thase & Page, 1977).

Techniques for Using Open- and Close-Ended Questions

The types of questions used during an interview are usually selected to obtain specific information or to encourage clients to express themselves more fully by elaborating on certain subjects, emotions, or events. The two options are the use of open- and close-ended questions. Research on these two types of questions suggests that open-ended questions facilitate emotional expression (Hopkinson, Cox, & Rutter, 1981), whereas close-ended questions have higher reliability and narrow the focus of the interview (Othmer & Othmer, 1989). Open-ended questions usually are formed with the words *tell me, explain more fully, what, how, when,* or *where.* For instance, "Tell me more about your work experiences" gives the client the opportunity to select the direction and subject of his or her response within the broad category of work experiences. Close-ended questions request more specific information; for example, "Have you served in the armed services?" Both types of questions are useful during an interview, as illustrated here:

COUNSELOR: How far did you go in school?

BEN: I quit in the 10th grade.

COUNSELOR: Why did you quit?

BEN: I don't know. I didn't like it.

Now the counselor turns to more open-ended questions in the interview.

COUNSELOR: What kind of problems did you have at school?

BEN: I couldn't get along with the teachers and the principal didn't like me, so I just quit.

COUNSELOR: Can you tell me more about your problems?

BEN: Well, I was absent a lot, and they must have known I was doing drugs and selling them, because they were always watching me. Man, I didn't do anything in school—I just quit.

In this case, the counselor quickly realized that there was more to the story about quitting school than Ben had suggested earlier. He shifted from questions used to get specific information to a free-response type, and Ben responded with pertinent information. Inconsistencies suggested by clients' statements or "mixed messages" can be clarified through the use of both open-ended and close-ended questions.

Techniques for Using Echoing, Restatement, or Paraphrasing

To focus attention on the cognitive or affective content of a client's statement, the counselor can use the techniques of echoing, restatement, or paraphrasing. One purpose of these techniques is to focus attention on the situation, object, person, or general idea of a statement. Paraphrasing or echoing the cognitive portion of a statement provides greater chances for obtaining a measure of the emotional tone associated with its content. Client affect may be expressed through nonverbal communication (gestures, facial expressions) or through descriptive words such as *sad, angry,* and *depressed* or *happy, affectionate,* and *supportive.* The degree to which affect is associated with the content of a client's statement provides counselors with important evaluative information. The following case illustrates this point:

KANISHA: My father thinks I should plan my life around a typical stereotyped role like homemaker, but—well, I've already told you that my father and I don't agree. He is just impossible!

COUNSELOR: You obviously do not agree with your father about future life roles.

KANISHA: On some things I guess I do, but most of the time, no.

COUNSELOR: You mentioned the role of homemaker.

KANISHA: I really don't know at this time. Most of my friends are going after a career and not worrying about marriage and kids. I guess I'd like to get married someday, but I'm not sure. Honestly, it depresses me to even think about it.

In this case, the counselor wanted to find out more about Kanisha's feelings about her father and particularly her feeling about the role of homemaker. The counselor was interested in determining whether there were perceived role conflicts that might influence career development. Kanisha seemed to be struggling with the message of her father's view of the appropriate role for women and with what friends were projecting as a role model. Such conflicts can inhibit ongoing career decision making well into the future.

Techniques for Using Continuation

Continuation is one of the so-called steering techniques used to encourage clients to go on with a topic and provide reinforcement that he or she is on the right course. Techniques used include nonverbal gestures such as keeping eye contact, nodding, staying silent, and using hand movements that invite the client to continue. Typical statements include "Go on," "Tell me more," "Hmm," and "What happened after that?" (Othmer & Othmer, 1989). An example follows:

COUNSELOR: What do you consider to be your major problem in selecting a career?

ABE: I don't know very much about different kinds of jobs.

COUNSELOR: Go on.

ABE: What's the future look like? What are the possibilities? I'm not sure what I like, but I know what I don't like.

COUNSELOR: Hmm. Tell me more.

ABE: How can you find out about all these things? Sometimes I feel like giving up and just taking any old job. But, then I may not be happy with it and have to start all over again. How does anyone really decide what to do?

In this case, the counselor steered Abe to elaborate on his lack of career information, interests, and decision-making procedures. Armed with such information as "What's the future look like" and "I'm not sure about what I like," the counselor is in a good position to obtain client agreement for specific career counseling goals.

Techniques for Staying on Track

Maintaining content focus is an effective technique for gainful productivity in a dyadic relationship. The counselor could have clients who are rather nonverbal, whose responses are short and abrupt, or clients who enjoy verbalizing. In both cases, keeping the conversation within the interview guidelines is one way of avoiding wasting time with irrelevant information.

Some clients have difficulty maintaining focus on a subject for a variety of reasons, including the defense mechanism of denial, lack of motivation to persist, and conflicting thoughts that make staying on track difficult. When clients have consistent patterns of difficulty maintaining focus on the subject of the discussion, referral for an in-depth analysis of the problem might be warranted. In those cases where clients deviate from the subject with unessential circumstantial information, abrupt and assertive action by the counselor may be necessary. The following case illustrates this point:

COUNSELOR: Tell me more about your interest in working with people.

KYUNG: I think I like people. My friend Julie was working in a day care center and the children there were okay. She got married and is taking a trip to the Bahamas. She and her husband like to swim and sail, they will probably go there every vacation and—

COUNSELOR: (*Interrupts*) Kyung, let's continue talking about *your* interests.

The process of interviewing clients for career counseling is a dynamic one and requires the skillful use of the techniques discussed in this section. Assessing and generating hypotheses about clients involves the possibility of a profound number of career-related problems. In the next sections, each part of the interview is discussed.

Current Status Information

General Appearance

General appearance is a generalized observation of the client's personal grooming, posture, facial expressions, and mannerisms. Forming a visual perception of the client's general appearance provides a reference point as the interview progresses. For example, appearance may provide some important clues about personality, awareness of social conventions, and ability to function in current life roles.

Attitude and Behavior

Attitude and behavior are also obtained through observation and, more specifically, through the quality of the interaction with the counselor. One client might relate easily and be cooperative, whereas another could be suspicious and guarded, requiring that the counselor offer reassurance and frequently refer to the confidentiality of the interview. Specific examples of a client's attitude and behavior should be recorded for later review. Some descriptive examples follow: articulate, avoids eye contact, shy, elated, depressed, relaxed, aggressive, anxious, tense, overbearing, alert, oppositional, self-righteous, sullen, insubordinate.

Affect and Mood

Affect is evaluated by observing the client's emotional tone during the interview, whereas mood is the client's current reported status. Affect is a momentary reaction to a current situation or conversation and might change as stimuli change. Mood, on the other hand, is self-reported for a specified period. Affect and mood can differ; for example, a client can appear happy (affect) when meeting the counselor but later report depression and despair (mood). Inappropriate affect refers to clients who demonstrate incongruence with the content of conversation, such as laughing inappropriately when a sad topic is discussed.

Demographic Information

Demographic information should include sex, ethnicity, age, and marital status. This information may be obtained by direct questioning or by self-report to questions on a structured form.

Work Experiences

Past work experience may also be recorded by the client or obtained through questioning. Report forms usually require listing both part- and full-time jobs. Other information commonly required on report forms includes likes and dislikes about jobs, career successes and failures, and jobs that may be considered for the future. Work roles are further discussed in the next section.

Medical and Educational History

Likewise, medical and educational history may also be obtained by direct questioning or by self-report. Both topics can have a significant effect on life roles. For example, physical and academic limitations are important factors to be considered in educational and career planning.

Family History

Family roles may be obtained by various methods, such as through career genograms. Gysbers and Moore (1987) describe these methods in detail. Another method referred to as an occupational family tree asks clients to list the occupations of grandparents, parents, aunts and uncles, and brothers and sisters. The respondent is questioned about his or her reactions to relatives' occupations in terms of pride or embarrassment. Other questions probe such subjects as family satisfaction with occupations and the benefits the family has received from specific occupations. The client is also asked to identify with any of the family members (Dickson & Parmerlee, 1980).

Direct questioning has the important advantage of observing client behaviors and emotional reactions. Therefore, even if a written self-report is used to obtain demographic data and work, medical, educational, and family history, a discussion of this information should be included in the interview.

Discovering the Significance of Life Roles and Potential Conflicts

An abundance of evidence, as suggested in Chapters 2 and 3, indicates that career counseling is not just concerned with strategies for selecting a career but is much broader in scope and content. Among others, Super (1990) has suggested an integrative approach to career counseling that focuses on the development of life roles over the life span, with emphasis on interrole congruence. The key to this concept is the effect of the development of one role on others. For instance, has the homemaker role inhibited career development or does the work role leave ample time for fulfillment of the citizen role? As Super (1980) pointed out, "Success in one facilitates success in others, and difficulties in one role are likely to lead to difficulties in another" (p. 287).

Hansen's (1996) Integrative Life Planning (ILP) model incorporates career development, life transitions, gender-role socialization, and social change. This model involves a "lifelong process of identifying our primary needs, roles, and goals and the consequent integration of these within ourselves, our work, and our family" (Hansen, 1990, p. 10).

The ILP model evolved from Hansen's (1978) *BORN FREE* project, which was designed to expand career options for both men and women. Hansen suggested that fragmented approaches to development place limits on decisions clients will make in their lifetimes. A more integrative approach recognizes that an individual's total development includes the broad spectrum of domains: social/emotional, physical, sexual, intellectual, vocational, and spiritual. Finally, in the context of our discussion, this model suggests that life roles are to be integrated in our planning and not isolated from the career decision-making process. The impact of decisions on lifestyle, including relationships, is a major part of a more comprehensive view of development.

The life roles to be evaluated in the interview include worker, homemaker, leisurite, and citizen. Included in the work role is work history, and included in the homemaker role is spouse and parent. Life roles increase and decrease in importance according to the individual's current status. For example, the student role is much more dominant in early life, even though career development is continuous and requires lifetime learning involvement. The potential complexity and variety of life roles over the life span can include a multitude of possible scenarios that warrant exploration. In the following paragraphs, each role is identified and examples of topics to be covered in the interview are presented.

Worker Role

Over time, the term *work* has generated many definitions and has meant different things to the individuals who do it. Also, the objectives people have for work can be quite different and might change as they pass through stages of career development. For example, some individuals work for the intrinsic enjoyment of it; for others, the primary objective might be as a way of making a living; and yet others work for social status or for self-identity. For many, a combination of objectives and other factors are equally important. Super (1984) suggested an inclusive perspective of the work role that covers most segments of lifestyle. Recently, the approach has shifted from a focus on work alone as a central life concern to an interest in the quality of life, life in which work is one central concern in a constellation of roles such as homemaking, citizenship, and leisure that interact to create life satisfaction. The terms work motivation and job satisfaction are now perhaps not displaced by, and certainly are incorporated into, the terms *quality of life* and *life satisfactions* (p. 29).

The different purposes individuals have for the work role concern us in the interview. Herr and Cramer (1996) suggested that the purposes of work can be classified as economic, social, and psychological. For example, a major economic purpose is to provide the individual with assets to satisfy current and future basic needs. In the social realm, friendships and social status are established through peer group affiliations where mutual goals are achieved. A work identity, self-efficacy, and a sense of accomplishment are examples of the psychological purposes of work.

The purposes and meanings of work are uniquely individualized. For example, a family-oriented individual who has strong needs to spend ample time with his or her children could be somewhat unhappy in a work role that limits family activities. A strong orientation for work leadership roles might inhibit an individual's needs associated with the life roles of citizen and leisurite. Although it may be difficult to satisfy the needs of all life roles, a greater balance of roles could enhance some people's quality of life. The following list of topics for discourse and samples of content for work-role interviewing represent only a few of the possibilities that can be discussed. Client needs should dictate the selection of subjects.

For a client making an initial choice of work role, the counselor should assess the following:

- Knowledge of life-role concepts
- Acceptance of the idea of different life roles
- Ability to evaluate how work roles affect other life roles
- Ability to project an ideal work role
- Ability to identify purpose of the work role
- Ability to project self into work roles
- Ability to identify future work roles
- Knowledge of personal characteristics
- Level of skill development

Although many of the variables considered in the initial choice might have to be reevaluated with individuals who wish to change careers, the degree to which the individual is able to do the following should also be explored:

- Adapt to changes
- Learn new and different skills
- Function under different management styles
- Assess reasons for career changes and work commitments
- Assess his or her abilities, limitations, interests, and values to adapt to work environment changes
- Use decision-making procedures
- Identify career resources and how to use them
- Identify sources of stress
- Apply methods of modifying behavior
- Identify educational and training programs

Homemaker Role

The role of homemaker has a wide spectrum of possibilities. For example, a 35-year-old single person might not consider this role a very important one, whereas a married 35-year-old who has children might consider homemaker a major role. A high school student could consider this role as something to be dealt with in the future, whereas a 50-year-old who has reared several children will place less emphasis on this role when planning a career change. The more recent phenomenon of the househusband and more emphasis on the male role as a homemaker adds to the diversity of possible interrole conflicts (see Chapters 11, 12, and 13).

The number of working mothers is expected to increase. There is a definite trend toward more working mothers who have children under the age of 6; for instance, 12% of such women were employed in 1950, whereas 57% were employed in the early 1990s (Chadwick & Heaton, 1992). Hoffreth and Phillips (1987) have suggested that 7 of 10 mothers with infants and young children will be employed before or by the end of the 1990s and this trend is expected to continue into the 21st century. A major concern about maternal employment is its effect on children, the family, and the working women themselves. In a comprehensive review of the literature concerning the effects of maternal employment on children, Herr and Cramer (1996) concluded that in general it does no harm to children (infants, preschoolers, and adolescents). Working mothers also seem to fare well, according to Ferree (1984), who conducted a national research study concerning satisfaction variables. She concluded that there were no significant differences in life satisfaction between working mothers and those who did not work outside the home. In a related study, results indicated that stress experienced by working women can be offset by spousal approval, dependable child care, and shared family responsibilities (Scarr, Phillips, & McCartney, 1989; Suchet & Barling, 1985).

The issues surrounding the homemaker role in families where both husband and wife work outside the home (dual-earner and dual-career) have major significance as a result of the expected increasing number of working mothers. In dual-earner and dual-career families, both husband and wife work outside the home, but dual-career families are characterized as more career-oriented and committed to career development on a continuous basis. Both types of families share some common goals as well as sources of stress, such as role conflict, role overloads, and decreased opportunity for leisure. The following is a list of subjects for general discourse:

- Degree of commitment to the role of homemaker
- Career now and homemaker later
- The woman as a homemaker and the husband as a breadwinner
- The reason both spouses may have to work
- The homemaker-worker connection
- Family life versus career commitment
- The significance of integrated life roles

Potential conflict issues such as the following should also be assessed:

- Decreased leisure
- Share of homemaker responsibilities
- View of traditional gender-based roles
- Stress from physical and emotional demands
- Multiple role demands
- Commitment to household chores
- Commitment to sharing child care responsibilities
- Commitment to development of spouse's career
- Nonsupport of spouse's career development
- Dissimilar levels of involvement in both work and family needs
- Decision-making procedures for such family matters as when to have children
- Expectations of family roles in dual-career marriages

Leisure Role

A number of clichés about the relationship of work and leisure have endured for generations. The primary message has been that a quality lifestyle is one in which there is a balance between time spent at work and time devoted to leisure activities. This message still prevails and has received renewed recognition as a means of fostering need satisfaction (Leclair, 1982). Within this frame of reference, quality of life is attained through a more holistic viewpoint of human and career development. Simply stated, individuals are to recognize that quality of life is associated with all life roles. Central to our concerns as career counselors is a balance of life roles that gives clients the freedom for self-expression to meet their needs. Moreover, when interrole conflicts are discovered, we have at our disposal a menu of suggestions designed to enhance all life roles.

The complementary role that leisure has to the work role is expressed by Kando and Summers (1971) as two-dimensional; that is, it reinforces positive associations that are also expressed in the work role (supplemental compensation) and provides activities to reduce stress associated with unpleasant work experiences (reactive compensation). Following this logic but with a somewhat different twist, Jackson (1988) suggested that individuals can receive psychological benefits from leisure, but only if they learn how to use the time spent in leisure in a purposeful manner. Remember that sources of stress found in work, such as competition, can also become sources of stress in leisure activities.

The availability of time that can be devoted to leisure for any one individual is situational. However, McDaniels (1990) advocated planning for different types of leisure as part of a counseling model. He also suggested that counselors act in an advocacy role to promote leisure activities in schools, workplaces, homes, and communities.

In sum, the leisure role should be assessed as a prolific means of complementing other life roles. The proportion of time a person allocates to leisure should be judged from the perspective of lifestyle. For example, the ambitious accountant might consider leisure activities as a luxury that has little current relevance, whereas the individual who is working full time as a bus driver and part time on two other jobs could view leisure as something that other, more fortunate people do. The *involvement* in leisure might simply be haphazard and left to chance. Although there is not a plethora of research suggesting the benefits of leisure activities, some research conclusions strongly suggest that effective participation in leisure can be therapeutic (Ragheb & Griffith, 1982) and can compensate for dissatisfaction found in work (Bloland & Edwards, 1981). Suggested subjects for discourse are the following:

- Benefits of leisure activities
- Purpose for planning activities
- Types of leisure, including intellectual, creative, social, and physical activities
- Resources for information on leisure activities
- How to become involved in a leisure/work model
- Perspectives of a holistic lifestyle
- Recognition of conflicts with other life roles
- The role of leisure and career development
- The advantages of balancing life roles with leisure
- Identification of needs and values associated with the leisure role
- Psychological needs satisfied through leisure activities
- The work/leisure connection
- Developmental tasks related to leisure development
- Development of a greater level of interest in leisure activities

Citizen Role

Similar to the leisure role's link to quality of life, the citizen role can serve as an additional or compensating source of satisfaction. Also, this role provides opportunities for fulfilling individual needs in a wide variety of activities found in most communities. Local civic organizations offer an abundance of opportunities for individuals to express civic responsibility as a way of responding to community needs. Although involvement in volunteerism was on the increase for community, state, national, and international projects in the late 1980s and the early part of the 1990s, the recent downsizing of the U.S. work force has created a different atmosphere in many communities. According to Rimer (1996), who reflects on a national poll sponsored by the *New York Times,* many communities now have fewer volunteers for community service. Workers who have lost their jobs are desperately searching for ways to maintain their lifestyle and no longer have the time or the inclination to volunteer for civic services. Thus, counselors need to observe the citizen role in the context of current conditions within communities.

The concept of balanced life roles implies that there are numerous opportunities to build a quality lifestyle. Individual work situations might not provide outlets to meet client needs associated with, for example, reading to blind students or being a tutor or hospital aide. Productive opportunities outside the work role are means of satisfaction that enhance interrole activities. That is, some needs that might otherwise be left unmet or that produce stress can be satisfied through civic activities.

Among others, Bolles (1993) has suggested that skills learned and developed through participation in civic organizations and activities can be used in career decision making. These skills can be matched with work requirements in career exploration (see Chapter 20). Also, volunteer experiences, along with education and other experiences, are considered in job placement (McDaniels, 1990).

In the interview, the counselor should assess the client for

- Perception of the citizen's role
- Knowledge of civic organizations
- Knowledge of benefits from participating in civic activities
- Knowledge of benefits from participating in volunteerism
- Evaluation of skills learned through participation in civic activities
- Knowledge of how skills can be transferred to work roles
- Degree of participation in civic organizations
- Desire to participate in civic organizations
- Reasons for lack of participation in community activities
- Likes and dislikes of civic activities
- Family involvement in civic activities

Supplement to the Interview: Discovering Problems That Interfere with Career Development

This part of the interview focuses on behavioral patterns of maladjustment. Identifying specific behavior domains that could contribute to conflicts in the work environment helps the career counselor identify goals and objectives for counseling intervention. For instance, individuals whose basic behavior style has been identified as overtly hostile and aggressive might respond to programs designed to manage anger and reduce aggression.

"Problems in living" and methods of coping with these problems need to be identified. This approach does not rule out psychiatric etiology as a source of work maladjustment but focuses more on the individual's ability to cope with work demands. Perhaps more important, mental disorders do not necessarily affect work behavior. Neff (1985) pointed out that the ability to function on a job is related to the nature of both an individual's mental health and his or her mental illness. More research is needed to establish the relationship between work maladaption and mental disorders.

Some research has suggested that career competence is not grossly affected by mental illness (character and affective disorders, severe psychoneurosis, and functional psychosis) when the mental illness subsides (Huffine & Clausen, 1979). The findings of this longitudinal research project suggested that developed competencies and socialization into the work world were not necessarily affected by the mental illness of the men studied.

The fourth edition of the *Diagnostic and Statistical Manual of Mental Disorders* (DSM-IV) (American Psychiatric Association [APA], 1994) has several categories of mental, social, and behavioral disorders. Although all these disorders can appear in the workplace, references to work impairment or dysfunctions are very generalized. The following quote from the DSM-IV (APA, 1994) is a guideline for how we must individualize our interpretation of mental disorders and the subsequent behavior associated with a disorder.

> In DSM-IV, there is no assumption that each category of mental disorder is a completely discrete entity with absolute boundaries dividing it from other mental disorders or from no mental disorder. There is also no assumption that all individuals described as having the same mental disorder are alike in all important ways. The clinician using the DSM-IV should therefore consider that individuals sharing a diagnosis are likely to be heterogeneous even in regard to the defining features of the diagnosis and that boundary cases will be difficult to diagnose in any but a probabilistic fashion. (p. xxii)

Behaviors That Can Lead to Work Maladjustment

One of our objectives in the assessment interview is to identify individualized behavior patterns that impair the work role. Table 5-1 presents symptoms of behavior and faulty cognitive functioning that can lead to work impairment. These symptoms were adapted from personality disorders and descriptions of depression found in DSM-IV (APA, 1994). The information can be used as guidelines for identifying similar patterns of behavior in clients being interviewed. The purpose of this table is not to classify clients according to any particular disorder but, more important, to serve as a guide for identifying behavioral contingencies and faulty assumptions that could lead to work impairment. A client identified as having poor social interaction skills, for instance, might also have difficulty relating to work affiliates and, thus, develop negative meanings associated with work.

Table 5-1 identifies disorders by behaviors, beliefs, and traits. The column "Work Impairments" suggests that some clients might have difficulty in the workplace when the behaviors, beliefs, or traits listed in the column are dominant and extreme. On the other hand, behaviors, beliefs, and traits associated with disorders do not necessarily lead to work impairment as suggested in the column "Other Work Role Observations." Using this logic, the interviewer attempts to determine

TABLE 5-1	WORK-ROLE PROJECTIONS

Identification	Behaviors, beliefs, traits	Work impairment	Other work role observations
Cluster A[1] Paranoid career client	Suspicious of others, especially authority figures Avoids participation in group activities Reluctant to self-disclose Hostile and defensive Strong need to be self-sufficient	Poor interpersonal relationships with boss and peer group.	May meet demands of work role because of high ambition, especially in work environments that are highly structured and nonthreatening.
Schizoid career client	Very indecisive Vague about goals Does not desire or enjoy close relationships Prefers solitary activities Often aloof	Work involving interpersonal interactions is difficult.	May work well in an environment that provides social isolation.
Cluster B[1] Antisocial career client	Truancy, vandalism, stealing Nonconformity to social norms Very aggressive Inconsistent work behavior Poor emotional control	Difficulty in sustaining productive work.	Clients who are identified as having only several characteristics of this disorder may be able to function successfully in a work role. However, full-blown antisocial career clients have considerable interference with work roles.
Borderline career client	Poor self-concept Difficulty in establishing long-term goals Difficulty with career choice Difficulty with identifying preferred values Impulsive Unstable interpersonal relations Uncertainty about life roles	Impulsive behavior interferes with work role functioning; poor commitment to work.	The instability and impulsive nature of borderline career clients presents considerable interference with most life roles, including the work role.

[1]Not all personality disorders are included in Clusters A, B, and C.

178

TABLE 5-1

WORK-ROLE PROJECTIONS *(continued)*

Identification	Behaviors, beliefs, traits	Work impairment	Other work role observations
Narcissistic career client	Exploits others Shows little concern for others Expects favorable treatment Excessive feelings of self-importance Constantly seeks attention	Poor interpersonal relationships; may pursue unrealistic goals while exploiting co-workers.	Because of a strong need for success and power, these clients are able to meet requirements and sometimes excel in work role functioning.
Cluster C[1] Obsessive-compulsive career client	Preoccupied with trivial details Seeks perfection in work tasks to the point that task completion is constantly delayed Has strong need for inflexible routines Avoids decision making Unnecessarily devoted to organizing tasks	Poor task completion. Poor productivity. Subject to stress because of indecision.	Because of excessive conscientiousness and extreme attention to detail, these clients are able to function in work roles that require highly organized procedures.
Avoidant career client	Poor interpersonal skills Avoids occupational activities that involve interpersonal contact Is preoccupied with being criticized or being rejected Is reluctant to take personal risks	Work role is affected by poor interpersonal skills.	Work role functioning is limited to environments that are nonthreatening and only require minimum social contacts.
Depressed[2] career client	Lacks interest and pleasure in most activities Has difficulty in concentrating on tasks Behavior is typically lethargic and shows loss of energy Has difficulty sleeping or sleeps excessively Expresses negative feelings toward and about self Dejected mood Low self-evaluations	In severe cases, clients are not able to function in work role.	In mild to moderate cases of depression, some interference can be expected, but not all clients are totally inefficient.

[1]Not all personality disorders are included in Clusters A, B, and C.
[2]The depressed career client is not considered a personality disorder.

SOURCE: Adapted from *Diagnostic and Statistical Manual of Mental Disorders*, 4th ed. rev., by the American Psychiatric Association, 1994.

the degree to which an identified behavior or trait affects the work role. For example, work involving interpersonal interactions might be difficult for some clients, but these clients have managed to become productive workers. Perhaps they could improve their potential with counseling designed to help them overcome this problem in all life roles, but their needs are not as obvious as are those of someone who simply cannot function effectively with others. In sum, the severity of the identified needs determines the course and extent of intervention strategies.

In the DSM-IV, personality disorders are grouped into three clusters—A, B, and C—to accommodate the commonalities found among them. For example, career clients who resemble the characteristics, traits, and behaviors found in the Cluster A group might appear strange, peculiar, and bizarre. Likewise, those career clients who resemble the characteristics associated with the Cluster B group could appear highly emotional and dramatic. Those identified with Cluster C might appear anxious and fearful. The commonalities and overlap of symptoms found in personality disorders suggest that clients can demonstrate behaviors, beliefs, and traits of more than one personality disorder.

In an attempt to organize qualities of work behavior that lead to failure in work, Neff (1985) identified five types or patterns of work psychopathology using classifications ranging from Type I to Type V, as shown in Table 5-2. Individuals can be "typed" only when the characteristics listed predominate work behavior. Neff warns that not all clients will fit into these categories; some could have characteristics of several.

Lowman (1993) has attempted to devise a clinically useful taxonomy of psychological work-related dysfunctions, as reported in Table 5-3. One of his major premises is to illuminate the distinction between psychopathology and work dysfunctions, but he also reminds mental health workers that the two types of problems can coexist. For example, psychopathology may or may not affect work performance, and the presence of worker dysfunctions may or may not have an impact on psychopathology.

The disturbances in the capacity to work are useful categories for delineating worker dysfunctions. These patterns are summarized as follows. Underachievement is an apparent discrepancy between the individual's ability and performance. Possible causes are passive-aggressive behavior, procrastination, or periodic inhibition to work. Fear of success refers to intentional underachievement because of perceived negative consequences associated with being successful. Fear of failure suggests that an individual withholds work efforts for fear of not being successful.

Other disturbances in the capacity to work such as patterns of overcommitment (see Chapters 12 and 19), work-related anxiety (see Chapters 6 and 12), personality dysfunctions and work, life role conflicts (see Chapter 13), and transient, situational stress (see Chapters 6 and 20) will be discussed in these chapters and in other sections of this chapter. The last category in this section, perceptual inaccuracies, refers to differences between the individual worker's perception of the workplace and what actually exists.

Finally, category III, dysfunctional working conditions, refers to problems associated with the assigned job itself (such as too demanding or too difficult work), the quality or lack of supervision, and the possibility of poor interpersonal

TABLE 5-2	NEFF'S PATTERNS OF WORK PSYCHOPATHOLOGY

Type	Characteristics
I—Individuals who lack motivation to work	▪ Have a negative concept of the work role. ▪ Are indifferent to productive work. ▪ Will work if coerced. ▪ Meet minimum standards of work tasks. ▪ Resist work commitment. ▪ Require close supervision. ▪ Lack need or desire to work.
II—Individuals who experience fear and anxiety in response to being productive	▪ Feel incapable of being productive. ▪ Feel too inept to meet work demands. ▪ How low self-esteem. ▪ Competition at work is extremely threatening. ▪ Cooperative work efforts are difficult. ▪ Lack self-confidence. ▪ May retreat from work environment if severely threatened.
III—Individuals who are hostile and aggressive	▪ Underlying hostility is easily aroused. ▪ Peer affiliation is viewed as potentially dangerous. ▪ Are quick to quarrel with others. ▪ Relation with supervisory personnel is precarious and threatening. ▪ Work roles are often viewed as too demanding and restrictive. ▪ Have very poor interpersonal relationships.
IV—Individuals who are very dependent on others	▪ Early socialization convinces them that the way to self-preservation is to please others. ▪ Believe that the key to work success is pleasing authority figures. ▪ Have a strong need for constant approval, particularly from supervisors.
V—Individuals who display a marked degree of social naivete	▪ Have very little knowledge of work environment and demands of work role. ▪ Lack simple understanding of work role involvement. ▪ Have no perception of self as a successful worker to meet even minimal standards. ▪ Unable to project self into work role.

SOURCE: Adapted from Neff, 1985.

relationships. All these issues represent potential conflicts associated with working conditions.

The guidelines for identifying characteristics that could lead to work impairment or work dysfunctions associated with personality disorders, Neff's patterns of work psychopathology, and Lowman's taxonomy of psychological work-related dysfunctions must be used with caution. Identified characteristics must predominate to be significant. Moreover, work behavior is considered to be a

TABLE 5-3	TOWARD A CLINICALLY USEFUL TAXONOMY OF PSYCHOLOGICAL WORK-RELATED DYSFUNCTIONS

  I. Determining the relation between psychopathology and work dysfunctions
     A. Affecting work performance
     B. Not affecting work performance
     C. Affected by work performance
     D. Not affected by work performance
 II. Disturbances in the capacity to work
     A. Patterns of undercommitment
        1. Underachievement
        2. Temporary production impediments
        3. Procrastination
        4. Occupational misfit
        5. Organizational misfit
        6. Fear of success
        7. Fear of failure
     B. Patterns of overcommitment
        1. Obsessive-compulsive addiction to the work role ("workaholism")
        2. Type A behavior pattern
        3. Job and occupational burnout
     C. Work-related anxiety and depression
        1. Anxiety
           a. Performance anxiety
           b. Generalized anxiety
        2. Work-related depression
     D. Personality dysfunctions and work
        1. Problems with authority
        2. Personality disorders and work
     E. Life role conflicts
        1. Work-family conflicts
     F. Transient, situational stress
        1. Reactions to changes in the work role (e.g., new job) whose impact on the work role is time limited.
     G. Other psychologically relevant work difficulties
        1. Perceptual inaccuracies
III. Dysfunctional working conditions
     A. Defective job design (role overload, ambiguity, etc.)
     B. Defective supervision
     C. Dysfunctional interpersonal relationships

SOURCE: From *Counseling and Psychotherapy of Work Dysfunctions,* by R. L. Lowman, pp. 43–44. Copyright 1993 by the American Psychological Association. Reprinted by permission.

semiautonomous area of personality and, as such, might not be affected by personality disorders. On the other hand, work maladaption might be linked to personality disorders. In essence, work dysfunctions are the result of a complex interaction of personal characteristics and the workplace. In sum, these guidelines present examples of potential work behavior problems and should be used as such. In the next chapter, examples of methods of identifying potential work behavior problems are illustrated.

Faulty Cognitions

We are challenged to give more attention to cognitive processes in career counseling from the social-learning theory approaches to career development discussed in Chapter 2 (Mitchell & Krumboltz, 1996). Somewhat similar approaches to cognitive functioning are irrational beliefs (Ellis, 1962) and faulty reasoning (Beck, 1985). More specifically, the individual's perceptions of self and of people, events, experiences, and environment are seen as potential sources of mistaken and troublesome beliefs. Inaccurate information, faulty alternatives, and negative constructs derived from life experiences are sources of faulty cognitions.

Faulty cognitions inhibit systematic, logical thinking and can be self-defeating. For example, a client's expectations and assumptions can cause distorted perceptions and unrealistic thinking such as "There is only one career for me." Doyle (1992) presented the following examples of faulty cognition that he suggested can lead to false conclusions and negative feelings:

1. *Self-deprecating statements:* These expressions reveal poor self-worth, for example, "I'm not a good student" or "No one really likes me."

2. *Absolute or perfectionist terms:* When an individual sets up overly stringent guidelines for his or her behavior, the individual sets himself or herself up for self-criticism and a negative self-image. Conclusions that are absolute or perfectionistic often include the words *must, ought, should, unless,* or *until.* For example, "I should have been the one promoted" or "Unless I get an 'A,' I can't go home."

3. *Overgeneralization of negative experiences:* These are deductions based on too few examples of situations. Frequently, they are based on negative experiences that make clients think there are many obstacles making the future hopeless and bleak. For example, "Since I failed the first exam, I will fail the course" or "All the children in school hate me."

4. *Negative exaggerations:* These statements greatly magnify the true meaning of an event or reality. For example, "All professional athletes are greedy" or "You insulted my mother—you hate my family!"

5. *Factually inaccurate statements:* These remarks are based on inadequate or incorrect information. These erroneous data distort the client's perceptions of reality. For example, "You need an 'A' average to get into college" or "Autistic children are lazy."

6. *Ignorance of the effects of time:* These assertions ignore growth, maturation, and the effect that the passage of time can have on experience or events. For example, "He was a very poor student last year—he will surely fail this year" or "I have to go back to the lake and relive my vacation there" (p. 85).

Although faulty cognitions can lead to a multitude of personal problems, Mitchell and Krumboltz (1996) argued that the career decision-making process is most affected. Looking at it from a positive viewpoint, individuals with accurate, constructive beliefs will have fewer problems reaching their career goals. Moreover, realistic expectations foster positive emotional reactions to self and others.

In sum, this portion of the interview requires an assessment of the client's beliefs, generalities that cause a belief, other bases for a belief, and the actions that are a result of a belief (Mitchell & Krumboltz, 1987). Chapters 6 and 19 provide other criteria for evaluating faulty cognitions and also presents counseling intervention strategies designed to introduce more rational, productive ways of thinking.

Memory and Persistence

The client's ability to concentrate on tasks without being distracted by other stimuli is a prerequisite to more complex capabilities (Schwartz, 1989). In the context of career counseling, clients must be able to process information about work environments and themselves so they can make decisions in their best interests. The ability to attend selectively and to concentrate over time is a vital part of cognitive functioning necessary in the career decision-making process.

Some specific tasks for evaluating memory and concentration are reported in Hersen and Turner (1985), Craig (1989), and Othmer and Othmer (1989). Suggested techniques are straightforward, informal, and designed to screen clients for gross deficits in memory and concentration.

Memory is usually classified into three types: immediate (the client's ability to recall information he or she has just been told), recent (the client's ability to recall events that took place in the last several days, weeks, or months), and remote (the client's ability to recall events that happened several years in the past). Assessment for each type of memory provides important insights into each client's current cognitive-functioning capabilities. Memory impairment can indicate the client is easily distracted, preoccupied, confused, anxious, or depressed or has psychiatric disorders. The important point for the counselor to ascertain is the degree of severity of impairment in memory and concentration. The counselor will want to find out if the client is capable of adequately attending to the tasks of a selected career counseling program. The rule of thumb here is, when in doubt, seek assistance from other professionals. A client with significant deficits in concentration or memory should be referred for a formal inquiry (Rosenthal & Akiskal, 1985).

Memory can be evaluated during the interview in an informal manner. For example, one way to check immediate recall is to spell your name or the name of the school or a city and ask the client to repeat the spelling. To check recent memory, ask the client to give directions to a well-known location or to your office. Remote memory can be evaluated during a discussion of past events (Othmer & Othmer, 1989). A more formalized method of evaluating memory is described in Hersen and Turner (1985).

ASSESSING IMMEDIATE RECALL.   To assess immediate recall, the client is asked to remember three things that are presented verbally; for example, pen, blue, and the number 14. After the client successfully repeats the items, he or she is instructed to keep remembering them, because the counselor will ask for a repetition in approximately 5 minutes.

In another assessment technique, the client is instructed to listen carefully to a series of numbers; he or she will be asked to repeat them immediately after the presentation. For example, "Listen carefully and repeat these numbers after I'm finished." (Present them at the rate of one each second.) "2–7–9." After each successful answer, the number of digits is increased, 1–5–4–7, and so forth. When the client is no longer able to recall the digits in proper sequence, the process is repeated with the instructions to recall the digits in backward order, starting with two numbers and increasing the number of digits each time. Individuals with normal intelligence and without any organic impairment can usually repeat six digits forward and five in reverse (Hersen & Turner, 1985).

ASSESSING RECENT MEMORY.   You can measure recent memory by asking clients about verifiable information that has transpired within a few days. Some example questions are these:

What did you eat for lunch yesterday?

Who was the presidential candidate who spoke at the municipal auditorium this week?

Tell me what you saw on TV news last night.

What national holiday did we celebrate on Wednesday?

ASSESSING REMOTE MEMORY.   Remote memory can be evaluated by asking clients to assess recollections of significant historical events. The ability to cognitively select and recall significant events in the past is a measure of remote memory. Some examples are:

Where were you born?

Where did you go to high school?

What was the Great Depression?

What was your first job outside the home?

What was Watergate?

What was Desert Storm?

ASSESSING CONCENTRATION AND TASK PERSISTENCE.   Concentration and task persistence refer to the ability to sustain focused attention sufficiently to complete tasks commonly found in career counseling programs. For example, can the client sustain focused attention to complete such tasks as gathering information; generating, evaluating, and selecting alternatives; and formulating plans to implement decisions? According to Hersen and Turner (1985), deficiencies in concentration and memory can be observed through serial subtraction.

For assessment of concentration, the client is asked to subtract 3 from 100, then 3 from that number, then 3 again, and so forth. If this task is done correctly for five or six subtractions, then the client is asked to subtract 7 from 100, and so forth. The counselor will need to determine whether an inability to perform these calculations is due primarily to educational level and calculating ability or to the inability to concentrate. For example, if a client has a college degree and is unable to calculate beyond one subtraction, the counselor could probably conclude that the ability to concentrate has been adversely affected.

Summary

1. Recently, more attention has been directed to personal problems and faulty cognitions that can adversely affect career decision making.

2. Deficits in cognitive clarity require intervention other than career guidance. Because career problems are often an integral part of personal problems, intervention strategies deal with both simultaneously.

3. The intake interview is designed to identify client needs for career counseling or other career needs that could interfere with career development and life role functioning.

4. The intake interview includes gathering current status information, discovering problems that interfere with career development, discovering the significance of life roles and potential conflicts, and developing goals and objectives.

5. Techniques for interviewing include establishing rapport, observation, self-disclosure, open- and close-ended questions, echoing, continuation, and staying on track.

6. General appearance is a generalized observation of the client's personal grooming, posture, facial expressions, and mannerisms.

7. Attitude and behavior are observed through the quality of the interaction with the counselor.

8. Affect and mood are evaluated by the client's emotional tone and reported status.

9. Demographic information and work, medical, educational, and family history are obtained by self-report or through direct questioning.

10. Life roles selected for interviewing include worker, homemaker, citizen, and leisurite. Life roles are considered an integral part of each individual's development. Success in one life role enhances success in another.

11. Behavior patterns that impair the work role are identified in the intake interview as needs that determine intervention strategies.

12. Faulty cognitions inhibit systematic, logical thinking and can be self-defeating. Sources of faulty cognitions are primarily from life experiences.

13. Memory is classified as immediate, recent, and remote. Memory can be evaluated during the interview through informal questioning and by more formalized procedures.

Supplementary Learning Exercises

1. Develop a list of reasons to support intake interviewing for career counseling. Give specific examples to support your reasons.

2. Present two examples of irrational beliefs that could interfere with career decision making.

3. Develop interview objectives for a specific ethnic client. Justify your rationale.

4. Discuss how work history can identify work maladjustment. Build two cases to illustrate.

5. Defend or criticize the following statement: Life roles are to be considered a significant part of career development.

6. Develop two examples to illustrate how self-disclosure can or cannot be effective in the interview.

7. Present several examples of dialogue to illustrate the effective use of open- and close-ended questions.

8. Have the benefits of leisure activities been overemphasized? Defend your arguments to classmates.

9. Develop a list of intervention strategies that could be used to encourage shared responsibilities in the home for dual-earner families.

10. Give several examples of behavior that could be identified with career client personality disorders in Table 5-1. Explain how these identified behavior patterns would or would not interfere with the work role.

For More Information

Brown, D., & Brooks, L. (1991). *Career counseling techniques*. Boston: Allyn & Bacon.

Doyle, R. E. (1992). *Essential skills and strategies in the helping process*. Pacific Grove, CA: Brooks/Cole.

Cormier, W., & Cormier, L. S. (1991). *Interviewing strategies for helpers: Fundamental skills and cognitive behavioral interventions* (3rd ed.). Pacific Grove, CA: Brooks/Cole.

Gysbers, N. C., & Moore, E. J. (1987). *Career counseling, skills and techniques for practitioners*. Englewood Cliffs, NJ: Prentice-Hall.

Ivey, A. E., & Ivey, M. B. (1999). *Intentional interviewing & counseling* (4th ed.). Pacific Grove, CA: Brooks/Cole.

Lowman, R. L. (1993). *Counseling and psychotherapy of work dysfunctions*. Washington, DC: American Psychological Association.

Neff, W. S. (1985). *Work and human behavior* (2nd ed.). Chicago: Aldine.

Othmer, E., & Othmer, S. (1989). *The clinical interview*. Washington, DC: American Psychiatric Press.

6

Career Counseling Intake Interviews: Case Studies

Chapter Highlights

- *Problems that interfere with career development*
- *The Case of What Was Left Unsaid*
- *The Case of Faulty Cognitions*
- *The Case of the Confused Decision Maker*
- *The Case of the Anxious Computer Technician*
- *The Case of the Forgotten Work Address*
- *The Case of the Fired Plumber*
- *The Case of the Unfulfilled Worker*
- *Five-step process of using assessments results*
- *Developing goals and objectives for career counseling examples*

I
N THE PRECEDING CHAPTER, THE RATIONALE FOR INTERVIEWING CLIENTS
for career counseling pointed out the need for developing an intake interview to
determine appropriate intervention strategies. Embedded in this rationale is the
recognition that some career clients may not fully benefit from career decision-
making procedures for a variety of reasons, including illogical thinking, irrational
beliefs, other faulty cognitions, or severe psychological problems. What is needed
are methods of identifying potential problems that inhibit clients from making decisions in their best interests. For example, clients who cannot reason in a rational
manner have erroneous perceptions of work roles and are unable to accurately
process career information because of false beliefs; they would best be served by
intervention programs to correct these problems before continuing in career decision making.

We cannot, of course, deal only with factors that inhibit career decision making. We must also deal with contingencies that contribute to work role maladjustment and potential problems associated with family, homemaker, citizen, and
leisure roles. The assumption that life role development is the outcome of the long
process of personal and interpersonal development gives credence to the position
of focusing attention on each client's perception of the interrelationship of these
roles. For example, poor interpersonal skills found as limiting factors in the work
role can also impair the development of the citizen role (interpersonal relations in
civic clubs) and the leisure role (activities involving others). Although life roles are
discussed as separate entities, problems in one life role can affect development in
another. In essence, the career counselor's ability to effectively tease out problems
that inhibit positive growth is a necessary skill in using the intake interview.

In the first section of this chapter, an intake interview closely follows the sequence for interviewing suggested in Chapter 5, starting with current status information. The second section discusses problems that interfere with career
development; these problems are illustrated with case studies. Part three covers
life roles and potential conflicts. Finally, we discuss the development of goals and
objectives.

Current Status Information

Techniques for observing clients were illustrated in Chapter 5; therefore, in this
section, we will emphasize the value of demographic information and work, medical, and educational histories.

THE CASE OF WHAT WAS LEFT UNSAID

Ida, a 36-year-old woman, was referred by a mental health agency to a state-supported
agency that provided career counseling. The information sent with the referral contained
demographic data, a sparse educational history, a diagnosis of clinical depression, and
prescribed medication. The following notes were made by the career counselor as she interviewed Ida.

A. General appearance
Client was appropriately dressed.
Hair had not been recently washed.
Wore little or no makeup.
Wore glasses.
Gait was normal.
Movements were without tremor.
Carried envelope and placed it on desk.

B. Attitude and behavior
Introduced herself.
Eye contact was appropriate.
Showed no evidence of unusual behavior.

C. Affect and mood
Said she was depressed but did not look it.
Appeared rather lifeless.
Stated that she was somewhat nervous about being interviewed.
Stated she "felt good" especially when she was alone.
Said she didn't like "being around a lot of people."
Was vague when expressing herself.

D. Demographic information
Said she was married four times, but could not remember the sequence of
birth of four children or which marriage they were from.
High-pitched voice used during discussion of marriages.
Currently living with a cousin who helps care for her children.

E. Work experiences
Difficulty in recalling work experiences.
Held part-time job in fast-food restaurant during senior year in high school.
Held part- and full-time jobs in fast foods for several months after graduation.
Waitressed in different local restaurants.
Was a receptionist in accounting firm for about four months.
Disliked restaurant work.
Enjoyed work as a receptionist; claims she left because she was hospitalized.

F. Medical history
Stated that she was in good health until age 29 when she was hospitalized
for depression. Stayed in a psychiatric hospital for five days. Has been
treated as an outpatient with medication for several years but was unable to
specify exactly how long.
Felt that failure in marriage was a major cause of depression.
Reported problems with sleeping.
Reported no other significant illnesses.

G. Educational history
Finished high school with average grades.
Did not finish a course in computer programming. Said she had a strange
feeling "that she should not finish this course."

During the interview the counselor became concerned about vague references to past history. Even with further questioning, she could not get appropriate feedback:

COUNSELOR: Ida, could you tell me more about the feeling you experienced that convinced you not to finish the computer programming course?

IDA: I don't know how to explain it—it was just like something told me not to finish.

COUNSELOR: Something told you not to finish?

IDA: Yeah, I can't explain it.

Another example was expressions about work experiences.

IDA: I quit working with them because my uncle told me to.

COUNSELOR: Does your uncle often give you advice?

IDA: He helps me a lot—he just seems to know what's best.

The counselor decided to end the interview and get more information about Ida's past history. Another appointment was set to continue the interview. In the meantime, a complete report was received from a mental health agency, which contained a signed release, a social history, and psychological workup. Ida had been diagnosed as a schizophrenic, undifferentiated type, and had been hospitalized on three occasions in the last five years.

When Ida was asked why she didn't mention the hospitalization, she responded with a shrug. The counselor also discovered that the uncle who was currently advising Ida had died ten years earlier.

In the case of severe psychiatric problems, there is usually evidence of marked impairment of life role functioning, particularly in the work role and homemaker role. The client's suggestion of a "sixth sense" telling her to abruptly quit an educational program and the fact that she felt controlled by someone else was enough evidence to request more in-depth information. Because the psychiatric and psychological evaluation was three years old, the counselor requested a complete update.

One of the major learning outcomes of this case is the importance of obtaining all available client information. The documented history of severe psychological problems does not always translate into suspending career counseling but may require an up-to-date evaluation of current psychological status.

Discovering Problems That Interfere with Career Development

Faulty Cognitions

Examples of faulty cognitions from Doyle (1992) offer a sound basis for assessing a faulty deductive-thinking process. Doyle's (1992) six examples are ways of thinking that reflect negative feelings about oneself. Irrational expectations of career counseling, as suggested by Nevo (1987), are examples of faulty cognitions and irrational thoughts often found in prospective clients:

1. There is only one vocation in the world that is right for me.
2. Until I find my perfect vocational choice, I will not be satisfied.
3. Someone else can discover the vocation suitable for me.
4. Intelligence tests would tell me how much I am worth.
5. I must be an expert or very successful in the field of my work.
6. I can do anything if I try hard, or I can't do anything that doesn't fit my talents.
7. My vocation should satisfy the important people in my life.
8. Entering a vocation will solve all my problems.
9. I must sense intuitively that the vocation is right for me.
10. Choosing a vocation is a one-time act.

The goal for the interviewer is to help clients identify maladaptive thinking. Using "choosing a vocation is a one-time act" as an example, the counselor asked the client to explain this expressed belief in the following case.

THE CASE OF FAULTY COGNITIONS

CLIENT: I want to find my lifetime job now and get it over with so I can go on to other things.

COUNSELOR: What kind of job did you have in mind?

CLIENT: I thought that's what you're supposed to help me with . . . anyway, I want a job that I can start in when I graduate.

The counselor then asked the client to describe the basis for his belief.

COUNSELOR: Do you think you will stay with the job you choose now for the rest of your life?

CLIENT: Well, I guess so. My father has worked as a bookkeeper as long as I can remember.

COUNSELOR: Was he always a bookkeeper?

CLIENT: Umm, come to think of it, he did work somewhere else.

COUNSELOR: Do you think you might also have other job opportunities in the future?

CLIENT: I never thought of that, but I guess I will.

The counselor was now in a position to explain the idea of career development over the life span and the importance of learning career decision-making techniques. In addition, he could help the client analyze faulty reasoning and false assumptions. The path to a more logical approach to career decision making had been established.

Doyle (1992) suggested a technique for helping this client work through faulty reasoning. The client writes out beliefs and conclusions and the assumptions on which they are based. For example:

All bankers are rich.

Once you are a banker, you drive a big car.

The only way for me to get rich is to become a banker.

The rationale for this exercise is based on the premise that faulty reasoning and faulty logic usually have underlying faulty assumptions. Having clients write out their assumptions in this manner assists them in recognizing that their beliefs may be inaccurate.

Yet another way of helping clients identify faulty cognitions is through the *Career Beliefs Inventory* (CBI) (Krumboltz, 1991) discussed in Chapter 4. If a counselor strongly suspects that a client has developed faulty assumptions that are measurable with the CBI, this instrument could prove to be a valuable counseling tool. Career counselors should be familiar with such inventories, particularly those that help clients expose false beliefs that interfere with wise decision making.

Another technique used to help clients recognize that they have some control of their destiny is concept of locus of control (Rotter, 1966). In sum, counselors arrange learning situations that prove clients can gain control of their lives through appropriate actions.

Behaviors That Can Lead to Work Maladjustment

Observing current behavior and recording behavioral patterns from past events is a means of studying life experiences and their relationship to how clients have learned to behave. In this part of the interview, the focal point is on clients who manifest maladaptive behavior and methods to teach them appropriate ways to behave. Two case summaries are used to illustrate how behaviors can lead to work maladjustment.

THE CASE OF THE CONFUSED DECISION MAKER

Kris, a 17-year-old high school student, asked for help in choosing a career. She reported to the counselor's office with one of her older brothers. She stated, "I cannot decide what to major in at college."

Kris was neatly dressed and well groomed. Her speech was fluent and of normal rate and rhythm. She tended to speak very softly. She seemed to be somewhat anxious about making a career decision. She did not appear to be depressed. She constantly looked to her brother for approval.

In the top 10% of her class, Kris had a record of being a very capable student. She had good rapport with teachers as well as with her peer group. She strongly identified with several girls her age at the high school.

Kris had five brothers, and her father was a meat inspector in a local plant. He worked hard to maintain the family. Her mother had never worked outside the home.

When the counselor asked Kris to come into his office alone, she seemed very uncomfortable and asked if her brother could attend the session with her. The counselor reassured her that they would have ample time to talk with her brother later. She reluctantly agreed to begin the interview.

From the description Kris gave of her home environment, the counselor assumed it was very traditional. Moreover, the chores assigned to the children were typically based on what the parents considered appropriate work for boys and for girls. There seemed to be strict stereotypical roles embedded in Kris's perception of traditional work roles for women. She appeared to be very passive and gave the impression that she expected someone else to make decisions for her.

When discussing future objectives, Kris seemed quite confused when the counselor suggested she consider all careers including nontraditional ones. At one time she had expressed an interest in architecture but considered it to be for men only and therefore decided against it as a possible choice.

Kris's behavior pattern reflected little confidence in her own abilities and deference to others for decision making. She appeared to be quite uneasy when she was asked to leave her brother and constantly referred to him as giving her good advice and reassuring her of what was best for her. The following dialogue demonstrates her dependency needs.

KRIS: My parents will help me choose the right kind of work.

COUNSELOR: Could you tell me more about your parents' choosing the right kind of work for you?

KRIS: My mother and father usually help me with most of the things that I decide on, and if they don't, my older brothers do.

From these excerpts, it seemed clear that Kris was quite dependent on others for decision making. Kris's background and behavior patterns closely matched Neff's (1985) Type IV pattern of individuals who are very dependent on others. The counselor feared that Kris might make career decisions based on what her family considered best for her, rather than on her own interests, values, and abilities. Also, the counselor suspected that if Kris's current behavior patterns continued as is, she would suffer the consequences of a Type IV worker and develop work-related dysfunctions as outlined by Lowman (1993).

The counselor's strategy consisted of building greater rapport with Kris and establishing a basic trust, using the following guidelines:

1. Be respectful and genuine.

2. Focus on developing self-awareness by using reflective procedures.

3. Assist her in understanding how environmental circumstances influenced her behavior.

4. Help her establish alternative ways of thinking and behaving.

5. Assist her in recognizing how she can control her own destiny by illustrating the concept of locus of control; that is, how external and internal people think.

6. Help her recognize the relevance of her values and interests in a career decision-making mode.

7. Introduce career decision-making steps as discussed in Chapter 4.

To promote more realistic goals for career decision making, especially toward self-direction, the counselor chose a cognitive behavioral-intervention strategy (Corey, 1991; Ellis, 1971). The first step included techniques to help Kris separate rational beliefs from irrational ones. Second, the counselor assisted Kris in modifying her thinking, especially the thoughts associated with stereotypical gender-role development. Third, the counselor challenged Kris to develop a greater self-awareness and a more realistic philosophy of integrated life role development. To help her reduce stereotyping in career options, Kris was also scheduled to view the *BORN FREE* series (Hansen, 1978).

THE CASE OF THE ANXIOUS COMPUTER TECHNICIAN

A 28-year-old male computer technician named John sought the services of a career counselor in private practice. His major complaint was a recent upsurge in anxiety when a new group of workers was assigned to his department. He felt threatened by them and, as he saw it, was treated as an outsider and definitely not as part of their group. He feared that he would be fired and considered resigning and finding a different job or asking for reassignment to another department.

John appeared to be anxious; he moved around in his chair and the pitch of his voice changed, particularly when talking about this new group of people. He constantly moved his arms and hands and clenched his fists. He did not appear to be depressed and stated that he felt very anxious.

John had never seriously considered marriage; he saw himself as a "loner." Furthermore, he had few friends and spoke of himself as being shy with limited social contacts.

John evaluated his educational background as average or above in academics. He had received computer training from a local community college. He was currently taking more courses. John characterized his student life in much the same way as his current situation—that is, few social activities and a feeling of isolation.

He interpreted his role as citizen as voting in most elections; he did not participate in any civic activities. He expressed a feeling of rejection by the individuals he had met in organizations. John collected musical records from the Big Band era and enjoyed listening to them when he was alone. He occasionally attended movies, visited his parents, and watched TV.

When expressing work role experiences, his anxiety seemed to peak, as observed by increased motor activities. Earlier trends of isolating himself from contact with others continued in the current work environment; he ate by himself in the cafeteria and did not join bull sessions during breaks. He did not have a "good" friend among the peer group. He characterized his work role as quietly getting the job done.

John's symptoms of anxiety seemed to be related to a long-standing pattern of difficulty with social interactions. Low self-esteem, feelings of rejection, and avoidance of social activities were embedded in most of his statements. These characteristics are found in Neff's (1985) Type II work psychopathology, in Cluster A personality disorders, and in Lowman's (1993) work-related anxiety work dysfunction taxonomy (see Chapter 5). However, John does not exhibit all of the Type II characteristics; likewise, he cannot be identified with any one personality disorder but has characteristics of two or more. This example could be quite typical of many career clients and supports the assumption that identified behaviors, actions, beliefs, and thinking can be generically evaluated as contingencies that could lead to work maladjustment. In sum, John had a history of being an acceptable worker. His life roles could be enhanced with better social skills and more positive self-concepts as a worker and social being. John wanted to change jobs for the wrong reasons. The counselor suggested that he could explore other career opportunities and simultaneously participate in a counseling program designed to help him recognize sources of stress. Other intervention strategies selected were anxiety-management training, social skills and assertiveness training, and relaxation training. In addition, thought-stopping techniques (Cautela & Wisock, 1977; Doyle, 1992) were used to eliminate inappropriate thinking, negative self-concepts, and worry-oriented thinking.

The counseling intervention strategies proposed for John were based on the following premise: Emotions are often the result of how we think, and a change in John's thinking process could reduce or eliminate emotional disorders and dysfunctional behaviors (Ellis & Grieger, 1977; Lazarus, 1989; Trower, Casey, & Dryden, 1988). There are many sources of stress in the work environment, as discussed in Chapter 19, including poor communications between management and workers and between peer groups. Techniques for group-counseling procedures are recommended.

Memory and Persistence

This part of the interview is used when there is sufficient evidence to suspect problems with immediate, recent, or remote memory. Typical examples of memory loss include forgetting names, telephone numbers, directions, and so forth. In more severe cases, memory loss can interfere with social and occupational functioning. Excerpts from a case history are used to illustrate the identification of memory loss and persistence.

THE CASE OF THE FORGOTTEN WORK ADDRESS

A 52-year-old man named Jack was accompanied by his wife to see a career counselor in private practice. She stated that she wanted her husband to get a steady job with a guaranteed salary.

Jack was neatly dressed and groomed. He had short combed hair and was freshly shaven. He appeared confused and was somewhat bewildered about why he was there and what he was to do. His speech patterns suggested he had difficulty in recalling words to complete sentences. He stated that he felt well and was looking forward to being "talked to." There had been no indications of depression. Jack had been married on two occasions. His first marriage lasted only about 18 months because, as he put it,

"I was very young." He has two children from his current marriage of 20 years. He lives with his wife in a home they own. One child is currently attending college

For more than 20 years, Jack's main occupation was cafeteria manager in a small town. Approximately a year ago, he was fired from his job and was currently selling cosmetics as a door-to-door salesman. When asked why he was fired, Jack stated that they told him he was not capable of doing the work anymore. When asked what he would like to do in the future, he replied "I like to read a lot and wouldn't mind working in a bookstore."

Jack appeared to be in good health and was of medium build and weight. He stated that he did have hypertension, which was controlled by medication.

Jack had gone to the local high school and received a B.S. degree from the state university. He had above-average grades in high school and college. When asked why he had planned to change jobs, Jack responded by asking that his wife be allowed to come in and describe his current condition. Jack's wife mentioned that he had been an effective cafeteria manager until about 18 months ago, when he started having difficulty remembering chores that he'd done automatically in the past. He misplaced cash receipts, forgot to make assignments of the personnel (causing chaos in the cafeteria), and forgot the address of the cafeteria. Jack was given a second chance but was not able to improve his work efficiency. He had now taken a sales job selling cosmetics and had not been too successful. His wife also pointed out that he had difficulty coordinating his clothing; he selected conflicting color combinations and at times put his T-shirt on backward. He also stumbled frequently, and when he mowed the yard, he made criss-cross patterns, leaving part of the lawn unmowed. At night when he got up to go to the bathroom, he would return to the wrong room.

At this point, the counselor got agreement from the couple to evaluate Jack's memory. When Jack was asked to repeat the spelling of the city in which he lived, he was able to spell it only with prompting. He also failed to repeat other spellings that were presented. When asked, Jack was unable to give directions to several well-known locations within the city. The counselor then asked Jack to listen carefully to a series of numbers and repeat them immediately after presentation. He was unable to respond correctly after two trials with only three digits. He was not able to recall any digits backward.

The procedure used for assessing recent memory was as follows: When Jack was asked what he had for lunch yesterday, he responded with a typical luncheon menu, but his wife stated that this was not the food that she served him. When he was asked what he saw on the TV news the night before, he simply responded by saying "the same old thing."

The assessment of remote memory was more encouraging. Jack was able to state his birthdate, where he went to high school, and where he obtained his first job outside his home. The counselor concluded that he had poor immediate and recent recall but that his remote memory was fairly well intact.

Jack's wife verified that he had difficulty concentrating and following tasks through to completion. She gave several examples in which he had difficulty maintaining focus on a particular task, like mowing the yard or going to a local store to purchase a single item. It seemed that Jack would easily leave a task without giving much thought to the consequences of his actions.

The counselor referred Jack to a neurologist, who discovered Jack had a brain tumor. An operation followed shortly thereafter, and the tumor turned out to be benign.

Several months after rehabilitation, Jack returned to the counselor's office ready to search for a new occupation. He had decided during his recovery time that he wished to follow his desire of working in a bookstore. The counselor began the assessment interview once again.

Discovering the Significance of Life Roles and Potential Conflicts

Life roles are considered significant determinants of an individual's lifestyle (Super, 1990) and, as such, constitute a formidable influence on career development. Intake interviews also help discover whether clients have significant role conflicts and the degree to which such conflicts inhibit career development. However, the evaluation of life roles for this interview should be based on individual needs and interests. For example, not everyone needs or wants to participate in a civic organization. What is significant, however, is to identify a need that can be fulfilled in civic activities. Life roles should be viewed as having individualized meanings and purposes and as developmentally linked to career development; conflicts in one role can hamper the development and satisfaction of other roles. The following excerpts from interviews illustrate the significance of life role evaluations.

THE CASE OF THE FIRED PLUMBER

Yuri, a 40-year-old plumber, requested career counseling to change jobs. "I don't like this plumbing work anymore," he said. He was dressed in soiled work clothes and hadn't shaved for several days. Yuri appeared to be anxious; he constantly moved in his chair, raised his arms, and clenched his fists. He was grossly overweight and asked that he be given permission to smoke. His speech was fluent and of normal rate and rhythm.

Yuri completed high school but had no other formal training. He claimed to be an average student and never failed a grade. During on-the-job training, he learned the skills to become a licensed plumber.

Starting at the lowest level in plumbing, he had advanced to the master plumber status and had been employed as a plumber for 12 years. He was recently fired for disruptive behavior and fighting with two fellow workers.

Yuri reported no serious medical problems and had no history of psychiatric treatment. He had been a tobacco smoker for 15 years and occasionally drank alcohol.

For leisure, Yuri watched sports on TV and enjoyed renting movies for home viewing. He also enjoyed watching his son play Little League baseball and regularly practiced with him. Short family vacations consisted of visiting relatives and camping.

Yuri was not active in civic affairs, other than annually helping organize the local Little League. He claimed that he had such little time off from his work that it would be difficult for him to actively participate in civic organizations.

Evidently Yuri felt that household duties were "woman's work," and even though his wife worked full time outside the home, he did not help with such tasks as cooking, shopping, washing, or housecleaning. He did mow the yard and water the grass. Yuri complained that his wife had recently demanded his help with household chores, which resulted in several major arguments that lasted for days. Yuri and his wife were not on very good terms and had seriously considered divorce. Shortly after his wife chose to spend several days with her mother to "sort things out," Yuri was fired for fighting on the job.

The fact that Yuri had worked for the same plumbing company and with most of the same peer affiliates for 15 years indicated that he had the skills necessary to interact appropriately within the work environment. It was also clear that Yuri's relations with his wife were in turmoil. Although it was difficult for the counselor to determine at this time whether serious marital problems had existed for a long time, it was clear that Yuri's refusal to help with household chores precipitated the most recent problems. Yuri admitted that he enjoyed working as a plumber, but the stress associated with dual-earner problems had probably influenced how he felt about his current work environment.

This case is a good example of how one life role affects another. The major problem was conflict between husband and wife who both worked full time outside the home, not Yuri's wanting a job change. The counselor's plan was to have Yuri and his wife commit to counseling with emphasis on sharing responsibilities and household tasks.

The techniques suggested were based on Hansen's (1996) Integrative Life Planning Model, which encourages couples to move away from dominate-subordinate relationships toward being equal partners. Among other changes suggested in this model are movement from the position of "job to life roles, and from achievement only to achievement and relationships for both women and men" (Hansen, 1991, p. 84). Career decision making for a different job would be deferred for the time being. Yuri agreed to relocate to a different company as a plumber.

Work and family are not separate worlds, and the case of the fired plumber illustrates how conflict in the homemaker role influenced Yuri's behavior in the work role. Other problem areas that can contribute to conflicts include the following:

Shift work

Separation and travel

Relocation

Work spillover (preoccupation with work role)

Relationships with supervisors

Relationships with co-workers

THE CASE OF THE UNFULFILLED WORKER

Gui, a 42-year-old married woman, was self-referred to a career counselor in private practice because, as she put it, "I really don't know what's wrong with me. I like my job and I'm happy with my marriage and my family, but something is missing in my life." Gui was very attractive and neatly and appropriately dressed. She had a new hairdo and made an outstanding appearance. She was very fluent and her speech was of normal rate and rhythm. Although Gui had a positive attitude about her work and many other factors of her life, she still felt that she could improve her lifestyle. She expressed dismay at not being able to be more specific about what was troubling her. She seemed to be somewhat depressed but stated that she was feeling well.

Gui had married twice. Her first marriage lasted only a short period, and, as she put it, she married when she was very young and made a mistake. She'd been married the second time for more than 20 years and had one child from this marriage. Her child was now attending college. Her husband was a professional engineer and had a good income.

Gui had several odd jobs while in high school and college working in fast-food places and dress shops. She was currently managing a local dress shop and had had this job for at least six years. She felt very comfortable in this work and enjoyed meeting people and doing the usual tasks that were involved in running and managing the shop. She expressed no particular desire to get another job but would be willing to if she were able to fulfill her needs better.

Gui stated that she was in excellent health and had never had significant problems with bad health. She was of medium height and weight.

Gui had received an A.A. degree at a local community college and was currently taking courses at a nearby college. She hoped to receive a degree in business management in the near future.

Gui and her husband, a dual-career couple, seemed to have worked out a very satisfactory relationship in their homemaker roles. Her husband participated in household tasks and assumed responsibilities that gave Gui more time to take care of her work and attend classes at college. She expressed no problems with her marital life and stated that her husband also seemed to be very happy.

As stated earlier, Gui felt that her work role was satisfactory. She had dreamed of managing a dress shop while she was an employee several years ago, and now the opportunity had been given to her. The dress shop she currently managed had been very successful, and she had received several awards from the parent company for exceptional sales. She claimed to relate well to both employees and customers. She was taking a business management course to improve her skills in management.

Because of the strong commitment to upgrade their careers, both Gui and her husband devoted little time to leisure activities. They exercised together in the morning by jogging or walking and attended various events in the community such as theater, movies, and art exhibits. Gui stated that they took the usual vacations, had taken their son to national parks, and had visited historical places.

When asked about participation in civic activities, Gui seemed somewhat bewildered and stated that she simply wouldn't have time to participate in these activities because of her full schedule. She was not aware of activities in local civic organizations and had not considered volunteerism.

The counselor returned to Gui's statement, "Something's missing in my life." The counselor asked her to express this feeling more fully:

GUI: I don't know how to really explain it, and I feel guilty about even talking to someone about this. For gosh sakes, I have a great husband and a marvelous child and a very good job. I can't put a finger on what's wrong with me, but I seem to have a feeling that I want to do other things that I'm not doing at this time.

COUNSELOR: Tell me more about the feeling that you want to do "other things."

GUI: Well, I have to give that some thought, but I guess what I really mean is I have a lot of interests and I haven't been able to fulfill many of them.

COUNSELOR: Tell me more about your interests.

GUI: The first one that strikes my fancy is that I had dreams of being an artist, but when I took art classes and started painting, I quickly realized that I didn't have the talent to go on. But, I'm still interested in art and miss being around arts-and-crafts people.

COUNSELOR: Have you ever thought of taking an art class in college?

GUI: Yes, I've had several of those, but I don't want to continue taking art classes.

As the conversation continued, the counselor felt that a values inventory might help Gui clarify needs she could not identify. The counselor recalled that values tend to remain fairly stable and endure over the life span. She felt that this might be an area that would help Gui come to some realization of what she would like to do in the future.

The counselor decided to use the Five-Step Process for Using Assessment Results developed by Zunker (1994). The steps are paraphrased as follows:

Step 1: Analyzing Needs

In this step, the counselor ascertains the client's perception of her need for information to foster self-knowledge. In evaluating Gui's lifestyle, the counselor decided that work climate, family responsibilities, and leisure time had been committed, but rewarding activities in the community had been given little attention.

COUNSELOR: Gui, you've expressed a very positive viewpoint of your work, family, and leisure activities. In fact, you had no negative thoughts concerning these life roles. It seems to be that other areas of your lifestyle may be lacking—what do you think?

GUI: You're probably right, but the only thing that you've mentioned so far has been civic activities, and as I told you, I know very little about them.

COUNSELOR: Okay, well, I can give you more information about them, but at the same time I would like to know more about your needs and how you might fulfill them. Since we cannot identify specific needs at this time, let's agree that we want to identify some unknown need that gives you the feeling that something is "missing in your life."

Step 2: Establishing a Purpose

Following the needs analysis, the counselor and the client decide on the purpose of testing. Both should recognize that testing cannot be expected to meet all identified needs. In Gui's case, however, the counselor was thinking of only one or two tests to foster self-knowledge. The purpose of each test and inventory should be explained in terms that the counselee can understand. In the following dialogue, the counselor attempts to link the purpose of the test to Gui's needs.

COUNSELOR: As you recall, we've been talking about a number of needs that you feel have not been satisfied or, as you put it, fulfilled. Would you agree that an exploration of your values would be helpful?

GUI: Yes, I do, but what kind of test do you have in mind?

COUNSELOR: Well, I was thinking of a values inventory that would help us establish priorities of values and also introduce sets of values for dialogue.

Step 3: Determining the Instrument

The client and the counselor agree on the type of assessment instrument to be administered. The counselor relates the characteristics of the test and the kinds of information that it will provide.

GUI: Well, I think it would be great to take a values inventory, but I don't quite understand how it's going to help.

COUNSELOR: You expressed a need to fill a gap in your life, and I think a values inventory that provides such measures as ability utilization, aesthetics, altruism, creativity, and lifestyle would be helpful.

GUI: Oh, that sounds great! Maybe they will tell me just what I need to know.

COUNSELOR: A word of caution, Gui. These tests will help us discover some life career values, but they are not designed to tell you what to do in the future. They will provide us with some information to discuss.

Step 4: Using the Results

The counselor interprets the test scores in a manner that the client can understand and relates the results to the established purpose of testing.

COUNSELOR: Gui, here is a profile of your scores. You will notice that you have high scores in aesthetics, creativity, and social interaction. A high score in aesthetics means . . .

As the counselor went through an explanation of scores, she made certain that Gui understood that test scores from a values inventory are not necessarily more valid or accurate than her own perceptions of her problems. However, the results do provide new ideas and opportunities for specificity in the counseling dialogue. In Gui's case, this was important because she had been very vague about what she felt were her unfulfilled needs. As they discussed the results of the test, Gui agreed with the results from the standpoint that she did have a very high value in aesthetics; perhaps this was one area that was lacking in her life. It could provide other opportunities and interesting social interactions and creative endeavors.

Step 5: Making a Decision

The final step is to make a decision based on the assessment's results. Gui decided that she would set aside more time to become involved as a volunteer at the local art museum. She also felt that it would be a good idea to eventually become a docent. She would seek agreement for her plans from her husband and son. The counselor was to see Gui after she had established herself at the art museum to continue dialogue and evaluate her progress.

Developing Goals and Objectives

The unique and distinct information obtained from an intake interview is used to generate individualized goals for career intervention counseling. The information that emerges about how clients interact in their environment and function in a diversity of life roles provides a clearer understanding of needs and subsequent counseling strategies and interventions. In an informative discussion of the goals of career intervention, Spokane (1991) suggests that clients become more positive about their abilities to obtain major life goals as follows: "The goal of career intervention is to enhance the mobilization of persistently constructive attitudes, emotions, and behaviors that will improve the client's career attainment" (p. 56).

As part of a strategic planning model for practitioners and human service organizations, Kurpius, Burrello, and Rozecki (1990) recommend systematic planning as a necessary element to improve effectiveness, and part of this model includes a section that addresses the formulation of goals and objectives (p. 5):

1. Specify objectives.
2. Generate strategies.
3. Implement action plans.
4. Recycle.

Brown and Brooks (1991) recommend the following sequence for goal setting:

1. Identify client goals.
2. Determine the feasibility of goals.
3. Establish subgoals.
4. Assess commitment to goals.

Using the case of the unfulfilled worker, we will apply the sequence for goal setting recommended by Brown and Brooks (1991). Gui's identified goals were

1. Identify sources of anxiety
2. Identify resources for a more balanced lifestyle
3. Identify values and their application to unmet needs

The feasibility of these goals was established as being realistic:

1. The client was highly motivated to explore and discuss solutions.
2. There was mutual agreement about the overall goal of lifestyle direction.
3. There was mutual agreement about subgoals such as assessing values.

Subgoals were established as follows:

1. Assess values.
2. Visit the local art museum.
3. Share plans with family.

The commitment to goals was established by a mutually agreed-on systematic plan that the counselor carefully and fully explained. Her systematic approach enhanced Gui's willingness to participate. The key ingredients were identifying needs and mutually agreed-on goals with systematic plans for action.

Summary

1. Specially designed intervention programs are most useful for identifying clients who cannot reason in a rational manner, have erroneous perceptions of work roles, or have false beliefs.

2. Work role maladjustment behaviors are also identified and modified through intervention programs. Attention should be focused on life role development and the interrelationships of these roles.

3. "The Case of What Was Left Unsaid" points out the importance of obtaining all client background information available.

4. "The Case of Faulty Cognitions" illustrates the rationale that faulty reasoning and faulty logic are based on false assumptions.

5. "The Case of the Confused Decision Maker" illustrates how sex-role stereotyping can influence behavior and career decision making.

6. "The Case of the Anxious Computer Technician" illustrates how fear and anxiety can interfere with work behavior and other life roles. Counseling intervention strategies focused on helping the client recognize the sources of stress.

7. "The Case of the Forgotten Work Address" illustrates how memory can be evaluated with clients who demonstrate the inability to do routine work tasks.

8. "The Case of the Fired Plumber" illustrates how one life role can influence behavior in another role.

9. "The Case of the Unfulfilled Worker" is an example of how an unidentified need can be clarified through a five-step interpretation procedure using a values inventory.

Supplementary Learning Exercises

1. Using "The Case of What Was Left Unsaid," specify how the interviewer could have probed for more background information. Identify clues to the client's problems.

2. Suggest intervention strategies to deal with the following beliefs: "Psychological tests can tell me what to do in the future" and "I am destined to have only one vocation."

3. How can the concept of locus of control be effectively used to assist clients in controlling their futures? Identify symptoms of behavior that would support the use of this procedure.

4. Develop a profile of behaviors that indicate stereotyped gender roles. Suggest intervention strategies.

5. What are the major symptoms of interpersonal relationship problems? Develop goals and objectives for modifying behavior.

6. Develop a supportive argument for the idea that life roles have individualized meanings.

7. Present examples of how one life role affects another. Give suggestions for identifying such problems in the interview.

8. Develop a case that illustrates how a narcissistic career client might behave in the workplace.

9. Illustrate the five steps for using assessment results with an interest inventory and an abilities test.

10. Present suggestions for detecting serious psychological problems in the interview. Illustrate with examples.

For More Information

Brammer, L., & McDonald, G. (1996). *The helping relationship: Process and skills.* Boston: Allyn & Bacon.

Brown, D., & Brooks, L. (1991). *Career counseling techniques.* Boston: Allyn & Bacon.

Egan, G. (1997). *The skilled helper* (5th ed.). Pacific Grove, CA: Brooks/Cole.

Krumboltz, J. D. (1991). *Career beliefs inventory.* Palo Alto, CA: Consulting Psychologists Press.

Littrel, J. (1998). *Brief counseling in action.* New York: Norton.

Morse, P., & Ivey, A. (1996). *Face to face: Communication and conflict resolution in the schools.* Thousands Oaks, CA: Corwin.

Nevo, O. (1987). Irrational expectations in career counseling and their confronting arguments. *Career Development Quarterly, 35,* 239–250.

7

Using Standardized Assessment in Career Counseling

Chapter Highlights

- *Problems associated with selecting standardized assessment instruments*

- *Suggestions for evaluating adapted and accommodated versions of standardized tests*

- *Achieving equity in assessment*

- *Assessing the acculturation level of multicultural groups*

- *Unearthing career beliefs*

- *Identifying skills, proficiencies, and abilities*

- *Identifying academic achievement*

- *Identifying and confirming interest levels*

- *Discovering personality variables*

- *Determining values*

- *Exploring career maturity variables*

- *Using computer-assisted career guidance assessment*

- *Resources for evaluating assessment instruments*

T HE DEVELOPMENT OF STANDARDIZED TESTS AND ASSESSMENT INVENTORIES has been closely associated with the vocational counseling movement. As early as 1883, the U.S. Civil Service Commission used competitive examinations for job placement (Kavruck, 1956). Multiple aptitude-test batteries developed during the mid-1940s have been widely used in educational and vocational counseling (Anastasi, 1988). Scholastic aptitude tests used as admission criteria for educational institutions were implemented through the Educational Testing Service (ETS) established in 1947 and the American College Testing Program (ACT) established in 1959.

Recently, more emphasis has been placed on skills identification through informal techniques (Bolles, 1993; Healy, 1990; Holland, 1992; Zunker, 1990). The growing popularity of informal methods of identifying skills strongly suggests that some assessment of individual aptitudes, skills, and other individual characteristics is vitally important in the career decision process, despite the controversy surrounding standardized aptitude tests and job success predictions. Healy (1990) has also suggested encouraging clients to develop self-assessment skills as a way of focusing more fully on career options. What seems to be the major issue is how assessment results can be used most effectively in career counseling programs. A good approach considers assessment results as only one facet of individuality to be evaluated in the career decision process. More specifically, career decision making is seen as a continuous counseling process within which all aspects of individuality receive consideration. Skills, aptitudes, interests, values, achievements, personality characteristics, maturity, contextual interactions, and salient cultural variables are among the more important aspects that can be evaluated by assessment measures. Thus, assessment results constitute counseling information that can provide the individual with an awareness of increased options and alternatives and encourage greater individual exploration in the career decision process.

The career counseling models discussed in Chapter 4 suggest that all relevant information be included in the career decision process to encourage greater individual participation and consideration of a wider range of career options. Furthermore, the more knowledge counselor and client have of individual characteristics, the greater assurance we have of a balance of considerations in career decision making. Career counseling programs that are designed to incorporate all relevant information should lessen the chances that career decision making could be dominated by any one factor.

Recognizing the increasingly growing diverse groups in our society for whom tests were not developed, standardized, or validated, the Association for Assessment in Counseling (AAC) issued a document in 1993 entitled *Multicultural Assessment Standards: A Compilation for Counselors* (Prediger, 1994). This document contains vital information for selecting assessment instruments, administration and scoring, and interpreting assessment results. In 1988, a joint committee on testing practices sponsored by the American Psychological Association (APA) published a document entitled *Code of Fair Testing Practices in Education* (see the APA Web site in Appendix D). This document details the responsibilities of test users and test developers. These publications clearly point out the necessity of all counselors to select and use assessment instruments that are appropriate for each client. For instance, extreme caution should be taken when selecting tests for and interpreting test scores to individuals who were not adequately represented in the normative sample.

This chapter will include some suggestions for the appropriate use of standardized assessment results. In Chapter 8, self-assessments and other methods of assessing variables that can be used in career exploration and career decision-making are introduced. The first section of this chapter briefly discusses some psychometric procedures used for standardizing tests; validity and reliability are briefly reviewed. These concepts are assumed to be covered in other courses, thus the emphasis here will be assessment use in career counseling. In the next section, we will discuss some issues associated with achieving equity in the use of assessment. Finally, goals of assessment are introduced with example assessment instruments.

Psychometric Concepts for Selecting Assessment Instruments

The career counseling models discussed in Chapter 4 suggest a variety of uses of assessment in career counseling. Although testing does not dominate counseling procedures in all counseling models, assessment usually has an important role for information gathering, accurate client self-assessment, problem identification, interventions, and outcome evaluations. The unique characteristics and identified traits of each client provide the direction for identifying options and guide the structure of intervention strategies that are tailored to meet individual and special needs. There are many other uses of assessment in career counseling, but these examples underscore the importance of selecting appropriate instruments that will result in valid and reliable results for all groups, including diverse groups. Counselors are to be knowledgeable about psychometric concepts that are necessary in selecting and using assessment instruments.

Reliability

The coefficient correlation of reliability is the degree to which a test score is dependable and consistent; repeated trials will yield approximately the same results. Clearly, the consistency and dependability of a test score determines its role in the counseling process. Although measurement errors can reduce reliability, the intended use of assessment results should be the determining factor for a final judgment of test reliability. For instance, when test scores are used in high stakes decisions, such as placement in a special program, each test should be carefully scrutinized according to its purpose, content, appropriate use, and validity and reliability; valid and reliable test results are critically important. For the individual exploring several occupational options suggested by an interest inventory, a more moderate reliability coefficient may be acceptable. Keep in mind that the test developer has the major responsibility for providing evidence that reliability is sufficient for its intended use (Drummond, 1992).

Finally, reliability coefficients are obtained by test-retest (same test is given twice with certain time intervals), alternate forms (equivalent tests are administered within certain time intervals), and internal consistency (results of one test are divided into parts referred to as split-half). The stability of a test is determined by coefficients of correlation that remain high over long intervals. Factors that effect stability are summarized by Peterson, Sampson, and Reardon (1991, pp. 127–128) as follows:

(a) The stability of the human trait itself; for example daily moods have low stability, whereas verbal aptitude has high stability

(b) Group differences, such as gender or ethnic background

(c) Individual differences within groups, such as genetic endowment, age, and learning

(d) The nature of performance; for example whether it is a maximum effort, as in an achievement test, compared with rating what is generally true, as in an interest inventory

(e) The internal consistency of the test itself

Validity

According to the Standards for Educational and Psychological Testing (APA, 1985) validity refers to the meaningfulness and usefulness of certain inferences based on a test score derived from a test in question. Counselors need to answer whether a test measures what it purports to measure. For instance, does a nationally administered aptitude test measure success for the freshman year in a particular college when predicting that the chances are "good" a certain client will make a grade of "C" or better? This question and more should be asked about validity and more specifically, content validity, criterion validity, and construct validity.

Content validity involves opinions of experts about whether the items of a test or inventory represent the content domain of characteristics being measured. For instance, do test questions adequately sample measures of skills, abilities, values, interests, or personality? Measures of human traits such as personality, values, and interests require considerable understanding of traits that are to be measured and considerable skill in developing questions that successfully tap the universal content domain of such human traits.

Criterion validity is determined by the degree to which test scores predict success on an outcome criteria. In predicting success in college, as cited earlier, aptitude test scores are related to the behavior (earned grades) during the first semester in college. Criterion-based interest inventories relate an individual's score with a normative group, such as geologists and ministers, that are satisfied and stable in their occupations. The rationale is that individuals who have similar scores will experience satisfaction in those occupations.

Constructs developed from theory and research, such as cognitive ability and anxiety states, are related to test scores that are derived from tests or inventories developed to measure the defined construct. The results, construct validity coefficient of correlation, provide the evidence that the interpretation of scores is associated with the theoretical implications of the construct label (APA, 1985). For example, the construct of intelligence may include one's ability to build colored block designs within time intervals. This part of an intelligence test contributes to an overall score from which the IQ is derived. The point here is that counselors should carefully evaluate the focus of the construct and the items that are used to measure it.

In sum, selecting assessment instruments requires an understanding of psychometric concepts used in the development of standardized tests. As client and counselor collaborate on selecting tests, counselors should be able to explain the purpose of a test, what the test is designed to measure, why a certain test could be useful, how and why a test is considered a valid and reliable instrument, and how the results can be used to assist the client. Finally, the counselor must be certain that the test administration is appropriate for the client and the results fully account for the client's background and diversity.

Issues in Achieving Equity in Assessment

The changing demographics during the last quarter of the 20th century have changed American society into a more diverse culture. More members of our society speak a second language other than English in their homes, and in 1995, more than 5.5 million children entered school without English-language skills (Garcia, 1995; Sandoval, 1998b). Clearly, the clientele of career counselors is changing and will continue to change as the national workforce grows more diverse.

Standardized tests must be used with caution or not used at all when assessment techniques, content, and norms are not applicable "because of an individual's gender, age, race ethnicity, national origin, religion, sexual orientation, disability, language, or socioeconomic status" (APA, 1992, p. 1601). It is not clear at this time how test publishers will effectively deal with the issues of diversity, but it should be clear to test users that each test must be carefully chosen for each client. In the meantime, some helpful suggestions for counselors are briefly reviewed in the following paragraphs.

Carefully read the test manual to determine if the client is a member of a group that has been included in the normative sample used for validity and reliability analysis. This information is often included in a separate publication from the test administration manual and is usually referred to as a technical information manual. Specifically, evaluate the test-taking sample and make notes about its composition.

Counselors should also know the relevant background information about their clients. For instance, whether English is their dominant language, and their socioeconomic status, ethnicity, gender, and other variables. If there are language differences, counselors determine if a test version in the client's dominant language is available. You might have to contact test publishers for this information (Geisinger, 1998).

Be aware of information the test publisher should provide about translated, adapted, and accommodated versions of a test. A translated version is usually accomplished by translating the instrument from the original language to the target language, and this is followed by a "back translation": a second translator translates the version of the target language back to the original version. The degree to which they are comparable can best be assessed during this process; significant differences in word meanings can change the nature of a test and make it invalid. Keep in mind that cultural differences among individuals who grew up in different language environments can lead to different interpretations of what test questions are intended to evaluate (Geisinger, 1998).

Adapted and accommodated versions of a test can provide information that is helpful to the counselor, although there are numerous problems that must be solved. Adapting or accommodating a test usually refers to changes made in the test administration, scoring, or norms to accommodate special groups. Counselors should make certain that the nature of the test has not been changed by an adaptation. For example, when a typical paper-and-pencil test is given verbally or by audio tape or the test time has been increased, one must evaluate its effect on the test results. If the scores are derived from norms from the entire population, counselors must determine if a significant proportion of members from the client's ethnic group were represented. It is often helpful if special population norms are given, for instance, a separate test given to a representative group of Hispanics, that can be compared with the national norms (Geisinger, 1998). The major purpose here is to make test results as equitable as possible for all groups. One should be cautious, however, when interpreting scores from a sample of Hispanics or any other ethnic-racial group. It must be remembered that ethnic-racial groups such as Hispanics may share some cultural values and environmental influences, but they are not necessarily a homogenous group.

In sum, counselors should be skilled in evaluating assessment instruments and, more important, have resources available for this purpose. Most test-publishing companies now have 800 numbers, e-mail, and Internet access. Published materials can also be helpful, and a list is provided near the end of this chapter. Counselors should also be skilled in evaluating the unique characteristics of each client's environmental background. All clients have been shaped by cultures that are organized according to unique roles, rules, cultural values, behavior patterns, expectations, and interpersonal history (Okun, Fried, & Okun, 1999). Understanding how clients construct personal meanings from past experiences provides counselors with vital information for establishing the goals of assessment and counseling.

Acculturation

Finally, there is an important central concept, acculturation, that counselors should use in selecting and using assessment. This term refers to the adoption of beliefs, values, and practices of the host culture (Comas-Diaz & Grenier, 1998;

Westermeyer, 1993). We will discuss this concept more in Chapter 8—but in this context, acculturation contains contextual developmental issues that should be considered in assessment.

Table 7-1 displays a list of contextual assessment areas that should help assess a client's cultural transition, adaptation, and acculturation. An evaluation process of contextual areas is referred to as an ethnocultural assessment (Comas-Diaz & Grenier, 1998) about a client's maternal and paternal cultures of origin, heritage including countries of origin, religions, social class, languages, gender roles, sociopolitical factors, family roles, and biological factors such as genetic predisposition to certain health problems. As our society continues to become more diverse, we can expect an increase of intermarriage and blending of cultures. A practical tool such as ethnocultural assessment should prove invaluable for establishing an assessment plan and should guide appropriate interpretation of assessment results.

Assessment Goals in Career Counseling

According to Thorndike (1997), there were more than 3000 tests in English for sale in 1994. That number appears to be growing, which points out the difficulty of selecting tests but is also encouraging because so many choices are available. In this section, assessment goals will be followed by examples of assessment instruments on the current market. These examples should not be considered as endorsements of instruments for use with all clients. With advancing technology, we can expect continuous changes in how we use assessment. No doubt, many of the well-known and highly used instruments will continue to be popular and will be updated for use with all clients. Counselors should remain alert to new tests that have proved to be valid and reliable.

The use of assessment usually follows the initial interview in which, among other goals, a client-counselor relationship of collaboration has been established. The role and implications of assessment should be clearly delineated; counselors should make it clear that clients will be actively involved in the assessment process. Active involvement includes selecting assessment instruments and client self-assessment as discussed in Chapter 8. In the first stages of career counseling, the counselor determines if the client needs personal counseling, either through an interview or an inventory that measures career beliefs and dysfunctional thinking.

Goal 1: Unearthing Career Beliefs

The inventories and questionnaires used for this purpose reveal some of the client's beliefs about careers, decision-making styles, identity issues, maladaptive behaviors, degrees of anxiety, fear of failure, and reasons why people are undecided. Some of the inventories used are the following:

Career Beliefs Inventory
Consulting Psychologists Press
3803 E. Bayshore Drive
Palo Alto, CA 94303
800-624-1765

This inventory is used as a counseling tool to help clients identify career beliefs that can inhibit their abilities to make career decisions that are in their best interests. The results are computed for 25 scales under the following five headings: My Current Career Situation, What Seems Necessary for My Happiness, Factors That Influence My Decisions, Changes I Am Willing to Make, and Effort I Am Willing to Initiate. Norms are available for junior high school students, and separate norms are available for male and female employed adults. Scores can be interpreted in percentile ranks for each scale.

TABLE 7-1	CONTEXTUAL ASSESSMENT AREAS

1. Ethnocultural heritage
2. Racial and ethnocultural identities
3. Gender and sexual orientation
4. Socioeconomic status
5. Physical appearance, ability or disability
6. Religion when being raised and what now practicing, spiritual beliefs
7. Biological factors (genetic predisposition to certain illness, etc.)
8. Historical era, age cohort
9. Marital status, sexual history
10. History of (im)migration and generations from (im)migrations
11. Acculturation and transculturation levels
12. Family of origin and multigenerational history
13. Family scripts (roles of women and men, prescriptions for success or failure, etc.)
14. Individual and family life cycle development and stages
15. Client's languages and those spoken by family of origin
16. History of individual abuse and trauma (physical; emotional; sexual; political including torture, oppression, and repression)
17. History of collective trauma (slavery, colonization, Holocaust)
18. Gender-specific issues such as battered wife syndrome
19. Recreations and hobbies, avocations, and special social roles
20. Historical and geopolitical reality of ethnic group and relationship with dominant group (including wars and political conflict)

SOURCE: From "Cultural Considerations in Diagnosis" (pp. 159–160) by L. Comas-Diaz, in F. W. Kaslow (Ed.), *Handbook on Relational Diagnosis and Dysfunctional Family Patterns,* Wiley. Copyright 1996 by John Wiley & Sons, Inc. Reprinted by permission.

Career Thoughts Inventory
Psychological Assessment Resources, Inc.
P.O. Box 998
Odessa, FL 33556
800-331-8378

This inventory is designed to measure the degree of a person's dysfunctional thinking and how that can affect the career decision-making process. The inventory consists of 48 items and 3 scales: Decision-Making Confusion, Commitment Anxiety, and External Conflict. The total score is an indicator of an individual's overall dysfunctional thinking. This inventory can be used for high school, college, and adult clients. The reading level is 6th grade, and the inventory takes about 7 to 15 minutes to complete.

My Vocational Situation
Psychological Assessment Resources, Inc.
P.O. Box 998
Odessa, FL 33556
800-331-8378

This inventory consists of three scales—Lack of Vocational Identity, Lack of Information or Training, and Emotional or Personal Barriers that can cause problems. It can be completed in less than ten minutes.

Identifying problems by assessment plays a major role in establishing rapport and determining intervention strategies during the first phase of counseling. Counselors decide if the client can proceed with career counseling or should be referred for psychological counseling. In some models the career counselor serves a dual purpose and provides the necessary "personal" counseling while beginning career counseling.

Goal 2: Identifying Skills, Proficiencies, and Abilities

Aptitude tests primarily measure specific skills and proficiencies or the ability to acquire a certain proficiency (Cronbach, 1990). More specifically, aptitude test scores provide an index of measured skills that is intended to predict how well an individual may perform on a job or in an educational or training program. In addition, aptitude test scores indicate an individual's cognitive strengths and weaknesses; that is, differential abilities that provide an index to specific skills. For example, a measure of scholastic aptitude tells us the probability of success in educational programs. A clerical aptitude test score provides an index of ability to perform clerical duties. In the former example, we are informed of combinations of aptitudes that predict scholastic success, whereas in the latter we are provided with more specific measures of skills needed to perform well on a specific job.

Aptitude tests may be purchased as batteries measuring a number of aptitudes and skills or as single tests measuring specific aptitudes. Combinations of battery scores provide prediction indexes for certain educational or training criteria, as well as performance criteria on certain occupations that require combinations of skills. An example of an aptitude battery is the *General Aptitude Test*

Battery (GATB) published by the U.S. Department of Labor (1970b). This test was originally developed by the U.S. Employment Service for state employment counselors. The *GATB* measures the following nine aptitudes: intelligence, verbal, numerical, spatial, form perception, clerical perception, motor coordination, finger dexterity, and manual dexterity.

Other aptitude tests published as single-test booklets measure a wide range of specific skills including dexterity, mechanical comprehension, occupational attitude, clerical aptitude, design judgment, art aptitude, and musical talent.

Although aptitude tests primarily provide a basis for predicting success in an occupation or in training programs, they can also be used as counseling tools for career exploration. In this approach, measured individual traits provide a good frame of reference for evaluating learning needs. The following sample cases illustrate the use of aptitude test batteries:

- Susan is a senior in high school and does not plan to attend college. She is interested in obtaining work after graduation from high school. Her academic record indicates she is an average student with no particular strengths evidenced by academic grades. Her interests have not crystallized to the point at which she would be able to specify a particular occupational interest. Several assessment inventories were administered including a complete battery of aptitude tests. These scores were used to discover areas of specific strengths and weaknesses for inclusion in Susan's career exploration program. Identification of specific aptitudes was seen as a stimulus for discovering potential career considerations.

- Ron is returning to the work force after a serious head injury received in a car accident. During several months of recovery, his previous job in construction work was terminated. He is now interested in "looking for other kinds of work." An aptitude battery was administered to determine possible deficits resulting from the head injury. As the counselor suspected, the test scores indicated poor finger and manual dexterity. Jobs requiring fine visual-motor coordination had to be eliminated from consideration in career exploration.

In Susan's case, aptitude scores provided the stimulus for the discussion of measured aptitudes along with other materials used in career counseling. Susan was provided with a specific focus in career exploration. Ron's deficiencies were found and considerable time in career exploration was saved. Following are representative examples of multiple aptitude test batteries available on the market today.

The Differential Aptitude Test (DAT)
G. K. Bennet, H. G. Seashore, and A. G. Wesman
The Psychological Corporation
555 Academic Court
San Antonio, TX 78204-2498
800-211-8378

This test consists of eight subtests: verbal reasoning, numerical ability, abstract reasoning, space relations, mechanical reasoning, clerical speed and accuracy, spelling, and language usage. The entire battery takes more than three hours to administer. This battery was designed primarily for use with high school and college students. When verbal and numerical scores are combined, a scholastic aptitude score is created. Other subtests are used for vocational and educational planning.

The General Aptitude Test Battery (GATB)
United States Employment Service
Washington, DC 20210
(Call your regional employment agencies)

This battery is composed of 8 paper-and-pencil tests and 4 apparatus tests. Nine abilities are measured by the 12 tests: intelligence, verbal aptitude, numerical aptitude, spatial aptitude, form perception, clerical perception, motor coordination, finger dexterity, and manual dexterity. This test is administered to senior high school students and adults. Testing time is two and a half hours. Test results may be used for vocational and educational counseling and placement.

Flanagan Aptitude Classification Tests (FACT)
J. C. Flanagan
SRA-McGraw-Hill
220 East Daniel Dale
De Soto, TX 75115
800-843-8855

This test consists of 16 subtests: inspection, coding, memory, precision, assembly, scales, coordination, judgment/comprehension, arithmetic, patterns, components, tables, mechanics, expression, reasoning, and ingenuity. Each test measures behaviors considered critical to job performance. Selected groups of tests may be administered. The entire battery takes several hours. This test is designed primarily for use with high school students and adults.

Armed Services Vocational Aptitude Battery (ASVAB)
U.S. Department of Defense
Washington, DC 20402
408-655-0400

The *ASVAB* form 19 consists of 9 tests: coding speed, word knowledge, arithmetic reasoning, tool knowledge, space relations, mechanical comprehension, shop information, automotive information, and electronics information. These tests combine to yield three academic scales: academic ability (word knowledge, paragraph comprehension, and arithmetic reasoning), verbal (word knowledge, paragraph comprehension, and general science), and mathematical (math knowledge and arithmetic reasoning). Four occupational scales are also checked: mechanical and crafts (arithmetic reasoning, mechanical comprehension, and auto, shop, and electronics information); business and clerical (word knowledge, paragraph comprehension, mathematics knowledge, and coding speed); electronics and electrical (arithmetic reasoning, mathematical knowledge, electronics information, and general science); and health, social, and technical (word knowledge and paragraph meaning, arithmetic reasoning, and mechanical comprehension).

Goal 3: Identifying Academic Achievement

Achievement tests are designed primarily to assess present levels of developed abilities. Current functioning and basic academic skills such as arithmetic, reading, and language usage are relevant to planning for educational intervention strategies. Academic proficiency has long been a key factor in career planning for individuals considering higher education; however, basic academic competencies are also major determinants in qualifying for certain occupations. For example, identified academic competencies and deficiencies are major considerations for placement or training of school dropouts. Achievement test results provide important information to be included in programs for adults who are entering, returning to, or recycling through the work force. Changing technology and economic conditions will force many workers to enter programs to upgrade their skills or to train for completely different positions. Assessment of present levels of abilities will be needed to determine the possible scope of career exploration for these individuals.

For our use in career counseling programs, we will consider achievement tests in three categories: (1) general survey battery; (2) single-subject tests; and (3) diagnostic batteries. The general survey battery measures knowledge of most subjects taught in school and is standardized on the same population. The single-subject test, as the name implies, measures knowledge of only one subject/content area. Diagnostic batteries measure knowledge of specific proficiencies such as reading, spelling, and arithmetic achievement.

The use of achievement tests in career counseling is illustrated in the two cases that follow. In the first example, achievement test results are used to assist a student in determining a college major. In the second example, a diagnostic battery is used to assist a woman who is returning to the work force after several years of being a homemaker.

- Juan is a senior in high school who is considering college, but he cannot decide between biology and chemistry as a major. All other factors being equal as far as career opportunities are concerned, the decision is made to determine which is Juan's strongest subject area. The counselor and Juan selected single-subject tests in biology and chemistry, as these tests are relatively more thorough and precise compared with the general survey battery and the diagnostic battery. Thus, single-subject achievement tests provide a more thorough evaluation of specific subject abilities for Juan's consideration.

- Betty quit school when she was in the sixth grade. After several years of marriage, she was deserted by her husband and is seeking employment. Other test data reveal that she is of at least average intelligence. After careful review of alternatives by counselor and client, a diagnostic battery was selected for the specific purpose of determining basic arithmetic skills and reading and spelling levels. Both client and counselor were especially interested in determining academic deficiencies for educational planning; that is, consideration should be given to upgrading basic skills for eventual training for a high school equivalency. This information was seen as essential for both educational and career planning.

Because of the wide range of achievement tests on the market today, individual tests will not be listed here. Instead, following are representative major publishers of achievement tests.

CTB-Macmillan-McGraw-Hill
Publishers Test Service
20 Ryan Ranch Road
Monterey, CA 93940
800-282-0266

Educational Testing Service
P.O. Box 6736
Princeton, NJ 08540
609-406-5050

Houghton Mifflin Company
222 Berkeley Street
Boston, MA 02116
800-225-3362

The Psychological Corporation
555 Academic Court
San Antonio, TX 78204-2498
800-211-8379

SRA-McGraw-Hill
220 East Daniel Dale
De Soto, TX 75115
800-843-8855

Goal 4: Identifying and Confirming Interest Levels

In recent years, a considerable body of literature has concerned itself with gender bias and unfairness in career interest measurement. Diamond (1975) has a number of the most relevant articles under the sponsorship of the National Institute of Education (NIE). The NIE publishes guidelines that identify gender bias as "any factor that might influence a person to limit—or might cause others to limit—his or her consideration of a career solely on the basis of gender" (Diamond, 1975, p. xxiii).

According to Diamond (1975), the guidelines have led to some progress in reducing gender bias in interest inventories by calling for fairness in the construction of item pools ("Items such as statements, questions, and names of occupations used in the inventory should be designed so as not to limit the consideration of a career solely on the basis of gender"), fairness in the presentation of technical information ("Technical information should include evidence that the inventory provides career options for both males and females"), and fairness in interpretive procedures ("Interpretive procedures should provide methods of equal treatment of results for both sexes" [p.xxiii]). Generally, the guidelines are aimed at encouraging both sexes to consider all career and educational opportunities and at eliminating sex-role stereotyping by those using interest inventory results in the career counseling process.

More recently, the debate about sex bias in interest inventories has focused on the question of whether men and women have different interests. According to Harmon and Meara (1994) and Hansen, Collins, Swanson, and Fouad (1993), men and women still differ in the way they endorse interest inventory items. Thus, interest inventory results might not reflect actual differences between men and women for occupational groups of specific occupations (Fouad & Spreda, 1995). Counselor and client should evaluate interest inventory items to determine if they appropriately represent interests of both genders (Zunker & Osborn, 2002).

Interest inventories have long been associated with career counseling. Two of the most widely used are the *Strong Interest Inventory (SII)*, originally developed by E. K. Strong (1983), and the Kuder interest inventories, developed by G. F. Kuder (1963). More recently, Holland's (1992) approach to interest identification (as discussed in Chapter 2) has received considerable attention. For example, a number of interest inventories—including the *SII*, the American College Testing Program Interest Inventory, and the *Self-Directed Search* (Holland, 1987a)—are constructed to correspond with Holland's personality types and corresponding work environments. In most inventories, interests are primarily designated by responses to compiled lists of occupations and lists of activities associated with occupations. The rationale is that individuals having similar interest patterns to those found in an occupational group would probably find satisfaction in that particular group.

Two methods commonly used for reporting results are direct comparison (likes and dislikes) with specific occupations and comparisons with themes or clusters of occupations. Interest inventories that provide direct comparisons with specific occupations usually include a numerical index for comparative purposes. For example, the *Kuder Occupational Interest Survey* (Kuder, 1966) provides a coefficient of correlation as an index for comparing an individual's response with an occupational group—that is, higher correlations indicate similar interest patterns to certain occupational groups (Kuder, 1963). The *SII* provides a standard score for this purpose. In addition, a number of inventories provide profiles that indicate whether interests are similar or dissimilar to those of occupational criterion groups. For example, an individual might give interest responses very similar to those of accountants and very dissimilar to those of social workers.

Clusters of occupations are presented in a variety of schemes. Some clusters are based on the *Dictionary of Occupational Titles (DOT)* models of people, data, and things. The *Kuder General Interest Survey* (Kuder, 1964) yields ten interest scales as follows: outdoor, mechanical, computational, scientific, persuasive, artistic, literary, musical, social service, and clerical. The *SII* yields six general occupational theme scales taken from Holland's (1992) six modal personal styles and matching work environments. The cluster systems index a group of occupations rather than a single occupation, although the individual can derive specific occupations from the clusters. For the nonreader, picture interest inventories are used to determine occupational interests. These inventories depict occupational environments, individuals at work, and a variety of job-related activities. Individual response is recorded by circling numbers or pictures or by pointing to pictures. Picture interest inventories also provide a basis for discussion about career exploration.

Following are some representative examples of interest inventories.

Kuder Occupational Interest Survey
Publisher Test Service
CTB-Macmillan-McGraw-Hill
20 Ryan Ranch Road
Monterey, CA 93940
800-282-0266

This survey is computer-scored and consists of 77 occupational scales and 29 college-major scales for men, and 57 occupational scales and 27 college-major scales for women. Recommended uses of the inventory include selection, placement, and career exploration. The survey is untimed, usually taking 30 to 40 minutes. Norms are based on samples of data from college seniors.

Self-Directed Search (SDS)
Psychological Assessment Resources, Inc.
P.O. Box 998
Odessa, FL 33556
800-331-8378

This interest inventory is based on Holland's (1992) theory of career development. It is self-administered and self-scored, as well as self-interpreted, and takes approximately 30 to 40 minutes to complete. The scores are organized to reveal an occupational code or a summary code of three letters representing the personality types and environmental models from Holland's typology: realistic, investigative, artistic, social, enterprising, and conventional. This inventory is used with high school and college students and with adults.

Strong Interest Inventory
Consulting Psychologists Press
3803 E. Bayshore Dr.
Palo Alto, CA 94303
800-624-1765

This inventory combines the male and female versions of the *Strong Vocational Interest Blank* into one survey. The interpretation of scores is based on Holland's typology. The interpretation format includes six general occupational themes, 23 basic interest scales, and 124 occupational scales. Administrative indexes include an academic-orientation index and an introversion-extroversion index. The time to complete is about 30 to 40 minutes. Both male and female occupational scale scores are available.

Career Assessment Inventory (CAI)
C. B. Johansson
National Computer Systems
P.O. Box 1416
Minneapolis, MN 55440
800-627-7271

This computer-scored inventory can be administered in approximately 45 minutes. It is designed for 8th-grade students through adults. General occupational theme scales, basic interest scales, and occupational scales are reported. This inventory is primarily used with noncollege-bound individuals.

Wide Range Interest and Opinion Test
Guidance Associates of Delaware, Inc.
1526 Gilpin Avenue
Wilmington, DE 19806
302-658-4184

This test consists of 150 sets of three pictures from which the individual is asked to indicate likes and dislikes. The pictures depict activities ranging from unskilled labor to the highest levels of technical, managerial, and professional training. The test evaluates educational and vocational interests of a wide range of individuals, including the educationally disadvantaged and the developmentally disabled.

The Campbell Interest and Skill Survey (CISS)
NCS Assessments
P.O. Box 1416
Minneapolis, MN 55440
800-627-7271

This instrument is part of a new integrated battery of psychological surveys that currently includes the *CISS*, an attitude-satisfaction survey, and a measure of leadership characteristics. Two other instruments, a team development survey and a community survey, are being developed and will complete this integrated battery. The *CISS*, developed for individuals 15 years and older with a 6th-grade reading level, has 200 interest and 120 skill items on a 6-point response scale. The results yield parallel interest and skill scores: orientation scales (influencing, organizing, helping, creating, analyzing, producing, and adventuring); basic scales (29 basic scales, such as leadership, supervision, counseling, and international activities); occupational scales (58 scales, such as financial planner, translator/interpreter, and landscape architect). Special scales measure academic comfort and extroversion.

Goal 5: Discovering Personality Variables

Major career theorists have emphasized personality development as a major factor to be considered in career development. For example, Roe (1956) postulated that early personality development associated with family interactions influences vocational direction. Super (1990) devoted considerable attention to self-concept development. Tiedeman and O'Hara (1963) considered total cognitive development in decision making. Holland's (1992) system of career selection was directly related to personality types and styles. The case for the use of personality inventories in career counseling programs seems well established; however, there is a lack of evidence that personality inventories are being widely used in career counseling programs.

The development of the *Sixteen Personality Factor Questionnaire (16 PF)* by Cattell, Eber, and Tatsuoka (1970) led the way for integrating personality inventories into career counseling programs. Vocational personality patterns and occupational fitness are considered major components of this questionnaire. The 16 factors measured by the *16 PF* are "source" traits or factors, which are derived from distinct combinations of an individual's personality traits (Cattell, Eber, & Tatsuoka, 1970). These traits are compared with occupational profiles and provide vocational observations and occupational fitness projections. *Vocational observations* include information concerning the individual's potential for leadership and interpersonal skills and potential benefits from academic training. *Occupational fitness projections* rank how the individual compares with specific occupational profiles from extremely high to extremely low. Specific source traits are recorded for each occupational profile available (currently there are 24), providing a comparison of characteristic traits common to individuals employed in certain occupations. The *16 PF* is singled out because a major portion of the inventory development was devoted to vocational personality patterns and occupational fitness projections. Throughout this text, references are made to the importance of satisfying individual needs associated with work, family, and leisure. As we assist individuals in career exploration, we must consider the individuality of each person we counsel. Within this frame of reference, individual personality patterns greatly assist in identifying and clarifying each individual's needs. As needs change over the life span, our goal is to help individuals clarify their needs for effective planning and goal achievement. Personality inventories provide valuable information for identifying needs and providing a stimulus for career exploration. The following examples demonstrate the use of personality inventories in career counseling programs.

- Ahmed reports that he is quite frustrated in his present working environment and is considering changing jobs. His unhappiness has caused family problems and social problems in general. His performance ratings by his superiors were high until the last two years, when they dropped to average. Assessment results indicate that he is interested in his current job as accountant. A personality inventory indicated a strong need for achievement. Group discussions that followed brought about a consensus that Ahmed was still interested in the field of accounting, but in his current position, he was not able to meet his needs to achieve. Earlier these needs were apparently met from positive reinforcement received from high ratings by his superiors. At this point in his life, he is searching for something more than "just doing a good job of bookkeeping." Recognizing his source of frustration, he decided to stay in accounting but moved to another division in the firm.

- Shayna had definitely decided that she was interested in an occupation that would provide her with an opportunity to help people. A personality inventory indicated that she was very reserved and nonassertive and deferred to others. She agreed with the results of the personality inventory and further agreed that these characteristics would make it difficult for her to accomplish her occupational goal. Shayna became convinced that she would have to modify these personality characteristics through a variety of programs, including self-discovery groups and assertiveness training.

In these cases, personality inventory results provided the impetus and stimulation for action to meet individual career needs. In the first example, Ahmed recognized a motivational drive that he had repressed for years as the major source of his frustrations. Fortunately, he was able to meet his needs to achieve in another division of the firm in which he was employed. In the second example, Shayna chose to keep her career goal but increased her chances of success in that career with further training. These examples provide only two illustrations of the use of personality inventories in career counseling but clearly establish their potential usefulness. Personality inventories provide important information that can be incorporated into group or individual counseling programs to assist individuals with career-related problems.

Following are representative examples of personality inventories.

California Test of Personality
CTB-Macmillan-McGraw-Hill
20 Ryan Ranch Road
Monterey, CA 93940
800-282-0266

Five levels of the test are available: primary, elementary, intermediate, secondary, and adult. The test assesses personal and social adjustment. Subscale scores are provided for the two major categories. The test is used primarily in career counseling to assess measures of personal worth and of family and school relations.

Minnesota Counseling Inventory
The Psychological Corporation
555 Academic Court
San Antonio, TX 78204-2498
800-211-8378

This inventory was designed to measure adjustment of boys and girls in grades 9 through 12. Scores yield criterion-related scales as follows: family relationship, social relationship, emotional stability, conformity, adjustment to reality, mood, and leadership. Scales are normed separately for boys and girls. These scores provide indexes to important relationships and personal characteristics to be considered in career counseling.

Sixteen Personality Factor (16 PF)
Institute for Personality and Ability Testing
1602 Coronado Drive
Champaign, IL 61820
800-225-4728

This instrument measures 16 personality factors of individuals 16 years or older. A major part of this questionnaire has been devoted to identifying personality patterns related to occupational fitness projections. These projections provide a comparison of the individual's profile with samples of occupational profiles. The instrument is hand-scored or computer-scored. Four forms have an average adult vocabulary; two forms are available for low-literacy groups.

Temperament and Values Inventory
Charles B. Johansson
Interpretive Scoring Systems
A Division of National Computer Systems, Inc.
P.O. Box 1416
Minneapolis, MN 55440
800-627-7271

This inventory has two parts: (1) temperament dimensions of personality related to career choice, and (2) values related to work rewards. The inventory has an eighth-grade reading level and is not recommended for use below the ninth grade. The inventory is untimed and computer-scored. Scores help determine congruence or incongruence with an individual's career aspirations.

Myers-Briggs Type Indicator
Consulting Psychologists Press, Inc.
3803 East Bayshore Road
Palo Alto, CA 94303
800-624-1765

This inventory measures individual preferences by personality types: extroversion or introversion; sensing or intuition; thinking or feeling; and judging or perceiving. Scores are determined according to the four categories. The publisher's manual provides descriptions of the 16 possible types (combinations). Occupations that are attractive to each type are presented in the appendixes. This inventory provides direct references to occupational considerations based on one's personality type.

Goal 6: Determining Values

During the last two decades, much has been written about beliefs and values. Some argue that we have experienced significant changes in our value systems during the last 20 years. There is the ongoing debate about differences in values between the so-called establishment and the younger generation. Much of the concern has centered on lifestyle and the work role. Questioning the social worth of one's work has motivated many to reformulate their life goals. As career counselors, we must be concerned with individual beliefs and values in the career decision-making process. An important function is to act as agents who provide methods for clarifying values. In this frame of reference, we are concerned not only with work values but also with values per se as we help others find congruence with the inseparables—work and life.

For counseling purposes, we classify values inventories into two types: (1) inventories that primarily measure work values, and (2) inventories that measure values associated with broader aspects of lifestyle. Work value inventories, as the name implies, are designed to measure values associated with job success and satisfaction (achievement, prestige, security, and creativity). Values found to be high priorities for the individual provide another dimension of information that can be used in career exploration. In our second category, values are considered in much broader terms but can be related to needs and satisfactions associated with life and work. Thus, both types of inventories provide information that can be especially helpful for clarifying individual needs associated with work, home, family, and leisure. Two examples of the use of a value measure follow.

- Ngo, a middle-aged, married man with five children, was employed for five years as a salesman in a local furniture store. He is currently seeking a change in employment and sought out a state agency for assistance. As part of the assessment program, he took the *Survey of Personal Values* (Gordon, 1967). The results of the inventory clearly indicated that Ngo was very goal-oriented; that is, he preferred to have definite goals and plan precisely for the future. However, he felt that he had no real control over his life, particularly because in his past job as a salesman his commissions had fluctuated greatly from month to month. He expressed frustration and despair. The major focus of the group discussions that followed centered on identifying those variables through which individuals can exert control over their lives. Ngo was encouraged to recognize his past experiences as assets for his future in the job market. Exploring potential careers by identifying skills from previous work experiences gave him the confidence he lacked in the past. More important, Ngo learned of several jobs for which he was qualified that gave him the opportunity to set goals and plan for the future.

- Rosa was considered an outstanding student in high school and was very active as a member of the student council. She expressed a deep concern to the career counselor about her inability to identify a working environment in which she felt she could find satisfaction. There were no particular role models, organizations, or occupations that seemed to have the potential to satisfy her needs. In the *Work Values Inventory (WVI)* (Super, 1970) administered to her, she rated intellectual stimulus, creativity, and job placement very high. These values were incorporated into further discussions that provided her with a starting point from which she was able to launch a career exploration. Potential occupations were partially evaluated to determine how they could satisfy her work values identified by the *WVI*.

In the first example, a values inventory identified Ngo's major difficulty in career planning as stemming from a need to identify sources of discontentment with his past job. Once the unsatisfied value was revealed—a desire to have control over his life—Ngo was encouraged to identify past job skills that were applicable to new jobs over which he could have more control. In the second example, the identified work values served as a stimulus in launching a study of careers from the perspective of finding a career that could meet Rosa's needs. Once one is able to consider careers from an individual viewpoint, more realistic decisions usually follow. Following are representative examples of work values inventories.

Work Environment Preference Schedule
The Psychological Corporation
555 Academic Court
San Antonio, TX 78204-2498
800-211-8378

This inventory measures an individual's adaptability to a bureaucratic organization. It is untimed and self-administered. A total score reflects the individual's commitment to the sets of attitudes, values, and behaviors found in bureaucratic organizations. Separate norms by sex are available for high school, college, and Army ROTC students.

Work Values Inventory (WVI)
Houghton Mifflin Company
222 Berkeley Street
Boston, MA 02116
800-225-3362

This inventory measures sources of satisfaction individuals seek from their work environments. Scores yield measures of altruism, aesthetics, creativity, intellectual stimulation, independence, prestige, management, economic returns, security, surroundings, supervisory relations, value of relationship with associates, way of life, and variety. Norms are provided by grade and sex for students in grades 7 through 12. The scores provide dimensions of work values that can be combined with other considerations in career counseling.

Following are representative examples of broader values inventories.

Study of Values
Houghton Mifflin Company
222 Berkeley Street
Boston, MA 02116
800-225-3362

This is a self-administered inventory that measures individual values in six categories: theoretical, economic, esthetic, social, political, and religious. Norms are provided by sex for high school, college, and various occupational groups. The measured strength of values (indicated as high, average, or low) provides points of reference for individual and group counseling programs.

Survey of Personal Values
SRA-McGraw-Hill
220 East Daniel Dale
De Soto, TX 75115
800-843-8855

This inventory measures values that influence how individuals cope with daily problems. Scores yield measures of practical-mindedness, achievement, variety, decisiveness, orderliness, and goal orientation. The inventory is self-administered. National percentile norms are available for college students, and regional norms are available for high school students.

The Values Scale
Consulting Psychologists Press, Inc.
3803 East Bayshore Road
Palo Alto, CA 94303
800-624-1765

This scale measures 21 values: ability utilization, achievement, advancement, aesthetics, altruism, authority, autonomy, creativity, economic rewards, lifestyle, personal development, physical activity, prestige, risk, social interaction, social relations, variety, working conditions, cultural identity, physical prowess, and economic security. The measures are designed to help individuals understand values in relation to life roles and evaluate the importance of the work role with other life roles. Scores are interpreted by using percentile equivalents. Norms are available for high school and university students and adults.

Goal 7: Exploring Career Maturity Variables

Career maturity inventories—also referred to as career development inventories—measure vocational development as specified dimensions from which one is judged to be vocationally mature. The dimensions of career maturity are derived from career development concepts. That is, vocational maturity, like career choice, is a continuous development process that can be segmented into a series of stages and tasks (Crites, 1973, pp. 5–7; Super, 1957). Super put the process of career choice on a continuum, with "exploration" and "decline" as endpoints (as discussed in Chapter 2). Career maturity is considered the degree of vocational development measurable within this continuum. Super measured career maturity within several dimensions: orientation toward work (attitudinal dimension), planning (competency dimension), consistency of vocational preferences (consistency dimension), and wisdom of vocational preferences (realistic dimension). These dimensions identify progressive steps of vocational development and determine the degree of development relative to normative age levels.

Thus, career maturity inventories are primarily measures of individual career development. For example, attitudinal dimensions reveal individual problems associated with career choice. Competence dimensions provide measures of an individual's knowledge of occupations and planning skills. Career maturity inventories provide a focus for individual or group programs. They also evaluate the effectiveness of career education programs and curricula and help identify other career guidance program needs. Following is a list of representative career maturity inventories.

Career Development Inventory
D. E. Super, A. S. Thompson, R. H. Lindenman, J. P. Jordaan, and R. A. Myers
Consulting Psychologists Press, Inc.
3803 East Bayshore Road
Palo Alto, CA 94303
800-624-1765

This inventory is a diagnostic tool for developing individual or group counseling procedures; it can also be used to evaluate career development programs. Scores yield measures of planning orientation, readiness for exploration, information, and decision making. The reading level is 6th grade, and the inventory applies to both sexes. Both cognitive and attitudinal scales are provided.

Career Maturity Inventory (CMI)
Psychological Assessment Resources, Inc.
P.O. Box 998
Odessa, FL 33556
800-331-8378

The 1995 edition of the CMI yields three scores: Attitude Scale, Competence Test, and overall Career Maturity. The test can be both hand-scored and machine-scored. The CMI is designed to be used with students from grade 6 through 12 and with adults.

Cognitive Vocational Maturity Test (CVMT)
B. W. Westbrook
Center for Occupational Education
North Carolina State University
Raleigh, NC 27607

This test is primarily a cognitive measure of an individual's knowledge of occupational information. Scores yield measures of knowledge of fields of work available, job selection procedures, work conditions, educational requirements, specific requirements for a wide range of occupations, and actual duties performed in a variety of occupations. This inventory provides important information about career choice abilities and can be used as a diagnostic tool for curricula and guidance needs.

Adult Career Concerns Inventory
Consulting Psychologists Press, Inc.
3803 East Bayshore Road
Palo Alto, CA 94303
800-624-1765

Three major purposes are listed for this inventory: career counseling and planning, needs analysis, and measuring relationships between adult capability and previous, concurrent socioeconomic and psychological characteristics. Scores are related to career development tasks at various life stages as follows: exploration, establishment, maintenance, disengagement, retirement planning, and retirement living. Norms are available by age, starting at 25, by combined sexes, and by age groups and sex.

The Salience Inventory
Consulting Psychologists Press, Inc.
3803 East Bayshore Road
Palo Alto, CA 94303
800-624-1765

This instrument, a research edition in developmental stage, is designed to measure five major life roles: student, worker, homemaker, leisurite, and citizen. Inventory results provide counselors with an evaluation of an individual's readiness for career decisions and exposure to work and occupations.

Goal 8: Using Computer-Assisted Career Guidance (CACG) Assessment

During the last three decades, the use of CACG assessment has steadily increased. One primary reason for the growth is that results are immediately available to clients. Computer-based assessment programs also interpret results to clients by occupational fit with lists of career options. However, some concerns about the validity of instruments in computer-based assessment have been expressed by independent researchers (Sampson, 1994; Sampson & Pyle, 1983) and by professional organizations such as the American Psychological Association (1985, 1986). In this section, we will review some of the advantages and disadvantages of six computer-based assessment processes.

The six different assessment processes associated with CACG (Sampson, 1994) are as follows:

1. *Responding to an on-line instrument.* This process increases validity of the instrument but also increases the time clients must spend on-line.

2. *Inputting scores from an instrument completed off-line.* The obvious advantage is that clients spend less time on-line. The distinct disadvantage is that clients might not be fully aware of how assessment results relate to occupations.

3. *User-controlled on-line self-assessment.* Clients using this system may judge variables *they* consider most important. However, considerable on-line use is a disadvantage.

4. *A system-controlled on-line self-assessment.* Simplifying assessment by reducing options is considered an advantage for some clients. The disadvantage is a significant reduction in the client's control of the system.

5. *Prestructured off-line self-assessment.* More students will have access to the system, but they may be overwhelmed with the comprehensive nature of some guidebooks used with this program.

6. *User-controlled on-line sequence of self-assessment, clarification, and reassessment.* The goal of this system is to improve the client's acceptance of using self-assessment, especially with clarification material available. However, more on-line time is needed for this process.

Other problems associated with CACG assessment include various forms of instrument validity, scoring, search, and interpretative functions. Be aware that validity of CACG assessment systems should meet the same set of standards used for other psychometric measures. For instance, the validity of scoring standardized instruments includes weighting items into scales and ensuring error-free scoring. However, errors in these two processes are difficult to identify in computer-based assessment. Thus, career service providers might not be aware of potential errors and subsequent misleading results.

Finally, interpretative statements generated by computer-based testing systems should be carefully evaluated for their validity. One must ask for some proof that interpretative statements have been carefully evaluated and are indeed valid results that clients can fully understand and apply to their search processes.

As computer-based assessment continues to grow, career service providers must insist that system developers and independent researchers meet the testing standards that have been clearly defined by the American Psychological Association. Evidence of valid testing standards should be clearly delineated in promotional materials, as well as in professional manuals.

Information About Assessment Instruments

Numerous publications can help you gather information about career assessment instruments, including these:

Kapes, J. T., Mastie, M. M., & Whitfeld, E. A. (Eds.). (1994). *A counselor's guide for career assessment instruments* (3rd ed.). Alexandria, VA: National Career Development Association.

Mental Measurements Yearbook
The Buros Institute of Mental Measurements
The University of Nebraska Press
135 Bancroft Hall
Lincoln, NE 68588-0348

Test Critiques
Test Corporation of America
330 West 47th Street
Kansas City, MO 64112

Test in Print
The Buros Institute of Mental Measurements
The University of Nebraska Press
135 Bancroft Hall
Lincoln, NE 68588-0348

Tests
Test Corporation of America
330 West 47th Street
Kansas City, MO 64112

Summary

1. Standardized tests and assessment inventories have been closely associated with career counseling. Skills, aptitudes, interests, values, achievements, personality characteristics, and vocational maturity are among the assessment objectives of career counseling.

2. The use of standardized assessment procedures in career counseling provides the client with increased options and alternatives, subsequently encouraging greater individual involvement in the career decision process. In career counseling programs, assessment scores are used with other materials to stimulate and enhance career exploration.

3. There is a growing concern about the appropriate use of assessment results for diverse groups that were not included in a test's standardization and validation. Professional groups have issued guidelines to assist test users and developers.

4. Reliability and validity are two psychometric concepts that counselors must evaluate when selecting assessment instruments.

5. Issues involved in achieving equity in assessment include a wide range of variables that must be considered in test selection and use for diverse groups. Test manuals containing technical information should be carefully reviewed to make certain all assessment information is appropriate for each client.

6. The goals of assessment include evaluating traits for career exploration and career decision-making. It is most important to establish a client-counselor relationship of collaboration to select tests and set goals for using them. Inventories that measure career beliefs are used as measures of dysfunctional thinking.

7. Aptitude tests primarily measure specific skills and proficiencies or the ability to acquire a certain proficiency. Measured aptitudes provide a good frame of reference for evaluating potential careers.

8. Achievement tests primarily assess present levels of developed abilities. The level of basic academic skills such as arithmetic, reading, and language usage is relevant information that should be included in planning for educational or training programs.

9. Interest inventories are relevant counseling tools because individuals having interest patterns similar to those of people in certain occupations will probably find satisfaction in those occupations. Interest inventories can effectively stimulate career exploration.

10. Personality development is a major factor in career development because the individuality of each counselee must be considered. Personality patterns are integral in identifying and clarifying the needs of each individual.

11. Assessment and clarification of beliefs and values are important com-
     ponents of career counseling. Two types of values inventories are (a) in-
     ventories that primarily measure work values and (b) inventories that
     measure dimensions of values associated with broader aspects of
     lifestyles.

12. Career maturity inventories measure the dimensions from which one is
     judged to be vocationally mature. Super identified dimensions of career
     maturity as orientation toward work, planning, consistency of voca-
     tional preferences, and wisdom of vocational preferences. Career matu-
     rity inventories have two basic purposes: (a) to measure an individual's
     career development and (b) to evaluate the effectiveness of career edu-
     cation programs.

13. Computer-assisted career guidance assessment has steadily increased.
     Validity of instruments and the proper reporting of meeting usual test-
     ing standards has been a chief concern of researchers and professional
     organizations.

Supplementary Learning Exercises

1. Visit a state rehabilitation office to determine the assessment programs
    used for rehabilitation programs. Summarize the purpose of assessment
    in this context.

2. Administer and interpret one or more of the tests and inventories dis-
    cussed in this chapter. Summarize the results and discuss strategies for
    using the results in career counseling.

3. Interview a personnel director of an industrial company and discuss the
    company's assessment program for placement counseling. Identify the
    rationale for each assessment instrument used.

4. Review AAC's *Multicultural Assessment Standards: A Compilation for
    Counselors*. Present your review to the class.

5. Interview a high school or a college counselor concerning his or her
    assessment programs for career counseling. Identify the counseling
    strategies underlying the use of assessment instruments.

6. Request permission from a university counseling center to take (or self-
    administer and interpret) their battery of tests and inventories used in
    career counseling. Summarize the results.

7. Review the evaluations of an aptitude test; an achievement test; and
    one interest, values, personality, and career maturity inventory in the
    Mental Measurements Yearbook.

8. Write an essay defending this statement: Assessment results can be ef-
    fectively used in career counseling programs for diverse groups.

9. Choose one or more of the following situations and develop an assessment battery that can be incorporated in career exploration programs:

   a. A middle school in a socioeconomically deprived neighborhood
   b. A senior high school from which 70% of the graduates enter college
   c. A community college in a large city
   d. A small four-year college
   e. A large university
   f. A community agency providing career counseling for adults
   g. A rehabilitation agency
   h. A private practice in career counseling

10. Select at least two of the references for evaluating assessment instruments and compare the information obtained.

For More Information

American Psychological Association. (1985). *Standards for educational and psychological testing*. Washington, DC: Author.

American Psychological Association. (1986). *Guidelines for computer-based tests and interpretations*. Washington, DC: Author.

Betz, N. E., & Fitzgerald, L. F. (1995). Career assessment and intervention with racial and ethnic minorities. In Frederick T. L. Leong (Ed.), *Career development and vocational behavior of racial and ethnic minorities* (pp. 263–277). Mahwah, NJ: Erlbaum.

Brown, D., & Brooks, L. (1991). *Career counseling techniques*. Boston: Allyn & Bacon.

Fouad, N. A., & Spreda, S. L. (1995). Use of interest inventories with special populations. *Journal of Career Assessment, 3,* 453–468.

Harris-Bowlsbey, J., Dikel, M. R., & Sampson, J. P. (1998). *The Internet: A tool for career planning*. Columbus, OH: National Career Development Association.

Lowman, R. L. (1991). *The clinical practice of career assessment: Interests, abilities, and personality*. Washington, DC: American Psychological Association.

Sandoval, J., Frisby, C. L., Geisinger, K. F., Scheuneman, J. D., & Grenier, J. R. (1998). *Test interpretation and diversity: Achieving equity in assessment*. Washington, DC: American Psychological Association.

Zunker, V. G., & Osborn, D. (2002). *Using assessment results for career development* (6th ed.). Pacific Grove, CA: Brooks/Cole.

8

Self-Assessment and a Model for Using Assessment

Chapter Highlights

- *Using self-assessment as an alternative in career counseling*
- *Learning how to self-assess*
- *Self-assessment through self-observations*
- *Autobiography*
- *Focused questions to uncover specific variables*
- *Nontraditional interest identification*
- *Card sorts*
- *Lifeline—A career life planning experience*
- *Guided fantasy exercise to increase self-awareness*
- *Self-assessment of skills*
- *Using assessment results, including standardized tests*
- *Seven-stage model for using assessment results*
- *The future of assessment*

T HE TERM SELF-ASSESSMENT HAS BEEN USED IN CAREER COUNSELING TO SIG- nify that an individual's personal traits as assessed are important variables in the choice process. Traditionally, individuals were administered a variety of tests that were designed to measure aptitudes, intelligence, interests, values, and personality, among other traits. Self-assessment has also been considered as a method that encourages individuals to estimate the level or the degree of their personal traits. Recent examples include self-estimates of abilities by Harrington and O'Shea (1992) in their career decision-making package, McKinlay (1990) who developed a questionnaire for identifying skills and interests, and Bolles (2000) who recommends self-estimates of developed skills as a vital step in career decision making.

In this chapter, we focus on assisting individuals to self-assess by using non-traditional methods of self-estimates. We also focus on assisting individuals in recognizing how their personal traits were shaped and developed within environmental and contextual interactions. Clients who are actively involved in the process of self-assessment are empowered to determine the direction the stage of assessment takes in a career counseling model (Healy, 1990). Clients are also made aware of salient messages they received in their environment that have influenced their career development.

This chapter includes a rationale for self-assessment that includes support information from career theorists. In the second section, some examples of self-assessment are described. In the third section, learning to self-assess is introduced. The fourth section presents a model for using assessment results that includes both standardized tests and self-assessment through self-estimates. Finally, future assessment is briefly described.

Rationale for Self-Assessment as an Alternative

In his seminal work in social learning theory, Bandura (1986) emphasizes the role of thoughts and images in psychological functioning. One of his major positions is that as we learn from environmental interactions, we also learn to evaluate or estimate a sense of self. This process is known as a triadic reciprocal interaction system that includes (1) contextual environmental interactions with (2) an individual's beliefs, self-perceptions, memories, prediction, anticipation, and (3) behavioral actions. At the core of this triad is the self-system—composed of cognitive structures and self-perceptions—that directs behavior. The self-system includes self-awareness, self-inducements, self-reinforcements, and self-efficacy. A major point is that development of self is greatly influenced by social interaction variables within one's environment over the life span.

In a related study, Sigelman (1999) suggests that the goodness of fit between an individual and environment greatly influences such factors as self-awareness and self-efficacy. For instance, if an individual perceives that he or she is valued by society, that is, there is a goodness of fit to social expectations, certain behaviors are reinforced. The individual is conditioned to believe that these behaviors, such as sex-typed activity and the level of prestige of an occupation, are appropriate. However, if messages from environmental variables change, the individual might reevaluate beliefs.

In another study, Newman and Newman (1999) suggest a list of interacting factors that affect sex-role socialization and the career decision-making process as shown in Figure 8-1. Although several factors are involved in this schemata, they could be grouped under the Bandura triadic interaction system. The point here is that there appears to be solid agreement that cognitive, situational, and behavioral factors are involved in forming a sense of self that influences an individual's career development and subsequent choice process.

In the career development theories discussed in Chapters 2 and 3, self-knowledge is frequently mentioned as a key concept in the career choice process. The term self-knowledge, in this context, is often reflected in other frequently mentioned constructs as self-concept, self-awareness, self-perceptions, self-efficacy, and self-esteem. In one way or the other, the terms represent a sense of self that we are interested in assessing for career counseling. In the following summations of career development research, we see more evidence to support the importance of discovering the foundations from which one's self-knowledge influences career choice.

Closely related to our discussion of self-knowledge is the social-learning model, as discussed in Chapter 2, which emphasizes the importance of learning experiences and their effect on occupational selection. Krumboltz and Nichols (1990) suggest that self-knowledge is accumulated over time through complex cognitive systems that involve information processing and memory processes. From a learning theory perspective, self-observation generalizations and task approach skills are fundamental to constructing individuals' belief systems about themselves. These beliefs are the foundation from which individuals set goals and make choices; beliefs are primarily formed from the individual's unique learning experiences, genetic endowments, and environmental conditions and events.

Within this conception of learning, individuals form self-generalizations based on numerous experiences. Some may be fairly accurate whereas others are faulty and harmful to the individual's development. Individuals also develop work habits, performance standards and values, problem-solving methods, and emotional responses that are referred to as task-approach skills. The key point is that individuals can develop new self-generalizations and task approach skills over time as they learn from new and different experiences (Mitchell & Krumboltz, 1996). Self-assessment in this context enables clients to identify limitations and advantages of contextual interactions and evaluate the validity of their rationale in making occupational choices or to changing career directions.

In the cognitive approach to career counseling discussed in Chapters 3 and 4, self-knowledge is considered a significant element in cognitive information processing. Self-knowledge involves interpretation and reconstruction. The interpretation process is based on matching current situations with episodes stored in long-term memory. Similar to the learning theory approach, reconstruction occurs according to an existing schemata: individuals reconstruct past events to accumulate new data (Peterson, Sampson, & Reardon, 1991).

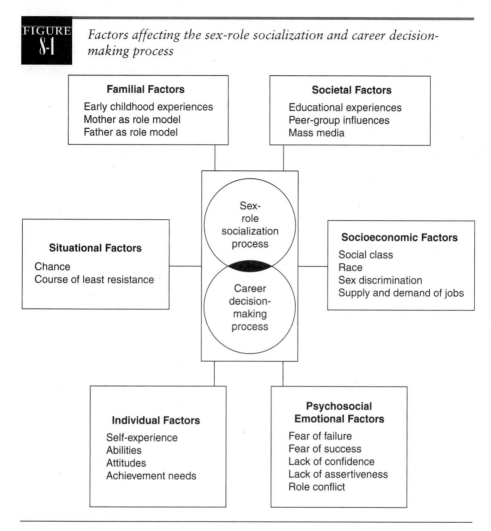

FIGURE 8-1 *Factors affecting the sex-role socialization and career decision-making process*

Familial Factors
Early childhood experiences
Mother as role model
Father as role model

Societal Factors
Educational experiences
Peer-group influences
Mass media

Situational Factors
Chance
Course of least resistance

Sex-role socialization process

Career decision-making process

Socioeconomic Factors
Social class
Race
Sex discrimination
Supply and demand of jobs

Individual Factors
Self-experience
Abilities
Attitudes
Achievement needs

Psychosocial Emotional Factors
Fear of failure
Fear of success
Lack of confidence
Lack of assertiveness
Role conflict

SOURCE: From *Development Through Life: A Psychological Approach*, by B. M. Newman & P. R. Newman. Copyright 1999 by Brooks/Cole–Wadsworth Publishing Company, a division of International Thomson Publishing, Inc.

Self-concept theory, according to Super (1957) and Super, Starishesky, Matlin, & Jordaan (1963), suggests that self-concept plays an important role in occupational selection. Super's position has been that individuals go through developmental stages in which the self-concept is cultivated. According to Krumboltz and Nichols (1990), Super did not specify how self-concept was refined, but he did recognize that the development of self-concept was a result of experiences. Thus, there appear to be significant similarities between Super's self-concept theory and learning theory by Krumboltz and Nichols (1990); both theories assume learning from contextual interactions.

In Holland's (1985a) typology model, self-evaluation is a broader and more general assessment that is used to find congruence with a work environment characterized by six general orientations. He has emphasized, however, that a satisfactory occupational choice depends on an individual's self-knowledge and accurate occupational knowledge. Those clients who possess a high degree of self-awareness are generally viewed as having a greater chance of finding congruence in a work environment.

Similar to Holland's approach, accurate self-knowledge improves one's chances of finding congruence with a work environment and its reinforcement potential in the trait-and-factor and person-environment-fit model. An in-depth analysis of one's abilities, interests, values, and personality style is needed to match congruent work environments. The individual projects self into the work environment in search of fulfillment and to satisfy achievement needs. The greater your knowledge and understanding of your unique traits is, the better the chance you have of meeting personal goals.

Tiedeman and O'Hara (1963) developed a career decision-making model that refers to self-in-situation from the earliest awareness of self to when an individual becomes capable of evaluating experiences, anticipating and imagining future goals, and storing experiences in memory for future reference. The logic of the Miller-Tiedeman (1988) model is that one must view life as a learning process; let life teach you (Wrenn, 1988). The "inner wisdom" implied is the driving force of optimal career selection.

Gottfredson (1996), as reviewed in Chapter 3, especially stressed the importance of self-concept as gender self-concept that develops into a strong need that influences career choice. In general, both sexes develop self-sophistication and discrimination through cultural and socioeconomic conditions learned in their environments. Although Gottfredson did not describe how people learn, she points out that career choices are limited as a result of environmental situations and contextual interactions such as quality of education, availability of libraries, neighborhood, and family background(Krumboltz & Nichols, 1990).

Understanding human development in a contextual model, introduced in Chapter 3, suggests that development is ever-changing and an ongoing interplay of forces. Thus, self-assessment provides clients with a greater understanding of forces that have influenced the development of skills and interests and at the same time points out the direction of future learning and growth needs. Assisting clients to improve their self-assessment techniques will enhance their abilities and desires to assess who they are and the dynamic interactions within contexts that influenced them.

In a multicultural career counseling model, contextual issues receive a high priority. Self-generalizations may be limited because of a lack of experiences, exposure to learning opportunities, and discrimination. Clients who are led to focus on limitations they have experienced through self-assessment should be encouraged to use this information to develop strategies for more exposure to occupations and self-improvement. Multicultural counseling encourages clients and counselors to thoroughly evaluate each client's environmental background, including unique contextual variables that have contributed to the development of each individual's worldview.

In sum, self-assessment can enhance a client's understanding of the purpose of assessment and empower clients to manage the appraisal process and their career search (Healy, 1990). Contextual interactions are recognized by many career theorists and model developers as a major focus in the career counseling process and are highlighted when clients self-assess their environmental backgrounds. Two important questions that can aid in placing career search in greater perspective to an individual's needs are (1) how and why certain skills were developed, and (2) what lifestyle events influenced the development of interests can aid in placing career search in greater perspective to an individual's needs. Clients might also discover that a lack of exposure to the work world has dampened their outlooks for the future. Finally, clients could recognize that numerous variables should be considered in making a choice. The logic associated with self-assessment provides a pathway for clients to assume an active role in a collaborative client-counselor relationship that, in turn, enables clients to become more involved in the entire counseling process.

Learning to Self-Assess

Self-assessment is a means of learning more about oneself through self-observation of current and previous learning experiences or through nontraditional measuring instruments and exercises. For example, learning experiences involve numerous sources, such as family (nuclear or extended), school, peers, work experiences, hobbies, religious affiliation, leisure activities, community involvement, media, role models, and many other events and activities. A link between one's interest in an occupation may be traced to a combination of influence variables. Knowledge of this link provides a basis for evaluating how an interest is developed and its validity. For instance, when a student was asked why he choose geology as a major he replied, "Because my friends did." In his search for a different major, he recognized that he chose geology for the wrong reasons and was now prepared to begin a career choice process based on his interests and abilities. In most cases clients can find significant relationships from salient messages received from their environment. Some of the messages may limit career choices, some may have positively influenced their career choices, whereas other messages have contributed to indecisiveness. Self-assessment through self-observation should be focused to increase one's self-awareness and provide a direction to expanding its growth.

The use of self-observation in a variety of counseling programs provides some guidelines for its use in career counseling. For instance, self-monitoring as used in self-management strategies is a means of identifying problems that can interfere with an individual's ability to appropriately maintain a self-managed lifestyle (Beck, 1976; Brammer, Abrego, & Shostrom, 1993; Cormier & Cormier, 1991; Cormier & Hackney, 1987). The overarching goal of self-management is to promote enduring client changes through self-directed behavior. Clients are taught to self-monitor certain key behaviors by self-observation and self-recording. Kanfer

(1980) points out that clients who self-assess or self-observe and record their behaviors do develop a greater sense of awareness of those focused behaviors and more concrete information about their frequency and influence. The outcomes of self-management through self-monitoring are quite relevant to the objectives and goals of career counseling models.

To strengthen clients' involvement in the career counseling process, self-management strategies can be adapted in a self-assessment process designed to provide clients with skills to manage career life changes. Clients also learn to evaluate influences from contextual interactions within their environments through self-observation and self-assessment. The potential of unearthing significant events, conditions, and traits from a client's contextual interactions has not been fully appreciated in career counseling models (Bingham and Ward, 1996; Healy, 1990; Subich, 1996). Clients become active participants by maintaining a daily log that charts information about activities and their situational antecedents and consequences, as well as their thoughts and feelings during these interactions. This information can be used for problem identification as well as provide a baseline for evaluating certain traits such as interests, abilities, values, and personality style.

Counselors should assist clients in identifying any themes that emerge from self-observation and self-assessment. Such themes can be confirmed through further assessment. During the review, the counselor guides the client in identifying events and influences that were dominant. For example, Aldo, a legal resident for two years, was working part time and wanted a full-time job, but was undecided. His daily log contained such activities and statements as these:

"The boss asked me to arrange the shelves so that the workers could find what they need."

"I wish the boss would tell me more about what he expects."

"I don't like for him to change my work assignment."

"My father told me to get a regular job with regular hours so you know what to expect."

(next day) "I am happy!" "Today I do what I usually do and I like to have everything ready for the crew to pick up the materials they need." "I look at the list and count the number of things they want and I put exactly that amount in the bag."

"Tonight we did what we usually do each week—we go to hear some music and then we ate at Lugi's."

"I feel good tonight."

The pattern of statements and observations recorded by Aldo for an entire two-week period reflected an interest and a need for work environments and leisure time to be well-organized, precise, and routine and in which the work tasks and time commitments are clearly defined. Aldo confirmed these observations; however, the counselor was concerned that Aldo had not been exposed to many other work environments and informed him that work could change in the future. The counselor and Aldo agreed that he would observe several different jobs by job shadowing. The counselor and Aldo agreed that it would be helpful to evaluate his educational achievement level for the possibility of training for targeted work environments in the future.

Another example illustrates Aya's frustration with deciding on an occupation. Her statements reflected an interest in music with several log entries about attending musical concerts and listening to musical programs. Her favorite place to go during free time was the record and music store; however, she never mentioned any musical related careers as possible choices. When asked about her musical interests, she replied that she had learned to play the piano from her uncle but never considered music as a career. Further probing indicated that Aya did not believe a musical career was appropriate for her because her family considered it as amusement only and not the work for a woman. She also mentioned that a music career would require college and that "my family does not go to college." She also confided, however, that she would be thrilled to be a music teacher.

Using this information, counselor and client approached the family for a meeting to discuss Aya's future. Both realized the family must give their blessing to a career that would require a college degree and a significant change in their perception of what was appropriate work for a female member of their family. Another hurdle would be to convince her family that college is for everyone who is capable, including women.

These two cases illustrate the importance of client's participation in the career choice process. By recording their self-observations Aldo and Aya were actively involved in resolving their problems. Counselors are in a much better position to assist clients in understanding personal preferences and unique experiences that influence and limit career choice when clients present their own interpretations of their behavior. Self-assessment provides an entry into understanding the significance of salient messages each individual receives from his or her environment.

In a related discussion of environmental influences, Healy (1982) suggests that counselors should lead clients to realize the importance of personal connections with others. Current personal associations can be compared with past ones from different periods in an individual's life span. Feelings about relationships per se can be further explored by having the client reflect on work-related associates, such as a mentor, respected supervisor, and a subordinate. As the client's history unfolds, other important information can be discussed, such as skill development of strengths and accomplishments that can be used in the career search.

Self-assessment through self-observation can also assist clients in recognizing dysfunctional beliefs. In this process, clients become aware of distortions in their thinking processes. Counselors need to fully prepare clients for such exercises. Meichenbaum (1977) suggests that two critical factors in self-observation are the client's willingness to participate and his or her ability to do what Meichenbaum refers to as "listen to themselves." Peterson, Sampson and Reardon (1991) suggest that clients should be presented with both negative and positive data about themselves and about occupations to challenge their modes of thinking. Counselors can also use examples of faulty cognitions, such as those by Nevo (1987) and Doyle (1992) found in Chapters 5 and 6, as examples for recognizing how irrational thinking can limit and hamper career search. Finally, clients learn a new internal dialogue through self-talk, referred to as cognitive restructuring. As clients refocus their self-talk from negative to positive thoughts and statements about themselves, they continue to observe themselves and assess outcomes.

In sum, self-assessment involves clients in self-observations that focus on their unique learning experiences and environmental conditions and events. Salient messages that influenced or limited career choice are the central focus of such an exercise. Counselors should fully inform clients of the purpose and techniques of self-observation and self-assessment. The outcome of this process should enable clients to have greater control and direction of the career counseling process.

Self-Assessment Procedures for Career Counseling

This section will provide some examples for encouraging and stimulating self-assessment. Counselors should use these methods as examples from which they can develop their own procedures to meet the unique needs of each client. Clients who can conceptualize the purpose of self-assessment should be more willing to participate in the process. Counselor and client agree to purpose and need of each procedure; therefore, clients also collaborate in the selection process of non-traditional assessment measures.

Autobiography

Counselors may find that an autobiography helps to complement the intake interview. The autobiography is usually written, but can be given orally. Counselors instruct clients to simply "write an autobiography of your life," with no further instructions. The unstructured autobiography has the advantage of leaving the subject of the response up to the client. The disadvantage is that clients may choose to avoid subjects that could be significant. Counselors may also suggest a structured outline to follow in composing the autobiography, or they may suggest that the client write a work autobiography.

Focused Questions to Uncover Specific Variables

Counselors may develop specific questions that can be used to tap subjects of importance revealed in the interview or from other background information. Counselors can introduce clients to such questions by pointing out the value of discussing significant influences from contextual variables. Some examples follow:

How did you become who you are?

What does your family want you to do?

Father? Mother? Siblings? Uncle and Aunt? Others?

Who has been the most influential person in your life? How?

What do you predict will be your career (job) (work) in the future?

What have others (friends, family, teachers, etc.) told you your career should be?

In outline format, trace the development of you interests and abilities.

What were some of the major events in your life?

Make a list of your likes and dislikes and relate them to your experiences.

Compose a list of your most significant problems. Circle those that are most troublesome.

Such probing questions and exercises were designed to focus attention on relevant contextual interactions and the messages the client received from them. Clients self-assess the major influences and relate them to interests, skills, personality, and vocational identity for further evaluation.

Interest Identification

Goodman (1993) presents an intriguing method of assessing interests adapted from Simon, Howe, and Kirschenbaum (1972). Goodman suggests that activities she has devised stimulate clients to want to know more about their interests.

Clients are instructed to write 20 things they like to do. They can list activities done at work; leisure activities, such as movies, parties, and reading; or taking classes. The following code is assigned to each interest listed.

1. Put a T next to the activities that you would enjoy with additional training.

2. Put an R next to each item that involves risk—physical, emotional, or intellectual.

3. Put a PL beside those items that require planning.

4. Indicate with an A or a P or an A/P whether you prefer to do the activity alone, with people, or both.

5. Next to each activity, put the date when you last engaged in it.

6. Star your five favorite activities.

SOURCE: From "Using Nonstandardized Appraisal Tools and Techniques." Presentation to Michigan Career Development Association Annual Conference. April 29, 1993 at Kalamazoo, MI. Reprinted by permission of J. Goodman.

Each activity provides counselor and client with relevant subjects for discussion and evaluation of its significance. Clients are encouraged to draw conclusions from each statement through self-assessment and relate them to interests.

Other examples of techniques used to encourage clients to self-assess interests include the following:

1. Develop a list of at least ten role models. Explain why you selected each model and relate your choices to interests.
2. List five occupations you like and five you do not like.
3. List the types of activities you enjoy.
4. List the school subjects you like most and least.
5. List your favorite TV programs, magazines, and books.

In sum, interests can be identified through a variety of questions and exercises that require clients to be active participants. Many of the suggested exercises can be done in groups and have the advantage of group interactions; however, some clients may be more comfortable when relating environmental contextual interactions to counselors who have established a trusting relationship with the client.

Card Sorts

Card sorts are another method of determining interests. Clients sort cards that have the name and description of an occupation on them into three categories: "Would Not Choose," "Would Choose," and "No Opinion." Counselor and client discuss all categories and identify common themes that emerge. Clients relate interests and common themes to their backgrounds.

Lifeline—A Career Life Planning Experience

This exercise requires the client to draw a line from birth to death and indicate on it key life experiences and present position. The major purpose of this exercise is to actively involve clients in concentrating on future tasks and life planning. The following exercise was used at Colorado State University to prompt self-awareness and the recognition that each individual has certain responsibilities in developing his or her future.

Exercise	Purpose
Lifeline	To identify past and current situations in life
Identifying and stripping of roles	To become free of all previous roles by temporarily discarding them.
Fantasy time	To develop more self-awareness when free of identified roles
Typical day and a special day of the future	To further crystallize self-awareness and individual needs for the future when free of identified roles
Life inventory	To identify specific needs and goals with emphasis on identifying each individual's positive characteristics.
News release	To further clarify specific interests and future accomplishments desired
Resume goals	To clarify or reformulate goals while reassuming originally identified roles
Goal setting	To set realistic short-term and long-term goals

This exercise has been recommended for use with groups primarily for the purpose of group interaction. An example of this lifeline exercise with a hypothetical group is discussed in Chapter 18.

Guided Fantasy—An Exercise to Increase Self-Awareness

Brown and Brooks (1991) point out that guided fantasy is not to be used with all clients because some may be unwilling to participate for a variety of reasons. In a literature review, however, Skovalt, Morgan, and Negron-Cunningham (1989), as cited in Brown and Brooks (1991), report that guided fantasy has been successfully used for more than sixty years with clients of different age levels, sexes, and races, including Afro-Americans.

One of the major purposes of guided fantasy is to uncover subconscious material that can be used in career decision making (Skovholt, Morgan, & Negron-Cunningham, 1989). Spokane (1991) suggests that mental imagery does increase self-awareness and encourages expressions of aspirations that could go undetected. The purpose and procedure for this exercise suggests that clients will freely express their needs and desires when they are free of perceived restraints. The procedures for guided imagery include the following:

1. Induce relaxation through Jacobson's (1938) relaxation techniques
2. Establish the fantasy itself, such as, a day on the job or my workplace in the future
3. Discuss the reactions to the fantasy

Skills Identification

Skills identification through self-assessment techniques has received renewed attention recently (Bolles, 2000; Brown & Brooks, 1991; Holland, 1992). The focus is on identifying skills from previous experiences in a number of activities including work and hobbies. The identification of transferable skills is discussed with an example in Chapter 20.

The *Self-Directed Search* (Holland, 1992) includes a section in which clients evaluate themselves on 12 different traits based on previous experience. In addition, Brown and Brooks (1991) suggest several methods involving self-assessment of skills.

Some computerized career counseling programs are designed to identify client skills by having clients self-rate their abilities. An example can be found in DISCOVER (American College Testing Program, 1987). Using the following scale, clients rate themselves on several skills including leadership, sales, manual dexterity, reading, and spatial abilities.

5 = High (top 10% of persons my age)
4 = Above average (upper 25%)

3 = Average (middle 50%)

1 = Low (bottom 10%)

Skills are used to identify strengths and abilities. Obviously, clients who have limited opportunities to use their skills could have some difficulty in ranking themselves in the examples from *DISCOVER*. However, knowledge of this problem provides an entry to intervention strategies that are designed to give clients the opportunity to try out and improve their skills and learn new ones.

In sum, counselors can personalize numerous nontraditional methods of self-assessment to meet the unique needs of their clients. These procedures do provide an alternative assessment process when standardized assessment is not appropriate. Nontraditional methods can also be used as an initial assessment to assist clients in recognizing additional evaluation needs. Finally, the results of self-assessment should focus on problem identification.

Model for Using Assessment Results

Flexibility is the key to a successful assessment model. A model should be structured to meet the needs of all clients and have the flexibility to blend with traditional career counseling models. Both standardized and self-assessment techniques can be used and, in fact, are to complement each other. Assessment does not dominate the career counseling process when both client and counselor negotiate its use.

The use of an assessment model that is built on a collaborative client-counselor relationship does not decrease counselors' responsibilities but, in fact, requires counselors to sharpen their assessment knowledge and skills. When sharing assessment information with clients, counselors should be proficient in effectively relating to clients the necessary components of assessment that will make results meaningful. Effectively relating to clients requires skills to (a) assess the level of information-processing clients will understand, and (b) communicate to clients from a knowledge base of psychometric theory and practice. Being fully prepared for each client requires the counselor to be resourceful. The following paragraphs include some suggestions.

Counselors should be prepared to evaluate psychometric evidence of validity, reliability, and appropriate norms for each standardized test. Counselors are to be aware of current references that evaluate standardized instruments. Counselors can also consult with test publishers and consultants for advice on selecting and using assessment instruments.

Counselors should use caution when using nonstandardized assessment instruments or exercises that are used to complement or replace standardized instruments. For example, guided fantasy should not be used by counselors who have not been trained or supervised in its administration and use. The rule to follow is that all instruments and exercises require training and supervision.

Counselors should have a working knowledge and an understanding of the theoretical concepts from which career counseling models were developed. An assessment model that is flexible can be adapted to enhance the agenda of a career counseling model and complement its purpose. The point here is that counselors should be able to explain how assessment is to be used and what the client's role will be in the process. Clients who understand and are active in the counseling process are empowered to participate in setting the counseling agenda.

Counselors need to inform clients how to self-assess. The increasing diversity of backgrounds of clients now and in the future requires that counselors evaluate contextual interactions in an attempt to make assessment use and interpretation meaningful. From this vantage point, clients assess what they have and have not learned, what human traits they have or have not cultivated, what advantages and limitations they have experienced, and how and why they have or have not set goals for the future. Of course, there are many other reasons for clients to evaluate contextual interactions, but these examples provide viable opportunities to focus on problem identification and subsequent purposes of assessment.

A model designed to incorporate both standardized and self-assessment is conceptualized as a useful tool within the purposes, goals, and procedures of a career counseling model. The pathway of a career counseling model determines the overall role of assessment; however, assessment is prescribed and tailored when client and counselor have established its purpose. Thus, career counseling does not begin with a battery of tests that are automatically administered to all clients; rather, assessment enhances a major focus of problem identification emphasized in career counseling models. Although assessment is an important component of career counseling models, it should not detract from other important counseling steps and stages (Healy, 1990).

A model for using assessment results has seven stages that are outlined here and followed by an explanation of each step.

Stage 1. Client and counselor should maintain a collaborative relationship.

Stage 2. Client and counselor should negotiate the client's role in assessment.

Stage 3. Counselors should describe the principles and purpose of standardized tests and self-assessment techniques.

Stage 4. Client and counselor should specify client's assessment needs from information in the intake interview.

Stage 5. Client and counselor should select appropriate assessments instruments.

Stage 6. Client and counselor should reevaluate and identify client's problems.

Stage 7. Client and counselor should formulate goals.

The first stage in this model is designed to maintain the collaborative client-counselor relationship that was established in the intake interview. The major focus of assessment is determined by its role in the career counseling model chosen by client and counselor. Career counseling models that call for pre-counseling inventories, such as the multicultural model, actually begin with assessment. Pre-counseling inventories should receive the same evaluation as any other assessment instrument, that is, client and counselor discuss the purpose and agree that these instruments could be helpful.

The client's role in assessment as negotiated in Stage 2 should be character-ized as a partner who collaborates and negotiates need, purpose, selection, and use of each instrument or exercise that follows the script of the career model being used. Obviously, some clients will be able to assume a greater responsibil-ity in this process than others will; however, an informed client should be more responsive and active in the entire counseling process. In any case, counselors should inform clients of the purposes of career counseling and the role of assess-ment. In most assessment models reviewed in Chapter 4, assessment results are used to plan for further evaluations and to develop intervention strategies.

In Stage 3, the principles and purposes of assessment and especially self-assessment are introduced. A review of goals of standardized assessment in Chap-ter 7 will provide some suggestions for principles and purposes of standardized instruments. Self-assessment in this context begins by involving the client in devel-oping tentative conclusions about self-identity from background data, especially contextual interactions. Clients assess their identities as they recall observations of self-in-situation and how they learned to refine and cultivate such traits as interests, values, personality, and skills. The salient messages that were received from contex-tual interactions are very important. Clients might not be aware that they have un-wittingly eliminated certain career paths by assimilating contextual influences. Through self-assessment, clients filter out these problems and prepare themselves for their roles in career counseling, that is, to be open to considering all careers of interest. Self-assessment measures and exercises are an extension of this process. Self-assessment becomes a means of identifying and confirming client's observa-tions, and these findings can be used as data to identify significant problems.

Client and counselor may opt to use standardized instruments or self-assessment instruments or both in the process of exploration and discovery. For example, standardized assessment instruments may be used to verify or confirm tentative conclusions reached by means of self-assessment. Obviously, all assess-ment instruments must be appropriate for each client. This bring us to Stage 4, of specifying client needs. Motivated clients should be active in developing a list of needs that will help overcome barriers and reach goals. Specifying needs means just that, for example, client and counselor agree that a client's level of reading and math skills will provide a starting point for improving them. For instance, a criterion-referenced test will inform both client and counselor of specific defi-ciencies in reading and math. In addition, client and counselor agree that a mea-sure of interests would assist the client in an exploration exercise.

Once the needs have been established, client and counselor review standard-ized instruments and self-assessment procedures to determine the appropriate type and kind in Stage 5. Counselors must make certain that a collaborative rela-tionship is maintained. Clients should be encouraged to express their opinions and be active in the selection process; clients advance their careers by taking charge of actions that offer promising directions. Appropriate assessment instru-ments should equip them with information that illuminates pathways to career exploration and direction. A client who suddenly discovers a work environment that appears to be amiable, for instance, might also be interested in finding other work environments of interest. Clients who are equipped to understand the im-portance of assessment results can initiate appraisals they believe to be important.

In Stage 6, client and counselor identify any problems that surfaced during the initial appraisal. Some problems may require additional assessment whereas others can be processed through career interventions. Identified problems are dissected into needs, and those requiring further assessment are to be recycled in the assessment model. Outcomes of some intervention strategies may also require further evaluation.

Finally, client and counselor formulate goals as designated by Stage 7. This stage refers to possible future assessment of intervention outcomes. For example, after a client has completed an intervention strategy designed to develop certain skills, an appropriate assessment instrument may be used to evaluate progress.

Formulating goals is an important next step for clients who have successfully completed the assessment stage and are moving on to the next stage in the career counseling model. The client's objective is to complete the career decision process. Counselors and clients should recognize that the use of assessment is one step in a career counseling model and, most important, not necessarily the dominant step. A major focus of future career counseling research may involve assessment, but surely will involve the effectiveness of intervention strategies and other model components.

In sum, an assessment model should be flexible enough to blend with career counseling models built from different career development orientations. An assessment model should be designed to meet the needs of all clients, including those from diverse groups. Assessment should be considered as one step or stage in the career counseling process, but it should not dominate career counseling. An assessment model suggests that both standardized tests and self-assessment instruments can be used in combination to complement each other. Assessment should be personalized, that is, it is used when established needs have been discovered by client and counselor. In fact, client and counselor must maintain the collaborative counselor-client relationship established in the intake interview. Counselors equip clients to become active agents in the assessment process and empower them to establish goals and the directions career counseling should take to meet their needs.

A Glimpse at the Future of Assessment

The first edition of this book was written by hand and dictated onto tape that a secretary used to produce the first draft. This process was tedious, expensive, and time consuming. A typing error often required the retyping of a complete page, and making corrections to a manuscript was devastating!

The differences in how we produce books today compared with yesterday may mimic significant changes we will observe in assessment in the future. Paper and pencil tests may largely be replaced by advances in technology associated with computers. Computerized test administration and interpretation should significantly increase in the near future. Computer adaptive testing is now on line; Graduate Record Examinations may be taken by computer adaptive format. This format selects test questions from a bank of items stored in the computer by how the test taker responds to items. For example, if a question is answered incorrectly, the new item selected may have the same degree of difficulty and measures the same construct. When enough information has been collected for a construct, the program selects items designed to measure another construct. Thus, two individuals may take the same test but respond to different items. The advantage is shorter testing time, accessibility, and immediate feedback (Sandoval, 1998a).

Problems involved in computer-assisted career guidance assessment programs were briefly mentioned in the last chapter. We will probably see a continuation of these instruments, however, and we can expect innovative ideas for additional testing and its use in the future.

Through multimedia a wider range of test items will be available. Sandoval (1998a) suggests that computerized administration and scoring of *performance* assessments are being developed. Being able to respond to video tapes of current and changing work environments explained in the language of your choice has some exciting possibilities. The potential of assessment by multimedia virtual reality is only beginning. Currently this is being used to evaluate aircraft pilots.

Perhaps the development of new and different assessment techniques will give the client even greater control over his or her assessment plan. Let us hope that equity of assessment interpretation will be a major focus of future instruments. Finally, our future clients may be able to create their ideal careers through multimedia exposure that is appropriate for their use and be offered potential congruent work environments. Such a program may no longer just be a futuristic dream.

No doubt there should be many new formats for assessment in the future; however, counselors also need to be aware of safeguards and approval of their professional associations for all future assessment instruments.

Summary

1. Self-assessment has been used in a variety of ways in the career counseling process. Healy (1990) has called for reforming career appraisals by using more self-assessment in career counseling.

2. Several career development theories refer to self-knowledge as an important ingredient for selecting a work environment. Self-assessment attempts to uncover the contextual interactions that have influenced individuals in both selecting a career and in limiting careers considered.

3. Self-assessment also empowers clients to negotiate with counselors to determine the benefits of assessment and the direction career counseling will take. Clients become personal agents for developing their careers.

4. Self-assessment includes autobiographies, lifeline exercises, focused questions, interest identification exercises, guided fantasy, and skills identification.

5. A seven-stage model for using assessment may be used in traditional career counseling models. This model is designed to enhance a collaborative client-counselor relationship.

6. Advancing technology should provide new and different formats for future assessment. Computer adaptive and computer scored and interpreted assessment will continue to expand. Multimedia and virtual reality on computers provide opportunities for developing innovative assessment techniques.

Supplementary Learning Exercises

1. What do you consider to be the major advantages and disadvantages of (a) standardized tests and (b) self-assessment instruments.

2. Develop a rationale for using self-assessment in career counseling. Explain your major points.

3. Develop a list of reasons that you would support evaluating a client's environmental contextual interactions. Compare them with those of your classmates.

4. Explain the importance of self-knowledge in career counseling.

5. Develop at least five focused questions to uncover developed skills.

6. Search the career counseling literature for at least five exercises that provide interest evaluations.

7. Research the advantages and cautions of using guided fantasy.

8. Give as many reasons as you can for maintaining client-counselor collaborative relationships in an assessment model.

9. Describe the principles and purposes of standardized tests and self-assessment.

10. Outline the client's role in the assessment process.

For More Information

Anastasi, A. (1988). *Psychological testing* (6th ed.). New York: Macmillan.

Comas-Diaz, L. (1996). Cultural considerations in diagnosis. In F. W. Kaslow (Ed.), *Handbook on relational diagnosis and dysfunctional family patterns* (pp. 159–160). New York: Wiley.

Comas-Diaz, L., & Grenier, J. R. (1998). Migration and acculturation. In J. Sandoval, C. L. Frisby, K. F. Geisinger, J. D. Scheuneman, & J. R. Grenier, *Test interpretation and diversity* (pp. 213–241). Washington, DC: American Psychological Association.

Fouad, N. A. (1995). Career behavior of Hispanics: Assessment and career intervention. In F. T. L. Leong (Ed.), *Career development and vocational behavior of racial and ethnic minorities* (pp. 165–187). Mahwah, NJ: Erlbaum.

Geisinger, K. F. (1998). Psychometric issues in test interpretation. In J. Sandoval, C. L. Frisby, K. F. Geisinger, J. D. Scheuneman, & J. R. Grenier (Eds.), *Test interpretation and diversity* (pp. 17–31). Washington, DC: American Psychological Association.

Kapes, J. T., Mastie, M. M., & Whitfield, E. A. (1994). *A counselor's guide to career assessment instruments* (3rd ed.). Alexandria, VA: National Career Development Association.

Peterson, G. W., Sampson, J. P., & Reardon, R. C. (1991). *Career development and services: A cognitive approach.* Pacific Grove, CA: Brooks/Cole.

Sandoval, J. (1998). Testing in a changing world: An introduction. In J. Sandoval, C. L. Frisby, K. F. Geisinger, J. D. Scheuneman, & J. R. Grenier, *Test interpretation and diversity* (pp. 3–17). Washington, DC: American Psychological Association.

Sandoval, J. (1998). Test interpretation in a diverse future. In J. Sandoval, C. L. Frisby, K. F. Geisinger, J. D. Scheuneman, & J. R. Grenier, *Test interpretation and diversity* (pp. 387–403). Washington, DC: American Psychological Association.

Zunker, V. G., & Osborn, D. (2002). *Using assessment results for career development* (6th ed.). Pacific Grove, CA: Brooks/Cole.

9

Using Computers for Career Counseling

Chapter Highlights

- *Guidelines for using computer-assisted career guidance systems*
- *Advantages of computer-assisted career guidance systems*
- *Development of career information systems*
- *Using DISCOVER—an example case*
- *Brief review of SIGI PLUS*
- *Steps in using computer-assisted career guidance programs*
- *How to use the Internet appropriately for career guidance*
- *Examples and Web locations of current programs*

NEW TECHNOLOGY, AUTOMATION, COMPUTER SCIENCE, AND INCREASED SPE-cialization have brought about numerous changes in occupational structure and job demand in the last three decades. The pace of change is ever-increasing; jobs that existed a few years ago no longer exist. The career counselor has traditionally been faced with an overwhelming amount of career information that must be organized to be useful—always requiring an enormous time commit-ment. Keeping abreast with basic occupational information itself is very time-consuming. In addition, career counseling has broadened in scope as more em-phasis is focused on the variables involved in career life planning. The traditional primary role of occupational information provider is now only part of most ca-reer counseling programs. By necessity, the time once allocated to organizing, editing, and classifying occupational information has been reduced by the increas-ing demand for broad-scope career-related programs. Nevertheless, the effective career counselor must be provided with current occupational information and re-sources reflecting the ever-changing labor market.

Today's sophisticated student demands up-to-date projections on the work force and uses this information as a major factor in making career decisions. Current job search strategies must include projections of the labor market as well as current job descriptions. Therefore, keeping abreast with changing occu-pational trends remains a very important part of the career counseling program.

It is not surprising that the career counseling profession has for the most part emphatically endorsed the development of computer-assisted career guidance sys-tems. The fast-paced development of both hardware and software systems has created very attractively designed programs for different populations and for dif-ferent purposes. The easily accessible up-to-date career information on computer-based programs has given the career counselor a very powerful tool to help meet the needs of our society in the current job market. Other developments such as on-line assessment and interactive career guidance software systems have greatly added to the flexibility of programming. Clearly, career counselors will periodi-cally need easily accessible information to stay abreast with future developments.

The first part of this chapter contains some relevant research about computer-assisted career guidance systems, including a brief discussion of the disadvantages and advantages of using these systems. This discussion is followed by a section that describes system components. The third section covers the development of Career Information Delivery Systems (CIDS), and the fourth section illustrates how DISCOVER (the college and adult version) might be used to counsel a col-lege student. The fifth section provides some sources of labor market and job in-formation on the Internet. Finally, the last section describes how to use and implement a computer-assisted career guidance system.

Some Implications of Research

Evaluating the effectiveness of computer-assisted career guidance systems is an ongoing process undertaken by many counseling professionals, including the

Center for the Study of Technology in Counseling and Career Development at Florida State University. The purpose of this center is to provide continuing support for the improved professional use of computer applications in counseling and career guidance. In recent years, the center has contributed a great deal of research for this effort.

In a study comparing the effectiveness of three computer-assisted career guidance systems—DISCOVER (American College Testing Program, 1984), System of Interactive Guidance and Information (SIGI) (Katz, 1975), and SIGI PLUS (Katz, 1993)—the center found that clients who used these systems responded favorably to the career options generated (Peterson, Ryan-Jones, Sampson, Reardon, & Shahnasarian, 1987). In a related study, Kapes, Borman, Garcia, and Compton (1985) compared user reactions to DISCOVER and SIGI. Specifically, the researchers evaluated the reactions (ease of use, quality of information provided, and total effectiveness) of undergraduate and graduate students and found no significant differences among the ratings of the two systems. Perhaps more important, both systems were rated as highly useful.

In a study of general satisfaction of computer-assisted career guidance among undergraduate students at a medium-size Southern university, Miller and Springer (1986) found that students rated DISCOVER as a worthwhile counseling intervention that helped them meet their career exploration needs. In another study analyzing the effectiveness of SIGI, Maze and Cummings (1982) found that the users needed very little assistance with various components. Splete, Elliott, and Borders (1985) have successfully used DISCOVER II and SIGI in their Adult Career Counseling Center at Oakland University.

A study by Roselle and Hummel (1988) compared the effectiveness of using DISCOVER II with two groups of college students, who were separated according to levels (high versus low) of intellectual development as measured by a standardized instrument. To evaluate how effectively they used the system, the students were observed and audiotaped as they interacted with DISCOVER II. The evaluation criteria included how well they learned about career possibilities, integrated career information, reached a career decision, and took appropriate action. The results supported the hypothesis that effective interaction with DISCOVER II is related to intellectual development. These results may not be surprising, but they did suggest that students with low intellectual development need more structure and opportunities for discussion with a counselor during and after their interaction with computer-assisted career guidance systems.

In a related study, Kivlighan, Johnston, Hogan, and Mauer (1994) posed the question, Who benefits most from computer-assisted career guidance systems? This group of researchers used vocational identity to evaluate the effects of SIGI PLUS on 54 college students. They discovered that those students who had a sense of direction and purpose benefited most when exposed to a computer-based career program. These results suggest that strategies used to address clients' purpose and direction are productive methods of assisting them to gain maximum benefits from computer-assisted career guidance systems.

In a study of user evaluation of computer-assisted career guidance system effectiveness, Peterson, Ryan-Jones, Sampson, Reardon, and Shahnasarian (1994) had 126 university students evaluate a career guidance system they had completed.

Students filled out a career guidance evaluation form that measured effectiveness of information about occupations including occupational rewards and demands. The general attractiveness of the system that was used was also evaluated. The results indicated that significantly more students rated systems positively on all dimensions of the evaluation form.

In another study, Zmud, Sampson, Reardon, Lenz, and Byrd (1994) examined responses from 112 university students who used a computer-assisted career system. More specifically, the students' attitudes toward computers, user satisfaction with human-computer interface, satisfaction with decision and task support, and general satisfaction with computer-assisted career guidance systems were evaluated. The results revealed that the students' attitudes toward computers are favorable; students perceived computers to be enjoyable, nonthreatening, and easy to use. Students were also very satisfied with the computer systems' quality, information of occupational recommendations, and increased self-knowledge they experienced.

In general, these studies indicate that users react positively to computer-assisted career guidance systems. Moreover, the results suggest that these systems are worthwhile counseling tools that can help clients meet career exploration needs. Therefore, career counselors should be computer literate enough to understand the development, rationale, and purpose of computer-assisted career guidance systems and be able to use them on a daily basis.

Some Cautions When Using Computers

A major concern with the use of computers in career counseling is that of confidentiality (Harris-Bowlsbey, Dikel, & Sampson, 1998; Sampson, 1983). Confidentiality abuses are more likely with electronic data storage systems than with traditional approaches. Velasquez and Lynch (1981) maintained that this problem can be solved with identification codes, passwords, and general restrictions on individuals who may access client information, but career counselors must assure each client of the specific methods used to maintain confidentiality.

When using the Internet the potential for violation of confidentiality is increased through inappropriate access to client records, e-mail correspondence, client case notes, and client assessment information. Two solutions include changing passwords frequently and converting messages into code (Harris-Bowlsbey, Dikel, & Sampson, 1998). Counselors must constantly monitor security measures.

Counselors should also be aware that computer-assisted career guidance assessment instruments should meet the same standards used to evaluate traditional psychometric measures. Validity and reliability must be established for the instruments' use within the computer career guidance system. Particularly, scrutiny should be given to the possibility of scoring errors and subsequent weighting of psychometric scales that can lead to misleading results. Most important, the counselor must have substantial evidence that the interpretative statements generated by computer-based testing are valid. Finally, counselors should be certain that each client fully understands the implications of computer-generated interpretative statements when applying them to the career search process (Zunker & Osborn, 2002).

Another fear among some career counseling professionals is that computerized systems will be the sole source of career guidance programming. Computer-assisted career guidance systems should supplement, but not replace, the counselor. Although software programs are becoming more user-friendly, the career counselor must structure and sustain the client throughout the career guidance sequence, especially in choosing career related programs on the Internet. Computers do allow for independent and individualized courses of action but do not remove the career counselor's responsibility for direction and structure.

Finally, the counselor must address the problem of user anxiety. Inadequately prepared users can easily become discouraged with computerized systems. Personnel must be available to instruct users during the initial stages, assist users through various phases of the system, and follow up with users who have used the system (Sampson & Pyle, 1983).

Advantages of Computer-Assisted Career Guidance Systems

The interactive capability of computerized systems allows users to become more actively involved in the career guidance process. It is hoped that this active involvement will encourage users to ask more questions of the process itself. Second, user motivation is sustained through the unique use of immediate feedback. Third, the opportunity to individualize the career exploration process provides opportunities to personalize career search strategies. Fourth, computer-assisted career guidance systems provide systematic career exploration and career decision programs that may be accessed at any given time. Finally, access to large databases of up-to-date information for local, state, national, and international locations is immediately available.

Types of Computer-Assisted Career Guidance Systems

The most common types of computer-assisted career guidance systems are information systems and guidance systems. Information systems provide users with direct access to large databases on such subject areas as occupational characteristics (work tasks, required abilities, work settings, salary) and lists of occupations, educational and training institutions, military information, and financial aid.

Guidance systems are typically much broader in scope. They contain a variety of available modules, such as instruction in the career decision process, assessment, prediction of future success, assistance with planning, and development of strategies for future plans. Many computer-assisted career guidance systems contain an information system as well as a guidance system. Many systems are directed toward certain populations, such as students in junior high school, high school, and college; some systems are for people who work in organizations; and some address the needs of retirees.

Computer-assisted career guidance systems have undergone vast changes during the last decade. Future modifications could come even more quickly as these systems are designed to meet the needs of an ever-changing work environment and the skills associated with rapid technical change.

Understandably, many of the computer-assisted career guidance systems have similar components and are accessed through menus that provide some flexibility for individual needs. The following components are found in most systems:

1. Occupational information
2. Armed service information
3. Information about postsecondary institutions of higher learning
4. Information on technical and specialized schools
5. Financial aid information
6. Interest inventories
7. Decision-making skills

Other common components include the following:

1. Local job information files
2. Ability measures
3. Value inventories
4. Methods of predicting academic success in college
5. Job search strategies
6. Resumé preparation information
7. Information on job interviews
8. Components for adults

The Development of Career Information Delivery Systems

The growth of CIDS was a direct result of funding from the National Occupational Information Coordinating Committee (NOICC) through its State Occupational Information Coordinating Committees (SOICCs). Improved microcomputer technology in the 1980s resulted in a movement away from mainframe delivery systems and significantly reduced the cost of implementing such a system. Career information is organized in most systems on a national and state basis. Some of the national commercial systems include options to develop state and local information (McCormac, 1988).

Since its beginning in the late 1980s, CIDS has become a very popular tool that has been used effectively within comprehensive counseling programs in schools and colleges and by adults seeking further training, education, or different jobs. It is estimated that in 1994, more than 40 states had CIDS users as official state systems, and more than 9 million people used them at about 20,000 different sites (Mariani, 1995-96).

The four components common to most CIDS are assessment, occupational search, occupational information, and educational information. On-line assessment includes instruments that measure values, interests, skills, aptitudes, or experiences as they relate to career choice. Many systems will accept results from additional assessment instruments, such as the *Self-Directed Search, ASVAB, Strong Interest Inventory,* and *GATB* (discussed in Chapter 7).

Skills assessment is a relatively new tool to help students and experienced workers identify skills desired and needed in the current work force. The American College Testing Program's *Work Keys System* is designed to help learners make transitions from school to work or from job to job. It assesses the skills individuals possess, determines the skills that jobs require, and provides instructional support to help learners improve their skills. The process includes a comparison of skill levels required for particular jobs with learners' skill levels (American College Testing Program, 1996a).

The CIDS occupational search is very innovative. Users can generate lists of occupations from assessment results. As users choose search variables from a list, the level of congruence the user gives to each variable is used by the computer to generate lists of occupations. If a user is not satisfied and wishes to explore other occupations, the system allows users to change the criteria used in the original search. Finally, a user may simply select an occupation for review.

The occupational information component contains key information about a large number of occupations, such as the nature of the work, working conditions, numbers employed, job outlook, education and training requirements, recommended school courses, earnings, related occupations, physical demands, common career ladders, and sources for more information. Many CIDS programs include state and local information about occupations.

The educational component includes information on vocational and technical schools, two- and four-year colleges, and, in some systems, graduate schools. Included in this component are admission requirements, programs of study, types of degrees offered, school affiliation, community setting, tuition and fees, financial aid information, total enrollment, housing information, athletic programs and other student activities, student body characteristics, military training opportunities, special programs, and sources for more information (Mariani, 1995-96).

Career development programs in schools use CIDS in many innovative ways. For example, counselors use printouts of occupational descriptions in grades 3 and 4 to illustrate the kind of information that can be found in their local CIDS.

In a related type of program, students in elementary schools are asked to make a list of occupations that interest them. The counselor then provides printed descriptions of the requested occupations. Both programs are used as an introduction to CIDS that primes the students to use the career exploration program individually when it is available to them.

The extent of CIDS use in secondary schools often depends on the number of staff or computers available. In some schools, peer counselors or adult volunteers introduce students to CIDS.

CIDS is also integrated into the curriculum in some junior and senior high schools. Some schools offer career exploration programs that include CIDS. Others infuse career exploration into existing courses, such as a major writing project in an English class on one's career choice.

Universities and colleges usually incorporate CIDS in their career center as a part of a total career exploration system. Credit courses in career exploration are also offered at some postsecondary institutions. Some instructors require that students do a career search as a part of a course requirement or assign projects that include the use of CIDS.

CIDS are also used at other sites, such as employment and training offices, vocational rehabilitation offices, state job services, public libraries, prisons, and public businesses. Also, the federal government has established one-stop career centers in several states. As Mariani (1995–96, p. 22) put it, "Some people may find themselves choosing a career, getting a job, and buying a new wardrobe all at the local mall."

More information can be obtained from state CIDS directors and from the following sources.

National Occupational Coordinating Committee
2100 M Street NW, Suite 156
Washington, DC 20037
202-653-5665

Association of Computer-Based Systems for Career Information
c/o National Career Development Association
5999 Stevenson Avenue
Alexandria, VA 22304-3300
703-823-9800, ext. 309

National Career Development Association
4700 Reed Road
Suite M
Columbus, OH 43220
888-326-1750

Center for the Study of Technology in Counseling and Career Development
Florida State University Career Center
5408 University Center, 4th Level
Tallahassee, FL 32306-1035
904-644-6431

Using DISCOVER

The original DISCOVER system was designed to assist high school and college students in making career choices. DISCOVER for colleges and adults, published by the American College Testing Program (1987), contains the following modules:

1. Beginning the career journey
2. Learning about the world of work
3. Learning about yourself
4. Finding occupations
5. Learning about occupations
6. Making educational choices
7. Planning next steps
8. Planning your career
9. Making transitions

Although users are advised to proceed through the modules in a sequential order, certain modules can be accessed on demand. For example, an individual seeking information about educational institutions can access two-year or four-year college lists. In the example of Yasmin, a freshman who is undecided about a major or a career, the sequential order is most desirable.

Case 9-1: THE CASE OF AN UNDECIDED FRESHMAN

YASMIN: In high school, I never gave too much thought to a career, even though my parents tried to persuade me to make up my mind. I guess I just didn't get around to it. I hope you can help me decide.

COUNSELOR: We have several ways to help you. First I'll explain the various materials we have, the usual sequence students go through, and the time involved.

After the counselor informed Yasmin of the career guidance programs, he obtained a time commitment from her.

COUNSELOR: I want you to understand that you will have to spend considerable effort and time to find the answers to your questions. If you agree to that, I believe we can help you make a good decision about your future.

Yasmin chose the DISCOVER program from the range of options offered by the counselor.

YASMIN: I actually like to work with computers. In high school, we used computers in several of our courses.

The counselor informed Yasmin of the various components of DISCOVER, their purpose, and how to access them. Yasmin began with Module I. She was asked to respond to questions as follows:

3 = I already know this
2 = I know something about this, but not enough
1 = I don't know this at all

The first group of questions concerned the world of work. For example, Yasmin was asked whether she knew that academic majors can be grouped in a logical way, and how choices of academic majors are related to occupations. In the second group of questions, she was asked about herself; that is, if she had knowledge about her abilities, interests, or work-related values. In the third section, she was asked to explore occupations in terms of how they related to her interests, abilities, values, and experiences. Other questions dealt with learning about occupations, making decisions about education, planning next steps, planning a career, and coping with transitions.

After Yasmin completed these questions and the computer compiled the information, the counselor requested a printout to determine what direction Yasmin should take. In Yasmin's case, the greatest needs seemed to involve knowing about the world of work, herself, and which occupations to explore. From this list, the counselor and Yasmin decided that she would take the ability, interest, and value inventory offered in the system.

Yasmin began with the interest inventory offered in Career Planning Task Two. She received the following instructions: Consider whether you would like or dislike doing each of the activities listed, not your ability to do it. For each of the 90 activities, use the following key. Circle your choice.

> L = If you LIKE the activity
> I = If you are INDIFFERENT (don't care one way or the other about the activity)
> D = If you DISLIKE the activity

Then Yasmin moved on to the abilities inventory, where she was asked to rate herself in comparison with other persons her own age. She was instructed to use the following scale:

> 5 = High (top 10% of persons my age)
> 4 = Above average (upper 25%)
> 3 = Average (middle 50%)
> 2 = Below average (lower 25%)
> 1 = Low (bottom 10%)

Yasmin was asked to rate her ability in meeting people and helping others; that is, whether she was good in sales, leadership, organization, and clerical or mechanical tasks. She was asked about her manual dexterity and her numerical, scientific, creative/ artistic, creative/literary, reading, language usage, and spatial abilities.

On the values inventory, she was instructed to read each value carefully, mark one of the choices provided, and rank-order the values from 1 through 9. An example of one value is listed here.

1. Creativity in a job means: discovering, designing, or developing new things, and/or being inventive in your job, and/or finding new ways to make or do things

   What opportunity for creativity do you want in a job?

   > 4 = High
   > 3 = Medium to high
   > 2 = Medium
   > 1 = Skip this value

After completing this module, Yasmin made an appointment to see the counselor. Meanwhile, Yasmin could investigate science careers on her own. The combination of her scores on the inventories suggested that she was interested in ideas and things, rather than people and data. (The DISCOVER World-of-Work Map depicts 12 regions of work represented by general areas of work or job families and a second dimension of work by Data/Ideas and People/Things. A third dimension refers users to Business Contact, Business Operations, Technical, Science, Arts, or Social Services.) Yasmin was directed toward Region 9, Natural Science and Mathematics, and Region 8, Medical Specialties, Technologies, Engineering, and Related Techniques. Her second dimension was Ideas and Things, and the third dimension was in Science. At the next counseling session, the following exchange took place.

COUNSELOR: You seem to have a definite interest in the sciences and medical specialties, Yasmin. What do you think?

YASMIN: All I can say is, I did well in biology, chemistry, and math in school. Maybe that's the reason I ended up in this area.

As the conversation continued, it became clear that Yasmin needed more information about occupations because her work experience was very limited. She decided to go to Career Planning Task 6: Selecting Occupations. In this module, she was asked to select desirable characteristics of occupations. For example, in selection of a work setting she responded to the following:

Work Setting (where you'd work)—I want to work:

a. Indoors in an office
b. Indoors other than in an office
c. Outdoors
d. Combination of indoors and outdoors

Other characteristics Yasmin evaluated were "employment outlook," "work hours," "supervision of others," "travel required," "unusual pressure," "beginning income," and "educational level."

Yasmin wanted a job projected to have openings by 2005. She also preferred working indoors rather than outdoors and wanted a regular shift of seven to eight hours a day. Yasmin also indicated that she would be willing to earn a bachelor's degree or continue with graduate work, if necessary, to meet her goal. She was interested in a starting salary of about $30,000 per year.

After providing the program with a measure of interests, abilities, values, and characteristics of desired occupations, Yasmin was presented with a list of occupations for consideration. She asked the counselor to assist her in evaluating these findings.

YASMIN: I have a long list of occupations here, and I'm not sure what to do with all of them.

COUNSELOR: That's not all bad because now you have a list to choose from that provides a lot of options. As you review each career you may want to eliminate some immediately and explore several others more thoroughly. Remember, you can get a printout for those careers that are of interest and review them at your convenience.

Yasmin then selected some occupations from the list. One of her selections was Medical Technologist. She requested a detailed printout that included a description of the work tasks, work settings, tools and materials used, related civilian occupations, related military occupations, education or training possibilities, special requirements, personal qualities needed, the career ladder, salary potential, projected demand for new workers, the advantages and disadvantages, and where to get more information. In addition, the code for the *Dictionary of Occupational Titles* was given along with the code for the *Standard Occupational Classification* and the *Guide for Occupational Exploration*.

In subsequent counseling sessions, Yasmin concluded that medical technology was of great interest, and she decided to explore this field further. To gain more information, she visited a local hospital where medical technologists were employed. In the course of considering this career, Yasmin discovered that medical technology matched her interests, values, abilities, work tasks, and desired work setting. She was also pleased to discover that the starting salaries for medical technologists generally met her financial requirements. Yasmin later returned to the computer for more information concerning training sites and financial aid.

DISCOVER provided meaningful interactive tasks and information modules to help Yasmin make a career decision. The on-line assessment program provided an effective method of evaluating interests, abilities, and values. The flexibility of this program made it possible to access relevant tasks and data as needed, such as job descriptions and education-training information. Using the job description, the counselor encouraged Yasmin to seek more information from other materials and from an on-site visit.

Counselors should be aware that computer-based programs are changing rapidly. DISCOVER is an on-line program that is very script-driven and may be replaced with more interactive programs. In the meantime, the counseling sessions with Yasmin provide a good introduction to currently used computer-based career programs.

DISCOVER Multimedia

DISCOVER Multimedia has recently been introduced as a new version of DISCOVER in compact disc-interactive (CD-i) format. It should not be confused with CD-ROM. This new system does not require a computer, as it can be used on a color TV and a disc player.

DISCOVER Multimedia consists of three discs. Disc 1 is entitled "Learning about Yourself" and allows users to visually identify occupations that match specific interests and abilities. Six video sequences that illustrate the World-of-Work Map are also available.

Disc 2 contains detailed information about approximately 500 different occupations through a slide show that enhances the text for each occupation. There is a 15- to 20-second narrative for each occupation, accompanied by color photographs.

Disc 3 contains a two-year and four-year college search sequence. A narrative is accompanied by two photographs of most four-year institutions.

The publishers of this program suggest that DISCOVER Multimedia will encourage young people, especially those who are accustomed to playing video games, to learn more about career information. The major rationale for this new program is that photographs and full-motion video will make career planning not only more enjoyable but also more realistic.

System of Interactive Guidance and Information (SIGI) and SIGI PLUS

Another major computerized system is SIGI and SIGI PLUS developed by Katz (1975; 1993). There are five SIGI subsystems as follows:

1. Values
2. Locate
3. Compare
4. Planning
5. Strategy

These subsystems were developed to assist college students by clarifying values, locating and identifying occupational options, comparing choices, learning planning skills, and developing rational career decision-making skills.

SIGI PLUS contains nine components as follows:

1. Introduction
2. Self-Assessment
3. Search
4. Information
5. Skills
6. Preparing
7. Coping
8. Deciding
9. Next Steps

This system was developed to include adults in general and those who are seeking information about organizations. Katz (1993) suggests that individual needs determine the level of motivation in the career search and, as such, are considered as domains of self-understanding. Thus, needs are centered around values, interests, temperament, and attitudes that should be assessed as important variables in the search process. One of the outstanding features of this program is the special needs of adults in transition; it is designed to assist adults who may be changing occupations, moving into new occupations, or reentering the labor force. Reardon, Peterson, Sampson, Ryan-Jones, and Shahnasarian (1992) found that students liked both systems, SIGI and SIGI PLUS, but preferred the latter because of its greater flexibility. Evidently, students opted for more control of a system that is user friendly to their individual needs.

Steps in Using Computer-Assisted Career Guidance Programs

Throughout this chapter, several direct references have been made about the use of computer-assisted career guidance programs. My primary purpose has been to emphasize the computer's role in meeting the career exploration needs of individuals and groups. Structured procedures that use components of computerized programs as a career counseling assistant are a major advantage. Computer-assisted career guidance programs are a major component of a total career guidance program. As such, they are coordinated with other components, materials, and procedures; they are not the *sole* delivery system. Individual needs may dictate the use of several components including computerized systems, or in some cases, computerized systems alone may meet client needs. Within this framework, I advise following these steps for using computer-assisted career guidance programs:

1. *Assessment of needs.* Individualized needs of each student should determine the direction of program use and the components accessed. For example, one student might need only information on financial aid programs. A student moving to a distant state could be seeking information on two-year and four-year colleges within driving distance of his or her future residence. Others, like Yasmin, can be helped in determining their career directions.

2. *Orientation.* Each student or group of students should be given a thorough orientation to the purpose, goals, and demonstrated use of computerized systems.

3. *Individualized programs.* Each individual should follow a preconceived plan based on needs. This plan can be modified as needed; the flexibility of computerized programs can be a distinct advantage when plans change.

4. *Counselor intervention.* The individualized plan should provide for counselor intervention. For example, an appropriate point may be a discussion of the results of one of the inventories. Providing sources of additional occupational information and discussing tentative occupational choices are good strategies in the career exploration process. The point is that individuals should not be "turned over to the computer" without any planned intervention from a counselor.

5. *On-line assistance.* Provisions should be made to assist individuals in various stages of career exploration. How to return to the main menu or how to access various components can be frustrating experiences for the computer novice. The following questions can be anticipated: "How can I get this printed?" "I need to stop now and go to class—what should I do?" "I hit the wrong key, can you help me?"

6. *Follow-up.* As in all phases of career exploration, individual progress should be monitored. Career counselors should help individuals sustain their motivation, evaluate their progress, and evaluate the effectiveness of programs.

These activities are designed to develop the individual's decision-making skills. The counselor should assist the student at various stages, including helping the student and accessing different areas of the system. Most important, the counselor should make use of the information obtained from the computer for more effective career counseling.

Using the Internet

The Internet may be described as a proverbial sleeping giant that has enormous potential for the career counseling profession. We are beginning to tap the resources that are available now, but the future use of the Internet will be an important subject of the career counseling profession in the generations to come. Harris-Bowlsbey, Dikel, & Sampson (1998) have developed a guide for using the Internet in career planning. This guide contains sample Web sites for assessment, searching databases, education and training opportunities, financial aid, internship opportunities, job openings, career information, education and training information, military information, and career counseling programs. In sum, Web sites can assist individuals with self-assessment including interests, skills, abilities, values, intelligence, and personality. Web sites also provide information for (a) exploring occupations, (b) educational institutions, (c) scholarships, (d) financial aid opportunities, and (e) job openings. Some Web sites provide free information whereas others charge a fee. Still other Web sites provide information resources that link occupations, educational institutions, and other opportunities with trade journals, government agencies, professional organizations, and so on. You can also locate chat rooms and support groups, or post a resumé for job placement. Many other networking possibilities can be used to meet individual needs.

Strong words of caution in using the Internet are also contained in the Harris-Bowlsbey et al. guide. First, the competencies of Internet providers significantly varies—from those who have little formal training to those with an excellent background. In other words, some are capable of providing valid services, but it is most difficult to determine who they are especially for first-time users. Second, Chapters 7 and 8 point out the necessity of using valid and reliable assessment instruments. But the problem does not stop there; one must also interpret the results according to the prescribed use of the instrument. Invalid interpretation of results can lead to invalid conclusions and subsequently to invalid decisions. Third, the Web site database must be periodically updated to provide valid information. A major concern involves the quality of the Web site resources and services. Finally, the readiness of the client for decision making focuses on unique individual needs that may require personal individual counseling. This precaution is not just directed to clients who may need psychotherapy but also for those individuals who need counselor guidance and direction to overcome barriers that prohibit appropriate career decision-making techniques. A major point is to have available user support when needed (Harris-Bowlsbey, Dikel, & Sampson, 1998).

Figure 9-1 illustrates an appropriate use of the Internet in career planning and in the decision-making process. Six steps are illustrated: In the first step, individuals realize a need to decide. Learning about and or reevaluating self, step two, suggests that clients be alert to their personal attributes and limitations. In step three, occupational information is presented in a manner "that facilitates the transition of self-information into occupational alternatives" (Harris-Bowlsbey, Dikel, & Sampson, 1998, p. 2). The next three steps are used to refine the identified alternatives into possible tentative choices by using the vast amount of database information available on the Internet. Finally, the individual decides to seek more information and eventually selects the new alternative (Harris-Bowlsbey, Dikel, & Sampson, 1998).

To assist counselors in appropriately providing services through Internet-based career resources and services, the National Career Development Association (NCDA) and the National Board for Certified Counselors (NBCC) have published guidelines. (See Appendix D for NCDA Web sites that list guidelines.) The following book is a valuable resource for Internet use by career counselors:

> *The Internet: A Tool for Career Planning*
> Harris-Bowlsbey, J. H., Dikel, M. R., & Sampson, J. P.
> National Career Development Association
> 4700 Reed Road, Suite M
> Columbus, OH, 43220
> Phone (888) 326-1750, Fax (614) 326-1760

Following are some examples of current programs:

> *America's Job Bank*
> http://www.ajb.dni.us

Currently one of the most widely used sites, this is a computerized network that links 2000 state employment offices and contains a national pool of active job opportunities.

> *America's Labor Market Information System (ALMIS)*
> http://www.ecu.edu/-lmi.html

This site provides information about various projects, such as the latest developments on job banks and technology resource centers.

> *U.S. Department of Education*
> http://www.ed.gov

This site is designed to help parents, teachers, and students. Information on such topics as financial aid, grants, and educational software packages can be reviewed, and some of it can be downloaded.

> O*NET (a replacement for the *Dictionary of Occupational Titles [DOT]*) U.S.
> Department of Labor Office of Policy and Research/ETA/O*NET
> 200 Constitution Avenue, NW Mail Stop N5637
> Washington, DC 20210

Career Planning Process

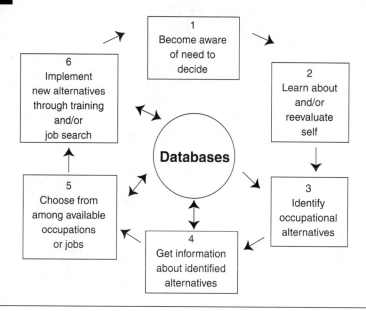

SOURCE: From *The Internet: A Tool for Career Planning*, by J. Harris-Bowlsbey, M. R. Dikel, & J. P. Sampson, 1998, p. 2. Copyright 1998 by the National Career Development Association. Reprinted with permission of NCDA.

The timetable for O*NET's completion can be obtained from the following Web site:

www.doleta.gov/programs/onet

Training Technology Resource Center (TTRC)
http://www.ttrc.doleta.gov

This site offers information on federal and state employment and training activities. Information about state agencies, including CIDS programs, can be obtained from this site. Be aware that many other public and commercial sites are available for career-related information. Some sites include lists of employers, colleges, and government job sources. Others include career-related associations and organizations as well as career libraries. Still others include job listings from city newspapers and the international job market. You could also submit your resumé to a database, or you might want to participate in an on-line job fair. Here are examples of two sites that are helpful:

BOX
9-1

BOX 9-1 CACG Implementation Problems

Inadequate planning

- Use of "ad hoc" or "no planning" approaches
- Inadequate linkage between computer use and organizational needs
- Inadequate needs assessment prior to computer use
- Adoption of systems overly influenced by funding or administrators
- Piecemeal rather than systematic adoption of systems
- Limited staff participation in decision making about CACG

Poor integration of CACG systems within career services

- Lack of suitable context for clients to process their use of information resources
- Lack of counselor intervention for clients who need assistance
- Lack of evaluation data for demonstrating accountability and for improving CACG integration
- Scheduling problems
- Inconsistent support from CACG developers

Occupational Outlook Handbook
http://stats.bls.gov:80/ocohome.htm

Resources for Minorities
http://www.vjf.com/pub/docs/jobsearch.html

This brief introduction to the Internet suggests that computerized career-related programming has only begun to surface. We can expect to see a growing list of innovative ideas that will build to a comprehensive linked system of the future. One goal of the Internet is to build a nationwide talent bank to help employers and prospective employees make initial contacts (Woods & Ollis, 1996). The unique career-related programs developed at this time should serve as the foundation for the continuing evolution of computerized career-related programming.

Implementing a Computer-Based Program

It has often been said that the first steps in implementing a new program are the most important ones. This cliché certainly applies to implementing a computer-

> **BOX 9-1 CACG Implementation Problems** *(continued)*
>
> ### Inadequate staff training
>
> - Imbalance between training expenditures and hardware/software expenditures
> - Inadequate training with respect to
>   hands-on experience with systems
>   a conceptual basis for comparing and selecting systems
>   integrating CACG with various service delivery models
> - Unrealistic expectations about the performance of computer applications
> - Unrealistic expectations about the time needed for implementation
> - Confusion regarding the role of the counselor and the role of the computer
>
> ### Staff anxiety and resistance concerning CACG
>
> - Concern over changes in the workplace
> - Negative staff attitude as a result of implementation problems
>
> *Note:* Staff anxiety and resistance are negatively influenced by planning, integration, and training problems described above.
>
> SOURCE: From *Effective Computer-Assisted Career Guidance: Occasional Paper Number 2,* by James P. Sampson, 1994. Center for the Study of Technology in Counseling and Career Development, Florida State University. Reprinted by permission.

assisted system for career guidance. Systematic planning for computer-assisted systems is highly related to their effectiveness and acceptance by students, faculty, and community (Sampson, 1994). In this section, we will review an implementation model, but first we will discuss implementation problems.

The information contained in Box 9-1 identifies problems associated with implementing a computer-assisted career guidance (CACG) program. Some of these identified problems suggest a lack of effective planning, whereas others are associated with inadequate staff training and a lack of integration with other career services. For instance, staff must be aware that CACG does not take the place of counselor intervention with clients and that clients need assistance with linking information found on CACG to their career search and other assistance. The significant danger here is the false assumption that CACG is the sole career service component!

Sampson (1994) makes a very important point that implementation problems could very easily limit CACG's long-term effectiveness. Furthermore, all parties must be educated to the effective use of CACG *before* it is selected and put on-line. Proper implementation ensures that CACG is an important component of career services.

The process of implementing CACG includes the following seven-step implementation model developed by Sampson (1994):

1. Begin with a program evaluation to determine how well current guidance services meet clients' needs. If the evaluation discloses unmet needs, the staff should highlight the purpose and goals regarding how a computer-based system can close the gap. To accomplish this goal, establish a selection committee.

2. Have the committee identify desired software products that will meet clients' needs. After reviewing systems, the committee should determine appropriate software and hardware.

3. Software integration involves comprehensive plans for how a system will be implemented. This implies that committee members have become very knowledgeable about the chosen system. Plans include how to mesh the system with the overall guidance program and to specify roles of staff members, operational procedures, and evaluation systems.

4. The next step involves comprehensive staff training. The effectiveness of a computer-assisted guidance program is strongly related to a working knowledge of the system.

5. The trial use determines how well the staff has done its homework and how students react to using the system. The system begins operation after successful trial evaluations.

6. The system becomes operational.

7. Evaluation of service delivery is seen as an ongoing process. Evaluation feedback suggests that there should be continual refinement. Fast-paced development of hardware and software probably means that computer-assisted programs could change every year.

The seven-step implementation program was developed by Sampson (1994) of Florida State University, Center for the Study of Technology in Counseling and Career Development. Anyone seeking information about computer-assisted career guidance programs should contact this center.

Summary

1. The rationale for computerized career counseling stems from the need for up-to-date information and the unique capabilities of the computer to satisfy this need. A number of computerized counseling systems with different combinations of computer hardware and software and different sets of objectives have been developed.

2. Recent research indicates a positive reaction to computer-assisted guidance systems by users. Moreover, the results suggest that the systems evaluated are worthwhile for counseling intervention and help individuals meet career exploration needs.

3. The most common types of computer-assisted career guidance systems are information systems and guidance systems.

4. Career Information Delivery Systems (CIDS) were developed with the assistance of NOICC and the SOICCs. One of the major purposes was to give states the opportunity to develop state and local data.

5. The DISCOVER program and SIGI and SIGI PLUS for colleges and adults are examples of systems that include on-line assessment programs, job descriptions, and educational information, all of which are easily accessible.

6. The Internet has tremendous potential for the career counselor. Currently, information on the Internet includes self-assessment programs, searching databases, and career development resources.

7. A seven-step implementation model should be followed when implementing a computer-based program.

Supplementary Learning Exercises

1. Visit a school, college, or agency that has a computer-based career information system. Request a preview of the system, and identify the major components in a written report.

2. Outline and discuss the advantages of having a computer-assisted career guidance system in one or more of the following: a high school, a community college, a four-year college, and a community agency providing career counseling to adults.

3. Form two groups and debate the issues relating to the following statement: Computer-assisted career guidance systems will replace the career counselor.

4. Develop a local visit file (individuals in selected occupations who agree to visits by students) that could be included as a component in a computer-assisted career guidance system. Describe the advantages of a visit file.

5. Interview a career counselor who has substantial experience in using computer-assisted career guidance systems. Write a report on the systems used and summarize the counselor's evaluation of the systems.

6. Describe the advantages of having a statewide occupational information data bank of job openings and labor forecasts. How could you incorporate this information in career counseling programs in high schools,

community colleges, four-year colleges or universities, and community programs for adults?

7. Decide what is meant by an interactive computer-assisted career guidance system. Illustrate your description with your own version of an example script.

8. What do you consider to be the major components of a computer-assisted program for adults? Defend your choices.

9. Compare the DISCOVER subsystems with the SIGI-PLUS subsystems. What are the major differences? What would you adopt for a community college? Give your reasons.

10. Explain your conception of the future role of the Internet as a counseling tool. Focus on the advantages and limitations.

For More Information

Brammer, L. M., Abrego, P. L., & Shostrom, E. L. (1993). *Therapeutic counseling and psychotherapy* (2nd Ed.). Englewood Cliffs, NJ: Prentice-Hall.

Cormier, L. S., & Hackney, H. (1987). *The professional counselor: A process guide to help*. Englewood Cliffs, NJ: Prentice-Hall.

Gati, I. (1994). Computer-assisted career counseling: Dilemmas, problems, and possible solutions. *Journal of Counseling and Development, 73*, 51–57.

Harris-Bowlsbey, J., Dikel, M. R., & Sampson, J. P. (1998). *The Internet: A tool for career planning*. Columbus, OH: National Career Development Association.

Healy, C. C. (1982). *Career development: Counseling through life stages*. Boston: Allyn & Bacon.

Healy, C. C. (1990). Reforming career appraisals to meet the needs of clients in the 1990s. *The Counseling Psychologist, 18*, 214–226.

Jones, L. K. (1993). Two career guidance instruments: Their helpfulness to students and effect on student's career exploration. *School Counselor, 40*, 191–200.

Kivlighan, D. M., Johnson, J. A., Hogan, R. S., & Mauer, E. (1994). Who benefits from computerized career counseling? *Journal of Counseling and Development, 72*, 189–192.

Mariani, M. (1995–96, Winter). Computers and career guidance: Ride the rising ride. *Occupational Outlook Quarterly, 39*, 16–27.

McCormac, M. E. (1988). Information sources and resources. *Journal of Career Development, 16*, 129–138.

Sampson, J. P. (1994). *Effective computer-assisted career guidance: Occasional paper number 2*. Center for the Study of Technology in Counseling and Career Development, Florida State University.

Sampson, J. P., Kolodinsky, R. W., & Greeno, B. P. (1997). Counseling on the information highway: Future possibilities and potential problems. *Journal of Counseling and Development, 75*, 203–212.

Skovalt, T. M., Morgan, J. I., & Negron-Cunningham, H. (1989). Mental imagery in career counseling and life planning: A review of research and intervention methods. *Journal of Counseling and Development, 67,* 287–292.

Spokane, A. R. (1991). *Career intervention.* Englewood Cliffs, NJ: Prentice-Hall.

Wilson, F. R. (1995). Internet information sources for counselors. *Counselor Education and Supervision, 34*(4), 369–387.

Zunker, V. G., & Osborn, D. (2002). *Using assessment results for career development.* Pacific Grove, CA: Brooks/Cole.

PART TWO

Career Counseling for Special Populations

10

Career Counseling for Multicultural Groups

Chapter Highlights

- *Definitions of culture*

- *Four major cultural groups: Asian Americans, African Americans, Hispanic Americans, Native Americans*

- *Cultural variability*

- *Cultural differences in work-related activities*

- *Review of immigrants' problems and adjustments to a new and different culture*

- *Learning how to be culturally competent*

- *How to interview multicultural groups*

THE NEED TO DEVELOP CAREER GUIDANCE STRATEGIES FOR MULTICULTURAL groups will increase throughout this century. An article, "Minority Numbers" (U.S. Bureau of Census, 1993), based on a report from the Population Reference Bureau of the U.S. Census Bureau, suggested that by the middle of the next century, the United States will no longer be a predominately white society. The more appropriate reference will be "a global society," in which half of all Americans will be from four ethnic groups: Asian Americans, African Americans, Hispanic Americans, and Native Americans. These projected demographics of diversity will present significant challenges to all the helping professions. As more multicultural groups gain access to opportunities for education and higher-status jobs, the career guidance profession should be prepared to assist them.

Career counselors are intent on developing career counseling objectives and strategies that will assist individuals of various ethnic groups to overcome a multitude of barriers including prejudice, language differences, cultural isolation, and culture-related differences. Because this group is composed of persons from a wide variety of ethnic backgrounds, counselors are being challenged to become culturally aware, evaluate their personal views, and understand that other people's perspectives may be as legitimate as their own (Sue & Sue, 1990).

We begin this chapter with an introduction to the meaning of culture as it relates to career counseling. Second, four major cultural groups are briefly discussed. Third, cultural variability and worldviews are examined. Fourth, culturally related work values are explored. Fifth, the challenge of becoming culturally competent is presented. Sixth, immigration and its sequelae is reviewed. Finally, some suggestions for interviewing multicultural groups are unearthed.

What Is Culture?

Cultural diversity is an important topic for all counselors, and especially for the career counselor. In many respects, we have not addressed the issue of culture in the counseling profession. For example, researchers have paid little attention to appropriate intervention strategies and assessment instruments for specific ethnic groups (Betz & Fitzgerald, 1995), which are among the many issues and questions to be resolved. Because of the variety of ethnic groups found in the United States today, we may find the answer to these issues and questions to be very evasive and quite complex. In the meantime, the career counselor must give high priority to cultural variables that influence career development.

Returning to the question of identifying culture, perhaps each of us could offer an explanation of what culture means. We would be able to illustrate our definitions with examples of cultural aspects, variables, customs, and perceptions of different individuals from a variety of "cultures." We could describe activities associated with a culture, we could refer to heritage and tradition of cultures, we could describe rules and norms associated with cultures, we could describe behavioral approaches associated with cultures, and we could describe the origin of cultures. These are examples of different meanings associated with the definition of *culture* and the different interpretations we use to identify people of different cultures. Thus, culture is a complex concept that can refer to many aspects of life and living. Matsumoto (1996) defines *culture* "as the set of attitudes, values, beliefs, and behaviors shared by a group of people, but different for each individual, communicated from one generation to the next" (p. 16). Ogbu (1990) defines culture as follows:

> Culture is an understanding that a people have of their universe—social, physical, or both—as well as their understanding of their behavior in that universe. The cultural model of a population serves its members as a guide in their interpretation of events and elements within their universe; it also serves as a guide to their expectations and actions in that universe or environment. (p.523)

These definitions, although leaving a lot to be said about culture, provide a good fit for the career counselor's use of the word. For example, *sharing* implies the degree to which an individual holds the values, attitudes, beliefs, norms, or behaviors of a particular group. Furthermore, the emphasis is on cognitive processes of psychological sharing of a particular attribute among members of a culture. Although culture can be conceptualized in different ways, there appears to be agreement that language, family structure, environment, and traditions are most influential in determining group differences (Okun, Fried, & Okun, 1999). The lesson to be learned is that even within cultures, each individual should be treated as such rather than from a stereotypical viewpoint that one has about a particular culture. We must be alert to cultural diversity among members of any ethnic group; for instance, Wehrly (1995) points out that 56 ethnic groups identify with their own culture and have their own language in Mexico. The point is that one should not assume that any ethnic group is homogenous.

Culture is a learned behavior. Therefore, two people from the same race may share some values, attitudes, and so on but might also have very different cultural makeups. How much has been *acculturated* from racial heritage through socialization varies even within the dominant cultural group of a country (Triandis, 1992, cited in Matsumoto, 1996). Therefore, we must not make assumptions from cultural stereotypes—as we have heard so often in counseling, we enter into counseling relationships with *individuals*.

Four Major Cultural Groups

Governmental agencies have grouped individuals by culture for a variety of reasons but especially for the national census. Our discussion will include the most recent groupings as African Americans (black is often used), Asian and Pacific Islanders (Asian and Asian Pacific Americans are often used), Hispanic (Latino/a is often used) and Native Americans. The data in Figure 10-1 reveals percentage of our total population by race from 1990 and projected to 2050. It is estimated that almost 50% of the population in the United States will be minorities by the year

Percentage of population by race

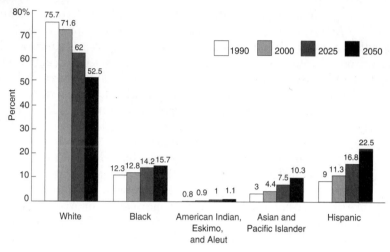

Adapted from U.S. Department of Commerce, Bureau of Census 1996.

2050 (U.S. Department of Commerce, 1996). More specifically, there will be an estimated increase from 12% to 15% in African Americans, from .8% to 1% in Native Americans, from 3% to 10% in Asian and Pacific Islanders, from 9% to 22% in Hispanics, and a decrease from 76% to 52% in white Americans. These data indicate that we must continue to rethink our counseling theories, models, and materials to meet the needs of this increasingly diverse population.

For the most part, African Americans remain socially isolated in church, school, and work. Even though there appears to be justification for the construct of human universal issues common to all people, we must also remember that each individual is shaped by unique contextual experiences. This message has been repeated often throughout this text.

African Americans

The largest racial minority group in this country is African Americans. Most African Americans live in urban areas and have assumed a moderate position in our society. For the most part, they have been wage earners rather than being self-employed. In essence, they have been blue-collar workers rather than managers or proprietors. African American men have achieved greater career mobility than African American women have. Although some of both sexes have managed to achieve upward mobility to professional occupations, the overall success of upward movement of African Americans is minimal. Those who have attained middle-class status are also in position to take advantage of educational opportunities and career mobility. Others, particularly those classified as underclass—primarily from three-generation families on welfare—are without job skills and lack motivation to change their status (Axelson, 1993; Smith, 1983).

Many African Americans are made to feel as outsiders in public schools, according to Vontress (1979) and, more recently, McBay (1992). Even after several decades of integration, they are treated differently than whites are. More important, African Americans continue to receive inferior educational opportunities compared with whites. What is implied here is that African Americans have reached or soon should reach the point of not being considered so unlike whites; thus, special expertise to counsel or teach them may not be warranted. In the meantime, they remain socially isolated in church, school, and work.

Achievement and motivation among African Americans in college have been found to be equally high for both men and women. This finding suggests that African American women have high expectations for work and a sense of responsibility to contribute to family income. They tend, however, to choose the more traditional feminine professional occupations at about the same rate as white women do (Woody, 1992). The message to the counselor is twofold: Encourage and enhance the high level of achievement motivation of African American women and encourage more to consider nontraditional, professional occupations.

The National Science Foundation (1989) gathered statistics on the number of African Americans enrolled in graduate courses in doctorate-granting institutions as a percentage of total graduate enrollment: 1.7% in both computer sciences and life sciences, 1.3% in physical sciences, and 1.4% in mathematical sciences. The number of doctoral degrees awarded to African Americans from 1975 to 1989 in physical sciences, life sciences, and engineering ranged from a low of 101 in 1980 to a high of 133 in 1978 (Vetter, 1989). In a more recent survey in 1994, 13% of African Americans who are age 25 or over obtained a bachelor's degree, compared with only 8% in 1980 (Bennett & DeBarros, 1995).

Finally, Malcolm (1990) suggested that we must encourage more African Americans to major in mathematics and the sciences by engaging children in these subjects early in their educational experience and by encouraging parents to influence their children in this direction. In essence, we must encourage African Americans to choose majors in a wider variety of career fields.

In a survey of African American workers, Taylor (1990) suggested that the major reasons for fewer job prospects for African Americans are related to industrial decentralization and shifts from manufacturing to service industries. These events have significantly reduced job prospects for unskilled and semiskilled workers and have had devastating effects on the poorly educated. However, Johnson (1990) reported that underemployed and underpaid African Americans have developed coping strategies to maintain self-worth and self-esteem through personal and familial achievements.

In a related study, Woody (1992) researched work patterns of African American women and found that many lack requisite skills to compete for technical work and will fail to qualify for higher-level jobs. She argued that African American women have severe job limitations, and many are restricted to low-end jobs because of discrimination. She suggested that there is a "women's work subculture" that may be alleviated only through an improved national employment policy.

Asian and Pacific Americans

The U.S. Bureau of the Census (1993) has grouped Asian Pacific Americans into nine categories: Chinese, Filipino, Japanese, Asian Indian, Korean, Vietnamese, Hawaiian, other Southeast Asians (Cambodian, Laotian, Thai, and Hmong) and, finally, other Asian and Pacific Islanders, which includes Samoans, Guamanians, Tongans, and all other Asian and Pacific Islands ethnicities. Many Asian American groups place a high value on education. Sue and Okazaki (1990) suggested that Asian Americans perceive education as a means of upward mobility and are highly motivated to remove barriers that could limit them. However, Leong and Serafica (1995) argued that Asian Americans are often victimized by discriminatory employment practices. Asian women are given especially low status and are exploited in the working world (Chu, 1981; Kumata & Murata, 1980). Hsia (1981) argued that Asian Americans are hindered in the job market because of poor communication skills, which accounts for their tendency to choose jobs such as engineering, computer science, and economics. In evaluating counseling processes as a source of conflict for Chinese Americans, Sue and Sue (1990) made several pertinent observations: (1) Chinese American students inhibit emotional expression and do not actively participate in the counseling process, (2) Chinese Americans are discouraged from revealing emotional problems by their cultural conditioning, and (3) Chinese American students react more favorably to well-structured counseling models. Sue's conclusions emphasize the importance of understanding cultural influences when counseling Chinese Americans.

Fernandez (1988) argued that Southeast Asian students should be counseled using behavioral approaches. She considered it inappropriate to use counseling techniques that require clients to verbalize excessively. Evanoski and Tse (1989) have successfully used bilingual materials and role models in workshops directed toward parents of Chinese and Korean children that exposed them to methods of accessing a variety of occupations. The basic assumption was that these parents have a tremendous influence on their children.

The following special needs and problems associated with Asian Americans in counseling are summarized from suggestions by Kaneshige (1979), Sue (1992), and Ivey (1986).

1. Asian Americans are very sensitive about verbalizing psychological problems, especially in group encounters.

2. Asian Americans tend to be inexpressive when asked to discuss personal achievements and limitations.

3. Asian Americans tend to misinterpret the role of counseling in general and the benefits that may be derived from it.

4. Asian Americans can be perceived as very passive and nonassertive with authority figures, but in reality they are reacting to cultural inhibitions that discourage them from being perceived as aggressive.

5. Asian Americans may strongly resist suggestions to modify behavior that is unassuming and nonassertive.

In recent years, Vietnamese have presented particular problems for career counselors who have assisted them in relocating in this country. The needs and problems of this adult cultural group are good examples for illustrating limitations of employment for first-generation Asian Americans. In addition to the need to learn English, other problems and difficulties are (1) recognizing the importance of transferable skills, (2) considering past work history as relevant, (3) understanding the concept of career ladders, (4) locating information about unemployment, and (5) recognizing the importance of resumé preparation and interview skills training.

As a group, Asian Americans have the lowest rate of unemployment (Smith, 1983). In general, Asian Americans are very industrious workers, seem to value education, and have taken advantage of higher education to enhance their career development. They are also known to do well in business administration, engineering, and sciences. However, the stereotype of the Asian American as being good in sciences but lacking in verbal skills could limit their access to careers that require communication skills. Even though the most recent immigrants from Asia are mainly employed in service occupations, many Asian Pacific Americans can be found as workers in the professions, in office and clerical jobs, and as service workers.

Finally, among traditional Asian cultures, offering what is considered to be desirable help includes giving advice and suggestions but avoiding confrontation and direct interpretation of motives and actions. When discussing personal issues, it is more appropriate to be indirect, and the counselor should do most of the initial verbalization with a rather formal interactive approach (Sue, 1994).

Hispanic (Latinos/as) Americans

Hispanic Americans are thought to compose the second largest minority group in this country (Axelson, 1999). The states with the largest Hispanic populations are California, Texas, New York, and Florida. Most Hispanics live in metropolitan areas (Axelson, 1993; Smith, 1983). According to Axelson (1999), in the next 25 years the Hispanic population will become the largest minority in the United States, and by 2025, the Hispanic population will reach 39 million.

According to Ivey and Ivey (1999), some groups of Hispanic Americans prefer to be recognized as Mexican American, Cuban American, and Puerto Rican American. By far the largest group of Hispanics are from Mexico (64.3%) followed by Hispanics from Central and South America (13.4%), Puerto Rican (10.6%), Cuba (4.7%), and other Hispanics (7%) (Peterson & Gonzalez, 2000).

Although Ponterotto (1987) reported that Hispanics underuse counseling services in both mental health and academic settings, there is good evidence that they could benefit from these services, especially when intervention strategies meet special needs. Rodriguez and Blocher (1988) found that interventions with academically and economically disadvantaged Puerto Rican women produced positive results by raising their levels of career maturity and developing beliefs that they can control their own destinies.

Social factors such as social-class membership, environment of the home and school, and the community in which the individual resides significantly influence career perspectives and attitudes toward work (Osipow, 1983; Pietrofesa & Splete, 1975). Arbona (1995) supported this conclusion by debunking the idea that cultural traits have restricted Hispanics in career choices. Instead, socioeconomic status and lack of opportunity have restricted Hispanics from access to higher education and subsequently to their occupational aspirations. Hispanics, however, are not a homogeneous group; there are important differences between subgroups and between Hispanics from different socioeconomic backgrounds (Arbona, 1995).

It is not a good idea, however, to overgeneralize about the Hispanic students in our schools today; many are acculturated and fit into the mainstream of society. One can expect, for example, to find diverse value systems among Hispanics. There are, however, those Hispanics who cling to their traditional heritages and, consequently, may have difficulty in adjusting to an Anglo-dominant school and culture. Caught between conflicting cultures, the adolescent Hispanic seeks the support of peers who are experiencing similar conflicts. As a result, there is usually less interaction with other groups of students and, typically, school becomes a low priority.

The Mexican American family, in particular, has been characterized as a closely knit group that greatly influences the values of its members. For example, Axelson (1999) suggested that Spanish-speaking children are generally taught to value and respect family, church, and school as well as masculinity and honor. Families are primarily patriarchal (as far as the center of authority is concerned) with a distinct division of duties; that is, the father is the breadwinner, and the mother is the homemaker. Spanish is the primary language spoken in the home and in the barrio. However, it appears that traditions, including family solidarity, are breaking down among younger Hispanics (Axelson, 1999).

Fouad (1995) recommends several career intervention strategies for Hispanics. Researchers are encouraged to assess these recommendations and to aim their research efforts toward examining the career behavior of Hispanics. The following career counseling recommendations have been paraphrased from Fouad (1995, pp. 186–187).

1. Consider the cultural context of all clients, including Hispanics. Some Hispanics have retained traditional value systems, whereas others may not be traditional. When we are not certain about the client's cultural background, we need to be creative or, as Leong (1993) has labeled it, to have "creative uncertainty." Using this approach, we are to guide our counseling efforts toward the client's willingness to inform us of how culture has influenced his or her life.

2. Be flexible in the career counseling process, especially when we incorporate familial and environmental factors in decision making.

3. Choose assessment instruments with care relative to what is appropriate for Hispanic cultures.

4. Use immediate intervention to retain Hispanic students in school. Career information should include reasons for taking math and science courses.

5. Develop strategies to include self-efficacy as a key to future career success.

6. Provide Hispanic females with a wide variety of career information, including information on nontraditional careers.

Native Americans

The American Indian and Alaska Native population in the United States is estimated at 1.9 million (U.S. Bureau of the Census, 1990). More than 1.5 million American Indians, also referred to as Native Americans, live in the United States. Approximately half of them live on Native American lands and some 275 reservations. Of those Native Americans who live outside the reservations, the largest concentrations are in Los Angeles, San Francisco, and Chicago, but Minneapolis, Denver, Tulsa, Phoenix, and Milwaukee also contain significant numbers. The states with the highest numbers of Native Americans are Oklahoma, California, Arizona, New Mexico, Alaska, Washington, North Carolina, Texas, New York, and Michigan. According to the Bureau of Indian Affairs (1993), there are 318 recognized tribes, plus 200 Alaska Native tribes. Each tribe may have a different language, religious beliefs, and social characteristics that are common to that tribe. Almost two-thirds of Native Americans live in urban areas for training, college, or employment. Many keep in close contact with their family and friends who live on the reservations (Johnson, Swartz, & Martin, 1995).

On the reservations, many are involved in farming, ranching, fishing, and lumber production. Off the reservations, Native Americans work in factories, on farms, and as skilled craftsworkers. Some tribes are engaged in various enterprises, such as motel management; others offer bingo and lottery games to the general public (Axelson, 1993).

An important variable in the career development of Native Americans is the degree to which they adhere to cultural customs, language, and traditions (Johnson, Swartz, & Martin, 1995). The degree of cultural heritage is described on a continuum by Ryan and Ryan (1982, cited in LaFromboise, Trimble, & Mohatt, 1990), as follows:

1. *Traditional:* Speak only native language and observe traditions.
2. *Transitional:* Speak both native language and English and may question traditions of the past.
3. *Marginal:* Speak of themselves as Indian but identify with roles in dominant society.
4. *Assimilated:* Have generally embraced the dominant society.
5. *Bicultural:* Are accepted by dominant society but also identify with tribal traditions and culture.

As with other ethnic groups, we should not stereotype Native Americans but, rather, focus on the degree to which each client adheres to cultural customs, language, and traditions. Significant differences between individuals within cultural groups must be addressed in the career counseling process. But we should also remember that old traditions should be respected, and some may be used to foster career development; the use of role models and experientially related activities are recommended (Johnson, Swartz, & Martin, 1995).

Martin (1995) has developed the following initial intervention strategies for Native Americans that include cultural and contextual variables.

1. Obtain information about the Native American client. For instance, the counselor should have information about the client's tribe and reservation community and should visit the reservation, if possible. Relevant information includes tribal history, customs, and family systems. As in all career counseling strategies, the counselor should have up-to-date educational and career information and as much information about workplace affiliates as possible.

2. Establish communication with the client. The counselor should use what is referred to as cultural/environmental/contextual focusing; this "includes not only knowledge of and respect for the values of other cultures, but comfort with and knowledge of one's own values and ethnicity" (Betz & Fitzgerald, 1995, p. 263). Perspectives of presenting problems are better understood by both counselor and client within this context.

3. Be aware that extended families play an important role in the decision-making process. A major goal is to gain the family's support and provide clients with specific methods that will assist in the career development process.

4. Obtain an evaluation of the client's English ability, preferably from an educational institution that offers courses in English for Native Americans.

5. Use strategies to increase the client's knowledge of the world of work. Recommended are structured reading-discussion techniques using current occupational resources. Video resources may also be used, and group guidance can be an effective technique with Native Americans.

6. Help your Native American client to obtain firsthand knowledge of an occupation by job shadowing (spending time in the workplace with an individual engaged in a particular occupation), interviewing individuals on job sites, or enrolling in an on-the-job training program are recommended.

Most of the counseling strategies discussed in this chapter are often referred to as specially focused interventions (Betz & Fitzgerald, 1995). The name certainly applies to ethnic groups who have special needs that counselors must become increasingly aware of, especially for Native Americans. Bowman (1995) argues that it is impossible for career counselors to be aware of all variables within a culture; let us acknowledge that fact, but the proper attitude is to be open to continued learning about cultural diversity.

Another variable to be considered in counseling approaches is that tribes differ in value orientations and individuals differ within tribes. Thus, as in all minority groups, general recommendations for counseling have to be modified to meet individual needs. Thomason (1991) pointed out that a major consideration is the degree of acculturation in the dominant society. Furthermore, he suggested that the client's set of beliefs about how changes occur is an important consideration for developing intervention strategies for Native Americans.

Herring (1990) argued that there are many career myths about Native Americans; he believes that we simply do not have the necessary research results to draw many conclusions about their career development. Like other minority groups, Native Americans have not been exposed to a wide range of careers and have limited opportunities to attend college because of high unemployment rates. He suggested that Native Americans be introduced to more nontraditional occupations and be provided with career information using Native American role models to expand their career considerations.

Many Native Americans have a strong desire to retain the symbolic aspects of their heritage, much of which is different from the dominant culture. The challenge for counselors is to assist Native Americans in preserving the positive aspects of their heritage while encouraging them to modify some behaviors. For example, the ability to enjoy the present should be combined with planning skills, and the ability to share with others should be combined with assertive behavior. The value orientation of Native Americans is a sensitive issue for career counselors.

Native American resistance to counseling in general is exemplified by the group's underuse of existing mental health services. According to Manson (1982), Native Americans are the most neglected group in the mental health field. Miller (1982) suggested that more Native Americans would take advantage of counseling relationships if appropriate counseling strategies were used. Trimble and LaFromboise (1985) summarized Miller's strategies as follows:

1. Personal ethnic identity in itself is hardly sufficient for understanding the influence of culture on the client.

2. The client's history contains a number of strengths that can promote and facilitate the counseling process.

3. The counselor should be aware of his or her own biases about cultural pluralism—they might interfere with the counseling relationship.

4. The counselor should encourage the client to become more active in identifying and learning the various elements associated with positive growth and development.

5. Most important are empathy, caring, and a sense of the importance of the human potential. (p. 131)

Cultural Variability and Worldviews

In general terms, worldview refers to the individual's perception and understandings of the world (Sue & Sue, 1990). Okun, Fried, and Okun (1999) point out that worldviews include, among other variables, perceptions of basic human nature, the roles of families, relationships with others, locus of control, orientation of time, work values, and activities. Worldviews, in this context, are developed both through individual experiences that are nonshared and through shared experiences and events. Nonshared experiences account for much of the variability within cultures, whereas shared experiences reflect worldviews that are common among members of a specific culture. For instance, *individualism* and *collectivism* are often used to explain cultural differences (Triandis, 1994). In individualistic cultures such as those in Europe and North America, a great amount of value is placed on individual accomplishment. The individual strives for self-actualization. The rugged individualist is revered for his or her autonomy and independence; individuals are empowered to achieve and become individually responsible.

In collectivist cultures such as those in Africa, Asia, and Latin America, the individual's major function is focused on the welfare of the group for their collective survival. Individuals strive to build group solidarity. In these societies, individual uniqueness is not rejected, but more emphasis is placed on being identified with one's social group. The needs of the group take precedence over self-interests. What is important here is sharing, cooperation, and social responsibility. For example, an individual may conceptualize a career choice from the perception of what is best for the family group rather than from an individualistic perspective. In many collectivist cultures, family is more important than the individual.

When counseling individuals from different ethnic groups, counselors should evaluate the degree and nature of acculturation by how it has effected the client's worldview. For instance, Axelson (1999) suggests that some cultural values breakdown as the younger generations assimilate the values of the dominant white culture. In this context, *acculturation* refers to the extent to which a client has assumed the beliefs, values, and behaviors of the dominant white society. It is not unusual for some clients to make an attempt to adjust to local environments whereas others live biculturally or multiculturally; that is, they adopt some behaviors of the white dominant culture and retain values from their own culture and the cultures of others they have come to know. Many experience conflicts, especially between generations, when older members of a family want to retain cultural rules, scripts, and roles, while the younger generation adopts those of the dominant white society. For example, honor of the family conditions one to never oppose collective family decisions, but members of the younger generation might prefer that the locus of control shift from a collectivist to an individualist position. They wish to express themselves independently and make decisions based on their individual needs and self-interests.

Among some cultures, differences in time orientation from the dominant society can present barriers to effective career planning and other time commitments that are normally assumed in career counseling. In traditional career counseling, the client is expected to be on time for appointments and abide by a set of time rules to complete certain career interventions. In cultures of color, individuals are not as obsessed with being on time and maintaining a strict time commitment. A Navajo Indian woman asked me if the next meeting would be "Indian time" or "American time." She explained that "Indian time" is "whenever we get together that is convenient." Being on time for most counselors is viewed as a positive value, and lateness is often misunderstood as a symptom of indifference or a lack of basic work skills. In this case, I learned that time orientation has different meanings for different cultural groups.

Hall's (1971) theory on concept of time has often been cited. In his conceptualization, time is divided into *polychronic* and *monochronic* categories. People engage in and are highly involved in tasks at any given time in the polychronic time category. Activities are rather unstructured, and individuals are more spontaneous and consider appointments as easily changed. In the monochronic category, time is viewed as fixed, and one task is undertaken at a specified time. Schedules are considered very important, and appointments are viewed as almost sacred (Okun, Fried, & Okun, 1999). Collectivistic cultures tend to favor polychronic time whereas individualistic cultures opt for monochronic time.

Another worldview perspective, how different groups view human nature, is an important concept for career counselors to understand when working with multicultural groups. African Americans and European Americans consider human nature as both good and bad. In African American cultures, good and bad behavior are determined by their benefits to the community. European Americans judge good and bad as a part of each individual; good and bad are two sides of human nature that are in opposition and conflict (Diller, 1999).

The belief that human nature is basically good and that human beings can be trusted to have positive motives is shared by Asian, Native, and Latino/a American cultures. Following this logic has subjected these groups to being judged by the dominant society as naïve and gullible in the workplace. The perception is that individuals who follow such a logic need to "wise up" to reality. Career counselors need to assist individuals from different cultures to be aware and alert to workplace associations, which might require them to modify their conceptualizations of human nature.

Finally, personal space and privacy are also considered to be culturally oriented. Individuals from different cultures tend to invade each other's personal space without being aware of it. Triandis (1994) suggests that you invade personal space by walking into it, staring into it, and even through smell by wearing a strong perfume. This invasion is culturally determined; for instance, North American and Arabic cultures expect others to look them in the eye when talking whereas Asians consider direct eye contact to be insulting. Hall (1982) claims that Arabs expect to stand very close to each other when engaged in a serious conversation. Thus, conversational distances are often determined by language and culture, for example, Latino/as usually stand closer to each other than Anglo-Americans do when conversing. Counselors need to be alert to any signals of discomfort with regard to space and adjust distances accordingly.

In sum, individuals are socialized and shaped by their societies and contextual interactions within their environments. Thus, it is not surprising that one cultural group may generally view a behavior as being appropriate, but members of a different culture may view that same behavior as gross or insulting. The point here is that we as counselors must attempt to understand our clients in terms of their origins, assimilation, and acculturation; we should learn to appreciate differences that exist in the way others think and behave. We must resist stereotyping clients by their culture. It is important to recognize that there are different worldviews within cultural groups. In essence, worldviews are to be considered as unique for each individual. Worldviews are basically developed within each individual's ethnic and racial heritage. Finally, worldviews can be modified through experiences with other cultures.

Cultural Differences in Work-Related Activities

Many clients have different work values, including people from different cultural backgrounds. Value orientations to work can be sources of serious conflict and misunderstanding in the workplace. One of the most provocative studies of work-related values was done by Hofstede (1984). His study included 50 different countries in 20 different languages and 7 different occupational levels (Matsumoto, 1996, 2000). His aim was to determine dimensions of cultural differences of work-related values. His findings are paraphrased as follows:

1. *Power distance.* This dimension attempts to answer the basic hierarchical relationship between immediate boss and subordinate. In some countries, such as the Philippines, Mexico, Venezuela, and India, individuals tended to maintain strong status differences. In countries such as New Zealand, Denmark, Israel, and Austria, status and power differentials were minimized. In the United States, there was some degree of minimizing power differences.

2. *Uncertainty avoidance.* This term is used to describe how different cultures and societies deal with anxiety and stress. On a questionnaire designed for this study, countries that had low uncertainty avoidance indexes differed significantly from countries that had high scores. Examples from those with low scores were that workers had lower job stress, less resistance to change, greater readiness to live by the day, and stronger ambition for advancement. Examples of high uncertainty avoidance scores were fear of failure, less risk taking, higher job stress, more worry about the future, and higher anxiety.

3. *Individualism/collectivism.* This dimension attempted to answer the question about which cultures foster individual tendencies rather than group or collectivist tendencies. In this study, the United States, Great Britain, Australia, and Canada had the highest scores for individualism. Peru, Colombia, and Venezuela were most collectivistic. People in high individualistic countries were characterized as placing more importance on employees' personal lifestyle, were emotionally independent from the company, found small companies attractive, and placed more importance on freedom and challenge in jobs. People in countries with low individualism were emotionally dependent on companies, frowned on individual initiative, considered group decisions better than individual ones, and aspired to conformity and orderliness in managerial positions.

4. *Masculinity.* This dimension is thought to be an indicator of which cultures would maintain and foster differences between sexes in the workplace. However, most employees who answered the questionnaire were men, so the conclusions drawn here should be considered tentative. People in countries that had high scores on this variable were characterized as believing in independent decision making, having stronger achievement motivation, and aspiring for recognition. People in countries that had low scores on this variable were characterized as believing in group decisions, seeing security as more important, preferring shorter working hours, and having lower job stress.

These results appear to suggest that culture does have an important role in work-related values. Moreover, we can conclude that employees' perceptions of work roles—as well as of other life roles—are influenced by culture-related values. Differences between cultures help us understand employee attitudes, values, behaviors, and interpersonal dynamics. Nevertheless, we must remember that differences between countries, as outlined in this study, need not necessarily correspond with similar differences on the individual level. The cultural differences found in this study suggest that we use them as general guidelines to understand how cultural dimensions influence work-related values, to see that they can lead to conflicts in the workplace, to be aware that cultural differences are legitimate, and to challenge us to recognize that individual differences exist within cultures (Matsumoto, 1996, 2000).

The Challenge of Becoming Culturally Competent

During the last two decades an increasing number of publications have addressed the need for counselors to become culturally competent, that is, to develop the ability to provide appropriate services cross-culturally. Sue, Arredondo, and McDavis (1992) have developed nine competence areas as basic for a culturally skilled counselor. The three overarching dimensions are (1) understanding own assumptions, values, and biases; (2) understanding the worldview of the culturally different client; and (3) developing appropriate intervention strategies and techniques. The three dimensions are broken down into subgroups of beliefs and attitudes, knowledge, and skills, and each of the subgroups are delineated in self-explanatory statements. Information about competencies can be obtained from the American Counseling Association Web site (listed in Appendix D).

In another publication addressing cultural competence, Cross, Bazron, Dennis, and Isaacs (1989) developed individual cultural competence skills. They suggest five skill areas that have some overlap with the nine competence areas reported in the previous paragraph. Growth in each of the five skill areas can be measured separately, but growth in one area tends to support growth in the others. They include (1) awareness and acceptance of differences, (2) self-awareness,

(3) dynamics of difference, (4) knowledge of the client's culture, and (5) adaptation of skills. Each of these skill areas will be discussed separately in the paragraphs that follow.

The first skill area, awareness and acceptance of differences, is essential for counselors to begin the process of becoming culturally competent. In addition to recognizing individual and unique differences with every client, counselors are to become more aware of cultural differences that exist in worldviews and work-related activities that were discussed earlier. This first step is essential for developing an appreciation of cultural diversity.

When discussing awareness of differences, Sue and Sue (1990) suggested that current mental health practices cannot be applied universally to culturally different populations without recognition of significant cultural differences. Sue and Sue implied that counselors who are unaware of different worldviews (psychological orientation, manners of thinking, ways of behaving and interpreting events) are essentially ineffective; counselors must learn to accept the worldviews of others. The following characteristics are necessary to be a culturally effective counselor (Sue, 1978):

1. An ability to recognize which values and assumptions the counselor holds regarding the desirability or undesirability of human behavior

2. Awareness of the generic characteristics of counseling that cut across many schools of counseling theory

3. Understanding of the sociopolitical forces (oppression and racism) that have influenced the identity and perspective of the culturally different

4. An ability to share the worldview of his or her clients without negating its legitimacy

5. True eclecticism in his or her counseling (p. 451)

Sue and Sue implied that counselors can use their entire repertoire of counseling skills as long as they accept different views and are cognizant of the experiences and lifestyle of the culturally different. These researchers emphasized that counselors must be alert to the influences of different views and environmental factors. Finally, counselors must be cautious not to impose their values on others.

The second skill area, self-awareness, requires the counselor to recognize any prejudice that would make it difficult to empathize with people of color. Counselors are to view the role of culture in their own lives as a backdrop for appreciating how and why others may be different. The recommended outcome is for an appreciation of how a variety of cultural variables shapes human behavior. To develop this skill area, one is required to develop sufficient self-knowledge of culture specific factors that influence behavior and a personal awareness of one's own cultural background. In short, counselors must recognize their limitations and expertise. An evaluation of racial attitudes, beliefs, and feelings may well be assessed by a white racial identity developmental model such as the one built around the work of R. T. Carter (1995) and Helms (1990b). Their conceptualizations of an identity model that represents that of a white member of the dominant society contains five stages as follows:

1. *Contact stage:* Is unaware of any biases associated with his or her race and racial identity.

2. *Disintegration stage:* Acknowledges a white identity that often results in confusion and conflict.

3. *Reintegration stage:* Devalues other races and idealizes whiteness.

4. *Pseudo-independent stage:* Intellectualizes the understanding and acceptance of other races and is somewhat tolerant.

5. *Autonomy stage:* Becomes nonracist and internalizes a multicultural identity.

This model enlightens counselors to the behavioral characteristics that occur at various stages of identity development for both the counselor and the client. The process should not be conceived as a linear progression but, rather, as continuous and cyclical involving interactions with individuals from diverse cultures that lead to adaptive changes. Counselors should continually evaluate their progress of awareness as racial and cultural beings.

Axelson (1993) suggested basic points of self-awareness for improving counseling in a multicultural society, including cultural-total awareness, self-awareness, client awareness, and counseling procedure awareness. These basic points of awareness lead to focusing on the client's needs. Needs are most appropriately conceptualized from a broad base of human experiences to more discrete distinctions. The broad base of human experiences includes common human experiences, specific cultural experiences, individual experiences, and the unique individual. This approach to counseling in a multicultural society consists of the following four steps:

1. Recognize that all human beings possess the like capacity for thought, feeling, and behavior.

2. Be knowledgeable in several cultures; study differences and similarities among people of different groups and their special needs and problems.

3. Gain an understanding of how the individual relates to important objects of motivation, what his or her personal constructs are, and how they form his or her worldview.

4. Blend steps 1, 2, and 3 into an integrated picture of the distinctive person as experienced during the counseling process. (p. 18)

The third skill area, the dynamics of difference, also relates to self-awareness. This skill is seen as a counselor's knowledge of subtle differences between cultures in the way they interact and communicate. For instance, eye contact has different meanings; some cultures avoid eye contact and others may expect it while conversing. Counselors can communicate an awareness of differences between cultures by adopting appropriate cultural counseling techniques.

The fourth skill area, knowledge of the client's culture, suggests that counselors be prepared for counseling by familiarizing themselves with the client's culture. Suggested topics include country of origin, sociopolitical context, preferred language, religion, family role, gender roles, cultural assumptions of appropriate behavior, cultural values and ideologies, class definitions if any, power in relationships, work roles, customs, and traditions. Knowledge of the client's culture is most relevant in the counseling process, especially in the development of appropriate collaborative relationships between client and counselor that are essential for productive counseling outcomes.

The adaptation of skills, the fifth skill, is the process of altering counseling programs and intervention strategies to better fit the client's cultural values. Again, the counselor must be familiar with the client's cultural background. For example, clients from collectivistic cultures may expect their families to participate in all decisions, and counselors who ignore this basic need may be quite ineffective. Counselors need to carefully evaluate the career counseling process from the perspective of how methods, procedures, and materials can be adapted to make certain they are culturally appropriate.

Counselors who become familiar with the terms *etics, emics,* and *ethnocentrism* will fully appreciate the need to adapt their counseling methods, materials, and procedures. The term etic suggests that there are universal truths across cultures. The basic assumption, for example, is that one can evaluate behavior and motivation by universal cultural norms. Thus, counselors' own culture has relevance for people of all cultures. In essence, the etic perspective is from outside the group (Wehrly, 1995). The term emic considers truths as culture specific. The basic assumption is that we should judge an individual's behavior by the values, beliefs, and social mores of his or her particular culture. The emic perspective is from within the culture (Wehrly, 1995). When counselors insist on strictly using their own background of biases, values, and beliefs to interpret culturally different actions and behaviors, they are suggesting that their race is superior, and that is known as *ethnocentricism.* (Matsumoto, 1994). As Okun et al. (1999) point out we expect all others to think and act as we do.

In a provocative publication on multicultural counseling, Speight, Myers, Cox, and Highlen (1991) suggest that counselors will be overwhelmed with current approaches to counseling individuals from different cultures if they are expected to base counseling only on culture specific differences. Furthermore, these researchers suggest that culture-specific counseling is impractical and results in fragmentation of efforts. This research team has suggested a much broader approach to multicultural counseling that includes not only cultural specificity but also human universality and individual uniqueness. Human universality involves constructs applicable to all cultures. For example, counselors would explore a variety of worldviews from different cultural groups for the purpose of discovering common themes among them. Such themes would be used with specific cultural information as a backdrop for incorporating individual uniqueness as a third dimension in career counseling.

Self-knowledge is emphasized in optimal theory as a means of understanding and appreciating others. Awareness of one's worldview is important for recognizing feelings, assumptions, and biases from which one views others. The major task of this process is to become alert to personal and sociopolitical meaning of one's culture and ethnicity. Thus, counselors discover themes that are universal in scope

FIGURE
10-2

Influences on worldview

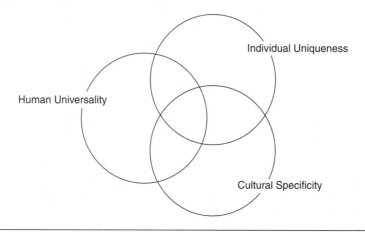

Human Universality

Individual Uniqueness

Cultural Specificity

SOURCE: From "A Redefinition of Multicultural Counseling," by S. Speight, L. Myers, C. Cox, & P. Highlen, 1991, *Journal of Counseling & Development, 70,* 29–35. Copyright by the American Counseling Association. Reprinted with permission.

and are common to racial, ethnic, and cultural groups. Figure 10-2 illustrates the development of worldview from the perspective of a more holistic approach that includes individual uniqueness, cultural specificity, and human universality.

In sum, the optimal theory approach is multidimensional in nature and differs from culture specific approaches by stressing the influences that shape worldviews as being more holistic. Therefore, counselors would build an understanding of how (a) specific cultures influence the development of worldview, (b) the human universality of themes cut across cultures, and (c) the uniqueness of the individual is developed. Within this theory, interrelationships are interconnected from which emerge values, beliefs, and actions. This redefinition of multicultural counseling should attract research and debates that will take time to delineate.

In a related publication, Diller (1999) argues that our traditional counseling services have been based on Northern European cultural values, ideals, and beliefs that are referred to as Eurocentric. Duran and Duran (1995) strongly suggest that we cannot meet the needs of individuals that are culturally different by the exclusive use of Eurocentric-based career counseling theories, practices, and materials. The call is for career counseling to not be culture-bound, that is, we must move away from only using Eurocentric approaches and be more sensitive to different cultural values and assumptions. Again, we can adapt our counseling approaches to gain more relevant culture specific information and develop culturally appropriate interventions as demonstrated by the Multicultural Career Counseling Model for Ethnic Women in Chapter 4.

Skill and competency development are most important in meeting the challenge of becoming culturally competent. However, counselors must also evaluate their basic assumptions about career counseling, that is, can contemporary theory and practices meet the needs of an increasingly diverse population? What is implied here is that counselors not only need to build skills for cultural competency, but they must also rethink the underlying principles of current theories and practices. The following paragraphs, which outline the assumptions for a multicultural counseling theory, suggest that we use both western and non-European systems of helping.

Recognizing that a theory for multicultural counseling and therapy was long overdue, Sue, Ivey, and Pedersen (1996) have proposed a multicultural counseling and therapy theory (MCT). These authors have suggested that contemporary theories of counseling and psychotherapy do not adequately deal with the complexity of culturally diverse populations, and we assume that this conclusion includes career development theory and counseling. Specifically, current theories do not describe, explain, or predict current cultural diversity. But even more important, the shortcomings in current contemporary theories and practices will not adequately prepare the mental health profession to meet the needs of an increasingly diverse population, in which current minorities will become a numerical majority within several decades.

Following is a summary of other underlying assumptions that prompted the development of MCT:

1. Individualism should not dominate the mental health field (consider self-in-situation and people-in-context discussed in Chapter 3).

2. Learning occurs within a cultural context.

3. Cultural identity is changing.

4. Culture should be defined inclusively and broadly.

5. Counselors must possess an understanding of the culture and sociopolitical context of a client's behavior before they can develop appropriate intervention strategies and use appropriate assessment instruments.

6. To develop multicultural competence, the counselor must increase his or her own self-awareness.

7. Multicultural training will be necessary to increase the skills and perspectives needed in the future.

The comprehensive nature of this metatheory should promote a large body of research well into the 21st century. In fact, Sue et al. (1996) have developed suggestions for various research approaches for their theory. They have suggested that past researchers focused on social biases of Eurocentric society and subsequently have not addressed the positive attributes and characteristics of racial and ethnic minority groups.

The MCT theory has many implications for the future of counseling, but its main focus is on changing conventional counseling. As we learn from the research that this theory will certainly promote, we will be in a better position to consider counseling strategies to meet the needs of culturally diverse groups. Here are some of the suggested changes at this point (Sue et al., 1996):

1. *Balance the focus of counseling.* We are to move away from the traditional focus on the individual and pay more attention to family and cultural issues. Thus, a balance is needed between self-oriented help and self-in-relation help.

2. *Expand the repertoire of helping responses.* Some of the helping responses that counselors now use—and, in fact, their approach to helping responses—may be inappropriate for culturally different clients. For example, passive attending and listening skills could confuse some clients from different cultures.

3. *Identify indigenous helping roles.* Dealing with human problems is quite different from one culture to another. Counselors should be trained to understand different culturally based roles and that traditional healers found in some cultures are viewed with high credibility.

4. *Develop alternatives to the conventional counseling role.* New and different counseling roles may require that counselors practice outside of their offices, such as in the community or in organizations. Counselors should become more externally focused—that is, advocate changes in the community, enhance job opportunities, and intervene on behalf of the client. In sum, counselors need to become advisors, advocates, facilitators of indigenous support systems, consultants, and change agents.

Immigration and Its Sequelae

Immigrants have arrived in this country under a variety of circumstances. Some are exiles such as the immigrants from Southeast Asia, Central America, and Cuba among others. Some immigrants have come to find work and enjoy the privileges of a free society, and many have come for both political and financial reasons. The first great wave of immigrants came from Northern and Western Europe circa 1820–1880, and the second wave came from Southern and Eastern Europe circa 1881 to 1929. After World War II, the current increase in immigrants began and continues into the 21st century. The largest numbers have come from Mexico, Asia, Cuba, Central and South America, and the Middle East (Axelson, 1999).

That migration experience can be a very stressful one is probably a gross understatement of what some individuals have experienced. Adjustment to a new culture involves multiple factors that include transitions and transformations. Transition involves reconstructing social networks and adjusting to a new socioeconomic system and a different cultural system (Rogler, 1994). The transformation process, although similar to transition, encompasses ethnic identity issues of acculturation and assimilation or gradual inclusion of values and social mores from the dominant culture. Some modify their ethnic identities; others strive to maintain cultural beliefs shaped in their homeland.

Counselors evaluate an immigrant's migration experience to uncover such information as country of origin, sociopolitical context, education, and socioeconomic status, belief systems, types of migration, occupational history, culture shock, support systems, and medical history. The post migration evaluation process should include level of acculturation, language skills and preferred language, level of adjustment, and impact on identity (Comas-Diaz & Grenier, 1998). The postmigration adjustment process is greatly affected by the host country's attitudes toward the immigrant, the level of family adjustment, the geographical region of relocation, and acculturative stress experienced by individuals and the family as a group.

The most pressing need for most immigrants is finding work for their financial support. Those who cannot speak and understand English and lack job skills usually are forced to accept low-level work and the minimum wage scale. More educated and sophisticated immigrants have found successful careers in a variety of occupations and professions; however, recent immigrants are usually found in low-paying service and manufacturing jobs. Not surprisingly, skill and educational level of immigrants greatly determines their job placement and their experiences in assimilation.

A common experience among immigrants is cultural shock, especially for those who locate in geographical areas where they are isolated. As they confront a different cultural environment they face isolation, loneliness, and loss of support from their families. Those who relocate in enclaves where they live with other members of their culture who have recently migrated collectively experience the angst of a different cultural environment. According to Okun et al. (1999), minorities are tolerated if they conform to the dominant culture and are expected to assimilate white values and lifestyle.

Development of children and adolescents is especially interrupted and may remain in a discontinuous state for long periods. Their self-identity is challenged severely by new and different peer groups. Learning a new language for many immigrants poses significant problems for obtaining work, in educational programs, and in social activities. Counselors should evaluate the acculturation level to determine the degree of adoption of beliefs, values, and lifestyle of the host culture. Developmental issues of adjustment to cultural differences and the host cultures' sex roles are important variables related to developmental tasks of immigrant children and adolescents. As immigrants lose some of their original cultural identity and acquire a new identity in a second culture, they may alternate between wanting to "belong" and resistance to "belonging"; their developmental process can be most difficult.

The need to assimilate values and lifestyle of the host culture has become a growing conflict. Multiculturalists suggest that there should be a model of partial assimilation in which immigrants retain some of their customs, beliefs, and language. There is pressure to conform rather than to maintain their cultural identities, however, and these conflicts are greatly determined by the community to which one migrates (Okun et al., 1999). These experiences are not new; many Europeans experienced exclusion and poverty during the first two waves of immigration in the 19th and 20th centuries. Eventually, these immigrants transformed this country with significant changes that included enlightenment and acceptance of diversity. People of color, however, continue to struggle for acceptance. Once again, the challenge is to recognize that other cultures think and act differently and that they have the right to do so. Perhaps, in the not too distant future, immigrants will no longer be strangers among us (Suro, 1998).

Evaluating and understanding an immigrant's identity development can be at least partially assessed by a Minority Identity Development model by Sue (1981) and Atkinson, Morten, and Sue (1993). This model describes the psychosocial development of minority group members. Stages of development and transitions between stages are expressed in terms of the minority members' attitude toward self, others of the same minority, others of a different minority, and the dominant society or groups.

Stage 1: Conformity. The individual is self-deprecating and prefers to be identified with dominant cultural values.

Stage 2: Dissonance. The individual develops conflicts about the dominant system and is in a state of cultural confusion.

Stage 3: Resistance and immersion. The individual is more self-appreciating and rejects the dominant society.

Stage 4: Introspection. The individual carefully evaluates his or her attitude toward self and the dominant society.

Stage 5: Synergetic articulation and awareness. The individual accepts his or her cultural identity and develops selective appreciations of the dominant culture.

In addition to providing guidelines for career guidance activities, this model also provides counselors with a greater understanding of the stress and adjustment problems of immigrants. Excerpts from an interview described in Box 10-1 illustrate a migrant's acculturation and adjustment to the dominant society.

BOX 10-1　An Immigrant's Experiences

During the pre-interview stage, the counselor and Zoila agreed that the Multicultural Career Counseling Checklist (Ward & Bingham, 1993) and the Career Counseling Checklist (Ward & Tate, 1990) would be helpful for organizing background information and identifying problems. After discussing several items on both checklists, the counselor was encouraged that rapport had been established. Both counselor and client felt comfortable with discussing racial issues and differences in cultural groups.

Zoila was raised a Catholic and noted that all members of her family in Mexico were Catholics. She became a Protestant when she married her Mexican-American husband about one year after arriving in this country and has been active in church work. She has been married for 20 years and has two children, ages 19 and 15. The oldest child, a girl, is attending college, and the youngest is in his sophomore year in high school.

BOX 10-1 An Immigrant's Experiences *(continued)*

When she arrived in this country, Zoila could not speak a work of English. She attended an adult education program for three years before she became proficient. Thus, in her early years she could only socialize with other Hispanics. She felt that this was the limiting problem she faced as an immigrant. She did not feel that the local Hispanic community was prejudiced and did not experience overt discrimination in the community. However, she does harbor the feeling that many people "think that those who come from Mexico are not good." She remembers being "homesick" for her family, especially her mother. She also missed holiday celebrations and traditions in Mexico. She occasionally returned to Mexico to visit her family but plans to remain in the local community and make a life for her family in this country.

Zoila left Mexico primarily because there was little work for women in Mexico, especially where she lived. She claims that she has always wanted to work in a situation where she could advance. She felt that her chances in Mexico for such an opportunity were practically nil. She recognized early that upward mobility meant education or training, and she set out to get it. She took several jobs in local industries and also worked as a care giver in a home for the mentally retarded and saved her money for an education. After receiving a GED Certificate she enrolled in college to take business courses. She feels that the course that helped her the most was public speaking during which she was able to improve her English skills.

In the meantime, she raised two children who have also done quite well in their educational programs. She speaks English in her home except, as she put it, "when I get angry." Her daughter has a greater link to Mexican traditions and customs than does her son, who Zoila characterizes as being "Americanized."

Zoila now owns and operates a small business that employs three other individuals. Her business has been successful for seven years. She has managed to purchase the building in which her business is located and rents out part of it to a retail outlet. She is mostly accepted by both Hispanics and members of the white community. She is a member of the local Chamber of Commerce. Her friendly and pleasing personality attracts many to her business.

When Zoila was asked about her lifestyle here, she replied that she had been raised to believe that the man of the house was to make the living while she raised the children. "This is the way in Mexico," she stated. However, she felt the need to work in this country to provide more opportunities for her children. Even though she enjoys her work and interactions with the public, she would prefer to be "just a housewife." She stated, "If you want to get ahead here, you don't have the choice."

In sum, the story of Zoila illustrates a relatively successful process of immigration. This true story continues to unfold.

Some Suggestions for Interviewing Multicultural Groups

Developing a greater sensitivity to culturally diverse clients has become increasingly important for career counselors; we must foster specific counseling techniques to accommodate the human diversity that exists in our society. The core dimension of interviewing is effective communication between clients and counselors. Also, during the interview, counselors form opinions and assumptions about clients from both verbal and nonverbal communications. Because of cultural and ethnic differences between counselor and client, the counselor must be alert to a wide spectrum of ethnic and cultural characteristics that influence behavior. Some cultural groups conceptualize their problems differently from those of the dominant white culture and seek solutions based on these assumptions. For instance, a client who believes he is being ostracized because of race might be much more interested in finding immediate employment than in pursuing a program for identifying a long-term career goal. Another client might be reluctant to share her personal problems with someone outside the family circle and, in fact, might interpret direct questioning as an infringement of her privacy.

Although it is difficult to generalize techniques suggested for different cultural groups, it seems feasible to first determine the level of acculturation by socioeconomic status, language preference, place of birth, generation level, preferred ethnic identity, and ethnic group social contacts (Ponterotto, 1987). Questions must be carefully selected and presented to not offend the client. For example, directness may be judged as demanding, intrusive, or abrupt by some cultural groups. Furthermore, an open person can be seen by some cultures as weak, untrustworthy, and incapable of appropriate restraint (Copeland & Griggs, 1985). Here are some other points to remember when interviewing people from other cultures:

- General appearance can be quite distinctive for some subcultures and should be accepted on that basis.
- Attitude and behavior are considered difficult to ascertain. Major belief themes of certain cultures influence members' attitudes about themselves and others. Their perceptions of the world may be quite different from those of the counselor.
- Affect and mood are also related to cultural beliefs and to what is considered appropriate within a culture. The meaning given to gestures often differs by culture. Work experience may be quite limited because of lack of opportunity. Also, in some cultures, it is considered very immodest to speak highly of yourself and the skills you have mastered.
- Life roles, and particularly relationships, are unique to cultural socialization. In some cultures, females are considered equal to males, whereas in others females are expected to be subservient.

These examples illustrate the necessity of building an extensive body of resources for interviewing ethnic minorities. Other general recommendations include

(1) use straightforward, slang-free language, (2) become familiar with cultural life-role models, (3) identify a consultant who can provide helpful information, and (4) become familiar with support networks for different cultural groups.

In Chapter 5 a career counseling intake interview outline contains a list of topics that can be followed, with some modifications, for interviewing individuals from culturally diverse groups. The information contained in the preceding paragraphs include some significant suggestions for career counselors. Most important is to remember is that cultural groups are not to be stereotyped as homogeneous. Thus, with our focus on the uniqueness of individuals, we should begin by establishing a collaborative working relationship with each client. A trusting relationship is essential for productive interviewing. The Multicultural Career Counseling Model for Ethnic Women (Bingham & Ward, 1996) discussed in Chapter 4 suggests that a *Multicultural Career Counseling Checklist* (Ward & Bingham, 1993) and the *Career Counseling Checklist* (Ward & Tate, 1990) be administered as an aid in *establishing rapport.* Selected items from both checklists can be used as an entry to discussing problems that are related to cultural diversity.

The acculturation level of the client should be assessed in the *second step* as delineated by Ponterotto (1987) in the previous paragraphs and repeated here:

- Language preference
- Place of birth
- Generation level
- Socioeconomic status
- Preferred ethnic identity
- Ethnic group social contacts

This information may be used to determine the individual's level of assimilation in the transformation process of balancing values, beliefs, and traditions brought from the country of birth with new ideas of lifestyle and traditions of the host country. The stage of identity development should also be evaluated. Additional focus areas should include the following:

- Neighborhood contextual experiences
- Quality of housing
- Experiences with racism
- Religious beliefs

When interviewing a culturally different individual, significant differences in techniques should be observed. Such a list has been compiled by Ivey and Ivey (1999). Each technique has been listed with an explanation, an illustration, or both. The following suggestions for managing an interview with a culturally diverse individual should be used in conjunction with the suggested sequence for an interview as displayed in Chapter 5 and illustrated in Chapter 6.

Eye Contact. In Native American and Latino/a cultural groups, direct eye contact, especially by the young, is considered disrespectful. Okun et al. (1999) note that in many cultures individuals are forbidden to look directly at others who have more power. It is inappropriate in Muslim cultures for women to make direct eye contact with a nonfamily male. Obviously, direct eye contact is interpreted differently among cultures; some cultures consider it to be an invitation to a sexual liaison, whereas others consider it an invitation to conflict.

Touch. Guidelines for touching across gender lines is clearly defined in some cultures. For instance, in many societies, especially in the Middle East and among Asian groups, women do not touch or shake hands with unrelated men. The counselor should let the client initiate the greeting and ending of a counseling session.

Probing Questions. In some cultures, especially among some Asian groups, asking for more in-depth information is considered as very rude and intrusive. Being aware of this potential problem, counselors restructure their questions to focus on the topic the client has initiated, as shown in the following samples:

COUNSELOR: How do you think you could best help the situation with your brother?

COUNSELOR: What can you tell me about the relationship?

The counselor has a delicate balancing problem with Asian groups who respect individuals that demonstrate proficiency in their profession, but resent those who appear to be too intrusive.

Space and Distance. Be alert to cultural differences in what is considered to be an appropriate distance from another individual when interviewing. Remember that the British prefer more distance than do North Americans (more than an arm's length), Latino/a people like being closer, and those from the Middle East prefer to be "right in your face."

Verbal Style. "I" is not a word in Vietnamese; individuals are defined by their relationships: Son (I) asks Father (you) for permission, Mother speaks to children (them).

Restrictive Emotions. Many cultural groups are taught to mask their emotional feelings. Thus, they might appear to be disinterested and preoccupied. This is particularly true of Native Americans who consider masking of emotional responses as a sign of maturity. In most cases you can expect African Americans and Latino/a people to openly express emotions.

Confrontation Issues. Ivey and Ivey (1999) comments that "confrontation needs to be used with great sensitivity to individual and cultural differences" (p. 201). He suggests that extreme confrontational statements may not be helpful with certain groups, especially in the opening stages of interviewing. Counselors must remember that personal and family honor are almost sacred among some cultural groups, especially in Asian cultures. Direct confrontive techniques may be perceived as being ill-mannered by some groups. Counselors can learn to be careful and flexible in how they construct questions, such as, "tell me more about your feelings when that event took place." "What is your son's typical story of that behavior?" Use the principles of supportive empathic confrontation to construct questions, and sometimes silence can be helpful to give the client time to struggle with a problem.

Self-Disclosure. This technique is quite paradoxical in that it is most essential when establishing rapport for a trusting client-counselor relationship and can be most damaging to the counseling relationship if the counselor is perceived as being immature. For instance, self-disclosure at the initiation of the interview can be helpful for building trust: "I grew up in the South and I'm white and you are an African American." "Do you think we can work together?" However, counselors who focus too much time on their own personal lives and intimacies can lose face with their clients. Again, a delicate balance must be maintained.

Focus on Self-in-Relation and Self-in-Context. The point has been made that in North America we tend to focus on the "I." In many other cultures, the focus is on family or solidarity of groups. In making career decisions the focus can be directed to include the family. The individual perceives himself or herself as a self-in-relationship and makes decisions that meet the needs and approval of the family. Family honor and loyalty may be the driving force that the counselor must recognize.

In sum, what one is expected to remember about the differences between cultures and what are considered to be acceptable and culturally appropriate verbal and nonverbal techniques is sometimes overwhelming. This points out, however, the necessity of preparation for counseling and interviewing encounters, especially with individuals from culturally diverse groups. Counselors must also remember that they are interviewing unique individuals who share some cultural values with others but who have also been shaped by nonshared experiences. The techniques that we have just reviewed are generalized suggestions that might not apply to all members of a particular culture. Nevertheless, the career counseling profession must prepare itself for diversity to be effective in the 21st century.

Summary

1. Culture is a very complex concept that can refer to many aspects of life and living. Culture is a learned behavior. Two people from the same race could share some values, attitudes, and so on but might also be very different in their cultural makeups. Counselors should be alert to value orientation when working among different cultural groups.

2. Four major cultural groups include African Americans, Asian Pacific Americans, Hispanic Americans, and Native Americans. Currently, the largest racial minority group in this country is African Americans. They will soon be surpassed by the Hispanics. Culturally different African Americans tend to remain social isolates in church, school, and employment. Many Asian Americans place a high value on education. Asian Americans tend to inhibit emotional expression, and so many do not actively participate in counseling programs. In general, Asian Americans are reluctant to admit personal problems because of their cultural conditioning. Asian Americans tend to misinterpret the role of counseling and its potential benefits. The second largest minority group in this country is Hispanic Americans. General cultural characteristics of Hispanic

Americans appear to distinguish them as the least "Americanized" of the ethnic groups. The Hispanic family is typically a closely knit group that greatly influences the value systems of its members. Native Americans are culturally conditioned to view life from a different perspective than that of the dominant white culture. Native Americans are generally not motivated to achieve status through the accumulation of wealth. The lifestyle of most Native Americans is extremely democratic, and their culture promotes egalitarianism.

3. Culture variability of worldviews includes constructs of individualism and collectivism. Examples of other differences in cultures are time orientation, view of human nature, and personal space and privacy. Worldviews should be considered unique for each individual.

4. Culture does have an important role in work-related values. Differences between cultures help us understand employee attitudes, values, behaviors, and interpersonal dynamics.

5. Effective counselors have knowledge of and are sensitive to different cultural orientations when establishing rapport in counseling relationships. To be effective with populations of different cultures, counselors must be aware of different worldviews (the psychological orientation of thinking, behavior, and interpretation of events). Counselors must be careful not to impose their values on others. Necessary skill areas include awareness of differences, self-awareness, knowledge of client's culture, and adaptation of counseling method, materials, and procedures.

6. Optimal theory is multidimensional in nature and emphasizes how (a) specific cultures influence the development of worldviews, (b) the human universality of themes cut across cultures, and (c) the uniqueness of the individual is developed.

7. A multicultural counseling and therapy theory (MCT) was developed because, as the authors suggest, contemporary theories of counseling do not adequately deal with the complexity of culturally diverse populations. We must balance the focus of counseling, expand the repertoire of helping responses, identify indigenous helping roles, and develop alternatives to the conventional counseling role.

8. Immigrants have special needs that involve the premigration process as well as the adjustment process in a new and different culture. Adjustment to a new culture includes transitions of reconstructing social networks, adjusting to a new socioeconomic system, and learning a different cultural system.

9. Counselors must develop a greater sensitivity to culturally diverse clients when conducting an interview. Technique issues include eye contact, touch, probing questions, space and distance, verbal style, restrictive emotions, confrontation, self-disclosure, and focus on self-in-relation and self-in-context.

Supplementary Learning Exercises

1. Define your cultural background and that of a classmate. Compare differences and similarities.
2. How would you explain the differences between individualism and collectivism? What socialization variables influenced the differences between them?
3. Do you believe the multicultural counseling and therapy theory (MCT) is necessary? Support your conclusion.
4. Take one or more of the four major cultural groups discussed in this chapter and develop culture specific issues that should be addressed in career counseling.
5. Write an essay about how cultural worldviews are developed. Include differences between other cultures and the white dominant culture.
6. Describe how different cultural work values can be sources of conflict and misunderstanding in the workplace.
7. Debate the pros and cons of counselors becoming culturally competent.
8. What do you consider to be the most difficult culturally competent skill to learn? Explain.
9. Interview a culturally different person. Share your experience with the class.
10. Which of the following two methods do you consider to be the most effective for career counseling? Support your conclusions.
    a. Use culture specific information.
    b. Use human universality information.

For More Information

Axelson, J. A. (1999). *Counseling and development in a multicultural society* (4th ed.). Pacific Grove, CA: Brooks/Cole.

Betz, N. E., & Fitzgerald, L. F. (1995). Career assessment and intervention with racial and ethnic minorities. In Frederick T. L. Leong (Ed.), *Career development and vocational behavior of racial and ethnic minorities* (pp. 263–277). Mahwah, NJ: Erlbaum.

Bingham, R. P., & Ward, C. M. (1996). Practical applications of career counseling with ethnic minority women. In M. L. Savickas, & W. B. Walsh (Eds.), *Handbook of career counseling theory and practice* (pp. 291–315). Palo Alto, CA: Davies-Black.

Comas-Diaz, L. (1996). Cultural considerations in diagnosis. In F. W. Kaslow (Ed.), *Handbook on relational diagnosis and dysfunctional family patterns* (pp. 159–160). New York: Wiley.

Comas-Diaz, L., & Grenier, J. R. (1998). Migration and acculturation. In J. Sandoval, C. L. Frisby, K. F. Geisinger, J. D. Scheuneman, & J. R. Grenier, *Test interpretation and diversity* (pp. 213–241). Washington, DC: American Psychological Association.

Diller, J. V. (1999). *Cultural diversity: A primer for the human services.* Pacific Grove, CA: Wadsworth.

Hofstede, G. (1984). *Culture's consequences: International differences in work-related values.* Newbury Park, CA: Sage.

Ivey, A. E., & Ivey, M. B. (1999). *Intentional interviewing & counseling* (4th ed.). Pacific Grove, CA: Brooks/Cole.

Matsumoto, D. (2000). *Culture and psychology* (2nd ed.). Belmont, CA: Wadsworth.

Okun, B. F., Fried, J., & Okun, M. L. (1999). *Understanding diversity: A learning practice primer.* Pacific Grove, CA: Brooks/Cole.

Speight, S. L., Myers, L. J., Cox, C. I., & Highlen, P. S. (1991). A redefinition of multicultural counseling. *Journal of Counseling and Development, 70,* 29–35.

Sue, D. W., Arredondo, A., & McDavis, R. J. (1992). Multicultural counseling competencies and standards: A call to the profession. *Journal of Counseling and Development, 70,* 477–486.

Sue, D. W., Ivey, A. E., & Pedersen, P. B. (1996). *A theory of multicultural counseling and therapy.* Pacific Grove, CA: Brooks/Cole.

Sue, D. W., & Sue, D. (1990). *Counseling the culturally different: Theory and practice* (2nd ed.). New York: Wiley.

Suro, R. (1998). *Strangers among us: How Latino immigration is transforming America.* New York: Knopf.

Wehrly, B. (1995). *Pathways to multicultural counseling competence.* Pacific Grove, CA: Brooks/Cole.

11

Special Issues in Career Counseling for Women

Chapter Highlights

- *Career development theories relating to women*
- *Women's special needs for career guidance*
- *Multicultural perspectives when working with women*
- *Implications for career counseling of women*
- *Some intervention components for career counseling of women*
- *Counselor bias when counseling women*
- *Gender bias and gender fairness of interest assessment of women*

A FEW SHORT YEARS AGO, CAREER COUNSELING PROGRAMS FOR WOMEN consisted of exploring the traditionally held working roles. The choices were narrowed to such occupations as clerk, teacher, or nurse. One of the first questions asked was, "How will this job fit into your husband's occupational goal?" The message to women was quite clear: You have only a few jobs to choose from, and your career is secondary to your husband's or other family obligations. Currently, career counselors find that women are rearranging their career priorities—planning for a lifelong career in a wide range of occupations has become the highest priority. A career first and marriage maybe or later is the new order of preference for many. In this post–women's movement era, women continue to look beyond the traditional feminine working roles. The women who embark on this career course will find that a variety of barriers still remain. First, the bias associated with sex-role stereotypes in the working world still exists (McBride, 1990; Rider, 2000; Wentling, 1992; Wood, 1994). Second, the woman who gives her career development equal status with her husband's will find acceptance of her role personally challenging, with little support from many men and women (Betz & Fitzgerald, 1987). Male and female counselors might also resist accepting women's changing career priorities (Harway, 1980; Unger & Crawford, 1992). In essence, there continues to be resistance in our society—albeit somewhat less since the women's movement—to the role of women in the working world from men and women at all levels of the work force, from managers and professionals to blue-collar workers. A number of professional counselors and organized groups have recommended developing counseling programs to assist women who are strongly committed to pursuing full-time careers. For many other women who are unable to perceive themselves as career-oriented but who wish to break away from traditionally feminine roles, the need for counseling programs might be even greater. For these women, the consideration of a lifelong career is entirely new and conflicts with the concepts developed in their early socialization; that is, women were primarily "socialized" to see themselves as homemakers while men pursued careers (Betz, 1994a; Smith, Smith, Stroup, & Ballard, 1982). The rapidly changing values regarding traditional sex roles in the United States suggest that several additional factors influence the type and magnitude of critical career decisions women are currently making. For example, the decline of motherhood as a full-time occupation is becoming increasingly prevalent in our society ("Chipping Away," 1991; "Charting the Projections," 1995); consequently, women feel freer to consider full-time careers outside the home. In addition, families' current financial needs have made it necessary for both husband and wife to work, and jobs traditionally allocated to men are now available to women (U.S. Department of Labor, 1992–1993). Finally, research has shown that we have not adequately addressed the role of women in our work force or the special needs of women who work (Gianakos & Subick, 1986; Patterson, 1996; Siltanen, 1994).

In this chapter, we discuss women's special career counseling needs and describe several career counseling components. The chapter is divided into six sections: the first part reviews women's career development patterns; the second part identifies and discusses special career counseling needs; career counseling and career counseling programs for girls and women are discussed in the third part; the fourth part describes some career counseling components that meet the special needs identified in part two; counseling bias is discussed in the fifth part; and finally, issues of gender bias and gender fairness in interest assessment are reviewed.

The term *gender roles* will be used from here on instead of the more familiar *sex role*. Although many researchers have used these terms synonymously, Money (1982) pointed out that an individual's sex role is a component of his or her gender role; the sex roles are physiological components of sex-determining role sets for men and women. The more inclusive term, *gender role,* is composed of nonphysiological components of sex, including behaviors, expectations, and roles defined by society as masculine, feminine, or androgynous (Unger, 1979).

Career Development Theories and Women

Women's career development has received only cursory attention by career development theorists (Osipow, 1983). The need for career development theories free of gender-role stereotyping has been suggested by Betz and Fitzgerald (1987). Super (1990) is one of the major career development theorists (discussed in Chapter 2) who addressed women's career development patterns, which he classified into seven categories: stable homemaking, conventional, stable working, double track, interrupted, unstable, and multiple trial. Still significant is Super's double-track career pattern, which establishes homemaking as a second career. Conflicts between homemaking and career remain a concern that must be addressed in career counseling programs (Wilcox-Matthew & Minor, 1989).

Ginzberg (1966) considered three lifestyle dimensions for women that may be used in career counseling approaches: (1) *traditional* (homemaker-oriented), (2) *transitional* (more emphasis on home than on job), and (3) *innovative* (giving equal emphasis to job and home). These dimensions seem to represent realistic lifestyles found among today's working women, with the addition of a *career-oriented* dimension—one in which the highest priority is given to the development of a career. It is difficult for many women to move toward the innovative dimension, primarily because of psychological barriers; some women might be reluctant to become more career-oriented for fear of losing the stereotypical female identity so readily accepted by our society. For many, the loss of this identity is indeed threatening and deters a serious focus on career development.

According to Betz and Fitzgerald (1987), occupational choices for women are greatly influenced by home and family responsibilities. Betz and Fitzgerald suggest that social class, plus attitudes generated by marriage, financial resources, educational level, and general cultural values of past and immediate families, are major determinants influencing occupational choice. Furthermore, women's occupational choices are not made independently of other variables in our society. Women do indeed have special needs that must be addressed in career counseling programs.

In a related research program beginning with 3000 sixth graders in southeast Michigan and tracking 2000 of them well into early adulthood, Eccles, Barber, and Jozefowicz (1999) report some interesting findings. They suggest that numerous mediators developed from contextual interactions are involved in career choices among women. For instance, occupational aspirations are mediated by expectancy beliefs and values that are referred to as achievement-related choices. Women who expect to do well in particular occupational environments tend to aspire to such careers. Furthermore, gendered socialization experiences lead to the development of core personal values and self-identity, which are instrumental in establishing long-range goals. Gender roles influence the kind of activities women want to participate in regarding an occupation and lifestyle. Career roles for women are also influenced by a culture's definition of female roles, which include parenting and spouse-support. Finally, mediation developed from individual experiences of cultural interactions modify career aspirations.

Zytowski (1969) denoted the vocational development patterns of women as (1) mild vocational, (2) moderate vocational, and (3) unusual vocational. These patterns closely follow the lifestyle dimensions developed by Ginzberg in that each category is progressively more occupationally oriented. According to Zytowski, the modal life role for women in our society is that of homemaker. Through vocational participation, a woman may change her modal lifestyle. Patterns of vocational participation for women are determined by age at entry, the length of time the woman works, and the type of work undertaken. Further determinants of vocational patterns for women are individual motivation, ability, and environmental circumstances, such as financial needs. Of significance to our considerations is that women do differ and have special needs to be included in career development programs.

Sanguiliano (1978) emphasized the theme of different and special needs of women. Although she agreed that women do follow a serial life pattern, there are unique times of hibernation, renewal, postponement, and actualization. She contended that life-stage theorists such as Erikson (1950), Havighurst (1953), Kohlberg (1973), and Levinson (1980) reveal significant shortcomings in describing the development of women. Stage theorists do not account for the unexpected, critical events and the myriad of unusual influences that shape feminine life patterns. Sanguiliano suggested that a woman's life cycle does not follow a rigid progression of developmental tasks but is similar to a sine curve representing the impact of unique experiences and critical events.

According to Sanguiliano, the formulation of self-identity is one fundamental difference between men's and women's developmental patterns. Women's self-identification is significantly delayed because of the conflicting expectations ascribed to feminine identity. Men learn their masculinity early and are better prepared to adapt to changes, but women do not have comparable, clearly defined boundaries and images of appropriate gender-linked roles. Men are reinforced in their efforts to attain clearly defined masculine roles; women depend on loosely defined feminine roles and have few support systems.

Sanguiliano's principal argument is that women's individual life patterns require special consideration. Attention should focus on unique paths women take to break away from gender-role stereotyping. Individual progress toward self-identity is germane to Sanguiliano's approach to determining counseling components for women.

Spencer (1982) supports Sanguiliano's denial that women's development follows the rigid progression suggested by life-stage theorists. Spencer contends that feminine developmental tasks are unlike masculine tasks and that women follow unique patterns of development. Using Levinson's life-cycle sequence and transitional periods of men discussed in Chapter 12, Spencer compared women's development with the men's model: early transitions (ages 17–28), age-30 transitions (ages 28–39), midlife transitions (ages 39–45), and late-adult transitions (ages 65–?).

The early transitional period, the time when one reappraises existing structures, begins the search for personal identity (Erikson, 1950; Levinson, Darrow, Klein, Levinson, & McKee, 1978). Spencer contended that separating from the parental home is more difficult for the young woman than for the young man; women receive less encouragement and experience less social pressure to become independent. Furthermore, women do not have adequate support systems to encourage self-expression in a society that presents conflicting messages. In essence, women have a more difficult time developing self-identity.

During the age-30 transitions, marital conflicts are prevalent in women who look for new directions. For example, women who want to spend time in career development often find difficulty forming egalitarian marital relationships. The frustrations women face in dual family/career commitment are often misunderstood. On one hand, women are socialized to think of themselves only as homemakers, but, on the other hand, they have a strong need to express themselves in a career. Women have to struggle to realize that greater freedom and satisfaction are options.

Midlife transitions are periods of reappraising the past and of continuing the search for meaning in life. This period is marked by an increased awareness that some long-held beliefs might not be valid. For women, successful appraisal of life accomplishments is usually reflected in what others (husband and children) have done (Troll, Israel, & Israel, 1977). Therefore, when their children leave home, women have difficulty creating new identities and new life purposes.

The late-adult transition is a continued reappraisal of self in society. According to Spencer, the primary task of this period is to gain a sense of integrity in one's life. Spencer (1982) concluded that women rarely achieve the developmental goal of ego autonomy—"They are doomed from the start" (p. 87).

Spencer (1982) and Sanguiliano (1978) suggested that women have different developmental patterns than men do: (1) Women experience intense role confusion early in their development; (2) women are more inhibited in their self-expression; (3) women tend to delay their career aspirations in lieu of family responsibilities; and (4) women's developmental patterns are more individualized. These unique and individualized developmental patterns may present significant problems in career decision making. Career counselors should carefully consider self-concept development and value assessment in career decision-making programs for women.

Chusmir (1983) identified characteristics and background traits of women in nontraditional vocations (construction trades, skilled crafts, technical fields, science, law, engineering, and medicine). He suggested that women who choose nontraditional occupations have personality characteristics usually attributed to men. For example, they tend to be more autonomous, active, dominant, individualistic, intellectual, and psychologically male-identified than do women who choose traditional careers (social work, nursing, teaching, and office work). Motivational characteristics of women who choose nontraditional occupations are also similar to those attributed to men: achievement orientation, status seeking, and strong need for self-regard and recognition. Examples of background traits of women in nontraditional occupations are better education, better mental health, fewer or no children, eldest or only child, postponed marriages, fathers who were younger and in management roles, well-educated fathers, and enrollment in women's studies courses.

Chusmir suggested that personality and motivational traits of women who choose nontraditional occupations are formed by the time they are teenagers. Clearly, the research focuses on the importance of feminine early developmental patterns. Intervention strategies designed to expand occupational choices for girls should be introduced during elementary school years.

In each of the career developmental patterns of women briefly reviewed, emphasis was placed on the woman's role as homemaker, and the special needs of women interested in developing careers were stressed. Women who give at least equal emphasis to job and home were considered "innovative" (Ginzberg, 1966) or "unusual" (Zytowski, 1969) because they differed in lifestyle from the "typical" homemaker. These terms are very misleading today, however, as predictions from the U.S. Department of Labor are that numbers of women job seekers will slowly increase (Peterson & Gonzalez, 2000). Even more important are the considerations we should give to women as individuals, free of gender-role stereotyping, in an expanding job market.

The general developmental patterns of women suggest that a woman's life cycle does not follow life-stage models developed from the study of men. Compared with men, self-identity is slower to develop, primarily as a result of gender-role stereotyping. Our society accords a secondary priority to career choice as well as to career development for women. Women's difficulty with career decision making is closely associated with role confusion and the lack of role models and support systems.

More recently, career development theorists have given some attention to women's career development. For example, some gender issues are addressed in the individual developmental constructs in the theory of work adjustment and person-environment-fit counseling (Dawis, 1996) discussed in Chapter 2. Although gender is not considered as a defining variable in the theory, gender becomes important when it influences work skills and work needs that have not been identified. The point here is that women have not been given an opportunity equivalent to that of men to develop the full range of work skills required in the world of work. Therefore, what reinforces women in a number of work environments is unknown. However, this theory considers gender as an important "background" variable that could account for personality structure, style, and adjustment style of workers. Therefore, when more gender variables are identified in the world of work, more emphasis can be given to gender as a defining variable.

Gottfredson (1996) makes an interesting observation about gender concerning group differences, for instance, how gender, ethnic, and social groups and how group membership per se might shape career aspirations (see Chapter 2). Gottfredson asserts that group-based identities influence and shape one's preference for place and fit in the social order. Moreover, the theory of circumscription and compromise "assumes that most young people orient to their own gender and social class when contemplating careers" (p. 202). Gottfredson stresses that orientation to sex roles in early childhood (ages 6 to 8) results in a concern for individuals to do what is considered appropriate for one's sex, particularly in vocational aspirations.

In the theory of sociological perspectives on work and career development discussed in Chapter 2, Hotchkiss and Borow (1996) suggest that long-standing social inequities constrain females' work-related achievements. Although there is some evidence of decline in gender segregation of occupations (Roos & Jones, 1993), there is much more to do to reduce gender barriers to the work world.

In an outstanding article, Fitzgerald and Betz (1994) suggest that women's career development is affected by discrimination and sexual harassment, cultural constraints as occupational gender stereotypes, and gender-role socialization, in addition to the "motherhood mandate." One point well taken is that women's abilities are not being fully used both in education and in occupations; thus, many women are functioning in jobs for which they are overqualified. Fitzgerald and Betz suggest that, first, each career development theory should determine its applicability to particular groups, such as gender and ethnic groups. Second, information should be given about the applicability of a theory for groups or how people's characteristics affect the predictive validity of a theory. Third, each theory should be scrutinized for its conceptualization of structural and cultural factors and how they relate to important theory variables. Using structural and cultural factors as a measure of a theory's effectiveness will provide new perspectives for career theories, particularly for greater insights into women's career development.

Finally, the fact that men and women differ in many dimensions gives credence to a multifactorial model of development. For more than 30 years of gender research, Spence (1999) concludes that numerous sets of dimensions determine masculinity and femininity. Furthermore, even though males and females of any given age differ by identified gender-related behaviors, these attributes vary among individuals within each gender; they are thought to be influenced by contemporary contextual interactions. What Spence and other researchers are emphasizing is that gender roles are most complex in development; they are multidimensional and multifactorial. There is no overaching unitary or single dimension or sets of dimensions that determine masculinity or femininity. There are however, numerous factors whose interaction is extremely complex in determining one's gender role identity development. One's gender-related behaviors can be modified or sustained by contemporary experiences.

The answer to the question of why men and women differ in their choices is viewed as differences in values, goals, and self-perceptions. Thus, educational and occupational choices are guided by the following according to Eccles, Barber, and Jozefowicz (1999): "(a) one's expectations for success on and sense of personal efficacy for various options, (b) the relation of the options to both one's short- and long-range goals and one's core self-identity and the basic psychological needs,

(c) one's gender-role-related schemas, and (d) the potential cost of investing time in one activity rather than another. All these psychological variables are influenced by one's experiences, cultural norms, and the behaviors and goals of one's socializers and peers" (pp. 158–159). Thus, a much broader multifaceted and multidimensional approach to women's development has the promise of unearthing more information about career aspirations of women.

Identifying Women's Special Needs

Our society has seen a significant number of women go to work in nontraditional jobs during times of emergency. For example, during World War II, women assumed many jobs that were then considered reserved for men. The concept of the working role of women during this time was well exemplified in the then-popular song, "Rosie the Riveter" because most people saw the situation of women in nontraditional jobs as somewhat humorous and temporary. The trend today is toward equalization of job opportunities, particularly those jobs that were predominantly held by men. That the number of women working in skilled occupations (as defined in the Bureau of Census Classifications) has significantly increased underscores that attitudes toward working women are changing.

The emerging trend toward equalization suggests a number of special needs for women. One need is for information resources about nontraditional occupations for women. To make a wider range of choices available to women, several federal agencies have sponsored programs to inform women of nontraditional jobs. These programs will be expanded into public schools, two- and four-year colleges, and relevant federal, state, and local community agencies.

One program, Women in Nontraditional Careers (WINC) (Alexander, 1985), is designed to help women consider nontraditional occupations. This model consists of three major components: (1) training school staff to alert them to the need for broadly based career planning and how occupational choice affects lifetime earnings, (2) classroom instruction that provides students with information about the labor market and other topics that is free of gender bias, and (3) the establishment of nontraditional job exploration in the community. In addition, the program activities include women working with other women who are employed in nontraditional occupations.

Federal Law Requirements

Women need to be made aware of the federal laws under Title VII of the Civil Rights Act of 1964 and Title IX of the Educational Amendments of 1972. These laws prohibit discrimination on the basis of gender in employment, payment received for work, and educational opportunities, and they assist women in attaining equal opportunity in these three important areas. Title VII applies to all employers with 15 or more employees, employment agencies, and labor organizations. Discrimination is prohibited against employees on the basis of race, color, religion, gender, or national origin. The policy on discrimination applies to hiring, upgrading, promotion, salaries, fringe benefits, training, and all other terms and conditions of employment. Title IX refers to all educational agencies and institutions receiving federal assistance. This law prohibits discrimination against students and employees on the basis of gender, including the admission and recruitment of students, the denial or differential provision of any aid, benefit, or service in an academic, extracurricular, research, occupational, or other educational program or activity, as well as in any term, condition, or privilege of employment (including hiring, upgrading, promotion, salaries, fringe benefits, and training).

Career Information

Through affirmative action and other programs, women are more frequently considered for leadership positions previously reserved for men. However, the number of women in doctoral training programs and in certain scientific fields has remained relatively out of proportion (Betz & Fitzgerald, 1987). Clearly, women need career information that encourages them to consider a wide variety of careers—especially those previously pursued only by men. Women who have the interest and ability to pursue assertive, managerial careers need direction and encouragement, as do women who are interested in skilled labor and technical occupations.

Dual Roles

Economic conditions have greatly contributed to an increase in the number of married women who are employed full time. For many families, it has been essential that both parents work to fulfill financial responsibilities. Today's husband and wife consider their work efforts a joint venture. The family stereotype of homemaking mother and breadwinning father is no longer typical. In greater numbers, women are assuming a dual role of homemaker and worker. Managing both roles has caused conflicts for many women, particularly in meeting their own individual needs (Hansen, 1990). Although the dual role of working women has found greater acceptance, personal contradictions that need clarification persist in the working woman's life (Nadelson & Nadelson, 1982). Today's women need to more fully value an independent lifestyle and clarify their self-concepts. More specifically, counseling should help women identify their abilities and skills and provide them with the same opportunities given to men in making use of their talents in our society.

An Integrative Life Planning (ILP) model by Hansen (1996) incorporates career development, life transitions, gender-role socialization, and social change. This model is designed to expand career options for both men and women because fragmented approaches to development and life roles place limits on decisions clients will make in their lifetimes. A more integrative approach to career development recognizes that an individual's total development includes a broad spectrum of domains. The impact of decisions on lifestyle, including relationships, is a major part of a more comprehensive view of development.

As women make a greater commitment to education and training, their willingness to accept full responsibility for household tasks, including childrearing, is decreasing (Benin & Agostinelli, 1988). The increasing pressure for an equitable division of household responsibilities focuses on what men actually do in the home. Coleman (1988) found that men spend more than 50% of their time in play with their children, whereas women spend only 10% of their time in this way. Some evidence suggests, however, that women are frequently reluctant to delegate household tasks to men (Bernardo, Shehan, & Leslie, 1987). See Chapter 13 for more information on dual-career families.

Child Care

Although this topic is considered relevant for both parents, research has shown that mothers shoulder the greater burden with regard to child care issues (Lott, 1994). The enormity of child care problems is evidenced by the fact that the percentage of married women with children under the age of 6 has increased from 12% in 1950 to 57% in 1992 (National Commission on Children, 1993). Child care providers include caretakers in the home, day care centers, adult members of the household, older siblings, and no provider at all—some children are left to look after themselves. More recently, some organizations have provided on-site day care centers (Gilbert, 1993; see Chapter 13 for more information on child care sites).

Many work, family, and personal difficulties for women evolve from child care problems. Examples of work-related problems are arriving late for work, leaving early from work, scheduling problems, missing work, and having difficulty concentrating on work tasks. Family-related problems primarily focus on family conflicts over child care arrangements. Personal problems usually involve stress and the conflict that results between the need to achieve in a work situation and the need to be a responsible parent. Some women decide not to take a promotion because the new position could interfere with child care. Others decide not to return to work after childbirth because child care problems cannot be resolved to their satisfaction. The problems of child care are exacerbated for workers who have less money to budget for it (Fernandez, 1986).

Working Environment

The working environment is relatively unknown to women who have considered themselves primarily homemakers. Because a significant number of women will work outside the home (U.S. Department of Labor, 1992–1993), programs that inform women about what typically can be expected in work settings are needed more than ever. Employee expectations, effective communication with peers and supervisors, promotional policies, and authority relationships are examples of items requiring clarification.

Needs of Displaced Homemakers

This group is usually identified as comprising women over the age of 35 who have been out of the labor force for an extended period of time. They are ineligible for unemployment insurance and do not qualify for various government aid programs, such as Aid to Families with Dependent Children (AFDC). Many of these women may have to turn to public support for assistance (Lott, 1994). Because of their previous lifestyles, many displaced homemakers lack job search skills and are completely unprepared for entry into an occupation.

Needs of Divorced Women

Similarly, divorced women are often unprepared for self-sufficiency and often have children who depend on them. Not only are many forced to seek employment, but they also have the sole responsibility for rearing their children. This new lifestyle requires balancing the responsibilities of parenthood and home management with the responsibilities of work. In addition to the recommendations for the displaced homemaker, other possible counseling components may cover day care centers, transportation information, and quick, efficient methods of food preparation. These women must learn to set priorities to effectively meet both home and employment responsibilities.

Internal Restrictions

Of major importance are the internal restrictions women experience when considering full-time careers or nontraditional roles. To project oneself into an occupational environment dominated by men can indeed be a difficult task for many women who grew up under the influence of traditional gender stereotyping of occupations. Women who have considered only traditional jobs such as teacher, nurse, or clerical worker find the contemplation of many other careers foreign to them. On one hand, early socialization has instilled identification with certain society-sanctioned gender roles (Spence, 1999); on the other hand, women are being told to break away from the traditional gender role. Indeed, many find this dichotomy too great to bear. In general, some women lack confidence and self-esteem, which tends to limit their career choices. There is also evidence that gender-role orientation adversely affects achievement motivation (Eccles, 1987; Eccles, Barber, and Jozefowicz, 1999; Frenza, 1982; Wood, 1994).

Need for Leadership Roles

Other inhibiting barriers prevent women from reaching their full potential in the world of work. Epstein (1980) suggested that our cultural heritage does not encourage women to excel in business-related occupations. In our culture, the model for a business manager is typically masculine (Lindsey, 1990). Through social conditioning, men are perceived as leaders and better able to carry out demanding tasks (Cejka & Eagly, 1999). Women who have taken on leadership roles are often regarded merely as tokens, and their abilities and skills are questioned, even by their colleagues. Women are often made to feel like outsiders in organizations and are ostracized by the existing formal and informal structures. Wood (1994) contends that women need more experience (access to formal and informal structure) and exposure to feminine leadership role models to encourage a greater degree of motivation to attain leadership positions.

The Glass Ceiling

The so-called glass ceiling is an invisible barrier that consists of subtle attitudes and prejudices that have blocked women and minorities from ascending the corporate ladder (Reskin & Pakavic, 1994). For example, one method used to block women and minorities from top-level corporate jobs is to insist that senior executives have 25 years' experience. Another method used to exclude women is to groom them for either lower-level positions or for those positions not on track for senior-level positions. Garland (1991) reported that white males most often prefer mentoring other white males. *Nations Business* magazine ("Chipping Away," 1991) pointed out that although women and minorities account for 50% of the nation's work force, only 5% hold senior-level management positions. According to this same source, women are chipping away at the glass ceiling and will have more success in industries where the customer base is women. Through affirmative action policies, the government is also attempting to break the glass ceiling (U.S. Department of Labor, Bureau of Labor Statistics, 1991).

The Trials and Tribulations of Women Who Want to Climb to the Top

Wentling (1992) suggested that the following actions are necessary for women to attain senior-level management positions:

1. *Educational credentials:* Obtain at least an MBA or equivalent.
2. *Hard work:* Be ready and willing to work at least 54 hours per week at the office and take work home.
3. *Mentors:* Find and network with the most qualified mentor.
4. *Interpersonal/people skills:* Female executives have several common characteristics, including the ability to manage people.
5. *Competency on the job:* Expect to be more thoroughly evaluated and screened than men are.
6. *Willingness to take risks:* Be innovative and initiate projects.

Women and Entrepreneurship

In 1992, women owned 5.4 million businesses, and in 1990, they employed 11 million people. Also, women own 30% of *small businesses,* and it is predicted that their share will increase to 40–50% by the year 2000 (Aburdene & Naisbitt, 1993). Despite substantial gains in business ownership and the increases projected for the future, women entrepreneurs face barriers not usually encountered by men. As suggested by Gould and Parzen (1990), (1) women lack socialization to entrepreneurship in the home and society; (2) women have been excluded from business networks; (3) women lack capital and information about how to obtain it; (4) women suffer from discriminatory attitudes of lenders; and (5) women are often ostracized in the business community because of gender stereotypes, which in turn influences expectations of women as entrepreneurs.

Clearly, women need more assistance in learning about pathways and barriers to owning their own business. However, a very encouraging fact is that so many women have successfully ventured into the world of entrepreneurship. Federal support programs include the Women's Business Ownership Program, the Women's Network for Entrepreneurial Training (a national training program), and the Women's Business Ownership Act of 1988, which offers incentive loans.

Sexual Harassment

The issue of sexual harassment has been well documented in the workplace for several years. For example, in 1980 the Working Women's Institute concluded that sexual harassment was the single most widespread occupational hazard women face in the work force (Lott, 1994). The attention given to sexual harassment was dramatically increased by (1) the 1991 Senate hearings involving Supreme Court nominee Clarence Thomas and his accuser, Anita Hill; and (2) the U.S. Navy Tailhook scandal involving the mistreatment of women by U.S. Navy personnel.

What constitutes sexual harassment has been the central issue of several recent court cases. The "reasonable woman" standard was applied as the appropriate legal criterion for determining whether sexual harassment had occurred: If a reasonable woman would consider behavior offensive even though a man would not, the court would rule that sexual harassment had occurred (Fitzgerald & Ormerod, 1991). Sexual harassment does indeed occur, according to Barnett and Rivers (1996) (cited in Peterson & Gonzalez, 2000); more than 50% of working women will experience sexual harassment in their jobs.

Other factors used to determine when a behavior is considered offensive are (1) if the behavior was judged extreme, (2) if the victim was responsible for what happened, (3) if the perpetrator was a direct supervisor of the victim, and (4) if there was significant frequency of occurrence (Kail & Cavanaugh, 1996).

In a *Newsweek* poll in October 1992 (Lott, 1994), 21% of women respondents claimed they had been harassed, and 42% said they knew someone who had. More recently, Rider (2000) suggests that roughly two-thirds of women report some form of sexual harassment at work. Some descriptions of harassment are sexual remarks, suggestive looks, deliberate touching, pressure for dates, letters and calls, pressure for sexual favors, and actual or attempted rape.

Beginning more than a decade ago, many large organizations developed policies, procedures, and programs to define sexual harassment, to decide what to do about it, and to determine how to prevent it. In June 1992, 81% of Fortune 500 companies offered their employees sensitivity training programs designed to make them more aware of acts that constitute sexual harassment (Lott, 1994). Recently, Fernandez (1999) has developed training programs that are needed to enhance gender relations in corporate America. Aamodt (2000) also suggests that training to eliminate sexual harassment in the workplace should be a primary target of employers. Sexual harassment continues to be a problem in the workplace that must be addressed to make certain women have equal access to employment and career advancement.

Multicultural Perspectives When Working with Women

On several occasions in this chapter and more often in the previous chapter, the point has been made that women are socialized in a particular culture. By incorporating ethnicity in career development of women we gain a greater understanding of multiple facets of influence that shape values, beliefs, actions, and worldviews of women. A most important point to remember is that one's development does not take place in isolation but is greatly influenced by salient messages received within the environment. The ethnic-related messages are integrated with other variables that greatly affect the gender role development. We will briefly examine ethnicity and gender of African American women, Southeastern Asian women, Hispanic women, and Native American women.

African American women have a long history of doing menial labor as cooks, housemaids, nannies, and other low-pay-scale jobs (Harley, 1995). More recently, African American women are found in professions largely as a result of federal legislation and affirmative action policies (Higginbotham, 1994). An increasing number of African American women have been successful in owning their own businesses (Ballard, 1997). Most of career growth has been in the public sector, however; women of color continue to be subject to discrimination in the private sector.

The collective strengths of African American women are in social networks of other women and relatives such as sisters. Many regularly participate in sororities, church women's groups, and women's social clubs. In essence, female friendship is a strong support system for African American women. Women support each other in difficult times and remain loyal to their churches. African American women have a strong spiritual commitment that is used to counteract the unfairness and hardships of oppression and racism. Some of the challenges facing African American women are health problems such as systemic lupus erythematosus and HIV/AIDS. Hunter (1996) noted that number of HIV/AIDS cases are increasing among African American women and children. Poverty and homelessness are also growing problems. Teenage pregnancy among African Americans is declining, but the problem remains a challenge.

Career counseling for ethnic women was discussed and illustrated in Chapters 4 and 10. Career counselors must recognize that there is diversity in any subgroup. Thus, African American women are not to be considered as a homogeneous group.

Winbush (2000) suggests, however, that job training and child care are two primary needs of many African American women.

Southeastern Asian American women have received little attention in the research literature. This population includes women from Vietnam, Laos, and Cambodia. Since 1975, more than one million Southeastern Asian refugees have migrated to the United States (Zaharlick, 2000). Of this group, the Vietnamese are the best educated and most fluent in English and have the most experience in professional and technical occupations. There is much diversity among this subgroup of people; however, some values are shared. Southeastern Asian women feel a strong devotion to their children and to family continuity, they strive to avoid actions that would bring shame to the family, and they have strong self-control (Zaharlick, 2000).

A couple I know owned and operated a restaurant and also worked on the midnight shift in a local weaving plant. When asked about their schedule, they replied that they were financially supporting their first son who is attending a university, and they wanted him to spend most of his time studying. They did not seem to feel that what they were doing was anything special and showed great pride in their son's achievement. Obviously, in this case, family and devotion to their children was of major importance.

Southeastern Asian women have difficulty in witnessing current breakdowns in family honor as their children adopt more of the values and lifestyle of the dominant culture. Their children are learning from a new and different peer group that individualism is the contemporary lifestyle. Children disobeying family rules is a growing problem for Southeastern Asian Women. Their children seemed to be inspired to improve their status, however, and are in most cases willing to devote time and effort necessary for upward mobility.

Hispanic women are a very diverse group who have migrated here from a vast number of different countries; however, they too have some common background variables such as religion preference. Most are Christian and members of the Catholic Church, although in recent years some have joined Protestant groups. Hispanic women learn from their religion that they are to view their chief roles as mothers and wives (Burgos-Ocasio, 2000). They are primary care givers and center their lives around family needs.

Hispanic women also need information about HIV/AIDS because the number of cases among Hispanics is rising. Their health needs are traditionally taken care of by home remedies and other women in the family, and they use indigenous healing systems by referring individuals to a *currandismo* (Mexican folk healer). Although more information about the benefits of current medical practices may be needed, all nontraditional methods, remedies, and healers should be recognized (Sue, Ivey, & Pedersen, 1996).

Ortiz (1996) points out that Hispanic women are increasingly migrating and joining the labor force. Most have few skills, little education and end up finding work as maids, factory workers, or non-skilled jobs. Their major goal is to send their earnings back to their country of origin to support their families. Short-term goals include finding a place to live and a job. Long-term goals usually include becoming legal citizens and bringing their children and families to join them.

Neal (2000) also reminds us that there is great diversity among the customs and cultures of Native Americans. "The roles of women varied from tribe to tribe, geographical region to geographic region" (p. 166). Native American women have historically been influential within their tribes. This tradition continues in many tribes; for instance, Wilma Mankiller was the Chief of the Cherokee Nation of Oklahoma in 1985 (Mankiller & Wallis, 1993). Other Indian nations have also elected women as chairpersons or chiefs. Some tribes have a council of women elders that has control of ceremonial life and businesses operated by the tribe. However, the traditional primary role for Native American women, similar to so many other cultures, is care of the family.

Of most significance to Native American women as homemaker and care giver is that Native American families are the poorest socioeconomic group (Neal, 2000). The most impoverished families in this country are Native American families with no husband present. The source of strength among Native Americans is their biological family and the extended community family. They also find spiritual strength from their traditional ancestral homelands.

Implications for Career Counseling

Thus far, we have identified or implied several career counseling needs for women. More specifically, these needs include (1) job search skills, (2) occupational information, (3) self-concept clarification, (4) strategies and role models for managing dual roles—homemaker and worker, (5) assertiveness training, (6) information about a variety of working environments, (7) lifestyle clarification, and (8) development toward a value of independence. These needs suggest specially designed intervention programs for women in program content, techniques, and subject matter. For example, many job search skills are universal for all job seekers, but women, especially those of other cultures, have a special need to develop strategies for negating employer discrimination. Other examples of specific intervention programming needs include providing a more complete understanding of job search techniques, teaching women to use occupational information, encouraging women to evaluate a wide range of careers, and alerting them to the stereotyping of female workers. Programs designed to assist women with managing dual roles, child care, and lifestyle skills may be accomplished in a variety of counseling settings, including groups of women or with their spouses. Multicultural issues are covered in Chapters 4 and 10.

Intervention Components for Counseling Women

In the next section of this chapter, we present four counseling intervention components that partially meet women's needs. Not included is assertiveness training, which is discussed in the next chapter but which can also be used to meet the needs of women. These intervention strategies (as shown in Table 11-1) can be incorporated within career counseling models illustrated in Chapter 4 and should be considered to be strategies that meet unique needs of individual women and applied as such. For example, women who are identified as needing information on discriminatory employment practices might find group discussions with other women very helpful. The suggested technique options do not exhaust all possible methods of accomplishing the specific tasks, and what follows is only a brief explanation of each intervention component.

Intervention Component I—Job Search Skills

A specially designed job search skills strategy can help women deal with potentially discriminatory practices. The primary purpose of this component is to prepare women to apply for nontraditional jobs, although the skills learned can be applied to any job search. The point is that women need special assistance with preparing applications for jobs that are primarily reserved for men. Displaced homemakers and culturally diverse females especially need this component because many have little experience in applying for a job. To be effective, women must not only learn the general skills needed for interviewing and resumé writing, they must also be prepared to deal with discriminatory practices associated with gender-role stereotyping and race. For example, in typical gender-role stereotyping of black females, they are considered best suited as a maid or cook. When these women work, it is assumed to be a necessity, as the man is perceived to be the primary breadwinner. Thus, men are typified as leaders who make decisions; women are seen as passive, cooperative, and unable to rise to leadership positions in the work world. In essence, traditional gender-role stereotyping implies that women are generally inferior in marital roles and work roles (Reschke & Knierim, 1987; Wood, 1994).

The technique options suggested to accomplish the goals of this intervention strategy are workshops, group or individual counseling, and resource exploration. As with other counseling strategies, combinations of the technique options are recommended. Three representative resources that can be used to build resource exploration and other parts of the program are *Exercises for the Résumé Workshop: A Program for Women, Résumé Preparation Manual—A Step-by-Step Guide for Women*, and *Launching Your Career* (all available from Catalyst, 220 Park Avenue South, New York, NY 10003, Fax 212-477-4252).

Intervention Component II—Working Climate

The purpose of this intervention strategy is to prepare women for typical gender-role stereotyping found in many working environments. Unfortunately, gender-role stereotyping has been prevalent in many sectors of our society. For example, advertising often portrays women as being very dependent and almost helpless (Comstock, with Paik, 1991; Wood, 1994). There is also evidence of stereotyping in textbooks and in teachers' interactions with students (Basow, 1992). One of the

TABLE 11-1 INTERVENTION COMPONENTS FOR COUNSELING WOMEN

Strategy component	Technique options	Specific tasks
I. Job search skills	1. Workshop 2. Group and/or individual counseling 3. Resource exploration	1. Evaluate and clarify purpose of the interview. 2. Require that each counselee demonstrate interview skills. 3. Evaluate and clarify purpose of resumé. 4. Require that each counselee demonstrate resumé preparation skills. 5. Clarify potential discriminatory employment practices. 6. Clarify federal laws that prohibit discrimination on the basis of gender in employment, pay, and education. 7. Clarify possible strategies for combating employer discrimination.
II. Working climate	1. Workshop 2. Group and/or individual counseling 3. Role-clarification exercises	1. Identify typical stereotyping of female workers by peer affiliates. 2. Clarify competitive nature of working environment. 3. Identify and clarify interpersonal skills associated with peer affiliates. 4. Identify and clarify interpersonal skills associated with supervisors. 5. Increase understanding of work setting.
III. Lifestyle skills	1. Workshop 2. Group and/or individual counseling 3. Role-clarification exercises	1. Clarify goals and specific needs associated with potential career. 2. Identify methods of jointly meeting family and personal needs. 3. Identify and require that each counselee demonstrate an understanding of the dynamics associated with dual careers. 4. Identify and require that each counselee demonstrate assertiveness skills. 5. Identify and clarify the implications of early socialization and needs for establishing a value of independence. 6. Clarify the concept of implementing one's self-concept into a career.
IV. Support and follow-up	1. Group and/or individual counseling support 2. Follow-up visits	1. Identify and clarify problems associated with working environment. 2. Identify and clarify problems associated with family. 3. Identify and clarify problems associated with personal goals.

most serious problems facing working women is the large gap in earning power between men and women. Fundamental to this problem are sex-based wage discrimination and occupational sex segregation (Lott, 1994). It appears that women continue to select occupations from a more restricted range of options and continue to see fewer suitable occupations (Fitzgerald & Betz, 1994; Poole & Clooney, 1985). Thus, women need special assistance to cope with typical stereotyping of women workers.

Basow (1992) presents the current picture of the barriers women face to reach the top-ranked jobs as rather discouraging: Women confront a "glass ceiling" when trying to reach top-ranked jobs. In 1990, fewer than 3% of the 6502 top jobs at Fortune 500 companies were held by women, although this is improved from 1% a decade before. At the current rate of increase, gender equity will be reached in the executive suite in the year 2466 (p. 264). Evidence suggests that women continue to be underrepresented in top positions in the workplace as we enter the 21st century (Rider, 2000). For example, Kail and Cavanaugh (2000) reviewed current research on women in top positions in the workplace in the 1990s and found that the "glass ceiling" exists in private corporations, government agencies, and nonprofit organizations.

A combination of role plays, discussion groups, and effective use of audiovisual material is recommended for accomplishing the specific tasks of this intervention. A speaker who is willing to share experiences can also be effective. "How to listen" exercises and clarification of differences among assertiveness, nonassertiveness, and aggressive behavior are important segments of this strategy. Other learning outcomes include (1) effective methods of communicating in a working environment, (2) identifying and understanding authority lines in typical organizations, (3) effective group decision-making techniques, (4) factors contributing to good worker-supervisor relationships, (5) understanding the role of the informal group in a typical organization, and (6) effective methods of establishing rapport with peer affiliates.

Following are some representative resource materials that may be used for this intervention component:

Corporate Quality Universities: Lesson in Building a World-Class Force
Jeanne C. Meister
American Society for Training and Development
1640 King Street
Box 1443
Alexandria, VA 22313-2043

Gendered Lives: Communication, Gender, and Culture
Julia T. Wood
Wadsworth Publishing Company
Belmont, CA 94002

Women and Corporations—Breaking In Women and Corporations—Moving Up
(two videotapes)
National Innovative Media Co.
Route #2 Box 301B
Calhoun, KY 42327
800-962-6662

Women in Business (videotape)
Cambridge Educational
P.O. Box 2153
Charleston, WV 25328-2153
800-468-4227

Intervention Component III—Lifestyle Skills

To learn that every person is unique and should be considered as an individual who has certain aptitudes, interests, and aspirations is the primary purpose of this intervention strategy. Women especially have more control over their lives than ever before. We have not yet reached the ultimate androgynous society, but we have taken giant steps away from gender-role stereotypes. The time has come for all women to consider their individual needs in determining their lifestyles. What should be communicated is that every woman is an individual who has certain strengths and weaknesses and, like everyone else, is unique. The challenge is to clarify the uniqueness (self-image, skills, and aspirations) and to project those characteristics into work, family, and life planning.

In this intervention component, special attention is directed toward goal setting from an individualized frame of reference. Identifying and clarifying individual strengths and weaknesses through self-concept exercises is recommended. Assertiveness training with emphasis on interpersonal work relationships is another technique for accomplishing the tasks of this strategy. Individual personality development could be explored through discussion of background experiences, including those involving family, peers, school, and other life events.

Special consideration should be given to the task of identifying and clarifying dual-career family problems (Pleck, 1985). Rapoport and Rapoport (1978) identified five areas of stress common to couples who are both pursuing full-time careers and have at least one child: (1) *overload dilemmas* (the management of household and child-rearing activities), (2) *personal norm dilemmas* (conflicts arising from what parents consider proper lifestyle and what other individuals consider proper), (3) *identity dilemmas* (intrinsic conflicts associated with life roles), (4) *social network dilemmas* (conflicts associated with relatives, friends, and other associates), and (5) *role cycle dilemmas* (conflicts associated with family life cycles such as birth of a child, child leaving home, and other domestic issues that produce stress on career development). Suggested solutions include shared responsibility exercises, time-management techniques, and effective planning between parents who have discussed and established individual and family priorities.

The following representative materials may be used for this component:

The Three-Career Couple: Mastering the Art of Juggling Work, Home, and Family
Peterson's Guides
202 Carnegie Center
P.O. Box 2123
Princeton, NJ 08543-2123

Planning for Work
Catalyst
220 Park Avenue South
New York, NY 10003
Fax: 212-477-4252

Sex, Career and Family
Sage Publications, Inc.
2455 Teller Rd.
Thousand Oaks, CA 91320

American Lifestyles
Vocational Biographies, Inc.
Sauk Centre, MN 56378
Phone: 800-255-0752
Fax: 320-352-5546

The Best Jobs in America for Parents
Ballantine Books
201 E. 50th St.
New York, NY 10022
Phone: 800-733-3000
Fax: 212-872-8026

Working Parents: Balancing Kids and Careers
(videotape)
The Learning Seed
330 Telser Road
Lake Zurich, IL 60047

Intervention Component IV—Support and Follow-Up

A follow-up intervention strategy provides support through either group participation or individual visits. The primary purpose of this strategy is to reinforce
those skills learned from other intervention components. The need for this component is underscored by research that suggests that women have difficulty finding acceptance of their abilities to contribute significantly in a working
environment. In fact, more than likely they will experience rejection and isolation, which often leads to withdrawal and the subsequent assumption of a more
passive position (Wilcox-Matthew & Minor, 1989). In addition, women who are
actively expressing their needs through a career might also receive negative reactions from spouse, family members, relatives, and friends (Sigelman & Shaffer,
1995). Research indicates that the chances are high that a woman will experience difficulty in attaining fulfillment in a career because many of her associates
will strongly suggest that she change her position. Because of the potential negative feedback from associates, friends, relatives, and spouse, reinforcement is
considered an essential strategy in counseling women.

The specific task suggests that problems that could be encountered ought to
be identified and clarified. In the process of clarification, a recycling through one

or more of the intervention components may prove valuable. For example, more effective methods of home management might be needed, or a reformulation of goals might be required. The follow-up intervention strategy provides support as well as problem identification associated with work, family, and personal goals. Exercises that promote problem identification and provide subsequent alternative solutions are recommended.

Counselor Bias

During the 1970s, there was an explosion of research concerning counselor bias—more specifically, that is, gender bias that frequently occurs in career counseling by both male and female counselors. The problem centered around the charge that counselors of both sexes dissuade women from choosing a traditionally masculine role. Betz and Fitzgerald (1987) conducted an excellent review of the literature from the 1970s through the mid-1980s and concluded that the methodology and other factors make the results less than definite. The authors suggest that some sex-role bias among counselors did exist during this time, but the research results do not necessarily substantiate this conclusion.

Although all research findings do not point to gender discrimination among counselors, there appears to be sufficient evidence that counselors need to give more consideration to an androgynous model (counseling free of gender roles) in their career counseling approaches. More specifically, all career options in educational programs should be made available as a viable part of career exploration for all individuals, regardless of their genders. Counselors should be challenged to evaluate their personal views of the world of work and to understand that others may have legitimately different views.

The federal law requirements in Titles VII and IX, identified earlier in this chapter, should be carefully reviewed by career counselors for their counseling implications. One major implication is that women must be informed about the equal opportunities provided by these acts. More explicitly, women should not be dissuaded by counselors from considering any career for which they are qualified. In addition, women should be encouraged to feel free to pursue jobs that were traditionally reserved for men only. Finally, women should be encouraged to seek admission to educational or training programs for which they qualify. Clearly, counselors should be supportive of women and foster equal opportunities in employment, wages, and educational/training programs.

Gender Bias and Gender Fairness of Interest Assessment

Since the mid 1970s, a considerable body of literature has been published on issues of gender bias and unfairness of career interest measurement. A major issue has been the limited career options available for women forecast by the results of interest measures. In the meantime, the American Psychological Association

(APA) has addressed sex bias in its publication of ethical principles (APA, 1990). This prestigious national association focused on "individual and role differences" in mental health practices—more specifically in this context, "role differences" associated with gender. Much earlier, in the 1970s, the National Institute of Education (NIE) voiced its concern about sex bias found in interest inventories; this group argued that occupational options are limited primarily on the basis of gender (Diamond, 1975). Thus, the concern about sex bias has been pervasive in the mental health professions and continues to be the focus for career service providers when using interest inventory results.

As the debate about sex bias in interest inventories continues to evolve, the issues have remained basically the same. First, do men and women have different interests? Fouad and Spreda (1995), Harmon and Meara (1994), and Hansen, Collins, Swanson, and Fouad (1993) all agree that men and women *still differ* in the way they endorse interest inventory items. For instance, women are influenced to endorse items according to their socialization—that is, by what is considered appropriately feminine, such as nurturance, caring, warmth, and expression of emotion—the results of which may reinforce traditional occupations for women (Betz, 1994a). Thus, interest inventory results might not reflect actual differences between men and women for occupational groups or for specific occupations (Fouad & Spreda, 1995). Therefore, specific items on interest inventories require careful scrutiny to determine whether they appropriately represent interests of both genders. Second, are interest inventories constructed with the assumption that work is dichotomized into man's work and woman's work or, in the language of measurement, is there content bias? For instance, items that encourage role stereotyping, such as "salesman" or "policeman," should be omitted (Hackett & Lonborg, 1994). As Betz (1992a) points out, the main problem of sex restrictiveness in interest inventory results is that different score patterns for men and women encourage gender-stereotypic occupations.

Other psychometric qualities, such as the internal structure of inventories, could be another source of bias. For example, how raw scores are converted to norms used in profile interpretation could contribute to bias (Hackett & Lonborg, 1994). In recent years, publishers have restructured and revised their inventories to lessen this problem. Although improvements have been made in the psychometric quality of tests, however, this does not automatically translate into using the results of instruments in a fair manner.

A related issue is whether to use raw, same-sex, or sex-balanced inventory scores. According to Holland, Fritsche, and Powell (1994), the role of interest inventories is to provide a reflection of the current interests men and women have; when standardized scores are used, the interests become modified and reality becomes obscured. Spokane and Holland (1995) obviously endorse raw scores as a most effective method of interpreting the results of interest inventories. Fouad and Spreda (1995) and Prediger and Swaney (1995) argue that whereas raw scores might reflect reality, they might also endorse occupational segregation for women or sex-restrictive options. It appears that the argument boils down to the suggestion that raw scores should be used because they accurately reflect vocational aspirations of men and women that could differ because of their life histories, whereas Fouad and Spreda (1995) and Betz (1992a) suggest that other methods be used to increase a wider range of options for women.

Yet another issue involves the norm reference groups used for interpreting completed interest inventories. More explicitly, the prevailing question is whether sex bias in interest inventories can be most effectively overcome through separate norms (reference group by gender, often referred to as same-sex norms) or combined-gender norms (reference groups combining males and females). Same-sex norms have the advantage of having one's score compared with patterns of interest of others who have similar gender-related socialization experiences. For instance, a woman can view her scores in reference to both male and female samples. Also, same-sex norms provide more options for exploration of interests (Hansen, 1990). Separate sex norms for men and women have been developed for the *Strong Interest Inventory* (SII) and the *Kuder Occupational Interest Survey*. Both inventories plan to expand the number of feminine occupational scales as more data become available about women in different occupational roles.

Finally, the argument about whether to use gender-based norms or raw scores may simply be negotiated by the *purpose* of the assessment. For instance, if the purpose of assessment is to increase an individual's options by including those typically underrepresented by his or her gender, then one would use gender norms and explain the purpose of their use to the client. Conversely, if the purpose of assessment is to measure congruence with respect to individuals in an occupation or a major field of study, then one could use raw scores. In this respect, both men and women are provided with a broader range of options, and thus gender bias is not viewed as exclusively a matter of women's interests.

According to Prediger and Swaney (1995), one way of reducing sex bias in interest inventories is by using sex-balanced scales found in the UNIACT, an interest inventory published by the American College Testing Company. This instrument was designed to measure basic interests common to occupations while "minimizing the effects of sex-role connotations" (Prediger & Swaney, 1995, p. 432). This inventory included items that were considered typical of male and female role socialization; items that produced an appreciable difference in response by gender were eliminated. The rationale is that sex-balanced items will elicit similar responses from men and women, thereby eliminating different sets of scales. Prediger and Swaney argued that different sets of occupational scales for men and women perpetuate sex-role stereotyping because such tests inherently suggest that some work is typically male-oriented and other work is typically female-oriented.

What we have here are difficult decisions for the career counselor regarding which inventory is most appropriate for specific clients. Perhaps a compromise is the best solution. Betz (1993) suggests that the counselor use both a same-sex norm inventory and a sex-balanced inventory. The basis for this recommendation is that using both sets of norms will likely provide more options for career exploration (Zunker & Osborn, 2002).

Summary

1. Women are reassessing their career priorities and are looking beyond the traditional feminine working roles. Even though women are being

given greater opportunities to expand their career choices, however, barriers to the changing role of women in the working world still exist.

2. Super was one of the major career development theorists who addressed career development patterns of women. Ginzberg denoted three lifestyle dimensions—traditional, transitional, and innovative—in career counseling approaches for women. Zytowski labeled vocational developmental patterns of women as *mild vocational, moderate vocational,* and *unusual vocational.* Sanguiliano suggested that a woman's life cycle does not follow a rigid progression of developmental tasks and that attention should focus on unique paths women take to break away from gender-role stereotyping. Spencer supported Sanguiliano's denial that women's development follows the rigid progression suggested by life-stage theorists. Spencer contended that feminine developmental tasks are unlike masculine tasks and that women follow a unique pattern of development. Chusmir suggested that personality and motivational traits of women who choose nontraditional occupations are formed by the time they are teenagers.

3. The emerging trend toward equalization suggests specially designed career counseling programs for women. Special career counseling needs for women are job search skills, occupational information, self-concept clarification, help managing dual roles, assertiveness training, information on a variety of working environments, lifestyle clarification, and development toward a value of independence. Women are socialized in a particular culture, so we should incorporate ethnicity in career development of women and into counseling strategies.

4. The family stereotype of a homemaking mother and a breadwinning father is no longer typical. In greater numbers women are assuming the dual roles of homemaker and worker. Managing both roles has created conflicts for women, especially in meeting their own individual needs.

5. Career counseling approaches should be androgynous; that is, free of gender-role stereotyping. Counseling intervention components include job search skills, working climate, lifestyle skills, and support and follow-up. Career counseling should also include approaches designed to integrate needs of ethnic women.

6. Developmental strategies for girls prepare them for career-related events that are highly probable during their life spans. Counseling intervention components can assist girls in overcoming gender-role stereotyping and can include identifying successful career women as role models and mentors.

7. Issues of gender bias and gender fairness of interest assessment are indeed complex and involve numerous technical problems such as test item development and norm references, as well as issues concerning societal changes. Guidelines developed for assessing gender bias and gender fairness in career interest inventories primarily encourage both males and females to consider all career and educational opportunities.

Supplementary Learning Exercises

1. Support or disagree with Spencer's contention that feminine developmental tasks are unlike masculine tasks. Back up your arguments through interviews with at least two women.

2. Interview a woman who has had a successful career. Identify her reactions to the gender-role stereotyping of women and to the barriers that still exist for the woman in the working world. If she is married, ask her how she has managed the dual career of homemaker and career woman.

3. Write to the Women's Bureau (Employment Standards Administration, U.S. Department of Labor, Washington, DC 20402) and request materials developed to promote equalization for women in the work force. Indicate how several examples of materials may be used in career counseling programs for women.

4. Divide the class into three groups and identify and clarify dual-career family problems. One group considers problems associated with the husband, another group considers problems associated with the wife, and the third group considers problems associated with other family members. Build counseling components for solving the identified problems.

5. Visit a women's center and obtain descriptions of career-related counseling programs. Summarize your findings and point out the potential use of the women's center as a referral source.

6. Develop a list jointly or independently of the early socialization processes that promote gender-role stereotyping. Explain how this information can be used in career counseling programs for women.

7. Develop a scenario to be used for emphasizing gender-role stereotyping in a work setting. Present it to the class for critique.

8. Develop a list of questions that women are typically asked in a job interview. Provide guidelines for answering these questions.

9. Interview at least two women who are currently holding nontraditional jobs. Summarize the problems they have faced and their recommendations to other women.

10. Using the counseling components developed for women in this chapter, develop strategies for one or more components designed to accomplish the specific tasks.

For More Information

Basow, S. A. (1992). *Gender: Stereotypes and roles* (3rd ed.). Pacific Grove, CA: Brooks/ Cole.

Eccles, J. S. (1993). School and family effects on the ontogeny of children's interests, self-perceptions, and activity choices. In Gilbert, L. A. (1993). *Two careers/one family.* Newbury Park, CA: Sage.

Eccles, J. S., Barber, B., & Jozefowicz, D. (1999). Linking gender to educational, occupational, and recreational choices: Applying the Eccles et al. Model of achievement-related choices. In W. B. Swann, J. H. Langlois, & L. A. Gilbert (Eds.), *Sexism and stereotypes in modern society* (pp. 153–192). Washington, DC: American Psychological Association.

Hansen, L. S. (1997). *Integrative life planning: Critical tasks for career development and changing life patterns.* San Francisco: Jossey-Bass.

Lott, B. E. (1994). *Women's lives: Themes and variations in gender* (2nd ed.). Pacific Grove, CA: Brooks/Cole.

Philpot, C. L., Brooks, G. R., Lusterman, D., & Nutt, R. L. (1997). *Bridging separate worlds: Why men and women clash and how therapists can bring them together.* Washington, DC: American Psychological Association.

Rider, E. A. (2000). *Our voices: Psychology of women.* Pacific Grove, CA: Wadsworth.

Spence, J. T. (1999). Thirty years of gender research: A personal chronicle. In W. B. Swann, J. H. Langlois, & L. A. Gilbert (Eds.), *Sexism and stereotypes in modern society* (pp. 255–290). Washington, DC: American Psychological Association.

Wood, J. T. (1994). *Gendered lives: Communication, gender, and culture.* Belmont, CA: Wadsworth.

12

Special Issues in Career Counseling for Men

Chapter Highlights

- *Influences on gender-role development issues of men*
- *Men's special needs for career counseling*
- *Some multicultural perspectives when working with men*
- *Implications for career counseling of men*
- *Some intervention components for career counseling of men*

THE PREVIOUS CHAPTER EXAMINED THE RECENT CHANGES IN WORKING roles for women. It stands to reason that when there are role changes for one sex, pressure develops toward changes for the other. Since the beginning of the feminist movement, men have reexamined their roles, beliefs, and values regarding their relationships with women. Basow (1992), Wood (1994), and Rider (2000), among others, suggest that men do not have an easy time adjusting to the egalitarian movement toward equal rights for women in the workplace and in other areas in our society.

To change their perspective of what is an appropriate masculine role, men will have to modify their beliefs that they are supposed to dominate women. Moreover, the change in lifestyle for men will be difficult because they are the products of a socialization process that mandates that men should be aggressive and competitive, acting as protectors and providers. It is no surprise, then, that men are confused when faced with a new set of values suggesting that the traditional masculine role should be significantly modified.

In this chapter, we examine the socialization process that has shaped men's lives and influenced their perspective on appropriate masculine roles. We attempt to understand why men have adopted stereotyped behavioral roles that are not conducive to equality and cooperation in the working environment. We attempt to analyze why men behave so aggressively in their attempts to gain career achievement and success. The answers to these questions are related to career counseling procedures designed to help men meet the demands of their career and their life roles in a changing society.

We begin this chapter with a discussion of the influence of parents, school, and media on gender-role development. Next, the special needs of men are identified and discussed. In the final part, four intervention components are presented and analyzed.

Influences on Gender-Role Development

This section examines three sets of influences on gender-role development: parents, the schools, and the media.

Parental Influence

The purpose of this section is to determine whether parents treat boys and girls differently and the effects, if any, that parents' reactions to children have on gender-role stereotyping. An introduction to research studies that attempt to answer these questions is a good starting point for understanding the socialization process children experience from interaction with important adults in their environment. Insights into potential reasons that individuals behave the way they do is relevant information for career counselors.

According to Basow (1992), the preference for male children over female children is a worldwide phenomenon. In some cultures, female infants are swiftly disposed of following birth (French, 1992; Neff & Levine, 1997). Thus, it should not be surprising that many pregnant women place a higher value on giving birth to a boy than to a girl. These parental attitudes are relayed to children as gender stereotypes that affect children's development (Rider, 2000). For example, Lindsey (1990) supports the concept of differential parental attitudes toward infants, finding that parents regard boys as sturdier than girls and tend to play more roughly with baby boys. Evidence supports the contention that parents expect sons to be more active and aggressive and daughters to be passive and nonassertive (Basow, 1992).

Solomon (1982) contended that the growing boy is surrounded by a multiplicity of social influences, including parental attitudes, that facilitate his internalization of the masculine role. For example, parents tend to choose different types of toys for boys than for girls (Wood, 1994). Although this method of gender typing has decreased in recent years, parental choice of toys continues to be based on perceived appropriate gender roles (Lytton & Romney, 1991).

Differential parental expectations of boys and girls may, to some extent, influence career choices and other roles children envision for themselves. Parents as models and children's tendencies to identify with same-sex parents are powerful gender stereotypes that lead children to prescribe to certain roles they have observed. Boys are vigorously socialized into gender by their fathers; fathers and men in general appear to enforce appropriate roles on children more intensely than women do (Chodorow, 1989; Wood, 1994). For example, fathers tend to attribute independence and aggressiveness to boys and passivity and dependence to girls. Boys look to their fathers as role models that define manhood for them; they emulate fathers' examples to become masculine.

According to cognitive development theory, once gender identity is developed, much behavior is organized around it (Lindsey, 1990). Parents who have been gender-role socialized provide models for their children, who actively seek identification with the same-sex parent. As boys learn gender concepts, there is an increasing agreement with adult stereotypes (Leahy & Shirk, 1984). Thus, home tasks that parents consider appropriate for boys and girls reinforce learned gender-role concepts. Rosenwasser (1982) suggested that although there are changes in mothers' perceptions of appropriate tasks for girls and boys, tasks still tend to be gender typed.

School Influence

The process of formal education further reinforces expectations learned in the home. Elementary school is often described as being very feminine in that most teachers are women, thus providing feminine models for children (Rosenwasser, 1982; Tracy, 1990). Moreover, evidence suggests that teachers in elementary school treat boys and girls differently (Sadker & Sadker, 1994). After reviewing research on this subject, Doyle (1983) found that boys were encouraged to be more aggressive than girls were, whereas girls were more likely to be noticed for dependent, clinging behaviors. Boys are portrayed as being resourceful, brave, and creative, whereas girls are portrayed as passive, helpless, and dull (Scott, 1981).

According to Etaugh and Liss (1992), our educational system has a significant influence on the development of gender-stereotyped work roles. "Feminine-appropriate" courses are language, home economics, and typing; boys are encouraged to take math and science courses. Sadker and Sadker (1994) argue that teachers respond differently to boys and girls in all grade levels, K–12, partly because teacher-education training books are gender biased.

Wood (1994) also suggests that schools reinforce gender-role stereotypes in their curriculum by making women's achievements invisible. For instance, men's accomplishments are highlighted in curricular materials, whereas women's roles are often excluded. Thus, more attention given to males emphasizes that males are more important than females and that they are more able than females to lead and exert influence. Following this logic, men are to be the chief executive officers, whereas women are more suited for supportive roles.

The appropriate future work role is made clear by educators and counselors, who further socialize boys and girls to conform to the established norms society has fostered. Teachers and counselors who endorse traditional gender-role behavior directly influence the choice of career options, and the message is clear to the boy that much more is expected of him in career achievement.

Media Influence

Television

By 1991, most U.S. households (98.3%) owned a television, and approximately two-thirds of households owned one or more sets. In addition, 60.2% had installed cable television (Television Bureau of Advertising, 1991, cited in Wood, 1994). Although many children and adolescents watch television on the average of 2 to $3\frac{1}{2}$ hours a day, some watch as much as 7 hours (Nielsen Media Research, 1989). Relevant here is that masculine and feminine roles children observe on television programs can affect their perceptions of reality and of what is appropriate for adults to do in the real world (Signorielli & Lears, 1992). As Wood (1994) points out, media are the "gatekeepers of information and images" (p. 231). Furthermore, the media greatly influence how we perceive gender roles (Thompson & Zerbinos, 1997).

Several researchers have charged that television programs continue to reiterate the gender stereotyping of women as dependent and passive, as needing to look good to please men, and as greatly involved in relationships or housework (Davis, 1990; Heaton & Wilson, 1995; Pareles, 1990; Skill, 1994; Woodman, 1991). Conversely, children's television shows typically portray men as aggressive, dominant, and involved in masculine accomplishments. Men are also seen in high-status positions, whereas women are expected to be younger, very physically attractive, and less outspoken than males. In sum, children see more males in significant roles, whereas females are usually relegated to minor roles with little responsibility concerning the outcome of a story (Spicher & Hudak, 1997; Wood, 1994).

Television commercials also contribute to children's perceptions of appropriate gender-role stereotypes (Jones, 1991). Products advertised by men represent a broad variety of uses and depict men in more dominant roles or as tough and rugged, as in the "Marlboro man." On the other hand, women have been used to advertise products used in kitchens or bathrooms (Furnham & Bitar, 1993).

Books

Substantial evidence indicates that boys and girls are highly stereotyped in children's books as well (Nelson, 1990). St. Peter (1979) reviewed 206 children's books and grouped them into the following three categories: books published before the women's movement, books published since the women's movement, and books selected from nonstereotyped lists (*Little Miss Muffett Fights Back*) of books about girls. Her results revealed that boys were the central character twice as often as girls were in the first two categories of children's books. Furthermore, boys were pictured more often—a 3:2 ratio—on the covers of the books reviewed. The titles of books in the first two categories used boys more often than girls by more than 2:1. Interestingly, St. Peter found that, with the exception of books from nonstereotyped lists, the proportion of boys to girls on the covers of children's books has increased since the women's movement. An examination of the character roles portrayed in children's books indicated that girls were more expressive than boys, whereas boys were more likely to be portrayed as fulfilling goals.

In a more recent study of children's books, Purcell and Stewart (1990) concluded that significant differences still appear in how male and female roles are presented. Males continue to be presented as clever, brave, adventurous, and as primary breadwinners, while females continue to be presented as passive, victimized, and goal-constricted (Allen, Allen, & Sigler, 1993). Basow (1992) argues that because males have greater visibility in children's readers and are given more active roles than females are—especially in occupations—stereotyped gender roles are reinforced.

Identifying Men's Special Needs

The emerging trend toward androgyny will create a need for counseling programs to help men reevaluate their roles, beliefs, and values in all areas of their lifestyles, including their relationships with women in the home and workplace. Rabinowitz and Cochran (1994) and Lott (1994), among others, point out that the idea of androgyny has freed both men and women to consider alternative lifestyle behaviors and gives both the opportunity to acknowledge their masculine and feminine qualities. Career counselors need to be especially concerned with social changes that affect career development and interpersonal relationships in the home and at work.

Fear of Femininity

Researchers seem to agree that men's fear of being perceived as feminine has been indoctrinated through gender-role socialization (O'Neil, 1982, 1990; Solomon, 1982). Gender-role socialization has created a masculine/feminine polarity, as found by a prominent research group (Levinson et al., 1978) and more recently by Levinson (1996). O'Neil (1982) summarized the roles associated with masculine/feminine polarity as follows. Masculinity is associated with the following:

1. Power, exercising control over others; (and being recognized as) a person of strong will, a leader who "gets things done"

2. Strength, bodily prowess, toughness, and stamina to undertake long, grueling work and endure severe bodily stress without quitting

3. Logical and analytical thought, intellectual competence, understanding of how things work

4. Achievement, ambition, success at work, getting ahead, earning one's fortune for the sake of self and family

Femininity is associated with the following:

1. Weak, frail, submissive, and unassertive behavior; victimized by others who have more power and are ready to use it exploitatively; limited bodily resources to sustain a persistent effort toward valued goals

2. Emotions, intuition; likelihood of making decisions on the basis of feelings rather than careful analysis

3. Building a nest, taking care of needs of husband and children

4. Homosexuality (pp. 21–22)

According to the Levinson research team (Levinson et al., 1978; Levinson, 1996), the integration of masculine/feminine polarity is usually achieved during midlife because younger men tend to identify strongly with the stereotypic masculine characteristics and are reinforced by cultural conditions. The Levinson studies suggest that evolving tasks in early adulthood make it difficult for men to deviate from learned masculine roles.

Other investigators have concentrated on problems associated with fear of femininity (Cochran, 1994; O'Neil, 1982, 1990). O'Neil (1982) suggested that the fear of femininity among men contributes to their obsession with achievement and success and is associated with (1) restrictive self-disclosure (fear their thoughts and actions will be associated with femininity), (2) health problems arising from conflicts, and (3) stress and strain.

Skovholt (1990), who researched gender differences in self-disclosure, concluded that men tend to avoid emotional intimacy with one another. Furthermore, he suggested that women were more willing than men were to disclose to intimates. Another of these conclusions suggests that fear of femininity is one of the major factors that contributes to men's avoidance of emotional intimacy. Clearly, the fear of femininity is an appropriate topic in helping men understand the effects of their gender-role socialization.

Placing Achievement and Success in Perspective

According to Russo, Kelly, and Deacon (1991), men are conditioned to perceive career success and achievement as primary measurements of manhood and masculinity. These researchers suggested that a man's work represents his status in society and is the primary base for measuring success over the life span. Basow (1992) pointed out that men are conditioned to be overly competitive, ambitious, and status-seeking because these are the qualities associated with successful men. Furthermore, a man's obsessive work behavior stimulates him to seek power and control and to become overly aggressive (Tannen, 1990). Men who exhibit obsessive patterns of work behavior clearly need counseling assistance to help them place achievement and success in perspective.

Learning to Relax

Highly valued masculine traits (such as competitiveness, independence, and self-reliance) make it difficult for men to learn to relax (Solomon, 1982). Masculinity is associated with work that consumes energy and imposes stress. Being passive is considered feminine and drives men to constant activity. Solomon (1982) suggested that men's leisure activities are not always conducive to relaxation. For example, a "friendly" game of tennis or golf often turns into a highly competitive activity that is not compatible with relaxation.

Learning to relax during leisure time appears to be an important need for men who are overly ambitious and competitive. Kail and Cavanaugh (2000) suggested that when there is a balance between work and leisure, leisure is a definite source of need satisfaction. Herr and Cramer (1996) contended that choice and control of leisure is important to self-esteem and holistic health. Career counselors can provide a valuable service by helping individuals determine practical, satisfying, and relaxing sources of leisure. Leisure counseling, as suggested by Leclair (1982) and McDaniels (1990), is a productive activity for professional counselors. Leisure counseling activities include (1) value clarification of work and leisure, (2) interest and attitude clarification, (3) identification of leisure opportunities, and (4) application of decision-making skills.

Restrictive Emotionality

As a result of research in the 1970s (Skovholt, 1978) and more recently (Skovholt, 1990), Skovholt has determined that emotional expression and self-disclosure are serious problems for men. Lindsey (1990), while concentrating on the social perspective of gender-role development, contended that expression of grief, pain, or weakness is perceived to be unmanly. The fear of being perceived as unmanly makes many men resist being open, honest, and expressive, for such expressions are considered an open admission of vulnerability and loss of control so important to the masculine role (Rabinowitz & Cochran, 1994). O'Neil (1982) believed that restrictive emotionality is one of the leading causes of poor interpersonal relationships between men, between men and women, and between men and children. These authors suggest that men and women have developed two different styles and levels of communication: Men deemphasize interpersonal relationships in communication, whereas women tend to be more expressive and more concerned with interpersonal processes. Different levels and styles of communication can lead to misunderstandings and conflicts in many social situations, including interactions in the home and the workplace.

Dealing with Competition

Some men have been socialized to be highly competitive; winning is perceived as important to maintaining the masculine role (Smith & Inder, 1993). In other words, men validate their masculinity through competition at work. Intense competition among men in the workplace can result in some men being very reluctant to be honest with their peers and having difficulties in developing interpersonal relationships. That is, intense competition among men may be highly related to stressful work environments and work anxiety (Lowman, 1993; O'Neil, 1982).

As discussed in Chapter 19, work environments in the United States have changed dramatically. Workers at all levels are worrying about survival as more organizations downsize their work force. Men as well as women feel stress from occupational insecurity in the workplace climate. Many are competing by working longer hours and for less pay to maintain job status (Roskies & Louis-Guerin, 1990). Future organizations could require more cooperation among workers, and workers will be required to deal with a wider variety of assignments and other workers (Hammer & Champy, 1993). In such work environments, openness and honesty with peer affiliates are important qualities to foster.

Learning to Recognize Self-Destructive Behavior

Closely related to issues of dealing with competition are behaviors that lead to health care problems. One pattern of work overcommitment is the widely studied Type A behavioral pattern. Friedman and Rosenman (1974), and more recently Strube (1991), conceptualized a model of how men behave in the workplace and designated the two masculine styles of functioning as Type A and Type B. Type A persons have an accelerated overall lifestyle, with involvement in multiple functions. They are overcommitted to their vocations or professions, have an intense drive for achievement, and develop feelings of guilt when relaxing. Other characteristics include excessive drive, impatience, competitiveness, restlessness; abrupt speech; nervous gestures; and rapid walking, eating, and moving. Type B persons are the opposite. They are characterized as serene, having the ability to relax, and lacking a sense of time urgency.

According to Thompson, Grisanti, and Pleck (1987), there is more Type A behavior in males than in females. Greenglass (1991), however, found that professional women were predominantly Type A. Type A behavior has been linked to cardiovascular problems; workers who experience stress may have a higher rate of heart disease than non–Type A workers (Baker, Dearborn, Hastings, & Hamberger,

1988; Houston & Kelly, 1987). More recently, a five-year study at the Duke University Medical Center found that mental stress could hold the key to future heart problems. The major conclusion is that reducing abnormal responses to mental stress can lead to a reduction of cardiac problems (Jiang et al., 1996).

In the workplace, Type A individuals have an intense sense of time urgency and attempt to participate in most tasks, job assignments, and events that are ongoing in the workplace. Type A individuals give the impression that they can meet all challenges and successfully cope with any challenge, especially at work. Goldfried and Friedman (1982) suggest a program of cognitive restructuring as an effective intervention to modify Type A behavior. In cognitive restructuring, individuals learn to recognize behaviors that are self-destructive by acknowledging unrealistic and irrational beliefs that have reinforced their Type A behavior patterns. Counseling sessions, designed to promote cognitive restructuring, help them identify anxiety-arousing situations so they can take steps to modify their behavior (Doyle, 1992). Relaxation training, developed by Wolpe (1958), is another method of helping Type A individuals deal with anxieties.

Changing Male Roles in Dual-Career Homes

In a provocative study of dual-career couples, Wilcox-Matthew and Minor (1989) pointed out some concerns, benefits, and counseling implications. Because men have been socialized to play the role of "king of the hill," they can have difficulty sharing family roles and feeling comfortable in a nurturing role. One major issue is the management of household tasks. Counselors need to encourage men to share household duties, particularly in dual-career homes. The concept of shared responsibility is a step toward accepting new learning patterns that might require shifting roles for both husbands and wives in dual-career homes. (Chapter 13 discusses men in dual-career marriages in more depth.)

Needs of Househusbands

In the 40-year span from 1940 to 1980, the percentage of employed mothers with children under age 18 rose from 8.6% to 56.6% (Hoffman, 1983). Another dramatic social change is the fact that, in 1950, 12% of married women with children under age 6 worked outside the home, and in 1991 that figure reached 57% (Chadwick & Heaton, 1992).

These figures underscore the possibility of more involvement among men in primary and shared household/child care activities. A significant question involves how men react to the role of househusband. In the scanty literature that exists, there is evidence of resentment among fathers involved in paternal caretaking (Lamb, Frodi, Hwang, & Frodi, 1982). Russell (1982) reported that fathers involved in shared care giving were bored with their roles, desired adult interaction, and were pressured by male peers. On the other hand, Russell (1982), Radin (1983), and Sagi (1982) found that shared caregiving fathers experienced an enhanced father-child relationship.

Perhaps men need to be made aware of the benefits of primary and shared responsibility for household/child care activities. In a study of 16 fathers who had assumed 50% or more of the responsibility of child care and household tasks, Rosenwasser and Patterson (1984) found that all but one indicated that they would recommend their lifestyles to other men. The results of this study provide some encouragement for men who assume the role of househusband.

As we learn more about the problems men face with child care and household tasks, appropriate guidelines for counseling consideration should emerge. In the meantime, counseling considerations for househusbands can include methods for dealing with ridiculing peers, boredom, household management, role conflict, and balancing household tasks with career.

Needs of Divorced Men

In the preceding chapter, the needs of divorced women were identified and discussed. Divorced men have similar needs. In particular, men who have dependent children will find that balancing the responsibilities of parenthood and managing a home with the responsibilities of work is a definite need. Halle (1982) studied 26 men whose wives filed for divorce and identified the following problems these men experienced: depression, self-blame, suicidal ideation, rage, jealousy, stress of new demands, vulnerability, being judged less of a man, and needing help with child-rearing. As with divorced women, men must learn to cultivate composure to effectively meet both home and employment responsibilities.

Men in Nontraditional Careers

Nontraditional occupations, as identified by Chusmir (1990), are those that have less than 30% of the same-sex workers. For example, four careers that are female-dominated (57% women) are social work, nursing, elementary school teaching, and office work. Although there is greater acceptance of men in nontraditional careers, there continue to be prejudice, ridicule, and negative perceptions of the men who choose them. It appears that gender typing of careers is still prevalent in our society, and those who deviate experience the scorn of those whose thinking is dominated by gender-role stereotyping.

The career counselor should make it clear that all careers can be considered in the decision-making process. Both negative and positive aspects of choosing an atypical career should be discussed. The negative aspects have been mentioned; the positive ones include faster opportunities for promotion, upward mobility, and increased compensation (Chusmir, 1990).

Multicultural Perspectives When Working with Men

There is a noticeable absence of research on career development of culturally diverse men. Therefore, our discussion in this section is limited in scope. To begin our discussion, it is most important to remember that there is more diversity within groups than between groups (Rider, 2000). Thus, generalizations about people of color and, in this context, men of color, does not apply to all men that can be identified as members of a certain subgroup being discussed. We can perceive some generalizations as being shared by a culture, but not necessarily by every client from that culture. We are more justified in viewing each client as a unique individual.

Parham (1996) makes the point that African American men value treating others with respect, kindness, and decency. He infers that African American men have not received reciprocal treatment in this country by the white dominant society. He suggests that counselors become active advocates to change discriminatory practices in communities. Furthermore, he suggests that counselors address the oppressions associated with racism and white supremacy directly with the client. Most important, is for counselors to assist African-American men to develop a self-awareness or self-knowledge such that they develop an ability to grow and express themselves openly and freely. Finally, we must "help African-American clients more fully understand, appreciate, and express, their African-ness" (Parham, 1996, p. 188). In essence, selected developmental strategies to help African-Americans include assisting self-concept development, developing more internally directed behavior, becoming more aware of job opportunities, clarifying motivational aspirations, and dealing with ambivalence toward whites.

When the needs of Asian American men are addressed as a group, the tremendous diversity within this group of people should be kept in mind (see Chapter 10). According to Leong (1996b), however, individualism and collectivism are key variables for understanding differences between Asian Americans and Euro-Americans. This is especially true for Asian-Americans who are less acculturated. Asian American men consider family honor more important than personal goals. Decisions are based on what is best for the family.

Client-counselor relationships, especially among less acculturated men must be carefully balanced. For example, Asian Americans expect a hierarchical relationship with counselors. Thus, Asian American men expect a professional relationship rather than an egalitarian one. Other suggested developmental strategies for Asian American men are learning to understand organization systems and bureaucracies, improving communication skills, and learning to understand work environments. Counselors may find that using Asian Americans as role models will enhance the effectiveness of counseling goals.

All Latino subgroups, such as Mexican, Cuban, and Puerto Rican, are quite nationalistic. Gender identity for men is associated with the term machismo, which generally stands for arrogance and sexual aggression in Latino/Latina relationships. Machismo is also associated with men having firm control of their families. This stereotype portrayal of men suggests that more value is placed on boys than on girls in Latino/a culture. However, the reverence of motherhood for women has influenced the trend toward equalization of sexes in the Hispanic cultures (Altarriba & Bauer, 1998; Arredondo, 1996).

Because of the great diversity among Hispanics, counselors should spend considerable time learning about specific cultures from the clients. Suggested developmental strategies for Hispanic American males include learning about effective communication skills, work environments and organizations, the use of career information, job search strategies, and interpersonal relationships. Other suggestions include learning goal-setting and problem-solving skills, developing working-parent skills, and improving financial management of resources.

Native Americans are also a very diverse group of people who have been grossly misunderstood. Native American men have very often been stereotyped as drunkards who sit around the reservation and do little work. This reputation has unfortunately been widespread in this country and in Canada. The most devastating aspect is that the complete blame for alcoholism has been placed on the Native American. One needs to investigate the history of relationship between the U.S. government and Native Americans to fully understand the extent of their losses individually and collectively.

LaFromboise and Jackson (1996) suggest that we return the principle of empowerment to the Native American so that he or she can control his or her own lives: "People are capable of taking control but often choose not to do so because of social forces and institutions that hinder their efforts" (LaFromboise & Jackson, 1996, p. 196). The following strategies are designed to help Native American men maintain their cultural heritage while introducing concepts of career development of the dominate society:

1. Use parents and relatives as counseling facilitators. The rationale for this approach is embedded in the strong family ties of Native Americans.

2. Use Native American role models. They should assist in helping break down resistance to counseling objectives. Native Americans should react more favorably to other Native Americans.

3. Emphasize individual potential in the context of future goals. Identity conflicts make it difficult for Native Americans to project themselves into other environments, including work environments.

Implications for Career Counseling of Men

The preceding sections identified some effects of gender-role conflicts in men. These conflicts are important considerations in counseling men on career development, maintenance, and lifestyle orientation. Particularly valuable are programs that foster the idea that both men and women are gender-role socialized. Generally speaking, men resist self-disclosure more than women do, suggesting a greater need for men to understand socialization processes. The importance of learning about leisure and relaxation techniques suggests programs designed to assist men in identifying and planning for appropriate leisure activities. The problem many men have with putting work achievement in proper perspective and learning to deal with competition suggests programs that delineate differences between aggressiveness and assertiveness. Finally, the concept of dual-career roles needs clarification.

Culturally diverse men have some shared characteristics that need to be addressed in career counseling. Counselors can prepare for these men by learning as much as they can about the client's culture and acculturation level. Counselors should discuss racial issues with clients to learn more about an individual's background. Counselors are encouraged to approach each client as a unique individual who has some shared characteristics with his or her cultural group but also nonshared experiences that have influenced values, beliefs, and interests.

Intervention Components for Counseling Men

The four intervention components that follow (outlined in Table 12-1) address general and specific career issues that arise from gender-role conflicts in men. Within each strategy are specific tasks that can be selected as counseling objectives to meet specific needs or interests of groups or individuals. Likewise, each intervention component may be selected for its special appeal to specific individuals or groups; the interventions need not be offered in any particular sequence. The technique options do not exhaust all possible methods of accomplishing the specific task.

Intervention Component I—Expressiveness Training

The two goals of this strategy are to help individuals identify situations in which it is appropriate to express their emotions and learn that it is acceptable to freely express emotions in those situations. Dosser (1982) reported that men have a more difficult time experiencing their emotional feelings than do women. Specifically, men have more difficulty expressing emotions of happiness, sorrow, tenderness, delight, sadness, and elation. Jourard (1964), who initiated studies of self-disclosure, suggested that men reveal less information about themselves than women do. Research has shown that there is a high correlation between self-disclosure/self-awareness and interpersonal functioning (Dosser, 1982). In general, men devalue what they perceive as feminine traits of gentleness, expressiveness, and responsiveness (O'Neil, 1982; Solomon, 1982). In the work environment, men tend to be much more guarded than women are against revealing weaknesses to fellow workers and resist certain cooperative tasks that could expose their vulnerability (Lindsey, 1990). Inexpressiveness can become highly dysfunctional in many relationships, including those with peer affiliates in the working environment, children, spouse, and friends.

Counselors should recall that some cultural groups, especially Asian Americans and Native Americans, consider someone who shows emotions to be weak or immature. Special considerations should be given to these groups by explaining differences between other cultures and American males who have a European background.

The workshop described for this intervention component should incorporate all or most of the other technique options. For example, inexpressive behavior can be succinctly illustrated through videotaped presentations or other video media. Role clarification exercises can be used to demonstrate the impact of inexpressive behavior on interpersonal relationships. Videotaped feedback can help individuals perceive how others see them. Homework assignments can be quite varied and inclusive and may include an assignment of recording one's behavior for a week and reporting back to a group, or keeping records of the behavior of others. Individual goals and strategies should be identified, and group counseling may be used to provide the counselee with feedback from his peers regarding his progress toward accomplishing established goals. Peer-group interaction is also a valuable means of support for individual and group efforts.

The specific tasks for this intervention component can be sequenced to meet the needs of individuals or groups. The tasks of identifying and clarifying inexpressive behaviors are especially important for men because they have been socialized to regard their inexpressiveness as an appropriate masculine trait. Indeed, these tasks may be used at various times to provide the framework from which men can learn to identify the differences between inexpressiveness and expressive behavior and to judge their progress toward becoming more expressive.

Other tasks to be emphasized by the career counselor are those that direct attention to behaviors that interfere with establishing appropriate interpersonal relationships with fellow workers, family, and friends; expressiveness is an important characteristic for establishing relationships at work, in the home, and during leisure time.

Intervention Component II—Assertiveness Training

Assertiveness training has become immensely popular during the last 20 years, providing a basis for research in the scientific community and training programs for the general public. Programs for women have included assertiveness training to help them achieve individual goals for improving interpersonal relationships. Recognition of the need for special programs for men has led to a reexamination of several existing programs for women—including assertiveness training. Research indicates that men also benefit from programs designed to help them become more assertive (Dosser, 1982; Goldberg, 1983). Wolpe's (1973) discussion of assertive behavior suggested that men generally need to be more assertive when expressing affection, admiration, and praise. Wolpe also suggested that differences between hostile/aggressive behaviors and assertive behaviors need to be delineated. Wolpe pointed out that some individuals might experience embarrassment when expressing affection, admiration, and praise. Goldberg (1983) suggested that men need to learn how to become less competitive and aggressive when interacting with colleagues and spouses.

The specific tasks of this strategy are primarily designed to assist men in clarifying the differences between aggression and assertiveness. The technique options provide several strategies to help men recognize the benefits of appropriately expressing their emotions, thoughts, and beliefs in a direct and honest manner. Assertiveness training can provide behavioral guidelines for men to use in modifying their aggression when interacting with peer affiliates on the job and with their families at home. Examples of appropriate verbal and nonverbal behaviors help men target specific situations in the process of modifying their behaviors. Dosser (1982) suggested that it is advantageous to concentrate on the expression of

TABLE 12-1 INTERVENTION COMPONENTS FOR COUNSELING MEN

Strategy component	Technique options	Specific tasks
I. Expressiveness training	1. Workshop 2. Group and/or individual counseling 3. Role clarification exercises 4. Videotaped feedback 5. Homework assignments	1. Clarify how men's behavior has been shaped through socialization. 2. Identify and clarify inexpressive behavior. 3. Require that each counselee demonstrate an inexpressive behavior. 4. Clarify the advantages of expressive behavior and disadvantages of inexpressive behavior. 5. Clarify the advantages of a less rigid masculine role. 6. Clarify potential problems of inexpressive behavior in the working environment. 7. Clarify potential problems if inexpressive behavior in the home, with colleagues, and with friends. 8. Identify and discuss factors that prohibit expressive behavior. 9. Clarify strategies for becoming more expressive. 10. Demonstrate consequences of inexpressive and expressive behaviors in the work environment. 11. Clarify the differences between self-control and inexpressive behavior. 12. Role-play/rehearse expressive behavior.
II. Assertiveness training	1. Workshop 2. Group and/or individual counseling 3. Role clarification exercises 4. Videotaped feedback 5. Homework assignments	1. Clarify the differences between assertive, aggressive, and unassertive behavior. 2. Develop a philosophy of assertiveness (i.e., one's assertive bill of rights). 3. Identify behavioral expressions that are assertive. 4. Identify behavioral expressions that are aggressive. 5. Identify positive assertive responses to interpersonal situations with friends, fellow, employees, and strangers. 6. Identify the differences between aggressive and passive behaviors. 7. Clarify factors of socialization that inhibit assertiveness. 8. Identify and clarify the concept of self-disclosure.

TABLE 12-1

INTERVENTION COMPONENTS FOR COUNSELING MEN (continued)

Strategy component	Technique options	Specific tasks
III. Dual-career roles	1. Workshop 2. Group and/or individual counseling 3. Role clarification exercises 4. Videotaped presentations 5. Homework assignments	1. Clarify the concept of dual careers. 2. Clarify reasons women have the same rights as men in developing a career. 3. Clarify reasons men have the same rights as women in nurturing their families. 4. Clarify how socialization has determined gender roles in our society. 5. Clarify the concept of an egalitarian marriage. 6. Identify and discuss methods of sharing household management and tasks. 7. Clarify how husband and wife can look on their dual career and work roles as a joint venture. 8. Clarify the role of a "liberated" husband in a dual-career marriage. 9. Identify and clarify fears about possible loss of status or self-esteem among men when adjusting to changing roles in dual-career families. 10. Identify and clarify changing styles of interaction between spouses who both support dual-career concepts. 11. Identify changing attitudes in relation to work and responsibilities in dual-career families. 12. Clarify the family-nurturing role for men in dual-career marriages.
IV. Support groups	1. Group and/or individual counseling 2. Role clarification exercises 3. Videotaped presentations 4. Homework assignments	1. Identify the concept of androgyny. 2. Identify and clarify problems associated with the modification of masculine roles. 3. Identify and clarify problems associated with reactions to the women's movement. 4. Increase understanding of the masculine socialization process. 5. Increase understanding of the feminine socialization process. 6. Identify stereotyped work roles for men and women. 7. Identify and clarify problems men will encounter when they adopt a more androgynous role. 8. Identify and clarify problems associated with maintaining modified behaviors of expressiveness, sharing in dual-career homes, and assertiveness. 9. Identify and clarify the purpose of men's consciousness-raising groups.

positive feelings in assertiveness training. Rich and Schroeder (1976) compiled a list of suggested techniques and procedures for assertiveness training, including developing a philosophy of assertiveness, role playing, role reversal, response practice, constructive criticism, modeling, relaxation, exaggerated role taking, postural and vocal analysis training, and homework assignments. Most of these suggested procedures can be accomplished with the technique options recommended for this intervention component.

Intervention Component III—Dual-Career Roles

In Chapter 11, we learned that an increasing number of women are planning lifelong careers in a wide range of occupations. In their life plans, women are giving career development a higher priority than or at least equal status to other priorities, such as marriage and family. Dual-career families are becoming less novel in the 2000s, but the increased prevalence of this lifestyle has not been accompanied by changes in the values, beliefs, or behavior of many of the men or women in these marriages. Men may have difficulty making the transition from traditional attitudes of man-at-work/woman-at-home to that of negotiating dual-career and family roles. These entrenched attitudes and perceptions of appropriate masculine roles will die slowly because of the long-standing socialization process that has stereotyped gender-role models. The process of change requires recognizing deeply rooted patterns of masculine role behavior and attitudes toward women in general. However, recent evidence indicates that when men are challenged to modify their behavior in dual-career families, they change their attitudes and actions (Biernat & Wortman, 1991; Wilcox-Matthew & Minor, 1989). The recent shift of roles in dual-career families gives this intervention component credibility for helping husbands make adjustments in their attitudes toward their wives' career aspirations, demonstrating advantages of fathers' being able to participate in their children's lives more directly, and encouraging men to assume a greater role in household management responsibilities.

The specific tasks in this strategy are designed to clarify the concept of dual-career families and to introduce changes in male role models. Special attention should be given to identifying and clarifying dual-career family problems as discussed in Intervention Component III—Lifestyle Skills for Women in Chapter 11. Other suggested solutions contained in this strategy for women, such as shared responsibility and role-coping exercises, can also be used in this intervention component for men.

Intervention Component IV—Support Groups

Other counseling considerations may evolve as men begin to reexamine their roles as males. During the process of reexamination, some men may experience a sense of loss of status and self-esteem when confronted with the prospect of egalitarianism. At the beginning of the transition process, husbands might make pseudo attempts at conforming to newly established goals of sharing, but they might continue to consider their wives as being primarily responsible for fulfilling household and family needs. Counselors can use a combination of role playing and discussion groups to encourage men to share these responsibilities. Other special issues that may be addressed include the following: (1) men might place more importance on their careers because they have considered themselves the primary breadwinners, (2) men might react negatively toward women who are successful and strong, (3) men might experience difficulty in changing and modifying the nature of adult relationships, and (4) men might have difficulty adopting different male roles in work and recreation (Stein, 1982). These issues clearly indicate the need for career counselors to provide support groups for men to express their needs in career-related issues and lifestyle concerns. Stein (1982) suggested that support groups for men provide an effective environment for addressing gender-role and career-related issues.

The technique options and specific tasks for this strategy provide the opportunity for men to freely express their emotions. Men should be encouraged to recognize and express emotions and behaviors that are usually associated with the feminine role, such as gentleness, sadness, caretaking, and nurturing. Conversely, they should also be encouraged to express typical masculine role traits of assertiveness, dominance, and competitiveness when appropriate. Both activities provide a rich source for learning how men react and relate to each other when assuming feminine and masculine role models. These experiences should be designed to help men establish caring and empathic interpersonal relationships in the work environment. In essence, men should be encouraged to modify traditional, stereotyped patterns of behavior to build personal relationships that do not require that they resort to rigid, masculine role models.

A men's support group also provides the opportunity to introduce specific topics of interest, such as difficulties in parenting, excessive need to achieve, expressing emotions, sharing household tasks, and competitiveness in the work place. The group can be divided into dyads and triads to discuss specific topics of interest.

The general goal of a men's support group is to change rigid, gender-role masculine behavior so men can build better relationships with women and other men. The peer interaction in men's groups should lead to greater flexibility in all interpersonal relationships. Counselors may want to structure groups by cultural background and let men converse in their native tongues.

Summary

1. Recently, men have begun reexamining their roles, beliefs, and values regarding their relationships with women. Boys exhibit traditional gender-role appropriate behavior at a very early age. The learned framework of societal expectations intensifies in early childhood through social learning from parents, the schools, and the media.

2. Parents expect sons to be more active and aggressive and daughters to be passive and nonassertive. Parents' treatment and expectations of children in early childhood foster developmental patterns that might determine future role behavior.

3. The process of formal education further reinforces expectations of gender-role behavior learned in the home. Our educational system fosters the development of gender-typed work roles.

4. Television programs and commercials, children's books, and comic strips foster the development of gender-typed roles.

5. Special career counseling needs of men include fear of femininity, placing achievement and success in perspective, learning to relax, restrictive emotionality, dealing with competition, learning to recognize self-destructive behaviors, changing roles in dual-career homes, support for househusbands and divorced men, difficulties in nontraditional careers, and culturally related characteristics.

6. Career counseling approaches should be free of gender-role typing. Counseling strategy components include expressiveness training, assertiveness training, dual-career families, and support groups.

Supplementary Learning Exercises

1. Develop a counseling component to help individuals identify typical masculine aggressive responses.

2. Review several history textbooks and identify descriptions of strong, masculine characters.

3. Develop a script that demonstrates the "Sturdy Oak" gender role.

4. Develop a list of masculine roles that interfere with cooperative efforts in the work environment.

5. Interview a husband and wife of a dual-career family to determine the extent of sharing of household planning and duties. Include couples from diverse cultures.

6. Using the dimension of the masculine role descriptions, develop a list of behaviors that are detrimental to career fulfillment, including for people of different cultures.

7. While observing several television programs, develop a list of characters that represent the dimensions of the role appropriate behavior.

8. List your experiences in school that influenced gender-role appropriate behavior.

9. Develop a counseling component that is designed to help men modify their masculine role behavior in the work environment.

10. Develop counseling strategies that could be used to help men deal with competition.

For More Information

Andronico, M. P. (Ed.) (1996). *Men in groups: Insights, interventions, and psychoeducational work.* Washington, DC: American Psychological Association.

Beymer, L. (1995). *Meeting the guidance and counseling needs of boys.* Alexandria, VA: American Counseling Association.

Geary, D. C. (1998). *Male, female: The evolution of human sex differences.* Washington, DC: American Psychological Association.

Horst, E. A. (1995). Reexamining gender issues in Erikson's stages of identity and intimacy. *Journal of Counseling and Development, 73,* 271–278.

O'Neil, J. M. (1982). Gender role conflict and strain in men's lives: Implications for psychiatrists, psychologists, and other human-services providers. In K. Solomon & N. B. Levy (Eds.), *Men in transition.* New York: Plenum.

O'Neil, J. M. (1990). Assessing men's gender role conflict. In D. Moore & F. Leafgren (Eds.), *Men in conflict* (pp. 23–38). Alexandria, VA: American Association of Counseling and Development.

Pleck, J. H. (1981). *The myth of masculinity.* Cambridge, MA: MIT Press.

Rabinowitz, F. E., & Cochran, S. V. (1994). *Man alive: A primer of men's issues.* Pacific Grove, CA: Brooks/Cole.

Skovholt, T. M. (1990). Career themes in counseling and psychotherapy with men. In D. Moore & F. Leafgren (Eds.), *Men in conflict* (pp. 39–56). Alexandria, VA: American Association for Counseling and Development.

Solomon, K. (1982). The masculine gender role: Description. In K. Solomon & N. B. Levy (Eds.), *Men in transition.* New York: Plenum.

13

Special Issues in Family Systems Featuring Issues for Dual Careers

Chapter Highlights

- *How to identify the nuclear family and the extended family*
- *Current trends of change in family systems and family relationships*
- *Case example of a dual-career couple in conflict*
- *Issues facing dual-career families*
- *Implications for career counseling*
- *Appropriate counseling interventions for the case example*

THE FAMILY'S INFLUENCE ON CAREER DEVELOPMENT HAS BEEN A SIGNIFI-
cantly relevant issue for a number of career development theorists. Roe (1956), and more recently Roe and Lunneborg (1990), directed considerable attention to the developmental period of early childhood in their study of parent-child relations. Super (1990) projected the homemaker role as a major life role in the life-span, life-space approach to career. Gottfredson's (1996) treatise on sex-role orientation emphasizes the role of family influence. Mitchell and Krumboltz (1996) suggest that environmental conditions and events are factors that influence career paths. In sociological perspectives on work and career development, family effects on career development are considered a major variable: "The focus is on how family structure (intact, not intact) and maternal work roles influence development of work-related attitudes and choices of youth" (Hotchkiss & Borow, 1996, p. 284).

Many other factors of parental actions and behaviors—such as parents' expectations for their children's success and parents' perceptions of their children's competence, interests, skills, and activities (Eccles, 1993)—are potential causal factors of career development. These examples, among others, suggest that more emphasis should be given to the study of familial variables to determine the degree to which these variables affect career development. As we begin the 21st century, we are encountering a different world in which traditional family systems have been altered, transformed, and reconstituted. Furthermore, determining the degree to which such variables as single parents, dual-worker parents, divorce, and remarriage shape career development is a challenge for professionals from several academic disciplines. These changes in family systems suggest that career development might also be changing its course. To fully delineate career development, the career counseling profession will likely require a closer alliance with other academic disciplines that view the work role as a pervasive variable in the lives of current and future generations.

In recent years, both parents often have to work to fulfill financial responsibilities, but it should be recognized that many women *choose* to work and pursue a career. In greater numbers, women are assuming the dual role of homemaker and worker. Families in which both parents work are referred to as either dual-career or dual-earner households. Both types share some common goals and common issues. The term *dual career* is usually reserved for families in which both spouses hold professional, managerial, or technical jobs. Most of our discussion will be devoted to dual-career families.

As more women have changed roles, men also have changed by assuming a larger share of the homemaker role. But sharing responsibilities, particularly in the home, has caused role conflicts. In this chapter, we will discuss some aspects of family dynamics in a changing world and the challenges that face couples in dual-career roles. More specifically, in the first part of the chapter we discuss the family as a system and some aspects of family relationships. In the second part of the chapter, issues facing dual-career families, some of which relate to dual-earner families, are covered. Finally, implications for career counseling are presented.

The Family as a System

In this chapter, the family is conceptualized as a social system. Any system, whether a corporation, a city government, or a family, comprises interdependent elements that have interrelated functions and share some common goals. In this perspective, we view individuals in families as interconnected elements, each of whom contributes to the functioning of the whole. Thus, we cannot wholly understand the system by focusing on the component parts because each is affected by every other part; the relationships of those parts result in a larger coherent entity. Families are viewed as composites of many factors, such as genetic heritage from parents, that are passed on to their children; members share common experiences and develop common perspectives of the future. The family system is embedded in larger social systems.

The nuclear family, most common in the United States, consists of husband/father, wife/mother, and at least one child. The extended family, the most common form around the world, is one in which parents and their children live with other kin. The sequences of changes in families are referred to as *family life cycles*. In this respect, the family itself is also a developing organism of roles and relationships that occur over the family life cycle (Kail & Cavanaugh, 1996; Sigelman & Shaffer, 1995).

Rowland (1991) points out that an increasing number of people do not experience the traditional family life cycle; social changes have altered the makeup of the typical family in a changing world. Sigelman and Shaffer (1995) suggest that the following trends of change in family systems alter the quality of family experience.

1. *Increased number of single adults.* Although more adults are staying single, more than 90% of today's young adults are expected to marry eventually.

2. *Postponement of marriage.* More adults are delaying marriage. The average age at first marriage for men is 26 and for women, 24.

3. *Decreased childbearing.* The average number of children in U.S. families is two. Adults are waiting longer to have children, and increasing numbers of young women are choosing to remain childless.

4. *Increased female participation in the labor force.* About 12% of married women with children under age 6 worked in 1950; the figure increased by the early 1990s to 57%.

5. *Increased divorce.* As many as 60% of newlyweds are expected to divorce.

6. *Increased numbers of single-parent families.* Projections indicate that about half of the children born in the 1980s will spend some time in a single-parent family. Fathers as single parents are increasing faster than are mothers as heads of single homes.

7. *Increased numbers of children living in poverty.* The increasing number of single-parent families has led to the increase in numbers of impoverished children.

8. *Increased remarriage.* About 75% of divorced individuals are remarrying. About 25% of U.S. children will spend some time in a *reconstituted family,* usually consisting of a parent, a stepparent, and children from another marriage.

9. *Increased years without children.* Adults are spending more of their later years without children in their homes for the following reasons: Some who divorce do not remarry, people are living longer, and couples bear children in a shorter time span.

10. *More multigeneration families.* Because people tend to live longer, more children establish relationships with grandparents, and some with great-grandparents. Parent/child relationships last longer, some for 50 years or more.

These trends of change in family systems pose some interesting questions concerning career development. For example, will perceptions of life roles including the work role be altered? What impact will family transitions have on career development? Gilbert (1993) found that some aspects of men's behaviors in the home appear crucial to children's developing self-concepts. Moreover, fathers in dual-career families are likely to model less stereotypic behaviors, thus providing children with a more positive role of being involved in parenting. Also, observing women as economically independent and having more choices and opportunities influences children's perceptions of what women can do and become (Gilbert, 1993). The point is that although these trends might not have negative effects on images that children form about career and life roles, we need to remain aware of potential causal factors that contribute to and influence career development in these rapidly changing times.

Family Relationships

Mothers have traditionally been the primary caregivers for children. But recent research indicates that mother-child relationships cannot be fully understood without the addition of the father's influence (Sigelman & Shaffer, 1995). Both parents indirectly affect their children through their own interactions—the way in which they influence each other. For example, mothers who experience a supporting relationship with their husbands tend to respond to children in a more sensitive manner (Cox, Owen, Henderson, & Margand, 1992). Fathers, on the other hand, are likely to become more involved with their children when their wives suggest that they have an important role in their children's lives (Palkovitz, 1984). Thus, in the family system, mothers, fathers, and children all affect one another in the socialization process.

The previous discussion of changing family systems suggests that U.S. children are being reared in a diversity of environments: in single-parent families, reconstituted families, and multigeneration families. Many other variables within family structures also account for more diversity, such as poverty or the number of children within a family system. Therefore, it is difficult to predict or develop a profile of a successful marriage for these diverse groups; however, longevity of marriage appears to have at least some relationship to marital satisfaction. Berry and Williams (1987) found that marital satisfaction is highest at the beginning, drops in satisfaction when children leave home, and rises in later life. Figure 13-1 illustrates the level of overall marital satisfaction from start of marriage to retirement from work.

Lauer and Lauer (1986, p. 385) interviewed women and men who had been married at least 15 years and compiled their reasons for staying married. The first seven responses were the same for both men and women, and they are listed here in order of frequency: (1) My spouse is my best friend; (2) I like my spouse as a person; (3) Marriage is a long-term commitment; (4) Marriage is sacred; (5) We agree on aims and goals; (6) My spouse has grown more interesting; and (7) I want the relationship to succeed.

In dual-career marriages, Newman and Newman (1995) report that the degree of marital satisfaction is related to agreement between husband's and wife's attitudes and aspirations. The way conflicts are expressed and negotiated and the manner in which resources are shared appear to be strong binding forces. Not

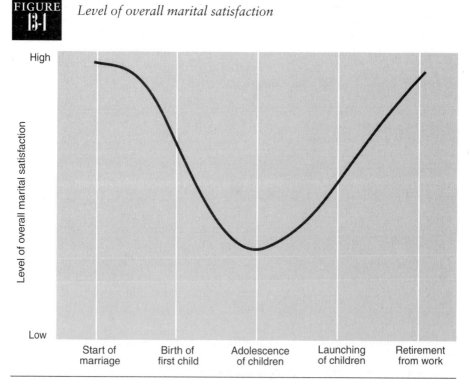

FIGURE 13-1   *Level of overall marital satisfaction*

SOURCE: From *Human Development*, by R. V. Kail and J. C. Cavanaugh. Copyright 1996 by Brooks/Cole Publishing Company, a division of International Thomson Publishing, Inc.

surprisingly, couples that have more traditional sex-role attitudes tend to experience greater stress in a dual-career marriage. This conclusion supports Gilbert's (1993) findings on dual-career families. For instance, husbands who witnessed their fathers in actual involvement in family work were more comfortable in assuming family roles. In the next section, dual-career families will be discussed, but first let us review a case example of a dual-career couple in conflict.

Case 13-1: A DUAL-CAREER COUPLE IN CONFLICT

A conversation between a hair stylist and her customer went something like this:

CUSTOMER: I just don't know how Jose and I can keep our sanity. He is gone most of the time, and now I have to leave for a few weeks. I hope the children will be okay.

STYLIST: Both of you sure travel a lot. I know Jose flies to New Orleans every week and now you are going overseas. When do you do fun things?

CUSTOMER: Fun things!! What's that?? All we ever do is argue about who is supposed to do what at the house and with the children.

STYLIST: You know, Maria, you have been telling me the same story every week. And I think you are depressed over the whole situation. I do hope you and Jose can work something out.

The customer, a married women named Maria, has two children, ages 9 and 5. The family lives in a fashionable home in an exclusive neighborhood. Almost everyone but the stylist views Maria and Jose's relationship as dynamic and exciting because of their prestigious career positions. Although their marriage situation is unusual in a number of ways, Maria was expressing typical problems associated with dual-career marriages.

Maria was reared on the West Coast with two siblings. Both parents were professionals. Her mother was a medical doctor specializing in internal medicine, and her father was an electrical engineer who had established his own consulting firm. Maria recalls that even though her parents were very busy with their careers, they made time for their children. They had a maid who also served as their nanny when they were small, but both parents shared in household tasks and driving Maria and her playmates to fun places.

Maria is now an internationally known architect employed by a prestigious international firm based in Phoenix. She is very pleased with her current position. Her husband Jose is a college professor currently employed at a university in a southern state more than 1000 miles from their home. Jose flies to his job every week, leaving on Monday and returning on Friday. He now has tenure and does not want to give up his current position.

Jose and Maria moved to Phoenix when a position opened in an architectural firm. Jose decided that if someone had to travel on a regular basis, it should be him. When Jose is asked about this decision, he usually replies, "It's best for the kids to have their mother with them." Maria is not particularly pleased with this response, however, as it indicates that Jose doesn't recognize her achievements and the fact that she had been selected after a highly competitive search by the firm. By his response, Jose seems to ignore the fact that she receives more than three times his pay and that they had agreed that most of her earnings would be set aside for the children's education. Maria doesn't expect Jose to tell every casual acquaintance about all these details, but she does expect more of an appreciation for a mutual decision that had been thoroughly discussed and agreed on.

Jose, on the other hand, feels that Maria overlooks his traveling time and the hardships associated with it. Maria seems to view his position as just another professor's job that is relatively unimportant.

The conversation in the salon continued:

STYLIST: I don't believe your husband gives you credit for all you have done.

MARIA: Well, sometimes he does, but it seems harder for him to express those kinds of feelings.

STYLIST: Why can't he do that? Why doesn't he just say it?

MARIA: Hmm . . . that's something I have to think about.

On the way home, Maria was worried. She was now having difficulty with her oldest son, who is losing interest in all school subjects. At home, he has refused to obey her on a number of occasions. When she discussed this situation with her mother by phone, Maria got the usual response: "Maybe you should give more attention to your children."

Jose grew up in a midwestern state with three siblings. Jose's father was a corporate lawyer and had built a reputable practice. His mother was a homemaker who had no intentions of working outside the home. Jose recalls the scrumptious meals his mother would prepare and that she always seemed to be there when he needed her. Jose's relationship with his father was one of respect, but there was never much affection expressed between the two, and his father was often too busy to spend time with him and his siblings. Jose describes his family system as a traditional one.

Jose and Maria met in graduate school. After a courtship of two years, they became engaged and were married soon after graduation. They lived in the Northwest and on the Atlantic coast. They moved to Jose's New Orleans teaching location when a position opened. Each move was made to improve Jose's career. Maria had taken jobs in nearby cities in each location, and her growing reputation as an outstanding architect finally gave her the opportunity to take "the job of a lifetime," and so the family moved to Phoenix.

It was Friday, and Jose was on his way home for the weekend. He had invited one of his male colleagues, Bob, to join him. They had planned for time to prepare a research project.

BOB: Jose, this is a nice flight, but doesn't it get tiresome to do this every week?

JOSE: I'm used to it by now, but I have to admit that there are times I would much prefer to stay at home. Actually, it's not the flight as much as it is the nights away from home that bother me.

BOB: Well, I hated to see you move. I still don't know why you had to do it.

JOSE: Maria just had to have this job, and I guess I had to cave in just this once. But I hope you understand that I get my way most of the time. Anyway, let's start talking over our plans for this research project. You know, Bob, I think this project could get us an international reputation.

The first year in Phoenix was a relatively happy one, as Maria tried her best to take most of the responsibility of managing the household. During the second year Jose began to argue about household tasks and spending time with the children on weekends, and he often refused to attend business-related events with Maria's firm. The small arguments seemed to get bigger, and Jose was often irritable. Both Jose and Maria felt they had reached a crucial stage in their marriage.

The next section addresses issues facing dual-career families. As you read this section, identify issues and potential sources of problems Maria and Jose are experiencing in their marriage. Following this discussion is a summary of Maria and Jose's case.

Issues Facing Dual-Career Families

The following issues are representative of current problems found among dual-career families, some of which apply to dual-earner families as well. This relatively new family structure was brought to the attention of researchers by the studies of British university graduates in the 1970s by Rapoport and Rapoport (1978). Following their work, many studies involving dual-career families contained serious methodological limitations, such as focusing on women only and using only academics as samples (Herr & Cramer, 1996). Nevertheless, the following issues emerged as potential career counseling concerns and should be viewed from the perspective that many more may come forth in future research.

Expectations and Intentions About Work and Family

In a study of university students, Gilbert (1993) found that young women and men reared in dual-career families were highly committed to a role-sharing marriage. In other words, children raised in dual-career families were more likely to develop positive views of integrating occupation and family work. This contrasts with the usual situation in traditional family structures, where the husband assumes the primary employment role and home roles are assumed by the wife.

These findings suggest that the kind and type of role sharing observed in the home by both women and men greatly influence their expectations of roles in marriage. Silberstein (1992) argues that a lack of agreement between expectations of roles in marriage has the potential to create interpersonal tension. The point is that role overload typically occurs between spouses when family roles are not clearly defined. For example, if the husband's occupational role is assumed to be primary, or if a wife views the husband's employment as a less important career, there is a greater potential for minimal sharing of household work.

Role Conflict

Role conflict is generally thought of as a system of competing demands from different roles; in the case of the dual-career family, the conflict is between family roles and work roles. Society has generally viewed the woman as the primary homemaker. The division of labor between spouses usually results in negotiating family roles, which are more complex when the family responsibilities include child care. When a husband does little sharing of household tasks, his wife may experience role overload. Role conflict results when husbands or both husbands and wives believe that men should continue to fulfill the traditional role of family breadwinner.

Evidence suggests that role conflict and role overload are decreasing somewhat in dual-career families; men seem to be increasing their willingness to share in household tasks and child care (Dancer & Gilbert, 1993). Some evidence also supports the position that, in heterosexual marriages, African American and Hispanic American men tend to spend more time doing household tasks than do European American men (Shelton & John, 1993). Although women have been somewhat relieved of household tasks during the past two decades, they continue to do the most work and assume the most responsibility for household tasks (Kail & Cavanaugh, 1996).

Klinger (1988) developed a model designed to delegate household tasks based on interests, aptitudes, and time available. This flexible model provides for changes in tasks and in who performs them as the situation or as economic factors change. It also addresses the fact that some tasks may be viewed as more desirable than others, so that the most-preferred and least-preferred tasks should be rotated between the spouses. The last part of the model provides for a "recycling" that ensures an equitable division of labor.

Part I—Formulate list of household tasks.

Part II—Agree on the frequency of the tasks (daily, biweekly, weekly, monthly, annually).

Part III—Agree on the person(s) responsible for accomplishing the task (considering each person's available time, interest, abilities). Highly desirable or highly undesirable tasks are rotated.

Part IV—Review of the tasks to determine the following:

a. Did the person(s) designated perform the task?

b. Was the task viewed as satisfactorily completed?

c. For "no" responses to questions a or b, what were the obstacles to completing the task?

d. What additional resources (time, dollars, people, or other factors) are needed to complete the task successfully?

Part V—Recycle: Add or delete tasks, change person(s) responsible for completing task if changes are necessary to maintain the perception of both persons that the division of labor is equitable.

The model can also be adapted to include child care. When the couple begins using the model, both partners should go through all the stages on a weekly basis. As they become familiar with the model, and if they are generally satisfied, then they can cycle through less frequently. The main determinant in how frequently the process is reviewed should be the level of dissatisfaction: the greater the level of dissatisfaction, the greater the need for the couple to recycle through the process.

Child Care

When both parents work, the care of children becomes a critical issue. Because more than half of the mothers in the United States work outside the home, child care has been an increasing concern. According to the National Commission on Children (1993, cited in Newman & Newman, 1995), there has been a steady increase in the use of day care since 1965. Forms of day care used include sitters, day care homes, and relatives.

Organizations have also recognized the need to provide for child care, and some offer one or more of the following alternatives:

Emergency care: The company provides temporary care when employees' regular arrangements fail.

Discounts: The organization arranges for a discount from national day care chains or pays a small portion of the fees.

Vouchers: Some organizations pay subsidies or offer special assistance to some low-paid employees.

Referral services: Organizations may offer employees a list of approved day care centers.

On-site day care: Day care centers are located on the organization's site.

Flexible benefits: Money paid to day care centers is deducted from each employee's salary, thus, it is not considered taxable income.

One of parents' major concerns is the potential negative effects on children who are placed in day care centers. Research indicates that day care infants are no different from infants who were reared in their homes on measures of cognitive, linguistic, and social development (Clark-Stewart, 1993). In fact, most studies suggest that children benefited from their day care experiences (Sigelman & Shaffer, 1995).

Geographic Moves

A pivotal point in dual-career families is a geographical relocation to enhance the husband's or the wife's career. First, a move could represent a sacrifice by one spouse. According to Silberstein (1992), usually the husband receives the major benefits from geographical moves; however, more couples are deciding to move to favor the wife's career. In some situations, a decision is made to commute so they can maintain the current residence.

Competition

Competition usually emerges when one spouse develops feelings of insecurity or frustration associated with his or her career (Silberstein, 1992). Feelings of competition might not be expressed directly but instead could result in debates about a variety of family or career concerns. For example, the tendency to address the issue of competition indirectly might lead to arguments about such issues as work schedules, vacation schedules, and child care commitments. The view that competition is largely inappropriate can cause dual-career partners to deny or avoid the issue.

Other Personal Factors

The need to dominate is a personality factor that influences how partners combine occupational and family roles. Typical of a dominating partner is to expect the other partner to take a secondary role in career aspirations and subsequent effort, thought, and time relegated to a career. For example, a dominating male may view his spouse as primarily responsible for raising children and the spouse's income as providing extra money. Or a deferring female may see her spouse as being the major breadwinner who must work full time, while she works part time and assumes the role of rearing children (Gilbert, 1993).

The attitudes, values, and subsequent views about women as professionals and about who should assume responsibility for which major roles in dual-career marriage can largely determine the degree of the partners' "fit" in dual-career home environments. For instance, do both spouses have a favorable attitude toward a role-sharing marriage? Do both agree to work full time and share financial responsibilities? In essence, how interested and committed are both partners to an egalitarian marriage?

The stages of career development of both partners are also important considerations. For example, one partner might have reached the point where career has become rather secondary in life's priorities and, as a result, might not support the other partner's career advancement. Second, personal factors could make one partner resist accepting nontraditional roles to provide time for the other partner's career efforts. In this case, one partner debunks the other partner's career aspirations and offers little in the way of role sharing for the other partner's career growth and productivity.

Relationship Factors

One very important aspect of dual-career relationships is the decision-making process within the family—more specifically, who is empowered to make decisions. This factor seems to boil down to the question of equity in the decision process. For dual-career families, it is particularly important to reach mutual agreement on both major and minor decisions. Otherwise, one partner may feel unjustly treated.

The sharing of decision making and subsequent agreement of common life goals can serve as a foundation of support for family roles. Likewise, the sharing of perceptions of women's and men's roles in dual-career marriages is considered significantly relevant to how partners combine occupational and family roles (Gilbert, 1993).

Family-Oriented Work Policies

The work situation itself might provide obstacles that become relevant issues in a dual-career marriage. Fortunately, many organizations are offering parents flexible work policies. The following is a summary of the information compiled by Gilbert (1993):

1. Telephone access is an organization's policy that permits parents to make personal calls to their children or receive them.

2. Parental leave is also provided by many organizations. This type of leave is different from maternity leave in that it is primarily for care of children who are seriously ill.

3. Flextime permits parents to choose arrival and departure times within a set range.

4. Flexible work arrangements permit arranging part-time work, job sharing, flexplace work (part of the day at home and part at the office), or telecommuting (work from home or satellite office).

Implications for Career Counseling

Clearly, one major problem of dual-career marriages is gender equity. The subtleties of male dominance that are often present in dual-career marriages lead couples to deal indirectly with their anxieties. Instead of attacking the underlying reasons for their frustrations, couples might resort to arguments over role assignments, child care, or other surface problems. In many instances, women might be searching for equity, while men might fear giving up power. The gap between expectations and reality for both spouses could be a productive intervention strategy, particularly if it is designed to clarify disparate expectations between spouses (Silberstein, 1992).

The major decision points in any marriage are crucial, but in dual-career marriages specific decision points can be identified. When or whether to have children can be particularly perplexing for spouses in dual-career marriages. This decision usually occurs during early career stages when women can more easily have children, which makes this decision a complex one. One method of resolving this issue is through negotiated compromises. Each spouse must share not only in this decision but also in actions and responsibilities that follow the decision.

Another major decision point that can provoke anxiety and stress in dual-career marriages is the necessity of moving to another location to foster one spouse's career. Again, who has the major role in being breadwinner? Decisions of this type highlight underlying questions that might have been avoided in the past. Counselors should be prepared to develop strategies that would prompt a reexamination of individual and collective priorities for both partners. The issues and individual feelings about work and family are indeed complex, and many couples may not be fully aware of personal issues involved in a geographic move to benefit one spouse's career. The counselor's task is to illuminate these issues for clarification. So far we have dismissed concrete issues such as management of household tasks and sharing of duties as if they have little relevance to the welfare of dual-career marriages. But it appears more appropriate to address the possibility of underlying and unresolved issues before the more concrete ones can be effectively dealt with. The idea of role sharing, planning for children, making time for leisure, and offering support to one's spouse are examples of viable topics for the career counselor. Finally, it is important to recognize that some couples may need to be referred to a marriage counselor to enhance marital satisfaction. Marital relationships might best be addressed in couples therapy.

Case 13-1:   (CONTINUED)

The case of Jose and Maria illustrates some of the stress associated with dual-career marriages. Both have highly advanced career positions that are quite demanding. Their high income level permits them to hire domestic help, but the responsibilities of managing a household and rearing children cannot be completely relegated to others outside the family system. The task of managing a two-career household has caused some of the following problems for Maria and Jose.

Gap Between Marital Expectations and Reality

For Maria and Jose, the gap between expectations and reality has led to some of their frustrations. Perhaps Maria, who was reared in a dual-career home, had not fully realized that family responsibilities cannot be fully delegated the way she had envisioned from her childhood experiences. It may have appeared easy for her mother, but in reality her mother was in a much better position than Maria is to control the demands of her workload and to keep a firm hand on household and family-related tasks.

Jose was not reared in a dual-career home; in fact, he was the product of a typical traditional system in which family roles were sex-role stereotyped. For the first years of marriage, Jose was happy; his expectations of married life, the roles of husband and wife, were mostly being met. Even though Maria was working full time, most attention was directed to his work-role advancement through geographical moves. And even though he had agreed to the fourth move for Maria's benefit, he expected the traditional role of husband and wife to continue, though perhaps with some modifications. When Maria had to ask for more of his support for household and child care activities, as well as support for her work, he felt betrayed.

Role Overload

For her part, Maria was an aggressive worker. She had multiple abilities and creative talents that needed to be expressed. Her work was now a challenge to her previously unused creativity, and it required that she devote most of her energy and cognitive skills to several ongoing projects. She would often arrive at home feeling fulfilled but also drained of energy. She also felt guilty when she was unable to devote more time to her children.

Competition and Empowerment Issues

Jose also experienced high levels of frustration associated with his career and his home life. The reality was that Jose was away from home and from his children on a regular basis. He also blamed commuting to work for his lack of productivity (research projects) in his academic discipline. Jose could very well have developed a fear of losing empowerment in his home. These two assumptions on Jose's part were troublesome ones. Being away from home four days a week can be stressful for all family members. However, Jose had not let any distractions interfere with his academic productivity in the past.

Jose's high anxiety level was a product of fear associated with losing control over family matters. He had developed a strong need to be empowered to make decisions, and, more important, he expected most family decisions to agree with his perceived role as head of the family. When his family position was threatened, Jose fought back by competing with his spouse for career recognition.

The problems identified in this dual-career relationship are complex but typical of dual-career marriages. A closer look at the identified problems suggests that there was no significant indication of dysfunctional work, unsatisfactory work environments, or unstable peer and supervisory relationships. In fact, both spouses were well satisfied with their career positions. There were indications that some role sharing had been successful, and the family had functioned relatively well for several years. Their financial future was very promising.

The identified problems also reveal a gender equity battle between a highly successful wife and a successful husband. Some of the identified problems are typical of equity disagreements. For instance, their expectations of marriage were quite different.

Jose foresaw a more traditional marriage, with the husband assuming the primary work role, the wife working only for extra income, and the wife assuming the primary responsibility for house and child care. Maria had quite a different view of marriage—an egalitarian one of sharing and appreciating each other's independence. When these two different perspectives began to collide, stress, anxiety, and frustration were predictable outcomes.

The reactions of partners in conflict can vary considerably, but in this case—other than both being identified as having conflicting expectations of marriage—Maria's other problem was role overload. On the other hand, Jose's multiple problems are clearly a part of expectations of marriage and his views of gender roles.

The recommendations for intervention strategies in this case could include couples counseling designed to illuminate conflicting expectations of marriage and resulting conflicts. The major goal would be to address marriage roles of sharing and gender equity. The needs and problems of the children also need to be addressed.

In conjunction with couples counseling, the career counselor can provide (1) role-sharing strategies; (2) leisure time commitments, including family leisure time; (3) restatement of career goals, which center on agreement of plans for the future; (4) career development of children as a sharing venture; and (5) reformulation of life-span goals.

A number of outstanding counseling models are available for dual-career marriages, among them are the integrative strategies by Stoltz-Loike (1992). This integrative approach is based on the following assumptions:

1. A family has a variety of responsibilities that must be performed to function properly. How they are performed depends on the couple's skills, talents, and preferences.

2. Couples must communicate attitudes toward responsibilities. Conflicts need to be discussed and resolved.

3. Dual-career couples can effectively serve as models to help other couples balance career and family roles.

4. Communication, negotiation, and problem solving are to be viewed as ongoing processes over the life span.

5. Interventions are to be tailored to meet a variety of presenting problems among dual-career couples.

6. A spouse must balance his or her own family and work responsibilities with those of the other spouse.

7. Solutions to issues must be contextual to include each spouse's life, workplace, and community setting.

The major goal of this approach is to achieve balance of family and career equity. Helping couples recognize that role conflicts can occur at any time over the life span is another major goal. Because of overlapping roles and responsibilities, basic relationship skills of communication, negotiation, conflict resolution, and life-span success are stressed.

Summary

1. The families' influence on career development has been a significantly relevant issue for a number of career development theorists.

2. The family is conceptualized as a social system. The nuclear family is the most common in the United States. The extended family is the common form around the world.

3. Current trends in family systems include increased number of single adults, postponement of marriage, decreased childbearing, increased female participation in the labor force, increased divorce, increased number of single-parent families, increased numbers of children living in poverty, increased remarriage, increased years without children, and more multigeneration families.

4. The example presented of a dual-career couple in conflict is typical of issues involving struggles for gender equity of household and child care tasks and of work recognition.

5. Issues facing dual-career couples are expectations of work and family, role conflict, child care, geographic moves, competition, relationship factors, family-oriented work policies, and a number of personal factors.

6. Implications of career counseling include illuminating underlying issues of gender equity, couple communication, sharing exercises, family and career status, and conflict resolution.

Supplementary Learning Exercises

1. Does the nuclear family or the extended family have more influence on a child's career development? Defend your position.

2. What strategies would you suggest for a single parent who is concerned about a child's career development?

3. Defend the following statement: Mother-child relationships cannot be fully understood without the addition of the father's influence.

4. Which two trends in changing family systems do you consider to be the greatest threat to the traditional U.S. family system? Defend your choice.

5. What are the major differences between dual-career and dual-earner families? Of the two, which would have the greater difficulty with role conflicts?

6. Explain how expectations of marriage influence behaviors in dual-career marriages. Give at least five examples.

7. Give three examples of how parents in a traditional marriage influence their children's perceptions of dual-career marriages.

8. How can agreement on life-span goals affect a dual-career marriage? Give at least three examples.

9. Explain how you could assist a dual-career couple negotiate a geographic move that will benefit the wife's career.

10. Interview one couple in a dual-career marriage and one in a dual-earner marriage. Explain the similarities and differences.

For More Information

Barnett, R. C., & Rivers, C. (1996). *She works, he works: How two-income families are happier, healthier, and better off.* San Francisco: Harper.

Dreman, S. (1997). *The family on the threshold of the 21st century: Trends and implications.* Mahwah, NJ: Erlbaum.

Frone, M. R., Russell, M., & Barnes, G. M. (1996). Work-family conflict, gender, and health-related outcomes: A study of employed parents in two community samples. *Journal of Occupational Health Psychology, 1,* 57–69.

Gilbert, L. A. (1993). *Two careers/one family.* Newbury Park, CA: Sage.

Goldenberg, H., & Goldenberg, I. (1994). *Counseling today's family.* Pacific Grove, CA: Brooks/Cole.

Karambayya, R., & Reilly, A. H. (1992). Dual earner couples: Attitudes and actions restructuring work for family. *Journal of Organizational Behavior, 13,* 585–601.

Matthews, L. S., Conger, R. D., & Wickrama, K. A. S. (1996). Work-family conflict and marital quality: Mediating processes. *Social Psychology Quarterly, 59,* 62–79.

McHenry, P. C., & Price, S. J. (1994). *Families and change: Coping with stressful events.* Thousands Oaks, CA: Sage.

Rider, E. A. (2000). *Our voices: Psychology of women.* Pacific Grove, CA: Wadsworth.

Silberstein, L. R. (1992). *Dual-career marriage: A system in transition.* Hillsdale, NJ: Erlbaum.

Taylor, R. J., Jackson, J. S., & Chatters, L. M. (1997). *Family life in black America.* Thousands Oaks, CA: Sage.

14

Career Counseling for Individuals with Disabilities

Chapter Highlights

- *The Americans with Disabilities Act*
- *Special problems and needs of individuals with disabilities*
- *Implications for career guidance*
- *Rehabilitation programs*
- *Case study: client at a state rehabilitation center*
- *Career education and a module for individuals with disabilities*
- *Group counseling program for individuals with disabilities*
- *Assessment instruments for individuals with disabilities*

REHABILITATION SERVICES AND SPECIAL EDUCATION PROGRAMS ON CAREER counseling for persons with disabilities have recently received considerable attention. Innovative career-related educational programs and counseling strategies have been developed to assist individuals with disabilities in making the best possible life and work adjustment. These programs emphasize maximizing each individual's potential for employment. Career counseling programs for individuals with disabilities have elements in common with traditional career counseling programs; however, the diversity of needs requires specially designed assessment instruments, career counseling techniques, materials, and career-related educational training programs.

The terms used to describe people with disabilities have been changed to negate stereotypes and false ideas. The major objection was labeling individuals with demeaning names. For example, a spastic does not describe a person but refers to a muscle with sudden involuntary spasms. It is much more acceptable to think of a disability as a condition that interferes with an individual's ability to do something independent such as walk, see, hear, or learn. Thus, it is preferable to say "people with disabilities" rather than "the disabled"; "Joe is a wheelchair user," rather than "confined to a wheelchair"; "has a hearing impairment" rather than "is deaf-mute"; and "persons with mental retardation" rather than "the mentally retarded." The focus should be on the unique identity of a person rather than on a label that implies that everyone with that particular label is alike and has a separate status. A person's identity should be an individual matter that focuses on a unique condition, and the words we use should convey this message.

In this chapter, we first focus on the Americans with Disabilities Act (ADA). The second section describes special problems and needs of individuals with disabilities. Implications for career guidance and the role of state rehabilitation agencies are then discussed. An actual counseling case of an individual with a disability who sought services from a state rehabilitation agency is described in the next section. A career education program for students with disabilities is covered in the next section, followed by a description of a group counseling program for individuals with disabilities who have been hospitalized. Finally, assessment instruments for individuals with disabilities are discussed.

The Americans with Disabilities Act

The ADA, signed into law on July 26, 1990, is a comprehensive law. For example, Title III regulations require public accommodations (including private entities that own, operate, or lease to places of public accommodation), commercial facilities, and private entities to make reasonable modifications of policies, practices, and procedures that deny equal access to individuals with disabilities. Box 14-1 provides an overview of requirements in public accommodations.

The ADA identifies individuals with disabilities as follows:

> An individual with a disability is a person who has a physical or mental impairment that substantially limits one or more "major life activities," or has a record of such an impairment, or is regarded as having such an impairment.

Americans with Disabilities Act Requirements in Public Accommodations Fact Sheet

General

- Public accommodations such as restaurants, hotels, theaters, doctors' offices, pharmacies, retail stores, museums, libraries, parks, private schools, and day-care centers may not discriminate on the basis of disability. Private clubs and religious organizations are exempt.

- Reasonable changes in policies, practices, and procedures must be made to avoid discrimination.

Auxiliary aids

- Auxiliary aids and services must be provided to individuals with vision or hearing impairments or other individuals with disabilities, unless an undue burden would result.

Physical barriers

- Physical barriers in existing facilities must be removed, if removal is readily achievable. If not, alternative methods of providing the services must be offered, if they are readily achievable.

- All new construction in public accommodations, as well as in "commercial facilities" such as office buildings, must be accessible. Elevators are generally not required in buildings under three stories or with fewer than 3,000 square feet per floor, unless the building is a shopping center, mall, or a professional office of a health care provider.

- Alterations must be accessible. When alterations to primary function areas are made, an accessible path of travel to the altered area (and the bathrooms, telephones, and drinking fountains serving that area) must be provided to the extent that the added accessibility costs are not disproportionate to the overall cost of the alterations. Elevators are required as described above.

SOURCE: U.S. Department of Justice, Civil Rights Division, 1991. *Americans with Disabilities Act Handbook*, Coordination and Review Section.

Examples of physical or mental impairments include, but are not limited to, such contagious and noncontagious diseases and conditions as orthopedic, visual, speech, and hearing impairments; cerebral palsy, epilepsy, muscular dystrophy, multiple sclerosis, cancer, heart disease, diabetes, mental retardation, emotional illness, specific learning disabilities, HIV disease (whether symptomatic or asymptomatic), tuberculosis, drug addiction, and alcoholism. Homosexuality and bisexuality are not physical or mental impairments under the ADA. "Major life activities" include functions such as caring for oneself, performing manual tasks, walking, seeing, hearing, speaking, breathing, learning, and working.

Individuals who engage in the illegal use of drugs are not protected by the ADA when an action is taken on the basis of their current illegal use of drugs (U.S. Department of Justice, 1991, pp. 3–4).

Of interest to the career counselor are the ADA's requirements concerning employment of individuals with disabilities and transportation accessibility. Box 14-2 includes a fact sheet prepared by the U.S. Department of Justice on employment and transportation requirements and the effective dates of these requirements.

One major issue covered in this act is employment discrimination. The ADA prohibits discrimination in all employment practices including job application, hiring, firing, advancement, compensation, training, and other terms and conditions of employment. Also included are advertising for employment, fringe benefits, and tenure. Employers are free, however, to select the most qualified applicant available and to make decisions based on reasons unrelated to a disability. For example, two individuals apply for a typist job and one is able to accurately type more words per minute. Thus, the employer can hire the better typist even though that particular person does not have a disability and the other does. The key to such decisions appears to center around job performance needs, and in this case, typing speed is needed for successful performance of the job.

Other subjects covered in the ADA that interest the career counselor are job descriptions, job application forms, job application process, interviews, testing and medical examinations, hiring decisions, benefits, working conditions, raises and promotions, and reasonable accommodations. More information about the ADA can be obtained at the following address:

Office on the Americans with Disabilities Act
Civil Rights Division
U.S. Department of Justice
P.O. Box 66118
Washington, DC 20035-6118

Special Problems and Needs of Individuals with Disabilities

The problems and needs associated with disability are inclusive and pervasive. Career counselors address adjustment problems associated with disability as well as career choice and career development factors. The severity of functional limitations and the individual's adjustment to his or her limitations are the most important factors to consider in career counseling. The special problems and needs of individuals with disabilities discussed in this section should be considered as representative examples from a diverse population.

BOX 14-2

Americans with Disabilities Act Requirements Fact Sheet

Employment

- Employers may not discriminate against an individual with a disability in hiring or promotion if the person is otherwise qualified for the job.

- Employers can ask about one's ability to perform a job, but cannot inquire if someone has a disability or subject a person to tests that tend to screen out people with disabilities.

- Employers will need to provide "reasonable accommodation" to individuals with disabilities. This includes steps such as job restructuring and modification of equipment.

- Employers do not need to provide accommodations that impose an "undue hardship" on business operations.

Who needs to comply

- All employers with 25 or more employees must comply, effective July 26, 1992.

- All employers with 15–24 employees must comply, effective July 26, 1994.

Transportation

- New public transit buses ordered after August 26, 1990, must be accessible to individuals with disabilities.

- Transit authorities must provide comparable paratransit or other special transportation services to individuals with disabilities who cannot use fixed route bus services, unless an undue burden would result.

- Existing rail systems must have one accessible car per train by July 26, 1995.

- New rail cars ordered after August 26, 1990, must be accessible.

- New bus and train stations must be accessible.

- Key stations in rapid, light, and commuter rail systems must be made accessible by July 26, 1993, with extensions up to 20 years for commuter rail (30 years for rapid and light rail).

- All existing Amtrak stations must be accessible by July 26, 2010.

SOURCE: U.S. Department of Justice, Civil Rights Division, 1991. *Americans with Disabilities Act Handbook,* Coordination and Review Section.

Adjustment

Individuals whose disabilities result from physical trauma might have difficulty adjusting to and accepting disability, which can interfere with motivation to seek retraining and employment. Cook (1981) and Salsgiver (1995) postulated that individuals might experience the feeling that they have done something sinful and are being punished resulting in shock, depression, and denial before accepting and adjusting to a disability. Psychological denial of a disability is discussed frequently in rehabilitation literature. Failure to accept its limitations can impede counseling assistance; the individual will not be open to retraining or to experiences provided by rehabilitation agencies or educational institutions.

Wright (1983) and more recently French (1996) contended that individuals with physical disabilities are given an inferior status position in our society. The frustrations produced from a physical disability can be accompanied by shame and feelings of inferiority. The acceptance of one's physical condition is often linked with one's total self-esteem. Careful consideration should be given to the sources of poor self-concept, ways of reacting to physical disability, and ways of adjusting to it. Counselors need to assist clients in understanding prejudice and discrimination of individuals with disabilities and how it affects self-image.

Attitudinal Barriers

Individuals who are labeled *handicapped* or *disabled* face attitudinal barriers to employment. Employers are reluctant to hire individuals with disabilities because of erroneous assumptions: more sick leave will be required, insurance rates will be affected, safety on the job will be endangered, and plant modifications will be mandatory. People with mental retardation especially are considered to need constant supervision and are perceived as incapable of learning. In general, employers have stereotyped views of individuals with disabilities, resulting in discrimination (Daniels, 1981; Mackelprang & Salsgiver, 1999).

Wright (1980) suggested that one of the most successful methods of improving employers' hiring attitudes is through placement of individuals with disabilities who turn out to be successful workers. An advocacy role through personal contact with potential employers is also an effective method for building positive attitudes. The importance of the advocacy role in career counseling is underscored by Neff (1985), who contended that individuals with disabilities face an impressive array of negative social attitudes, prejudice, and other social barriers. Noble (1992) suggests that a disability should be seen as a diversity and not a deficiency; thus, clients are viewed as individuals rather than patients.

Generalizations Formed as a Result of Being Labeled *Disabled* or *Handicapped*

Being identified as disabled or handicapped may limit one's access to the job market. For example, the label *amputee* might conjure up an image of someone who has lost a leg because of amputation and is severely restricted. Another individual who has had successful open heart surgery might be perceived as sickly and weak. Such generalizations inhibit opportunities for employment, especially for individuals who have minor functional limitations because of an amputation or illness. The career counselor should emphasize that each individual is to be judged on his or her own merits; a disability is only one individual characteristic to be considered in the employment process.

Lack of Models and Norm Groups

The current lack of visibility of individuals with physical disabilities working successfully in a broad spectrum of career fields reinforces low self-esteem and negative attitudes about labor market potential. Negative attitudes about potential work environments can also be reinforced by employment personnel who exhibit feelings of discomfort when interviewing individuals with a disability (Bryan, 1996). Another problem with employment personnel involves standardized tests and inventories that are not always normed for those with physical disabilities, resulting in conflicting or misleading assumptions concerning employment potential (Bolles, 1991).

Kriegel (1982) addressed problems of societal acceptance of individuals with disabilities. He suggested that they are often perceived as second-class citizens, and he contended that society ignores the reality of having a disability: "The terms of our visibility have been created not by us but by those who see what they want to see rather than what is there" (p. 55). Kriegel also appealed to individuals with disabilities to learn to accept their disabilities and to make the most of their assets. Those who have accomplished these goals are good role models.

Onset of Disability

The age at which a disability occurs is a relevant factor to be considered in career counseling. Stone and Gregg (1981) suggested that the effects of a childhood disability can result in parental or community overprotection. In early onset of a disability, an individual's exposure to occupations is limited and career development is usually delayed (Curnow, 1989). The type of disability is also a factor for consideration; adolescents with hearing impairments are more limited in career development than are hearing adolescents.

Early onset of disability can greatly influence career choice. For example, juvenile diabetes might later result in heart disease or visual impairment that could limit an individual's ability to function in occupations requiring keen vision or physical exertion (Stone & Gregg, 1981). Finally, Smith and Chemers (1981) suggested that individuals can be deficient in assertiveness and in independence if they have experienced early onset of a disability.

Onset of disability in adulthood often requires that career counselors introduce the process of career redevelopment. By assessing the realities of their functional limitations, individuals may be required to change career direction. In sum, later onset of disability (1) can have disturbing effects on personal adjustment,

(2) can be related to lower levels of educational or vocational aspirations (Thurer, 1980), and (3) can be related to indecisiveness in career choice, especially with individuals whose medical conditions will be improved or stabilized in the future (Roessler & Rubin, 1982).

Social/Interpersonal Skills

Persons with disabilities have special needs, including a restrictive view of career opportunities. Misconceptions about disabilities have limited intervention strategies that would usually be considered in career development theories (Curnow, 1989), such as social skills training. Fine and Asch (1988) suggested that social and psychological problems for persons with disabilities should receive greater than or at least equal attention to the disability itself.

Individuals with disabilities tend to limit their social lives to interactions with other persons with disabilities. Curnow (1989) suggested that they are reluctant to develop friendships outside the disabled community. Positive reinforcement received from peer groups is especially important. Strategies to assist these individuals to develop more inclusive interpersonal relationships is an important counseling component.

Self-Concept

Disabling conditions have the potential to create a poor self-concept (Humes, Szymanski, & Hohenshil, 1989; Mackelprang & Salsgiver, 1999). Individuals with disabilities tend to report lower self-esteem. A life associated with constant rejection and being labeled as different can potentially create a poor self-image. "Who am I?" may indeed be a difficult question to answer positively. Our goal in this context is to assist individuals in accurately assessing strengths and weaknesses to help them modify their self-perceptions. Programs that include components to help develop positive self-images are very important in meeting the needs of these individuals.

Skills for Independent Living

Individuals with disabilities need special help in developing skills for independent living. For some, the greatest problem is learning to accept limitations that could restrict their ability to become fully independent. For others, increasing their desire to be independent could be the counseling challenge. In essence, some individuals might be unrealistic about their ability to be fully independent, whereas others might lack the motivation to become independent, preferring to maintain their dependence on others. The following special problems and needs were compiled from *Barriers and Bridges* (California Advisory Council on Vocational Education, 1977):

1. Architectural barriers place limits on the mobility of people with ortho-pedic disabilities. Inaccessible transportation, training, and workplaces will eventually be overcome by legislation, but progress is slow.

2. Employers' bias and reluctance to hire people with disabilities limit placement opportunities.

3. There is a lack of trained personnel in vocational education to deal effectively with special problems of people with disabilities.

4. The general public's lack of knowledge concerning the needs and problems of people with disabilities creates barriers to employment.

5. Families of persons with disabilities, who are often the main source of physical and psychological support, often fail to understand the problems and needs of the person with a physical disability. Without professional training, family members may find it difficult to determine whether to foster acceptance of limitations or motivation for independence.

Multicultural Issues

We have learned in our discussions about other special populations in the imme-diate preceding chapters that diversity is multifaceted and multidimensional. Fe-males who are African-American, for instance, are considered to have a double minority status. Following this logic, an African American female who has a dis-ability might be labeled as having a triple minority status. The point here is that we cannot isolate significant variables by their impact on career development (Szymanski, Hershenson, Enright, & Ettinger, 1996). For example, onset of dis-ability, severity of disability, self-image, support networks, and so on are vari-ables that interact with cultural and gender factors that are interrelated and interconnected in unique environments. All variables are unique individual char-acteristics that provide direction or pathways to intervention strategies and goals of career counseling.

Of the 49 million U.S. citizens who have been estimated to have a disability, those between the ages of 15 and 64 include 9.6% Asian and Pacific Islanders, nearly 17% Hispanics, approximately 21% African Americans, and approxi-mately 27% are American Indian, Eskimo, or Aleut (McNeil, 1995). Peterson and Gonzalez (2000) suggest that these individuals more than likely will have to overcome double and triple minority status in their job searches, thus their chances of obtaining employment are reduced. Counselors need to be advocates in their communities by reminding employers that they cannot discriminate against qualified individuals with disabilities in their hiring practices.

Finally, it is generally agreed that career counseling of individuals with disabili-ties is very challenging especially for culturally diverse clients. In the case example later in this chapter, a rehabilitation counselor goes through the steps of developing an Individualized Plan of Employment for an Hispanic female who has a disability. This carefully designed comprehensive program included problem identification, psychological and physical evaluations, development of a comprehensive plan, financial assistance, college enrollment, job search counseling, and follow-up evaluation. Roessler & Rumrill (1995) suggest that postemployment services should be extended beyond 60 days to meet additional needs involved in career adjustment, pay and opportunities equal to other workers, and support to maintain employment.

Implications for Career Guidance

The problems associated with the career development of individuals with disabilities exemplify the need for career counselors to adopt advocacy roles. In addition to directly assisting the client with physical disabilities, career counselors should support community education and training programs to foster acceptance in the work world. Programs that assist educators, families, and employees in working with individuals with disabilities can be invaluable in reducing the physical and psychological barriers that currently exist. People with disabilities face negative attitudes, prejudice, discrimination, and other social barriers. As a consequence, counseling programs should provide more positive roles and role models. Developing positive self-images and interpersonal relationship skills are important intervention strategies. Finally, the advocate role implies considerable dedication to removing social barriers and to providing supportive counseling. Above all we are to help persons with disabilities to understand themselves and become self-advocates (Blotzer & Ruth, 1995; Tower, 1994).

Rehabilitation Programs

This section focuses on programs for individuals with disabilities sponsored by state rehabilitation agencies and on rehabilitation centers sponsored by the private sector.

State Rehabilitation Agencies

State rehabilitation agencies provide career counseling and other services to individuals who meet two eligibility requirements: (1) The person must have a disability that results in a substantial handicap to employment, and (2) vocational rehabilitation services must reasonably be expected to benefit the person relative to employability (Texas Rehabilitation Commission, 1994). The disabling conditions among populations served by state agencies are extensive and inclusive. Rehabilitation services have been extended to individuals with mental illness, orthopedic problems, mental retardation, visual and hearing problems, circulatory problems, amputation of limbs, and other disabling conditions such as alcoholism, cancer, epilepsy, kidney disease, multiple sclerosis, muscular dystrophy, and cerebral palsy (Porter, 1981).

To meet the needs of such a diverse group of individuals, state rehabilitation agencies have developed numerous and varied programs designed to assist individuals reentering the work force or maintaining their chosen occupations. Parker and Hansen (1981) have compiled a list of services provided by state rehabilitation agencies: (1) counseling and guidance; (2) medical and psychological evaluation; (3) physical and mental restoration services; (4) prevocational evaluation and retraining; (5) vocational and other training services; (6) expense allowances; (7) transportation; (8) interpretive services for the deaf; (9) reader, orientation, and mobility services for the blind; (10) prostheses and other technical aids and devices; (11) work adjustment and placement counseling, (12) job placement services; (13) occupational license, tools, equipment, and so forth; and (14) other goods and services to benefit the client in achieving employability.

Privately Supported Rehabilitation Agencies

Among the most widely known, privately sponsored, nonprofit rehabilitation agencies are Goodwill Industries, Salvation Army, Jewish Vocational Services, St. Vincent De Paul Society, National Society for Crippled Children and Adults, United Cerebral Palsy Association, Volunteers of America, and Deseret Industries. Although these organizations and other national, state, and local private rehabilitation agencies sponsor a diversity of programs, Goodwill Industries of America serves as a good example of a national network of programs for individuals with disabilities. Goodwill Industries of America is generally recognized as the world's leading privately sponsored agency for training individuals and with facilities for individuals with disabilities.

Local Goodwill Industries are autonomous, having their own boards of directors, and are affiliated with the national organization, Goodwill Industries of America of Bethesda, Maryland. Goodwill Industries conducts a wide range of activities, including classroom instruction, sheltered workshops, encounter sessions, therapy (physical, occupational, or speech), counseling, and placement. Many local Goodwill Industries collect donated clothing, furniture, household goods and appliances, books, art objects, radios, and televisions for repairing, refurbishing, and rebuilding by individuals with disabilities. These items are sold in a network of bargain retail outlets. Another method Goodwill Industries uses to provide jobs is to subcontract with private industries and with state and federal government agencies for assembling and manufacturing of goods, janitorial, grounds maintenance, and other services.

Goodwill Industries also provide educational skills training programs. For example, Goodwill Industries of San Antonio provides the following services: psychological testing, vocational evaluation, personal and social adjustment, work adjustment, prevocational training, special academic instruction, therapeutic recreation, skills training, and job placement. The individualized services offered by this agency are funded from service fees charged to referring agencies, such as the Texas Rehabilitation Commission, the Commission for the Blind, local independent school districts, the City of San Antonio Manpower Consortium, the Veteran's Administration, and private insurance firms.

Most age groups can be served by privately supported, nonprofit rehabilitation agencies. Services include provisions for assistive devices such as artificial limbs, braces, wheelchairs, glasses, and hearing aids. Assistance is also given to help individuals develop independent living skills through programs in which individuals share supervised apartments. The Salvation Army and Volunteers of America have emphasized programs for homeless individuals with alcohol or psychological problems.

Career counselors need to be aware of the goals, objectives, and services of private rehabilitation agencies in their community or local area. Programs that help prepare individuals with disabilities for employment (such as work-adjustment seminars, prevocational classes, personal counseling, medical management, and mobility training) are valuable referral resources for career counselors. Sheltered workshops, supported by a number of private rehabilitation agencies, provide a workplace for individuals who are unable to meet work requirements in the competitive job market. Career counseling for disabled individuals is greatly enhanced through a wide variety of programs offered by rehabilitation programs supported by the private sector.

Case 14-1:   Counseling Program

The following is an actual case of an individual who received rehabilitation services from a state agency. Names, dates, and other information have been changed to protect client confidentiality. This example illustrates rehabilitation services provided by a state agency in a small town of about 25,000 people. The following steps in the rehabilitation process are covered in this case: (1) initial contact, (2) diagnostic workup, (3) evaluation and certification, (4) vocational assessment, (5) service planning, (6) placement, and (7) postemployment services.

Initial Contact

The purposes of the initial contact are to establish a counseling relationship, provide the client with information about the state agency, and obtain information from the client to determine eligibility for rehabilitation services. In this case, Sam, the rehabilitation counselor, interviewed the client to obtain personal/social information, educational background, past work experiences, physical limitations, and financial needs. Excerpts from the case file are used to illustrate examples of information recorded from the initial contact.

Dora was a self-referred high school graduate and had never received rehabilitation services. She was 40 years old, divorced approximately three years ago, and had two children. Her older child was married and living nearby, but the younger had chosen to live with her. Dora had married at age 18 and had lived in several cities and states with her salesman husband. Sam noted in his report that her mood was very flat and that she seemed remorseful and lethargic. She became extremely emotional when she referred to her marriage, stating, "I resent that my husband left me because of my arthritis."

Dora reported that she had suffered serious problems with arthritis for the past ten years, requiring five surgical procedures on her hands. During the interview, she demonstrated lack of finger flexibility and restricted hand mobility. She was taking two prescribed medications.

Dora's only source of income was $600 monthly child support, and she had no savings. She was unable to insure her five-year-old automobile, and her current rent and utility bills totaled $310. Dora's work experience was very limited; she had worked as a teacher's aide for approximately nine months but was unemployed at the present time.

Sam decided that Dora was a good candidate for rehabilitation services and had her fill out an official request form. She was then scheduled for a medical and psychological evaluation. Sam had to verify reported physical problems, and he wanted a full report on potential psychological disturbances associated with the emotional instability he had observed. Sam also requested reports of previous medical diagnosis and treatment.

Diagnostic Workup

The orthopedist's report indicated that Dora had a severe case of rheumatoid arthritis. After carefully studying the medical report, Sam arrived at the following functional limitations and vocational handicaps.

1. Can stand for short periods of time only (Orthopedic report from Dr. Bone)
2. Unable to lift anything over 10 lbs. on a repetitive basis (Orthopedic report from Dr. Bone)
3. Unable to push or pull (Client's statement)
4. Cannot bend for prolonged periods (Client's statement)
5. Has limited finger dexterity (Orthopedic report from Dr. Bone)

The psychological report discussed results of intelligence, achievement, personality, and several aptitude tests. Sam summarized Dora's assets from the psychological evaluations as follows:

1. Normal intelligence
2. Good clerical skills
3. Ability to learn and retain new information
4. Good reading skills
5. Good oral expressive skills
6. Average academic achievement for her educational level
7. Potential for college-level training

In addition, Sam summarized Dora's limitations:

1. Diagnosed as depressive reaction
2. Poor self-concept
3. Lacks confidence
4. Subject to mood swings

5. Limited work history
6. Poor manual dexterity
7. Easily fatigued

Evaluation and Certification

After reviewing medical and psychological reports, Sam approved Dora's request for re-habilitative services. The results of her disability as well as the degree of her handicap were evaluated. In this case, her physical disability was considered severe enough to merit services. Psychological problems associated with the depressive reaction would also be considered in planning services for her. In developing a rehabilitation plan, Sam was required to address all services that would help Dora reach her rehabilitation goal. Dora was notified of her acceptance, and an appointment was set for the following day.

In preparation for the next counseling appointment, Sam carefully reviewed the material that had accumulated in Dora's file. He paid particular attention to medical problems resulting in functional limitations. The psychological report clearly indicated that Dora would need supportive counseling; however, he decided that his first goal was to establish a vocational objective.

Vocational Assessment

In the counseling sessions that followed, limitations and assets were thoroughly dis-cussed. Although Dora had strongly considered teaching as a vocational objective, she agreed that an interest inventory would help verify her interests and introduce other career considerations. Dora was given a computer-scored inventory, and a date was set for the next counseling session.

The vocational assessment phase of the rehabilitation process continued with an interpretation and discussion of interest inventory results and the test data contained in the psychological report. Dora decided that she would like to explore a career in either elementary school teaching or social work. With these two careers in mind, Sam directed her to references describing these occupations in detail. Dora spent consider-able time reviewing job descriptions and requirements. At Sam's suggestion, she made on-site visits to a school and a social welfare agency. Shortly after these visits, Dora de-cided that she would prefer a career as an elementary education teacher.

Service Planning

Sam developed a comprehensive vocational plan for Dora. This plan, known as the Individualized Plan of Employment (IPE), contains the following aspects of action:

1. The rehabilitation goal and immediate rehabilitation objectives
2. Vocational rehabilitation services
3. The projected date of initiating services and the anticipated duration of services
4. Objective criteria, evaluation procedures, and schedules for determining whether the rehabilitation goal and intermediate objectives are being achieved

5. Explanation of availability of a client assistance program (Roessler & Rubin, 1982, p. 132)

Sam postulated that Dora would need assistance with medical and emotional problems during the course of her college training. He also recognized that he would have to assist Dora in obtaining grants and other benefits that might be available to her. Excerpts from Sam's service plan suggestions follow: (1) enrollment in a local college with financial assistance for tuition, fees, and transportation; (2) other financial assistance through grants and Social Security benefits; (3) physical treatment to be continued as necessary; and (4) regular counseling sessions necessary to address reported psychological problems. Sam decided to provide supportive counseling and, if necessary, refer Dora to a college counseling center or local mental health unit.

Thomas and Butler (1981) and more recently, Mackelprang and Salsgiver (1999) suggested that rehabilitation clients often need extensive personal counseling designed to assist them in accepting their disabilities, adjusting to reactions of others to their disabilities, reintegrating their self-concepts, and adjusting to changes in relationships with family and others in their lives. Career counselors need to evaluate different counseling theories and techniques in meeting the needs of different types of clients. In essence, individuals with disabilities may require extensive personal adjustment counseling.

During the next four years, Dora made remarkable academic progress despite recurring physical and psychological problems. She had three operations on her hands to improve flexibility, and the regular supportive counseling provided by Sam helped her overcome the depressive reaction. Financial assistance provided by the state and other agencies helped Dora maintain subsistence. During her final year in college, Sam directed Dora to attend seminars on resumé preparation and job interview skills.

Placement

In a conference with Sam, Dora decided that she wanted to remain in the area. Sam evaluated the local job market for teachers and found it to be keenly competitive for elementary school teachers; however, he decided that he could improve Dora's chances of obtaining a position by assisting her in job interview preparation. Sam also helped Dora develop a list of alternate school systems to which she could apply.

Postemployment Services

Sam plans to follow Dora's work for at least 60 postemployment days. He will focus on her adjustment to the new job and adaptations she must make in her daily schedule. Finally, Dora will be notified that if services are needed in the future, he can reopen her case.

Dora's case illustrates the comprehensive nature of rehabilitation counseling for individuals with disabilities. The services offered involved considerable client contact and coordination of functions provided through training programs, financial assistance resources, and medical treatment. Although state rehabilitation programs follow a general pattern, there are variations in services given.

Nevertheless, rehabilitation counselors must possess numerous skills and considerable knowledge to foster client career development.

Career Education for Students with Disabilities

Brolin and Gysbers (1989) have developed the Life-Centered Career Education Curriculum (LCCE) for individuals with disabilities. This program has been widely adopted in school systems in several states and in some foreign countries. This curriculum focuses on 22 major competencies that students need to succeed in daily living, personal/social, and occupational areas after leaving school. For daily living, competencies include buying and preparing food, managing finances, and caring for personal needs. For personal/social skills, competencies include achieving self-awareness, achieving independence, and making adequate decisions. Finally, for occupational preparation, competencies include selecting and planning occupational choices and obtaining a specific occupational skill. This model is competency based and specifies counselor time for carrying out guidance activities in each component.

Counselors are provided with a trainer/implementation manual, activity books, and an inventory to assess competency levels. The suggested competencies for this model are infused into the kindergarten through grade 12 curriculum. Some school systems have used this model to facilitate and improve community awareness of students' needs and increase parent participation in learning activities. The LCCE has also been used for staff in-service training to make staff aware of the model's structure and purpose.

Brolin and Gysbers (1989) suggest that career awareness, career exploration, and preparation are major benefits of this model. The career awareness phase is very important during the elementary years. Programs that focus on helping students with disabilities should emphasize developing self-worth, socially desirable behaviors, communication skills, positive attitudes toward work, and desirable work habits.

The career exploration phase includes guidance activities that explore abilities, needs, and interests. The use of work samples, simulated job tasks, and community jobs are important hands-on experiences. In addition, this phase includes experiences with the work roles of homemaker, family member, volunteer and with individuals engaged in productive avocational/leisure activities.

The preparation phase includes guidance activities that help clarify personal/social and occupational competencies. Interests, aptitudes, and skills are further clarified. Lifestyle and career choices are more clearly delineated. Many students with disabilities require more than the usual amount of time to prepare for an occupation.

One issue that needs to be addressed in the 21st century is the place of proficiency tests required for graduation in many states. Should all students with disabilities be required to take and make acceptable scores on these tests? Perhaps more important, what kind of criteria should be used for students with disabilities to determine high school graduation? Finally, can the stereotypes and negative attitudes toward individuals with disabilities be erased from many professionals, including some members of the counseling profession? No doubt, some students with disabilities need individual attention, but counselors need to view these students' needs in perspective rather than in a stereotypic manner. As with other special populations, students with disabilities should receive career counseling, first, by identifying their individual needs and, second, by building programs to meet them (Brolin & Gysbers, 1989).

A Module for Specific Needs of People with Disabilities

Counseling considerations for people with disabilities were developed by Ettinger (1991): focusing on special needs, making the school-to-work transition, and assessing the impact of federal legislation on future programming. The authors suggested four major areas that should be included in the career development plans of persons with disabilities:

1. Career information, such as an understanding of the roles, responsibilities, and the realities of the workplace.
2. Learning strategies to enable individuals to master the information they need to know.
3. Prevocational skills, such as responsibility, initiative, punctuality, care of materials, and task completion.
4. Social skills, with an emphasis on job interviewing, accepting and providing criticism, and relating to authority figures. (Ettinger, 1991, pp. 9–13)

In making the school-to-work transition, persons with disabilities often need assistance in establishing and clarifying goals. This transition also involves a change in environment, which is sometimes difficult for people with disabilities. The counselor's role here is to help the individual change roles from student to employee. This task could involve group discussions of self-concept, developing communication and interpersonal skills, and learning the expectations in the work world.

Ettinger (1991) points out that career counselors in schools are essential advocates for assisting students in making the transition from school to work. This transition period refers to the first year of employment after high school, postsecondary education, or training. Transition services are defined in the Individuals with Disabilities Education Act of 1990 (IDEA) (U.S. Department of Education, 1990) as a coordinated set of activities for a student, designed within an outcome-oriented process, which promotes movement from school to postschool activities, including postsecondary education, vocational training, integrated employment (including supported employment), continuing and adult education, adult services, independent living, or community participation. The coordinated set of activities shall be based on the individual student's needs, taking into account the student's preferences and interests, and shall include instruction, community experiences, the development of employment and other postschool adult living objectives, and when appropriate, acquisition of daily living skills and functional vocational evaluation [Sec. 602 (a) (19)].

School-to-work transition has been an extremely popular topic for workshops and seminars since the early 1990s. The National School-to-Work Learning and Information Center opened in Washington, D.C. in August 1995. This office serves as a training center and an information resource facility. (See Chapter 17 for more information on school-to-work programs.)

A Group Counseling Program for Individuals with Disabilities

The following counseling program illustrates a group counseling procedure for individuals with disabilities. The descriptions include excerpts that illustrate relevant counseling techniques. The counseling activity sequence consisted of four highly structured meetings, shown in Table 14-1. The clients were hospitalized male patients who were accepted as clients for a vocational rehabilitation project. John had been injured in a car accident and was almost totally paralyzed. The other clients had been injured in industrial accidents. Rex's right leg was amputated below the knee. Roberto had lost three fingers and developed a staph infection. Harold's injury prevented him from bending his left leg.

Several days before the first counseling meeting, each client completed a vocational counseling inventory that was to be used as a counseling tool for each of the group meetings.

Session I: Personal/Social Adjustment Counseling

The counselor began the first session with the usual self-introductions. The counselor briefed the clients on the purpose of the counseling session.

COUNSELOR: We're going to have four meetings to talk about some problems that you might experience when you return to the work force. Today we're going to cover some personal problems that you might experience in readjusting to a work role and general factors that influence the performance of workers who have similar problems.

The next excerpt illustrates the use of the previously completed vocational counseling inventory and the importance of group interaction. The counselor selected items to stimulate discussion. For example, the item, "Now that I have a disability, life is going to be difficult," generated considerable discussion.

HAROLD: I've thought about this a lot since I've been in the hospital, and things are really going to be different when I get out.

TABLE 14-1	VOCATIONAL REHABILITATION-COUNSELING ACTIVITY SEQUENCE

Title	Activity
Personal/social adjustment counseling	Briefing on the purpose of counseling session; discussion of problems of workers with disabilities, personal/social adjustment problems, and factors influencing work performance
Peer group affiliation	Counseling session on the importance of good peer relations, factors influencing peer group affiliation, the give-and-take of working with others, and the influence of the working environment on job satisfaction
Worker-supervisor affiliation	Counseling session on the factors determining good relations with a supervisor, the role of the supervisor, and the influence of good worker-supervisor relations on work proficiency and job satisfaction
Job attitude	Counseling session on factors determining vocational success, factors influencing attitudinal development, and the influence of job attitude on work proficiency and job satisfaction

ROBERTO: Well, I've been here for almost two months, and I've learned to accept the fact that I probably will be doing a different kind of work than I did before. By the way, what kind of work did you do? (*looking at Harold*)

HAROLD: I was a foreman on a construction job, and I had to go around the different jobs for this contractor I worked for.

ROBERTO: Well, you might be able to do the same kind of thing.

During this meeting, it was difficult for John to enter into the discussion, for he had been recently injured and was almost completely paralyzed. However, toward the end of the session he spoke.

JOHN: I used to play in a band before I had this car accident, but I don't know what I am going to be able to do now. Anyway, I'm going to this Warm Springs Foundation, and I hope I will get some feeling back in my body and I will find out something.

John's response had a great impact on the entire group because his message was quite clear; here was someone who still had hope even though his injury had the potential of being much more restrictive than those of the other members of the group.

Session II: Peer Group Affiliation

The next excerpt illustrates how group interaction enhanced Session II. This meeting began with the counselor's question, "What kind of people did you like to work with on previous jobs?" During the course of exchanging ideas, several opinions were expressed. It became apparent to the counselor that all but one member of the group seemed to have a fairly healthy attitude toward peer workers. The counselor used several key questions and phrases to stimulate discussion: "Are most people you work with easy to talk to during breaks?" "Some people feel like an outsider on the job." "A friend of mine prefers working alone." "Are most of the people you have worked with friendly?"

Through group interaction, the point was made that good peer relations are most important for the worker with a disability. Examples of statements from group members follow:

JOHN: Some people are going to try to pity me because I've got a disability, while some are going to be very uncomfortable when I'm around.

REX: To have a friend, you have to be a friend, and you can also do that as a disabled person.

HAROLD: Not everybody you work with is going to be friendly, but it sure helps if *you* try.

Session III: Worker-Supervisor Affiliation

The excerpts from this session illustrate how the counselor took advantage of the experiences of one group member to enhance the discussion. Harold had been employed in a supervisory position before his accident but was rather hesitant in communicating his viewpoint as a supervisor. The counselor began this session by having each member of the group discuss his relationships with a past supervisor or a boss. Each client stated that he had very little difficulty in worker-supervisor relationships. However, the counselor suspected that the relationships between employee and supervisor were not as compatible as expressed by the clients. Therefore, the counselor introduced several topics, hoping to elicit further responses from the group. An example of the exchange among group members follows:

COUNSELOR: I've had some bosses that I would have worked harder for had they been a little more friendly. How about the rest of you?

ROBERTO: I remember a few guys like that, and we used to really chew them up during our bull sessions.

JOHN: Yeah, sometimes bosses give too many orders and are not really interested in you.

HAROLD: *(Finally responding)* Well, when I was the boss, sometimes I had to get on people to make them work. Look at it this way, bosses have bosses, and they also have pressure to get the job done.

REX: I never thought of it that way!

JOHN: Yeah, I guess everybody has to answer to someone.

The discussion continued, centering on how one's perception of a supervisor influences personal reactions to the work environment.

Session IV: Job Attitude

The following excerpt illustrates how the counselor continued with the very productive previous counseling session and related the previous topic of discussion to the purpose of this final meeting.

COUNSELOR: Well, last time we raked bosses over the coals, but we finally agreed that bosses and supervisors do have a pretty tough job, and they are generally good guys if you act like you want to work with them and do a good job. This will be especially important as a worker with disabilities.

The counselor then asked each group member to restate what he had learned from the previous meeting.

COUNSELOR: Each of you has illustrated how your attitudes about a supervisor influence your perception of the work environment. Now, let's direct our attention to how your attitudes will affect your return to the work force as a worker with disabilities.

ROBERTO: If you have a good attitude about your boss and people you work with, you will probably like your job too.

JOHN: We have gotta think positive or we'll lose hope.

HAROLD: Sometimes it's going to be hard to have the right attitude—but you only hurt yourself.

This group counseling program encouraged group interaction by sharing concerns about new and different lifestyles as persons with disabilities. Programs like this one emphasize (1) personal/social adjustment problems that might be encountered by each member of the group when he or she returns to the work force, (2) retraining that could be necessary for a different occupation, (3) peer affiliation and supervisor relationships as a person with disabilities, and (4) the influence of one's attitudes on work proficiency and job satisfaction.

Assessment Instruments for Individuals with Disabilities

Micro-Tower—A Group Vocational Evaluation System

The *Micro-Tower* system of vocational evaluation was developed by ICD Rehabilitation and Research Center of New York City. The original instrument, *Tower,* is an acronym for Testing, Orientation, and Work Evaluation in Rehabilitation. *Tower* is an evaluation system consisting of 94 work samples that are individually administered. The *Micro-Tower* system is a group of 13 work samples that can be administered in a group session lasting three to five days. The *Micro-Tower* (1977) work samples are objectively scored and are considered to be performance tests. Work samples are measures of aptitude for a number of unskilled and skilled occupations grouped according to five broad areas of aptitude:

Primary aptitude	Work sample tests
Motor	Electronic connector assembly; bottling, capping, and packing; lamp assembly
Clerical Perception	Zip coding; record checking; filing; mail sorting
Spatial	Blueprint reading; graphics illustration
Numerical	Making change; payroll computation
Verbal	Want-ads comprehension; message taking

A third- to fourth-grade reading level is required to take the *Micro-Tower* system test. Work samples can be administered to an individual who is seated but do require the use of at least one hand. The individual must understand spoken English. A unique feature of the *Micro-Tower* system is the involvement of the clients in group discussions that explore their interests, values, lifestyles, and so on. A separate manual is provided, which has specific procedures and variations for the discussion groups. One major objective of the discussion group is to improve the client's motivation for job placement. Discussion groups are also used as an entrée for the testing period in an effort to make the testing situation as non-threatening as possible.

Several sets of normative data are available, including sets for groups who are in general rehabilitation, are Spanish-speaking, are left-handed, have physical disabilities, have psychiatric disturbances, have brain damage, have cerebral palsy, are in special education, are of a different culture, are ex-drug abusers, are ex-alcoholics, and are adult offenders. Interpretive materials for the *Micro-Tower* system are elaborate and thorough. The results are plotted on a graph from weak to strong for the skill area and specific work samples. Additional reports for the counselor include (1) behavioral observations made during testing, (2) a summary of the client's interest and perceived performance, (3) a client data sheet, (4) a summary report that includes a narrative of the test results, (5) a recommendation summary sheet that covers such areas as special training recommended, (6) referral recommendations, and (7) vocational recommendations (*Micro-Tower*, 1977).

The *Micro-Tower* system grew out of a need for a work evaluation instrument that could be administered to a group in a relatively short period. The evaluation system may also be used as a screening device to determine which clients would benefit from a more extensive evaluation of specific aptitudes. A manual is provided to help counselors convert *Micro-Tower* scores into estimates of *DOT* aptitude levels. The variety of norms available for interpretation increases the usefulness of the instrument.

Valpar Component Work Sample System

The *Valpar Component Work Sample System* (*VALPAR*) (Peterson, 1982) was developed by the Valpar Corporation of Tucson, Arizona, for disabled and nondisabled in all age groups. Its purpose is to assess vocational and functional skills through a series of 16 work samples. Each work sample measures a certain universal worker characteristic. The work samples involve hands-on tasks; some focus on general work characteristics, and others are related to specific job requirements. The following is a brief description of each of the work samples:

1. Small tools: Measures the ability to work with small hand tools, including screwdrivers and small wrenches.

2. Size discrimination: Measures visual discrimination by requiring that the individual screw correct-sized nuts onto threads mounted in a box.

3. Numerical sorting: Measures the ability to sort, file, and categorize by number code.

4. Upper extremity range of motion: Measures the range of motion of upper extremities and fatigue factors, finger dexterity, and sense of touch.

5. Clerical comprehension and aptitude: Measures the ability to perform certain clerical tasks and aptitude for typing.

6. Independent problem solving: Measures the ability to perform work that requires detailed visual comparisons of colored shapes.

7. Multilevel sorting: Measures the ability to sort according to number, letter, and color.

8. Simulated assembly: Measures the ability to do repetitive assembly tasks.

9. Whole-body range of motion: Measures gross motor abilities and fatigue factors.

10. Tri-level measurement: Measures the ability to perform precise measurements.

11. Eye-hand-foot coordination: Measures the ability to use eyes, hands, and feet simultaneously in a coordinated manner.

12. Soldering and inspection: Measures the ability to solder.

13. Money handling: Measures skills that are necessary in dealing with money and making change.

14. Integrated peer performance: Measures work behavior in interaction in small group assemblies.

15. Electrical circuitry and print reading: Measures the ability to understand and apply principles of electric circuits.

16. Drafting: Measures basic drafting skills and ability to learn drafting.

Each of the *VALPAR* work samples can either be used as a separate evaluation or integrated with a combination of other work samples or other testing instruments. The administrator gives the directions verbally, and each work sample can be completed in one or two hours. Modifications of the work samples are available for people with visual and hearing impairments. Norm groups include institutionally retarded, culturally disadvantaged, U.S. Air Force recruits, San Diego employed workers, low-income unemployed, hearing impaired, and what is described as employer workers that were unselected.

VALPAR is well designed and easy to administer and score. The value of work sample testing is the ease of associating the results with requirements of a particular job. Counselors who need work-sample evaluations should carefully consider the content of each work sample in the *VALPAR* system. The focus of this system is on physical skills and the ability to use eyes, hands, and feet in a coordinated manner (Peterson, 1982).

Other work-sample tests include the following:

Jewish Employment Vocational Service Work Sample System—JEVS
Vocational Research Institute
Jewish Employment and Vocational Service
1700 Sansom St.
Philadelphia, PA 19103

SINGER Vocational Evaluation System
SINGER Career Systems
80 Commerce Drive
Rochester, NY 14623

Vocational Information and Evaluation Work Samples—VIEWS
Vocational Research Institute
Jewish Employment and Vocational Service
1700 Sansom St.
Philadelphia, PA 19103

Social and Prevocational Information Battery (SPIB-R)

The *SPIB* (Halpern, Raffeld, Irvin, & Link, 1975) was designed for use with students with educable mental retardation (EMR) in junior and senior high schools. The *SPIB* is useful for EMR program identification, individual evaluation for placement in EMR programs, and monitoring progress and outcomes of EMR programs. The nine tests can be used to assess students' needs for social and vocational skills. The tests measure nine domains identified by the authors as part of five long-range goals for the EMR that should be achieved in secondary schools. These five goals are (1) employability, (2) economic self-sufficiency, (3) family living, (4) personal habits, and (5) communication skills. Tests have been developed to measure the objectives of each goal. The nine tests consist of 277 mostly true-or-false items that are administered orally. The authors identify the goal of economic self-sufficiency as one key objective necessary to postsecondary adaptation. The three domains set for this particular goal are (1) purchasing habits, (2) budgeting, and (3) banking. Test items were subsequently developed to measure self-sufficiency in these three domains. For example, in measuring purchasing habits, test items include measures of knowledge of sales tax, knowledge of types of stores, and effectiveness in using newspaper ads for best buys.

The *SPIB* can be compared with three reference groups. A junior high school–level conversion table permits comparisons from the derived raw scores with equivalent percentage correct scores and percentile ranks with junior high school–level students on each *SPIB* test. Likewise, a senior high school–level conversion provides comparisons with high school–level students on each *SPIB* test. The third conversion table is a combination of junior and senior high school–level normative samples.

The authors suggest a "task analysis" method of evaluating specific competencies within each domain *SPIB* measures. To accomplish this, each content area is divided into subcontent areas. For example, see how the domain of job-related behavior is divided into content and subcontent areas in Table 14-2. Each subcontent area defined provides the basis for developing instructional activities and measuring outcomes for each domain. In this way, the *SPIB* provides the foundation for establishing instructional programs for the EMR, as well as being a tool for measuring the outcomes of the instructional activities. The *SPIB* is a well-devised test battery for assessing and evaluating programs and provides the framework from which to build instructional programs for the EMR.

TABLE 14-2	CONTENT AND SUBCONTENT AREAS FOR THE DOMAIN OF JOB-RELATED BEHAVIOR	

Domain	Content areas	Subcontent areas
Job-related behavior	1. Knowledge of role and duties of a supervisor	a. Instruction b. Criticism c. Praise d. Hiring and firing e. Inspection of work f. Promotion g. Task assignment
	2. Knowledge of appropriate job-related communications	a. Job progress reports b. Relaying messages c. Reporting serious errors d. Requesting supplies e. Asking for help when needed f. Knowing whom to ask for help g. Asking for clarification
	3. Knowledge of what constitutes job completion	a. Importance of finishing a job b. Factors affecting job completion c. The effect of mistakes on job completion
	4. Recognition and knowledge of appropriate work relations with fellow employees	a. Compromising b. Cooperation c. Friendliness d. Showing appreciation e. Controlling temper f. Responsibility to others

SOURCE: From *Social and Prevocational Information Battery, Examiner's Manual,* by A. Halpern, P. Raffeld, L. D. Irvin, and R. Link, p. 3. Reprinted by permission of the publisher, CTB/McGraw-Hill, 2500 Garden Rd., Monterey, CA 93940. Copyright © 1975 by the University of Oregon. All rights reserved.

American Association of Mental Deficiency's (AAMD) Adaptive Behavior Scale

The *AAMD Adaptive Behavior Scale* (Nihira, Foster, Shellhaas, & Leland, 1975) is designed to replace the IQ test as a means of identifying individuals with mental retardation. The AAMD scale is primarily a rating scale for identifying adaptive behavior of individuals who have mental retardation and other special needs. The AAMD has endorsed this effort of using descriptions for identifying an individual's adaptive behavior, rather than using a single intelligence quotient (Nihira et al., 1975).

Of major importance in this approach is that adaptive behavior can be described from a developmental frame of reference. Thus, an individual is observed from an established standard that provides certain descriptive information about the individual's functioning. Using this technique, a more comprehensive and informative description of skills, habits, social expectations, and personal independence is provided.

The *AAMD Adaptive Behavior Scale* (Nihira et al., 1975) has two parts. Part I is a measure of 10 behavioral domains and 21 subdomains. The examiner is required to react to statements descriptive of behavior in certain identified situations. The examiner may circle a number representative of the individual being observed or may be required to check all statements that apply to the individual being observed. For example, in evaluating independence functioning, the examiner is required to rate individuals according to which statements may apply to them, such as "drops food on the table or floor" or "talks with mouth full" or "chews food with an open mouth." The behavioral domains evaluated include economic activity, language development, domestic activities, vocational activities, self-direction, responsibility, and socialization.

Part II is a measure of social expectations in 14 domains related to personality and behavioral disorders. The examiner is required to rate whether the individual occasionally or frequently is involved in a particular behavior. For example, in rating violent and destructive behavior, the examiner may be required to evaluate whether the individual occasionally or frequently "tears up magazines or books" or "rips or tears clothing." Other domains measured include antisocial and rebellious behaviors and unacceptable and eccentric behaviors.

The *AAMD Adaptive Behavior Scale* is designed to provide information that can be used to determine classroom instructional programs. A profile summary is provided for all adaptive behavioral domains measured by the rating scale. The scores are interpreted in percentiles and deciles. Percentiles are arranged according to age groups. Comprehensive information received from the scale should assist teachers in planning specific programs for individuals and groups according to behavioral domains. Thus, the behavioral domains can be used to formulate objectives to be achieved. Objectives can be systematically evaluated by periodic retesting. The adaptive behavior scale is an instrument that can serve many purposes: identify students for placement in certain programs, provide evaluation of ongoing special programs, assist in administrative decisions for students with special needs, and provide specific objectives for instructional planning.

Summary

1. The terms used to describe people with disabilities have changed to negate stereotypes and false ideas.

2. The passage of the ADA has focused more attention on career counseling programs designed especially to meet the needs of individuals with disabilities. The ADA is a comprehensive document that covers several subjects significant to the rights of individuals with disabilities, including fair employment practices and access to public accommodations and transportation.

3. Special problems and needs of persons with disabilities include difficulty adjusting to and accepting physical disabilities, attitudinal barriers, being labeled "disabled," lack of role models, onset of disability, social/interpersonal skills, self-concept, skills for independent living, and architectural barriers. Educational programs that develop a better understanding of the special problems are needed by both employers and families.

4. State rehabilitation agencies provide numerous and varied programs for persons with disabilities. An actual case of an individual who received rehabilitation services from a state agency included the following steps: initial contact, diagnostic workup, evaluation and certification, vocational assessment, service planning, placement, and postemployment services.

5. Privately supported rehabilitation agencies provide educational, work, and counseling programs. Among services offered are psychological testing, vocational evaluation, personal/social adjustment counseling, work adjustment, prevocational training, special academic instruction, skills training, job placement, and sheltered workshops.

6. A career education program for students with disabilities uses a Life-Centered Career Education Curriculum. Included are a career awareness phase, a career exploration phase, and a preparation phase.

7. A group counseling program that promotes the vocational rehabilitation of individuals with disabilities included activities in (a) personal/social adjustment, (b) peer group affiliation, (c) worker-supervisor affiliation, and (d) job attitude counseling.

8. The *Micro-Tower* system of vocational evaluation consists of 13 work samples and is used as a screening device to determine which individuals would benefit from more extensive evaluation of specific aptitudes.

9. The *Valpar Component Work Sample System* consists of 16 work samples used to measure certain universal worker characteristics. The focus of this system is on physical skills and the ability to use eyes, hands, and feet in a coordinated manner.

10. The *SPIB* was designed for use with students with EMR in junior and senior high schools. Nine tests are used to assess students' needs for social and vocational skills.

11. The *AAMD Adaptive Behavior Scale* provides a means of identifying individuals with mental retardation. It is primarily a rating scale for identifying adaptive behavior of individuals with mental retardation and other special needs.

Supplementary Learning Exercises

1. Interview a rehabilitation counselor and obtain program descriptions for individuals with disabilities.
2. Make several observations of a special education class. Compile a list of common problems based on your observations. Relate these problems to job placement.
3. Develop a list of rehabilitation journals that publish articles concerning career counseling programs for individuals with disabilities.
4. Visit an industry that employs individuals with disabilities. Compile a list of jobs performed and worker function activities.
5. Survey your campus to find physical barriers that restrict individuals with disabilities. Discuss how these barriers and others contribute to psychological barriers.
6. Using the *SPIB* goals and domains, develop a rationale for using assessment results of this type in career counseling programs.
7. Compile a list of audiovisual materials that can be incorporated in career counseling programs for individuals with disabilities. Review and report on at least two.
8. Develop counseling components designed to meet two or more special problems and needs.
9. Survey a community to determine programs available for individuals with disabilities. Using the survey results, develop plans for using these programs in a high school or community college counseling program.
10. Interview a personnel director of an industry that employs individuals with disabilities to determine common problems experienced by these workers. Develop counseling components to help individuals overcome the common problems reported.

For More Information

Bolles, R. N. (1991). *Job-hunting tips for the so-called handicapped or people who have disabilities*. Berkeley, CA: Ten Speed.

Brolin, D. E., & Gysbers, N. C. (1989). Career education for students with disabilities. *Journal of Counseling and Development, 68,* 155–159.

Curnow, T. C. (1989). Vocational development of persons with disability. *Career Development Quarterly, 37*, 269–277.

French, S. (1996). The attitudes of health professionals towards disabled people. In G. Hales (Ed.), *Beyond disability: Towards an enabling society* (pp. 151–162). London: Sage.

Mackelprang, R. , & Salsgiver, R. (1999). *Disability: A diversity model approach in human service practice.* Pacific Grove, CA: Brooks/Cole.

Roessler, R., & Rubin, E. (1982). *Case management and rehabilitation counseling: Procedures and techniques.* Baltimore: University Park Press.

Roessler, R. T., & Rumrill, P. D. (1995). Promoting reasonable accommodations: An essential postemployment service. *Journal of Applied Rehabilitation Counseling, 26*(4), 3–7.

Szymanski, E. M., & Parker, R. M. (Eds.) (1996). *Work and disability: Issues and strategies in career development and job placement.* Austin, TX: PRO-ED.

15

Career Counseling for Gay, Lesbian, and Bisexual Clients

Chapter Highlights

- *Sexual orientation as a factor in career counseling approaches*

- *Negative stereotypes attributed to homophobia*

- *Forms of discrimination at work: blackmail, ostracism, sexual harassment, exclusion, the lavender ceiling*

- *Identity issues and a homosexual identity formation model*

- *An holistic approach to identity development*

- *Cultural differences in sexual orientation*

- *Special needs of youth with same-sex orientations*

- *Six-stage model for career counseling gay, lesbian, and bisexual individuals*

IN THIS FINAL CHAPTER ON SPECIAL POPULATIONS IT SEEMS RELEVANT TO reflect on some of the statements made in several chapters concerning the needs of diverse groups. On several occasions the point was made that a single career development theory cannot account for all needs of all clients. Thus, career counseling models should be flexible enough to incorporate special provisions for special populations or groups that have unique needs. For instance, practitioners need intervention strategies that focus on meeting the needs of individuals who are experiencing multiple identities and multiple oppressions. Moreover, accounting for the needs of special groups is good reason for developing mini-theories for building counseling models. The previous five chapters in this section support that position and, with the addition of this chapter, we suggest even more consideration be given to the needs of special populations.

As we develop as a nation in the 21st century, the chances are that an even greater number of groups of individuals with special needs will emerge. Thus, what began as a humble counseling program in the 20th century to help immigrants with special needs should continue to expand its focus to include appropriate counseling models for other groups with special needs. The groups discussed in this chapter are no exception to that position.

In the first part of this chapter, the special needs of gay, lesbian, and bisexual persons (g/l/b) will be discussed. Gelberg and Chojnacki (1996) suggest this grouping to provide fluidity to the discussion of individuals who have special needs because of their sexual orientation. This grouping does not imply that g/l/b needs are the same and does not suggest a greater priority for any one group. Distinctions between groups and within groups will be highlighted throughout this chapter. In the first sections some general trends and counseling issues of g/l/b persons will be introduced. The sections that follow will include discrimination in the workplace of g/l/b individuals, identity issues, cultural differences in sexual orientation, counseling concerns of g/l/b youth, and career counseling suggestions for g/l/b clients.

Gay, Lesbian, and Bisexual Persons

It is difficult to arrive at a precise number of g/l/b persons living in this country; however, estimates range between 5 and 25 million individuals (Henderson, 1984; Kinsey, Pomeroy, & Martin, 1948; Michael, Gagnon, Laumann, & Kolata, 1994) and 7.5 to 25 million (Elliot, 1993). One problem in determining more precise numbers is the methodologies and definitions used for defining sexual orientation preference. We are safe in assuming, however, that there are a significant number of potential g/l/b clients who need career counseling.

There appears to be a growing trend for more open discussion about the effects of sexual orientation on career development. Kronenberger (1991) reported that more lesbian women and gay men are coming out of the closet and discussing issues they face, especially in the workplace. Evidence suggests that more companies are supporting gay and lesbian associations and networks, including Xerox, AT&T, Lockheed, Rand Corporation, Hewlett-Packard, Sun Microsystems, U.S. West Communications, and Levi Strauss. Many of these organizations have regarded gay men and lesbian women as another diverse group in the work force and are dealing with this group just as they do with multiethnic groups; they have added a sexual-orientation component to diversity training programs. However, the issues surrounding homosexuality in general and its effect on career development and bias in the workplace are far from being settled.

One major objective of g/l/b persons is to find acceptance in the workplace and remove barriers that discriminate and inhibit their career development. Hudson (1992) suggested that counselors should prepare for counseling g/l/b clients by building an extensive body of resources including specific information on those organizations and companies that support them as employees and a list of g/l/b professionals who could provide support and information. Eldridge (1987) provides the following recommendations for counselors: (1) keep in mind the subtle, insidious nature of heterosexual bias and use this knowledge as a reminder for reflection; (2) use gender-free language; (3) become familiar with models of g/l/b identity formation; (4) identify a consultant who can provide helpful information or feedback on working with g/l/b clients; and (5) become familiar with local support networks.

Some General Counseling Issues

The purpose of this section is to increase the counselors' knowledge and awareness of problems g/l/b persons face in career counseling and the workplace. The first issue that generally surfaces is that of *stereotyping* about the kind of jobs gay men and lesbian women commonly hold. For example, gay men are thought to occupy traditional female jobs such as interior decorator or hair stylist; lesbians are fire fighters, truck drivers, and auto mechanics. As has been emphasized throughout this text, clients should feel free to explore all occupations of interest, and counselors must avoid stereotyping g/l/b clients. Clients who have had their career aspirations limited because of stereotyping, that is, the jobs they consider appropriate because of their sexual orientation, especially need encouragement to consider all career options. Counselors need to take an active role in challenging stereotypes in an effort to expand a client's perception of what is an appropriate career, and in this context, sexual orientation should be viewed as only one factor to consider in career exploration and decision.

Homophobia has been described as "an irrational fear, hatred, and intolerance of g/l/b persons" (Gelberg & Chojnacki, 1996, p. 21). This feeling of fear, hatred, and intolerance has led to violence, discrimination, and rejection of g/l/b persons in society in general and the workplace in particular. This fear enhances negative stereotypes and is deeply embedded in our society and in many societies around the world. Currently, there are frequent reports of extreme violence resulting in physical and psychological harm to g/l/b persons.

Internalized homophobia refers to how g/l/b individuals are affected by societal beliefs as they react to salient messages received in their environments. In early identity development some g/l/b persons who are greatly affected by internalized homophobia reject themselves as appropriate individuals and form a dislike for self and a self-hatred for their feelings of attraction to members of the same sex. This is particularly true during early stages of awareness of their sexual orientation. Adolescents, for instance, might not fully understand the precise meaning of their differences in sexual identity but quickly learn that it is negatively regarded. They may be described as highly anxious, fearful, guilty, and self-loathing (Gelberg & Chojnacki, 1996; Gonsiorek, 1985). Gay and lesbian adolescents are particularly vulnerable to internal conflicts in coming to terms with their sexual orientation and challenges and threats from their peers and others in society (Hall & Fradkin, 1992).

Heterosexist assumptions are based on a culture that is biased toward heterosexuality (Eldridge & Barnett, 1991). In our society and in many others throughout the world, heterosexism is considered the only viable lifestyle (Obear, 1991). The point here is that counselors must be aware of their own homophobic and heterosexist bias when counseling g/l/b clients. Those counselors who want to become g/l/b affirmative must challenge their own assumptions when trying to understand the complexity of a sexual orientation different than their own. For instance, two same-sex partners who live together do not have the same rights as legally married individuals of the opposite sex do. G/l/b persons are not welcome in some work environments. The stigma associated with being a g/l/b person might continue over the life span. These examples suggest that g/l/b persons might view career life planning much differently than heterosexual individuals do.

The American Psychological Association (1991) has issued a published set of guidelines for avoiding *heterosexual bias in language*. Counselors should carefully choose proper words, especially gender-free nouns such as partner or significant other. Avoid the term *homosexual* that could imply a diagnostic category of mental illness. Use the term *sexual orientation* rather than *sexual preference*.

Discrimination of G/L/B Persons at Work

There are many forms of discrimination of g/l/b persons at work. One example is overt discrimination, which can lead to violence directed at g/l/b individuals. "Gay bashing," which is not always work related, has been often documented in newspaper articles in various geographical regions. Many incidents of "gay bashing" are not reported, however, primarily because the victim is reluctant to call attention to his or her sexual orientation. In many cases, violence is simply threatened as a means of harassing g/l/b persons at work.

"Hidden discrimination" is typically involved in hiring, promotion, and compensation (Friskopp & Silverstein, 1995). Known g/l/b persons are treated differently than are their peers and are given diminished opportunities for advancement.

This form of discrimination is subtle but effectively relays the message that this person is not wanted in an organization. Overt and hidden discrimination in a work environment obviously discourages g/l/b persons from making their sexual orientations known.

Other forms of discrimination are blackmail, ostracism, sexual harassment, exclusion or avoidance, termination, and the so-called "lavender ceiling." Openly gay managers may not have access to higher-level corporate positions because of their sexual orientation, and as a result, plateau early in their careers when they reach the "lavender ceiling" (Friskopp & Silverstein, 1995). The "lavender ceiling" for g/l/b persons like the "glass ceiling" for women, is a discrimination method that is often hidden.

Because discrimination at work, especially in a hostile work environment, has the potential of being very threatening to g/l/b clients, support groups may be helpful. Clients may find that networking provides important and relevant information to help determine if one should leave an organization or transfer to another more friendly and amiable division. For instance, when interviewing a gay man who had experienced threats of violence in an organization, Friskopp and Silverstein (1995) found that by networking he discovered that a different division in the organization was more g/l/b affirmative and friendly. Counselors should provide a list of company-based g/l/b employee groups that can provide information about specific organizations. Gay professional organizations by states is another valuable resource. Clients can also be directed to resources that provide the names and addresses of g/l/b friendly organizations as listed in the final section of this chapter. Finally, a resource file of individuals who have experienced work force discrimination as a g/l/b person and are willing to help others is a most valuable referral source.

Identity Issues

Concepts of identity development have a long-standing relationship with career counseling. Career development theorists such as Super (1957, 1990), have emphasized the importance and pervasive nature of self-concept development in career counseling. More recently, identity development literature has involved racial-ethnic and sexual orientation identity models. Reynolds and Pope (1991) argue, however, that there is a scarcity of research on issues of multiple oppressions and identities; Latina lesbians, for example, face more complexities in the identity development process than do white, middle-class females. Unearthing identity issues involved in developing g/l/b sexual orientations will take considerable extensive research in the future. In the meantime, Cass (1979, 1984) has developed a gay identity model entitled Model of Homosexual Identity Formation (HIF) that contains six stages and is discussed in the following paragraphs. After reviewing the research on the HIF model, Levine and Evans (1991) note that it has empirical evidence to support its constructs.

Stage I: Identity Confusion

Stage II: Identity Comparison

Stage III: Identity Tolerance

Stage IV: Identity Acceptance

Stage V: Identity Pride

Stage VI: Identity Synthesis

Identity Confusion, Stage I, may be described as an awareness stage in which the individual recognizes that his or her feelings and behaviors indicate a same-sex sexual orientation. This is a period of soul searching and internal conflicts and a process of clarifying self-concept in adolescence (Erikson, 1963) during which coming to terms with sexual identity is an integral part of development. In Stage II, Identity Comparison, the individual acknowledges the possibility of being attracted to the same sex, feels different, and develops a sense of social alienation; the individual has difficulty in identifying with family and peer groups. During Stage III, Identity Tolerance, the individual tolerates rather than accepts an identification of an individual whose sexual orientation is different; however, the individual begins to contact other g/l/b persons to counter isolation. Identity Acceptance, Stage IV, is characterized by continued contacts with other g/l/b persons to validate a new identity and a new way of life. The individual accepts a g/l/b sexual orientation as an alternate identity. In Stage V, Identity Pride, the individual takes pride in disclosing an identity as a g/l/b person and rejects heterosexuality as the only appropriate lifestyle. In the final stage, Stage VI, Identity Synthesis, the individual is able to integrate a g/l/b identity with other aspects of self and develops compatibility with both heterosexual and g/l/b worlds.

This model provides points of reference for many factors that are significant to career counseling and career decision-making, starting with problem identification during the intake interview. Individuals who have not fully developed their sexual orientation identity might have difficulty in projecting their self-concept into a work environment. They might limit their occupational choices or appear indecisive during times of anxiety, confusion, and instability. For instance, those who have reached the Stage IV of identity acceptance might not be fully prepared or able to integrate their unfinished identity development within a career. Role confusion, emotional instability, irrational thinking, and indecisiveness can all be related to identity formation suggested in the HIF model. A word of caution—more than likely other related variables and factors also warrant consideration in problem identification, including examples that are discussed in the following paragraphs.

When using this model as a framework for career counseling, the counselor should be aware of the following four points: (1) some g/l/b individuals may recycle through the model depending on experiences and encounters within contextual interactions in the environment and particularly in the work environment; their progress might not be continuous; (2) the time it takes to move through the different stages in the identity model can vary enough that there are significant differences and might involve other factors not accounted for in the model; (3) there appear to be developmental differences between g/l/b persons, that is, gay men, lesbian women, and bisexuals could have different patterns of identity development; and (4) sexual orientation is only one variation in human development and other variables might account for individual variation (D'Augelli, 1991; Fassinger & Schlossberg, 1992; Fox, 1991; Gelberg & Chojnacki, 1996; Pope & Reynolds, 1991; Sophie, 1986).

Some related issues that point out the limitations of stage identity models are relevant to developing career counseling interventions. First, stage identity models suggest that sexual identity development has only one outcome; these models fall short of accounting for diversity of experiences during the developmental process (Brown, L. S., 1995). Individuals develop multiple identities that must be integrated with other group memberships and identities. A bisexual person, for instance, who is uncertain about how to interpret his or her sexual attractions to both men and women might be very apprehensive about making a career commitment. Second, individuals from different ethnic backgrounds could reflect a completely different viewpoint of sexual concepts and identity. Some cultural groups may inhibit certain forms of sexual expression and prescribe others (Rust, 1996).

Also, as suggested in Chapter 10, identity development is not a segmented process and should therefore be considered more comprehensive and inclusive (Myers, Speight, Highlen, Cox, Reynolds, Adams, & Hanley, 1991). As a more holistic approach, identity development is viewed as a multidimensional process that includes multiple oppressions based on race, ethnicity, sexual orientation, sex, and age. For an ethnic minority lesbian, all oppressions must be considered to fully understand the process of identity development. This comprehensive viewpoint suggests that we should not isolate variables but, rather, assist individuals in conceptualizing the totality of the process of self-identity development. For example, individuals are not to be socialized into a worldview that leads to a fragmented sense of self. Furthermore, for an individual to feel positive about being a g/l/b person requires that individual to repudiate external stereotypes of g/l/b individuals. Although an optimal theory of identity development suggests that current identity models have limitations (Myers et al., 1991), the HIF model does provide some guidelines for relevant information that can be included in the career counseling process.

In sum, unique development can account for differences among each type of sexual orientation. For instance, the unique needs of lesbian women could result in different patterns and timing of development than would be typical of gay men or bisexual individuals (Sophie, 1986). Etringer, Hillerbrand, and Hetherington (1990) suggest that lesbians are less uncertain about making a career decision when compared with gay men, heterosexual men, and women. The researchers conclude, "the degree of uncertainty regarding one's career choice and degree of dissatisfaction with that choice vary by sex and by sexual orientation" (p. 107). The causes of uncertainty among g/l/b populations have not been fully determined but are thought to be associated with employment discrimination and self-disclosure of sexual orientation. Lesbian women, for example, might be more reluctant to self-disclose in career decision-making than gay men are (Sophie, 1986).

A good characterization of g/l/b identity development is a gradual process of discovery rather than a sudden awakening during childhood. Children might sense a feeling of being different, and this perception can provide sexual meaning during puberty. Periods of confusion might be followed by anxiety that usually takes years to resolve. Progress from one stage to another is usually not orderly, but sporadically individuals move to and from stages of development as they struggle with self-awareness (Coleman & Remafedi, 1989). Thus, counselors who can identify a client's progress in the HIF model have significant information concerning self-awareness and other important factors relevant to career decision-making.

Some research identifies when the awareness of same-sex feelings and attractions take place. For gay males, this is during early to mid-adolescence and for lesbian women, around the age of 20 (Anderson, 1994). Other findings include a survey of 13 Japanese American gay males in which half of them reported that they began to experience same-sex feelings during the early teens and the remainder in their late teens and early twenties (Wooden, Kawasaki, & Mayeda, 1983). A survey of onset of sexual orientation of 120 lesbian women and gay adolescents suggested they experienced same-sex feelings between 4 and 18 years of age (Telljohann & Price, 1993). Finally a study by Uribe and Harbeck (1992) reported same-sex experiences for gay males occurred at an average age of 14, but much later for lesbian women. These studies suggest that onset of same-sex attractions can vary for individuals but usually begins during adolescence. Gay males experience same-sex activities earlier than lesbian women do. The amount of time that it takes an individual to progress through stages does not appear to be clear cut nor is the age when gay men and lesbian women reach the final stage of identity in Cass's model. One could conclude that progress through the HIF is not necessarily linear but could be characterized as cyclical as individuals cycle-regress-recycle through stages. This argument is supported by McDonald (1982), who suggests that the developmental process of gay men and lesbian women could extend well into adulthood.

Cultural Differences in Sexual Orientation

In this section, we focus on differences in sexual orientation by culture. The research in this area is very sparse; counselors should watch for more in-depth research and analysis in the near future. More than likely new themes and patterns of cultural differences in sexual orientation will emerge early in the 21st century. In the meantime, this discussion of cultural differences in sexual orientation provides a means of discovering special needs of Asian Americans, African Americans, Latina and Latino Americans, and Native Americans.

According to Chung and Katayama (1999), there are significant differences between Asian and American cultures toward acceptance of the different sexual orientation of g/l/b individuals. Chung and Katayama point out that heterosexism and homophobia are more prominent and intense in Asian cultures and suggest three overarching reasons why homosexuality is not accepted in Asian cultures: First is the philosophy of harmony and complementary of the Chinese "Yin-Yang," which has similar versions in other Asian cultures such as Korea and Japan. This philosophy represents a natural order of life that prescribes that persons of the opposite sex are to be unified; thus, it is against nature to have a same-sex orientation. Second, because traditional gender roles and family systems in most Asian cultures are so highly honored, same-sex orientations are unacceptable. As a result, g/l/b activities and relationships are closely censored. Third is the prominence of agrarian societies in Asian countries. Farmlands are passed on from one traditional family to the next. Same-sex orientation works against a long-established tradition. These traditions and philosophy of a "natural life," according to Yin-Yang, does not allow for an open same-sex orientation lifestyle. Because the consequences of disclosing a same-sex orientation are so severe, most g/l/b persons remain in the closet. As a result, the concept of g/l/b identity is not recognized in many Asian cultures (Chung & Katayama, 1999).

Asian American g/l/b persons have found a somewhat more compatible environment in America, especially in certain geographic regions. Being aware of the mores, traditions, and lifestyles of the g/l/b's mother country and its society, however, provides counselors a greater understanding of identity development and contextual messages individuals receive from their environment in this country. Evidence also indicates that Asian lesbian and gays have difficulty in being accepted in white and middle-class-oriented gay communities (Chan, 1989; Newman & Muzzonigro, 1993). In this context they are considered, like other minority ethnic groups, to have a double minority status. As Chung and Katayama (1999) put it, their "efforts involve the parallel psychological processes of developing integrated ethnic and sexual identities" (p. 166).

In a study by Chan (1989), 19 women and 16 men between the ages of 21 and 36 who identified themselves as lesbian, gay, and Asian Americans were interviewed and filled out a questionnaire. Most of the sample was Asian Americans who were born in Asia. The results suggested that most of these first-generation individuals preferred to identify themselves as lesbian and gay rather than as Asian Americans, but others in the sample refused to identify as one or the other, preferring instead to identify with both. This latter group felt that it was as difficult to be accepted by the gay and lesbian community as by the Asian community. Chan (1989) concluded that stage of identity development largely determined whether an individual was more closely identified with being lesbian or gay or Asian American. Disclosure as lesbian or gay in this sample usually occurred by informing a sister rather than parents. It appeared that most felt their parents would not accept their sexual orientation and feared rejection.

In a more recent study, Chan (1997) points out that modern homosexual identities are Western constructs. East Asian cultures have no comparable sexual identities. Discussions about sexuality are taboo and considered highly embarrassing even among friends. An individual's sexual orientation is considered to be private. Sexuality issues are not usually expressed in public. Moreover, the concept of individual identity does not exist; there is only group identification as a family member. Thus, cultural differences in identity development, especially among Asian Americans, need further exploration and analysis.

In a study of gay issues among black Americans, Loiacano (1989) found similar results to those reported by Asian g/l/b persons. Black American lesbians are largely considered incompatible with role expectations in a black community (Lorde, 1984). Furthermore, gay and lesbian communities do not offer the same level of affirmation to blacks that they do to their white members. Black gay men were viewed as inferior as members of gay communities and do not receive the same level of affirmation that white members do (Icard, 1986). Loiacano (1989) confirmed these findings in an interview with a small sample of three males and three females. Later, he suggested that three themes emerged from his interview: (1) finding validation in the gay and lesbian community, (2) finding validation in the black community, and (3) needing integrate identities (Loiacano, 1993). Although his study is considered as only providing tentative data, it seems to verify the idea of a double minority status among black gays and lesbians.

A study of 20 older African American gay men living in New York city, whose average age was 56, presents some interesting data. The authors of this study conclude that being an African American gay was different than being white and gay primarily because of the interpretation of race and color in our society (Adams & Kimmel, 1997). In the African American community gay men are perceived negatively as wanting to be female and cross-dressers and threaten family child-rearing responsibilities. Gay men are also perceived as traitors to African American families and their race. The lesbian and gay community is viewed as a white establishment that ignores the needs of people of color. These attitudes and stereotypes make it difficult for African American gay men to feel accepted in both the African American community and the gay and lesbian community (Adams & Kimmel, 1997). The results of this study should be interpreted as characteristic of this sample only; however, similar conclusions were reached by Icard (1986), Lorde (1984), and Loiacano (1993).

Finally, a study of the results of an anonymous questionnaire of 1,400 African American gay men and lesbian women from various geographic regions in the continental United States was reported by Peplau, Cochran, and Mays (1997). Significant conclusions of relevant information for career counseling include the findings that interracial partners were relatively common among the respondents and that same-sexual activities are often more hidden in the African American community than in white gay and lesbian communities. These conclusions suggest that African American gay and lesbians have little support for their sexual orientation within their communities, which makes it more difficult to integrate identities for career development and to focus on traditional career and life planning issues.

Espin (1987) found similar results with Latina lesbian women. This group of lesbians also feared rejection in the Hispanic community and received marginal support in the gay and lesbian community. Espin found that it was difficult to determine if ethnic identity or sexual orientation identity was considered most important by the women studied. She concluded that her respondents had varying degrees of success as identifying as both lesbian and Latina.

Morales (1992) depicts the Latino and Latina community as being excessively homophobic and thus having little tolerance for gay and lesbian lifestyle. He suggests that Latino gay men and Latina lesbians exist in three worlds: the gay and lesbian community, the Latino and Latina community, and the white heterosexual mainstream society. Choosing which of the three to identify with presents challenges and conflicts that are indeed complex. In the beginning of the choice process Latino gay men and Latina lesbians might resort to denial of conflicts. Using the unrealistic logic of denial, they might naively choose a gay and lesbian lifestyle with the hope that they will find a utopian lifestyle free of discrimination and conflicts they encounter in their own communities and in the dominant culture.

A second choice might focus on coming out as a bisexual rather than as gay or lesbian. This choice avoids being labeled and categorized as gay, or in Spanish by maricon and thus, might be more acceptable to individuals who have difficulty in identifying with gay and lesbian communities. In a third choice, Latino gay men and lesbian women choose to live independently in all three communities and not "mix" the three. The conflicts in allegiances that soon develop usually lead to high levels of anxiety and fears of betrayal and most come to the conclusion that some form of unity is desirable (Morales, 1992).

In the final stages of establishing priorities, the integration process becomes the central focus. But the integrating process of being identified within three communities as gay or lesbian can result in fear and anxiety of the future and the recognition that such an identity will be a constant challenge. These circumstances expose Latino gay men and Latina lesbians to risks of loosing career opportunities that are already limited because of their minority status (Morales, 1992). Like other minority groups, Latino gay men and Latina lesbians should be helped throughout this entire process by support groups and relevant information about prospective employers and their hiring policies.

To understand the gay and lesbian world of Native Americans, we must digress in a few sentences to the mid-eighteenth century. French missionaries at that time report finding Native American men who dressed in women's clothing, assumed female roles and accepted other men as sexual partners. The French word *berdache,* meaning male homosexual, was given to these men and also to women who assumed the role of warrior and hunter and wore male attire. Among the Native Americans in which this behavior was observed, the berdache were not only tolerated, but well accepted in some tribes. The berdache phenomenon was evidently widespread in the major cultural groups in North America, in some tribes in Mexico and South America, and among the Alaskan Eskimo (Mondimore, 1996).

According to Tafoya (1997) the berdache phenomenon is a part of a Native American's worldview of a "Two-Spirited tradition." In this context, Native Americans are not comfortable with identifying themselves as g/l/b persons but, rather, as individuals who possess both male and female spirits. As Tafoya (1997) explains, "gay can be seen as a noun, but Two-Spirit as a verb" ("This is meant as a metaphoric statement, meaning that a noun is a person, place, or thing, whereas a verb deals with action and interaction") (p.5). What is emphasized here is that the

Native American tradition stresses transformation and change that is too flexible to fit the categories of gay or straight. Masculine and feminine concepts of Native Americans are quite different from European concepts. There is a greater spectrum of acceptable sexual behavior among Native Americans, and there is less stigma associated with women who assume male roles and men who assume female roles (Highwater, 1990).

The berdache phenomenon and the Two-Spirited person might not be well known among many young Native Americans, especially those who have attended federal boarding or missionary schools. However, a visit to the Lakotas and Sioux in the Northern Plains in 1982 found that the berdache tradition was still practiced but modified from what was described as the "old ways" (Williams, 1993). Contemporary practices are more secretive and are not enthusiastically endorsed by young Native Americans; however, Native Americans in general have great tolerance and respect for personal choice. In this context, the Native American community might be more accepting of individuals who identify as Two-Spirited in Native American terms or as g/l/b in the dominant society. Nevertheless, g/l/b individuals must also face a dominant society that is less tolerant and discriminates against individuals who are identified as having a same-sex orientation. Native Americans are also subject to stereotyping as discussed in Chapter 10.

In sum, one could conclude that ethnic minority gays indeed have a double minority status. A lesbian ethnic minority could be given a triple minority status. Both ethnic minority gays and lesbians struggle with parallel psychological processes of identity; ethnic identity and sexual orientation identity development complement or complicate self-awareness and self-concept development. In addition, lesbians must also overcome gender-role socialization that can limit career development.

Throughout this text it has been emphasized that we must identify unique individual needs for career counseling direction. In this section some needs have been identified that can be generalized to most ethnic minority g/l/b groups. In other words, ethnic minority g/l/b persons share some general needs such as protection against discrimination, but each group of ethnic minorities also has special needs. Within these groups, individual needs must also be unearthed. In essence, all the unique needs of individuals who seek career counseling should be addressed.

Counseling G/L/B–Oriented Youth

Counselors have often been reminded that adolescents most need their services. In the context of working with g/l/b–oriented youth, the complex task of sexual identity can be very disruptive. A counselor who is aware of the issues surrounding the development of self-concept in career development must also be alert to the special problems brought about by sexual minority status during adolescence. Many g/l/b adolescents Coleman and Remafedi (1989) interviewed had abandoned their friends, were rejected by their families, had failing grades, and were involved in substance abuse. Furthermore, half of the sample had run away from home, had been arrested, or had a sexually transmitted disease. A smaller minority of the group had attempted suicide, accepted money for sexual favors, or been sexually victimized. Other studies by Bell and Weinberg (1978), Saghir and Robins (1973), and Jay and Young (1979), found that sexual orientation was a precipitating factor in suicide attempts among g/l/b persons and that most attempts at suicide occurred before the age of 21.

Counselors should also recognize that overall health is a most important component of career counseling and that it is not unusual for many individuals during adolescence to take health for granted in a rather cavalier way. Their attitude about HIV infection might be reflected as a gay's problem; however, we now know that the risks of becoming HIV infected among sexually active adolescents has significantly increased for both heterosexual and g/l/b persons. Although the leading cause of transmission of HIV to women has changed to heterosexual activities, most modes of transmission reported through 1999 were through g/l/b activity (Centers for Disease Control and Prevention, 1999). According to Hein (1988), HIV transmission to adolescents was twice as common by g/l/b activity than by needle sharing. The point here is the need to inform all adolescents including g/l/b persons of the probability of HIV infection through sexual activity and the sharing of needles. Moreover, the risks appear greater for all adolescents who have not received instructions of risk-reduction guidelines.

What we must make clear here is that HIV/AIDS is not solely a g/l/b disease. Here are some facts to digest (Winfeld & Spielman 1995):

1. One in every 250 Americans is HIV positive.
2. Two hundred people are infected daily (in 1994).
3. There are more than 6,000 full-blown AIDS cases among children.
4. In 1992, heterosexual sex became the leading transmission route of HIV in women.
5. More young men, gay and straight, are starting to show signs of a second epidemic in the age group of 16 to 25 (p. 145).

Winfeld and Spielman (1995) have proposed an HIV/AIDS education program for the workplace that could be modified and used for other groups as well, including adolescents. Some topics that are relevant to our discussion here are the following:

- Theories of the origin of AIDS
- What are HIV and AIDS?
- How are HIV and AIDS transmitted?
- How are HIV and AIDS not transmitted?
- Who is at the greatest risk?
- Risk reduction guidelines

Counselors who recognize the influence of sexual orientation on career development will create an atmosphere in which sexuality can be openly discussed. Counselors must be prepared to convey full acceptance of g/l/b clients. Counselors are not to assume that every client is heterosexually oriented or that certain clients are g/l/b by stereotypical suggestions. The adolescent especially needs to feel comfortable in expressing sexual orientation issues. The counselor should convey a nonjudgmental attitude. The uncertainty, ambiguity, cultural stigma, and fears of the future are viable topics to be integrated in preparing adolescents for career decision-making.

Career Counseling for G/L/B Persons

Although g/l/b persons bring unique issues to career counseling, Gelberg and Chojnacki (1996) suggest that these issues can be resolved in current career counseling models. Furthermore, these researchers suggest adapting career counseling approaches to meet specific needs of g/l/b clients. The Multicultural Career Counseling Model for Ethnic Minority Women outlined and discussed in Chapter 4, provides some guidelines for meeting the special needs of the g/l/b population. Within that model, steps designed to meet the special needs of ethnic minority groups provide examples for meeting the special needs of g/l/b persons. For instance, g/l/b persons locate their stage of identity development. Counselors explore their biases of g/l/b persons. The contextual interactions of g/l/b should be fully explored. Standardized tests that have not included sexual orientation as a variable in their development should be used with caution. Some g/l/b individuals might have limited their career choices because of stereotyped perceptions of what is considered appropriate work for gay men and lesbian women. The use of allies as mentors in the career decision process and job search is suggested by Gelberg and Chojnacki (1996). All these issues and more should be resolved in current career counseling models to meet the unique needs of g/l/b individuals. The following six stages are designed for g/l/b persons, and most important, can be included within contemporary career counseling models.

Stage 1, *Pre-counseling Preparation,* requires the counselor to evaluate his or her awareness of the g/l/b worldviews and cultures. Counselors must challenge their own assumptions about g/l/b sexual orientation. Counselors may want to use consultants to assist them in the preparation process. The basic assumptions of counselors who are affirmative g/l/b helpers are characterized by an adaptation of the work of Schwartz and Harstein (1986) and quoted from Gelberg and Chojnacki (1996, p. 17) as follows:

1. Being gay, lesbian, or bisexual is not a pathological condition.
2. The origins of sexual orientation are not completely known.
3. G/l/b persons lead fulfilling and satisfying lives.
4. There are a variety of g/l/b lifestyles.
5. G/l/b persons who attend counseling without a desire to change their sexual orientation should not be forced into change.
6. G/l/b–affirmative individual and group counseling should be available.

Individuals who are g/l/b ethnic minorities should be perceived as having double or triple minority status. Counselors may also want to include steps that are a part of the Multicultural Career Counseling Model for Ethic Minority Women discussed in Chapter 4. For example, in Stage 1, counselors may want to administer the Multicultural Counseling Checklist (Ward & Bingham, 1993) and the Career Counseling Checklist (Ward & Tate, 1990) both of which are displayed in the appendix. Gender issues may also be included for female clients who are considered as having a triple minority status.

Stage 2, *Establishing an Affirmative Trusting Relationship*, may require considerable time and effort beyond one counseling session. Counselors can expect g/l/b clients to be reluctant to express themselves freely until a trusting relationship has been established and maintained. A collaborative relationship in which the counselor is an ally is recommended as a viable affirmative approach (Gelberg & Chojnacki, 1996). To be an effective ally, counselors need to become knowledgeable about g/l/b issues, limitations of career choice, and the influence of homophobic attitudes expressed by important others in g/l/b individuals' career development. Affirmative career counselors not only assist g/l/b persons with career decision-making but remain as allies and resources if and when discrimination is encountered in hiring and in the workplace.

As discussed in Chapter 4, a culturally appropriate counseling relationship also consumes time and is most necessary for effective counseling with ethnic minority g/l/b persons. Counselors should also create a counseling environment that is conducive to discussing worldviews that may be quite different than their own. The client-counselor relationship can be facilitated by early discussions of ethnic/racial information (Bingham & Ward, 1996).

Stage 3, *Client Identity Issues*, involves the client's place of development on the six stages of the Cass (1979) HIF model. This information is to be used with career development issues to evaluate the readiness of the client to make career decisions. It is also a point of reference for counseling interventions of personal counseling or psychotherapy. For instance, some clients may need further assistance with developing their identities before career counseling or in conjunction with it. Client identity issues can also be related to problems with irrational thinking and emotional instability. Difficulty with progression through identity stages can also result in client indecisive behavior. The following excerpts from a case of a female senior high school student illustrates how identity problems interfere with career decision-making.

In her senior year in high school Liz was asked by her parents to see a career counselor. Her speech patterns were very stilted, and she was hesitant to express herself openly, seemingly saying only what was absolutely necessary. Her counselor changed the subject to a known interest of Liz's, horseback riding, and spent the major portion of the first counseling session discussing this topic. On her next visit to the counseling center, Liz was much more relaxed and warmly greeted the counselor. After a few minutes of small talk, the counselor suggested that they begin the interview. This session and the following session were productive as they discussed demographic information and educational attainment. When future plans were introduced, Liz stated that her parents want her to follow a lifestyle pattern that she is not sure she wants. "Go to college and meet a nice boy you can marry," she stated as she mocked her parents. This was the beginning of a long story Liz told that focused on her confusion with sexual identity, rebellion, and a general indecision about what the future holds for her. The more she expressed her thoughts, the more certain the counselor became that Liz was greatly confused about her identity as a woman and was far from being ready to make career choices. The counselor proceeded with personal counseling directed at identity development.

Counselors need to create a counseling climate in which the client feels free to express identity development issues. Counselors should encourage discussion of contextual interactions that may assist the client in understanding sources of confusion and negative feedback. Specific issues that are ethnically/racially related are most appropriate for multicultural groups. Counselors may want to use a mentor who can participate as an ally in helping the client resolve issues. Counselors should offer support and be an affirmative confidante. The following case illustrates the use of an ally in the career counseling process with a ethnic minority gay man.

Julio was born in Texas to immigrant parents from Mexico. He often visited Mexico and was fluent in both English and Spanish. His stated need for career counseling went something like this: "I need a steady job so I can go to college for a better one." As Julio discussed his background, he revealed that he was openly gay, which made him the subject of jokes on the job. He needed advice about how to manage his sexual orientation with his family and fellow workers. Julio had not met many gays in his new community and felt uncomfortable talking to "straight" men about his problem. The counselor took this opportunity to tell Julio of a gay Mexican man who would be willing to act as an ally to help solve Julio's problems.

After several visits with the ally, Julio informed the counselor he felt much more at ease when talking about his personal problems to an interested gay man. He felt that he had gained a better understanding of what to expect when he is identified as a gay person from members of the local Mexican American community. He also was given the names and addresses of local business places and organizations that were considered gay and lesbian friendly.

In this case the counselor felt that Julio would react most positively to someone who could realistically share his problems and provide him with advice from real life experiences. The counselor had learned that it is most difficult to convince an ethnic minority who is gay that the counselor understands the minority's problems. Clearly, one who has experienced similar problems as an ethnic minority and also has a gay sexual orientation can help clients by sharing personal experiences.

Stage 4, *Identify Variables That May Limit Career Choice,* suggests that discrimination, bias, and stereotyping are negative influences that limit career choices for all g/l/b persons, including ethnic minority individuals. A thorough discussion of these three variables should center on how each might have influenced clients to not consider certain careers. The major basis for their decisions to eliminate certain careers could be flawed such that appropriate careers seem to be only those that are stereotyped for either gay men, lesbian women, and ethnic minorities. Obviously, clients should conclude that any and all careers can be considered in the choice process. In essence, the client takes back what has been taken away.

Stage 5, *Tailored Assessment,* should follow the assessment model described in Chapter 5 and outlined as follows:

Step 1. Maintain a client-counselor collaborative relationship.

Step 2. Maintain the role of assessment in the counseling model used.

Step 3. Negotiate the client's role in assessment.

Step 4. Describe the principles and purposes of standardized and self-assessment.

Step 5. Client and counselor specify the client's assessment needs from information in the intake interview.

Step 6. Client and counselor select appropriate assessment instruments.

Step 7. Client and counselor reevaluate and identify problems.

Step 8. Client and counselor formulate goals.

In the next stage, career counseling models typically proceed to problem identification and the establishment of counseling goals (see Chapter 4). After completing these steps, clients proceed to the decision model that is most appropriate for them. During this process g/l/b specific career resources should be provided. No doubt more career information will be developed specifically for g/l/b persons in the future, but in the meantime two MBA graduates, Friskopp and Silverstein (1995), have a good reference list that includes locations of organizations with nondiscrimination policies, addresses for employer policies, gay employee groups, and gay professional organizations.

Other resources include the following:

National Gay and Lesbian Task Force Policy Institute
Listing of Corporations, Organizations, Unions, and Educational Institutions
Offering Domestic Partner Benefits
Publications Department
2230 17th St, NW
Washington, DC 20009

Standing Committee for Lesbian, Gay, and Bisexual Awareness
VCU
907 Floyd Ave.
Box 842032
Richmond, VA 23284-2032
Attn: John Leppo

Growing American Youth (G.A.Y.)
c/o Our World Too
11 South Vandeventer
St. Louis, MO 63108

National Advocacy Coalition on Youth and Sexual Orientation
1025 Vermont Avenue, Suite 200
Washington, DC 20005

Parents, Friends, Families of Lesbians and Gays (PFLAG)
Box 18901
Denver, CO 80218

Stage 6, *Job Search Strategies,* prepares clients for developing their resumés and the job interview and locating g/l/b affirmative organizations. Counselors should emphasize to clients the importance of assessing work environments. This process for g/l/b clients involves more than finding job opportunities. In some respects the process adds another dimension to the person-environment-fit constructs; g/l/b persons should locate a work environment that is actively g/l/b affirmative. Counselors can help g/l/b clients avoid many problems they could face in a hostile work environment by providing direction for locating a friendly environment in the job search process. The key is having up-to-date resources.

Two excellent resource books that should be added to the affirmative counselor's list are *Cracking the Corporate Closet* (Baker, Strub, & Henning, 1995) and *The 100 Best Companies for Gay Men and Lesbians* (Mickens, 1994). Updated editions of these books should be available in the near future. Some of the criteria used in these resources to determine if an organization is g/l/b affirmative are anti-discriminatory policies that include sexual orientation, domestic partner benefit policies, diversity training that includes sexual orientation, and existence of g/l/b employee groups. Both resources also use other criteria to evaluate overall "gay friendliness."

For clients who are interested in other work sites, the national edition of the *GAYELLOW PAGES* (Green, 1994) is a good resource and should be regularly updated. This publication provides a list of business places and services that are g/l/b friendly. Also included are associations for g/l/b persons. A list of specific regional work locations is provided in the publication *Out! Resource Guide* (1994). Resources can also be found in Brooks (1991), Dworkin and Gutierrez (1992), Friskopp and Silverstein (1995), Gelberg and Chojnacki (1996), Vargo (1998), and Winfeld and Spielman (1995).

Finally, a most important resource is the networks that provide advice for g/l/b persons. Counselors would be wise to compile a list of local available networks that offer assistance to g/l/b persons. In addition, counselors should recruit and train local gay men and lesbian women to assist other g/l/b persons who need help in locating an affirmative workplace.

Another unique issue for g/l/b persons involved in the job search process is the question of whether the client should reveal his or her sexual orientation. This decision has many implications for g/l/b clients. Winfeld and Spielman (1995), Gelberg and Chojnacki (1996), and Friskopp and Silverstein (1995) suggest that coming out is a multidimensional process involving a number of factors and variables that include the following: the client's identity development; the g/l/b affirmative status of the employing organization; the knowledge of the client's sexual orientation by family, friends, and associates; the status of the client's partner and what "coming out" would mean to him or her; and the readiness of the client to face the workplace as a known g/l/b person. Keep in mind that identity development is an ongoing continuous process that is more cyclical than linear as individuals move up and down the parameters of the HIF model. Counselors can assist clients in making this decision through discussions of the implications of many variables that are both external and internal. Clients may be helped by other g/l/b persons who have gone through this process. Counselors may also suggest that clients network with g/l/b employees in the organizations of interest.

Some suggestions for coming out at work include extensive planning. One must lay the foundation for a positive reception, which includes having an outstanding job performance and building credentials that support and enhance job assignment. Allies who are supportive also need to be identified. Clients who also recruit heterosexuals as allies will usually have a stronger support base. Clients may also be instructed to test the waters by dropping clues about their sexual orientations, for example, by suggesting they support gay people and their rights. Reactions to such statements provide clues about what one might encounter in coming out (Friskopp & Silverstein, 1995).

Vargo (1998) suggests that gay men and lesbian women must be prepared for coming out at work by being fully aware of the reasons why one should take this step. Relevant questions include what the client's short-term and long-term goals for coming out are and how these goals can be reached. For instance, should one come out to only a few selected workers and gradually inform other key persons? Will coming out enhance the chances of advancement or detract from it? Clients should be encouraged to anticipate problems that might emerge and how these problems can be solved.

There appears to be strong supporting evidence from professional gay men and lesbian women that the benefits of coming out at work are far greater than are those of remaining in the closet (Friskopp & Silverstein, 1995; Vargo, 1998; Winfeld & Spielman, 1995). Some problems reported that arise from remaining in the closet are fear of exposure, problems in socializing, lower self-esteem, and vulnerability to harassment such as blackmail. In addition gay men and lesbian women experienced resentment for having to censor thoughts, even words, and, of course, actions that might reveal one's sexual orientation. Professional gay men and lesbian women who experienced coming out, strongly suggested that being in the closet is a very painful and disturbing experience (Friskopp & Silverstein, 1995; Signorile, 1993). For instance, Ike felt relieved that he could now be honest and "above board" with his fellow workers. Ann was tired of a double life and felt much better about herself and her relationships at work after coming out. The major personal benefits from coming out appear to be self-acceptance and self-actualization. However, each individual should be encouraged to thoroughly evaluate his or her work environment for the consequences of coming out as well as for his or her ability to manage pressure and discrimination that could result from coming out.

The experiences of coming out at lower level jobs or nonprofessional work might be more perilous and risky, especially in highly conservative environments (Vargo, 1998). Clients should be encouraged to evaluate each work environment for its openness shown by other gay employees and the advantages and disadvantages of announcing one's sexual orientation in that environment. Vargo (1998) reports that the trend is for more gays and lesbians to come out at work primarily because of formal policies that protect them from discrimination.

Being closeted at work or coming out at work are viable topics for g/l/b persons; however, more research is needed with an in-depth analysis of the psychological antecedents and subsequent consequences of this process. In the meantime, the references previously mentioned provide insights into this process and cover such topics as managing a g/l/b identity at work. Clients should confer with other g/l/b persons in the work force for guidelines in making decisions involving g/l/b issues of coming out at work.

In sum, g/l/b persons have special needs that are to be addressed in the career counseling process. Career counseling can proceed within existing career counseling models for g/l/b persons with some adaptations and modifications. Special needs may be included in career counseling models as additional components that are relevant to the stages and steps of existing models. Counselors must also account for individual differences and subsequent needs of individuals within groups. For instance, an ethnic minority lesbian should be viewed as an individual with a triple minority status. All ethnic minority g/l/b persons receive an additional minority status that may reflect unique needs of their ethnic minority identification.

Summary

1. G/l/b persons have special needs because of their sexual orientation that should be addressed in career counseling.

2. There are estimates of between 5 and 25 million g/l/b persons in this country.

3. More organizations and companies are supporting gay and lesbian associations and networks. Many regard gay men and lesbian women as another diverse group in the workplace.

4. Individuals with a sexual orientation of g/l/b continue to be stereotyped about the kinds of jobs they should hold, are threatened by violence often resulting from homophobia, form a dislike for themselves through internalized homophobia, and generally receive negative feedback from a society that views heterosexism as the only viable lifestyle.

5. Discrimination in the workplace can involve threats, lack of promotions, blackmail, ostracism, sexual harassment, exclusion or avoidance, termination, and the "lavender ceiling."

6. Sexual orientation is considered an important component of identity development. Identity development may follow a five-stage process that varies by sex and race, sexual orientation, and other developmental factors associated with individual environments. Individuals progress through stages at different rates, and the age when g/l/b persons reach the final stage in an identity model varies.

7. Ethnic minority gay men have a double minority status. A lesbian ethnic minority may have a triple minority status. Ethnic minorities suggest that they are only marginally received in g/l/b communities.

8. Adolescents who are g/l/b oriented face a complex task of developing a sexual identity. They might be abandoned by friends and rejected by their families. Among major problems are suicide ideation and HIV infection.

9. Unique issues g/l/b persons bring to career counseling can be resolved in current career counseling models with some adaptations and modifications. Six stages that can be included within current career counseling models are pre-counseling preparation, establishing an affirmative trusting relationship, client identity issues, identify variables that can limit career choice, tailored assessment, and job search strategies.

Supplementary Learning Exercises

1. Develop an informative program about HIV/AIDS that could be used in schools at all levels.

2. Choose three special needs of g/l/b clients and develop appropriate intervention strategies.

3. Develop a list of topics that could be used with adolescents who are in the process of developing a sexual orientation of gay, lesbian, or bisexual.

4. Develop a list of publications that could be used by g/l/b clients in conjunction with career counseling.

5. Develop a career counseling program that would specifically meet the needs of a triple minority status woman.

6. Visit an organization that is g/l/b affirmative. Obtain published materials that state the organization's policies. Share this with your class.

7. Interview a gay, lesbian, or bisexual person. Make note of his or her workplace experiences.

8. Identify the topics you would use in an intake interview with g/l/b persons. Specify how you would introduce selected topics.

9. What are some methods you would use to inform the public that you are a g/l/b affirmative counselor? List some problems you might experience.

10. Debate the following issues as either pro or con:
    (a) G/l/b persons should have equal rights.
    (b) G/l/b persons do not choose their sexual orientation.
    (c) G/l/b persons should be restricted from choosing certain occupations.

For More Information

Cass, V. C. (1979). Homosexuality identity formation: A theoretical model. *Journal of Homosexuality, 4*(3), 219–235.

Cass, V. C. (1984). Homosexuality identity formation: Testing a theoretical model. *Journal of Sex Research, 20*(2), 143–167.

Chan, C. S. (1997). Don't ask, don't tell, don't know: The formation of homosexual identity and sexual expression among Asian American lesbians. In B. Greene (Ed.), *Ethnic and cultural diversity among lesbians and gay men* (pp. 240–249). Thousand Oaks, CA: Sage.

Chung, Y. B., & Katayama, M. (1999). Ethnic and sexual identity development of Asian American lesbian and gay adolescents. In K. S. Ng (Ed.), *Counseling Asian families from a systems perspective* (pp. 159–171). Alexandria, VA: American Counseling Association.

Friskopp, A., & Silverstein, S. (1995). *Straight jobs, gay lives.* New York: Scribner.

Gelberg, S., & Chojnacki, J. T. (1996). *Career and life planning with gay, lesbian, & bisexual persons.* Alexandria, VA: American Counseling Association.

Mondimore, F. M. (1996). *Homosexuality.* Baltimore: Johns Hopkins University Press.

Rust, P. C. (1996). Managing multiple identities: Diversity among bisexual women and men. In B. A. Firestein (Ed.), *Bisexuality* (pp. 53–84). Thousand Oaks, CA: Sage.

Vargo, M. E. (1998). *Acts of disclosure: The coming-out process of contemporary gay men.* New York: Haworth

Winfeld, L., & Spielman, S. (1995). *Straight talk about gays in workplace.* New York: AMACOM.

16   Implications of Development Patterns
and Research for Career Counseling in Schools

Career Counseling in Educational Settings

16

Implications of Development Patterns and Research for Career Counseling in Schools

Chapter Highlights

- *Early childhood studies*
- *Havighurst's developmental tasks*
- *Piaget's stages of cognitive development*
- *Erikson's stages of psychological development*
- *Self-concept development according to Super and Gottfredson*
- *Play as a factor in career development*
- *Influence of cultural and socioeconomic diversity on childhood development*
- *National career guidelines in three areas of career development*
- *Stages of development and developmental tasks for middle/junior school students*
- *Cognitive and physiological development of adolescents*
- *Implications for career guidance programs in elementary school, middle/junior school, and senior high school*

UMAN DEVELOPMENT IS NOT AN ISOLATED, DETACHED, OR UNRELATED series of events in life; rather, it is a blend of diverse elements including psychosocial and economic variables. These interacting elements formulate life stages and cover the entire life span. Understanding human development is one essential ingredient leading to a greater comprehension and interpretation of career development stages and tasks.

In this chapter, we discuss selected models of human development and related research. Our discussion focuses on issues that may be used to develop career guidance programs for elementary school children and adolescents in junior and senior high schools.

The vast number and variety of human development studies include many research models and theoretical orientations from several academic disciplines, including developmental psychology. Understandably, there are differences of opinion about how to interpret this accumulated wealth of information and how to apply it to programs and practices in career guidance. The interrelationships between human and career development are becoming more clear, however, as investigators carry out more complete and sophisticated experiments and apply their results to more comprehensive sets of principles. Of course, more research is still needed to provide definitive evidence of relationships between career and human developmental models, but meanwhile human developmental models and selected research provide career counselors with a greater understanding of their tasks of building goals and developing career guidance programs.

This chapter is divided into three sections that explore the developmental patterns of and selected research on elementary school children, junior high school students, and senior high school students. At the end of each section, we present implications for career guidance programs.

Studies of Early Childhood Development

Early childhood, especially the first three years, has been previously designated as the most formative years in human development (White, 1959). Before the 1970s, child development specialists seemed convinced that the first three years greatly determined a person's future motives, drives, and behavior. More recently, this viewpoint has gradually shifted to a more adaptive view of human development over the life span. Moreover, each stage of development has its own set of unique tasks to be accomplished for a smooth transition.

In studying human development over the life span, Biehler and Hudson (1986) reviewed several longitudinal studies:

1. Early personality tendencies can be diverted by the experiences one has during subsequent stages of development.

2. Predictions of adult adjustment based on child behavior were often found to be inaccurate. Individuals have a profound adaptive capacity at various stages of development.

3. Even the negative impact of infant deprivation does not have a permanently negative effect for all children.

These results suggest that *all* stages of human development are important. Infancy might be better viewed as a very important and sensitive period in an individual's development, rather than one necessarily having a permanent impact on later behavior. Moreover, the impressive adaptive capacity found in human development longitudinal studies illustrates the importance of developmental tasks at different stages of the life span.

Stages of Development and Developmental Tasks for Elementary School Children

Stage theorists have concentrated on developmental patterns of accomplishments, events, and psychological, physiological, and sociological changes in human development. During the transition process from one stage to another, developmental tasks provide a description of requirements or actions that are necessary to pass successfully through a stage of development. This perspective suggests a foundation for building effective career guidance programs. Only selected theories and research are summarized here; more in-depth coverage of these subjects can be found in developmental psychology textbooks.

Boxes 16-1 through 16-3 summarize the continuity of development by stages, ages, grades in school, and the developmental tasks assigned to stages. Erikson's (1963) developmental stages are a good example of the stage theorists' approach;

 BOX 16-1   Havighurst's Developmental Stages

Developmental tasks of infancy and early childhood

1. Learning to walk
2. Learning to take solid foods
3. Learning to talk
4. Learning to control the elimination of body wastes
5. Learning sex differences and sexual modesty
6. Forming concepts and learning language to describe social and physical reality
7. Preparing to read
8. Learning to distinguish right and wrong, and the beginning of conscience development

Havighurst's Developmental Stages *(continued)*

Developmental tasks of middle childhood (ages 6 to 12 years)

1. Learning physical skills necessary for ordinary games
2. Building wholesome attitudes toward oneself as a growing organism
3. Learning to get along with peers
4. Learning an appropriate masculine or feminine social role
5. Developing fundamental skills in reading, writing, and calculating
6. Developing concepts necessary for everyday living
7. Developing morality, a conscience, and a scale of values
8. Achieving personal independence
9. Developing attitudes toward social groups and institutions

Developmental tasks of adolescence (ages 12 to 18 years)

1. Achieving new and more mature relations with peers of both sexes
2. Achieving a masculine or feminine role in society
3. Accepting one's physique and using the body effectively
4. Achieving emotional independence from parents and other adults
5. Preparing for marriage and family life
6. Preparing for an economic career
7. Acquiring a set of values and an ethical system as a guide to behavior—developing an ideology
8. Desiring and achieving socially responsible behavior

Developmental tasks of early adulthood (ages 19 to 30 years)

1. Selecting a mate
2. Learning to live with a marriage partner
3. Starting a family
4. Rearing a family
5. Managing a home
6. Getting started in an occupation
7. Taking on civic responsibility
8. Finding a congenial social group

Developmental tasks of middle age (ages 30 to 60 years)

1. Assisting teenage children to become responsible and happy adults
2. Achieving adult social and civic responsibility
3. Reaching and maintaining satisfactory performance in one's occupational career

(continued)

4. Developing adult leisure-time activities
5. Relating to one's spouse as a person
6. Accepting and adjusting to the physiological changes of middle age
7. Adjusting to aging parents

Developmental tasks of later maturity (ages over 60 years)

1. Adjusting to decreasing physical strength and health
2. Death of a spouse
3. Adjusting to retirement and reduced income
4. Establishing an explicit affiliation with one's age group
5. Adopting and adapting social roles in a flexible way
6. Establishing satisfactory physical living arrangements

SOURCE: From *Developmental Tasks and Education*, 3rd ed., by R. J. Havighurst. Copyright © 1972 by Longman Publishing Group. Reprinted by permission of Addison-Wesley Educational Publishers, Inc.

Piaget's (1929) research illustrates cognitive development; and Havighurst's (1972) well-known work is a good example of developmental tasks over the life span. Other developmental stages and tasks will be discussed when relevant.

According to Havighurst, the developmental tasks expected of students before leaving the sixth grade reveal a set of physical and academic skills, social role development, and personalized values. Almost all of these tasks can be related to Super's (1990) concept of career development tasks (see Chapter 2). For example, during the growth stage (ages 0 to 14), according to Super's scheme of developmental stages and tasks, individuals go through numerous experiential learning activities while developing greater self-awareness. Directed experiences in elementary school that promote physical and academic growth, interpersonal relationships with members of the same and the opposite sexes, and self-concept development are important components of career development. Students who fail to achieve the developmental tasks in both Havighurst's and Super's steps could require special attention and direction.

Erikson (1963) suggested that the stage of development from ages 6 to 11 emphasizes industriousness; that is, children learn that productivity brings recognition and reward. In Erikson's view, children develop a sense of industriousness through their accomplishments, but they might be intimidated by the requirements of success and develop a sense of inferiority. Expressing success through academic

Piaget's Stages of Cognitive Development

Sensorimotor stage (0 to 2 years)

Individuals develop schemes through senses and motor actions

Preoperational stage (2 to 5 years)

During this stage, individuals develop symbolic images but have little ability to perceptualize viewpoints other than their own.

Concrete operational stage (6 to 12 years)

This is the beginning phase of understanding differences by means of stimuli. Children solve problems only by generalizing from concrete experiences.

Formal operational stage (adolescence)

At this stage, the ability to utilize hypothetical/deductive thinking provides many solutions to a problem rather than a single answer. Individuals are able to deal with abstractions and engage in mental manipulations.

SOURCE: Adapted from Piaget, 1929.

achievement, for example, is a major contributor to establishing industriousness in work-role and self-concept development. A sense of inferiority at this stage of development calls for individualized intervention strategies.

Learning Through Concrete Experiences and Observations

Piaget (1929), noted for his work in cognitive development, has provided a description of how humans think and the characteristics of their thinking at different stages of development. In early development, children cultivate "schemes" through their senses and motor activities. During the years from ages 2 through 5, children begin to develop conceptual levels but do not yet have the ability to think logically or abstractly. By the time children reach elementary school age, they have developed the ability to apply logic to thinking and can understand simple concepts. Through concrete experiences, children learn to make consistent generalizations. For example, children learn to classify persons or objects in more than one category (the Little League coach can also be a police officer).

BOX 16-3   Stages of Psychosocial Development

Trust versus mistrust (0 to 1 year)

Order in the environment and consistency in the quality of care lead to trust. Inconsistency and unpredictable care lead to mistrust.

Autonomy versus doubt (1 to 3 years)

Opportunities to explore or try out skills provide a sense of autonomy. Excessive rejection and lack of support lead to doubt.

Initiative versus guilt (3 to 5 years)

Freedom to express self through activities and language creates a sense of initiative, whereas some restrictions create a sense of guilt.

Industry versus inferiority (6 to 11 years)

Freedom to make things and to organize them leads to a sense of being industrious. Persistent failure to produce or to perform valued activities leads to a sense of inferiority.

Identity versus role confusion (11 to 18 years)

Through a multitude of experiences in different environments, the individual seeks continuity and sameness of self in search of an identity. Confusion may lead to a negative identity, perhaps a socially unacceptable one.

Intimacy versus isolation (young adulthood)

Commitment in terms of reaching out to others for a lasting relationship leads to intimacy. Isolation and a lack of close personal relationships is a result of competitive and combative behavior.

Generativity versus stagnation (middle age)

During this stage one concentrates on guiding and preparing the next generation. Focusing primarily on self creates a sense of stagnation.

Integrity versus despair (old age)

A sense of integrity is developed from acceptance of one's life and satisfaction with past achievements and accomplishments. Despair comes from the perception that life has been unsatisfying and misdirected.

SOURCE: Adapted from Erikson, 1963.

Encouraging and directing concrete experiences to promote increasingly abstract conceptual operations during this stage of development is a vital part of educational and career guidance programming in elementary schools. An example of an exercise illustrating this process would be asking students to identify one type of skill necessary for good schoolwork and then asking them to identify a job that requires a specific school subject.

Observation is also a contributing element to early cognitive development. Krumboltz's learning theory of career choice and counseling, discussed in Chapter 2, emphasizes the importance of observation learning attributed to reactions to consequences, observable results of actions, and reactions to others (Mitchell & Krumboltz, 1996). Children are particularly prone to adopting the behavior models they observe (Fagot & Leinbach, 1989). According to Bandura (1977, 1986), there are five stages of observable learning: (1) paying attention, (2) remembering what is observed, (3) reproducing actions, (4) becoming motivated (to reproduce what is observed), and (5) perfecting an imitation according to what was observed. Within this frame of reference, parents, teachers, teachers' aides, and classmates are potential models that elementary school children will imitate. Of course, models may come from other sources, such as television, movies, and books. The potential benefits of observational learning for career development of elementary school children are very important. Directed observable learning experiences involving work roles are an important component of early career guidance programs.

Self-Concept Development

In Chapter 2, we briefly mentioned Super's self-concept theory and its pervasive nature (Super et al., 1963). In a later publication, Super (1990) clarified his position on the nature and scope of self-concept in career development. Individuals, in Super's view, have constellations of self-concepts, or "self-concept systems," that denote sets or constellations of traits. In an elementary school setting, for example, an individual might have a different view of self as a student and as a member of a peer group. An individual might see himself or herself as gregarious but also as a weak student or not very intelligent.

Elementary students are formulating sets of self-concepts as they focus on class requirements; interrelationships with peers, teachers, and important adults; and the social structure in which they live and function.

In her theory of circumscription and compromise, discussed in Chapter 2, Gottfredson focuses on the development of self-images and occupational aspirations in four stages. In the first stage, Orientation to Size and Power (ages 3 to 5), children recognize adult occupational roles and exhibit same-sex preferences for adult activities, including employment. During stage two, Orientation to Sex Roles (ages 6 to 8), children focus on what is appropriate for one's sex; they now recognize that adult activities are sex-typed. As a result, children tend to dismiss occupations that are considered appropriate for the other sex. In stage three, Orientation to Social Valuation (ages 9 to 13), children rule out low-status occupations as preferences. As Gottfredson (1996) puts it, "they reject occupational alternatives that seem inconsistent with those new elements of self" (p. 193). Stage four is character-ized as an orientation to the internal unique self beginning at age 14. Individuals gain self-awareness and project self, sex-role, and social class into their perceptions of vocational aspirations.

Self-concept development is not a static phenomenon but an ongoing process, which changes sometimes gradually and sometimes abruptly as people and situa-tions change. In elementary school, children experience for the first time many as-pects of existence in an adult world, such as competition and expectations of productive performance. In play, they interact with peers and also assume roles in supervised and unsupervised situations. Self-esteem for some will be enhanced through academic achievement, whereas others will experience both positive and negative feedback in peer-socialization activities. Enhanced self-esteem encourages development of personal ideas and opinions of a positive nature; accurate self-concepts contribute to career maturity.

Play as a Factor in Career Development

Examining the period of childhood before age 11, Ginzberg and associates (1951) theorized that various occupational roles are assumed in play, resulting in initial value judgments of the world of work. Engaging in such activities is intrinsically rewarding for children, but their expressed occupational choices are made with little regard for reality. By the middle of the elementary school years, however, work orientation displaces play orientation. Similarly, Elkind (1981) and Gibson, Mitchell, and Basile (1993) suggested that children in the upper elementary grades have developed a more realistic view of the adult world—that is, a sense of inde-pendence and self-reliance.

Self-attributes become more prominent among children in upper elementary grades, causing them to intensify their focus on personal likes and dislikes.

Physical Development of Elementary School Children

Physical growth and maturation during the elementary school years play a major role in psychosocial development. Particularly significant is the noticeable differ-ence in growth rate between boys and girls. At age 6 years, girls are on average slightly shorter than boys, but by age 10, girls are as tall or taller than boys. The average age of puberty for girls is 12.5; for boys, 14 (Tanner, 1972). Many U.S. girls reach puberty before they finish the sixth grade.

Differences in growth and physiological changes between girls and boys in elementary school greatly influence social relationships and emerging self-perceptions. Learning appropriate masculine or feminine roles, according to Havighurst (1972) and Gottfredson (1996), among others, precludes greater equality between sexes, especially in occupational behavior. Particularly impor-tant are perceptions of appropriate behavior patterns—that is, patterns regarded as acceptable for a given sex. Sex-role stereotyping is fostered through observa-tion and imitation of male and female models. Other influences come through textbooks, other books, and popular television programs that describe and depict differences in roles for boys and girls. (See Chapters 11 and 12 for more detailed discussions.)

Influence of Cultural and Socioeconomic Diversity on Childhood Development

Our society is both economically and ethnically diverse; African American, Asian American, Hispanic American, and Native American children may have different developmental experiences than do children of the (now) dominant society of white European background (Sigelman & Shaffer, 1995). Differences within these groups vary considerably, primarily as a result of such factors as length of time in the United States, language usage, socioeconomic status, and level of acculturation (integration into mainstream society). Children of different cultures have been judged by the dominant society's standards for many years, but researchers have become more oriented to adopting a contextual perspective of human development (see Chapter 10 for more information on this subject).

Socioeconomic status (SES)—which is based on income, education, occupational status, and location of home—defines one's position in society (Brislin, 1993). But, according to Garbarino (1992), about one out of five children in the United States lives in poverty. Many of these are members of ethnic groups such as African Americans, Hispanic Americans, and Native Americans. Lower-SES parents are likely to have expectations for their children that are different from those of middle- and upper-SES parents. Parenting styles may differ significantly. Lower-SES parents expect their children to be like themselves; they emphasize conformity and obedience, and they expect their children will eventually work for a boss in a blue-collar job. Middle- and upper-class parents also expect their children to be like themselves; thus, they stress being independent, self-assertive, and creative and working for economic security, perhaps eventually owning their own businesses (Brislin, 1993). These examples of different expectations and subsequent parenting styles influence children's development and career aspirations. Children from different cultures have special needs, which was discussed in more detail in Chapter 10. In the meantime, we should learn to appreciate cultural diversity, be prepared to assist individuals in their career development, and become advocates for the special needs of all children. The adaptive capacity found in human development suggests that relevant strategies can also assist children from different socieoeconomic and cultural backgrounds.

National career development guidelines by the National Occupational Information Coordinating Committee (NOICC, 1992) include three areas of career development for students in elementary school:

1. Self-knowledge
   a. Knowledge of the importance of self-concept
   b. Skills to interact with others
   c. Awareness of the importance of growth and change

2. Educational and occupational exploration
   a. Awareness of the benefits of educational achievement
   b. Awareness of the relationship between work and learning
   c. Skills to understand and use career information
   d. Awareness of the importance of personal responsibility and good work habits
   e. Awareness of how work relates to the needs and functions of society
3. Career planning
   a. Understanding of how to make decisions
   b. Awareness of the interrelationship of life roles
   c. Awareness of different occupations and changing male/female roles
   d. Awareness of the career planning process

Implications for Career Guidance at the Elementary-School Level

The preceding recommended three areas of career development for students in elementary school, combined with other research reported in this section, suggest many ideas that can be applied to career guidance programs in elementary schools. Following is a representative list; related career guidance techniques will be reported in Chapter 17.

1. Self-concepts begin to form in early childhood. Because of the influence of self-concept formation on career development, there is strong evidence of how important directed experiences in enhancing self-concept are in elementary schools.

2. An important aspect of career development is building an understanding of strengths and limitations. Learning to identify and express strengths and limitations is a good way to build a foundation for self-understanding.

3. Elementary school children imitate role models in the home and school. Both parents and teachers can provide children with positive role models through precept and example.

4. Children learn to associate work roles by sexual stereotyping at an early age. Exposure to career information that discourages sex-role stereotyping will broaden the range of occupations considered available by children.

5. Community resources provide a rich source of career information, role models, and exposure to a wide range of careers. Students from families whose parents did not attend high school have a special need for community opportunities.

6. Self-awareness counseling is a major goal of the growth stage in elementary schools. Methods used to enhance self-awareness encourage

development of the ability to process and interpret information about self and others and about differences among people.

7. Learning to assume responsibility for decisions and actions has major implications for future career decisions. Some beginning steps include skills development that enables children to analyze situations, to identify people who can help them, and to seek assistance when needed.

8. Understanding the relationship between education and work is a key concept for enhancing career development. Skills learned in school and during out-of-school activities should be linked to work-related activities.

9. The idea that all work is important builds an understanding of why parents and others work. Reflection on the reasons for working fosters an awareness that any productive worker should be respected.

10. Learning about occupations and about people who are actually involved in occupations builds an awareness of differences among people and occupations.

Stages of Development and Developmental Tasks for Junior and Senior High School Students

Adolescence has been described as a period of turmoil resulting in a transition from childhood. Continuity of development is, for some, sporadic and chaotic. The key characteristic of this stage of development, according to Erikson, is the search for identity as one subordinates childhood identifications and reaches for a different identity in a more complex set of conditions and circumstances. The major danger of this period is role confusion; thus, this stage is often designated "Identity versus Confusion."

In Erikson's (1963) view, this is a critical period of development. As he put it, "These new identifications are no longer characterized by the playfulness of childhood and the experimental zest of youth: with dire urgency they force the young individual into choices and decisions which will, with increasing immediacy, lead to commitments for life" (p. 155).

According to Erikson, the choice of career and commitment to a career has a significant impact on identity. Given the current difficulty surrounding occupational choice because of rapidly changing job markets and impersonal organizations, Erikson suggested that many careers pose a threat to personal identity; as a result, some individuals avoid a firm career choice. Many adolescents delay commitment or place a psychological moratorium on the decision until further options are explored. Excerpts from an interview with Ted illustrate this point:

TED: My parents want me here so that I can choose a career. They don't like it that I haven't picked one.

COUNSELOR: As I said, we should be able to help you, Ted, but first, tell me more about jobs or careers you have considered.

TED: I thought about a few, like photography, but I really don't know what I want.

COUNSELOR: Tell me more about your thoughts on photography.

TED: A photographer like Mr. Brown is not what I want to be. I guess I'd like to work for a magazine.

COUNSELOR: You mentioned Mr. Brown. What don't you like about his job?

TED: I don't want to take pictures of weddings and things like that. To tell the truth, I don't really know much about what a photographer or any other worker does. I just wish my parents would leave me alone until I have more time. I'm going to community college next fall and I want to decide while I'm there.

A young person unable to avoid role confusion might adopt what is referred to as a "negative identity," assuming forms of behavior that are in direct conflict with family and society. Those who soon develop a more appropriate sense of direction can find this experience positive, but for others, the negative identity is maintained throughout adulthood. Identity diffusion, according to Erikson, often results in lack of commitment to a set of values and, subsequently, to occupations.

Likewise, Super (1990) and Crites and Savickas (1996) suggest strong relationships between identity and career commitment as variables of career maturity. Career maturity implies a stabilized identity that provides individuals with a framework for making career choices, a crystallized formation of self-perceptions, and developed skills. Career maturity is a continuous developmental process and presents specific identifiable characteristics and traits essential to career development. Characteristics of career maturity are decisiveness and independence, knowledge of occupational information, and skills in planning and decision making. (Chapter 7 reviews career maturity inventories that provide specific information about other dimensions of career maturity.)

Finally, defining appropriate sexual roles and achieving relationships with peers are crucial developmental tasks for adolescents (Havighurst, 1972). Success in accomplishing these tasks is essential to social adjustment at this stage of life. Socially responsible behavior implies that the first steps have been taken in achieving emotional independence from parents and other adults. According to Havighurst, social relationship patterns learned during adolescence greatly affect an individual's adjustment to the rules and life roles, including the work role, of the dominant society.

Cognitive Development During Junior and Senior High School

Following Piaget's (Piaget & Inhelder, 1969) cognitive developmental stages, as shown in Box 16-2, the transition from concrete operational thinking to formal thought is a gradual process beginning at approximately 12 years of age. During early adolescence, patterns of problem solving and planning are quite unsystematic. Near the end of high school, however, the adolescent has the ability to deal with abstractions, form hypotheses in problem solving, and sort out problems through mental manipulations. Linking observations and emotional responses with a recently developed systematic thinking process, the adolescent reacts to events and experiences with a newly found power of thought. In formal thought, the adolescent can direct emotional responses to abstract ideals as well as to people. Introspective thinking leads to analysis of self in situations, including projection of the self into the adult world of work (Elkind, 1968; Gillies, 1989; Keating, 1980; Piaget & Inhelder, 1969).

The cognitive development of formal thought introduces sets of ambiguities. On one hand, the adolescent is developing a systematized thinking process to solve problems appropriately. On the other hand, there is unrestrained theorizing, extreme self-analysis, and more-than-usual concern about the reactions of others. By virtue of concern for others, the peer group influence is particularly strong during adolescence. Self-analysis can lead to what Miller-Tiedeman and Tiedeman (1990) refer to as "I-power" as a means of self-development. Increased self-awareness is an essential part of the adolescent's development, particularly in clarifying self-status and individualized belief systems in the career decision-making process.

In the development of formalized thinking, adolescents do not simply respond to stimuli but also interpret what they observe (Bandura, 1977, 1986). In this connection, they will perceive stimuli in the environment as having positive and negative associations. An example of a negative association is a junior high student who believes that lawyers "rip you off because they are all crooks." In this sense, perceptions and values associated with occupations are developed through generalizations formed by experience and observations. Brown, Mounts, Lamborn, and Steinberg (1993) found that parents have the greatest influence on the long-range plans of adolescents, but peers are more likely to influence immediate identity or status.

Occupational stereotypes as perceived in career decision making may be generalized from interactions with both parents and peers as well as gained through other stimuli, such as films and books.

Physiological Development of Adolescents in Junior and Senior High School

A dramatic physiological change, sexual maturity, takes place for most boys and girls during junior and senior high school. Accompanying or preceding sexual maturity are dramatic bodily changes, such as increased muscle tissue and body stature, which permit the adolescent to perform adult physical tasks for the first time. Particularly important to the adolescent is physical appearance. In junior high school, concern for appearance reaches its peak as girls compare themselves to movie and television stars, females appearing in commercials, and professional models. Boys use the standards of strength and facial and bodily hair for judging early maturity (Biehler & Hudson, 1986). Feeling comfortable within the dominant peer group is highly related to being judged as "grown-up" or mature.

Reflecting on sexual maturity, Cal related the following incident:

I wanted to do everything I could to be grown up, but I was just a little twerp. I even tried to imitate how men walked. I guess I was 12 or 13 when I lit my first cigarette. Even though I coughed until I almost choked, I kept on smoking that cigarette! Yes sir, I wanted to be one of those "cool cats" with all the know-how.

But the worst of it was P.E. I didn't want to undress in front of anybody. I made up all kinds of excuses until the locker room was clear, and then I went home and showered.

You know, it was important then to be accepted by my friends. I guess I ended up being liked by most of them. Now when I look back, it seems we were all trying to fool each other.

Quiang, an early-maturing junior high school student, reflected on her experiences:

All of a sudden it seemed I had outgrown everyone—especially the boys. Some of the girls seemed as physically mature as I was, but they usually acted uneasy around me, and I certainly felt awkward around them. It was during this time that I made friends with some older girls. As far as the boys were concerned, there were mixed feelings. The older boys didn't accept me because I was "too young," while the younger ones were too little for me. I just felt out of place for a few years until everybody caught up.

After reviewing several longitudinal research projects to determine immediate effects of early and late maturity, Livson and Peskin (1980) reached the following conclusions:

1. Early-maturing males were most likely to be viewed more favorably by adults, thus leading to a greater sense of confidence and poise.

2. Late-maturing males exhibited attention-seeking behavior to compensate for feelings of inferiority.

3. Early-maturing girls were psychologically and socially out of sync with their peers.

4. Late-maturing girls who went through less abrupt physical changes were viewed as more petite and feminine and enjoyed popularity and leadership privileges.

The effects of early and late sexual maturity provide a frame of reference for counseling intervention. Evidence suggests that early maturing males are more than likely to receive approval and reinforcement for their behavior among male peer groups and adults. Late-maturing girls also enjoy acceptance and popularity (Livson & Peskin, 1980).

Simmons and Blyth (1987) confirm early and late maturity differences and their related benefits and costs, and they report some additional special effects:

- Early-maturing boys had more dates and dated more often than did late-maturing boys. Furthermore, early-maturing males were more positive about physical development and athletic abilities.

- Early-maturing girls had poorer grades in school and had more discipline problems. Also, they were more negative about their physical development.

Sexual maturity may be one basis for differentiating career guidance activities. Late-maturing males and early-maturing girls might experience a greater need for counseling intervention than do their peers. It seems that junior high school students benefit from guidance programs that inform them of the extent, type, and variation of physiological changes in early adolescence and that specifically address anxieties related to bodily changes (Richards & Larson, 1993; Thomas, 1973).

National career development (NOICC, 1992) includes three areas of career development for students in middle/junior high school as follows:

1. Self-knowledge
   a. Knowledge of the influence of a positive self-concept
   b. Skills to interact with others
   c. Knowledge of the importance of growth and change

2. Educational and occupational exploration
   a. Knowledge of the benefits of educational achievement to career opportunities
   b. Knowledge of the relationship between work and learning
   c. Skills to locate, understand, and use career information
   d. Knowledge of skills necessary to seek and obtain jobs
   e. Understanding of how work relates to the needs and functions of the economy and society

3. Career planning
   a. Skills to make decisions
   b. Knowledge of the interrelationship of life roles
   c. Knowledge of different occupations and changing male/female roles
   d. Understanding of the process of career planning

Implications for Career Guidance in Junior High Schools

The three recommended areas of career development for students in middle or junior high school, combined with research, yield numerous implications for career guidance programs in junior high school.

1. In many respects, junior high school is an educational transition from structured classroom settings to more specialized educational programs. Learning to relate acquired skills to educational and occupational goals promotes exploratory reflection and activities.

2. There appears to be a strong need to increase junior high school students' abilities to realistically appraise their own abilities, achievements, and interests. Minority students and students from homes where parents' education level is low need special assistance in understanding their strengths and limitations.

3. Students in junior high school have difficulty identifying and evaluating their interests in relation to total life experiences.

4. A limited knowledge of occupations makes it difficult for junior high school students to relate in- and out-of-school activities to future jobs. Exposure to jobs and career fields should be expanded to provide a basis for linking various activities to work.

5. The naiveté and limited knowledge of the factors necessary for evaluating future work roles suggest the desirability of introducing informational resources and teaching the necessary skills for their use. Learning about career options, for example, increases awareness of exploration opportunities.

6. Physiological development and sexual maturity during junior high school involve individual changes in self-perceptions and social interactions. Opportunities to explore, evaluate, and reflect on values seem to be very desirable activities for promoting a better understanding of self during this stage.

7. Junior high school students will greatly benefit from hands-on experience with skill activities associated with occupations. Basic and concrete experiences provide a means of learning skills used in work.

8. Because junior high school students should begin to assume responsibility for their own behaviors, they would greatly benefit from improved knowledge of planning, decision-making, and problem-solving skills.

9. Increased awareness of sexual differences among junior high school students suggests that emphasis be placed on learning how sex-role stereotyping, bias, and discrimination limit occupational and educational choices.

10. Students in junior high school who continue the process of awareness initiated in elementary school will recognize the changing nature of career commitment. The skills and knowledge learned to evaluate initial career choices will be used to evaluate others over the life span.

The Need for Career Guidance in High Schools

The results of a recent Gallup survey sponsored by the National Career Development Association and reported by Hoyt and Lester (1995) strongly suggest that high schools should give more attention to career development, help all students plan careers, help all students develop job skills, help all students find jobs, and help work-bound students develop work skills. More specifically, the respondents suggested the changes reported in Table 16-1.

It is interesting to observe that responses from both women and men did not differ very much in recommended changes. In fact, none of the responses between men and women were significantly different. The results also indicate that slightly

TABLE 16-1	PERCENT OF SUGGESTED CHANGES AMONG WOMEN AND MEN CHOOSING "NOT ENOUGH ATTENTION"		
Suggested change		% Women	% Men
Place high school dropouts and graduates into jobs		64.1	64.1
Help students choose their careers		50.8	51.0
Help students who do not go to college develop skills so they can get jobs after graduation		56.8	62.6
Help students develop skills in identifying jobs that are open in their communities		54.5	53.0
Help students learn how to use occupational information about salary and working conditions		54.7	58.8
Help students develop the skills they need to get jobs such as job interviewing techniques		59.4	55.2
Prepare students for college		37.8	36.0

Note: N = 1,046

SOURCE: Reprinted from *Learning to Work: The NCDA Gallup Survey,* by K. B. Hoyt and J. N. Lester, p. 63. Copyright 1995 by The National Career Development Association. Reprinted with permission of NCDA.

more than one-third of both women and men answered "not enough attention" was given to prepare students for college, whereas more than 64% of both men and women answered that there was not enough attention given to placing high school dropouts and graduates into jobs. Also, more than 55% of both men and women felt that more help was needed in developing job skills and job interviewing techniques. Adults were asked whether they believed that the high schools in their community were sufficiently preparing students in seven areas related to the recent emphasis on school-to-work skills. Specifically, the adults were asked whether high schools pay enough attention to helping students (1) choose careers, (2) develop job skills, (3) learn how to identify local job openings, (4) obtain work after high school, (5) learn to use occupational information, (6) develop job-finding skills, and (7) prepare for college. The findings indicate that more than half of the adults surveyed said high schools were not doing enough to help students in all areas surveyed except in preparing them for college (37%).

Some of the questions asked of the respondents were very similar in nature, but the first data reported focused on the idea of career emphasis in secondary education reform, whereas the other reported results reflected the public's perception of the high schools' emphasis on school-to-work skills. We can conclude from the data, however, that some specific needs are not being met in high school career guidance programs.

Recently, comprehensive school guidance programs (Gysbers & Henderson, 1988) are being developed and considered for adoption by a number of school systems. Also "school-to-work" is a new approach to learning for all students, sponsored jointly by the U.S. Department of Education and Department of Labor. Yet another program is "planning for life," sponsored by the U.S. Army Recruiting Command with the support of the National Consortium of State Career Guidance Supervisors and the Center on Education and Training for Employment at the Ohio State University. These programs are mentioned here to show the growing demand for efficient career guidance programs in schools, including the high schools. These programs will be discussed in more detail in Chapter 17.

National career development guidelines (NOICC, 1992) include three areas of career development for students in high school:

1. Self-knowledge
   a. Understanding the influence of a positive self-concept
   b. Skills to interact positively with others
   c. Understanding the impact of growth and development

2. Educational and occupational exploration
   a. Understanding the relationship between educational achievement and career planning
   b. Understanding the need for positive attitudes toward work and learning
   c. Skills to locate, evaluate, and interpret career information
   d. Skills to prepare to seek, obtain, maintain, and change jobs
   e. Understanding how societal needs and functions influence the nature and structure of work

3. Career planning
   a. Skills to make decisions
   b. Understanding the interrelationship of life roles
   c. Understanding the continuous changes in male/female roles
   d. Skills in career planning

Implications for Career Guidance Programs in Senior High Schools

The preceding recommendations from NOICC (1992), combined with related research reported in this section, provide an abundance of implications for career guidance programs in senior high school.

1. Career guidance at the senior high school level must provide programs designed to meet the needs of students at various stages of career development. Establishing the career development needs of entry-level high school students and a means of monitoring their progress are relevant goals.

2. According to Super (1990), the exploratory age is characterized by a tentative phase in which choices are narrowed but not finalized. There-

fore, it is important for individuals to analyze their own characteristics relative to career decisions.

3. Senior high school students should benefit from information, activities, and modules that call for matching occupations with physical characteristics and skills. Programs designed to assist senior high school students entering the labor market for the first time are particularly important.

4. Senior high school students should understand the relationship between career choices and educational requirements. Educational awareness implies a working knowledge of educational opportunities available at specific institutions.

5. Teaching decision-making and planning skills involves guiding students through a series of steps as they formulate career goals. Refined self-knowledge—including interests, abilities, values, and occupational knowledge—is prerequisite to effective career decision making and planning.

6. Work-experience counseling provides individuals with insight into the work setting and prepares them to identify effective models. Work values, work environments, work habits, and other issues associated with work are particularly valuable to the novice.

7. Many senior high school students also need assistance in choosing an institution of higher learning. Knowledge of how to evaluate the advantages and disadvantages of these institutions is essential.

8. Community visits and interviews with individuals in different occupations are relevant activities for helping senior high school students relate their own personal characteristics to occupational requirements. Relating school subjects to jobs and describing sources of job information are pertinent goals for career development.

9. Students should be guided in creating a set of specific preferences and plans to implement after graduation.

10. Services to help prepare for the job search are offered through placement officers. Related activities may include resumé preparation, interview-skills training, preparation for employment tests, job testing, and listing of employment opportunities.

Summary

1. Research suggests that *all* stages of human development are important. Infancy should be viewed as an extremely important and sensitive period in human development, but one not necessarily having a permanent impact on later behavior.

2. Directed experiences in elementary school promote physical and academic growth, interpersonal relationships with members of both sexes, and self-concept development—all important components of career development. Students from diverse cultures may have special needs that need to be addressed. Students who fail to accomplish developmental tasks may require special attention and direction.

3. Erikson suggested that the stage of development between ages 6 and 11 emphasizes industriousness; that is, children learn that productivity brings recognition and reward.

4. Piaget described early cognitive development in children as cultivating "schemes" through motor activities and their senses. During the ages of 2 to 5, children begin developing conceptual skills but have not yet developed the abilities to think logically or abstractly.

5. Children are particularly prone to adopting the behavior of models they observe. Parents, teachers, teacher's aides, and classmates are potential models that elementary school children will imitate. Other models may come from television, movies, and books.

6. In elementary school, children experience many aspects of existence in an adult world for the first time, such as competition with others and expectations of productive performance. Differences in growth and psychological changes between girls and boys greatly influence social relationships and emerging self-perceptions. Sex-role stereotyping is quite evident in elementary school.

7. Implications of career guidance for elementary schoolchildren include the importance of self-concept development, building an understanding of strengths and limitations, providing appropriate role models, visiting community resources for career information and role models, developing self-awareness, learning to assume responsibility for decisions and actions, understanding the relationship between education and work, learning that all work is important, and learning about work environments and the people involved in occupations.

8. Adolescence has been described as a period of turmoil resulting in a transition from childhood. According to Erikson, adolescents search intensely for identity as they subordinate childhood identifications. The major danger is role confusion; thus, this stage is designated as "Identity versus Confusion." The choice of career and commitment to a career significantly affect identity.

9. According to Piaget, the transition from concrete operational thinking to formal thought is a gradual process beginning at approximately 12 years of age. During early adolescence, patterns of problem solving or planning are quite unsystematic, but near the end of high school the adolescent has the ability to deal with distractions and sort out problems through mental manipulations.

10. Parents have the greatest influence on long-range plans of high school students, although peers are more likely to influence current identity and status.

11. A dramatic physiological change, sexual maturity, takes place for the majority of boys and girls during junior and senior high school.

12. According to Havighurst, defining appropriate sexual roles and achieving relationships with peers are among the major developmental tasks of adolescents.

13. The effects of early and late sexual maturity provide a frame of reference for counseling intervention. The evidence suggests that early maturity for males has certain benefits in terms of appropriateness among male peer groups and adults. Late-maturing girls also enjoy acceptance and popularity. Late-maturing males and early-maturing females may experience a greater need for counseling intervention than do their peers.

14. Implications for career guidance in junior high school includes the importance of learning to relate acquired skills to educational/occupational goals. These students have a strong need to appraise their own abilities, achievements, and interests accurately. They should be given the opportunity to identify relationships between interests and total life experiences. Exposure to jobs and career fields should be expanded to provide a basis for linking various activities to work. Learning about career options increases awareness of exploration opportunities. Basic and concrete experiences provide a means of learning the skills used in work. Skills in planning, decision making, and problem solving are important for junior high school students. Finally, these students should understand that sex-role stereotyping, bias, and discrimination limit occupational choices.

15. A recent Gallup survey suggests high schools should give more attention to career development by helping all students develop job skills, all students plan careers, all students find jobs, and work-bound students develop work skills.

16. Recent career development programs for high schools include a comprehensive school guidance program, school-to-work programs, and planning for life programs.

17. Implications for career guidance programs in senior high school are numerous, and they indicate that programs should be designed to meet the needs of students at various stages of career development. Programs designed to assist senior high school students entering the labor market for the first time are particularly important. Senior high school students should understand the relationships between career choices and educational requirements. Learning decision-making and planning skills is essential. Learning more about work and what is required at work can

help senior high school students identify effective role models. Many senior high students need assistance in choosing institutions of higher education.

Supplementary Learning Exercises

1. Defend the following statement with examples to prove your point: Individuals have a profound adaptive capacity at various stages of development.
2. Construct at least two activities/strategies in which concrete experiences promote abstract conceptual operations.
3. Construct at least two activities/strategies of observational learning that would promote career development of elementary school-age children.
4. Survey a sample of elementary, junior, and senior high school students to determine their perception of appropriate career roles for their sex.
5. Develop a list of behavioral characteristics of an adolescent experiencing role confusion. Develop counseling strategies designed to overcome identified characteristics.
6. Identify standardized assessment instruments that measure self-concept development. Explain how you would use the results in career counseling.
7. Identify and interview a late- and an early-maturing adolescent. Present your findings to the class.
8. Describe your development from childhood. Identify significant transitions and their influences on your career.
9. Identify at least ten reasons such a significant number of senior high school students express a need for career guidance. Discuss these issues in class.
10. Using one or more of the implications for career guidance for the elementary, junior, and senior high school levels, identify specific career guidance needs and develop activities and strategies to meet them.

For More Information

Bandura, A. (1986). *Social foundations of thought and action: A social cognitive theory.* Englewood Cliffs, NJ: Prentice-Hall.

Bandura, A. (1989). Regulation of cognitive processes through perceived self-efficacy. *Developmental Psychology, 25,* 729–735.

Bronfenbrenner, U. (1995). Developmental ecology through space and time: A future perspective. In P. Moen, G. H. Elder, & K. Luscher (Eds.), *Examining lives in context: Perspectives on the ecology of human development*. Washington, DC: American Psychological Association.

Gardiner, H. W., Mutter, J. D., & Kosmitzki, C. (1998). *Lives across cultures: Cross-cultural human development*. Boston: Allyn & Bacon.

Kail, R. V., & Cavanaugh, J. C. (2000). *Human development* (2nd ed.). Belmont, CA: Wadsworth.

Newman, B. M., & Newman, P. R. (1999). *Development through life: A psychosocial approach* (7th ed.). Belmont, CA: Wadsworth.

Savickas, M. L. (1995). Current theoretical issues in vocational psychology: Convergence, divergence, and schism. In W. B. Walsh & S. H. Osipow (Eds.), *Handbook of vocational psychology* (2nd ed.) (pp. 1–34). Hillsdale, NJ: Erlbaum.

Savickas, M. L., & Walsh, W. B. (Eds.). (1996). *Handbook of career theory and practice*. Palo Alto, CA: Davies-Black.

Shaffer, D. R. (1999). *Developmental Psychology: Childhood and adolescence* (5th ed.). Pacific Grove, CA: Brooks/Cole.

Sharf, R. S. (1992). *Applying career development theory to counseling*. Pacific Grove, CA: Brooks/Cole.

Sigelman, C. K. (1999). *Life-span human development* (3rd ed.). Pacific Grove, CA: Brooks/Cole.

Thompson, C. L., & Rudolph, L. B. (2000). *Counseling children* (5th ed.). Belmont, CA: Wadsworth.

17

Career Counseling in Schools

Chapter Highlights

- *Comprehensive school guidance programs, including planning for life strategies*

- *Exemplary comprehensive school guidance programs in public schools*

- *Counseling children from different cultures*

- *Sample career goals and competencies for all school levels*

- *Strategies for developing self-knowledge, educational and occupational exploration, and career planning*

- *Examples of integrating career development concepts through classroom infusion*

- *Sources of career videos for educational purposes*

- *School-to-work programs*

- *Integrating academic and vocational education*

- *Goals of tech-prep programs*

- *Apprenticeship and future work*

- *Role of placement in the high school*

THIS CHAPTER COVERS SAMPLES OF COMPETENCIES AND SELECTED STRATE-gies for career guidance in elementary, middle/junior, and senior high school. In the first part of this chapter, we discuss a comprehensive school guidance program (K–12), then planning for life strategies that are a part of the comprehensive school guidance program. Next, suggestions for counseling children from different cultures are presented, followed by goals for the elementary, middle/junior, and senior high school. For each school level, we provide current career guidance objectives and student competencies followed by suggestions for how career counselors may fulfill their responsibilities. Specific strategies are followed by examples of infusion modules. In the next section, school-to-work programs and related programs of integrating academic and vocational education, tech-prep strategies, apprenticeships and the future work force are examined. Finally, we discuss placement in the secondary school.

Comprehensive School Guidance Programs

Gysbers and Henderson (1988) have developed detailed plans for developing, designing, implementing, and evaluating a comprehensive school guidance program. In an earlier conceptual treatise on comprehensive guidance programs, Gysbers and Moore (1987) pointed out that a comprehensive guidance model is not an ancillary guidance service; rather, it is a model in which all staff members are involved, including administrators, members of the community, and parents. Furthermore, these groups are involved in a common objective whose goal is the total integrated development of individual students. According to Gysbers and Henderson (1988), guidance programs should be viewed as developmental and comprehensive in that regularly scheduled activities are planned, conducted, and evaluated and comprehensive guidance programs feature a team approach. In essence, this means a full commitment to surveying current guidance programs within a district; establishing students' needs; establishing plans, activities, and staff to meet those needs; and recognizing that a comprehensive guidance program is an equal partner with other educational programs.

Human growth and development forms the foundation on which comprehensive guidance programs are built, especially within the domain of lifetime career development. The focus is the interrelationship of all aspects of life. For instance, the family role is not treated separately from other life roles. The life career developmental domains are characterized as follows: (1) self-knowledge and interpersonal skills (self-understanding and recognizing the uniqueness of others); (2) life roles, settings, and events (roles such as learner, citizen, and worker; settings such as community, home, and work environment; events such as beginning the work role, marriage, and retirement); (3) life career planning (decision making and planning); and (4) basic studies and occupational preparation (knowledge and skills found in various subjects typically offered in school curricula).

Counselor involvement and commitment in this approach is extensive. Counselors are involved in teaching, team teaching, and supporting teachers. A major innovation in this program is the development of student competencies and the methods used to evaluate them. For example, at the perceptual level, the acquisition of knowledge and skills related to selected aspects of community and self are evaluated as environmental orientation and self-orientation. The conceptual level emphasizes directional tendencies (movement toward socially desirable goals) and adaptive and adjustive behavior. The generalization level is the level of functioning students exhibit throughout the mastery of specific tasks. Each of these competencies is broken down into specific goals with identified competencies; student outcomes are specified by grade level and activity objectives.

Monitoring is accomplished using an individualized advisory system; each advisor has 15 to 20 students. The allocation of the counselor's time during the school day is suggested in percentages for participation in curriculum, individual planning, responsive services (recurring topics such as academic failure, peer problems, and family situations), and system support (consulting with parents, staff development, and compensatory programs).

The comprehensive school guidance program is a means of systematically implementing a program concept for guidance activities in kindergarten through grade 12. The value of this model is its comprehensive nature and the involvement of school professionals, selected members of the community, and parents. The program's flexibility allows for local development of needs. Another major advantage is the evaluation of student outcomes, professional effectiveness, and program design. The program centers around a life career development theme. The profound message to the career counseling profession is to recognize the importance of the interrelatedness of all life roles.

Planning for Life Strategies

A program called Planning for Life is sponsored by the U.S. Army Recruiting Command with the support of the National Consortium of State Career Guidance Supervisors and the Center on Education and Training for Employment at Ohio State University. This comprehensive guidance program provides a framework for improving the effectiveness of elementary, secondary and postsecondary programs; counselor education; and supervision and administration of career guidance programs. The special objectives of the National Consortium of State Career Guidance Supervisors is quoted as follows:

1. Provide a vehicle to enable states to join together in supporting mutual priorities, ongoing programs, and career development and prevocational services.

2. Promote the development and improvement of career guidance at all levels of education.

3. Involve business, industry, and government in creating and evaluating quality career guidance programs.

4. Serve as a clearinghouse through which states can seek assistance from public and private sources for program improvement and expansion.

5. Offer technical assistance to states in developing their annual and long-term plans related to career guidance and counseling. (National Consortium of State Career Guidance Supervisors, 1996, p. iv)

The Planning for Life Program complements the comprehensive guidance programs discussed earlier in this chapter. First, the Planning for Life program places career planning within the framework of the total school guidance program; career planning for all students is part of the comprehensive guidance plan. More specifically, elements of the Planning for Life Program are identified by the "seven C's":

1. *Clarity* of purpose is the sharing of the program's purposes with school, family, business, and community.

2. *Commitment* suggests that an investment of resources from all parts of the community is essential.

3. *Comprehensiveness* ensures that the program addresses all participants in the community with all career and educational opportunities.

4. *Collaboration* refers to the degree to which schools, family, business, and community share program ownership.

5. *Coherence* is the term used to make certain that there is a documented plan for all students and to see that specific assistance and program assessment is provided.

6. *Coordination* is the degree to which the program is interdisciplinary and career planning is developmental.

7. *Competency* is proof of student attainment.

Each year, outstanding programs are given national awards. The Omaha, Nebraska, public school system was one of two 1994 national award winners. The program is outlined in Box 17-1.

One outstanding feature of the Omaha public schools plan is collaboration. The schools obviously have the support of the community, which is an important part of any comprehensive guidance program. The comprehensive nature of this program is also impressive. Parental involvement in career education programs offers tremendous opportunities for supporting the school's efforts in career guidance. As is the case with most comprehensive career guidance programs, all students graduate with a career plan. Follow-up data on implementing these plans would provide yet another measure of overall effectiveness.

Finally, planning for life suggests that career and life are both ongoing processes that require individual and community commitment. Because of the very nature of our society, individuals must periodically reevaluate their circumstances to achieve a more productive life and career. The connections and links

Omaha Public Schools Comprehensive Guidance and Counseling Program

Grade Levels Kindergarten Through Twelve: Rural, Urban, Suburban

Overview

The Omaha Public Schools Comprehensive Guidance and Counseling Program provides a curriculum-based approach to address the career domain of student development.

- *Clarity of Purpose:* The career curriculum includes an agreed-upon written statement of purpose, philosophy, goals, and outcomes. All materials were developed by program committee members who include counselors, teachers, administrators, community agencies, and industry.

- *Commitment:* Teachers, community agency representatives, the business community, and counselors deliver the career program to all students. Personnel specializing in career planning are assigned to provide support and coordination for career planning in grades kindergarten through twelve. Advanced education planning specialist counselors are available in each high school.

- *Comprehensiveness:* The career planning guidance curriculum is delivered to all students beginning in kindergarten. All students graduate with a career portfolio. Assessments are utilized throughout the program. At least two advanced career education evening programs for parents and students are provided each year in all district high schools.

- *Collaboration:* Career planning program partnerships include: Urban League, University of Nebraska–Omaha, Metro Community College, Chamber of Commerce, Explorers, Nebraska Educational Planning Center, Gifted Education Instruction, vocational education and community relations agencies. The program has received over $100,000 in foundation grants each year for the past two years.

All goals and materials are designed and developed by committees representing various school departments, industry representatives and educational agencies. Advisory committees include parents/guardians, community and industry representatives, and counselors who monitor, evaluate, assess, and improve the career planning program. Parents have access to the student portfolio for comment and review.

- *Coherence:* All students begin to develop career/educational plans in seventh grade. Students annually update their portfolios each year through grade twelve. They use the portfolio to prepare a resumé and develop their career/education plan for after high school. All students graduate with a career planning portfolio.

■ *Coordination:* A written career planning curriculum is delivered to all students in grades K through 12. Specified outcomes and activities are developmentally sequenced for each grade level. Activities are delivered in conjunction with the academic curriculum. Career counselors formulate written plans that include activities, resources, and evaluation.

■ *Competency:* All students complete a career planning portfolio that includes goals, outcomes, and academic progress. Each component of the program is evaluated.

Commercial materials used:

■ IDEAS Interest, Determination, Exploration & Assessment System (IDEAS)
■ Self-Directed Search (SDS)
■ The Harrington-O'Shea Career Decision Making (CDM)
■ Myers-Briggs Type Indicator (MBTI)
■ True Colors
■ Guidance Information System

Noncommercial/local materials used:

■ *Look to the Future* Curriculum Guide for elementary school
■ Growing Through Developmental Guidance K–6
■ Growing Through Transitions: Career and Educational Planning Grades 7–12
■ Growing Through Counseling Curriculum Guide
■ Educational/Career Planning Portfolio
■ Parent Information Envelopes
■ Career Educational Planning Brochures

Program Features

The Omaha career program is an integral component in a total, comprehensive, competency-based guidance program. The inclusion of career planning in a total program emphasizes the importance of career development in the student's total development. The K–12 career guidance curriculum provides comprehensive, extensive activities to provide students with a developmentally appropriate classroom-based approach to career development and career planning.

For more information contact:
Stan Maliszewski, Guidance Supervisor
Omaha Public Schools
3215 Cuming Street
Omaha NE 68131
402-557-2704

SOURCE: From *Planning for Life: 1995 Compendium of Recognized Career Planning Programs.* National Consortium of State Career Guidance Supervisors, Center for Education and Training for Employment, 1900 Kenny Road, Columbus, OH 43210.

between lifestyle and career are clearly interwoven; we can hardly separate one from the other in program development. Thus, life planning programs suggest an important lesson: Planning for the future involves the interrelationship of both lifestyle and career.

Counseling Children from Different Cultures

Beginning in Chapter 4, different approaches to counseling multicultural groups were illustrated. In Chapter 10, which was fully devoted to multicultural counseling, the point was repeatedly made that individuals from different cultures may share some common beliefs, but the significant differences within groups suggest each client be treated as an individual. Counselors should, however, be aware of culture specific traits, beliefs, and customs from which counselors can vary their approaches. For instance, emotional boundaries of closeness of relationships are most difficult to observe (Thompson & Rudolph, 2000). Indo-Chinese, for example, only discuss problems with family members. In this context, counseling relationships might have to be carefully delineated to client and family.

Of utmost importance, counselors must evaluate the client's level of acculturation when determining how counseling will proceed. For instance, a fifth-generation Latina girl might aspire to a professional career, whereas, a Latina immigrant female might be conditioned to consider her role only that of a homemaker. The point here is not to stereotype individuals because of their cultural backgrounds, but, rather, to remain alert to modifying counseling to meet individual needs.

A review of Chapters 4 and 10 should assist counselors in preparing for delivery of individual and group career counseling programs for children from different cultures. Counselors might often have to offer nontraditional means of services to some clients. For instance, children who have been negatively affected by racism and oppression might react positively to spiritually oriented counseling programs to gain self-respect. Richardson (1991) suggests that counselors may find that African American churches can be a good resource for helping some students.

In sum, people of color might be reluctant to seek counseling because of a lack of understanding of its purpose and perhaps fear of its consequences. Some children, particularly Native American children, might feel that going to a counselor is a sign of weakness (LaFromboise & Jackson, 1996). And some children from Asian American cultures might view going to a counselor as shameful and embarrassing, that is, indicative of failure (Thompson & Rudolph, 2000). In general, children from different cultures have different worldviews from which they interpret relationships. For some, there is a need to avoid loss of face and for others subtle forms of communication are preferred (Leong, 1996a). Thus, it is essential that counselors learn about culture-specific variables in the lives of children from different cultures.

The Elementary School

Career guidance in schools generally includes the following processes: classroom instruction, counseling, assessment, career information, placement, consultation, and referral (Herring, 1998; National Occupational Information Coordinating Committee, 1992). Although elementary school counselors may be involved with most of these processes, consultation, classroom instruction, counseling, and career information resources present the greatest challenges. In this framework, elementary school counselors have the opportunity to influence the content of career-related programs and materials. Within most guidance programs, such as the comprehensive guidance program, proactive elementary school counselors can introduce an abundance of creative strategies and materials to teachers, parents, and administrators. Some suggested strategies and materials are discussed later in this section.

In Table 17-1, Paisley and Hubbard (1994) provide a sample of career goals and competencies for kindergarten through sixth grade. The overall goals are similar to the national career goals established by the National Occupational Information Coordinating Committee (NOICC, 1992) of self-knowledge, educational and occupational exploration, and career planning. However, the specificity of the competencies by grade level found in this table is unique and valuable information for counselors.

To reach most students in elementary school, classroom teachers must cooperate by agreeing to include career-related activities in classroom instruction. The overarching goal here is to provide exposure through the academic curriculum by infusing learning activities that focus on the career counseling goals established locally. In this context, elementary school counselors become a part of curriculum development through consultation. Thus, counselors' ability to work with classroom teachers is essential. The key to reaching this objective is creating innovative strategies and providing relevant materials. The following suggested activities are designed as strategies to promote self-knowledge, educational and occupational exploration, and career planning. These strategies can serve as a baseline for developing tailored ones that meet local needs.

⯈ Self-Knowledge Strategies

1. In a group discussion, ask students to use open-ended sentences, such as
   I'm happy when _____.
   I'm sad when _____.
   I'm afraid when _____.
2. Have students compile a list or draw pictures of people they talked to during the week. In groups, discuss types of relationships students have with the people they talked to.

TABLE 17-1	SAMPLE K–6 CAREER GOALS AND COMPETENCIES

Overall Goals

- Become aware of personal characteristics, interests, aptitudes, and skills
- Develop an awareness of and respect for the diversity of the world of work
- Understand the relationship between school performance and future choices
- Develop a positive attitude toward work

Competencies

Kindergarten students will be able to:
- Identify workers in the school setting
- Describe the work of family members
- Describe what they like to do

First-grade students will be able to:
- Describe their likes and dislikes
- Identify workers in various settings
- Identify responsibilities they have at home and at school
- Identify skills they have now that they did not have previously

Second-grade students will be able to:
- Describe skills needed to complete a task at home or at school
- Distinguish which work activities in their school environment are done by specific people
- Recognize the diversity of jobs in various settings

Third-grade students will be able to:
- Define what the term future means
- Recognize and describe the many life roles that people have
- Demonstrate the ability to brainstorm a range of job titles

Fourth-grade students will be able to:
- Imagine what their lives might be like in the future
- Evaluate the importance of various familiar jobs in the community
- Describe workers in terms of work performed
- Identify personal hobbies and leisure activities

Fifth-grade students will be able to:
- Identify ways that familiar jobs contribute to the needs of society
- Compare their interests and skills to familiar jobs
- Compare their personal hobbies and leisure activities to jobs
- Discuss stereotypes associated with certain jobs
- Discuss what is important to them

Sixth-grade students will be able to:
- Identify tentative work interests and skills
- List elements of decision making
- Discuss how their parents' work influences life at home
- Consider the relationship between interests and abilities
- Identify their own personal strengths and weaknesses

SOURCE: From *Developmental School Counseling Programs: From Theory to Practice,* by P. O. Paisley and G. T. Hubbard, 1994, p. 218–221. Copyright 1994 by the American Counseling Association. Reprinted with permission.

3. Ask students to describe a friend and then themselves. Discuss and describe individual differences.

4. Play "Who Am I?," with one student playing a role and others trying to guess the role.

5. Have students select magazine pictures of events, places, and people that interest them. Share interests.

6. Ask students to summarize ways in which individuals may be described. Then, ask students to select descriptions of themselves.

7. Ask students to answer the following questions in writing or orally: What do I do well? What goals do I have? What do I do poorly? Who am I like? What makes me different from others?

8. Have students make lists of "Things I like" and "Things I don't like." Compile the lists and discuss the variety of interests.

9. Form a "Who Am I?" group and meet once a week, during which each student describes a personal characteristic of an individual who performs a specific job. Compile a list for future discussions.

10. Ask students to list several interests and to describe how they became interested in an activity.

Ⅲ➡ Educational and Occupational Exploration Strategies

1. Arrange a display of workers' hats that represent jobs in the community. Have each student select a hat that indicates a job he or she would like to do someday and explain why the job is appealing.

2. Assign students to develop a list of skills for their favorite jobs and describe how these skills are learned.

3. Ask each student to pretend that a friend wants a certain job, and ask each to describe the kinds of skills the friend would need.

4. Have students make a list of activities their parents do at home and have them identify those that require math, reading, and writing.

5. Have students make a list of school subjects and identify jobs in which the skills learned from the subjects are used.

6. Referring to a list of occupations, have students describe what kind of person might like a particular occupation.

7. Have students make a list of occupations involved in producing a loaf of bread.

8. Ask students to find a picture from a magazine or newspaper that depicts a female and a male in nontraditional jobs.

9. Have students interview their parents about their work roles and discuss these roles with the group.

10. Ask each student to adopt the identity of a worker and list work roles. Discuss how work has a personal meaning for every individual.

⟾ Career Planning Strategies

1. Ask students to make a list of jobs/occupations they would use to describe their neighbors or acquaintances. Share with others.

2. Have students identify the kinds of people who work in a selected list of occupations. Emphasize likenesses and differences.

3. In a self-discovery group, discuss how people have different interests and enjoy different or similar activities.

4. Have students describe how workers in different activities are affected by weather.

5. Ask students to collect newspaper and magazine photos of different people and describe likenesses and differences.

6. Have students identify workers that visit their homes. Identify differences of work and occupations.

7. Assign students to write a short paragraph answering the question "If you could be anyone in the world, whom would you be?" Follow with a discussion.

8. Divide the class into groups of boys and girls and ask each group to make a list of jobs girls can and cannot do. Compare lists and discuss how women are capable of performing most jobs.

9. Have students describe in writing, orally, or both "someone I would like to work with." Make a list of positive characteristics that each student describes.

10. Discuss how people work together and demonstrate using the example of three people building a doghouse together. What would each person do?

Integrating Career Development Concepts—Infusion

The idea of integrating career development concepts into existing curricula is referred to as *infusion*. This technique requires that teachers expand their current educational objectives to include career-related activities and subjects. For example, teaching decision-making skills can be infused with traditional academic courses. Planning a class project with a designated time limit involves certain decisions, such as specifying the goals of the project, determining the possible approaches to the project, selecting the best one, and actually following through. Decision-making and planning skills are applicable to many—if not all—subjects and should be consciously taught as skills to be developed and refined. Infusion of career objectives requires that formal attention be given to career-related skills and tasks. An example of an infusion model for the elementary school follows:

The following career infusion module is designed to improve career awareness. This module provides rationale, objectives, description, place of activity, personnel required, cost, time, resources, and evaluation measures

Subject: Math, reading, language

Concept: Career awareness
Answering a Job Advertisement

Rationale: Students should have an understanding of the jobs described in want ads in order to develop an awareness of various occupations. Students should also learn about the requirements of various occupations and draw conclusions of whether they would like to work in the environment described by a want ad and during follow-up.

Objective: Students will describe in writing how different occupations are described in terms of salary, hours of work, training, and educational requirements.

Description:

1. Discuss the various ways people find out about openings in the job market.

2. Present a page from the local newspaper with want ads listed.

3. Have students select three careers in which they are interested and research the requirements, salary, training, and education necessary for the job being advertised.

4. Have the students write a description of the job that appeals to them the most and explain their choices.

5. Have students share their findings with classmates in a 3–5 minute report.

Where activity occurs: Classroom

Personnel required: Teacher

Cost: Cost of newspaper

Time: Discussion, one-quarter period; research and select careers, one and one-quarter periods; share with classmates, one-quarter period

Resources: Newspaper

Evaluation measures: Oral and written report

SOURCE: *Project Cadre: A Cadre Approach to Career Education Infusion,* by C. C. Healy & O. H. Quinn, 1977. Unpublished manuscript. Reprinted by permission.

Another important part of the elementary school counselor's role is that of keeping up-to-date on career resources that can be used effectively to meet career development goals. Materials that provide interactive programs can be very effective. For example, an interactive career CD-ROM program for grades 3 and up combines animation, photography, voice interviews, and music. Included in the package is a very simple self-assessment that matches answers by referring students to occupational clusters.

In another resource, students from grades 2 to 6 can take a video field trip in their classroom. Topics could include *Timber! From Logs to Lumber, The Fire Station, The Airport, The Dairy,* and others. For many such activities, complete lesson plans are available along with suggested additional activities.

Also a *Children's Dictionary of Occupations* is available on CD-ROM and in print. Student's activity packages for these publications are opportunities for interactive participation. These examples suggest that an abundance of relevant materials is available to assist teachers and counselors in meeting the goals of career development in the elementary school. The materials in the previous two paragraphs and in this one are published by

MERIDIAN Educational Corporation
236 East Front Street
Dept. K8-F98
Bloomington, IL 61701
800-727-5507

In sum, the elementary school counselor is charged with the responsibility of overseeing a career guidance program that includes improving each student's self-awareness and occupational awareness and learning basic life skills. In the process, students discover the relationship between education and life planning. They develop a positive attitude toward work. They become actively involved in their career development and involve their families in the career decision-making process. Finally, they learn the educational competencies that are necessary to survive in an ever-changing work environment (Herring, 1998). Counselors must work diligently with all school personnel, parents, and community to accomplish these goals. In this context, the elementary school counselor is a teacher, counselor, consultant, planner, and an expert resource person.

The Middle/Junior School

Students in middle/junior school should continue the career development goals that were initiated in the elementary school of self-knowledge, educational and occupational exploration, and career planning. The essential tasks learning about and exploring career-related information. A summary of career guidance goals for middle/junior school students has been compiled by Herring (1998), paraphrased as follows: (a) decision making skills, self-awareness by recognizing strengths and weaknesses, (b) educational awareness by recognizing the relationship between educational and work skills, (c) economic awareness by understanding how supply and demand influence job availability, (d) occupational awareness by learning about the content of jobs, and (e) work attitudes by recognizing the role of work in society. In middle/junior school, the students are encouraged to gain a greater depth of information about the work world and its relationship to life roles. Students also link skills learned in school with work requirements.

The following suggested activities are strategies designed to meet the objectives of self-knowledge, education and occupation information, and career planning. This continuation of what has been learned in the elementary school requires middle/junior school students to explore career information in greater detail, gain greater insight into self-concept and self-knowledge, and apply planning skills.

Self-Knowledge Strategies

1. Introduce the concepts of self-image, self-worth, and self-esteem. Assign small groups to discuss the relationship of these concepts to educational and occupational planning. Compile a list from these groups.

2. Ask students to complete a standardized or original personality inventory. Using Holland's (1992) classification system, have students relate personality characteristics to work environments.

3. Have students list courses in which they have excelled and those in which they have not. Ask students to relate skills learned to their personality characteristics and traits and interests.

4. Assign students to construct a life line in which they designate places lived in and visited, experiences in school and with peer groups, and major events. Have them project the life line into the future by identifying goals.

5. Have students discuss how different traits are more important for some goals than for others. Compile a list of jobs and corresponding traits.

Educational and Occupational Exploration Strategies

1. Ask students to write a description of the type of persons they think they are, their preferences for activities (work and leisure), their strengths and weaknesses, and their desires for a career someday. Discuss.

2. Have students list several occupations that are related to their own interests and abilities. Discuss.

3. Lead a class discussion by identifying relationships of interest and abilities to various occupations. Each student should explore one occupation in depth, including reading a biography, writing a letter to someone, or conducting interviews. The student should research training requirements, working conditions, and personal attributes necessary for the job.

4. Ask each student to visit a place in the community where he or she can observe someone involved in a career of interest. Have students discuss their observations, such as type of work, working conditions, or tools of the trade.

5. Have the students make a list of the school subjects that are necessary to the success of persons whose careers are being investigated. Discuss.

6. Ask students to research preparation requirements for several selected occupations. Have them identify one similarity and one difference in preparation requirements for each of the occupations listed. Discuss.

7. Assign students to write short narratives explaining why certain jobs have endured and others have disappeared. Discuss.

8. Have students classify ten occupations by abilities needed, such as physical, mental, mechanical, creative, social, and other. Have students select three occupations that match their abilities and interests.

9. Have students do a mini-internship program where they shadow a worker. Discuss and share with other students.

10. Have students write a story about the many jobs involved in producing a hamburger. Discuss.

ⅢⅢ➡ Career Planning Strategies

1. Present steps in a decision-making model and discuss the importance of each step. Ask students to identify a problem and solve it by applying steps in the model.

2. Organize students into groups and have them construct a list of resources and resource people who could help solve a particular problem.

3. In a group discussion, compare a horoscope from a daily newspaper with other ways of solving problems and making decisions.

4. Assign students to select three occupations and then to choose one using a decision model. Share and discuss in groups.

5. Have students prepare an educational plan for high school. Share and discuss in groups.

The middle/junior school is when students begin to make tentative plans and explore occupations on their own. In general, students tend to be more conscious of their self-characteristics and sharpen their relationship skills. Developing personal goals is a skill that requires middle/junior school students to become more aware of their personal attributes and how they could fit an occupational environment. Students should learn to discuss a number of job requirements and begin to appreciate the role of work in their futures. As they learn how to interpret information about career opportunities, students become aware of skills needed to find a job. Students should also learn more about local occupations, their requirements, and opportunities (Drummond & Ryan, 1995).

In sum, counselors need to provide the means by which middle/junior school students learn to make tentative choices. Such strategies that foster self-knowledge, exploration of careers, and career planning involve the counselor not only in individual and group counseling, but also in teaching, mentoring, consulting, and providing appropriate resources. Infusion of career development learning opportunities in the classroom should continue. The following example for a geography class is designed to include planning, decision making, and awareness of career opportunities in geography.

Subject: Social studies, geography

Concept: Planning and decision making
Career awareness
Chamber of Commerce Exercise

Rationale: Students should be exposed to different ways in which different groups make decisions, in order to improve their own decision making.

Objectives:

1. Students will be able to describe their part in the project to accord with teacher observation.

2. Students will list all the Republics of South America and at least one feature from the tourist bulletin for each.

3. Students will identify at least two ways in which their project activity corresponds to duties in two specific occupations.

Description: During a unit on South America, divide the class into six groups. Each group will be a Chamber of Commerce for a Republic of South America. Each group can plan a tourist bulletin with articles and drawings.

1. Students will tell how their group decided who would research information, write articles, draw pictures, etc.

2. Students will describe their responsibilities in preparing the tourist bulletin and tell how they think those responsibilities were like some they might have on a job.

3. Students will answer the question, "Can you see how assuming responsibility for something in this project might help you assume responsibilities in an adult occupation?"

Personnel required: Teacher

Cost: None

Time: 3 or 4 periods estimated

Resources: Maps and information on South America

Impact on regular offering/curriculum goals: Complement regular unit on South America; help students remember important information about the area

Evaluation measures: Paper/pencil test

SOURCE: *Project Cadre: A Cadre Approach to Career Education,* by C. C. Healy & O. H. Quinn, 1977. Unpublished manuscript. Reprinted by permission.

The High School

The time to make important decisions and the rights of passage are most relevant to this age of transitions. The high school years are truly a time of learning to prepare for the future. A listing of career goals and competencies by Paisley and Hubbard (1994), displayed in Table 17-2, suggests that students have now reached a time when they are expected to take more independent actions and accept responsibility for their decisions. A greater sense of awareness and knowledge of the world of work are guiding principles for the next great step in life. Moreover, students who have developed a positive attitude concerning the idea of a lifetime of learning, will recognize that a variety of options await them.

TABLE 17-2	SAMPLE OF GRADES 10–12 CAREER GOALS AND COMPETENCIES

Overall Goals

- Become aware of personal characteristics, interests, aptitudes, and skills
- Develop an awareness of and respect for the diversity of the world of work
- Understand the relationship between school performance and future choices
- Develop a positive attitude toward work

Competencies

Tenth-grade students will be able to:
- Clarify the role of personal values in career choice
- Distinguish educational and skill requirements for areas or careers of interest
- Recognize the effects of job or career choice on other areas of life
- Begin realistic assessment of their potential in various fields
- Develop skills in prioritizing needs related to career planning

Eleventh-grade students will be able to:
- Refine future career goals through synthesis of information concerning self, use of resources, and consultation with others
- Coordinate class selection with career goals
- Identify specific educational requirements necessary to achieve their goals
- Clarify their own values as they relate to work and leisure

Twelfth-grade students will be able to:
- Complete requirements for transition from high school
- Make final commitments to a career plan
- Understand the potential for change in their own interests or values related to work
- Understand the potential for change within the job market
- Understand career development as a life-long process
- Accept responsibility for their own career directions

SOURCE: From *Developmental School Counseling Programs: From Theory to Practice*, by P. O. Paisley and G. T. Hubbard, 1994, pp. 218–221. Copyright by the American Counseling Association. Reprinted with permission.

The role and scope of the high school counselor includes continuing to prepare students for a variety of life roles. As discussed earlier in the comprehensive career guidance programs, planning for life becomes more relevant for students in high school. The understanding of life roles and their interrelationship is a good perspective to foster.

The following strategies are designed to meet the goals of self-knowledge, educational and occupational exploration, and career planning in the high school.

⮕ Self-Knowledge Strategies

1. Have students list five roles they currently fill. Discuss in small groups and identify future roles, such as spouse, parent, and citizen. Discuss.

2. Discuss or show films on sex-role stereotyping. Have students identify how sex-role stereotyping prohibits many individuals from becoming involved in certain events, including work roles.

3. Assign students to select newspaper and magazine pictures and articles that illustrate societal perceptions of appropriate behavior and dress. Discuss.

4. Have students discuss physical differences among their peers. Emphasize how differences could affect individuals.

5. Discuss the value of cooperative efforts in the work environment. Have students develop a project in which cooperation is essential. Discuss.

6. Have students observe workers performing specific tasks and make notes of skills and time required to complete tasks. Discuss.

7. Have students discuss employer expectations compared with their own. Develop a consensus about how both are justified and can be attained.

8. Have students role-play a supervisor reacting to an employee's work performance. Discuss reactions of supervisors in a variety of situations.

9. Have students research the various causes of tardiness and absenteeism among workers. Discuss.

10. Ask students to interview at least three workers and three supervisors of workers on the subject of good work habits. Discuss.

⮕ Educational and Occupational Exploration Strategies

1. Have students identify geographical factors that can affect choice of a career (Geary, 1972). Obtain newspapers from urban and rural areas. Compare employment opportunities and contrast differences.

2. Have students identify high school courses required for entry into trade schools, colleges, or jobs (Walz, 1972). Discuss elements of required

courses and develop brochures that list jobs and corresponding high school courses required.

3. Help students understand how human values are significant in career decision making (Bottoms, Evans, Hoyt, & Willer, 1972). Develop a list of values that could influence selection of a career. Each student selects two values of importance and locates a career that would be congruent with those values. Discuss.

4. Help students understand the principles and techniques of life planning (Brown, 1980). In small groups, in eight 1-hour meetings, six components are presented and discussed: "Why People Behave the Way They Do," "Winners and Losers," "Your Fantasy Life," "Your Real Life," "Setting Goals," and "Short- and Long-Term Planning."

5. Help students prepare for entrance into college (Hansen, 1970). A college-bound club discusses in weekly meetings such topics as how to read a college catalog, how to visit a college campus, and college study.

6. Discuss the value of leisure activities. Have students report on the benefits involved in five leisure activities of their choice. Discuss.

7. Have students develop a list of leisure activities they enjoy and estimate the amount of time necessary to participate in each. Form groups to decide which occupations would most likely provide the necessary time and which ones would not.

8. Ask students to debate the pros and cons of selected leisure activities.

9. Assign students to develop a list of leisure activities they enjoy now and project which of these can be enjoyed over the life span. Have students collect and discuss brochures from travel agencies and parks.

10. Have students discuss the concept of lifestyle in terms of work commitment, leisure activities, family involvement, and responsibilities and share their projections of future life roles and lifestyle.

Ⅲ➡ Career Planning Strategies

1. Ask students to review several job search manuals. Discuss the steps suggested in the manuals and develop strategies for taking these steps.

2. Assign students to visit a state employment agency and describe its functions. Discuss.

3. Have students research newspaper want-ads and select several of interest. Discuss and identify appropriate occupational information resources.

4. Have students demonstrate the steps involved in identifying an appropriate job, filling out an application, and writing a resumé. Discuss.

5. Have students participate in a mock interview. Critique and discuss appropriate dress and grooming.

6. Help students develop planning skills (Hansen, 1970). A one-year course, taught as an elective, covers six major areas of study: (a) relating one's characteristics to occupations; (b) exploring manual and mechanical occupations; (c) exploring professional, technical, and managerial occupations; (d) relating the economic system to occupations and people; (e) exploring roles, clerical, and service occupations; and (f) evaluating and planning ahead.

7. Help students evaluate careers relative to standards of living and life-style (Sorapuru, Theodore, & Young, 1972a; Steidl, 1972). Students project themselves 10 to 15 years in the future and identify the kind of lifestyles they would like to have. Each student selects four careers and conducts research to determine if the projected lifestyle can be met through these careers.

8. Provide good job search procedures (Sorapuru, Theodore, & Young, 1972b). Students who have had part-time jobs explain how they got them. Groups investigate local organizations that help people find jobs. Students investigate telephone directories, school placement center files, and state employment agencies for leads to jobs. Students write resumés and "walk through" steps for applying and interviewing.

9. Help students understand the stressors of work responsibility (Bottoms et al., 1972). Students identify individuals who recently attained a position of prominence and compare changes in lifestyle (work, leisure, and family).

10. Involve parents in career planning and decision making in high school (Amatea & Cross, 1980). Students and parents attend six 2-hour sessions per week and discuss the following at school and at home: self-management and goal setting, elements in career planning and decision making, comparing self with occupational data, information gathering skills, and training paths.

Developing planning skills for future educational and vocational choices also involves a multitude of learning activities and guidance programs. Decision-making skills and knowledge of occupations and job placement are key factors to emphasize in career development infusion. The following infusion module for a high school English class should help students become more aware of the importance of decision making.

Subject: English

Concept: Planning and decision making
Decision making exemplified in literature

Rationale: Students should become more aware of the importance of decision making.

Objectives:

1. Students will arrange in order the steps in the systematic decision-making model discussed in class.

2. Students will analyze either a personal decision or a decision made by a literary character by listing the steps taken in making the decision; students will write in one page how that decision followed the steps in the model or, if it didn't, how it could.

Description: Read and hold a class discussion on Robert Frost's poem, "The Road Not Taken," having students express their thoughts about the importance of decision making and talk about experiences that led them to make an important decision or to change their minds after making one. Bring out the following points in the discussion:

1. It is important that the student make a decision systematically and participate in its formulation.

2. Before making a decision, one must examine the consequences of the decision, both pro and con.

3. To do this, one must try to get accurate information about each decision.

4. Decision making can be thought of as a series of steps: (a) set the goal; (b) figure out alternative ways of reaching the goal; (c) get accurate information to determine which alternative is best; (d) decide on an alternative and carry it out; (e) figure out if the choice was correct and why; and (f) if you did not reach the goal, try another alternative or start the process over again.

Personnel required: Teacher

Cost: None

Time: One period

Resources: Robert Frost's poem, "The Road Not Taken"

SOURCE: *Project Cadre: A Cadre Approach to Career Education Infusion,* by C. C. Healy & O. H. Quinn, 1977. Unpublished manuscript. Reprinted by permission.

Intervention Strategy for Understanding Sex-Role Stereotyping

All children need to be prepared for self-sufficiency in the future. One major challenge is to assist both boys and girls in overcoming the problems associated with sex-role stereotyping. Counseling-component modules for the classroom present one method of accomplishing this objective. The following case example uses a counseling module for junior high school.

Case 17-1: GROUP DISCUSSION OF SEX-ROLE STEREOTYPING

Jane, Sari, Bart, and John are in a junior high school self-discovery counseling group. The counselor asks each member to study an advertisement that uses a man or a woman on television and also to locate one in a magazine. Each will record the product being advertised and describe the individual in the ad.

Sari and John recorded the information for two ads, which were discussed in the next group session. Sari's notes included the following: "This woman was beautiful on television, in a long flowing dress with gorgeous hair blowing in the wind. She was advertising a soap to be used for the face and hands for keeping them soft and pretty."

John's notes were taken on a magazine ad: "This ad was on a full page in a magazine. It showed a man advertising cigarettes who had a tattoo on his hand. He looked like a cowboy with a weather-beaten face."

The counselor asked the group to discuss the characteristics of each character in the two ads. The adjectives used to describe each character were recorded. For the woman in the ad, the list included beautiful, graceful, clean, dainty, and sexy. The list for the man included macho, handsome, outdoorsman, self-assured, and rugged.

The counselor asked the group to discuss the appropriate roles in life for men and women implied by these advertisements. The apparent differences in roles were then extended to typical sex-role stereotypes such as women are to be pampered, dependent, and pretty, whereas men are strong, free to do as they please, and independent. The group discussed how these ads and other types of sex-role stereotyping have influenced their own perceptions of lifestyles for men and women and, subsequently, the careers they find appropriate for men and women. The counselor summarized the influence of sex-role stereotyping found in advertising and elsewhere in society. Finally, the changing role of women in general and specifically in the work force was emphasized.

Role models may also be used as a counseling component that can effectively emphasize the occupational potential of girls. Examples of women who have enjoyed successful careers provide girls with concrete evidence that women do have opportunities to develop careers in a working world thought to be dominated by men. Numerous techniques apply to such a component. One method is to have students interview working women and write a summary of their work-related experiences. Biographies of women may also be reviewed and discussed (*Vocational Biographies,* 1985). These examples should emphasize how women can overcome sex-role stereotyping and find equal opportunity in the job market. They also illustrate that women can effectively assume leadership roles in the world of work. Finally, role models provide support for girls seriously considering a career-oriented lifestyle and may also provide some potential mentors.

Locating a mentor from whom one can directly learn the skills of a given career is usually highly productive. Therefore, career education and career counseling programs that instruct girls on the values of mentor relationships are very useful. A mentor is usually an older person who is admired and respected and has tremendous influence on the young. Levinson (1980) suggested that women who aspire to professional careers have fewer opportunities to find a mentor than do men, primarily because there are fewer female mentors available. There is some evidence that cross-gender mentoring can be of value, but because some men have a tendency to not take career women seriously, there is the danger of increasing the chances of sex-role stereotyping.

Career Videos for Individual and Group Counseling

Some excellent career videos are available for educational purposes. Feller (1994) has collected a list of 650 career videos, 161 of which have been reviewed and rated by career development specialists. More information and a complete list of videos by Feller (1994) can be obtained in Zunker (1998) and from the following address:

Dr. Rich Feller
Colorado State University
School of Education
222 Education Building
Fort Collins, CO 80523-1588
Office: 970-491-6897
Fax: 970-491-1317
E-mail: feller@condor.cahs.colostate.edu

Strategies for Implementing Career Development Guidelines

Splete and Stewart (1990) reviewed the career development abstracts included in the ERIC database between 1980 and 1990. After their review, they made the following recommendations for how competencies could be achieved at various levels.

Elementary school level

- Involve more parents and community persons in presenting career information.
- Increase attention to self-knowledge activities, especially as they relate to the development of a positive self-concept.
- Increase media use (computer programs, videos, films).

Middle/junior high school level

- Place more emphasis on self-knowledge competencies.
- Get business persons involved with students to help them with educational and occupational exploration and career planning.
- Increase attention to the benefits of educational achievement as the amount of education for different occupations varies.
- Emphasize skills necessary to seek and obtain jobs.

High school level

- Emphasize activities related to awareness of interrelationship of life roles.
- Increase emphasis on understanding the relationship of work to the economy and how work influences lifestyles.
- Find opportunities for students to improve skills interacting with others, a needed workplace characteristic. (Splete & Stewart, 1990, pp. 1–36)

The strength of the NOICC competency-based program models is that they describe goals and objectives in terms of specific tasks. These competencies also lend themselves quite readily to task statements and activities devised to develop the skills necessary to complete each task. And perhaps most important, criteria for successful task performance can be specifically defined.

School-to-Work Programs

The U.S. Department of Education and the U.S. Department of Labor have jointly sponsored a work-based program known as school-to-work. This is considered a new approach to learning for all students in which students apply what they learn to real life and to real work situations. In 1994, the School-to-Work Opportunities Act was signed into law, offering the possibility for all sectors of a community to work together in making education a more meaningful experience. Every school-to-work system must contain the following three core elements (U.S. Department of Education, 1996):

1. *School-based learning:* Classroom instruction based on high academic and business-defined occupational skill standards.

2. *Work-based learning:* Career exploration, work experience, structured training, and mentoring at job sites.

3. *Connecting activities:* Courses that integrate classroom and on-the-job instruction; matching students with participating employers, training mentors, and building other bridges between school and work. (See Appendix E for a summary of a student's work experience in her own words.)

The major educational focus of this act is to assist students in making the transition from school to work. A work-based learning approach is designed to develop skills in critical thinking, problem solving, communications, and interpersonal relations. These skills are considered vital for all work roles.

Another major objective is to have students learn about job possibilities by shadowing existing workers and discussing work life and the workplace with someone while on a job. Experiencing multiple workplaces is stressed.

To apply academics to real tasks on a specific job, workplace mentors collaborate with classroom teachers. This rationale suggests that students will become more motivated in all academic programs when they are able to experience the connections and links between their schoolwork and what is required on a job.

Quality school-to-work programs must be expertly coordinated between the work site and the classroom. Thus, teachers must also be convinced of the program's benefits. Teachers, supervisors, and students must cooperatively plan academic content and skill development to ensure an appropriate learning experience.

Finally, it must be pointed out that school-to-work programs are not just another program for noncollege-bound students. On the contrary, this program allows students to participate in advanced academic courses while developing workplace skills. This national program recognizes that we are now part of a technological society that requires technical skills for practically all careers, including professional ones.

Integrating Academic and Vocational Education

Vocational educators have developed a vocational reform strategy system in which students achieve both academic and occupational competencies. The major goal is to improve the educational and employment opportunities of students who face new technologies and business-management systems that require high-level worker skills. Grubb, Davis, Lum, Plihal, and Mograine (1991) describe the following models for integrating academic and vocational education:

1. Incorporate more academic content in vocational courses (vocational teachers modify vocational courses to include more academic content).

2. Combine vocational and academic teachers to enhance academic competencies in vocational programs (a cooperative effort involves more academic content in vocational courses).

3. Make academic courses more vocationally relevant (academic teachers modify courses or adopt new courses to include more vocational content).

4. Modify both vocational and academic courses (change content of both vocational and academic courses).

5. Use the senior project as a form of integration (teachers collaborate in developing new courses around student projects).

6. Implement the Academy model (use team teaching of math, English, science, and vocational subjects for two or three years and then require other subjects in regular high school).

7. Develop occupational high schools and magnet schools (occupational schools have been more successful in integrating vocational and academic education than the magnet schools have).

8. Implement occupational clusters, "career paths," and occupational majors (students are encouraged to think about occupations early in high school).

The interest in integrating academic and vocational education has evolved primarily from a need to encourage vocational education students to take more rigorous academic courses. A strong academic background is essential for continuing education, which is a growing trend among vocational schools (Cetron & Gayle, 1991). The models described by Grubb and colleagues (1991) underscore the interest in making significant changes in vocational education.

Tech-Prep Programs

Tech-prep is a national strategy designed to ensure that students exit high school or a community/technology college with marketable skills for job placement, have academic credentials to pursue higher education, or have both of these options. In this context, *tech-prep* means integrated academics and technical training for secondary, postsecondary, and apprenticeship students, plus curriculum development to meet the skills requirements of advanced technology jobs. Also included is an innovative, up-to-date career counseling program about high-demand occupations, a comprehensive assessment program for students in middle/junior high school, and individualized high school graduation plans.

To accomplish the goals of tech-prep programs, school systems and cooperating colleges and universities have formed consortiums with industry. Through such organizations, education and industry can coordinate work-site-based training. In addition, follow-up assessment of graduates is enhanced.

Encouraging vocational education students to take more advanced academic courses is the major goal of tech-prep models. Typically, schools devise a variety of two-year technical curricula that include such subjects as applied mathematics, applied biology/chemistry, and principles of technology. There is often a working relationship with cooperating colleges that have agreed, by prior arrangement, to accept these courses for college credit or as entrance requirements.

Operationally, students concentrate on basic concepts during their first year and learn more about applications of the concepts during the second year. In principles of technology, for example, first-year students examine principles of force, work, energy, and power; in the second year, they apply these concepts in optical systems, radiation, and transducers. Many colleges that accept the principles of technology course count it as a laboratory-science requirement (Cetron & Gayle, 1991). The National Career Development Training Institute plans to incorporate the counselor's role in tech-prep programs in its training programs. We should hear a great deal more about these programs in the near future.

Apprenticeship and the Future of the Workforce

In recognition of the changing needs of the workforce, especially the need for technical skills, the U.S. Department of Labor has established a committee on apprenticeship. Like other work-based learning, training under the supervision of a master worker is a desirable learning experience. Building technical skills and observing how technical tasks relate to theoretical knowledge and interpretation is a major advantage of apprenticeship.

The Federal Committee on Apprenticeship suggests training strategies with the following eight essential components:

- Apprenticeship is sponsored by employers and others who can actually hire and train individuals in the workplace, and it combines hands-on training on the job with related theoretical instruction.

- Workplace and industry needs dictate key details of apprenticeship programs: training content, length of training, and actual employment settings.

- Apprenticeship has a specific legal status and is regulated by federal and state laws and regulations.

- Apprenticeship leads to formal, official credentials: a Certificate of Completion and journeyperson status.

- Apprenticeship generally requires a significant investment of time and money by employers or other sponsors.

- Apprenticeship provides wages to apprentices during training according to predefined wage scales.

- Apprentices learn by working directly under master workers in their occupations.

- Apprenticeship involves both written agreements and implicit expectations. Written agreements specify the roles and responsibilities of each party; implicit expectations include the right of program sponsors to employ the apprentice, recouping their sizable investment in training, and the right of apprentices to obtain such employment. (Grossman & Drier, 1988, pp. 28–63)

- Apprenticeships are independent of vocational-technical education programs, tech-prep programs, and cooperative education. This distinction is made because only apprenticeship produces fully trained journeypersons with the skills needed to perform effectively in the workplace. The concept of apprenticeships is important in meeting the ever- and fast-changing technical needs of the workplace.

Placement as Part of Career Planning

In this section, we cover the role of placement officers in secondary schools and also the role of the state employment agency.

The integration of career planning and placement services in many educational institutions has slowly evolved during the last three decades. A current suggestion is to eliminate the word *placement* as a part of the name of the center where career services are offered (Carter, J. K., 1995). This name change is the result of changing missions in educational institutions. For instance, many career centers have focused more on preplacement services, such as general information about educational programs, outreach programs, cooperative education and internships, part-time jobs, and computerized career guidance and information systems.

Placement should remain as a primary service offered by educational institutions, but in institutions where career planning and placement services have been combined into career centers, the services include a wide variety of programs that have received equal and in many cases more attention than placement has. Thus, a more appropriate name for locations that provide career-related services, including placement, is the more generic reference *career centers*.

The Purpose and Rationale for Career Centers

Career centers have been developed as a major component of career guidance programs. The management of programs and the use of occupational information material are major responsibilities of the career counselor. The counselor's understanding of how to use occupational information is highly related to the effectiveness of the career center. Counselors must also be well acquainted with the content of the various sources of career information. Program development for individual and group use of the center must be carefully planned.

Presentation of materials will vary according to the differing needs of groups and individuals. For example, a senior high school freshman class may be given an overview demonstration of the various resources in the center, whereas a group of high school juniors are presented with specific resources needed for a class project. Or a group of high school seniors may be given the assignment of researching the various careers in their declared majors.

Individual use of career information is highly personalized, and the counselor must recognize that different learning styles among clients call for flexibility in the use of career information resources. Moreover, Sharf (1984) pointed out that information-seeking behavior will vary from counselor to counselor. As counselors help individuals sort and assimilate information, they must also provide direction by generating questions concerning specific information that can be obtained from available resources. Just as career decision making is an individualized process, so too is the use and assimilation of career information.

In sum, the career center is used by individuals who are in various phases of career decision making; some are seeking information to narrow down choices, whereas others are searching for answers in the beginning phases of decision making. It is also a place where instructors can meet with groups of students or entire classes for a variety of career guidance objectives. Finally, the entire professional staff is encouraged to use the center as a resource for ongoing projects.

Several advantages of career centers are worth considering. First, a centralized location provides the opportunity to systematically organize all career materials into more efficient and workable units. The centralized facility also allows counselors to monitor materials on hand and simplifies the task of maintaining and selecting additional materials.

Second, students and faculty are attracted to centrally displayed materials that are easily accessed. Thus, a wider use of materials is usually assured, and in addition, attention is directed to programs offered by the career center. In essence, the career center brings into focus the career-related programs and the career resources offered by an institution.

A third consideration is the methods of promoting coordination and acceptance of career-related programs among faculty, staff, administration, students, and the community. A well-organized and well-operated career center will encourage a variety of members of an institution to participate in development, programming, and evaluation of career center materials and facilities. A commitment from a cross section of individuals will greatly enhance the career guidance efforts an educational institution offers.

A final consideration is programming innovations for the use of career materials and outreach activities, which are usually generated within the career center or sponsored by the career center. A well-planned facility can become the focal point in planning new programs and innovative activities for career guidance and career education. In essence, the career center should facilitate a wide variety of program development opportunities among staff and faculty.

The Role of Placement in Senior High School

A major component of the placement part of career planning involves job listings from local, state, regional, national, and international sources. The numerous federal and state programs that provide job placement for high school graduates and dropouts are valuable referral sources for secondary schools. A cooperative venture between the school, the business community, and federal and state agencies is essential in developing local sources of job listings. One of the most effective approaches is through a community advisory committee (Gysbers & Henderson, 1988). Local service clubs, chambers of commerce, federal and state agencies, and professional and personnel organizations are excellent resources for developing a local career advisory committee. As demand for hands-on experience increases, local career opportunities will be essential to the success of these programs. A viable listing of local part-time and full-time jobs will also enhance the popularity of the career planning and placement office.

Programs that enhance the transition from school to work should also be offered in senior high schools. In this respect, placement should be viewed as a vital function and a continuation of career guidance programs (Herr & Cramer, 1996). Some suggested program topics include how to prepare for an interview, write a resumé, locate job information, apply for a job, know if you are qualified for a job, and find the right job.

Finally, computer-assisted career guidance programs (discussed in Chapter 9) provide vital, up-to-date information about the current job market. The ability to generate local job information on available computer programs is extremely helpful to the job seeker. In fact, the fast-changing job market may very well require that computer capabilities keep up to date.

Placement services can also provide the vital link between academics and the working world. Career planning and placement services offered early in secondary programs should provide the student with knowledge of career skills to be developed in secondary education. Such programs should be established not to discourage future formal academic training but to provide relevance and added motivation for learning per se. Career planning and placement in this sense should be an ongoing program for students in various levels of secondary education, with the placement function playing a vital role in student services.

Placement by State Employment Agencies

State employment agencies consist of a network of local offices in cities and rural areas across the nation. This network is based on federal and state partnerships with the U.S. Employment Service, providing broad national guidelines for operational procedures in state and local employment offices. One principal source of job information has been compiled into what is referred to as a *job bank*. The job bank is a listing of all job orders compiled daily within each state. Microfiche copies are distributed daily to authorized users and all state employment offices. Those offices with computer terminals have direct access to the job bank. This up-to-the-minute job information is available to all job seekers, who are required to fill out an application and be interviewed before they are given access to the job bank.

The functions of state employment agencies, which have very active placement programs, are to help the unemployed find work and to provide employers with qualified applicants for job orders. Many state agencies divide their services into two categories: (1) placement for job seekers and (2) services to employers. For job seekers, state agencies offer the following services:

1. Job listings in professional, clerical, skilled, technical, sales, managerial, semiskilled, service, and labor occupations
2. Personal interviews with professional interviewers
3. Assistance with improving qualifications
4. Referral to training
5. Testing
6. Counseling
7. Service to veterans
8. Unemployment benefits (for those who qualify while they are looking for work)

Services offered to employers are as follows:

1. Screening for qualified applicants
2. Professional interviews
3. On-site recruitment and application taking
4. Computerized job listing in most areas of the state
5. Aptitude and proficiency testing
6. Labor market information on technical assistance
7. Technical assistance with job descriptions, master orders, and turnover studies
8. Unemployment insurance tax information

Job placement is the focus of state employment agencies, but career counseling is available when requested. State employment agencies also administer assessment instruments that are typically used in career counseling, such as aptitude and achievement tests. Individuals are regularly referred to state employment agencies by other state agencies. For example, rehabilitation agencies refer clients who have had extensive career counseling and are in need of job listings. The placement function is enhanced by computerized job banks and lists of qualified job applicants that provide a readily accessible matching system. Employment opportunities are quickly available to job seekers who need immediate placement.

Summary

1. Comprehensive school guidance programs are a means of systematically implementing a program concept for guidance activities in grades K–12. The value of this model is its comprehensive nature and involvement of school professionals, selected members of the community, and parents.

2. The Planning for Life Program complements comprehensive guidance programs. "Planning for life" suggests that career and life are ongoing processes that require individual and community commitment.

3. Counseling children from different cultures requires counselors to be knowledgeable about culture-specific variables but to base counseling goals on individual needs.

4. Elementary, middle/junior, and high school counselors provide guidance activities based on self-knowledge, educational and occupation exploration, and career planning. Counselors must be creative and innovative in developing a variety of strategies.

5. Intervention strategy for understanding sex-role stereotyping, career videos, and career development guidelines are resources that are available to assist school counselors.

6. A work-based program, known as school-to-work, assists students in making the transition from school to work. The rationale for this program suggests that students will become more motivated in all academic programs when they are able to experience the connections between schoolwork and what is required on a job.

7. Models for integrating vocational and academic education are designed to encourage vocational education students to take more rigorous academic courses.

8. Tech-prep programs have stressed the need to integrate academics and technical training. Students who opt for tech-prep would also qualify for higher education.

9. Other government-sponsored programs address changes in vocational education that place a greater emphasis on technology. Work-based programs and apprenticeships are being stressed.

10. Secondary placement offers a variety of programs to assist high school students in transition to work and entering college.

Supplementary Learning Exercises

1. Interview a representative from the business community for suggestions about how to establish collaborative efforts to meet school-to-work objectives. Summarize your recommendations.

2. Interview a school counselor to determine the role and scope of his or her career guidance program. Evaluate your findings and offer suggestions.

3. Develop objectives and strategies for introducing life planning concepts in the elementary school.

4. What strategies would you use to convince a middle/junior high class that life and career planning are important goals?

5. Develop a format that could be used to annually evaluate the career planning progress of high school students.

6. Interview at least two parents of school-age children who are willing to participate as career infusion models. Develop a format for presenting a program to a class.

7. Develop course objectives and goals for a minicourse on decision making for junior and senior high school students.

8. Visit a local industry to determine the kinds of on-site job experiences available. Write a description of at least five possible on-site jobs.

9. Develop at least five counseling strategies for middle/junior high school students to promote opportunities for reflecting on self-in-situation.

10. Develop at least five counseling strategies for senior high school students designed to help them choose a training program or a college.

11. Visit a senior high school placement office. Report your findings to the class.

For More Information

Beymer, L. (1995). *Meeting the guidance and counseling needs of boys*. Alexandria, VA: American Counseling Association.

Gysbers, N. C., & Henderson, P. (1988). *Developing and managing your school guidance program*. Alexandria, VA: American Association for Counseling and Development.

Gysbers, N. C., & Moore, E. J. (1987). *Career counseling, skills and techniques for practitioners.* Englewood Cliffs, NJ: Prentice-Hall.

Healy, C. C. (1982). *Career development: Counseling through life stages.* Boston: Allyn & Bacon.

Herr, E. L., & Cramer, S. H. (1996). *Career guidance and counseling through the life span: Systematic approaches* (5th ed.). New York: HarperCollins.

Herring, R. D. (1998). *Career counseling in schools.* Alexandria, VA: American Counseling Association.

LaFromboise, T. D. (1996). *American Indian life skills development curriculum.* Madison: University of Wisconsin Press.

Paisley, P. O., & Hubbard, G. T. (1994). *Developmental school counseling programs: From theory to practice.* Alexandria, VA: American Counseling Association.

Thompson, C. L., & Rudolph, L. B. (2000). *Counseling children* (5th ed.). Belmont, CA: Wadsworth.

18

Career Counseling in Institutions of Higher Learning

Chapter Highlights

- *Characteristics of college students*

- *How college affects career choice and development*

- *National goals for college career guidance programs*

- *Implications for career guidance programs in institutions of higher learning*

- *Career prep program at a community college consortium*

- *Module model of a curricular career information service*

- *Metroplex model for career counseling*

- *Life-planning workshops, including example case*

- *Work- and experienced-based programs for college and university students*

- *Role of college and university placement offices*

W E BEGIN THIS CHAPTER WITH A DISCUSSION OF CHARACTERISTICS OF COL-lege students and how college affects students' career choice and development. We also explore national goals for career guidance programs. Examples of career guidance programs in institutions of higher learning include representative models of innovative career counseling programs, such as a career prep program at a community college consortium, a curriculum module model, a metroplex model, a life-planning workshop, and work-experience models. Finally, we cover the role and function of college placement services.

Some Characteristics of College Students

Marcia (1967, 1980, 1991) described college students in terms of four identity statuses: the "foreclosed student," the "identity-diffused student," the "moratorium student," and the "achieved-identity student." These statuses were determined by the students' capacity for intimacy, moral awareness, respect for individual rights, and reliance on a universal principle of justice. The statuses also represent styles of coping with identity developmental tasks. For example, foreclosed students are closed off from self-exploration and limit their contacts and challenges. Identity-diffused students have few commitments to the future and are less mature than achieved-identity and moratorium students are. Moratorium students (described by Erikson as "delaying commitments") are able to effectively use the college experience to achieve their quest for identity. Achieved-identity students have successfully resolved ego identity, as evidenced by firmer commitments to future goals.

The diverse levels of development among college students, as revealed by Marcia's work, are not unexpected but do point out a wide range of career guidance needs. Mauer and Gysbers (1990) also determined the career concerns of college students (entering freshmen) from a study of 3600 undergraduates and grouped these concerns into the following categories:

1. *Anxiety:* Undecided about a career and confused about the process of career exploration
2. *Confidence:* Uncertain about an occupation
3. *Self-assessment:* Major strengths and weaknesses are unknown
4. *Occupational information:* Lacks knowledge of work and what workers do

The needs expressed in this survey suggest strategies that would greatly assist entering freshmen.

Recent evidence overwhelmingly supports career guidance programs in institutions of higher learning. More than 945,000 high school students responded to an American College Testing Program questionnaire during the 1994–1995 academic year, and 41% indicated that they needed help with educational and occupational plans (American College Testing Program, 1996b). Accomplishing the tasks required of the transition from Super's (1990) exploration stage to his establishment stage is not easy, as Healy (1982) observed. Almost half of all college students change majors, and even more change career goals while in college.

In addition, returning adult students are a growing population in institutions of higher learning. Hirschhorn (1988) reported that students over age 25 make up 45% of campus enrollments. The special needs of these students must be addressed by postsecondary career centers. Splete (1996) has been a leader in developing adult career counseling centers and has successfully built a model for such programs during the last 12 years at Oakland University. One goal of this center is to provide no-cost career exploration and planning opportunities to adults in the community. Splete (1996) has also supported research efforts in promoting effective career guidance practices for adults.

How College Affects Students' Career Choice and Development

During a 20-year-period, Pascarella and Terenzini (1991) conducted a comprehensive study of research findings on how college affects students. The following conclusions were paraphrased from the chapter on career choice and development.

1. Students frequently change their career plans.
2. Significant occupational status differences between high school and college graduates are sustained over the life span.
3. Individuals with bachelor's degrees are more likely to obtain high-status managerial, technical, and professional jobs.
4. College graduates are less likely to be unemployed than are high school graduates.
5. College graduates are less likely to suffer the effects of prolonged periods of unemployment.
6. Employers see college graduates as possessing requisite skills and values that make them more desirable for employment and advancement.
7. College graduates enjoy significantly higher levels of career mobility and advancement.
8. College experiences tend to produce conflicting influences on satisfaction with one's work. College tends to develop a capacity for critical judgment and evaluation that in turn provides sensitivity to shortcomings of jobs.
9. Maturity of career thinking and planning can be modestly improved through various career development courses.
10. Socialization in college increases student occupational aspirations.
11. College may enhance occupational success by facilitating development of traits that describe a psychologically mature person, such as symbolization (reflective intelligence), allocentrism (empathy and altruism),

integration (ability to combine a variety of views), and stability and autonomy.

12. For reducing unemployment, a college education was more important for non-whites than for whites.

The results of this study suggest that the benefits of a college education are quite significant in the world of work. This conclusion comes as no surprise but does give credence to recommendations counselors have made for years about the influence of higher education on lifestyle and future opportunities for career development. Not only does the college experience provide for career mobility and advancement, but it also increases occupational aspirations. In essence, the benefits of higher education improve the quality of life and the capacity to make appropriate judgments over the life span.

National Goals for a College Career Guidance Program

We include the national competencies and indicators (NOICC, 1992) for adults to underscore the necessity of preparing students for the work world and integrating life roles into a future lifestyle. These competencies and indicators present a significant challenge to institutions of higher learning and point out the importance of and need for an effective career guidance program. These competencies and indicators suggest not only the importance of educational and occupational exploration, but also the importance of work as it affects values and lifestyle. The far-reaching influences on college students suggested by these guidelines are quite apparent. To accomplish these goals will require a comprehensive program and commitment by the college or university.

Adult: Competencies and Indicators

Self-Knowledge

Competency I: Skills needed to maintain a positive self concept

- Demonstrate a positive self-concept.
- Identify skills, abilities, interests, experiences, values, and personality traits and their influence on career decisions.
- Identify achievements related to work, learning, and leisure and their influence on self-perception.
- Demonstrate a realistic understanding of self.

Competency II: Skills needed to maintain effective behaviors

- Demonstrate appropriate interpersonal skills in expressing feelings and ideas.
- Identify symptoms of stress.
- Demonstrate skills to overcome self-defeating behaviors.

- Demonstrate skills in identifying support and networking arrangements (including role models).
- Demonstrate skills to manage financial resources.

Competency III: Understanding developmental changes and transitions

- Describe how personal motivations and aspirations may change over time.
- Describe physical changes that occur with age and adapt work performance to accommodate these.
- Identify external events (for example, job loss, job transfer) that require life changes.

Educational and Occupational Exploration

Competency IV: Skills needed to enter and participate in education and training

- Describe short- and long-range plans to achieve career goals through appropriate educational paths.
- Identify information that describes educational opportunities (for example, job training programs, employer-sponsored training, graduate and professional study).
- Describe community resources to support education and training (for example, child care, public transportation, public health services, mental health services, welfare benefits).
- Identify strategies to overcome personal barriers to education and training.

Competency V: Skills needed to participate in work and lifelong learning

- Demonstrate confidence in the ability to achieve learning activities (for example, studying, taking tests).
- Describe how educational achievements and life experiences relate to occupational opportunities.
- Describe organizational resources to support education and training (for example, remedial classes, counseling, tuition support).

Competency VI: Skills needed to locate, evaluate, and interpret information

- Identify and use current career information resources (e.g., computerized career-information systems, print and media materials, mentors).
- Describe information related to self-assessment, career planning, occupations, prospective employers, organizational structures, and employer expectations.
- Describe the uses and limitations of occupational outlook information.
- Identify the diverse job opportunities available to an individual with a given set of occupational skills.
- Identify opportunities available through self-employment.
- Identify factors that contribute to misinformation about occupations.
- Describe information about specific employers and hiring practices.

Competency VII: Skills needed to prepare to seek, obtain, maintain, and change jobs

- Identify specific employment situations that match desired career objectives.
- Demonstrate skills to identify job openings.
- Demonstrate skills to establish a job search network through colleagues, friends, and family.
- Demonstrate skills in preparing a resumé and completing job applications.
- Demonstrate skills and attitudes essential to prepare for and participate in a successful job interview.
- Demonstrate effective work attitudes and behaviors.
- Describe changes (e.g., personal growth, technological developments, changes in demand for products or services) that influence the knowledge, skills, and attitudes required for job success.
- Demonstrate strategies to support occupational change (e.g., on-the-job training, career ladders, mentors, performance ratings, networking, continuing education).
- Describe career planning and placement services available through organizations (e.g., educational institutions, business/industry, labor, and community agencies).
- Identify skills that are transferable from one job to another.

Competency VIII: Understanding how the needs and functions of society influence the nature and structure of work

- Describe the importance of work as it affects values and lifestyle.
- Describe how society's needs and functions affect occupational supply and demand.
- Describe occupational, industrial, and technological trends as they relate to training programs and employment opportunities.
- Demonstrate an understanding of the global economy and how it affects the individual.

Career Planning

Competency IX: Skills needed to make decisions

- Describe personal criteria for making decisions about education, training, and career goals.
- Demonstrate skills to assess occupational opportunities in terms of advancement, management styles, work environment, benefits, and other conditions of employment.
- Describe the effects of education, work, and family decisions on individual career decisions.
- Identify personal and environmental conditions that affect decision making.
- Demonstrate effective career decision-making skills.
- Describe potential consequences of decisions.

Competency X: Understanding the impact of work on individual and family life

- Describe how family and leisure functions affect occupational roles and decisions.
- Determine effects of individual and family developmental stages on one's career.
- Describe how work, family, and leisure activities interrelate.
- Describe strategies for negotiating work, family, and leisure demands with family members (e.g., assertiveness and time management skills).

Competency XI: Understanding the continuing changes in male/female roles

- Describe recent changes in gender norms and attitudes.
- Describe trends in the gender composition of the labor force and assess implications for one's own career plans.
- Identify disadvantages of stereotyping occupations.
- Demonstrate behaviors, attitudes, and skills that work to eliminate stereotyping in education, family, and occupational environments.

Competency XII: Skills needed to make career transitions

- Identify transition activities (e.g., reassessment of current position, occupational changes) as a normal aspect of career development.
- Describe strategies to use during transitions (e.g., networks, stress management).
- Describe skills needed for self-employment (e.g., developing a business plan, determining marketing strategies, developing sources of capital).
- Describe the skills and knowledge needed for preretirement planning.
- Develop an individual career plan, updating information from earlier plans and including short- and long-range career decisions.

Implications for Career Guidance Programs in Institutions of Higher Learning

Several career guidance strategies in the senior high school apply to career guidance at postsecondary institutions. For example, career guidance must meet the needs of students at various stages of career development. Understanding the relationships between career choice and educational requirements is essential. College students must learn to relate their personal characteristics to occupational requirements. Career planning and decision-making skills are essential. College students need assistance in choosing graduate schools.

In general, college students should be assisted in systematically analyzing college and noncollege experiences and in incorporating this information into career-related decisions. In addition, career guidance services should help students select major fields of study and relate these to career fields. Career life planning that focuses on factors that influence career choices over the life span is a valuable concept to incorporate in career guidance programs. Placement offices should provide a wide range of services, including projected job markets and overall employment statistics, job search strategies, interview skills training, and job fairs.

Career guidance activities in institutions of higher learning must provide assistance in helping each student understand that career development is a lifelong process based on a sequential series of educational and occupational choices. Each student should be given the opportunity to identify and use a wide variety of resources to maximize his or her career development potential.

Examples of Career Guidance Programs in Institutions of Higher Learning

There are numerous career counseling programs in institutions of higher learning. Some institutions offer credit for 1- or 3-hour courses that are built around some aspect of career guidance. Others offer seminars or workshops that typically do not include credit hours. In some institutions, instructors assign projects that include career exploration, typically done in a career counseling center. Individual and group counseling is available at most institutions, and most institutions have a placement office or an employment services office available to students. One can expect to find computerized career guidance systems at most institutions of higher learning. Finally, some institutions offer career-related services to the community. In the following sections, examples of strategies designed to meet the needs of some students are presented. The first example is a tech prep consortium that has prepared a career prep handbook. The second is a curricular career information service module that covers a wide range of needs and contains modules for special population groups. The third is a career counseling program at a large metropolitan university that must serve not only its large student enrollment but also its alumni. The fourth example is a career life planning approach.

Career Prep at a Community College Consortium

In central Nebraska, 38 high schools have formed a consortium known as Central Nebraska Tech Prep Consortium. This consortium uses the combined expertise of its professional staff to develop materials and counseling strategies that are designed to accomplish their collective career guidance mission. Each spring, selected members of the career guidance staff from the consortium meet to revise their plans and materials. Counselors bring new ideas and materials that are evaluated and eventually distributed to the consortium members.

Each member of the consortium uses a student career preparation handbook that is designed to be used with all high school students. This handbook can be considered an extension of a comprehensive career guidance system that students have participated in during elementary, middle/junior, and high schools. The handbook is designed to continue the development of self-knowledge, educational and occupational exploration, and career planning. For example, a section entitled "Career Prep" is designed to help students make intelligent decisions about acquiring skills needed for careers in the 21st century. An informative section of the handbook describes the variety of two-year programs that are offered at local community colleges as well as four-year university programs in Nebraska.

Other interesting topics include employability skills, how education enhances employability, and 20 "Hot Track Jobs." As students proceed through the handbook they self-administer a career path assessment, identify their interests, and self-rate their abilities while reflecting on working conditions. On the basis of these results, students can investigate career clusters of Arts and Communication, Business, Management, and Technology, Human Services, Industrial and Engineering Technology, Natural Resources and Agriculture, or a combination of these. Each cluster is divided into specific jobs, for example, the Health Services section contains Laboratory Technology with listings of Pharmacists, Clinical Laboratory Technicians, Medical Laboratory Technicians, Pharmacy Technicians, and Ultrasound Technologists.

Academic expectations in community and technical schools and four-year institutions of higher learning and a directory of Nebraska postsecondary educational institutions are also provided. Internet addresses are given for Web sites that contain related information such as American Job Bank, National Career Search, Peterson's Education Center, Employment Opportunities, and many more.

Students can also review high school educational planning suggestions that include samples of curriculum requirements for different tech prep plans. Also included are postsecondary entrance test requirements, a senior year planning checklist calendar, postsecondary visitation features, application process, financial and scholarship information, budgeting tips, sample student resumés, and an example letter of application.

In sum, this program suggests that students have important decisions to make concerning their futures. What is stressed here is that intelligent educational decisions are going to be necessary now and in the future. In fact, students need to be prepared for a lifetime of learning new skills for new and different jobs in a global society. Students are encouraged to recognize the relationship between high school courses and the world of work. Students are to recognize that they have choices that include two-year associate degrees, vocational/technical training, and attending a four-year university. Moreover, the suggestion of starting a planning strategy now will be most important in meeting individual short- and long-term goals. This handbook supports the principles of what students have learned about themselves thus far in the educational process and suggests that more is to be learned about the future. The goal of a life learning approach is strongly endorsed and students are encouraged to continue career planning.

Curricular Career Information Service (CCIS): A Module Model

An innovative program for delivering educational and vocational information was initiated at Florida State University in 1975. The program emphasizes an instructional approach to career planning services. The CCIS is self-help-oriented, uses instructional models, and is multimedia-based; the program is delivered by paraprofessionals. The CCIS is an outreach program used in residence halls and the university student center. In addition, the modules have been used as the nucleus of a three-credit course in career planning offered by two academic departments at Florida State University. The instructional modules were conceptualized to meet specific counseling goals and are structured around behavioral objectives. Modules I through V are shown in Table 11-1; modules VI through XII can be found in Zunker (1998) and obtained from the following address:

Dr. Robert Reardon
Florida State University
The Career Center
Tallahassee, FL 32306-1035
Phone: 904-644-6431
Fax: 904-644-3273

After a brief interview, a typical student is directed to the first module, which begins with a 10-minute slide presentation outlining the goals and purposes of the CCIS. The second module provides an overview of variables considered desirable in career planning using slides and selected materials. The third module requires self-assessment, primarily accomplished through self-administration and self-interpretation of the SDS (*Self-Directed Search*) interest inventory (Holland, 1987b). The fourth module consists of a slide presentation of career information resources. The fifth module assists the student in locating careers related to academic majors. Other modules include employment outlooks, leisure planning, career planning for African Americans, career decision making for adult women and students with disabilities, and career interest exploration through work and occupational skills. The instructional approach to career planning used in the CCIS has potential application for all career counseling programs. Career counseling effectiveness can be better evaluated when behavioral objectives are specified as they are in these modules. Major and minor components of the instructional unit can be effectively evaluated through a systematic review process. Effectiveness of materials and of instruction techniques can be measured in relation to specific objectives. Thus, the system provides the opportunity for continuous modification and upgrading of each instructional component. As career-related materials and programs change rapidly in the future, the opportunity to systematically evaluate and subsequently upgrade them will be a major asset. Additional modules can be developed as needs are identified. As new program needs are identified, such as career assistance for minority groups, an instructional module can be built using materials already at hand and examples of existing modules. Thus, instructional modules are very flexible. Once the system of instructional modules has been established, the building of additional modules can be based on a review of needs identified by the professional staff. Also inherent in this process is the identification of additional career materials.

Instructional modules provide the opportunity for more effective choice of entry into career counseling for individuals seeking career decision assistance. The diversity of the learning activities provided through a series of career planning modules allows the individual a greater variety of options and a more effective means of choosing a point of entry. The development of modules for specific groups (such as adults, females, minority groups) represents a multifaceted approach to career counseling that eliminates the necessity of prescribing the same program for everyone. A diversity of programs also provides an attractive means of creating interest in career exploration activities. Career counseling programs that provide the opportunity to identify goals and desired outcomes have much greater appeal and assist the individual in identifying expectations of career planning experiences.

Library System for the CCIS

The CCIS Library has divided its material into two types: career planning information and occupational information. The career planning information is classified according to the Dewey Decimal Classification (DDC). The *Dictionary of Occupational Titles (DOT)* is used to classify all materials related to occupations (Reardon & Domkowski, 1977).

As material reaches the library, it is classified and assigned a DDC or *DOT* number. A cutter number is also assigned to each piece of material to distinguish it from materials with the same DDC or *DOT* number. Because the CCIS uses numerous materials that have *DOT* numbers printed on them, the classification process is greatly simplified. All material is classified by alphabetical order into one of three catalogs: (1) *DOT* index, (2) *DOT* subject, or (3) DDC subject.

Students are provided with step-by-step instructions in the use of the CCIS Library. For occupational information, the student uses Card Catalog 1 (*DOT* Index) and locates the *DOT* number. The number is used to locate the filed information and may also be used in Catalog 2 (*DOT* Subject Catalog) for information in books and tapes. For curriculum and career planning information, a student is referred to Catalog 3 (DDC Listing), in which information is filed alphabetically according to subject matter.

The CCIS adopted this system for flexibility of use and for ease of cross-referencing. Many students want easy access to files of occupational materials. Cross-referencing is considered very important because each brief, book, chapter, or pamphlet describing a certain occupation is contained in the subject catalog and is available to the student for his or her career search. Students thus have easy access to information from a variety of sources.

The CCIS is an inexpensive system for career information delivery. The use of paraprofessionals is recommended for on-line supervision and various outreach locations. A relatively small staff commitment is needed for module development and evaluation. The instructional modules developed for the CCIS have a flexible

TABLE 18-1 CURRICULAR CAREER INFORMATION SERVICES (CCIS) MODULES

Module	Title	Objectives	Activities
I.	Everything You've Always Wanted to Know About CCIS	1. To introduce you to the CCIS 2. To help you select activities that will assist you in solving your career problem.	a. Examine a Career Center brochure located on the yellow rack near the Career Center entrance to learn more about CCIS services and programs. b. Ask a Career Advisor to explain CCIS and the career advising process to you. c. Attend a Career Center tour. d. Browse the remaining module sheets on the yellow rack to learn more about some of the common concerns addressed through the career advising process.
II.	What's Involved in Making a Career Decision?	1. To dispel common misconceptions about career planning; 2. To help you identify areas that are important to consider development; and 3. To help you establish some guidelines for the process of career decision making.	a. Review the "What's Involved in Career Choice" sheet to gain a greater awareness of the career decision-making process. b. Review "A Guide to Good Decision Making" sheet to explore more effective ways to make career decisions. c. Review the "Career Choice Resources in CCIS" and/or books catalogued IA in The Career Center Library. d. Review materials in the Module II folder in the Mobile file (File 1). e. Attend a "Choosing a Major/Career" workshop in CCIS. f. With the assistance of a Career Advisor, complete the "Guide to Good Decision Making Exercise." g. Register for Unit I and II of the Introduction to Career Development Class MSDS 3340. A course syllabus is available for your review in the Module XVI section of the Mobile File (File 1).
III.	Looking at You	1. To help you examine some of your interests, values, and skills. 2. To help you identify some occupations or fields of study for further exploration.	INTERESTS a. Complete the Self-Directed Search (SDS). b. Complete the "Career Areas" topic in the Explore section of the CHOICES computer program. c. Complete the Interest Inventory in the "Learning About Yourself" module of the DISCOVER computer program. d. Complete the "Self-Assessment" section of SIGI PLUS. VALUES a. Interact with the SIGI PLUS computer program. b. Complete the Values Card Sort. c. Complete the Values inventory in the "Learning About Yourself" module of the DISCOVER program.

Module	Title	Objectives	Activities
			SKILLS
			a. Complete the aptitudes section in the CHOICES Guidebook.
			b. Interact with the Micro Skills computer program.
			c. Complete the Motivated Skills Card Sort.
			d. Complete the Abilities Assessment in the "Learning About Yourself" module of the DISCOVER computer program.
IV.	Information: Where to Find It and How to Use It	1. To help you locate all Career Center information related to your educational and career planning needs.	a. Perform a search using Career Key for the topic of interest to you.
			b. Review the diagram on the back of this sheet to locate various multimedia resources available in The Career Center Library.
V.	Matching Majors and Jobs	1. To help you learn how specific job titles relate to college majors or fields of study.	a. Review printed materials in the Module V "Matching Majors and Careers" folders in the Mobile File (File 1), specifically the "Match-Major" sheets.
			b. Read sections in these books or others found in Area IIC of The Career Center Library.
			IIC AA C7 The College Board Guide to 140 Popular College Majors
			IIC AA M3 What Can I Do With a Major in . . .?
			IIC AA N3 College Knowledge and Jobs
			IIC AA P4 College Majors & Careers
			IIC AA O2 The Occupational Thesaurus (Vols. 1 & 2)
			IIA 025 Occupational Outlook Handbook
			c. Perform a search on Career Key under the topic *Occupations by Major* to get a list of relevant CCIS resources. Ask a Career Advisor for assistance.
			d. Use the *College Majors Card Sort* to find majors and occupational opportunities.
			e. Review employment information in the *Undergraduate Academic Program Guide* for FSU majors.
			f. Use the SDS code assigned to a particular FSU major to search for occupations in the *SDS Occupations Finder* or the *Dictionary of Holland Occupational Codes* (IA G6).
			g. Examine materials on FSU academic programs in File 3.
			h. Review selected Employer Directories that list organizations by major, career, or geographical areas.
			i. Consult with Career Center staff members in Placement Services and Career Experience Opportunities (CEO).
			j. With assistance from a Career Advisor, explore opportunities on Career Key for informational interviews, extern experiences, and networking assistance with participating professionals and FSU alumni.

SOURCE: From *Curricular Career Information Service*, by R. C. Reardon, 1996. Unpublished manuscript, Florida State University. Reprinted by permission.

design and can be converted to computer-based career information systems. The most recent use of the CCIS was described by Peterson, Sampson, and Reardon (1991) and by Reardon (1996b).

Career Counseling at a Large University: A Metroplex Model

A large university located in a metropolitan area may have the added responsibility of satisfying heavy alumni demand for career guidance. Not only is the career center faced with a large volume of currently enrolled students choosing from diverse academic programs, but the center must also respond to a wide variety of alumni requests for career guidance. Alumni contemplating career changes with subsequent reentry into the work force represent a unique dimension of career counseling. The following examples of unique client needs exemplify the complexity of programs needed in such a career center: (1) individuals (young adults through middle age) anticipating a change of career direction; (2) individuals seeking relocation within their career field; (3) individuals desiring mobility within their career field through further educational training; (4) individuals seeking information about specific, current job market trends; (5) individuals seeking college reentry planning; and (6) individuals seeking second careers after early retirement from a primary career. In addition, many adults residing in the metropolitan area will seek assistance for career education planning before university enrollment. Thus, a career center metroplex model must be able to provide a wide range of services for currently enrolled students as well as for alumni and others in the community seeking assistance or career redirection.

The UCLA Placement and Career Planning Center is a good example of a metroplex model. Located in its own building, the center offers career planning and placement services to students and alumni from all University of California campuses. Along with several in-house programs, this center also offers outreach programs on a number of subjects. For example, in conjunction with the alumni association and various academic departments, the center offers specific career panels on a broad spectrum of career fields such as mental health, allied health, banking and investments, motion pictures, advertising, and marketing and sales. The programs are videotaped and available on request.

The results of a national survey by Hoyt and Lester (1995) of adults who were asked about what high schools should do to help individuals learn about work and work environments, suggests that there is a growing need for career centers to offer services to the general public. Another national survey conducted by the *New York Times* (Uchitelle & Kleinfield, 1996) underscored career information needs of adults found in the Hoyt and Lester (1995) study. The *New York Times* study results suggest that large numbers of U.S. workers have lost their jobs through downsizing of industrial corporations and now need career planning assistance. (Both surveys are discussed in detail in Chapters 19 and 20.) More recently, McGinn and Naughton (2001) report that there have been massive job cuts during an economic slowdown starting at the beginning of the 21st century. In fact, universities and colleges in most all communities can offer a valuable and needed service to community members.

Samples of career-related programs generally offered in heavily populated areas include direct job referral services, seminars on job search strategies, assistance with resumé preparation, interview skills training, job clubs (individuals engaging in similar job searches), life/work relationships, seminars on career decision making and problem solving, career information resources (including computer-based career information resources, both local and Internet), graduate school selection, and retraining for a different or related career. One way to determine the need for specific career-related programs is through a survey of alumni and community members.

Life-Planning Workshops

Life-planning workshops for college students have been conducted at Colorado State University since the early 1980s. These workshops were designed primarily to actively involve individuals in developing life plans through a highly structured step-by-step program. One key goal of these workshops is to promote self-awareness and the recognition that each individual has certain responsibilities in developing his or her future. Even though these programs were developed for college students, the format could easily be adapted for other groups, including adults who have finished or dropped out of college.

The life-planning workshops are usually conducted in one-day sessions lasting approximately seven hours. Each group of four persons has a facilitator. The program is highly structured, but each group may progress at its own pace. Because the structure of the program is set, facilitators need only minimal training. Group members remain together through the session.

The workshop format consists of eight structured exercises, as follows. Each exercise is shared in the group, and interaction is strongly emphasized. The first exercise, *life line,* requires that an individual draw a line from birth to death (life line) and indicate on it key life experiences and present position. These exercises are designed to involve the participants actively in concentrating on future tasks and life planning.

Exercise	*Purpose*
1. Life line	To identify past and current situations in life
2. Identifying and stripping of roles	To identify individual roles in life and share individual feelings as one strips roles
3. Fantasy time	To develop more self-awareness when free of identified roles
4. Typical day and a special day of the future	To further crystallize self-awareness and individual needs for the future when free of identified roles

5. Life inventory   To identify specific needs and goals with emphasis on identification of each individual's positive characteristics

6. News release   To further clarify specific interests and future accomplishments desired

7. Reassume roles   To clarify or reformulate goals while reassuming originally identified roles

8. Goal setting   To set realistic short-term and long-term goals

Identifying and stripping of roles, the second exercise, requires that each individual identify and rank in importance five different roles currently occupying his or her life. Each participant is encouraged to identify positive as well as negative roles. The next step is to start with the least important role and "strip" that role (no longer assume the role) and express feelings associated with freedom from that role. In this manner, each role is stripped until the person is role-free and subsequently able to express "freely" personal life-planning needs.

The third exercise, *fantasy time,* is a continuation of the second exercise, in which the individual is encouraged toward further introspection while being role-free. More specifically, the individual considers the influence of roles when developing future plans.

Once roles have been stripped, in the fourth exercise the individual outlines a *typical day and a special day of the future.* Now that the individual is able to visualize his or her life without the restrictions of roles, he or she can subsequently better consider ideal circumstances. This exercise is designed to provide an opportunity to consider how identified roles influence or actually block present and future need fulfillment.

The fifth exercise requires that each individual fill out a *life inventory,* which includes questions asking for greatest experiences, things done well and poorly, and desired future accomplishments. Each individual is directed toward developing specific needs and values while focusing attention on desired changes in the future. This exercise is designed to be a rebuilding process through identification of specific needs.

During the sixth exercise, *news release,* each individual considers his or her life line, as drawn in an earlier exercise, in relation to what the future should be. Each person writes a sketch of his or her life, projecting into the future while focusing on accomplishment and predominant roles. The major purpose is to promote the development of realistic future needs.

In the seventh exercise, *reassume roles,* the focus is on reassuming the roles that were stripped in earlier exercises. Each individual now must decide which roles should be kept and which should be discarded to reach his or her life goals. Reassumed roles may be rearranged in priority or replaced with new roles that provide greater opportunity for meeting goals. The emphasis is on the factors that can be changed to gain greater control of future life planning.

The final exercise, *goal setting,* requires that each individual describe specific behaviors that can bring about desired changes in his or her life. Again, the emphasis is on the individual's ability to make changes to meet life-planning goals.

Case 18-1:   LIFE-PLANNING WORKSHOP EXERCISES

The following example demonstrates the more specific activities involved in this program. Liang has been married for six years, has two children, and is currently employed as a high school biology teacher. Her family life has been stable for most of her marriage, but she has recently felt a need to change her career and life direction. As she stated to her counselor, "I'm not sure of what's happened; I just feel frustrated. I love my husband and children, but I am unhappy." After several counseling sessions, the counselor recommended that Liang participate in a life-planning workshop.

After being introduced to staff and members of the group, she heard an explanation of the purpose and goals of the exercises. The first exercise required that Liang construct a life line in which she included the results of important decisions and events, such as the birth of her brother, death of her father, meeting her husband, marriage, the births of her children, and so on. She jotted down her age at the time of each event and drew an arrow next to the more significant decisions. Valleys and peaks indicated the ups and downs in life.

Then Liang shared her life line with Chris, another participant.

LIANG: We have some similar experiences, I see.

CHRIS: Yes, but you have more work experience than I have. I wish I had more experiences so I could figure out what to do.

LIANG: I have worked since I was married and before, and yet I am confused. Come to think of it, I guess working helps you figure out some things.

CHRIS: Yeah, I would hope so.

LIANG: Mainly, what you learn is what you don't want to do.

CHRIS: Oh look, the major events in your life line are like mine; they center around family.

A general discussion of the purpose of a life line was led by the group leader, whose major focus was the value of previous experience in determining future goals.

The next exercise, identifying and stripping of roles, created considerable tension for Liang because she was not prepared to strip her roles as parent, spouse, teacher, homemaker, and friend.

LIANG: I don't want to dump my husband and children; it's hard for me to think of myself without them.

CHRIS: I know, but remember, this is make-believe.

LIANG: That's so, but I still feel it is difficult.

CHRIS: Go on, tell me what you would do.

LIANG: Well, I've always wanted a higher degree, but with the children, I don't have time for college.

CHRIS: Go on. I bet you would like a different job too!

LIANG: This sounds like bragging, but my college profs encouraged me to consider college teaching.

As Liang and Chris continued to strip away roles, they recognized the ambiguities associated with the exercise as well as the benefits of imagined freedom.

LIANG: I've wound up with quite a different lifestyle, and you have too.

CHRIS: If only I could do it. How many jobs do you have listed?

LIANG: Let me see. College professor, model, business owner, chief executive officer. Oh yeah, I want to live on the West Coast! But really, how could I realistically accomplish any of these?

After the third exercise, fantasy time, Liang outlined a "typical day" and a "special day" in the future.

Typical day
    Breakfast between 8:00 and 9:00
    Go to campus for class preparation 9–11
    Teach classes 11–12
    Have lunch at faculty lounge 12–1:30
    Office hours 2–3
    Play tennis 3–5
    Shop 5–6
    Dinner 7–8
    Attend play 8–10
    Bedtime

Special day (no time commitments)
    Wake up whenever I want in a plush room in a resort hotel
    Breakfast in bed
    Hike in the mountains
    Go skiing
    Meet friends around the fireplace at Happy Hour
    Dine and dance

As Liang fantasized a role-free lifestyle, she also recognized the meaningfulness of her current roles. She deeply cared for her husband and children and did not want to give them up under any circumstances, but she also came to the conclusion that something was missing from her life. Perhaps, she thought, it was the desire for more freedom with fewer time commitments. But everyone likes that, she mused, so what's new?

As she filled out the life inventory for Exercise 5, she was now faced with having to make significant decisions about the future. As she listed her greatest experiences and things she had done well and poorly, the items seemed to center around academic achievements and her family. Surprisingly, after considerable thought, Liang listed some of her teaching activities under tasks done poorly. "This is awful," she almost stated out loud, but it was true. She had to face it. Her heart had not been in it. What a mess, she loved her students, and yet, she was not giving them her best.

When Liang focused on changes for the future, she came to the conclusion that a career change was necessary, but accompanying this thought was the chilling reality of what this would mean. Her entire lifestyle and routine would have to be changed, she concluded. Is it worth it? How would her husband react? Liang's list of specific needs included the following:

- A greater commitment to my work
- A change to pursue my interest of more academic training
- A higher-level job in education
- More and better communication with my family—let my family know how *I* feel.

During this exercise, Liang heard the following exchange in her group.

DANTE: What's the sense of all this? These needs I have would disrupt my current lifestyle tremendously.

JIM: It might take that, Dante.

TED: It's not that simple. I would like to follow through on my needs, but I have to consider the needs of my family, too. I think we gotta negotiate.

As Liang listened to the members discuss the problems of implementing their needs list, she realized that she was not the only one experiencing frustration. It was comforting to know she was not alone in wanting something different, but she also realized that different personal situations required personal solutions. The conversation in the group continued.

JEAN: I never thought of getting older as an advantage, but my perspective of the future has fewer complications since my children left home.

LIANG: Would you follow through on your need list if your children still lived at home?

JEAN: Yes, I think so; in fact, I know I would, but everyone's situation is different.

Liang performed the sixth exercise, news release, while observing her life line. By looking at her life as a series of peaks and valleys, she realized that it was more important now to live a more directed life with a balance between life roles. She recognized that it was her choice to devote the major part of life to her family, but she also wanted more out of life at this point. Perhaps, she thought, there would be fewer valleys and more peaks in the future for everyone in the family.

As the group continued this discussion, Jean made another point.

JEAN: Being older also makes you realize that life goes by quickly. Just look at your life line—if it tells you anything at all, it is that opportunities are there for the taking. But if you don't, well, the line just keeps on moving.

As Liang began Exercise 7, she felt no aversion to reassuming roles and, in fact, realized that she wanted to retain her current life roles.

LIANG: There is no way I would give up my family. Through all of this, they still come first.

JEAN: I don't see that as a negative; in fact, I think it's great.

In the final exercise, goal setting, Liang felt that she had gained the confidence to follow through on some specific goals. It would take courage, she thought, to change career direction. It would disrupt everyone's life styles to do it, but the chances were that it would be worth it in the future. She would use negotiation as a means of restructuring family life while she attended the university. Putting some money aside each month for the next year would help finance graduate school, and meanwhile she could attend evening classes.

LIANG: I have decided that going back to the university is best for me and my family!

DANTE: That's not good enough, Liang. You're supposed to give specific behaviors to change things.

JEAN: Yes, that's too general.

LIANG: OK, let me see. I will have a meeting with my husband on Monday at 6:30. We will discuss the following topics: advantages of going to graduate school, financial arrangements, family arrangements, sharing household duties, and options for time of enrollment.

Liang's case points out the value of delineating and specifying the consequences of life roles. Individuals often become so involved in fulfillment of a particular role that other roles are ignored, and frustrations and stressful conditions that evolve are often left unidentified and unresolved. The interaction of group members often provides support for individuals to discover their own needs for career development.

The concept of career life planning as illustrated suggests that career programs should be constructed from a broad-based framework of life events, conditions, and situations over the life span. The major goal of career life planning is to help individuals cope with changing events and accomplish the tasks and transitions of developmental stages successfully.

Although the experiences of life teach us how to cope with certain events, the future is always challenging and unpredictable. More than 20 years ago, Lazarus (1980) suggested that past experiences can help one cope with future events. Calling this process "anticipatory coping," he proposed that the skills learned through successfully coping with experiences can help when encountering future events, and unsuccessful experiences can provide a basis for identifying behaviors that should be modified. Though all experiences are useful for future encounters, successful experiences tend to have a snowball effect by providing indexes to appropriate behaviors. The purpose of career life planning is to provide skills that may be applied in coping effectively with a variety of future events. Teaching clients skills that help them meet future events is one of the developmental goals of career life planning.

Work- and Experience-Based Programs

A growing trend in all levels of education seems to provide students the opportunity of work experience as a vital part of their educational programs. Although student teaching and a variety of intern and extern experiences are not novel ideas in institutions of higher learning, some innovations should interest the career counselor. One such innovation is the extern experience.

The extern model provides the student with an opportunity to observe ongoing activities in his or her major field of study and to interact with individuals on the job. The extern model differs from an internship in two ways: (1) the extern experience is of short duration usually during semester breaks, and (2) students usually do not receive course credit for an extern experience as most of their experiences involve observation and job shadowing. Generally, during senior year, students submit a proposal of their career goals with a statement of how the extern experience would help them meet these goals. Career centers or other administrative entities have agreements with host agencies to offer such experiences. Selected students will spend a specified time with a host agency during midsemester break or during an interim semester.

Intern models, on the other hand, provide students with the opportunity to spend more time in a workplace and are more work-experience-oriented than are extern models. In intern models, students actually do the work they are being trained to do. For example, junior-level students planning to become accountants may be chosen by an accounting firm to intern in one of its offices. Actual accounting work will be done under the supervision of a selected employee. The time spent in this experience is usually negotiated so that it doesn't interfere with the student's progress toward a degree.

Job shadowing also gives college students a window to view future work environments. In this program, college students explore an occupation by observing at a job site. As they observe, they ask questions and practice working with people while making valuable contacts for future use. This program requires colleges and universities to make arrangements with industry for students to job shadow. Formal programs include orientation (briefing students on program requirements), matching (students are matched with volunteers who have agreed to serve as a host), shadow (students spend several hours on the job with the host and may do hands-on work), and after shadowing (students write letters of thank you and reflect on what they have learned). Job shadowing usually takes place during semester breaks (Mariani, 1998).

The practice of providing college students with actual work experience related to their college majors should proliferate during the next decade. The length of the experience should also increase; students will find a longer time more beneficial than current extern programs allow. As colleges attempt to help students make more realistic career choices, more experience-based models will certainly emerge.

College Placement

The traditional placement service in our educational institutions has evolved into the career planning center. As suggested in the previous chapter, some professionals believe that the use of the word *placement* in the name, such as the "Career Planning and Placement Center," has become obsolete (Carter, 1995). The major argument centers around the students' perception of such a center: This is where you interview for a job. Thus, students overlook the fact that placement is only *one* of the services offered. The philosophical stance is that placement is subsumed in a center that offers a wide variety of career services that are of at least equal status with placement; therefore, the name of the center should reflect this change. What has been suggested are more generic names, such as Career Planning Center, Career Service Center, or simply Career Center. Regardless of the name, such centers should be student-service-oriented and should indeed offer a wide variety of services to all students—and in some cases, also to alumni or individuals in the community. In this context, placement continues to be an important part of services offered.

Partially to emphasize a changing philosophical position, national, regional, and local placement organizations have also undergone name changes. The national organization formerly called the College Placement Council is now the National Association of Colleges and Employers (NACE), a name change that reflects the broad-based approach of career service centers. Employers are now an important part of national, regional, and local organizations, and their participation in planning and sharing in all organizational matters has distinctly improved services to students. For instance, college representatives and employers have found a tremendous arena for exchanging information, such as salary surveys, job market information, internship programs, and workshops.

Don't be surprised if you continue seeing the term *placement* used in the names of centers and programs being offered, at least until students and faculty become more familiar with the current changes that are taking place. In the meantime, many of the following programs may be found at typical career planning and placement offices:

1. Full-time employment listings
2. Temporary-work files
3. Full-time vacation jobs
4. Job-search strategy meetings
5. Resumé-preparation workshops
6. Interview practice sessions
7. Career interest testing
8. Career exploration workshops
9. Individual and group counseling in career searching
10. Special programs such as minority recruiting opportunities for employers
11. Follow-up studies of previous graduates

Many colleges and universities have installed automated placement services. For a fee of $30 to $50, students can send resumés to regional, national, and international employment networks. Also, students can phone 24 hours a day to hear about full-time vacancy listings, to schedule interviews, and to receive information on part-time jobs, summer job vacancies, and internships (Herr & Cramer, 1996).

Technology may change how college students market themselves! Most college career centers are on-line and resumés can be sent to prospective employers through cyberspace. Telephone interviewing is a growing industry. Recruiters may use a telephone interview to narrow down a list of potential employees. Likewise, video conferencing is another way to interview anyone, even in remote areas, who is properly equipped. The increasing costs of travel could encourage the use of video conferencing technology in the future as a means of selecting applicants and screening them.

Interview Skills Training

The importance of training programs designed to improve interview skills is underscored by the fact that employers' decisions are often heavily based on their impressions of the interviewee. Also, many college students are, at best, only moderately experienced with interview procedures. Instruction has primarily been through role playing, videotape feedback, and mock interviews with personnel directors.

Using videotape has become a popular method of preparing individuals for an interview. Feller (1994) has compiled a list of commercial videos produced in the last decade, including ratings, reviews, and descriptions of 650 videos, some of which assist individuals in preparing for an interview.

Some videotapes that discuss interview preparation illustrate poor interview techniques and then follow with suggested changes and demonstrations of interviewee skills. Others demonstrate techniques, including establishing good eye contact; assuming the appropriate posture, voice level, and projection; closing the interview; following up; negotiating; and making a decision.

Videotapes can be used for individual training or in a workshop format, and they are also effective for group viewing—with or without discussion. For large groups, individuals can be divided into dyads or triads for practice interviewing. This procedure provides individuals with role-playing opportunities that can be videotaped for immediate feedback.

Snodgrass and Wheeler (1983) suggest that simulated interviews for videotaping could be derived from questions frequently asked during job interviews. One advantage of using videotape is that segments of the interview can be replayed and analyzed to afford greater flexibility of training.

Resumé Writing

As jobs become more competitive, personnel managers rely more heavily on resumés to select individuals for further evaluation. The resumé is the first criterion of the selection process, and its importance cannot be overstressed. The primary purpose of a resumé is to obtain an interview for the desired position. An effective resumé is one that "sells" the candidate's qualifications to the employer and thus provides the candidate the opportunity for an interview. Most effective resumés relate the candidate's skills, experiences, education, and other achievements to the requirements of the job. Resumés are essential for individuals seeking professional, technical, administrative, or managerial jobs and are often needed for clerical and sales positions. Preparation of a good resumé is an essential part of the job search sequence.

A functional resumé is designed to emphasize an individual's qualifications for a specific job. This type of resumé is often used by individuals who have had extensive work experience, particularly if they are applying for jobs in the same area in which they have had experience or for a job that is related to their experience. The functional resumé stresses selected skill areas that are marketable, and it allows the applicant to emphasize professional growth. Individuals can select guidelines from the following outline to prepare their resumés.

I. Personal data
    A. Name, address, and telephone number.
    B. Other personal data are optional, such as date of birth, marital status, citizenship, dependents, height, and weight.
II. Job or career objectives
    A. Prepare a concise statement of job objective and the type of position desired.
III. Educational history (If the previous work experiences are more closely related to the job objective, list them before educational history.)
    A. In reverse chronological order, list the institutions attended for formal education.
    B. High school can be omitted if a higher degree has been awarded.
    C. List dates of graduation and degrees or certificates received or expected.
    D. List major and minor courses related to job objectives.
    E. List scholarships and honors.
IV. Employment history
    A. In reverse chronological order, list employment experiences including
        1. Date of employment
        2. Name and address of employer and nature of firm or business
        3. Position held
        4. Specific job duties
        5. Scope of responsibility including most relevant experiences
        6. Accomplishments and highlights of background
V. Military experience
    A. List branch and length of service, major duties, assignments, rank, and type of discharge.
VI. Achievements related to job and career objectives (optional)
    A. List other assets, experiences, and skills significant to job objective. For example, knowledge of foreign language, volunteer activities, and special skills.
VII. References
    A. It is often not necessary to list references on the resumé. One may state that references are available on request.

    B. If references are listed, the name, position, and address of at least three persons is usually sufficient.

Here are some additional suggestions:

1. Because of affirmative action laws, many employers prefer that optional personal information (with the exception of citizenship) be deleted from the personal data section (I).

2. The job objective section (II) is designed to bind the parts of the resumé together into a common theme or direction and should be carefully stated.

3. The educational history section (III) should relate academic skills and achievements to the requirements of the job objective. Specific, relevant courses and experiences as well as degrees or specializations of formal education should be recorded.

4. The employment history (IV) should relate previously acquired working skills and accomplishments to the requirements and duties of the job objective. Voluntary as well as paid experiences should be included.

5. The military experience section (V) should relate skills and accomplishments acquired during military duty to the requirements and duties of the job objective.

6. The achievements (VI) listed should relate to the job objective, delineating any relevant special skills or accomplishments that were not recorded previously.

Examples of resumés are an important teaching instrument. The career counselor will want to accumulate copies of resumés from former students who have applied for different types of positions. A good model will help the novice write a resumé. There are many possible formats, and a number of publications on the market today provide examples of them. Such publications should be included in the counseling center's bibliography on job search strategy.

Computer-Assisted Career Guidance Programs

As discussed in Chapter 6, computer-assisted career guidance programs provide up-to-date information on the job market. Many of the systems contain local information about jobs. Computer-assisted programs also have components that provide information to students and notify them of other vital information that can be used in the job search. Employers can register job vacancies, salary, interview schedules, and so forth.

Computer-assisted programs also provide a quick method of matching qualified students and requests for job orders from prospective employers. For instance, an employer asks the placement office by phone or fax printouts for junior-level accounting majors who have at least a 3.0 grade point average and have plans to graduate in two semesters. Through prearranged agreements with students, the placement office can fax a list of students who meet the requirements. Speed may be important in the competitive job market, and placement offices that can quickly provide information to students as well as to prospective employers could have a significant advantage. Second, computer-assisted programs make current information easily accessible to the placement office staff. This is only one method of assisting students and employers through computer-assisted career guidance programs, but it points out the potential of these programs.

The Follow-Up

Follow-up information provides a valuable resource for multiple use by the college placement office. Here, however, we only cover the use of follow-up data as an aid in assisting college students in career planning. The overall employment status of graduates paints a realistic picture of the variety of jobs available to graduates from a particular institution. In addition, information on the current employment status of graduates according to majors can be most useful to the prospective graduate. Thus, follow-up is a very important resource that indicates employment trends and employment potential according to specific educational goals offered at the university level.

Follow-up is an important function of career centers, especially given the competitiveness of the job market. The information obtained from following up is valuable in helping students plan their education and careers. Even though the labor market may make abrupt changes, the follow-up has many implications for the job search strategy: (1) This information should aid the student in thinking about the type of organization in which he or she is likely to find employment with a particular degree; (2) a realistic salary is usually listed according to field of study; (3) the employment potential is better understood by field of study; and (4) the job satisfaction of working in a particular field is known. In essence, follow-up information should aid the individual in clarifying values and subsequently establishing goals; it also provides practical information concerning initial career search activities and probable geographical location of prospective jobs.

Most college and university career centers conduct an annual follow-up of the most recent graduating class. Some surveys report data in seven areas: (1) plans after graduation, (2) job commitment, (3) type of organization, (4) field of employment, (5) job satisfaction, (6) helpfulness of degree in employment, and (7) salary. Using this data, career center staff can compile information about jobs that graduates currently hold, including the graduates' field of study and employer, the nature of the job (part- or full-time), job satisfaction, salaries, plans for the future, and the satisfaction with the academic institutions's program.

Summary

1. Studies of the characteristics of college students suggest diverse needs for career guidance programs. Research has consistently shown that

almost one-half or more of college students desire help with educational and vocational planning.

2. College affects students' career choices and development by providing career mobility and advancement and by increasing career aspirations. The benefits of higher education can also lead to a fulfilling lifestyle and the capacity to make appropriate judgments over the life span.

3. National competencies and indicators are designed to enhance self-knowledge, educational and occupational exploration, and career planning for adults. These guidelines can be used to develop career guidance programs at institutions of higher learning.

4. Implications for career guidance include a wide variety of programs to maximize each student's career development potential.

5. A consortium of community colleges in Nebraska have designed a handbook that continues and extends the career guidance activities of comprehensive career guidance program in schools. Students are given more information about principles of self-knowledge, educational and occupational exploration and career planning.

6. The CCIS developed at Florida State University uses an instructional approach to career planning. The model is self-help–oriented, uses instructional models, and is multimedia-based. Several modules have been developed to help students perform a career search sequence; several other modules have been developed for special groups such as minorities and blind students. The diversity of learning activities provided through a series of career planning modules allows the individual a greater variety of options and a more effective means of choosing a career.

7. Career counseling centers located in metropolitan areas have heavy alumni demands for educational and career planning. The UCLA Placement and Career Planning Center is a good example of a metroplex model. This center is divided into several units to meet demands of currently enrolled students in undergraduate and graduate programs, as well as alumni and others in the community requesting educational and career planning assistance.

8. Life-planning workshops for college students have been conducted at Colorado State University for several years. The workshops are designed primarily to help students develop a life plan. Life-planning workshops (usually one-day sessions) consist of highly structured, step-by-step exercises.

9. The typical college placement office has drastically changed its image during the last 20 years. The intensification of the job search has led college placement centers to assume a wider scope of responsibilities. The placement office is no longer just an employment agency; it offers a variety of seminars and programs that assist students in planning for careers as well as in searching for jobs.

10. Typical programs being offered in career planning and placement centers in two- and four-year colleges include career search strategies, interview skills training, and instructions on writing resumés.

11. The demand for work- and experience-based programs for college students is increasing. Extern models provide the opportunity to observe ongoing activities in a major field of study. Intern models are more work-oriented and cover a longer time.

12. Computer-assisted career guidance programs provide the placement office with a wide range of options that allow staff to react quickly to employers' requests and student needs.

13. Follow-up studies serve as important resources for placement offices when they include (a) types of job opportunities available by geographical areas, (b) general employment patterns and fields of employment of graduates with specific majors and degrees, (c) employment potential within specific industries, and (d) current salary schedules. Follow-up information is being incorporated into career planning programs.

Supplementary Learning Exercises

1. Using the CCIS model, develop a module to introduce high school students to career information resources.

2. Develop a philosophical statement that includes the placement office as a vital part of the career guidance efforts in postsecondary schools.

3. Develop a strategy that would justify adult career guidance centers as an extension of college career guidance programs.

4. Write to several large universities located in metropolitan areas and request descriptions of their career counseling programs. Compare the programs for commonalities and innovative components.

5. Visit an industry to determine potential extern and job shadowing experiences available for college students. Compile the available experiences with recommendations for college majors that could benefit through an extern experience.

6. Survey a community to determine the number and kinds of agencies that are actively involved in career planning and placement activities. Develop plans to involve all agencies in a cooperative career planning and placement effort.

7. Develop plans and strategies that would focus on career planning and placement of school dropouts. Include in your plans the strategies you would use for encouraging dropouts to continue in an educational or training program.

8. Defend the following statement: Career planning and placement programs are essential in secondary schools and in two- and four-year institutions of higher learning.

9. What is the purpose of career life planning? Is it relevant in today's world? Discuss.

10. Describe what you consider to be the major advantages of life-planning workshops.

For More Information

Astin, A. W. (1984). Student values: Knowing more about where we are today. *Bulletin of the American Association of Higher Education, 36*(9), 10–13.

Brown, D., & Brooks, L. (1991). *Career counseling techniques.* Boston: Allyn & Bacon.

Figler, H. (1988). *The complete job-search handbook.* New York: Henry Holt.

Herr, E. L., & Cramer, S. H. (1996). *Career guidance and counseling through the life span: Systematic approaches* (5th ed.). New York: HarperCollins.

Marcia, J. E. (1991). Identity and self-development. In R. M. Lerner, A. C. Peterson, & J. Brooks-Gunn (Eds.), *Encyclopedia of adolescence: Vol. 1.* New York: Garland.

Mariani, M. (1994, Fall). The young and the entrepreneurial. *Occupational Outlook Quarterly, 38,* 2–10.

Pascarella, E. T., & Terenzini, P. T. (1991). *How college affects students: Findings and insights from twenty years of research.* San Francisco: Jossey-Bass.

Reardon, R. C. (1996). A program and cost analysis of self-directed career advising services in a university career center. *Journal of Counseling and Development, 74,* 280–285.

Reardon, R. C. (1981). *Developing career education at the college level.* Columbus, OH: ERIC Clearinghouse on Adult, Career, and Vocational Education. (ERIC Document Reproduction Service No. ED 205 775).

Reardon, R. C., Lenz, J. G., Sampson, J. P., & Peterson, G. W. (2000). *Career development and planning: A comprehensive approach.* Pacific Grove, CA: Brooks/Cole.

Spokane, A. R. (1991). *Career intervention.* Englewood Cliffs, NJ: Prentice-Hall.

Yost, E. B., & Corbishley, M. A. (1987). *Career counseling: A psychological approach.* San Francisco: Jossey-Bass

PART FOUR

Career Counseling in Work Settings and Career Transitions Throughout Life

21   Career Development of Adults in Organizations

19

Some Perspectives of Work

Chapter Highlights

- *Two examples of how work has changed*

- *What has happened to work in the United States*

- *Rethinking the idea of work*

- *Occupational projections for employment*

- *Work issues: Equal Opportunity/Affirmative Action, occupational insecurity, coping with joblessness, new entrepreneurial climate, work values, stress at work, violence, career burnout, healthful work, demand for increased quality of work, aging workers*

ORK IN AMERICA HAS A FASCINATING, EXTENSIVE HISTORY. WORK IS AT the heart of our concerns as professionals and individuals fortunate enough to live in a free society. Work can involve the most simple step-by-step procedures or be physically and mentally demanding, complex, interesting, boring, creative, or menial; or it can involve all the descriptions listed and many more. Throughout our history, work has fascinated researchers who have attempted to delineate the complexities of the labor itself and the problems of individuals who do it. Today, work has prevailed as a most viable subject within the scientific community and has occupied scholars from a variety of disciplines who dared venture into the complex arena associated with work.

In this chapter we cover the vast changes in the work force and the workplace. First, we discuss how work has changed, what has happened to work in America, and rethinking the idea of work. Next are occupational projections and how to focus on clients' needs. Several other perspectives of work are discussed, including Equal Opportunity and Affirmative Action strategies, occupational insecurity, coping with joblessness, the new entrepreneurial climate, work values, work commitment and work ethic, stress at work, violence in the workplace, career burnout, healthful work, the demand for quality of work, and aging workers.

Case 19-1: How Work Has Changed — The Secretary

Joan took a secretarial job that primarily required that she take shorthand, type, and make appointments. During most of her tenure of 15 years, the job requirements remained the same. But when the technology revolution arrived, the entire atmosphere of her office changed drastically. Joan was retrained to learn new skills, shorthand was no longer a requirement, typing was done on a computer, and appointments were made quite differently.

A person who filled a secretarial position 15 years ago may have been expected to type, take shorthand or dictation, manage files, make appointments, take telephone messages, and arrange for meetings, travel, or other appointments. Today, a secretary may be expected to perform all these tasks and, in addition, to use one or more software programs, usually including word processing, a spread sheet, and list processing. The secretary may be expected to maintain an interactive calendar, posting the calendar to a network of linked associates. The secretary may be required to use electronic mail to communicate with clients at remote locations, to post and retrieve information from electronic bulletin boards, and to keep abreast of software changes to upgrade the office system. In many offices, the secretary is also expected to be familiar with the basic operating principles of high-speed copiers, laser printers, and fax machines, at least enough to serve as the first line of defense when the system fails. (Newman & Newman, 1995, p. 576)

This example should serve as a point of reference for the work changes discussed in this chapter. It was chosen as an example of change because it is straightforward and easily understood. The complexity of changes in the many areas of the workplace are somewhat difficult to comprehend, however, especially for clients who have not experienced industrial organizations. The next example represents a much broader scope of change in the future workplace.

Case 19-2: HOW WORK HAS CHANGED—THE HUMAN NETWORK ORGANIZATION

Figure 19-1 illustrates how some future organizations may arrange their workplaces. Those individuals referred to as Front-Line Generalists will use portable computers (PCs) to access information for field sales and services. Many front-line generalists may work out of a home office. The front-line support groups are located in local offices and have access to back-line specialists who have up-to-date information on products. Central Management oversees the operation with a centralized database on mainframe or on supercomputers. This is referred to as a *client-server model* or, on the Internet, as the *browser-server model* (Dent, 1998). This model emphasizes the importance of service and specialized expertise in the future workplace. Most significant in the future workplace is that Front-Line Generalists are empowered with making critical decisions to meet the customers' needs; customer service is emphasized.

FIGURE 19-1 *Human network organization*

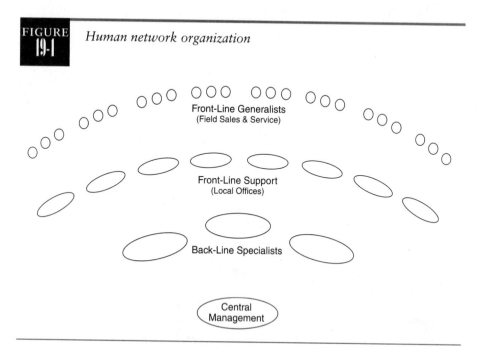

SOURCE: Reprinted with the permission of Simon & Schuster from *The Roaring 2000's: Building the Wealth and Lifestyle You Desire in the Greatest Boom in History* by Harry S. Dent, Jr. Copyright © 1998 by Harry Dent.

What Has Happened to Work in the United States?

As discussed in the opening paragraphs, the U.S. work force has changed significantly during the last 15 years. The U.S. Department of Labor estimates that 36 million jobs were eliminated in the United States between 1979 and 1993; a recent *New York Times* (1996) poll puts the number as high as 43 million through 1995. Although many of these jobs were eliminated by the development of new products and new procedures, the latest casualties are white-collar jobs that have been the victims of severe downsizing. A large percentage of total jobs lost were the result of contracting work with other companies. This type of job loss is referred to as "outsourcing" (Uchitelle & Kleinfield, 1996).

An astonishing development is that far more jobs have been added to the workplace than have been lost! Many of the newly created jobs offer fewer benefits and less pay, however, and many are part-time jobs. Individuals who are unable to find full-time work usually settle for temporary part-time work. The country's largest employer is Manpower, Incorporated, which "rents out" 767,000 substitute workers each year (Uchitelle & Kleinfield, 1996).

The problems associated with loss of jobs may continue according to Rifkin (1995), who surveyed 2,000 corporate executives from the world's most prominent organizations, reporting that 66% of them suggest that downsizing and re-engineering will continue in the future. As Reardon, Lenz, Sampson, and Peterson (2000) note, this may mean that increasing numbers of workers will experience unemployment or underemployment during their working lives.

The news is also not great for some who manage to find full-time work or become self-employed. Many take huge cuts in salary and benefits; for example, an executive who made $150,000 is lucky to make $50,000, and a manager who made $50,000 might now have a job that pays $25,000 (Uchitelle & Kleinfield, 1996). For literally millions of people in this country, the American dream of upward and onward is fading.

Chief executive officers who eliminate vast numbers of workers use the rationale that they must have leaner organizations to compete in the new global economy. Some of the hardest-hit organizations in the 1990s were AT&T, 123,000 jobs eliminated; Delta Airlines, 18,800 jobs; and Eastman Kodak, 16,800 jobs. Advancing technology has also taken some tasks away from human beings and given them to machines. For example, General Motors Corporation had 500,000 employees in the 1970s, but now can make the same number of cars with 315,000 workers (Uchitelle & Kleinfield, 1996). Many workplaces are in transition; the old certainties about work no longer apply. A summary of what has happened to two workers in the special report on downsizing by the *New York Times* written by Uchitelle and Kleinfield (1996) are good examples.

> A loan officer, age 51, who made $1000 weekly was told when he returned from a family vacation that he no longer had a job. The news was devastating, but the worst of it was yet to come. He pumped gas, was a guinea pig in a drug test, drove a car for a salesman, and, at the time the story was written, was currently employed as a

tour guide at $1000 per month. His wife divorced him, and his children shunned him, ashamed of a father who had lost his job.

This example might not be completely typical of all workers who lose their jobs, but it does point out the potential problems encountered by those whose jobs have been terminated by downsizing.

> Next is the story of a woman who lost three jobs because of downsizing. More specifically, this is an example of a woman, still in her forties, whose pay dropped each time she experienced downsizing. Her first job was in a meatpacking plant at $8.50 per hour, her second job was in a bank mailroom at $7.25 per hour, and her third job was at $4.75 per hour loading newspapers. She is currently employed at $4.25 per hour cleaning office buildings in Baltimore. She has not had a raise for three years. She has a high school diploma and studied one year at a community college.

This exemplifies the difficulty workers face at the lower end of the economic ladder. In addition to the personal/social problems faced by these individuals, they need assistance to find resources for training programs to upgrade their skills.

Rethinking the Idea of Work

Skills associated with organizational work grow more complex as advances in technology are usually followed by changes in the workplace. Organizations have had difficulty keeping job descriptions updated with the ever-changing needs of operating and competing globally. *Job restructuring* is the term organizations prefer to describe these changing perceptions of work and the skills that organizations currently consider necessary for efficient operation.

To add to the confusion, organizations are reorganizing and abandoning fundamental assumptions that underlie previous operating procedures; they are making significant changes in operational procedures as well as in job requirements to prepare for 21st-century capitalism (Reich, 1991). Some have labeled this process of change "reengineering the corporation" (Hammer & Champy, 1993). We will discuss this subject more in the next two chapters.

Many have attempted to explain the ongoing changes in a variety of media, but the career counselor might have little information to pass on to the client about what is actually happening in the real world of organizational work. Part of this problem is that the change process in job requirements is in its early stages. Second, the constant reconfiguration of the job market has been exacerbated by work force reductions through downsizing and subsequent retraining programs and ironically, in the late 1990s, an increasing need for skilled workers. Finally, as corporations reengineer or restructure their work forces—a move to compete for the global market—the emerging strategies to meet their goals will, in effect, provide them with a more discernible definition of job requirements in the future. However, the likely constant evolution of new and different products in our current and future organizations will subsequently require new and different skills from employees (Drucker, 1992). When the economy was as strong as it had been in the second half of the 1990s, unemployment remained low and there was greater competition among organizations for skilled workers. Thus, it is no surprise that economic conditions continue to be the driving force that determines labor demand and the increasing need for skilled workers. Rifkin (1995) suggests, however, that technological advances may actually decrease the number of jobs available in the future. The lesson to be learned here is that career counselors should be prepared to assist clients in an ever-changing job market.

In sum, the transformation of industries into smaller working units with vastly different operating procedures has created particular needs for individuals with certain types of skills. Meister (1994) identified six core workplace competencies employers require, as paraphrased here:

1. *Learning skills:* Organizations must adjust to new demands and improve their systems and processes to survive. Learning skills rank high in importance as organizations introduce changes. Employees must learn from a variety of sources, including co-workers, customers, suppliers, and educational institutions. The goal is for continuous improvement and to transform these skills into how an employee thinks and behaves.

2. *Basic reading, writing, computation, and cognitive reasoning skills:* Basic skills are a minimum requirement, but they are not narrowly defined as an ability to read, write, and perform mathematical computations. Employees must be able to apply information they read, for example, into action on a job.

3. *Interpersonal skills:* Good job performance in the past meant repeating tasks associated with each job. In current organizations, teams have become the vehicles of performance; thus individual performance is linked to well-developed interpersonal skills. The following skills are considered important: how to work in groups successfully and resolve conflicts, how to gain cooperation with peers, and how to network within the organization.

4. *Creative thinking and problem-solving skills:* The worker of today should be able to relate every phase of the production process, from obtaining raw materials to improving processes and procedures. Problem-solving skills should include being able to analyze situations, ask questions, seek clarification of what is not understood, and think creatively to generate options. The overall goal is for employees to develop skills that enable them to handle situations effectively without direction.

5. *Leadership (and visioning) skills:* In the emerging organizations, employees are encouraged to be active agents of change, rather than passive recipients of instructions. The employee today needs to develop abilities to envision improvement in work areas or establish a new direction and—perhaps most important—elicit the active commitment of others to accomplish his or her visions.

6. *Self-development (and self-management) skills:* These skills require that employees take charge of their careers and manage their own development. Employees must become aware of the changes in the workplace and be sure they have the requisite skills, knowledge, and competencies

for their current assignments and potential future ones. The management of one's career is considered to be a learned competence and a necessary and important condition in the emerging corporation structure.

Reich (1991) also delineated worker skills that will be necessary for the effective operation of current and future organizations. He framed these skills in what he refers to as the "new web of enterprise" (p. 87). Such organizations are referred to as high-value enterprises that resemble a spider's web. New connections from multiple locations on the globe will be spun continuously. Teams of workers will generate concepts of new products, how to produce them, and how they will be marketed. During the give and take of debate among team members, mutual learning will occur through shared insights, experiences, and solutions. Workers will learn from each other, learn about each other, and learn how to help one another perform better. Each point on the web will be unique and will represent its own combination of skills.

Within this frame of reference, three different but related skills will be needed by each team member. First are *problem-solving skills*. Problem solvers continuously search for new combinations and applications that might solve all kinds of emerging problems. Team members must have intimate knowledge of, say, semiconductor chips and what can be expected of them if they are reassembled or redesigned for a new product.

The second skill is referred to as *problem identification* or, as team members, *problem identifiers*. This skill requires an intimate knowledge of a customer's business and how a new and different product can give this customer the competitive edge. Instead of using the art of persuasion to sell a product, the operational procedure here is identifying new problems and possibilities to which a product could be applied.

The third skill requires that the worker play the role of *strategic broker*. This high-value position requires knowledge of specific technologies and markets to the point of foreseeing the potential for new products. This individual must coordinate the role of the *problem solver* and *problem identifier* and raise necessary funds to launch projects. These people are characterized as being continuously engaged in managing ideas.

What we see here is a recognition that survival in the 21st century will, in large part, depend on a well-trained work force. Newly acquired skills in problem solving and team building are designed to make improvements in job production, but work environments must also be redefined. The major goal appears to be the development of work environments that may be ever-changing, where workers conceptually understand their work and look for methods to improve it. The ideal organizational work environment promotes a culture of lifelong learning and a working atmosphere that encourages all employees to *want* to learn (Meister, 1994). Finally, we must remember that not all organizations have been restructured or reengineered. Some organizations, particularly government ones, have retained a bureaucratic structure. Some clients may find congruence within these structures rather than in the emerging ones, although Reich (1991) and Rifkin (1995), among others, point out that these older, structured organizations are decreasing in number.

Occupational Projections

The 1997–98 winter issue of the *Occupational Outlook Quarterly* ("Charting the Projections, 1996") has charted, through the year 2006, occupational projections developed by the Bureau of Labor Statistics. Following are some of the highlights of these projections.

Highlights of the Projections

The bureau's projections contain considerable detail about the structure of the economy, the demographic makeup of the labor force, and changes in employment in more than 500 occupations and 260 industries. The following trends are specially significant.

Occupational Employment

- Employment is projected to grow in occupations at all levels of education and training. On average, jobs usually requiring an associate degree or more education will grow faster than average. The majority of the numerical growth in employment, however, will be in the occupations requiring less education than an associate degree.
- Most health occupations will grow faster than the average. This growth will be driven by the rapidly growing health services industry, reflecting the close relationship between occupational employment growth and industry employment growth.
- Most computer occupations are projected to grow much faster than average. There is an increasing need in nearly all industries for workers with skills in computer technology. The rapidly growing computer services industry, which employs large numbers of these workers, will fuel this employment.

Labor Force

- Labor force growth will be slower over the 1996–2006 period than during the previous 10 years because of slowing population growth.
- As the baby-boom generation ages, the age distribution of the labor force will continue to shift upward. For example, the leading edge of the baby boomers will be in the 55- to 64-year-old group by the year 2006. Consequently, between 1996 and 2006, that age group will grow by 6.6 million and will increase its share of the labor force from 9% to 13%.
- The number of Hispanics and Asians in the labor force will continue to increase much faster than will the numbers of the black non-Hispanics and white non-Hispanics. White non-Hispanics, however, will still make up the majority—73%—of workers in 2006.

- The labor force participation rate will continue to increase for women while decreasing for men. As a result, women's share of the labor force will increase from 46 to 47%.

Industry Employment

- Industry employment growth will be concentrated in the service-producing sector of the economy. The services and retail trade industry divisions will account for 14.9 million new wage and salary jobs, about 85% of total growth between 1996 and 2006.

- Business services, which includes computer and data processing services, is the only industry division in which employment is projected to grow faster than average. Significant growth is projected in business services and health services.

- The goods-producing sector of the economy will decline slightly. The size of the decline is minimized by a projected increase in the number of jobs in the construction industry, the only goods-producing industry division projected to increase. Manufacturing will account for 13% of all wages and salary workers employed in 2006, down from 15% in 1996. (p.3)

The following figures from the Bureau of Labor Statistics present some interesting data. For example, the data in Figure 19-2, which projects employment changes for selected occupations, 1996–2006, points out that 15 of the 20 fastest growing occupations are associated with health services or computer technology.

Figure 19-3 presents occupations that have fast growth, high earnings, and low unemployment. These occupations are somewhat concentrated, with four each in computer technology, health care, and education fields. Finally, Figure 19-4 indicates that business services leads the service industry groups primarily because it is fueled by the fastest growing industry in the economy, computer and data processing services.

Counselors should remind clients that labor market forecasts may turn out to be inaccurate for many reasons including the following mentioned by Reardon, Lenz, Sampson, and Peterson (2000):

- Natural disasters—earthquakes, hurricanes

- World political events—war, trade agreements

- Changes in government spending—military base closures

- New welfare or student programs

- Technological inventions and breakthroughs

- New laws—balancing the federal budget (p.126)

The point here is that counselor and client should remain alert to a variety of circumstances that could affect economic policy and economic growth. Veneri (1997) points out, however, that most labor market projections under the direction of the U.S. Department of Labor have been accurate in the past.

FIGURE 19-2

Fifteen of the 20 fastest growing occupations are associated with health services or computer technology. Most have high earnings and low unemployment rates.

Projected employment change for selected occupations, 1996–2006
(percent)
VH = very high; H = high; L = low; VL = very low

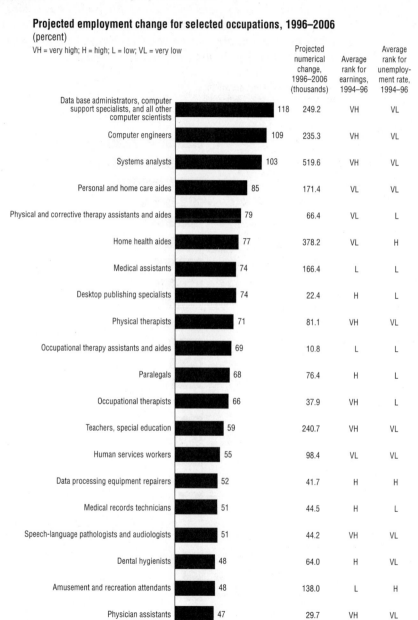

Occupation	Percent	Projected numerical change, 1996–2006 (thousands)	Average rank for earnings, 1994–96	Average rank for unemployment rate, 1994–96
Data base administrators, computer support specialists, and all other computer scientists	118	249.2	VH	VL
Computer engineers	109	235.3	VH	VL
Systems analysts	103	519.6	VH	VL
Personal and home care aides	85	171.4	VL	VL
Physical and corrective therapy assistants and aides	79	66.4	VL	L
Home health aides	77	378.2	VL	H
Medical assistants	74	166.4	L	L
Desktop publishing specialists	74	22.4	H	L
Physical therapists	71	81.1	VH	VL
Occupational therapy assistants and aides	69	10.8	L	L
Paralegals	68	76.4	H	L
Occupational therapists	66	37.9	VH	L
Teachers, special education	59	240.7	VH	VL
Human services workers	55	98.4	VL	VL
Data processing equipment repairers	52	41.7	H	H
Medical records technicians	51	44.5	H	L
Speech-language pathologists and audiologists	51	44.2	VH	VL
Dental hygienists	48	64.0	H	VL
Amusement and recreation attendants	48	138.0	L	H
Physician assistants	47	29.7	VH	VL

SOURCE: *Occupational Outlook Quarterly/Winter 1997–98.* U.S. Department of Labor, Bureau of Labor Statistics.

FIGURE
19-3

Of all the occupations expected to have faster than average employment growth, above average earnings, and below average unemployment, the 25 shown in this chart have the largest number of projected openings. These 25 occupations will account for 5 million new jobs, or 27% of all job growth. Eighteen of the 25 require at least a bachelor's degree. The occupations are somewhat concentrated, with four each in the computer technology, health care, and education fields.

Projected employment growth in selected occupations, 1996–2006
(thousands)

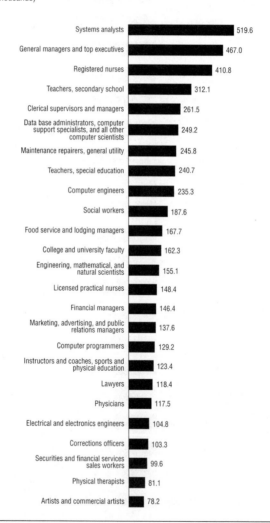

Systems analysts	519.6
General managers and top executives	467.0
Registered nurses	410.8
Teachers, secondary school	312.1
Clerical supervisors and managers	261.5
Data base administrators, computer support specialists, and all other computer scientists	249.2
Maintenance repairers, general utility	245.8
Teachers, special education	240.7
Computer engineers	235.3
Social workers	187.6
Food service and lodging managers	167.7
College and university faculty	162.3
Engineering, mathematical, and natural scientists	155.1
Licensed practical nurses	148.4
Financial managers	146.4
Marketing, advertising, and public relations managers	137.6
Computer programmers	129.2
Instructors and coaches, sports and physical education	123.4
Lawyers	118.4
Physicians	117.5
Electrical and electronics engineers	104.8
Corrections officers	103.3
Securities and financial services sales workers	99.6
Physical therapists	81.1
Artists and commercial artists	78.2

SOURCE: *Occupational Outlook Quarterly/Winter 1997–98.* U.S. Department of Labor, Bureau of Labor Statistics.

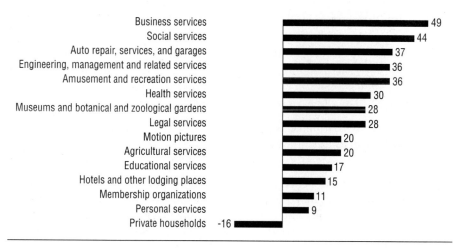

FIGURE 19-4

Services, which accounted for 37% of wage and salary employment in the service-producing sector in 1996, will account for 64% of new wage and salary jobs in the service-producing sector. Business services, the fastest growing industry group, is led by computer and data processing services, the fastest growing industry in the economy. Only membership organizations, personal services, and private households are projected to grow more slowly than average.

Projected change in wage and salary employment by major industry group within the services division, 1996–2006
(percent)

Industry group	Percent
Business services	49
Social services	44
Auto repair, services, and garages	37
Engineering, management and related services	36
Amusement and recreation services	36
Health services	30
Museums and botanical and zoological gardens	28
Legal services	28
Motion pictures	20
Agricultural services	20
Educational services	17
Hotels and other lodging places	15
Membership organizations	11
Personal services	9
Private households	-16

SOURCE: *Occupational Outlook Quarterly/Winter 1997–98*. U.S. Department of Labor, Bureau of Labor Statistics.

Focusing on the Client's Needs

Most clients will be looking at future work from a different perspective than in the recent past. Those not aware of changing work environments must be educated to view future work realistically. For example, some may want to follow the career path of their parents, who spent their entire careers with one organization, periodically moving up the career ladder, and enjoying health benefits and other rewards of long-term service. These workplaces may be more difficult to find in the future (Meister, 1994; Reich, 1991).

The career counselor who focuses on the client's needs provides each with the opportunity to express his or her individuality, desired life roles, and lifestyle and occupational plans. The pathways to finding the person-environment fit may contain roadblocks that justify intervention strategies of more in-depth career information, including descriptions of work changes and workplaces in the future. Obviously, not all clients will need this information.

Equal Opportunity/Affirmative Action

The importance of human resource management in organizations has received greater attention among organizational leaders during the last 50 years. Although some organizations have voluntarily adopted policies to hire more minorities, others have been forced to do so by federal mandates. The following federal laws have been passed to promote equal opportunity and affirmative action policies in American industry:

- Title VII of the Civil Rights Act of 1964, which prohibits discrimination in employment because of race, color, religion, sex, or national origin in companies of 15 or more employees
- The Age Discrimination in Employment Act of 1967, and the 1978 and 1986 amendments disallowing mandatory retirement
- The Equal Pay Act of 1963, which prohibits sex discrimination in pay
- The Rehabilitation Act of 1973, which was amended in 1978 to include alcoholism as a handicap
- The Americans with Disability Act of 1990 (see Chapter 14)
- The Civil Rights Act of 1991, an amendment to Title VII, which prohibits intentional discrimination in hiring based on race, religion, sex, national origin, or disability and removes the quota system of hiring and promoting minorities; also prohibits adjustment of test scores to increase hiring of minorities

Affirmative action policies have lead to a variety of strategies among organizations to hire a diverse work force; however, these strategies have not necessarily been motivated by hiring goals and quotas (Robinson, Allen, & Abraham, 1992). In general, some organizations have assumed the role of advocate and have become proactive in promoting hiring and offering advancement opportunities to a diverse work force. The strategies have centered around intentional recruitment of minority applicants (underrepresented groups are targeted for extensive recruitment), identification and removal of employment practices working against minority applicants and employees (such practices might involve company policies and supervisor attitudes), and preferential hiring and promotion of minorities (in companies where minorities are underrepresented, efforts are made to hire and promote qualified minorities) (Aamodt, 1999).

Federal laws have contributed greatly to helping minorities gain access to employment in organizations, although much more needs to be done. For instance, more effort needs to be directed toward training programs designed for minorities and all groups to improve their skills for the future work force. It seems plausible to conclude that those who do not receive proper training will be excluded from opportunities in the future. Counselors should remain alert to federal, state, and local laws and advocacy programs that provide employment and training opportunities for minority groups.

Occupational Insecurity

The massive downsizing of jobs, discussed earlier, has led to a new and unnerving workplace. Many workers who were considered middle class—following the typical American dream of job, home, and family—find themselves worrying about survival rather than about a new car, an addition to the house, or a second home. Dreams have faded with the cruel reality that one could be cast among the jobless at any time in today's workplace climate. Typical of this group is to worry about what was once taken for granted. The loss of home, retirement pensions, and health benefits are troubling thoughts that occupy many Americans. When they witness the plight of their fellow jobless workers, they are quick to recognize a loss of dignity that is often severe and pervasive.

A *New York Times* telephone poll conducted in December 1995 (Uchitelle & Kleinfeld, 1996) surveyed 1265 adults throughout the United States and found that many workers responding to their survey were struggling to adjust to downsizing. The majority polled stated they would work more hours, take fewer vacations, or accept lesser benefits to keep their jobs. These workers, almost desperately looking for job security, are willing to work harder and longer to maintain their occupational statuses.

The loss of control over one's future work role can lead to poor mental health (Roskies & Louis-Guerin, 1990) and subsequent devastating consequences to other life roles, such as family member and citizen. This lack of control also can take individual tolls, such as loss of self-esteem, which often leads to depression. Career counselors must recognize the potential conflicts that could result from occupational insecurity.

Coping with Joblessness

Closely related to occupational insecurity is the impact of unemployment. According to the 1997 U.S. Bureau of Census report, the unemployment rates by race, age, and sex in 1996 were as follows:

		Male %	Female %
White	35–44	3.5	3.8
	45–54	3.1	3.1
African American	35–44	7.8	6.9
	45–54	6.3	3.8
Hispanic	35–44	6.3	8.7
	45–54	5.1	7.2

According to these figures, African Americans and Hispanics have a greater unemployment rate than do whites; thus, an advocacy role for ethnic minorities should be a priority for career counselors.

The degree of negative effects of unemployment has been associated with both physical and psychological consequences such as withdrawal, decline of self-respect, loss of identity and affiliation, and disruptive behavioral reactions (Herr, 1989; Newman & Newman, 1999). Men and women seem to experience the same degree of distress following loss of a job (Leana & Feldman, 1991). According to Defrank and Ivancevich (1986), middle-aged men are more vulnerable to negative effects of job loss.

Among other counseling techniques, counselors should assume a supportive role while clients are involved in a new job search. The consequences of repeated job search failures can be devastating, and the career counselor may find that a long-term commitment to unemployed individuals may be necessary.

The New Entrepreneurial Climate

The opportunity to own your own business may increase in the new business climate of today's economy. Changes in operational procedures for organizations have created more opportunities for small businesses to offer their services and skills. One advantage of owning your own business is that you can operate out of your home and, in most cases, live where you are most comfortable.

The entrepreneur should be multifunctional; one may be required to develop marketing strategies, plan for finances, act as a salesperson, and maintain an office. The entrepreneur must be willing to spend long hours in launching a new business and must be willing to take chances and be innovative. It has often been said that the first steps are the hardest ones, and this is certainly true for the entrepreneur. However, the challenge of owning one's own business and the potential for economic rewards has been very satisfying for many who have entered this arena. The Internet has introduced new and intriguing opportunities for the emerging entrepreneurs.

The fall 1994 issue of *Occupational Outlook Quarterly* gives the following encouragement to future entrepreneurs (Mariani, 1994).

The Entrepreneurs Among Us

People who want a career working for themselves can develop their own businesses. The opportunities do exist. According to the Bureau of Labor Statistics, over 10 million members of the U.S. labor force (16 years and older) worked for themselves in their own unincorporated businesses in 1992. Another 3.5 million people head their own incorporated enterprises and can be considered self-employed even though, technically, they are salaried employees of their corporations.

Service occupations and executive, administrative, and managerial occupations had large numbers of self-employed workers in 1992, and self-employment is expected to increase much faster than average within these occupational groups through 2005. Marketing and sales occupations accounted for much self-employment, even though the number of self-employed workers in these occupations will grow much more slowly than average from 1992–2005. Two other large groups—professional specialty occupations and precision production, craft, and repair occupations—include many detailed occupations with a high share of self-employed workers. (p. 7)

Work Values

Cultural values can sometimes be difficult to separate from work values. As Rosenberg (1957) noted several decades ago, occupational choice is made on the basis of values, which are the principles that guide individuals in making decisions and developing behavioral patterns. Values are influential in determining individual goals and lifestyles and influencing work motivation, behavior, and satisfaction.

Attitudes toward work are also reflected in changing cultural values. Spindler (1955), who studied changing values in American mainstream culture after World War II, found significant changes from traditional values to what he called "emergent values." For example, the traditional value of future-time orientation or working toward future goals was contrasted with the emergent value of hedonistic, present-time orientation, which reflected a new focus on living for the present because the future is unknown. Following this logic, all work is perceived as temporary, with little value placed on longevity of the job, job identity, or the value of work itself.

Pine and Innis (1987) suggested that individual work values are influenced by a number of factors, including ethnicity, subcultures, historical cohorts, socioeconomic status, significant others, society, and economic conditions. Work values are influenced by changing conditions in our society, as illustrated by Schnall's (1981) study of longitudinal value shifts. Schnall found that basic belief systems in our society had shifted in stages during a half-century: (1) from the 1930s through the 1950s, more attention was paid to the welfare of others than self; (2) during the 1960s, the focus changed to self-indulgence and instant gratification with little regard for others; (3) during the 1970s, distrust for others was manifested in a strong movement toward self-reliance; and (4) during the 1980s, there was a shift back to concern for others with the growing need for individuals to experience self-fulfillment (Pine & Innis, 1987). Schnall's study clearly suggests that we have returned to some of the dominant values of the 1950s.

In a related study of value changes of college students, Astin (1984) suggested that students in the 1980s had value orientations similar to those of students in the 1950s: They wanted security, jobs that were indicators of success, and a home in the suburbs. Wall (1984), however, indicated that value orientations of college students in the 1950s and 1980s differed significantly because the possibility of moving up the career ladder, a foregone conclusion in the 1950s, was uncertain in the economically unstable 1980s.

The uncertain economic forecast changed the process of choosing careers from idealism to pragmatism—"where do I have the best chance of being employed?" and "how can I best market myself for that occupation?" Economic realities influence not only career choice but also how individuals work at jobs they otherwise might not have chosen. Self-fulfillment, which Schnall mentioned as a prevalent goal in the 1980s but not fully attainable in the uncertain economic conditions, might cause some people to withhold a firm emotional involvement in their work (Yankelovich, 1979).

The implications of observing work values in the context of changing cultural values and economic patterns in our society are profound. For example, career counselors should focus more on available opportunities than on individual psychology. This shift in emphasis implies that career counseling must become more realistic to be most effective. Finally, individual perceptions of work and commitment to work are inextricably connected with economic and societal forces. How these factors influence individual value systems must always be considered when counselors evaluate work values (Pine & Innis, 1987).

A Synthesis of Opinion About Work Commitment and Work Ethics

Growing evidence suggests that causes of job satisfaction and dissatisfaction are indeed complex issues. Just as intricate are the issues surrounding work commitment and work ethics. Some researchers have proposed that a common bond connecting these issues is rooted in our society. O'Toole (1981), among others, has postulated that low productivity is a cultural problem rather than the result of national economic policy. Yankelovich (1981a) suggested that our work ethic is an inextricable part of social issues. Both positions have common themes related to our national social development.

According to O'Toole (1981), overwhelming evidence indicates that culture is a fundamental determinant of our economic performance. He cited the past economic superiority of Germany and Japan as examples of cultures that encourage efficiency and productivity. He suggested that the Japanese especially have adopted managerial policies compatible with their culture. The answer is not simply to adopt another country's philosophy and orientation toward work but to develop policies that are compatible with our own culture. Furthermore, the major problem in the U.S. workplace today is that most of our current managerial and organizational policies and practices were developed in the 1940s and 1950s. These policies were compatible with the culture at the time, but during the last 30 years there have been dramatic social shifts. The rules for work commitment have been altered, and Americans simply are unwilling to do work under outdated mandates. The new work values are congruent with changes in the broader culture.

Yankelovich (1981b), in search of answers for self-fulfillment in work, has suggested that we need an ethic of commitment. He, like O'Toole, also addressed the changes of values in our culture, attacking in particular the self-psychology practices promoting the idea that sacredness lies within self. According to Yankelovich, the impact of the "duty-to-self" ethic has led to development of selfishness and hedonistic values. These self-indulgent values have subverted self-fulfillment. Yankelovich suggested that what is now needed is a new ethic that promotes a more cooperative attitude among workers and places less emphasis on competitiveness for personal gain.

Yankelovich contended that an ethic of commitment would emerge slowly over the next several decades. Changes in self-concept and attitude are key ingredients for self-fulfillment under the ethic of commitment. The first step is to discard the goals of the duty-to-self ethic and to concentrate on sharing, showing more concern for others, being cooperative, and striving to develop closer and deeper personal relationships. Relationships with others are to be simple, direct, and unencumbered by pursuit of status or financial rewards. Ultimately, more satisfying personal achievements will come from *sacred expressive values*. Sacred values include increased concern and dedication to improving community and country. Expressive values are personal, but they do not originate from me-first attitudes; they are broader in concept and allow for greater self-involvement and a closer connection to others.

Following the logic of Yankelovich (1981b), the shift in attitudes and values associated with the ethic of commitment will change workers' perspectives of their jobs and work environments. The primary motivation to work will not be based on moving up the career ladder at all costs. Commitment to work will be a sharing of producing, creating, and mutually expressive accomplishments. The work environment is to be one in which direct, honest, and straightforward communications are exchanged. The organization is to adopt leadership policies that are conducive to openness of communication between workers and supervisors and involve a caring interest in each worker. Work will continue to be an important commitment but will not be all-absorbing. Sufficient time to enjoy leisure and develop family relationships will be emphasized. Self-fulfillment is achieved when "one understands that the self must be fulfilled within the shared meanings of psychoculture."

Samuelson (1995) suggests that, as Americans, we expect such institutions as "big business" and "big government" to guarantee us secure jobs, rising living standards, clean environments, safe cities, and satisfying work, among other entitlements. As Samuelson puts it, "we feel entitled" (p. 4). Moreover, entitlement's fatal flaw is utopianism—that is, the false impression that we are working our way toward a perfect society. The problem is that we expect the perfect society to be handed to us; we also expect to assume little personal responsibility. This attitude is pervasive in all our life roles, according to Samuelson, including our work role. As individuals, we should expect to do more for ourselves and expect less from our government. In essence, we are to assume more responsibility for our own actions now and into the 21st century.

Stress at Work: Its Implications and How to Deal with It

One factor inherent in modern working life is stress, induced by work and the work environment. Stress in this context has been defined as a psychophysical response to various stimuli. Work-related stressor sources have been studied by a number of researchers (Ivancevich & Matteson, 1980; Kasl, 1978; Levi, 1984; Shostak, 1980). Sources of stress compiled by these researchers dramatize the complexity and variety of potentially stressful conditions most workers face:

1. *Conditions of work:* Unpleasant work environment, necessity to work fast, excessive and inconvenient hours
2. *Work itself:* Perception of job as uninteresting, repetitious, overloaded, and demanding
3. *Shift work:* Rotating shifts affecting bodily functions and role behaviors
4. *Supervision:* Unclear job demands, close supervision with no autonomy, scant feedback from supervisors
5. *Wage and promotion:* Inadequate income
6. *Role ambiguity:* Lack of clarity about one's job and scope of responsibilities
7. *Career development stressors:* Little job security, impending obsolescence, dissatisfaction over career aspirations and current level of attainment
8. *Group stressors:* Insufficient group cohesiveness, poor group identity in the organization
9. *Organizational climate:* Impersonally structured organizational policies
10. *Organizational structure:* Too bureaucratic or too autocratic

Job-Related Stress Is a Global Phenomenon

Job-related stress afflicts British miners, French nurses, and Australian government workers as well as U.S. executives. Blue-collar workers also experience job stress, perhaps because they have less control over their jobs and lives than do higher paid white-collar workers. An international survey conducted by the United Nations' International Labor Organization found that women suffer as much or more job-related stress than men do ("Job stress at work," 1993).

One reason suggested for the increase in job stress is that many workers are involved in a sort of electronic assembly line, which allows supervisors to evaluate them constantly during the workday. Perhaps more important are job demands that do not match a worker's current abilities, needs, or expectations. That is, there is a poor fit between workers and their work environments and subsequent requirements. Job-related stress has many roots and causes, but among the important ones are organizational management and work environment.

Magnuson (1990) suggested the following indicators of job-related stress:

- Low self-esteem
- Low motivation to work
- Poor concentration on work tasks
- Poor work relationships with peers and supervisors
- Poor communications with others on the job site
- Feelings of inadequacy and resentment
- Depression
- Excessive tardiness and absenteeism

More recently, Rice (1999) has suggested that job-related stress leads to dissatisfaction, burnout, and obsolescence. He considers psychological symptoms of work stress to include the following:

- Anxiety, tension, confusion, and irritability
- Feelings of frustration, anger, and resentment
- Emotional hypersensitivity and hyperactivity
- Suppression of feelings, withdrawal, and depression
- Reduced effectiveness in communication
- Feelings of isolation and alienation
- Boredom and job dissatisfaction
- Mental fatigue, lower intellectual functioning, and loss of concentration
- Loss of spontaneity and creativity
- Lowered self-esteem (p. 195)

Such symptoms, according to Rice (1999) can lead to several behaviors including lower performance, procrastination, work avoidance, aggression, depression, and increased alcohol and drug use and abuse. Work-related stress can lead to family problems, poor relationships with other workers and friends, and in very severe cases might be one driving force that leads to violence in the workplace.

Thus, the effects of stress are pervasive; work performance and interpersonal relationships are often affected. Stress has been linked to numerous physical problems, including cardiovascular diseases. Stress exists at all levels of the work force, from executives to blue-collar workers (Rice, 1999; Shostak, 1980). As organizations grow in complexity, potential stressor sources are expected to multiply.

Violence in the Workplace

In recent years headlines in newspapers and top stories on newscasts have featured incidents of workplace violence. For instance, the following incidents have been compiled by Muchinsky (1997) and Aamodt (1999) from the last decade:

- In Tampa, a Florida man shot three men who were his supervisors while they were eating lunch. He then wounded two other workers before committing suicide.
- After a female coworker turned down his romantic advances, a Sunnyvale, California, man shot and killed seven people in an office.
- After a car mechanic was fired, he returned to his workplace and fired into a crowd of workers killing two and wounding another.
- A Wendy's employee, in Tulsa, Oklahoma, fired 12 shots from a 38-caliber hand-gun, wounding six people including his supervisor. His boss had asked him to start work earlier.

- Four coworkers in the California Department of Transportation were killed by a fired former employee.

- In Houston, a supervisor was shot when he threatened to fire an employee.

These incidents point out workplace violence that centers around disgruntled employees and often involves individuals who have been fired from their jobs. Psychology of workplace violence is usually conceptualized as aggressive acts that are frequently retaliatory responses of individuals who see themselves as victims of injustice in the workplace. Such individuals conclude that they have been betrayed by organizations that have also violated the principles of procedural justice (Johnson & Indvik, 1994). In short, according to Aamodt (1999), violence against an employee or supervisor is considered to be an act of anger or vengeance.

The small amount of research on this topic has centered around studies of aggression and profiles of those who commit violence; however, violence in the workplace is indeed a complex phenomenon that contains many psychological antecedents. For example, many of the perpetrators of workplace violence have been known to have experienced interpersonal conflict and often have maladaptive personalities (Muchinsky, 1997). Moreover, aggression, especially in this context, should be conceptualized as a product of both individual and situational factors. For instance, such situational factors as noise, crowded conditions, heat, and alcohol usage can increase the likelihood of aggression (Pernanen, 1991).

This serious problem has led to the development of profiles of potential perpetrators of workplace violence. As Muchinsky (1997) points out, however, the characteristics among individuals who have committed acts of workplace violence could describe a number of individuals in the organization. The predictive accuracy of who will commit such acts is very difficult to attain; however, de Becker (1997) has developed "pre-incident indicators" that can be used by management to warn them of employees who are likely to act out violently. His work may well be a beginning of relevant research that will provide guidelines of warning systems that prove to be valid. Counselors should remain alert to research on this complex subject because we currently have more questions than answers.

In the meantime, organizations are beefing up security measures that include surveillance cameras, silent alarms, sophisticated locks, and security guards. Organizations are conducting more thorough background and reference checks of applicants. Management is learning to become more alert to high risk situations that could need immediate action. In general, employees and supervisors are being trained to recognize potential problems in the workplace that could lead to violence (Aamodt, 1999).

Career Burnout

In the early 1970s, the term *burnout* emerged in career counseling articles and in the popular media. Freudenberger (1974) is generally given credit for first using the term to describe certain kinds of career behavior (Herr & Cramer, 1996). Later, Freudenberger and Richelson (1980) defined *burnout* as the depletion of an individual's physical and mental resources caused by excessive attempts to meet self-imposed, unrealistic goals. A number of symptoms have been associated with burnout, including depression, fatigue, irritability, sleeplessness, and uncontrollable anger. Important to our discussion is that Freudenberger identified the work environment and work situation as precipitating factors that lead to symptoms of burnout.

A more precise explanation of burnout was discussed by Cherniss (1980, 1995), who concentrated on workers in the "helping" professions. Conceptually, Cherniss perceived burnout within the helping professions in three stages: (1) workers experience stress because of job demands, (2) workers experience strain because of emotional responses of anxiety and tension, and (3) workers attempt to cope defensively by changing their attitudes toward commitment to their jobs. For example, workers might treat clients in a manner that reflects an attitude of little concern for them. Cherniss observed that when helping professionals experience burnout, devotion to helping others is no longer a strong commitment. He suggested that in response to work-related stress and strain, workers in helping professions will actually disengage from their work. Other writers, such as Maslach, have come to similar conclusions concerning mental health workers (Maslach, 1976, 1981; Maslach & Jackson, 1981; Pines & Maslach, 1979).

Burnout has been used to describe a number of work-related behaviors. For example, Cordes and Dougherty (1993) describe burnout as a stress syndrome, characterized by emotional exhaustion, depersonalization, and diminished personal accomplishment. Burnout has been associated primarily with individuals in the helping professions such as teaching, social work, and health care. Similarly, the terms *burnout* and *stagnation* are used interchangeably to describe individuals who have lost enthusiasm for work (Edelwich & Brodsky, 1980). Another comparable term is *plateauing,* which is used to describe individuals who have reached their highest level in an organization (Drucker, 1992). In essence, burnout has not been delineated clearly and has received only preliminary and small-scale validation (Herr & Cramer, 1996). Therefore, the correlates of burnout described next should be considered to be preliminary observations in lieu of further research and delineation of the term.

Investigators generally seem to agree that burnout is not a single event but, rather, a process of gradual change in behavior, eventually reaching intense reactions and leading to crisis if left unresolved. Burnout has been associated with work overload, repetitive work tasks, boredom, ambiguity, lack of advancement opportunities, and time pressures (Forney, Wallace-Schultzman, & Wiggens, 1982). Schwab (1981; Rice, 1999) contended that burnout is highly related to role conflict. Farber and Heifetz (1981) and Emener and Rubin (1980) suggested that excessive work with very disturbed people is highly correlated with burnout. Other researchers suggested that off-the-job stress should also be evaluated when counseling individuals who exhibit symptoms of burnout (Pardine et al., 1981; Rice, 1999).

There appears to be a high degree of relationship between work-associated stress and burnout. Perhaps one strategy to use in dealing with individuals who exhibit symptoms of burnout is to evaluate work-related stressor sources, as outlined earlier. Support groups designed to foster self-acceptance and coping skills through the use of relaxation techniques are also recommended (Argeropoulos,

1981; Rice, 1999), and Gebhardt and Crump (1990) have proposed physical activity. The variety of strategies suggests that burnout is a viable counseling consideration for individuals throughout the life span.

Pines and Aronson (1988) suggested a four-step plan for dealing with career burnout: (1) Recognize the symptoms of burnout, (2) activate a plan for solving the causes of burnout, (3) distinguish between what can be changed and what cannot be changed, and (4) develop new coping skills and refine old ones. The first step is intended to promote awareness of stressors that cause individuals to believe they are helpless. Some, for example, may feel that burnout is "life's course" and that little can be done to change that course. Others try to ignore existing problems. Even though awareness may increase anxiety, it is a necessary first step toward solving career burnout problems. When individuals become aware of problems, they are usually willing to take action. For example, a worker who receives poor feedback on job performance from a supervisor may elect to either confront the supervisor or transfer to another work environment.

In many work environments, it is difficult to assess the causes of burnout, but to make progress toward change, the individual must carefully evaluate the underlying causes. Pines and Aronson (1988) pointed out that some bureaucracies cannot change their unresponsiveness to individuals; the system simply does not provide for it. For example, the work of a rehabilitation counselor is demanding and has many frustrating aspects. Even when success is attained, the counselor may only receive an increased client load as a reward. In this case, the counselor views the organizational changes to make the job more fulfilling as overwhelming; however, the counselor at least recognizes that the source of the problem is in the system rather than in himself or herself. In this scenario, the fourth step, developing coping skills, might include teaching the rehabilitation counselors to reinforce each other's work. This method promotes appreciation and respect for peers.

Other coping skills involve a careful evaluation of individual needs to solve a specific problem. Individuals may accomplish this through self-introspection or through professional help.

In conclusion, Pines and Aronson (1988) suggested that career counselors can help clients who could be experiencing burnout by (1) clarifying symptoms of burnout, (2) helping them develop the ability to distinguish sources of stress that they can control and those that are inherent in the work itself, and (3) developing tools for coping with stress by teaching clients how to focus on positive work aspects and develop positive attitudes.

Healthful Work

During the last decade, several publications have addressed the sources of job-related stress, whereas others have suggested methods of dealing with it. The relationship between job stress and disease has also been exposed as an ongoing problem that has been ignored in many workplaces. Recently, however, the connection between work and health has focused attention on designing more healthful workplaces. The physical, psychological, and psychosocial consequences of work are significantly related to job design (Aamodt, 1999; Karasek & Theorell, 1990). For example, bad job design fosters social isolation, little feeling of the social value of work, unrestrained job competition, sex-role conflicts, little or no freedom or independence, long periods of intense time pressures, and little autonomy for workers.

Jobs designed for the future and considered healthful work—that is, beyond the material rewards of work—are described by Karasek & Theorell (1990) as follows:

1. More jobs are to be designed to make maximum use of every worker's skill and provide opportunities to improve and increase skills.

2. More work freedom exists when workers are able to select their work routines and peer affiliates. Some work may be done in the home.

3. Workers are given equal status in making decisions as far as work demands are concerned. Jobs may require routine tasks, but they also provide new learning challenges.

4. Social contacts are encouraged to promote new learning and prevent work isolation. Advanced technologies are made available to encourage new learning.

5. Democratic procedures are prevalent in the workplace. Grievance procedures protect workers from arbitrary authority.

6. Workers receive feedback from customers, and in fact, customers and workers are encouraged to work together to customize products.

7. All workers are to share in family responsibilities and tasks, especially in two-earner homes. Time is set aside for family activities. (pp. 316–317)

In sum, healthful work reduces the sources of job stress prevalent in current work environments primarily by giving the worker more freedom and autonomy. Social interactions are encouraged to reduce threats associated with job competition. New learning is encouraged by making new technologies accessible to workers. Finally, more freedom of choice concerning work roles and greater autonomy in the workplace are recommended as key ingredients for designing jobs for the future.

Will There Be a Demand for Increased Quality of Work?

As we become more involved with global economics and multinational work forces, the quality of our products will become increasingly important. A quality product has been defined as one that is without defects or mistakes and is delivered on time. There have been significant signs that an international standard for certain products may be developing. The International Organization for Standardization (ISO) in Switzerland might provide the framework from which quality is assured ("ISO 9000," 1992). The ISO 9000 standard series explains fundamental quality concepts and guides organizations in tailoring and designing production systems to ensure quality. Other countries, including the United States (National Institute of Standards and Technology), also have organizations for standards.

Does this movement mean that there will be global supervision of products, and will these products only be exported and imported if they are registered under some system of standards? That question has yet to be answered, but changes in the workplace might follow adoptions of some system of standardization. Some U.S. chemicals and associated products are registered under the ISO 9000. Currently, few changes affect workers and management, but there has been some concern that this kind of standardization approach could evolve into a rating system affecting job security.

Workers' welfare and mental health will continue to concern us as counselors, and we will always be faced with ongoing changes that make our jobs a challenge. No doubt situations will continue to occur that create the need to develop new intervention strategies to assist individuals in making career decisions and adjusting to fast-paced changes in the workplace. The ISO 9000 approach to standardization could be a method of creating satisfaction among workers or a situation of change that creates more job-related stress. Within the next 10 to 20 years, we should have some answers.

Aging Workers

A question often considered in the hiring process is, Are aging workers more motivated to do good work than younger workers are? Research has shown that age per se is not a good predictor of how well a person will perform in either a blue-collar or a white-collar job. Older workers can be as competent as younger ones and typically have more positive attitudes toward their work. Furthermore, older workers seem to be more satisfied in their jobs, more involved in their work, and less interested in finding a different job (Warr, 1992).

As Sigelman (1999) points out, job performance of individuals in their fifties and sixties is not very different from that of younger workers. She notes that performance of older workers is not hindered by age-related physical and cognitive declines that are usually significant when one is much older. Also, the American Council on Education (1997, as cited in Kail and Cavanaugh, 2000) report that older employees make up the largest percentage of individuals taking courses designed to improve their technical skills. Perhaps older workers are also successfully competing for jobs through what is referred to as *selective optimization with compensation* (Hansson, DeKoekkoek, Neece, & Patterson, 1997). In this process, the older worker focuses on the skills needed to compete (selection), practices to keep those skills sharp (optimization), and compensates for skills he or she lacks.

One explanation for these findings is that older workers have found jobs that satisfy them, and they have accepted the downside of the job, realizing that it could be difficult to find a new job. The point here is that workers in their fifties and sixties can make good employees.

Summary

1. Changes in work requirements and skills have evolved with the technological revolution. As many as 43 million jobs were lost to downsizing
   by 1995 and more job losses are expected in the near future.

2. Organizations are reorganizing and abandoning fundamental assumptions that underlay previous operating procedures. Some skills
   individuals will need to compete are in the areas of reading, writing,
   computation, cognitive reasoning, interpersonal relations, creative
   thinking and problem solving, leadership, self-development, and self-
   management. In the "new web of enterprise," team members will function with problem solvers, problem identifiers, and strategic planners.

3. Health and computer occupations are projected to grow faster than
   average from 1996 to 2006. In general, however, labor force growth
   will be slower. Baby boomers will be in the 55- to 64-year-old age
   group by 2006. Labor force participation will continue to increase for
   women, Hispanics, and Asians. Industrial employment will be concentrated in the service-producing sector of the economy.

4. Equal opportunity and affirmative action programs have been adopted
   by organizations to promote hiring and advancement opportunities for
   minority groups.

5. Occupational insecurity can lead to mental health problems. All life
   roles can be affected.

6. Clients need assistance in coping with joblessness. Men and women can
   experience the same degree of stress.

7. The opportunities for entrepreneurs could be expanded by changes in
   organizational procedures and the development of the Internet.

8. Work values are influenced by several factors, including changing
   cultural values and economic patterns in our society. Career counselors
   should focus more on opportunities and choices that individuals perceive
   as available to them; career counseling must be realistic to be most effective. Individual perceptions of work and commitment to work are inextricably connected with economic and social forces.

9. Work commitment and work ethics could be cultural issues and related
   to our national social development. A new self-development ethic
   might be emerging that will change workers' perspectives of their jobs
   and the work environment.

10. Stress, defined as a psychophysical response to various stimuli, is inher-
    ent in modern working life. The effects of stress are pervasive: Work
    performance and interpersonal relationships are often affected. Stress
    affects all levels of workers, from executives to blue-collar workers.

11. The term *burnout* is used to describe several work-related behaviors.
    Burnout is a gradual process of behavioral change and is associated

with stress caused by work overload, boredom, repetitive work tasks, time pressures, and other work-related stressor sources.

12. Healthful work reduces the sources of job stress by giving workers more freedom of choice for work roles and autonomy.

13. The ISO may provide the framework used in organizations to ensure quality of work. The effects of change in the workplace could create opportunities for greater work-related satisfaction or change that creates job-related stress.

14. Workers in their fifties and sixties can be as competent as younger workers and typically have more positive attitudes.

Supplementary Learning Exercises

1. Describe your own work ethic and how it developed. Compare your description with a classmate's.

2. Develop a counseling component that is designed to help individuals overcome job stress.

3. Defend or criticize the following statement in writing or in a debate: Work ethics change because society changes.

4. How did teamwork displace assembly-line work that required one task to be repeated? Give an example.

5. What is the difference between the problem solver and the problem identifier? Which one has the most difficult task?

6. Explain the concept of a "new web of enterprise." How does it operate?

7. Give several reasons why the computer-related industries are among the fastest growing industries. Identify some specific jobs in this industry.

8. Develop counseling strategies for individuals who feel insecure in their occupation.

9. How would you assist an individual who has lost his or her job? Describe your procedures and their purpose.

10. Using the following source, write an essay on the changes in organizations that will be experienced in the early part of the 21st Century: Hammer, M., & Champy, J. (1993). *Reengineering the corporation: A manifesto for business revolution*. New York: HarperCollins.

For More Information

Aamodt, M. G. (1999). *Applied industrial/organizational psychology* (3rd ed.). Pacific Grove, CA: Brooks/Cole * Wadsworth.

Dent, H. S., Jr. (1998). *The roaring 2000's.* New York: Simon & Schuster.

Hammer, M., & Champy, J. (1993). *Reengineering the corporation: A manifesto for business revolution.* New York: HarperCollins.

Jackson, S. E., & Ruderman, M. N. (Eds.) (1995). *Diversity in work teams: Research paradigms for a changing workplace.* Washington, DC: American Psychological Association.

Meister, J. C. (1994). *Corporate quality universities: Lessons in building a world-class work force.* New York: Irwin.

Muchinsky, P. M. (1997). *Psychology applied to work* (5th ed.). Pacific Grove, CA: Brooks/Cole.

The New York Times (1996). *The downsizing of America.* New York: *New York Times.*

Reich, R. B. (1991). *The work of nations.* New York: Knopf.

Reskin, B. F. (1993). Sex segregation in the workplace. *Annual Review of Sociology, 19,* 241–270.

Reskin, B., & Pakavic, I. (1994). *Women and men at work.* London: Pine Forge Press.

Rice, P. L. (1999). *Stress and health* (3rd ed.). Pacific Grove, CA: Brooks/Cole.

Rifkin, J. (1995). *The end of work: The decline of the global labor force and the dawn of the post-market era.* New York: Putnam's.

VandenBos, G. R., & Bulatao, E. Q. (1996). *Violence on the job: Identifying risks and developing solutions.* Washington, DC: American Psychological Association.

20

Career Counseling for Adults in Career Transition

Chapter Highlights

- *Changing jobs case example*
- *National survey of working America*
- *New trend of workforce centers or one-stop career centers*
- *Issues facing adults in career transition*
- *Major themes in human development and implications of adult career development*
- *Basic coping skills for managing transitions*
- *Fictitious personal agency person as a model for personal development*
- *Intervention components for adults in career transition*

IN THIS CHAPTER, WE CONCENTRATE ON THE GROWING NEED FOR PROGRAMS and strategies to assist adults in career transition. Traditionally, career counseling programs have focused on strategies for initial career choices, giving only limited help to adults who change careers. In the last decade, however, greater attention has been focused on the development of counseling programs for individuals who choose to make a career change and for those who are forced into it. Changing work roles appears to be inevitable and most certainly unavoidable for many in the work force. As Drucker (1992) points out, we are in the middle of a transformation that is not yet complete. This transformation is rapid and highly discontinuous in nature; changes can be quite drastic and pervasive in scope. We are living at a time of a tremendous growth of knowledge through sophisticated research that has given us new technologies with vast potential for even more rapid changes in the near future. Billions-of-dollars mergers involving companies that can offer more programs through cable, for instance, are viewed by some as temporary leaders as even newer technological advances will provide bigger and better avenues to entertainment and the Internet. In the meantime our society is going through the pains associated with continuous change. Change in the world of work has been described as tumultuous, and its fallout will certainly have an effect on who will prosper in the future (Muchinsky, 1997).

Current speculation suggests that individuals who will prosper are those who are intelligent enough to learn new skills and, most important, those who are *willing* to experience new and different situations and have the capacity to relate to other people. Workers will no longer experience the luxury of a steady stream of continuous change but, on the contrary, will be required to adapt quickly to new and different ideas, goals, procedures, tools, and requirements. The career counselor's major contribution is to help individuals bridge the gap of uncertainty in a positive manner and accept the challenges of the unknown future.

We begin with the plight of an individual who has changed jobs several times. Next are examples of results from a national survey of working America. This is followed by a discussion of issues facing adults in career transition, Workforce Centers—One-Stop Centers, and then by a multidimensional model of career and individual development. The section "Major Themes in Human Development" is followed by implications of adult career development. Next, basic coping skills are presented for managing transitions, and the profile of the personal agency person is listed, followed by counseling components for adults in career transition.

Case 20-1: BEN IS CHANGING JOBS AGAIN

When Ben finished high school, he was referred to as a vocational educational student. Much of his course work was in woodworking and auto repair. Ben had always liked working with his hands, and he became a skilled cabinetmaker. He was first hired by a local builder, but he left this job after only a few months. His work history included a number of jobs in construction; he had also worked for several manufacturing firms and had lived in several states. When Ben reached the age of 41, he, along with several other employees, was dismissed from his current job. He and his fellow workers were told that the company was downsizing its work force.

When he returned to his home town, he informed his friends that he was tired of "drifting" from one job to another and was ready to settle down. The world of work was in the process of making rapid changes, however, as many industries were downsizing and restructuring job requirements. Even for Ben, who had developed several skills in different working environments, jobs were hard to find.

Ben was not aware of any local counseling assistance and turned to his friends for advice. They could offer little assistance—most were either unemployed themselves or were greatly concerned about keeping their jobs. For the first time in his life, Ben seriously worried about future employment. He began to consider strategies to find a job. He started by jotting down what he knew of the current changing conditions in the workplace:

- Many workers are being retrained because of new technology. Maybe I could be one of them.
- New skills are needed in the workplace.
- More corporations are having their products manufactured in foreign countries.
- I don't want to move again!
- They are referring to workers as labor pools that are contracted for certain jobs.
- A lot of workers are being replaced by robots.
- Job guarantees seem to be a thing of the past.

Ben began to explore the possibility of starting his own business. He had discovered that a number of firms were contracting for product assembly, rather than hiring a labor force to produce them. Ben recalled his work experiences, especially in the garment industry, where it was not unusual for goods to be partially assembled in several countries around the globe. His thoughts turned to products that could be manufactured locally. He realized that he could not compete with cheap labor in foreign countries that could handle certain products like garments or straw hats. He remembered hearing that some straw hats were woven in India, had the hat bands inserted in Thailand, and were shaped for shipping in the Philippines.

After several days of researching the needs of local firms, Ben found no leads. About the time when Ben was ready to give up the idea of becoming an entrepreneur, he made a startling discovery. When shopping, he found that a large department chain contracted for the production of some of their furniture and wooden cabinets. Ben knew he could build cabinets as good as and even better than the ones he saw. But there were many other factors to consider, including costs of raw products, building rentals, costs of production, and financial assistance. But Ben had learned that giving up easily was not very rewarding.

Ben's case illustrates how one individual used his past experiences and skills to become an owner of his own business. He had received little assistance with his career plans as a high school student and even less later when he was unemployed. This is typical of many adults in career transition today (Hoyt & Lester, 1995).

National Survey of Working America

The National Career Development Association (NCDA) sponsored a national survey of working America conducted by the Gallup Organization from September 27, 1993, through October 27, 1993. A national sample of adults ($N = 1046$) was surveyed by telephone. Of this group, 713 were working either full- or part-time. Some of the key findings (percentages were rounded to whole numbers) are in abridged form as follows:

1. When asked about sources of help and counseling they would use, the responses were

   40% would turn to friends or family.
   37% would go to a career counselor.
   17% would go to present employer.
   10% would return to community.
   8% would not know where to go for help.

The results also indicate that 68% of all adults sampled had *not* visited a professional school or college counselor. In contrast, 50% of the 18- to 25-year-olds *had* visited a professional school or college counselor.

2. When asked about career information sources they had used in the past, the responses were

   47% had used newspapers, magazines, and television.
   10% used college, university information centers, public libraries, public job services, or job training centers.
   7% used computerized career information systems (CIDS).
   33% used no job information sources.

When asked what they would do if they were given the opportunity to start over in search of a career, more than 70% of all adults surveyed stated they would try to get more information about career options. When asked how much special job training their employers had provided, approximately two-thirds indicated their employers had provided them with some type of training (Hoyt & Lester, 1995).

Returning to the story of Ben's efforts to find a work role, we discover that his problems were similar to those of many adults in the national survey. For example, he turned to friends for advice about job opportunities, and he was not aware of job information sources. Like 70% of the adults surveyed, Ben wanted more information about career options when he started a new career search. The next section covers some of these issues.

Issues Facing Adults in Career Transition

The first issue is a practical one: the unavailability of career counseling programs for adults. Adults are generally unaware of available jobs and lack directions in making satisfactory career changes. Furthermore, many adults have not developed career exploration skills, such as decision making, and do not know about resources that give job descriptions, requirements, and so forth (Brown & Minor, 1989). In essence, many adults are generally confused about future directions and where to find assistance (Hoyt & Lester, 1995).

Workforce Centers—One-Stop Career Centers

One answer to assisting adults in career transition are state sponsored workforce centers that are also known as one-stop career centers. This trend was initiated by the U.S. Department of Labor, and the Colorado Workforce Centers are a good example. Workforce centers have been designed to consolidate many components of state job services including employment and training services. A major goal of workforce centers is to assist job seekers as well as area employers. In some cases adjoining counties have consolidated into multi-county workforce centers, while some larger populated areas and some isolated areas have one-county workforce centers.

Career development services offered at the workforce centers include the following:

Self-help service available

- Career assessment
- Labor market information
- Information on training programs, education and schools
- Information on scholarships, financial aid and resources

Staff assisted services are available to dislocated workers, displaced homemakers, older workers, economically disadvantaged youth, adults, and other special program receipts. Although most of the services offered in workforce centers could be listed as subheadings under career counseling, they are presented separately to inform prospective clients of a variety of services.

- Career counseling
- Basic education and GED remediation
- English as a second language
- Career management assistance
- Financial assistance for basic education and career programs
- Referrals to supportive services and other community based organizations
- Career planning

- Supportive services to assist with training and program participation, based on need
- Computerized learning lab
- Internships and specialized work experience opportunities
- On-the-job training for permanent jobs with employers
- Workshops on goal setting, motivation, career planning and employability skills
- Job searching in the 21st Century
- Company information and profiles
- National job search sites via Internet
- Assistance with all stages of job search

In many of the workforce centers the following technological help is available:

- Self-help computer stations
- Fax machine
- Copier
- Scanner
- Phone room for professional inquiries
- Typing tutorials
- Computerized self-assessment
- Internet access
- Microsoft Office Program staff assistance available for use of resources

The workforce centers have been structured through a partnership between private industry and public agencies to meet the challenge of the global economy. What is viewed as a revolution in the workforce, education, and social policy has fueled changes that are driving American industry to search for ways to compete. A key element is the development of human resources. As American organizations integrate technology into all work processes, skill and job requirements will dramatically change. Thus, a workforce with technical expertise and the ability to analyze and solve problems, work in teams, and adapt to changes is crucial to the development of the future generation of organizations. Within this framework, the worker in career transition should be a primary target for the career counseling profession.

Organizational Changes Affecting Adults in Career Transitions

Counseling should do more than just supply exploration skills. The important components of career counseling not addressed in original career decisions (such as values, needs, goals, and developed skills) are major targets of career counseling for adults who have lost their jobs as a result of downsizing or changing work requirements. The issue here involves helping individuals reassess the contributing factors that led to the need for new and different skills and why a life learning approach to work in the future may be necessary. Schlossberg (1984, 1986), a major contributor to adult career development, suggests that adults should be treated as individuals who have different reactions to work transitions.

There are many reasons for the continuing retrenchment of organizations, such as strong overseas competition, declining manufacturing, declining energy and commodity prices, free trade policies, and deregulation. The globalization of U.S. companies, making them multinational enterprises, has also contributed to changes in work environments (Barnet & Cavanagh, 1994).

Reich (1991) presents the following example of how products are produced and marketed internationally: "Precision ice hockey equipment was designed in Sweden, financed in Canada, and assembled in Cleveland and Denmark for distribution in North America and Europe, respectively, out of alloys whose molecular structure was researched and patented in Delaware and fabricated in Japan" (p. 112). This example illustrates the mode of operation of multinational corporations, underscoring the fact that many organizations will lose their national identities.

These events have triggered a rethinking of bureaucratic assumptions about long-term employment commitments. As Kanter (1989) put it, "Climbing the career ladder is being replaced by hopping from job to job" (p. 299). The lack of certainty and clear direction for the future work role has generated many personal dilemmas. Adults who find themselves in career transition as a result of downsizing and changing skills need career intervention strategies that focus on establishing a career direction in the ever-changing workplace.

Along with evolving organizational structures, changes will come from the work force per se, that is, the workforce will be more culture and gender diverse. By the year 2000, white males no longer dominated the work force because the number of women, minorities, and immigrants has significantly increased. These new demographics offer challenges to supervisors and fellow workers as well as to the career development specialist. A greater sensitivity to such diverse populations in the workplace will become increasingly important. Evolving organizational settings will reflect the new demographics, and effective team members will have to be able to function well with all groups of people. Career counselors must be able to offer professional leadership to help individuals develop relational skills. (In this section, we will focus on cultural diversity; for more information on women, see Chapter 11.)

Organizations will also become more globally oriented, which translates into a greater potential for working with people from many cultures (Kanter, 1989). A multicultural work force could include natives of Mexico, Japan, Germany, and France, for example, and U.S. team members will have to understand the basic differences in cultural perceptions of work, in processing information, and in responding to tasks and fellow workers (Wigglesworth, 1992). Here are some examples of differences between cultures, as compiled by Harris and Moran (1991).

Nonverbal signals—the "A-OK" gesture

- In America, it means everything is fine.
- In Germany and Brazil, it is interpreted as obscene.

- The Japanese interpret it as money.
- To the French, it means "zilch" or zero.

Eye contact

- In America, poor eye contact translates into a "shifty" character.
- In Japan, children are taught to look at the tie knot or Adam's apple.
- In Latin America, prolonged eye contact can be considered disrespectful.
- Arabs look at each other squarely in the eye.
- The widening of the eyes in China is a danger signal and could indicate suppressed anger.

These few examples are indicative of the vast array of differences among cultures and underscore the increasing need for career counselors and their clients to become more culturally aware. Other differences include time factors, body language, physical distance, and what gives rise to conflict (Wigglesworth, 1992). The acquisition of skills necessary to be an effective worker in a diverse work force is long overdue and should be a high-priority focus for career counselors. For more information on multicultural groups, see Chapter 10. In the next paragraphs, we will discuss the relationships between workers and companies, among workers, and between workers and supervisors.

A survey done in 1993 by the *New York Times,* as reported in Chapter 19, found some interesting reactions from individuals who were in career transition. In what was labeled a National Economic Insecurity Survey, numerous tables were compiled from adults about the current job market and economic climate. The following are selected examples.

When asked whether companies are more or less loyal to their employees than they were ten years ago, 75% of all adults surveyed answered "less loyal." When asked whether workers are more or less loyal to their employers, 64% of all adults surveyed responded "less loyal." When asked whether most working people today cooperate more with one another at the place where they work or whether they compete more with each other, 70% of all adults surveyed answered "compete more." When asked whether they think the mood at many workplaces is more angry or more friendly, 53% of all adults surveyed answered "more angry." These results, providing some perceptions of the current workplace, give a rather dismal picture of its climate. That companies are less loyal to their workers and workers are less loyal to their employers than they were ten years ago could mean that some workers may have difficulty establishing any degree of trust with their employers. Many other negative reactions from employees and employers are possible within such an atmosphere.

The relationships among workers do not look any better from the results of the survey. Workers see their peers as being more competitive and more angry than in the past. These perceptions, whatever their cause, significantly add to insecurity in the workplace and to the potential of increased stress among workers and between workers and supervisors. The adult in career transition may indeed face a hostile work environment.

Finally, we must deal with the variety of expectations individuals have concerning their career choice. Many have enthusiastically entered a career with the expectation of a continuous, challenging, intrinsically rewarding work environment, only to experience something quite different. For these individuals, the realities of working somehow have been misinterpreted. Many see this as a broken promise of what they were led to expect from their careers, and they react as if in a crisis, ultimately seeking changes in their lifestyles. The conflicts between career and expectations are characteristically intense, leading many toward a search for a second career. Their message is quite clear—help us find fulfillment from life and work.

Career and Individual Development

As we consider a more integrated approach to career development, career issues and individual issues must be dealt with jointly (Hansen, 1996). Kram (1985) proposed a developmental model of career issues, displayed in Table 20-1, that reflects (1) *concerns about self*, including comparisons with peers and career role; (2) *concerns about career*, including work involvement and commitment; and (3) *concerns about family*, including family role and work-family conflict. These issues are examples of adult concerns that can serve as reference points for counseling intervention because this model presents multidimensional tasks at successive career stages.

TABLE 20-1	CHARACTERISTIC DEVELOPMENTAL TASKS AT SUCCESSIVE CAREER STAGES		
	Early career	**Middle career**	**Late career**
Concerns about self	*Competence:* Can I be effective in the managerial/professional role? Can I be effective in the role of spouse and/or parent?	*Competence:* How do I compare with my peers, with my subordinates, and with my own standards and expectations?	*Competence:* Can I be effective in a more consultative and less central role, still having influence as the time to leave the organization gets closer?
	Identity: Who am I as a manager/professional? What are my skills and aspirations?	*Identity:* Who am I now that I am no longer a novice? What does it mean to be a "senior" adult?	*Identity:* What will I leave behind of value that will symbolize my contributions during my career? Who am I apart from a manager/professional and how will it feel to be without that role?

TABLE 20-1	CHARACTERISTIC DEVELOPMENTAL TASKS *(continued)*		
	Early career	**Middle career**	**Late career**
Concerns about career	*Commitment:* How involved and committed to the organization do I want to become? Or do I want to seriously explore other options?	*Commitment:* Do I still want to invest as heavily in my career as I did in previous years? What can I commit myself to if the goal of advancement no longer exists?	*Commitment:* What can I commit myself to outside of my career that will provide meaning and a sense of involvement? How can I let go of my involvement in my work role after so many years?
	Advancement: Do I want to advance? Can I advance without compromising important values?	*Advancement:* Will I have the opportunity to advance? How can I feel productive if I am going to advance no further?	*Advancement:* Given that my next move is likely to be out of the organization, how do I feel about my final level of advancement? Am I satisfied with what I have achieved?
	Relationships: How can I establish effective relationships with peers and supervisors? As I advance, how can I prove my competence and worth to others?	*Relationships:* How can I work effectively with peers with whom I am in direct competition? How can I work effectively with subordinates who may surpass me?	*Relationships:* How can I maintain positive relationships with my boss, peers, and subordinates as I get ready to disengage from this setting? Can I continue to mentor and sponsor as my career comes to an end? What will happen to significant work relationships when I leave?
Concerns about family	*Family role definition:* How can I establish a satisfying personal life? What kind of lifestyle do I want to establish?	*Family role definition:* What is my role in the family now that my children are grown?	*Family role definition:* What will my role in the family be when I am no longer involved in a career? How will my significant relationships with spouse and/or children change?
	Work/family conflict: How can I effectively balance work and family commitments? How can I spend time with my family without jeopardizing my career advancement?	*Work/family conflict:* How can I make up for the time away from my family when I was launching my career as a novice?	*Work/family conflict:* Will family and leisure activities suffice, or will I want to begin a new career?

SOURCE: From *Mentoring at Work: Developmental Relationships in Organizational Life* by K. E. Kram. Copyright 1988 by University Press of America. Reprinted by permission of the publisher and the author.

In the early career stage, concerns of self include questions about one's competence at work and one's effectiveness as a spouse or parent. There is striving for identity, and key questions about occupational skills and aspirations are addressed. In this stage, the individual questions his or her commitment to an organization and the possible advancement pathways. The family role in the early career stage includes concern about establishing an appropriate lifestyle and about balancing work with family commitments. Middle career and late career stages contain similar questions that foster the idea of considering all life roles in developmental tasks at successive career stages.

Our level of awareness must increasingly be directed to the multidimensional nature of human and career development. We should not attempt to isolate one from the other in our development of counseling activities for all age groups, including the adult in career transition. As we converge our counseling processes to include all life roles and life's problems, we have a greater assurance that our effectiveness as counselors will be enhanced and—more important—will provide avenues for identifying clients' core problems. In the next section, major themes of human development provide further clues to adult development and subsequent issues facing adults in career transition.

Major Themes in Human Development

Human development research by a number of academic disciplines suggests that it is multidimensional as well as comprehensive in nature and scope (Sigelman, 1999). Career counselors should recognize that an abundance of published material suggests that human development is influenced by a number of factors and dimensions over the life span. In essence, human development is a unique process. We suggest that career counselors view each client as a unique person. In the following paragraphs we discuss some general themes of human development.

Adult life stage models were not used in this chapter because some observers have suggested either that these models have little relevance to practice (Courtenay, 1994) or that research concerning adult career development has reached only tentative conclusions (Herr & Cramer, 1996). We can, however, propose some implications of adult career development from the following general themes of human development, adapted from Sigelman (1999):

1. *We are whole persons throughout the life span.* Physical, cognitive, personal, and social development intermesh throughout the life span, and each individual's development has a distinctive and coherent quality.

2. *Development proceeds in multiple directions.* Individuals experience significant changes in development over their life spans, but these are viewed as gains and losses, rather than by the old notion of progression that consisted of growth and improvement up to adulthood, stability into middle age, and decline in old age. Within this framework of development, for every gain there is a loss. For example, the amount of

time spent on becoming an expert in a field means a loss of opportunity to develop other areas of specialization.

3. *There is both continuity and discontinuity in development.* The point here is that predicting the character of an adult from knowledge of the child is very risky. Continuity can continue from early childhood, but discontinuity can be fostered by events in one's environment, such as child abuse, inferior schools, or parental neglect.

4. *There is much plasticity in human development.* People can be adaptable throughout their life spans. Potentially harmful early experiences need not have a permanent effect on one's development.

5. *Nature and nurture truly interact in development.* There are multiple causal forces in human development; both nature and nurture interact in the change process. One or the other may be more influential in certain aspects of human development, but there are usually ongoing influences from both.

6. *We are all individuals, becoming even more diverse with age.* We do share common experiences with others, but we are indeed individuals and we accumulate our own unique histories of life experiences.

7. *We develop in a cultural and historical context.* We must recognize that human development takes place in different cultures, social classes, and racial and ethnic groups. Cultural variations in development should include contextual influences.

8. *We are active in our own development.* We create our own environment and influence those around us, but all participants are influenced in a reciprocal way.

9. *Development is best viewed as a lifelong process.* The linkages between early and late development are important connections to study. But it is also valuable to view behavior during each phase of life because development is a process. Understanding where we started from and where we are heading leads to an understanding of the processes involved.

10. *Development is best viewed from multiple perspectives.* Many disciplines have contributed to the understanding of human development. In this tradition, we must recognize that multiple theories are often integrated when we explain human development.

Implications of Human Development as Related to Adult Career Development

The intermeshing of physical, cognitive, personal, and social development that gives each period of the life span a distinctive quality should make us more aware of considering the overwhelming possibilities of an individual adult's development.

Perhaps we have been guilty of attempting to oversimplify development into categories that appeared to be more manageable.

The concept of multiple directions of development, with its gains and losses, challenges the older view of development as consisting of continuous growth and improvement into adulthood, stability, and decline. We must recognize that we give up something in almost every step we take toward specialization. One suspects that many adults do not view choices in this manner.

As humans, we have a remarkable capacity to change in response to experience. This translates into providing opportunities for growth even though an individual's past record is dismal.

The match between a person and his or her environment as a contributing factor of human development has overtones of several career development constructs (discussed in Chapters 2 and 3). When there is goodness of fit, positive things begin to happen.

The cultural and historical context in which one develops has enormous implications for counseling adults. This multicultural developmental position recognizes the centrality and primary importance of culture as an internalized subjective process that must be included in counseling programs developed for different ethnic groups.

There has been a greater recognition of individual agency in career development. We do indeed have an active role in our own development. Focusing adults' attention to this position will hopefully lead to more positive assertive action.

Finally, viewing development as a lifelong process reinforces the current importance placed on retraining and lifelong learning.

As we continue to view development from multiple perspectives, we are humbled by the comprehensive nature of human development itself. We can hope that the ongoing research efforts will provide more solid guidelines in the future. In the meantime, we can use what we have as tentative support for program development because the comprehensive nature of this subject will continue to provide more questions that need to be answered.

Basic Coping Skills for Managing Transitions

Brammer and Abrego (1981) developed a model for basic coping skills that assist adults in managing transitions (see Box 20-1). The first set of coping skills relates to perceiving and responding to transitions, such as developing self-control and a style for responding to change. The second set of skills relates to assessing, developing, and using external support systems. By developing a personal support system network, the individual can use friends and professionals in crisis situations. The third skill set is related to assessing, developing, and using an internal support system, such as assessing positive and negative attitudes and personal strengths and activating these strengths when needed. The fourth set involves reducing emotional and physiological distress through relaxation exercises and the verbal expression of feelings associated with distress. The fifth set, which involves

BOX 20-1 Basic Coping Skills for Managing Transitions

1 *Skills in perceiving and responding to transitions*
  1.1 The person mobilizes a personal style of responding to change. He or she
    1.11 Accepts the proposition that problematic situations constitute a normal part of life and that it is possible to cope with most of these situations effectively (perceived control over one's life).
    1.12 Recognizes the importance of describing problematic situations accurately (problem definition).
    1.13 Recognizes the values and limitations of feelings as cues to evaluate a transition (feelings description).
    1.14 Inhibits the tendency either to act impulsively or to do nothing when confronted with a problematic situation (self-control).
  1.2 The person identifies his or her current copying style (style of responding to change).
2 *Skills for assessing, developing, and utilizing external support systems*
  2.1 The person can assess an external support system. He or she can
    2.11 Identify his or her emotional needs during times of transition.
    2.12 Identify people in his or her life who provide for personal needs.
    2.13 Describe a personal support network in terms of physical and emotional proximity.
  2.2 The person can develop a personal network based on data from 2.1 or he or she can
    2.21 Seek sources (groups, organizations, locales) of potential support persons.
    2.22 Apply social skills to cultivate persons to meet identified needs.
  2.3 The person can utilize an established support network. He or she can
    2.31 Develop strategies for spending time with persons considered most helpful
    2.32 Apply skills for utilizing persons in his or her network when a transition is anticipated or arrives.
3 *Skills for assessing, developing, and utilizing internal support systems*
  3.1 The person can assess the nature and strength of positive and negative self-regarding attitudes. He or she can
    3.11 Identify personal strengths.
    3.12 Identify negative self-descriptive statements, as well as the assumptions and contextual cues that arouse such statements.
  3.2 The person can develop positive self-regard attitudes. He or she can
    3.21 Affirm personal strengths.
    3.22 Convert negative self-descriptions into positive descriptive statements when the data and criteria so warrant.

(continued)

BOX
20-1
Basic Coping Skills *(continued)*

   3.3 The person can utilize his or her internal support system in a transition. He or she can

      3.31 Construe life transitions as personal growth opportunities.

      3.32 Identify tendencies to attribute personal deficiencies as causative factors in distressful transitions.

4 *Skills for reducing emotional and physiological distress*

He or she can

   4.1 Practice self-relaxation responses.

   4.2 Apply strategies to control over-stimulation/under-stimulation.

   4.3 Express verbally feelings associated with his or her experience of transition.

5 *Skills for planning and implementing change*

   5.1 The person can analyze discrepancies between existing and desired conditions.

   5.2 The person exercises positive planning for new options. To the best of his or her abilities, the person can

      5.21 Thoroughly canvass a wide range of alternative courses of action.

      5.22 Survey the full range of objectives to be fulfilled and the values implied by the choice.

      5.23 Carefully weigh whatever he or she knows about the cost and risk of negative consequences that could flow from each alternative.

      5.24 Search intensely for information relevant to further evaluation of the alternatives.

      5.25 Utilize feedback to reassess his or her preferred course of action.

      5.26 Reexamine the positive and negative consequences of all known alternatives.

      5.27 Make detailed provisions for implementing or executing the chosen course of action including contingency plans.

   5.3 The person successfully implements his or her plans. He or she can

      5.31 Identify stressful situations related to implementing goals.

      5.32 Identify negative self-statements that interfere with implementing plans.

      5.33 Utilize self-relaxation routines while anticipating the stressful implementation of plans.

      5.34 Utilize self-rewards in goal attainment.

      5.35 Identify additional skills needed to implement goals (for example, anxiety management, training in assertiveness, overcoming shyness).

SOURCE: From "Intervention Strategies for Coping with Transitions," by L. M. Brammer and P. J. Abrego, 1981. *The Counseling Psychologist, 9*, p. 27. Reprinted by permission.

planning and implementing change, promotes planning various courses of action and formulating strategies for implementing them.

One example of applying these skills might be a man who is given the news that his job is to be terminated because of economic conditions. He can use self-control skills to perceive the current situation realistically. By recognizing he has time to make future plans before the termination turns into a financial crisis, he can call on friends for emotional support and for suggestions about how to conduct a job search. He can rely on skills used to develop inner strength to help him evaluate the current job market and make plans for the future.

Brammer and Abrego (1981) suggested that people often feel powerless to respond to change. Coping skills help adults in transition react more rationally when responding to changing conditions over the life span. Coping skills are often best taught in seminars or in small groups.

The Personal Agency Person

Throughout this chapter, references have been made to the worker of the future. Key descriptions have been used or implied, such as self-developing person, one who uses personal agency, or one who can adapt to change. There have been references to the fact that the worker of the future must develop new and different attitudes about work per se and about career development.

The idea of *positive uncertainty,* a term originated and recently discussed by Gelatt (1996), suggests that the future worker will shed obsolete beliefs and narrow views of the past to develop a future sense. Thus, limited thinking will change to prospective visions of what the future may offer. In essence, the uncertainty of the future should not inhibit but instead should challenge the worker to meet changes that will surely come.

The personal agency person has an evolving profile. First, we consider some basic assumptions. The true personal agency person may not exist. The profile of the personal agency person will change and evolve along with changing work environments and requirements. The degree to which a person matches the descriptions of the personal agency person does not guarantee success and satisfaction in the workplace, now or in the future. What we have are some descriptions of what is considered to be the future archetypal organization person (Kleinfield, 1996).

The Personal Agency Person Profile

Examples of basic shifts in thinking

- Does not feel entitled
- Assumes responsibility for the future
- Assumes a lifelong learning responsibility
- Dismisses obsolete beliefs about work

- Does not take any job for granted
- Assumes that personal involvement is key to success
- Is aware of and appreciates cultural differences
- Depends on own initiative
- Views the future with vision and imagination
- Has little fear of change
- Can deal with uncertainty
- Believes creativity is a basic requirement
- Focuses on innovation
- Considers change as both positive and necessary
- Believes good interpersonal relations is an employee's responsibility
- Is completely receptive to new ideas
- Assumes that there are few guarantees for the future
- Assumes that the organization does not owe anyone a career

Mode of action

- Is very functional in basic skills
- Creates effective changes in work assignments
- Cooperates with teams of workers and supervisor
- Strives for relationships to enhance career opportunities
- Strives for a balance between work, leisure, and spiritual needs
- Develops methods to improve effectiveness of job assignment
- Exhibits high levels of resourcefulness and imagination
- Takes advantage of opportunities to develop skills and learn more about job assignments
- Consciously strives to understand different races, ethnicities, and sexual orientations
- Develops overview and knowledge of total work environment and company purpose and policies
- Strives to perform to the best of his or her ability at all times
- Builds relationships with mentors
- Creatively demonstrates how product or products can be improved
- Assumes total responsibility for career development

Many characteristics of the personal agency person are not new qualities in an employee that an organization seeks, but, more important, the basic shifts in attitude and beliefs are key requirements of the future worker. The personal agency person accepts the future for what it is. One's career develops through individual effort, personal initiative, and self-development, with no future assurances from the organization. The mindset of the personal agency person is similar to that of a freelance performer who must sell himself or herself each day. Finally, the personal agency person believes that planning for unknown changes in the future is each person's total responsibility.

Career Counseling Intervention Components for Adults in Career Transition

Career counseling programs for adults in career transition have many elements in common with programs designed for initial career choice. However, there are enough different and distinct factors involved in career transition to merit the development of specific programs for adults considering career change. Major considerations are the individual adult experiences associated with work, leisure, family, and individualized lifestyle. Life's experiences provide both the counselor and the individual with a rich source of information from which to launch a career exploration. Identifying developed skills, interests, work experiences, and reformulated goals are examples of program strategies for the adult in career transition.

A counseling program for adults in career transition is outlined in Table 20-2. This program consists of seven intervention components referred to as *strategies*. Each intervention strategy has suggested technique options and specific tasks. The technique options suggested do not rule out other methods of accomplishing the specific tasks. In many instances, reference will be made to other chapters in this text and other publications for program considerations. Following are brief explanations of each intervention component.

Intervention Component I—Experience Identification

Valuable assets often overlooked in career counseling are work and life experiences. One of the main purposes of this component is to carefully evaluate past experiences in relation to potential use in career selection. Typically, the adult overlooks the value of developed skills or only casually considers them in career exploration. This component emphasizes providing the structure from which counselor and counselee can effectively evaluate an individual's background of experiences and relate them to interests, work requirements, and other variables associated with occupations.

The technique options suggested for this intervention strategy provide the counselor with alternatives to meet individual needs. In most instances, combinations of suggested options can be used. For example, after an individual writes an autobiography, the counselor can follow with an interview or work experience analysis or both. In other instances, only one of the options might be needed. This decision is often based on time availability and the educational level of the client.

TABLE 20-2 INTERVENTION COUNSELING PROGRAM FOR ADULTS IN CAREER TRANSITION

Strategy component	Technique option	Specific tasks
I. Experience identification	1. Interview 2. Autobiography 3. Background information format and guide 4. Work- and leisure-experience analysis	1. Identify and evaluate previous work experience 2. Identify and evaluate life experiences 3. Identify desired work tasks and leisure experiences 4. Assess familial relationships 5. Identify reasons for job change 6. Identify career satisfaction variables 7. Identify factors that contributed to job changes 8. Identify reasons for current interest in career change
II. Interest identification	1. Interest inventories	1. Identify and evaluate occupational interests 2. Identify specific interest patterns 3. Relate interest to past experience 4. Compare interest with identified skills 5. Relate interest to potential occupational requirements 6. Relate interests to avocational needs
III. Skills identification	1. Self-analysis of developed skills 2. Self-estimates of developed skills 3. Standardized measures of developed skills	1. Identify and evaluate developed skills from previous work tasks 2. Identify and evaluate developed skills from leisure learning experiences 3. Identify and evaluate developed skills from formal learning experiences 4. Identify and evaluate developed functional, technical, and adaptive skills
IV. Value and needs clarification	1. Value and needs assessment through standardized inventories 2. Values clarification exercises	1. Clarify values in relation to life and work 2. Determine level and order of needs in relation to life and work 3. Identify satisfaction and dissatisfaction variables associated with work

TABLE 20-2 INTERVENTION COUNSELING PROGRAM *(continued)*

Strategy component	Technique option	Specific tasks
		4. Identify satisfaction and dissatisfaction
		5. Identify expectations of future work and lifestyle
		6. Identify desirable work environments, organizations, and peer affiliates
		7. Realistically assess potential future achievements
		8. Assess potential movement within current work environment
		9. Identify work roles and leisure roles and how they interrelate with lifestyle
		10. Relate values to factors that contribute to obsolescence
		11. Identify personal factors associated with career decision
V. Education/ training planning	1. Published materials 2. Locally compiled information resources 3. Computerized system 4. Internet	1. Identify sources of educational/training information
		2. Identify continuing education programs
		3. Identify admission requirements to educational/training programs
		4. Investigate potential credit for past work experience and previously completed training programs
		5. Evaluate accessibility and feasibility of educational/training programs
		6. Identify and assess financial assistance and other personal assistance programs
		7. Relate identified skills to educational/training programs for further development

(continued)

TABLE 20-2 INTERVENTION COUNSELING PROGRAM *(continued)*

Strategy component	Technique option	Specific tasks
VI. Occupational planning	1. Published printed materials 2. Internet 3. Computer information systems 4. Visit files	1. Identify sources of occupational information 2. Identify and assess occupational opportunities 3. Relate identified skills and work experience to specific occupational requirements 4. Evaluate occupations from a need-fulfilling potential 5. Relate identified goals to occupational choice 6. Relate family needs to occupational benefits 7. Identify educational/training needs for specific occupations
VII. Toward a life learning plan	1. Decision-making exercises 2. Life-planning exercises 3. Making the transition to a Personal Agency Person	1. Learn decision-making techniques 2. Clarify short-term and long-term goals 3. Identify original and reformulated career goals 4. Contrast differences between original and reformulated goals 5. Identify alternative goals 6. Clarify goals in relation to family expectations 7. Develop a flexibility plan for life learning 8. Develop life-planning skills 9. Identify lifestyle preferences 10. Identify attitude and beliefs of the Personal Agency Person

The first technique option is the interview. The primary purpose of the interview is to assist the client in evaluating work and leisure experiences, training, and education in relation to potential occupational choices. The interview should focus on (1) specific work experiences, (2) specific educational/training experiences, (3) specific leisure experiences and preferences, (4) specific likes and dislikes of former jobs, and (5) special recognitions. In general, the interview should provide the basis from which the next step in the counseling program is determined. (See Chapters 5 and 6.)

The format for the autobiography can be either structured or unstructured. In the latter approach, the individual is instructed to write an autobiography without being given any specific guidelines. In the structured approach, the individual may be instructed to follow an outline or answer specific questions or both. The structured approach has obvious advantages for our purposes in that we are attempting to identify and evaluate specific information.

An autobiographical sketch can be used to identify developed skills (Radin, 1983). First, the individual is instructed to describe a significant accomplishment, such as starring in a dramatic production, being a leader in a scout group, or teaching photography. Descriptions of the accomplishment are analyzed to determine the use of functional, adaptive, and technical skills. Each autobiographical sentence is analyzed and later compiled and related to Holland's six modal personal styles. The following sentence is taken from a description of teaching photography and is analyzed for functional, adaptive, and technical skills:

"I started each class by demonstrating the proper use of a number of different cameras."

Functional	Adaptive	Technical
teaching	leadership	knowledge of cameras
communication	articulate	
	orderly	

Skills that are easily identifiable are those that are explicitly stated, whereas other skills are only implied, such as those needed to accomplish the task. In this case, teaching, communication, and camera knowledge are fairly explicit, while being articulate, orderly, and showing leadership are only implied.

The next option, background information, requires that the individual fill out a specified form. The information requested includes demographic data; marital status and family size; a list of jobs held and duties, education, and training completed; armed services experiences; honors and awards; leisure preferences; hobbies; and other related information. A variety of approaches may be used to identify satisfaction and dissatisfaction variables associated with work and other experiences. One technique is to ask the individual to rank-order or to list likes and dislikes of each past job held. Another option is to provide spaces for free-response reactions to work and other experiences.

Following the example of Bolles (1993), a work and leisure experience analysis form was designed (Figures 20-1 and 20-2), on which the individual lists specific work (Part I) and leisure experiences (Part II). In addition, the individual indicates likes and dislikes of the experiences listed. The objective is to identify tasks and experiences that may be considered in future career choices.

FIGURE 20-1   *Work experience analysis form*

Part I

Work experience	General duties	Specific tasks O over number if liked X over number if not liked
Bank Teller	Customer accounts Transactions	(1) Record + deposit receipts (2) Payout Withdrawals X Cash checks X Record transactions X Exchange Money

A review of the tasks for Intervention Component I suggests that the major objective is to identify specific desired work tasks, leisure experiences, family concerns associated with work, lifestyle, and potential reasons for job change. Using this information, the counselor and client should be able to identify a partial list of career satisfaction variables. The tentative conclusions and outcomes of this component will usually provide information for Component III, Skills Identification, but will also be integrated into other components of the program.

Intervention Component II—Interest Identification

Career counseling and interest identification have had a close association in their respective developments. Measured interests have been used primarily in predicting job satisfaction in career counseling programs. In our efforts to assist the adult in career transition, we must also be concerned with interests and their relationship to potential occupational choices. Conceptually, it is thought that interest identification can broaden and stimulate adults' exploratory career options. Adults should be in a relatively good position to identify individual interests, primarily from past experiences. Some are able, however, to identify uninteresting tasks and jobs but are unable to identify positive interests. For these individuals, interest identification is essential.

The suggested technique option for this component consists of interest inventories. Careful consideration should be given to the selection of the inventory; the counselor should assess the counselee's educational level, expectations of the future, reading level, educational and training potentials, cultural background, and

FIGURE
20-2

Leisure experience analysis form

Part II

Leisure experience
PTA Secretary

Specific tasks
O over number if liked
X over number if not liked

①Record Minutes
✗ Call roll
③ Read minutes

sexual orientation, among other factors. A number of inventories are also available for nonreaders. A list of inventories is provided in Chapter 7.

The task for Intervention Component II is to identify interest clusters or patterns as well as specific interest indicators. A major task is to relate identified interests to occupational variables and education/training opportunities in the following components to ensure that all components are well integrated.

Intervention Component III—Skills Identification

In recently developed career counseling programs by Bolles (1993) and Holland (1992) and several career-related computerized systems, skills identification has received special attention. The focus is on identifying skills developed from previous experiences in work, hobbies, social activities, community volunteer work, and other leisure experiences. (See examples of skills in Figures 20-3 and 20-4.) The rationale for this objective is that people, in general, fail to recognize developed skills and also do not know how to relate them to occupational requirements.

Skills-identification techniques have been used by Bolles (1993), Holland (1992), and Burton and Wedemeyer (1991). Bolles suggested that functional/transferable skills can best be identified by using a "quick job-hunting map." Holland provided a method to identify developed skills through self-estimates of ability. These methods along with career-related computerized systems concentrate on self-estimates of developed skills. Traditional standardized measures of skills and aptitudes may also be used.

The first technique option, self-analysis of developed skills, can be accomplished through the work and leisure experience analysis forms used in Intervention Component I. For example, the compiled specific tasks on this form provide sources for identifying developed skills. Following are some examples of this process.

Three steps are necessary to identify skills from the work and leisure analysis form: (1) list specific work tasks; (2) identify functional, adaptive, and technical

FIGURE
20-3

Skills identification form

Skills used in tasks

a. Functional	b. Adaptive	c. Technical
1. Clerical	1. Articulate	1. Accounting
2. Communication	2. Leadership	2. Knowledge of foreign money exchange
3. Editing	3. Diplomatic	
4. Organizational	4. Courteous	

skills for each work task; and (3) relate each functional, adaptive, and technical skill to one or more of Holland's six modal personal styles. For those skills that are difficult to identify with Holland's six modal personal styles, *The Occupations Finder* (Holland, 1987c) will help.

The second technique option, self-estimates of developed skills, can be accomplished by having the individual rate each functional, adaptive, and technical skill as good, average, or poor as illustrated in the previous example. These rankings provide self-estimates of skills within Holland's (1992) modal personal styles and corresponding work environments model.

A more traditional method of evaluating skills is through standardized testing, which is our third technique option. A variety of aptitude tests on the market today provide methods of evaluating skills based on normative data. Several aptitude tests were identified in Chapter 7.

The importance of specific skills identification is to encourage the client to consider skills developed from a variety of experiences as important factors in career exploration. By requiring that the individual identify skills in adaptive, functional, and technical groups, a more precise relationship to occupational requirements is understood, thus promoting a more realistic evaluation for future goals. This intervention strategy stresses the identification of skills from the individual's total lifestyle experiences.

Intervention Component IV—Value and Needs Clarification

The emphasis thus far has been on considering the "whole person" when counseling adults. This strategy correspondingly includes the adult's total lifestyle. Intervention Component IV focuses on the individual adult's values and needs. More specifically, these individualized values and needs are considered in relation to work, leisure, peer affiliates, and family. Each value and need must be considered in relation to the others. For example, work values are only one part of the value system that must be considered in career counseling programs for adults. Individuals

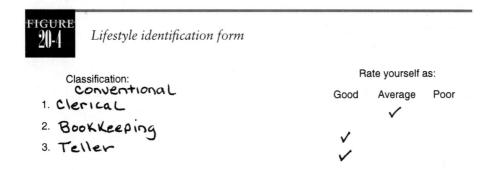

FIGURE 20-1 *Lifestyle identification form*

Classification:
    Conventional

Rate yourself as:

	Good	Average	Poor
1. Clerical		✓	
2. Bookkeeping	✓		
3. Teller	✓		

who are unable to clarify or satisfy their goals and needs concerning family might express dissatisfaction with work-associated tasks when the source of difficulty is actually unrelated to the work environment itself. Hence, the need for the lifestyle identification approach used in this component is established.

The first technique option is assessing values and needs through standardized inventories. Several inventories on the market today can be used for this purpose. Most inventories provide complete instructions for interpretation and counseling use. (See Chapter 7 for available inventories.)

Values clarification exercises are suggested as a second technique option. Values clarification may be accomplished in groups as well as in individual counseling programs. It is most important to select strategies that emphasize skills that assist individuals in identifying and developing their value systems. See the *Life Values Inventory* (Crace & Brown, 1996) for suggestions of value clarification strategies. The lifestyle component is indeed a broad, rather all-encompassing concept of career counseling. In this context, we consider the individual's entire system of values and needs associated with lifestyle. Individually developed values and needs may be thought of as an integrated system that determines satisfaction with life. We may dichotomize value systems for clarification, but eventually we must address the entire system of values. Our goal is to communicate to the adult in career transition that life is indeed multifaceted and that satisfactory solutions cannot be oversimplified. We must consider what we are, where we have been, and that our futures are relatively unpredictable. A change in career could reflect a desire to change lifestyle.

Intervention Component V—Education and Training

Education/training information was ranked as a high-priority interest among adults in career transition (Burton & Wedemeyer, 1991). The major purpose of this intervention is to assist adults in identifying sources of educational/training information and making the most effective use of those sources. As community colleges and four-year institutions offer a greater variety of continuing education programs, the working adult will be in a much better position to improve his or her occupational skills. Exposure to educational/training opportunities should enhance the career decision-making process.

This intervention strategy has four technique options. As with most intervention strategies, and particularly with this one, using all or combinations of the options is recommended. The first option suggests using published materials. One of the most important sources for working adults is locally compiled information resources, suggested as the second technique option. Educational/training programs within reasonable commuting distances provide opportunities for training while maintaining occupational and family obligations.

The third technique option for this intervention component is the computerized career information system. A number of interactive and information-oriented computer-assisted guidance programs are available today (as discussed in Chapter 9). Generally, three types of educational/training information files are available by computer: files containing programs for all states, files containing program information on a regional basis within states, and files of programs available nationally. Individual needs may dictate the need for localized programs.

The Internet, a fourth option, has the potential of providing relevant educational/training information files from local as well as state, national, and international sources. Read Chapter 9 carefully to determine the most appropriate use of the Internet.

The specific tasks for this component encourage a systematic approach to using educational/training information. Exposure to educational training opportunities will no doubt encourage many adults to consider methods of upgrading their skills for higher level job opportunities. Second, many adults will be encouraged to consider educational/training programs to keep from becoming obsolescent. Possible educational credit from past work experiences should also provide the incentive to enter continuing educational/training programs. Finally, we must encourage the fullest development of identified skills through educational/training opportunities delivered in this intervention.

Intervention Component VI—Occupational Planning

Occupational planning and the previously discussed educational/training component have many commonalities. Both focus on providing information to assist the adult in making the most effective use of occupational information. In fact, these two components are so closely related that they are often accessed at the same time (because occupational planning must take into account educational/training requirements). Therefore, many of the published materials combine educational/training requirements with occupational information.

Three of the technique options for this component suggest using published materials, computer-assisted programs, and the Internet. Computer-assisted programs and the Internet are discussed in Chapter 9. Most computer-assisted programs contain national occupational information files, but many provide occupational information on a local or regional basis within states. International occupational information can be located on the Internet. Many state and federal agencies provide labor forecasts and occupational information that should be incorporated into this intervention strategy.

The fourth technique option, visit files, can be an important segment for delivering relevant occupational information. A visit file provides the names of individuals or organizations who agree to visits and interviews by people interested in obtaining firsthand information about certain occupations. This file is usually compiled locally through personal contacts, and in some cases may be available through purchased programs. Many computer-assisted programs that provide localized and regional data contain visit files.

The tasks for this component suggest that occupational information is more than just information about a job. Indeed, occupational information should enable individuals to evaluate the variables that will influence their lifestyles. For example, personal goal satisfaction, family/financial needs, and use of identified skills are just some of the variables to consider when accessing occupational information. Of major importance are the potential need-fulfilling opportunities available in each occupation under consideration.

In 1987, the National Career Development Association (NCDA) commissioned the Gallup Organization to survey a sample of adults about their career planning processes and workplaces. One key finding is that six of ten adults would request more information if they were to begin another career search. Another one out of two adults did not know how to interpret and use career information (Brown & Minor, 1989). These findings suggest that a greater effort should be made to introduce adults to career decision-making techniques, with thorough instruction in how to interpret occupational information (see Chapter 4).

Intervention Component VII—Toward a Life Learning Plan

This component assists in the development of a life learning plan. Decision-making techniques and life-planning exercises provide two methods of developing effective planning. The rationale for life learning is based on a continuing need to develop planning strategies to (1) meet technological changes, (2) stay abreast of the information explosion, (3) upgrade skills, and (4) reduce the chances of becoming obsolete. In addition, and perhaps more important, changing individual needs and reformulated goals also create a demand for effective planning. The techniques and skills developed in this component enhance decision-making techniques for meeting both occupational changes and changing individual needs associated with work, leisure, and lifestyle. Furthermore, these skills not only provide methods for formulating current plans but also provide strategies for continued life learning-planning in the future.

The first technique option, decision-making exercises, helps individuals effectively decide on options related to their futures. As adults are faced with more options for continuing education/training and career choices, learning how to decide becomes a most relevant skill. In addition to the decision-making strategies discussed in Chapter 4, see *Career Decision Making* (Walsh & Osipow, 1988).

The second technique option promotes life-planning strategies. The specific task of establishing alternative plans for the future should be emphasized in this component. Skills identification and personal lifestyle preferences are integrated to provide the basis for alternative plans to meet future goals. Clarifying differences between original goals and reformulated goals is one way to show how changes in an individual's priorities change lifestyle patterns. Effective life-planning strategies help individuals in developing options and making effective decisions.

The third technique option suggests that adults can be greatly assisted by helping them make the transition to personal agency persons. By identifying the attitudes and beliefs of the personal agency person, the counselor introduces rich sources of information that can be used in group as well as in individual counseling sessions. Clients must be reminded that they must take full responsibility for their career development, which can start with their willingness to learn new work and relational skills.

The tasks for this component may suggest to the adult in career transition that the career counseling program has ended. On the contrary, a life learning plan should be viewed as cyclic; individual changes and external conditions may require the individual to recycle through one or more of the counseling strategies. A life learning plan should be viewed as continuous, with intermittent pauses. The important message is that the skills learned through these options will provide effective methods of finding and using resource information, clarifying individual needs, making decisions, and planning for the future.

Summary

1. Ben, a fictitious worker who had been the victim of downsizing, used past experiences and skills to become the owner of a business.

2. The results of a national survey of U.S. workers indicated that adults usually turn to friends for career advice. Among the findings was that many adults need sources of career information and career exploration skill training.

3. Workforce centers–one stop centers are designed to offer career development counseling, educational/training programs, and job placement services.

4. Current issues related to career problems among adults are (a) lack of available career counseling programs, (b) the downsizing of organizations, (c) the globalization of U.S. companies, (d) the multicultural work force, and (e) a potentially hostile workplace.

5. Career and individual development is a multidimensional model that includes concerns about self, family, and career.

6. Major themes in human development suggest that there are multiple directions of development, humans have a remarkable capacity to change in response to experiences, a match between person and environment is

an important factor, the importance of culture as an internalized subjective process must be included in counseling programs, individual agency in development is important, development is a lifelong process, and human development is a comprehensive process.

7. Basic coping skills are identified by sets of skills that assist in managing transitions.

8. Career counseling programs for adults in career transition have many elements in common with programs designed for initial career choice. There are enough different and distinct factors, however, to merit the development of specific programs for adults considering career change. Counseling intervention components that meet specific needs of adults include (a) experience identification, (b) interest identification, (c) skills identification, (d) values and needs clarification, (e) educational/training planning, (f) occupational planning, and (g) a life learning plan.

Supplementary Learning Exercises

1. Develop a list of the ten most dominant needs in your life at the present time. Share these with a colleague and project how these needs may change over your life span. Identify major sources of dissatisfaction and how these factors can cause you to become an unfulfilled individual.

2. What are your suggestions for counseling programs that would meaningfully interpret the realities of working? Obtain your suggestions by interviewing workers and by observing working climates.

3. Develop an outline for writing a work autobiography. Using the outline, write your own work autobiography.

4. Using the experience-identification component strategy, develop a counseling program to accomplish two or more of the specific tasks.

5. Compile a list of your own skills developed through previous work, leisure, and learning experiences. Relate these skills to specific kinds of occupations. Why is skills identification important for adults in career transition?

6. Develop a set of counseling strategies to clarify values and needs associated with expectations of future work and lifestyle. Why is it important for the adult in career transition to clarify values and needs?

7. Review several community college and four-year college catalogs' financial aid information. Compile this information and specify how you would use it in counseling adults in career transition.

8. Identify and list your personal goals and relate these to your career choice. Why is it important for adults to identify personal goals for career exploration?

9. Take any four major themes of human development and develop a list of implications for adults in career transition.

10. Debate the accuracy of occupational projections. Use references to support your position.

For More Information

Barnet, R. J., & Cavanagh, J. (1994). *Global dreams: Imperial corporations and the new world order.* New York: Simon & Schuster.

Gelatt, H. B. (1989). Positive uncertainty: A new decision-making framework for counseling. *Journal of Counseling Psychology, 36* (2), 252–256.

Gelatt, H. B. (1996). Developing a future sense. In R. Feller & G. Walz (Eds.), *Career transitions in turbulent times* (pp. 387–393). Greensboro, NC: ERIC Counseling and Student Services, University of North Carolina.

Hansen, L. S. (1997). *Integrative life planning: Critical tasks for career development and changing life patterns.* San Francisco: Jossey-Bass.

Leibowitz, Z., & Lea, H. B. (Eds.). (1986). *Adult career development, concepts, issues, and practices.* Alexandria, VA: National Career Development Association.

Muchinsky, P. M. (1997). *Psychology applied to work* (5th ed.). Pacific Grove, CA: Brooks/Cole.

New York Times. (1996). *The downsizing of America.* New York: *New York Times.*

Peterson, N., & Gonzalez, R. C. (2000). *The role of work in people's lives: Applied career counseling and vocational psychology.* Pacific Grove, CA: Brooks/Cole–Wadsworth.

Schlossberg, N. K. (1981). A model for analyzing human adaptation to transition. *Counseling Psychologist, 9*(2), 2–18.

Schlossberg, N. K. (1984). *Counseling adults in transition, linking practice with theory.* New York: Springer.

21

Career Development of Adults in Organizations

Chapter Highlights

- *How and why organizations are changing their management style modes*

- *Comparison of old organizational structure models and new evolving models*

- *Why organizations will no longer provide structure for careers*

- *How reengineering the corporation empowers workers*

- *Boundaryless organizations*

- *Corporate universities*

- *Postbureaucratic organizational advantages for multicultural groups*

- *Career development stages in organizations*

- *Theoretical model of vocational maturity in mid-career*

- *Employee assistance programs and outplacement counseling*

- *Retirement counseling*

- *How to evaluate an organization*

AREER COUNSELING PROGRAMS HAVE GROWN OVER THE LAST DECADE TO include a variety of new and different components. However, providing the individual with information about organizations has not been a major counseling effort. The center of attention has been on other occupational choice variables. Yet, experienced career counselors are well aware that career choices are often directed at organizations as well as at specific career fields. In addition, individuals tend to identify with organizations as well as with their occupations.

Despite the need for information about organizations, career guidance professionals have documented vast amounts of materials and programs aimed at helping students evaluate occupations, whereas little attention has been given to helping students evaluate organizations. Moreover, the industrial and management psychology literature suggests that a number of characteristics of organizations are important to consider in the career decision process (Hall, 1990). Thus, the relevant question for the career counselor is, "How can we make the assumption that individuals are making realistic and effective organizational choices?" Underlying this question is the obvious need for programs, procedures, and materials that build a better understanding of the organizations in which we work. The scope of the issues is indeed complex, but the career counseling profession greatly needs such efforts. Along with the growing list of career counseling concerns, organizations must also receive our attention.

In the 1990s, referred to as an age of transition, we experienced significant changes in organizational structure and, as we observed in the previous chapter, numerous operational changes in the work environment. Advances in technology, accompanied by competition from foreign markets, has led to downsizing and restructuring of the organization. Work itself will be different; many new jobs are being created and others will become obsolete. The counseling issues that evolve from vast changes must receive our attention.

In this chapter we introduce factors to consider in evaluating an organization and discuss how these factors can be incorporated into the career counseling process. This information may be used to assist individuals who are choosing an organization and those who are contemplating a career change. Many researchers, including Drucker (1992) and Kanter (1989), predict that the organization of the future will be vastly different. Most authorities seem to agree that major changes have begun to occur in management style and structure of the work environment. Middle management has been drastically reduced, and all workers are expected to learn new skills and develop positive attitudes for work on new and changing projects. The implications of these two changes greatly affect the career development of individuals who work in organizations. More specifically, some organizations will not offer predictable career paths and job security as in the past, and most will require continual retraining for employees to develop skills to meet ever-changing demands. Career development in organizations may indeed require greater initiative, interpersonal skills, and the ability to adapt to changing and different work environments.

We begin with a discussion of changing organizations and new concepts in career development. This discussion is followed by a review of changing organizational patterns, including reengineering the corporation and boundaryless organizations. Third, we discuss how postbureaucratic organizations may help multicultural groups. Fourth, the career development evolution in organizations is covered. The fifth part covers a variety of counseling programs in organizations. Finally, we include suggestions for evaluating organizations.

Changing Organizations and New Concepts in Career Development

In the 1970s and 1980s, career development in organizations was related to upward mobility with predictable promotions and job descriptions. An employee aspired to reach the top of the pyramid in an orderly progression of steps. However, numerous forecasts predict the replacement of the pyramidal organizational structure with a "flat" model, in which workers move laterally and use their skills for different projects. In this environment, workers are expected to learn new skills and adapt to the requirements of working with a team. Workers rotate to different projects and are required to initiate objectives that meet goals through innovation and learning. Management coordinates projects and participates directly in achieving these objectives. There appears to be a partnership between workers and managers and between workers and workers. Greater cooperation—sharing skills and mentoring—is encouraged. In sum, structural changes are already under way, accompanied by closer relationships between employees and employers and the reshaping of careers.

Tomasko (1987), and more recently Aamodt (1999), suggested that organizations' structure will have the following components: (1) a lean headquarters (limited staff); (2) networks, not conglomerates (workers can be rotated); (3) vertical disintegration and decentralization (no superstructures); (4) staff services that can be sold to others (once an efficient staff has been assembled they can be marketed to other users); (5) expert systems rather than experts (development of computer-based expert systems); and (6) greater human resource planning (switch from personnel administration).

The old models of organizational structure are compared with the new evolving models in Table 21-1. Included among the changes for workers are broader roles and more demanding skill requirements. The previous models had numerous job classifications that were narrowly focused. Currently, the term *multiskilling* is used to reflect the notion that many skills are to be learned in a lifelong learning program that may involve formal training as well as on-the-job training and job rotation. As discussed in the previous chapter, organizational training programs cover a variety of skills, including the basic skills of reading, writing, and computation; interpersonal skills; problem-solving skills; and leadership skills.

A smaller core of full-time employees is supplemented with part-time, temporary workers or contract workers. The work environment is highly automated, and workers who have learned several skills are used selectively. When necessary, short training programs for the core workers are used to improve quality practices.

The overall strategy of the evolving organizational model is lowering costs of operations while improving product quality. Organizations have increased the

TABLE 21-1	CHANGING ORGANIZATIONAL PATTERNS IN U.S. INDUSTRY	
	Old Model Mass production, 1950s and 1960s	**New Model** Flexible decentralization, 1980s and beyond

Overall strategy

▪ Low cost through vertical integration, mass production, scale economies, long production runs. ▪ Centralized corporate planning; rigid managerial hierarchies. ▪ International sales primarily through exporting and direct investment.	▪ Low cost with no sacrifice of quality, coupled with substantial flexibility, greater reliance on purchased components and services. ▪ Decentralization of decision making; flatter hierarchies. ▪ Multimode international operations, including nonequity strategic alliances.

Product design and development

▪ Internal and hierarchical; in the extreme, a linear pipeline from central corporate research laboratory to development to manufacturing engineering. ▪ Breakthrough innovation the ideal goal.	▪ Decentralized, with carefully managed division of responsibility among R&D and engineering groups; simultaneous product and process development where possible; greater reliance on suppliers and contract engineering firms. ▪ Incremental innovative and continuous improvement valued.

Production

▪ Fixed or hard automation. ▪ Cost control focuses on direct labor. ▪ Outside purchase based on arm's-length, price-based competition; many suppliers. ▪ Off-line or end-of-line quality control. ▪ Fragmentation of individual tasks, each specified in detail; many job classifications. ▪ Shopfloor authority vested in first-line supervisors; sharp separation between labor and management.	▪ Flexible automation. ▪ With directs costs low, reduction of indirect cost becomes critical. ▪ Outside purchasing based on price, quality, delivery, technology; fewer suppliers. ▪ Real-time, on-line quality control. ▪ Selective use of work groups; multiskilling, job rotation; few job classifications. ▪ Delegation of shopfloor responsibility and authority to individuals and groups; blurring of boundaries between labor and management encouraged.

purchase of quality components and services. For example, if a component can be produced better and cheaper elsewhere, the organization will contract for this component with another organization, which could be located in a foreign country.

We currently have many multinational organizations that produce some or all their products in foreign countries such as Mexico, India, Thailand, South

TABLE 21-1	CHANGING ORGANIZATIONAL PATTERNS *(continued)*

Old Model Mass production, 1950s and 1960s	New Model Flexible decentralization, 1980s and beyond

Hiring and human relations practices

▪ Workforce mostly full-time, semiskilled. ▪ Minimal qualifications acceptable. ▪ Layoff and turnover a primary source of flexibility; workers, in the extreme, viewed as a variable cost.	▪ Smaller core of full-time employees, supplemented with contingent (part-time, temporary, and contract) workers, who can be easily brought in or let go, as a major source of flexibility. ▪ Careful screening of prospective employees for basic and social skills, and trainability ▪ Core workforce as an investment; management attention to quality-of-working life as a means of reducing turnover.

Job ladders

▪ Internal labor market; advancement through the ranks via seniority and informal on-the-job training.	▪ Limited internal labor market; entry or advancement may depend on credentials earned outside the workplace.

Training

▪ Minimal for production workers, except for informal on-the-job training. ▪ Specialized training for craft and technical workers.	▪ Short training sessions as needed for core workforce, sometimes motivational, sometimes intended to improve quality control practices or smooth the way for new technology. ▪ Broader skills sought for all workers.

SOURCE: Office of Technology Assessment, U.S. Congress, 1990. *Worker Training: Competing in the New International Economy.* Washington, DC: Government Printing Office.

Korea, and many others. In the global web of organizations described in the previous chapter, products become international composites. Reich (1991) clearly illustrates this point:

> When an American buys a Pontiac Le Mans from General Motors, for example, he or she engages unwittingly in an international transaction. Of the $20,000 paid to GM, about $6,000 goes to South Korea for routine labor and assembly operations, $3,500 to Japan for advanced components (engines, transaxles, and electronics), $1,500 to West Germany for styling and design engineering, $800 to Taiwan, Singapore, and Japan for small components, $500 to Britain for advertising and marketing services,

and about \$100 to Ireland and Barbados for data processing. The rest—less than \$8,000—goes to strategists in Detroit, lawyers and bankers in New York, lobbyists in Washington, insurance and health-care workers all over the country, and General Motors shareholders—most of whom live in the United States, but an increasing number of whom are foreign nationals. (p. 113)

Organizations have also decentralized to speed up the process of taking action on relevant issues, such as making transactions with different entities in the manufacture of a Pontiac Le Mans. The emphasis in the evolving models is on simultaneous product and process development to get new products on line. There is a greater reliance on suppliers and contract firms, which has drastically changed working environments in organizations and the skills required of workers.

The implications for career development in restructured organizations are quite significant. Kanter (1989)and Muchinsky (1997), among others, have suggested that organizations will no longer provide highly structured guidelines for careers; the individual must be more assertive in developing his or her destiny. Self-reliance and the ability to adapt to new and different work circumstances are key factors in career development. The new workplace will require greater flexibility from employees and the ability to do several jobs; that is, in some cases, to be more of a generalist than a specialist. Competency in new skills—and, more important, the ability to anticipate future skills—will make individuals more marketable and secure. Although technical competence is extremely important, people skills and the ability to create synergy within a team will also have high priority.

Reengineering the Corporation

The standard pyramidal organizational structure has been replaced recently by what was earlier referred to as "flat models." New organizational structures are currently being developed from evolving operational changes to effectively meet the demands of doing business in a world that is also experiencing rapid and significant changes. There seems to be agreement that the massive bureaucracies of yesterday's organization were not structured to keep up with the fast pace of competitiveness U.S. corporations are facing today.

In bureaucratic organizations, labor was fragmented into specialized work. In reengineered corporations, work is more integrated and has shifted to teams of employees. Instead of one worker performing a particular task, now teams of workers as generalists complete the total process—assembling an automobile, for example.

The following illustration is an example of what influenced leaders to rethink standard organizational procedures: One company discovered that it took seven days to process an order; several steps in the process passed through layers of bureaucracy. It was quickly discovered that the person who took the order could "walk" it through this process in just a few hours, thus delivering the product to the customer in one day instead of seven. In developing organizations today, the renewed interest in serving the customer has caused changes in standard practices. According to Hammer and Champy (1993), the following "three

C's" are the driving force behind the changing organizations: *customers, competition,* and *change.* Today's customers expect products to meet their individual needs and are no longer satisfied with what the seller may have mass-produced to be only "good enough." High-quality goods are what today's more sophisticated consumer wants. *Price, selection,* and *service* are three key words used to describe customer satisfaction. Reengineering is about "starting over" in organizational design. It is basically a search for new models of work and new approaches to process structure (Hammer & Champy, 1993). The old models of bureaucratic organizations must be rejected along with the assumptions of the past. Focusing on labor, reengineering casts out hierarchical controls and divisions of labor. Focusing on process structures, such as research and development of new products and accounting, reengineering stresses creative use of information technology. Following are two examples that illustrate process structures.

A large U.S. camera manufacturing company discovered that its major rival in Japan had produced a 35mm single-use camera for which the U.S. company had no competitive offering. Traditionally, the product design process would take 70 weeks to produce a rival camera. Because this time lapse would give its competitor a huge advantage, the U.S. corporation decided to reengineer its product-development process. In the old model of development, some groups waited for earlier steps to be completed before their work began (referred to as "fragmented work").

In another design process, parts were designed simultaneously and then integrated. The major problem with this process was that all subsystems did not mesh, and the newly designed product could be significantly delayed. In this division of labor, the groups were not adequately communicating with each other.

To solve the problem, the organization developed a computer-integrated product design database. The database collects each engineer's work and combines it daily for an overall design review by the contributing engineers. Each group or individual can resolve problems immediately, instead of facing weeks or months of delay. The organization was successful in getting out its rival camera in 38 weeks.

Another example of reengineering is in the procurement process. In a large automobile manufacturing plant, the receiving clerk accepted deliveries of products without prior knowledge of an order for them. He had to assume they had been ordered, and he would let the accounts payable office handle any errors. Evidently, there were a large number of errors, for the accounts payable department had 500 employees.

The organization reengineered the procurement process that included the accounts payable function. Eventually, the procurement process produced three documents: the purchase order, the receiving document, and the invoice. Now the receiving clerk matches the three and is empowered to order payment. The organization currently has 125 people working in the vendor payment process (Hammer & Champy, 1993).

These two examples introduce changes that organizations are undertaking to successfully compete in the global marketplace. Even more changes are expected in the future. How many individuals will lose their jobs is unknown at this time. A better understanding of current organizational changes should assist counselors in developing a clearer perspective of this revolutionary process, which is expected to continue.

The Boundaryless Organization

To break the chains of organizational structure, Ashkenas, Ulrich, Jick, and Kerr (1995) have proposed yet another restructuring philosophy—a boundaryless organization. These corporate leaders have suggested methods of breaking through slow-moving bureaucracies to mobilize multiple constituencies for change. Identifying priorities for change includes methods for breaking through four boundaries that block success: *vertical, horizontal, external,* and *geographic.* The questionnaire on the next two pages was developed to determine how far each organization has progressed in breaking through the four boundaries, and the statements on the questionnaire also describe the behavior in boundaryless organizations. The 16 statements define general philosophical operational procedures in each boundary, and each boundary is evaluated by speed, flexibility, integration, and innovation.

The *vertical boundary* in boundaryless organizations has less to do with who has authority and rank and more to do with processing ideas and innovations. Most decisions are made "on the spot" at the workplace, and members operate more informally than in the lockstep methods of bureaucratic organizations. *Horizontal boundaries* refer to boundaries between functions found within organizations. For example, engineering, marketing, and accounting were functions that maximized their own goals, sometimes to the exclusion of organizational goals. In contrast to previous organizational structures, resources and innovative ideas move quickly across functions for more effective product lines. In the new scheme, products reach markets much more quickly.

The removal of *external boundaries* will hopefully lead to more effective communication with customers, suppliers, and other firms. Suppliers and customers are seen as strategic helpers to improve or develop new products.

Geographic boundaries have been disappearing quickly as the need grows for globally integrated products and services. Shared experiences across country lines and respect for local differences as sources of innovation have erased many of the roadblocks.

In sum, the boundaryless organization provides for significant changes in work procedures and work environments. Supervisors and managers become coaches rather than authority figures to whom workers must pledge their loyalty. The worker is given empowerment to make decisions and offer innovations directly to key people in the vertical structure. This empowerment was unheard of in the old organizational structure.

The process of advancement can come faster in the boundaryless organization, as more workers will have the opportunity to be innovative—by suggesting new product lines or new and different procedures in handling products, for example. There appears to be more freedom of expression and more opportunities to establish relationships with other personnel, customers, and suppliers.

A career counselor can use several methods to inform clients about the new organizational climate and the new skills required to function in this ever-changing workplace. The career counselor can provide a good reference, supply a videotape, organize a visit, have workers or managers from nearby organizations give presentations, or

Instructions: The following 16 statements describe the behavior of boundaryless organizations. Assess the extent to which each statement characterizes your current organization, circling a number from 1 (not true at all) to 5 (very true).

	Speed	Flexibility	Integration	Innovation	Total Score
Vertical boundary	Most decisions are made on the spot by those closest to the work, and they are acted on in hours rather than weeks. 1 2 3 4 5	Managers at all levels routinely take on front-line responsibilities as well as broad strategic assignments. 1 2 3 4 5	Key problems are tack-led by multilevel teams whose members operate with little regard to formal rank in the organizaton. 1 2 3 4 5	New ideas are screened and decided on without fancy overheads and multiple rounds of approvals. 1 2 3 4 5	
Horizontal boundary	New products or services are getting to market at an increas-ingly fast pace. 1 2 3 4 5	Resources quickly, fre-quently, and effortlessly shift between centers of expertise and operating units. 1 2 3 4 5	Routine work gets done through end-to-end process teams; other work is handled by proj-ect teams drawn from shared centers of experience. 1 2 3 4 5	Ad hoc teams represent-ing various stakeholders spontaneously form to explore new ideas. 1 2 3 4 5	

(continued)

QUESTIONNAIRE 1

STEPPING UP TO THE LINE *(continued)*

	Speed	Flexibility	Integration	Innovation	Total Score
External boundary	Customer requests, complaints, and needs are anticipated and responded to in real time. 1 2 3 4 5	Strategic resources and key managers are often "on loan" to customers and suppliers. 1 2 3 4 5	Supplier and customer reps are key players in teams tackling strategic initiatives. 1 2 3 4 5	Suppliers and customers are regular and prolific contributors of new product and process ideas 1 2 3 4 5	
Geographic boundary	Best practices are disseminated and leveraged quickly across country operations. 1 2 3 4 5	Business leaders rotate regularly between country operations. 1 2 3 4 5	There are standard product platforms, common practices, and shared centers of experience across countries 1 2 3 4 5	New product ideas are evaluated for viability beyond the country where they emerged. 1 2 3 4 5	
TOTAL SCORE					

SOURCE: From *The Boundaryless Organization: Breaking the Chains of Organizational Structure*, by R. Ashkenas, D. Ulrich, T. Jick, and S. Kerr, pp. 28–29. Copyright © 1995 by Jossey-Bass, Inc. Reprinted by permission of Jossey-Bass, Inc., a subsidiary of John Wiley & Sons, Inc.

introduce these topics in individual and group counseling. The wise career counselor may use a combination of two or more of these suggestions to accomplish this task effectively.

As Meister (1994) points out, however, "The skills and training required of both frontline workers and managers has changed significantly in the past two decades, and *will continue to change in the next*" [italics added for emphasis] (p. vii). What we clearly have are emerging rules, regulations, and procedures that have not been clearly defined in the new, forming organizational structures. We *do know* that lower-level employees are required to take much more responsibility and cooperate more closely. They must somehow learn to better understand how their jobs relate to the organizational mission. Employees will not repeat the same task over and over but will perform varied roles, so they must develop a broader set of skills.

Currently, there are at least 30 known corporate universities that provide training for their employees (Meister, 1994), as shown in the following list. Be aware, however, that changes in corporate training programs are greatly influenced by economic conditions. Counselors can alert clients to changes in corporations caused by mergers, downsizing, and re-locations. Educational training programs available in corporations should be a part of researching occupational information in the career counseling process.

Corporate Universities

Amdahl University
Amdahl Corporation
1250 East Arques Avenue
Sunnyvale, California 94088

American Express Quality University[SM]
American Express Travel Related
    Services Division
20022 North 31st Avenue
Phoenix, Arizona 85027

Apple University
Apple Computer, Inc.
20525 Mariani Avenue
Cupertino, California 95014

**Arthur Andersen Center for
    Professional Development**
Arthur Andersen & Co. SC
1405 North Fifth Avenue
St. Charles, Illinois 60174-1264

Banc One College
Banc One Corporation
100 Broad Street
Columbus, Ohio 43215

**Bristol-Myers Squibb Pharmaceutical
    College**
Bristol-Myers Squibb Company
P.O. Box 4000
Princeton, New Jersey 08543

CMDS Team University
Computer Management and
    Development Services
P.O. Box 1184
Harrisonburg, Virginia 22801

**Corning Education and
    Training Center**
Corning Incorporated
Corning, New York 14831

Dana Customer Training Center
Dana Corporation
8000 Yankee Road
Ottawa Lake, Michigan 49267

Disney University
The Walt Disney Company
P.O. Box 10,000
Lake Buena Vista, Florida 32830-1000

Federal Express Leadership Institute
Federal Express Corporation
3035 Directors Row
Memphis, Tennessee 38131

Fidelity Investments Retail Training
Services
Fidelity Investments
82 Devonshire Street
Boston, Massachusetts 02109

First of America Bank Corporation
Quality Service University
First of America Bank Corporation
108 East Michigan Avenue
Kalamazoo, Michigan 49007

Ford Heavy Truck University
Ford Motor Company
100 Renaissance Center
Detroit, Michigan 48243

General Electric Management
Development Institute
General Electric
Old Albany Post Road
Ossining, New York 10562

Hamburger University
McDonald's Corporation
Ronald Lane
Oak Brook, Illinois 60521

Hart Schaffner & Marx University
Hartmarx Corporation
101 North Wacker Drive
Chicago, Illinois 60606

Iams University
The Iams Company
7250 Poe Avenue
Dayton, Ohio 45414

Skill Dynamics, an IBM Company
IBM
500 Columbus Avenue
Thornwood, New York 10594

Intel University
Intel Corporation
2565 Walsh Avenue
Santa Clara, California 95051

KPMG Peat Marwick
Quality Institute
KPMG Peat Marwick
Three Chestnut Ridge Road
Montvale, New Jersey 07645-0435

MBNA Customer College
(MBNA America)
MBNA America Bank N.A.
400 Christiana Road
Newark, Delaware 19713

Motorola University
Motorola Inc.
1303 East Algonquin Road
Schaumburg, Illinois 60196

Saturn Training Center
Saturn Corporation
100 Saturn Parkway
Spring Hill, Tennessee 37174

Southern Company College
The Southern Company
64 Perimeter Center East
Atlanta, Georgia 30346

Sprint University of Excellence^{SM}
Sprint Corporation
2330 Shawnee Mission Parkway
Westwood, Kansas 66205

Sun U
Sun Microsystems
2550 Garcia Avenue
Mountain View, California 94043

Target Stores University
Target Stores
(Division of Dayton-Hudson Stores)
33 South 6th Street
Minneapolis, Minnesota 55402

Walton Institute
Wal-Mart Stores, Inc.
702 Southwest 8th Street
Bentonville, Arkansas 72716-8074

Xerox Document University
Xerox Corporation
P.O. Box 2000
Leesburg, Virginia 22075

Will Postbureaucratic Organizations Have Advantages for Multicultural Groups?

According to Fernandez (1999) more members of organizations will have opportunities to advance and be recognized, including minorities, in postbureaucratic organizations. He views the bureaucratic organization as an intensely political organization that has promoted informal rules and relationships through political maneuvering. Furthermore, the bureaucratic organization is inflexible and promotes homogeneity; that is, everyone is treated as if they were the same. Differences in ambitions, needs, lifestyle, and worldview are ignored. Simply put, Fernandez suggests that the bureaucratic organizations' mode of operation constitutes unfairness and creates inequities.

Within the new and different organizational structure that has been discussed in the preceding paragraphs, individuals become more empowered to make decisions. There are fewer layers of management and fewer status distinctions. Communication will be more direct and more workers will be recognized for their unique contributions. Workers will also be given the opportunity to rotate jobs and satellite offices will shuffle staff to accomplish goals. Diverse work teams should develop trust, respect, and mutual accountability. In such a work environment, team accomplishment is rewarded. The individual worker is valued for what he or she contributes to the team's performance regardless of race, color, creed, gender, or sexual orientation.

In an environment where there are diverse groups, each person should reflect on his or her own culture, respect other cultures, develop relationships with people of diverse backgrounds, learn to know others by interacting with them, learn to communicate effectively, become flexible, learn how to adapt, and, finally, adjust to the behaviors of others. Fernandez (1999) strongly suggests that postbureaucratic organizations may provide the environment in which individuals from different cultures can learn to work effectively together.

Evolution of Career Development in Organizations

Just as each developmental stage of career and human development is accompanied by a set of tasks necessary for completing the transition from one stage to another (see Chapters 2 and 3), stages of career development in organizations consist of tasks and transitions. Stages of development in organizations may be referred to as "employee socialization"; new employees are transformed from outsiders to participating, effective corporate members.

Feldman (1988) proposed a three-stage employee socialization process: *getting in* (the individual presents a realistic picture of self to the organization), *breaking in* (the individual is accepted by peer affiliates and supervisor), and *settling in* (the individual resolves conflicts between work life and home life and within the work environment).

Kram (1988) suggested the following four stages, based on individuals' personal needs.

Stage	Needs
Establishment	Support and direction
Advancement	Coaching, exposure, and role models
Maintenance	Making a contribution, sharing with others, serving as a mentor
Withdrawal	Letting go of work identity

These models form a frame of reference from which steps in career development can be observed. As individuals progress through stages, they learn new skills, are exposed to previously unknown jobs, become more self-aware, and find more opportunity for self-expression. Within this process, there is an ongoing search for job satisfaction, future career goals, and a direction for lifestyle preferences. Each developmental stage has unique and overlapping needs.

The stages in career development in organizations have been identified as entry, early, mid-career, and late career (Hall, 1990). Some researchers have focused on tasks needed to accomplish each stage relative to individuals' socio-emotional and psychological needs. Although these stages were developed during the old model of organizational structure, they still have relevance for individuals who are entering the evolving organizations. For example, individuals expect that they will identify with the new work force, workplace, and assignment of organizations. During the early career stage, workers become oriented to the organization and begin to acquire new skills. In mid-career, individuals are finding that they must balance life roles and find stabilization in their work roles. In late career, the individual maintains status in the organization but is also preparing to "let go" of responsibilities.

Entry Stage

Organizations and the counseling profession have paid little attention to how and why people choose organizations. Although individual career choice variables have occupied many researchers in the counseling profession, organizations have been more interested in selection variables to meet personnel needs. Yet both groups have researched the importance of matching individual traits to appropriate work environments. Meanwhile, the individual has little in the way of direction for organizational choice and less in the way of meaningful literature to review.

Work environments researched by Holland (1992) and Dawis (1996), among others, provide individuals with direction in matching their personal styles with occupational environments. Although the attraction of different occupational environments is indeed helpful in career decision making, the task of finding the appropriate work environment has not been fully delineated by organizations or career information materials.

We can only speculate that organizational choice is greatly influenced by an individual's expectations of what the organization is about and what it has to offer. Kotter (1984) compiled the following list of such expectations:

1. A sense of meaning or purpose in the job
2. Personal development opportunities
3. Amount of interesting work
4. The challenge in work
5. Empowered responsibility in the job
6. Recognition and approval for good work
7. The status and prestige in the job
8. The friendliness of people; the congeniality of the work group
9. Salary
10. The amount of structure in the environment
11. The amount of security in the job
12. Advancement opportunities
13. The amount and frequency of feedback and evaluation (p. 501)

These examples of expectations are primarily what make an organization attractive to an individual. The individual's effort in determining the likelihood of a match between an organizational climate and self is a very relevant factor in the selection process. However, final selection is usually based not only on organizational attractiveness but also on the individual's effort to join the organization (Kotter, 1984). Clearly, the career counseling profession needs to place more emphasis on guiding individuals in how to choose an organization. Some suggestions are given later in this chapter.

Early Career Stage

Early career experiences provide individuals with opportunities to establish themselves in organizations. For the beginning worker, it is an exciting time of entering the work force. For those who have been in the work force for some time, the content of their experiences may differ from those of the novice, but the developmental process will be very similar.

During early career, individuals demonstrate their ability to function effectively in organizations. The novice will be naive about the complexities of the work environment and will expend considerable effort in learning how to function within the organizational milieu. Employees who have worked in other organizations will concentrate more on learning the structure of the organization. Some individuals in both groups will move through early career in a few months, whereas others will take considerably longer; some may never become fully established.

The major tasks of early career, compiled by Campbell and Heffernan (1983), are as follows:

1. Become oriented to the organization.
    a. Learn and adhere to regulations and policies.
    b. Learn and display good work habits and attitudes.
    c. Develop harmonious relationships with others in the work environment.
    d. Integrate personal values with organizational values.
2. Learn position responsibilities and demonstrate satisfactory performance.
    a. Acquire new skills as tasks or position change.
    b. Take part in on-the-job training as appropriate.
3. Explore career plans in terms of personal goals and advancement opportunities.
    a. Evaluate current choice of occupation.
    b. Evaluate advancement opportunities.
    c. Develop a plan for advancement or position change.
    d. Consider alternatives in other occupations.
4. Implement plan for advancement or position change.

Although the pathway to a successful early career has pitfalls and stumbling blocks, there is a relatively well-defined direction. For example, building harmonious relationships in the work environment, becoming oriented to organizational rules and regulations, and demonstrating satisfactory performance are common concrete tasks of early career. The individual's personal reaction to advancement opportunities and acceptance of the values associated with organizational goals and peer affiliates are less tangible. Objective indexes (salary, merit pay, regulations, policies, and so on) and subjective indexes (meeting expectations, goal attainment, match between personal needs and organizational needs) are evaluative criteria the individual can use to determine future direction in the organization or change to another work environment.

In the following counseling session, Shanika, who has been with an organization for ten months, reflected a need to withdraw and find another work environment.

COUNSELOR: Yes, we do have some information about the organization you asked about. But first I would like to know about the one you are leaving.

SHANIKA: As you know, it's a well-known organization, and I was excited about the opportunity of working there. But I don't seem to fit in.

COUNSELOR: Could you be more specific?

SHANIKA: Well, the job assignment was not what I expected. The recruiter told me I would have a lot of responsibilities and interact with people at high levels, but in actuality there was little of either.

COUNSELOR: So it really wasn't the kind of job you expected?

SHANIKA: No, I was put off in a side office, and no one seemed to pay much attention to me. I did have a few assignments that seemed more like busywork than anything else.

COUNSELOR: Could this have been a part of the training program?

SHANIKA: Well, partly, but my supervisor hardly ever came around, and when he did, he seemed preoccupied.

In this case, reality shock and unused potential, as described by Hall (1990), were frustrating experiences for Shanika. She had high expectations from what she was told about the job and hoped to be challenged, but she experienced far less. There also appeared to be a communication gap between Shanika and her supervisor.

Wanous (1980) suggested that reality shock and lack of appraisal and appropriate feedback while in early career are major causes of withdrawal from an organization. In such cases, the career counselor must focus on the individual's perception of these two conditions and his or her level of sophistication in appraising them. Some individuals in early career will have unrealistically high expectations, whereas others may indeed find their jobs to be less than challenging and experience poor feedback from their supervisors.

Work environments in organizations also provide a variety of learning experiences that are relevant to career development. For example, exposure to unknown jobs could begin career direction for some members of an organization. In other cases, the individual's work experiences provide a meaningful sense of direction in career development. Developing harmonious relationships, for example, means learning effective communication skills, interpersonal relationships, and general modes of behavior that are easily transferable to other work environments.

Mid-Career

Mid-career has been identified as the middle phase of an individual's work life, with its own set of tasks and social-emotional needs (Hall, 1986). In terms of Super's vocational developmental stages, mid-career may be thought of as the beginning of the maintenance stage, which is characterized by a continual adjustment process to improve working position and situation. In Tiedeman's model of implementation and adjustment, mid-career is characterized by greater self-understanding and identification within the total system of a career field. Feldman (1988) labeled the mid-career experience as "settling in," characterized by resolution of conflicts and conflicting demands within the organization and in personal life. Mid-career is not necessarily age-related; individuals who make career changes may experience several mid-career stages.

The transitional process from early to mid-career has residual effects, as individuals establish themselves in an organization. In early career, the major course of change is the socialization process, but in mid-career, changes are from diversified sources, such as new and different technology, product demand, and changes in the labor market. Developing a perspective of positive growth orientation in organizations and encouraging individuals to adapt to changes is a healthy attitude to promote. Also, finding a meaningful area of contribution is part of the process of establishing an organizational identity. Individuals must distinguish between real barriers (no growth, slow growth, and organizational decline) and perceived barriers (role confusion, poor career identity, nebulous perceptions of career success and direction) that affect their abilities to reach personal goals.

The following dialogue demonstrates some sources of organizational and individual plateaus:

COUNSELOR: Tell me how you arrived at the decision to change jobs.

YING: Well, you know I've been with the company for twelve years, but I don't have the same enthusiasm for the job. I just can't put my finger on it.

COUNSELOR: Is the company doing well financially?

YING: That's a part of it; no promotion to speak of now.

COUNSELOR: Is this a company policy?

YING: No. John, a friend of mine, got one the other day. He's a lucky guy. He seems to always be in the right place at the right time.

COUNSELOR: Did you say that John was in your division?

YING: Yeah, he's always got something going. I don't understand how he does it. He went to this training program and six weeks later there he goes—up the ladder!

COUNSELOR: Tell me more about the training program.

YING: The company sponsored it. I could have gone, but I don't believe I like that kind of extra work. Besides, it would have interfered with the city golf tournament.

It appears from this conversation that Ying is not willing to be more assertive in his career development. The source of his plateau appears to be primarily a lack of a strong desire to advance. Perhaps Ying felt that he only needed to put in time for the next advancement. In mid-career, individuals may have difficulty balancing commitment to outside activities with intense competitiveness for promotions.

Mercedes, also in mid-career, tells how she discovered a career path in an organization:

MERCEDES: I kept looking in the want ads for a career in management after I finished college. I don't know how many times I was turned down. Finally, I took an entry-level job in this company just to tide me over. As I kept looking at the want ads, I also started meeting more people in the company. I began to realize that this wasn't such a bad place after all. But what really did it for me was when I met Linda. When she told what she was doing in the company, I knew I wanted to know more about it. Well, you know the rest of the story. I found out about several jobs I never knew existed, and I landed one I like very much. I guess I'll stick around.

In Mercedes' case, she was exposed to occupations and career opportunities she had never known before. An entry-level job provided the means to discover unknown opportunities, and after a successful socialization period, she discovered a career path that appealed to her.

In a more preconceived manner, Al began his career in a high-tech organization with the goal of reaching the management level.

AL: I started out as a computer salesman. After a few years, the company offered me a retail store management job in the eastern part of the state. My wife didn't want to move. That was a tough decision; the kids didn't want to leave either. We spent eight years there, but made the best of it. Meanwhile, I took advantage of every career development opportunity through a variety of training programs. I got good feedback from my supervisor, which really helped. During that process, I became familiar with many aspects of the company. It finally paid off when I was made regional manager a few years ago. It worked out well. I live near a lake now and in a delightful part of the state.

COUNSELOR: What are your future plans?

AL: I like what I'm doing, but I have become more interested in civic organizations and church work.

COUNSELOR: Do you have as strong a commitment to the organization as you once had?

AL: Yes and no. It's different than before. My wife is happy that I devote more time to other things, but I still get excited about the future. I enjoy working with these young kids. They have good management skills, and I enjoy helping them.

As shown in this interview, mid-career is a time when individuals develop an increased awareness of the long-term dimensions of a career and shift their focus from the work world to personal roles. Attention is focused not only on career maintenance but also on life issues, such as parenting, joining civic organizations, and caring for aging parents. Priorities between work roles and personal roles fluctuate according to circumstances. A healthy attitude to promote is a balance of roles, as career and life changes become increasingly connected.

Mid-career is also a time when individuals become more aware of life stages in terms of time spans and begin to view career in terms of implementing future opportunities, as shown in Super's (1977) model of vocational maturity in mid-career. Super's concept of vocational maturity defines life stages and tasks as interrelated in career development. His earlier studies of vocational maturity followed the vocational development of secondary students through adulthood (discussed in Chapter 2). More recently, he has been concerned with establishing the criteria of vocational maturity for older adults in mid-career. The developmental tasks associated with mid-career developed by Super (1977) are provided in Box 21-1. Super's model for adults has five basic dimensions of developmental tasks, similar to those in his adolescent model. The first dimension, *planfulness* or *time perspective*, focuses on the awareness of life stages and tasks. The second dimension, *exploration*, considers the tasks of exploring both goals and jobs for an eventual established position. *Information*, the third dimension, focuses on tasks dealing with the proper use of occupational sources, options, and outcome probabilities. The fourth dimension, *decision making*, considers skills, principles, and practices in decision making. The final dimension, *reality orientation*, considers the vocationally mature adult as having acquired self-knowledge, consistency, and stabilization in occupational preferences, choices, and work experiences.

The model provides a basis for determining which of the developmental tasks the adult has accomplished. It is useful for counseling because the identified dimensions and substages provide a frame of reference from which counseling

BOX 21-1   A Theoretical Model of Vocational Maturity in Mid-Career

I. Planfulness or time perspective
   A. Past: Exploration
       1. Crystallizing
       2. Specifying
       3. Implementing
   B. Present and immediate future: Establishment
       4. Stabilizing
       5. Consolidation
       6. Advancement
   C. Intermediate future: Maintenance
       7. Holding one's own
       8. Keeping up with developments
       9. Breaking new ground
   D. Distant future: Decline
       10. Tapering off
       11. Preparing for retirement
       12. Retiring
II. Exploration
   E. Querying
       1. Self
           a. In time perspective
           b. In space (organizational geography)
       2. Situation
           a. In time perspective
           b. In space (organizational geography)
   F. Resources (attitudes toward)
       3. Awareness of
       4. Valuation of
   G. Participation (use of resources)
       5. In-house resources (sponsored)
       6. Community resources (sought out)
III. Information
   H. Life stages
       1. Time spans
       2. Characteristics
       3. Developmental tasks
   I. Coping behaviors: Repertoire
       4. Options in coping with vocational development tasks
       5. Appropriateness of options for self-in-situation
   J. Occupational outlets for self-in-situation

BOX
21-1 **A Theoretical Model** *(continued)*

    K.   Job outlets for self-in-situation
    L.   Implementation: Means of access to opportunities
    M. Outcome probabilities
 IV. Decision making
    N.   Principles
        1. Knowledge of
        2. Valuation of (utility)
    O.   Practice
        3. Use of in past
        4. Use of at present
  V. Reality orientation
    P.   Self-knowledge
        1. Agreement of self-estimated and measured traits
        2. Agreement of self-estimated and other estimated traits
    Q.   Realism
        3. Agreement of self- and employer-evaluated proficiency
        4. Agreement of self- and employer-evaluated prospects
    R.   Consistency of occupational preferences
        5. Current
        6. Over time
    S.   Crystallization
        7. Clarity of vocational self-concept
        8. Certainty of career goals
    T.   Work experience
        9. Floundering versus stabilizing in mid-career
      10. Stabilizing or maintaining versus decline in mid-career

SOURCE: From "Vocational Maturity in Mid-Career," by D. E. Super. In *Vocational Guidance Quarterly,* June 1977, 25(4), p. 297. Copyright 1977 by American Personnel and Guidance Association. Reprinted with permission.

procedures can be built. The vocational maturity in the mid-career model should also provide the basis for informative research projects in the future.

Late Career

In late career, the major focus of an individual's life is on activities outside the organization. The individual builds outside interests and begins a gradual detachment from the organization. Activities within the organization may also shift from a power role to a minor role. Super refers to this stage as decline characterized by preretirement considerations. Within the organization, the individual is preparing to "let go" of responsibilities and pass them on to others. One major adjustment during late career is learning to accept a reduced work role and changing focus away from a highly involved work identity.

Emotional support in late career comes primarily from peers and particularly from old acquaintances. Moving away from the stress and turmoil associated with younger workers who are striving to move upward, late-career employees identify with peers and rekindle closer attachments to spouses. Having resolved many of the uncertainties of mid-career, they tend to focus on broader issues, such as the organization as a whole and the future of their profession or work (Kram, 1985).

Implications for Career Guidance Programs

The stages of career development in organizations provide guidelines for career guidance needs and program development. The need to assist individuals in organizational choice is apparent; however, the processes involved in organizational choice have not been clearly delineated by the counseling profession or by organizations. Thus, career counselors should encourage clients to carefully evaluate organizations on the basis of individual needs and realistic expectations. Assisting clients to learn about organizational life is an important component of counseling.

The stages of entry in early career are highlighted by the socialization processes that take place in each organization. The individual evaluates self-in-situation by observing the many facets of environmental working conditions, supervisor-worker relations, opportunities for advancement, and congruence with peer affiliates. During the socialization process, the individual needs support in developing a sense of direction in the worker social milieu, where he or she is also being observed and evaluated. Helping individuals assess the complexities associated with organizational life and establish an identity with a new organization are major counseling goals of this stage. For those who decide to withdraw and try again in a different organization, the decision process must include a careful analysis of the reasons for the desired change.

Learning to deal with competition is one of the major social-emotional needs of middle career, when individuals may need to reevaluate their career direction in organizations. As an individual integrates skills and becomes aware of organizational career paths, help in establishing a set of new goals is a relevant counseling objective. The hazards associated with obsolescence and "career plateaus" suggest that counseling programs encourage continuing education and training.

In late career, the individual is preparing to "phase out" or "let go" of major work responsibilities. Super (1990) used the term *decline* to indicate that a minor work role is imminent. Many people are reluctant to accept the fact that their work lives are almost over. For others, this stage has been eagerly anticipated as a time of freedom from work and obligations. Counseling strategies that help all workers prepare for this phasing out should include preretirement and retirement programs. More specifically, career programs should be designed to help individuals assess future needs, as discussed in Chapter 20.

Counseling in Organizations

The career counselor's role in organizations has not been fully determined or evaluated. However, Osipow (1983) has suggested that career counselors can fulfill definite needs in organizations. Some of his suggestions include programs to help individuals: (1) identify hazards in work, (2) identify work styles that match work sites, (3) deal with work-related stress, (4) deal with problems associated with dual-career roles, (5) deal with the effects of transferring to another job, (6) deal with interpersonal problems on the job, (7) deal with job loss, (8) deal with family problems, (9) deal with health care issues, and (10) prepare for retirement. The competencies necessary to meet the counseling needs of individuals in organizations suggest specialized training programs for career counselors.

Hall (1990) has suggested that organizations in general are not fully prepared to manage an individual's career development with resources and information materials. He suggested that individuals should be persuaded to assume responsibility for their own career development and to develop career competencies rather than job skills. The key word used by Hall to describe career competencies is *adaptability;* that is, learning to manage changes personally and tolerate the ambiguities of uncertainty. Organizations, on the other hand, should provide a supportive environment for career development by making it possible for individuals to use in-house human-management systems to explore various work roles and to experience various work sites in organizations.

Finally, Hall (1996) warns that a career with an organization might not offer a series of upward moves with steadily increasing incomes, power, status, and security. A sense of affiliation with one organization over a lifetime may be a relic of the past. If one redefines a career as a series of lifelong learning experiences, however, the idea of career will never die. Thus, the new career contract with an organization may include the *personal agency person* approach, as described in Chapter 20, which requires that individuals adapt quickly, learn continuously, and take responsibility for their own career development.

Employee Assistance Programs

During the last 20 years, organizations have been making greater use of employee assistance programs (EAPs). Recognizing the variety of counseling needs of their employees, especially on such problems as alcoholism and alcohol abuse, organizations are providing at least minimal services. McGowan (1984) has identified the reasons for the growing popularity of EAPs: (1) increased public sophistication about the interaction of psychological stress, work, and health; (2) limited availability of low-cost community mental health and family services; (3) increased concern about worker productivity and morale; (4) increased labor and management recognition of the value of maintaining a stable work force; and (5) repeated research findings that indicate that 15% to 20% of the working population have personal problems that could interfere with job performance.

Although varying significantly in different organizations, EAPs usually perform one or more of the following functions: (1) identification of employees with problems or potential problems, (2) intake and assessment counseling, (3) case coordination, (4) monitoring, information, and referral to other agencies, and (5) follow-up (Myers, 1984).

Some EAPs are part of the organization's personnel and human resources offices and are used primarily as referral services. Organizations also contract with EAP consortiums for services. A wide range of program service arrangements exist, and many have specified numbers of visits for counseling assistance. For example, some organizations pay for intake and diagnosis but the employee pays the charges for treatment services. Other organizations pay for five or six counseling sessions. EAPs are found in every type of organization and are staffed by social workers, psychologists, personnel administrators, educational counselors, alcohol counselors, and occupational program consultants (McGowan, 1984).

In a study of personal problems presented by employees to EAPs, Myers (1984) found the following problems to be most prevalent: (1) alcoholism and alcohol abuse, (2) compulsive gambling, (3) drug abuse, (4) employee theft, (5) family and marital problems, (6) personal finances, (7) legal problems, and (8) mental health problems and stress.

Career counselors should be aware of services available to employees and the specific services offered through EAPs. The evidence suggests that such programs will move increasingly toward comprehensive services while organizations develop new types of programs to meet the special needs of a variety of groups. For example, child care planning, health care planning for elderly relatives, preretirement counseling, and single-parent groups could be future EAP services.

The Emergence of Outplacement Counseling

The relatively new term *outplacement counseling* is used to define counseling services offered to employees terminated from industrial and governmental organizations and educational institutions. Outplacement counseling grew out of a need to help terminated employees assess individual strengths, evaluate career options, and learn effective job search strategies. The costs of outplacement counseling are absorbed by the terminating employer. There is little reference in the literature to outplacement counseling before the mid-1970s. This counseling service is expected to grow rapidly in the next decade.

Knowdell, McDaniels, and Walz (1983) have studied the contributing factors that led to the emergence of outplacement counseling:

1. *Technical change:* The increased use of computers and other technological changes have made many traditional employees obsolete. Robot systems are expected to replace many assembly-line positions in the near future.

2. *Corporate reorganization:* Rapidly growing corporations will have periodic reorganizations and power struggles. Many corporate executives will be terminated.

3. *Economic downturns:* Some organizations will find it necessary to periodically reduce staff because of changing economic conditions.

4. *Takeovers, mergers, and divestitures:* During the 1970s and 1980s, many corporations were merged, and as a result, executive officers were displaced.

5. *Stagnation and burnout:* Organizations have discovered that many executives have become ineffective because of various factors, including burnout, divorce, and identity crisis. These managers have difficulty focusing their energies on a job that they have had for a significant time.

6. *Obsolescence and overspecialization:* Many career specialists have difficulty finding use for their highly specialized skills when they are displaced from some organizations. For example, the space industry drew many workers into engineering positions that were highly specialized. As the aerospace industry declined, many of these individuals were displaced.

7. *Promotion to a level of incompetence:* It has been common practice to promote technically competent workers to managerial positions, but many have not had the necessary managerial skills and competencies. The result has been that many of these individuals are ineffective managers and need to be displaced.

8. *Changing value systems in society:* The stigma of being terminated by an organization is not as great as it once was. Tomasko (1987) suggests that downsizing organizations will result in more terminations of staff and executives.

Organizations have discovered that outplacement counseling provides them with many benefits. For example, most organizations want to keep a good public and community image, and they have resorted to outplacement counseling to help preserve this image. Also, organizations want to minimize lawsuits and grievance procedures (Drucker, 1992).

Counseling Strategies for Outplacement Counseling

Outplacement counseling is designed primarily to assist adults in career transition; therefore, most of the counseling components discussed in this chapter are relevant strategies for outplacement counseling. For example, the terminated employee will be encouraged to identify experiences and skills that are marketable in other organizations. Interest identification and value clarification are major counseling efforts. Decision-making exercises are relevant learning experiences for employees.

Among the special needs of displaced employees are strategies designed to help them deal with their anger and frustration. One useful strategy is helping displaced employees accept their anger as a normal reaction. Providing opportunities to express anger and frustration, individually or in groups, is considered helpful for adults in career transition. Resumé writing and developing interview skills are other needs to be addressed by the career counselor in outplacement counseling (Knowdell, McDaniels, & Walz, 1983).

Retirement Counseling

Throughout this book, career development has been presented as a continuous process over the life span. Career development is influenced by many variables: Some are externally generated (for example, economic crisis and job loss), others are internally generated (for example, perceptions of retirement), but all are integrated into the continuous career development process. Nevertheless, retirement counseling is often overlooked as part of the career development process and as a career counseling objective. As we prepare to meet the needs of individuals in the 21st century, the evidence suggests that retirement counseling will be a major component of the career development process. For example, Sheppard and Rix (1977) pointed out that 31 million Americans will be 65 or older by the year 2000 and 52 million will be that age by the year 2030, clearly indicating that over the next decades there will be significantly more retirees.

To meet this increasing need, organizations have developed preretirement programs (Morrow, 1985) that offer assistance in projecting pensions and other future benefits when the individual reaches retirement age. This type of preretirement program has often been referred to as a "probable inflation" model from which the individual can project his or her financial status at retirement. Other topics often addressed in organizational preretirement programs are optional retirement plans (such as partial retirement, which allows the individual to work part time), time management, financial planning, leisure alternatives, and marital and social relationships (Feldman, 1988).

Some organizations also offer planning services to individuals near retirement age. There are two types: limited and comprehensive. Limited retirement programs typically provide guidance in pension planning, Social Security and Medicare information, health insurance options, and information on retirement benefits at various ages of retirement. Areas included in comprehensive programs commonly include those covered in the limited programs plus the following: maintaining good health, marital/emotional aspects of retirement, leisure activities, relocation advantages and disadvantages, legal concerns (wills, estate planning, inheritance laws), family relations, employment possibilities, and lifestyle change.

Evaluating the Organization

This chapter has presented several suggestions about how we might help others evaluate an organization. These suggestions were offered in different contexts. You will recall that the purpose of this chapter is to build a frame of reference on organizational structure, leadership styles, motivation studies, and other factors that can help us evaluate an organization. We will, therefore, develop several key questions to help us in our evaluation. The questions that follow are, in most cases, very general and will be difficult to answer. They are only representative samples and do not include all that should be learned about organizations during the career search.

Our first question is, Can we evaluate an organization effectively enough to justify including organization evaluations as another step in the career exploration process? This and many of the questions we may pose concerning organizations are similar to those we attempt to answer about occupations. Admittedly, evaluating organizations will be difficult and time-consuming, but this is an important challenge; similar problems were faced by the early pioneers in vocational counseling in their quest for occupational information.

At this point, we have little research that might provide guidelines about how to effectively choose an organization (Hall, 1990). Therefore, our attempt here to develop a format and guidelines for evaluating an organization should be considered exploratory and tentative. Career counselors can select questions generated in the following paragraphs to assist clients in evaluating organizations.

We begin by reviewing the major components of this chapter to generate questions that may be used as an evaluation format. (The sequence of the major components addressed in an evaluation format need not be the same as that presented in the chapter.) One of our major concerns was organizational structure. This immediately led to a consideration of the authority relationships in the organization. Thus, we will first ask questions concerning the form of structure, policies, and formal control systems because these appear to be relevant to our observations. We will primarily want to consider how the structure of the organization influences the individual's role. Questions to be answered include the following:

- What is the pattern of the formal organizational structure?
- Where and by whom are organizational decisions made?
- What are the requirements for promotion in the organizational structure?
- What kinds of "movement" are available in the organizational structure?
- How would you characterize the organizational structure?
- Are the social systems compatible with my lifestyle?
- Will the entry point in the organization provide opportunities to meet goals and needs?

Our next major component for consideration is that of leadership style found in the organization. As you will recall, leadership style is a very important determinant of the role of subordinates. Another important point to remember is that some organizations take a contingency approach and determine a leadership style for each situational difference within the organization. These organizations could have combinations of differing approaches to leadership. Questions in this part of the evaluation include the following:

- Do the leaders appear to be task-oriented or people-oriented?
- What is the organization's philosophy or procedure for developing leaders?
- Do the leaders appear to be autocratic or democratic?
- What interaction, if any, takes place between leader and subordinate in the decision-making process?
- How are the goals and needs of the individual considered by the leaders?

- To what degree do leaders involve subordinates in sharing organizational goals?

Our third and final major component is our concern for work motivation in the organization. The evaluation of this component, like others, should be very individualized. Identifying individually developed goals and needs can be considered a prerequisite to evaluating this aspect of the organization. Major considerations are opportunities for satisfying needs for affiliation, achievement, power, status, recognition, actualization, and so on. In Chapter 2, we discussed Tiedeman and O'Hara's (1963) paradigm of decision making within which goals can be categorized as crystallized, reaffirmed, and integrated. Tiedeman postulated that an individual modifies goals or realigns them to find consistency in the working environment. Thus, the organizational work environment does provide a frame of reference within which certain individual considerations can be made. It is important to find congruency with as many organizational variables as possible to ensure a satisfactory work environment. Even though we may modify personally held goals, we should not be expected to change them completely. Finding a satisfactory work environment, like making an occupational choice, is an individual matter; both choices may be painstakingly difficult to make but are essential in satisfying individually developed goals and needs. Key questions about motivation include the following:

- Will the working environment provide a means of satisfying immediate goals?
- What job satisfactions can be realized in the organizational work environment? Do these opportunities satisfy my goals and needs?
- Will the social interaction satisfy my needs for affiliation?
- Will there be a fulfillment of my need for recognition and status with this organization?
- Will my need for achievement be met now and in the future?
- Are there adequate reinforcers provided by the organization and in what form?
- Can I find consistency between the organizational goals and my own values, beliefs, and attitudes?
- Do all persons have equal opportunities for achieving their individual goals?

Now that the questions have been generated, we must turn our attention to how they can be answered. Our first approach is to investigate published materials that might provide us with pertinent information. Because there have been such rapid changes in the last decade, we should attempt to obtain the most recent publications describing a corporation. One way to do this is to request information by using the list of corporate universities reported earlier in this chapter.

We should also consult the local library or career center for published information. However, publications can only partially help us evaluate an organization from the frame of reference we have established. They are generally designed to provide only a broad exposure to corporations and organizations, reporting some operational aspects, management procedures, and institutional structures. Information found on computerized programs and the Internet may have the same limitations, but, more than likely, they are frequently updated. We should not expect to fulfill our quest for evaluating organizations by using only published materials.

The suggested alternatives are visitation and interview. Career counseling programs have long suggested on-site job visits as valuable experiences during career exploration. From our frame of reference, assessment of occupational climate and other organizational variables are of equal importance. On-site visits also allow job seekers to interview a variety of individuals within the organization. When visitations are not practical, the interview becomes our primary method of evaluating an organization. In this context, the interview becomes a "mutual interview" in which the individual not only provides information but also receives information from organizational representatives. Both this method of evaluating an organization and the on-site visit method have obvious limitations. Organizational representatives are hired to project a "good image" of their organizations and may present a biased appraisal of organizational climate. On-site visits often do the same. Nevertheless, the individual with a good understanding of organizational structure, leadership styles, and organizational behavior will be in a much better position to evaluate an occupation within an organization during the career decision-making process. In the meantime, research is needed to develop more effective methods of evaluating organizational climate.

Summary

1. Organizations are changing from pyramidal structures to "flat models." Workers move laterally and use different skills for different projects.
2. Organizations no longer provide structured guidelines for careers; individuals must be more assertive in developing their destiny.
3. The term *multiskilling* is used to reflect the notion that many skills are to be learned in a lifelong learning program.
4. The role of manager is also going through transformation; a manager is now considered a coach or mentor.
5. In reengineered corporations, work is more integrated and has shifted from individuals to teams of employees.
6. Customers, competition, and change are driving forces behind organizational change of structure.
7. In the boundaryless organization, the following boundaries must be penetrated: vertical, horizontal, external, and geographic.
8. Multicultural groups may be given greater access to job advancement in postbureaucratic organizations.

9. Models of career development stages in organizations offer a frame of reference for observing the steps in career development. Each developmental stage has similar yet unique needs.

10. The major tasks of early career include becoming oriented to the organization, learning position responsibilities and demonstrating satisfactory performance, and implementing plans for advancement or position change.

11. Mid-career is a "settling-in" process characterized by resolutions of conflicts and conflicting demands within the organization and in personal life.

12. In late career, the individual turns his or her attention to activities outside the organization. One major adjustment is learning to accept a reduced work role and work identity.

13. Although the relationship between age and job performance is not clear, the type of work seems to be the most important variable.

14. The changing organization will bring about new concepts in career development. The individual must be more assertive in developing his or her destiny. Learning new skills and adapting to new and different work environments are key factors to success.

15. Organizations are using EAPs to meet the personal counseling needs of their employees. The primary functions of EAPs are identifying employees with problems or potential problems, intake and assessment counseling, and referring employees to other agencies for counseling.

16. Outplacement counseling is offered to employees terminated from industrial and governmental organizations and educational institutions. Outplacement counseling evolved from the need to assist terminated employees in assessing individual strengths, evaluating career options, and learning effective job-search strategies.

17. Retirement counseling is also being offered by organizations. Some organizations provide comprehensive programs, including information concerning leisure activities, legal concerns, and lifestyle change.

18. Procedures for evaluating an organization have not been fully developed. Important considerations include authority relationships in the organizations, leadership style found in the organization, and potential opportunities for satisfying individual needs. Publications, visitations, and interviews provide some means for evaluating organizations.

Supplementary Learning Exercises

1. Using the references listed in this chapter and others, develop strategies for evaluating an organization from published material. Explain how these evaluations could be incorporated into career counseling programs.

2. Develop a counseling component that gives an orientation to the realities of working in an organization.

3. Compare a bureaucratic organization structure with a boundaryless structure. Describe the differences in the workplace.

4. What kind of leader would you prefer in an organization? Describe the leader's characteristics and basic assumptions about the role of subordinates. List the reasons you consider leadership an important element to be considered in career counseling programs.

5. Interview an individual who has a leadership position in an organization. Focus your questions on relationships with subordinates. Develop a set of questions that could be used by your counselees to assess leader-subordinate relationships.

6. Interview an individual who has worked in an organization for several years to determine how that individual would evaluate an organization, based on past experience. Compare this evaluation with the questions listed in this chapter for evaluating an organization. What are your conclusions?

7. Develop at least five counseling strategies to meet the needs of individuals in early career. Discuss.

8. Compare the career development of an individual who works for an organization with someone who owns his or her own business. Discuss similarities and differences.

9. Develop a counseling component for individuals who are planning to retire.

10. Project what you consider to be an organization of the future. Focus on the roles of the worker, management, and the work force.

For More Information

Aamodt, M. G. (1999). *Applied industrial/organizational psychology* (3rd ed.). Pacific Grove, CA: Brooks/Cole * Wadsworth.

Ashkenas, R., Ulrich, D., Jick, T., & Kerr, St. (1995). *The boundaryless organization: Breaking the chains of organizational structure.* San Francisco: Jossey-Bass.

Drucker, P. F. (1992). *Managing for the future.* New York: Truman Talley Brooks/Dutton.

Fernandez, J. P. (1999). *Race, gender, & rhetoric.* New York: McGraw-Hill.

Hall, D. T. (1996). *The career is dead: Long live the career.* San Francisco: Jossey-Bass.

Hammer, M., & Champy, J. (1993). *Reengineering the corporation: A manifesto for business revolution.* New York: HarperCollins.

Hudson, F. (1991). *The adult years: Mastering the art of self-renewal.* San Francisco: Jossey-Bass.

Kirk, J. J. (1994). Putting outplacement in its place. *Journal of Employment Counseling, 31,* 10–18.

Appendix A

Multicultural Career Counseling Checklist

If you have a client of a different ethnicity/race than yours, you may wish to use this checklist as you begin to do the career assessment with your client.

The following statements are designed to help you think more thoroughly about the racially or ethnically different client to whom you are about to provide career counseling. Check all the statements that apply.

My racial/ethnic identity: _____

My client's racial/ethnic identity: _____

I. *Counselor Preparation*

 ❑ 1. I am familiar with minimum cross-cultural counseling competencies.

 ❑ 2. I am aware of my client's cultural identification.

 ❑ 3. I understand and respect my client's culture.

 ❑ 4. I am aware of my own worldview and how it was shaped.

 ❑ 5. I am aware of how my SES influences my ability to empathize with this client.

 ❑ 6. I am aware of how my political views influence my counseling with a client from this ethnic group.

 ❑ 7. I have had counseling or other life experiences with different racial/ethnic groups.

 ❑ 8. I have information about this client's ethnic group's history, local sociopolitical issues, and her attitudes toward seeking help.

 ❑ 9. I know many of the strengths of this client's ethnic group.

 ❑ 10. I know where I am in my racial identity development.

❑ 11. I know the general stereotypes held about my client's ethnic group.

❑ 12. I am comfortable confronting ethnic minority clients.

❑ 13. I am aware of the importance that the interaction of gender and race/ethnicity has in my client's life.

II. *Exploration and Assessment*

❑ 1. I understand this client's career questions.

❑ 2. I understand how the client's career questions may be complicated with issues of finance, family, and academics.

❑ 3. The client is presenting racial and/or cultural information with the career questions.

❑ 4. I am aware of the career limitations or obstacles the client associates with her race or culture.

❑ 5. I understand what the client's perceived limitations are.

❑ 6. I know the client's perception of her family's ethnocultural identification.

❑ 7. I am aware of the client's perception of her family's support for her career.

❑ 8. I know which career the client believes her family wants her to pursue.

❑ 9. I know whether the client's family's support is important to her.

❑ 10. I believe that familial obligations are dictating the client's career choices.

❑ 11. I know the extent of exposure to career information and role models the client had in high school and beyond.

❑ 12. I understand the impact that high school experiences (positive or negative) have had on the client's confidence.

❑ 13. I am aware of the client's perception of her competence, ability, and self-efficacy.

❑ 14. I believe the client avoids certain work environments because of fears of sexism or racism.

❑ 15. I know the client's stage of racial identity development.

III. *Negotiation and Working Consensus*

❑ 1. I understand the type of career counseling help the client is seeking (career choice, supplement of family income, professional career, etc.).

❑ 2. The client and I have agreed on the goals for career counseling.

❑ 3. I know how this client's role as a woman in her family influences her career choices.

❑ 4. I am aware of the client's perception of the woman's work role in her family and in her culture.

❑ 5. I am aware of the client's understanding of the role of children in her career plans.

❏ 6. I am aware of the extent of exposure to a variety of career role models the client has had.

❏ 7. I understand the culturally based career conflicts that are generated by exposure to more careers and role models.

❏ 8. I know the client's career aspirations.

❏ 9. I am aware of the level of confidence the client has in her ability to obtain her aspirations.

❏ 10. I know the client understands the relationship between type of work and educational level.

❏ 11. I am aware of the negative and/or self-defeating thoughts that are obstacles to the client's aspirations and expectations.

❏ 12. I know if the client and I need to renegotiate her goals as appropriate after exploring cultural and family issues.

❏ 13. I know the client understands the career exploration process.

❏ 14. I am aware of the client's expectations about the career counseling process.

❏ 15. I know when it is appropriate to use a traditional career assessment instrument with a client from this ethnic group.

❏ 16. I know which instrument to use with this client.

❏ 17. I am aware of the research support for using the selected instrument with clients of this ethnicity.

❏ 18. I am aware of nontraditional instruments that might be more appropriate for use with clients from this ethnic group.

❏ 19. I am aware of nontraditional approaches to using traditional instruments with clients from this ethnic group.

❏ 20. I am aware of the career strengths the client associates with her race or culture.

Appendix B

Career Counseling Checklist

The following statements are designed to help you think more thoroughly about your career concerns and to help your assessment counselor understand you better. Please try to answer them as honestly as possible. Check all of the items that are **true** for you.

- ❑ 1. I feel obligated to do what others want me to do, and these expectations conflict with my own desires.
- ❑ 2. I have lots of interests, but I do not know how to narrow them down.
- ❑ 3. I am afraid of making a serious mistake with my career choice.
- ❑ 4. I do not feel confident that I know in which areas my true interests lie.
- ❑ 5. I feel uneasy with the responsibility for making a good career choice.
- ❑ 6. I lack information about my skills, interests, needs, and values with regard to my career choice.
- ❑ 7. My physical ability may greatly influence my career choice.
- ❑ 8. I lack knowledge about the world of work and what it has to offer me.
- ❑ 9. I know what I want my career to be, but it doesn't feel like a realistic goal.
- ❑ 10. I feel I am the only one who does not have a career plan.
- ❑ 11. I lack knowledge about myself and what I have to offer the world of work.
- ❑ 12. I do not really know what is required from a career for me to feel satisfied.

❑ 13. I feel that problems in my personal life are hindering me from making a good career decision.

❑ 14. My ethnicity may influence my career choice.

❑ 15. No matter how much information I have about a career, I keep going back and forth and cannot make up my mind.

❑ 16. I tend to be a person who gives up easily.

❑ 17. I believe that I am largely to blame for the lack of success I feel in making a career decision.

❑ 18. I have great difficulty making most decisions about my life.

❑ 19. My age may influence my career choice.

❑ 20. I expect my career decision to take care of most of the boredom and emptiness that I feel.

❑ 21. I have difficulty making commitments.

❑ 22. I don't have any idea of what I want in life, who I am, or what's important to me.

❑ 23. I have difficulty completing things.

❑ 24. I am afraid of making mistakes.

❑ 25. Religious values may greatly influence my career choice.

❑ 26. At this point, I am thinking more about finding a job than about choosing a career.

❑ 27. Family responsibilities will probably limit my career ambitions.

❑ 28. My orientation to career is very different from that of the members of my family.

❑ 29. I have worked on a job that taught me some things about what I want or do not want in a career, but I still feel lost.

❑ 30. Some classes in school are much easier for me than others, but I don't know how to use this information.

❑ 31. My race may greatly influence my career choice.

❑ 32. My long-term goals are more firm than my short-term goals.

❑ 33. I have some career-related daydreams that I do not share with many people.

❑ 34. I have been unable to see a connection between my college work and a possible career.

❑ 35. I have made a career choice with which I am comfortable, but I need specific assistance in finding a job.

❑ 36. My gender may influence my career choice.

❑ 37. I have undergone a change in my life, which necessitates a change in my career plans.

❑ 38. My fantasy is that there is one perfect job for me, if I can find it.

❑ 39. I have been out of the world of work for a period of time and I need to redefine my career choice.

❑ 40. Making a great deal of money is an important career goal for me, but I am unsure as to how I might reach it.

❑ 41. My immigration status may influence my career choice.

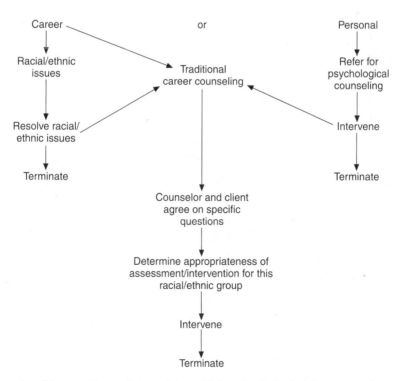

Career   or   Personal

Racial/ethnic issues → Traditional career counseling ← Refer for psychological counseling

Resolve racial/ethnic issues → Traditional career counseling ← Intervene

Terminate   Counselor and client agree on specific questions   Terminate

Determine appropriateness of assessment/intervention for this racial/ethnic group

Intervene

Terminate

Appendix D

Counseling Web Sites

The following professional associations and their Web sites provide an abundance of information about career counseling including competencies, ethical standards, and guidelines for using assessment.

American Counseling Association
http://www.counseling.org/

American Counseling Association Code of Ethics
http://www.counseling.org/resources/codeofethics.htm

American Psychological Association
http://www.apa.org

American Psychological Association Code of Ethics
http://www.apa.org/ethics/code.html

Association for Assessment in Counseling
http://www.aac.uc.edu/aac/index.html

Association of Computer-Based Systems for Career Information
http://www.acsci.org/

Competencies in Assessment and Evaluation for School Counselors
http://www.aac.uc.edu/aac/Resources/documents/atsc_cmptncy.htm

Ethics in Assessment
http://www.ed.gov/databases/ERIC_Digests/ed391111.html

Guidelines for the Use of the Internet for the Provision of Career Information and Planning Services
http://ncda.org/about/polnet.html

Multicultural Assessment Standards
http://www.aac.uc.edu/aac/Resources/documents/mcult_stds.htm

National Board for Certified Counselors Code of Ethics
http://www.nbcc.org/ethics/nbcc-code.htm

National Career Development Association
http://ncda.org

National Career Development Association Career Software Review Items
http://ncda.org/about/polsrg.html

National Career Development Association Ethical Standards
http://ncda.org/about/poles.html

Services by Telephone, Teleconferencing and Internet: A Statement by the
Ethics Committee of the American Psychological Association
http://www.apa.org/ethics/stmnt01.html

Standards for the Ethical Practice of Web Counseling
http://www.nbcc.org/ethics/wcstandards.htm

Appendix E

A High School Student's Experience in a Cooperative Education Program

The following account of a student's participation in a high school cooperative education program points out the values of work experiences.[1] Experiential activities involved money management, cooperative work activities with regular work staff, coping with work-related stress, and responsibility for work tasks. This student credits the cooperative education program as the single most influential aspect of her career education.

During my high school years, I was enrolled in a cooperative education program—I was a co-op student. As many people know, a co-op program is where a high school or college student earns academic credit and sometimes wages by working in the "real world" as part of a specified vocational curriculum. For example, a student in a retail merchandise program can earn credit and money through working in a department store. A food services student can work in a restaurant, a welding student can work for a sheet metal company, and so on.

I attended a high school that contained an areawide vocational skill center. Because I planned to attend college, I enrolled in the typical college prep courses, but I was also able to combine a college prep track with a vocational course (two hours a day for two years) that led to vocational certification by the State of Michigan. Early in my high school career, I had chosen elective courses from business: typing, shorthand, general business. I did quite well in these courses, and although I had no aspirations of becoming a business tycoon, I thought that having a background in business could prove helpful in the future, so I planned to take the Stenographer/Secretarial vocational program in my junior and senior years.

---

[1] From *My Vocational Experience*, by M. K. Wiinamaki, 1988. Unpublished manuscript, Southwest Texas State University. Reprinted by permission.

Immediately after finishing my sophomore year I was told of a co-op job—working in the County Treasurer's Office, which sounded more interesting than cleaning motel rooms (which I had done the previous summer). So I interviewed for, and subsequently landed, the position of clerk/"go-fer"/secretary in the Office of the County Treasurer of Chippewa County.

It was then that my real education began. As a 16-year-old, my work experience consisted of being a paper girl for two years, extensive babysitting, and cleaning motel rooms. I was now in an "adult" job, one full of responsibility and of learning a tremendous amount of information. During the two-and-a-half years I worked in that office, I learned more about the world of work than I did in any class I have ever taken—in high school, college, or graduate school.

The first major concept I learned was responsibility. I was required to be on time, day-in, day-out, even if I did not feel like going to work. However, my responsibility did not end with punctuality. I also had to *perform,* usually in pressure situations, under legal deadlines imposed by the State. I was responsible for accepting delinquent taxes and penalties and had to figure out the charges. At certain times of the year the office would become extremely hectic, but I was still expected to be accurate. After all, I was dealing with public funds.

Another area of my on-the-job education involved money management. For the first time in my life I was receiving a substantial amount of money in the form of a regular paycheck. Granted, it was only minimum wage, but working 20 hours per week during the school semester and 40 hours per week during summer, even minimum wage looked good to a high school girl with few expenses. I began to buy all my own clothes, my own gas, and was responsible for all of my entertainment expenses. Looking back, I believe both my parents and I appreciated this step of "economic independence."

Another crucial concept learned through my co-op experience was decision making, particularly the idea that decisions do have consequences and should be weighed before plunging head-first into one. I learned this in a variety of ways: first, by watching the adults with whom I worked, and second, by becoming aware of the political process around me. Decisions I made during those years still affect my life today.

The most generalizable skills I learned through co-op were interpersonal skills. I worked in an office with three women; though all of us had vastly different personalities, we had to cooperate and learn to co-exist peacefully, even when we did not agree. I also dealt with the public, people who were often paying delinquent land taxes, plus penalties, and who were generally unhappy about having to do so. I learned to be tactful, diplomatic, patient, and above all, to have a sense of humor about myself and about people. Working in such a stressful environment also taught me the importance of dealing with stress in a productive manner.

Time management was another skill I learned in my co-op job. When I began working regular hours, I was forced to use free time in a more productive manner—suddenly I had less time to goof off, do homework, and participate in household chores. I gained respect for adults who dealt with their job, spouse, children, and home. Life was more complicated than it had previously seemed.

In my position in the County Treasurer's Office, I had many occasions to talk to and become acquainted with a variety of people who held various city and county positions, such as county clerk, registrar of deeds, district attorneys, judges, and county commissioners. While students my age were learning about local politics in government class, I knew the officials by name and discovered what they actually did in their respective positions. Also significant was the fact that I had greatly increased my job experience during the time I worked as a co-op student. Many of the skills, such as typing, interpersonal skills, and problem-solving proved invaluable in subsequent positions. While all these skills and concepts were worthwhile, I think the most valuable benefit was a very positive increase in my self-esteem. I was now capable of working in the real world, of earning a living, of sticking with something that was not always pleasant. And that is a tremendous benefit.

So what happened after I left the County Treasurer's Office? During the time I worked there, I discovered some things about myself and the kind of environment I wanted to work in, and office work as a career was not what I envisioned. I learned that I did not enjoy the rigid structure, the routine, the repetition, but I did like working with people rather than with things. I entered college as a psychology major and thoroughly enjoyed the world of concepts, ideas, theories, and speculation. Throughout my years in college, I worked as a typist, a secretary in the Admissions Office, and as a word processor. Upon receiving a B.A. in psychology and realizing that graduate school was a necessity, I moved to Texas and promptly got a job as a word processor in a large law firm in Austin. Once again I was using the skills learned first in my co-op job as a high school student. In fact, that word-processing job supported me throughout graduate school, and also confirmed my decision to work in the field of counseling. I am glad to say that I am now working as a counselor, and I think I appreciate it more due to the years I spent in various secretarial jobs.

In summary, I learned a great deal about working, life, and myself through my experiences in cooperative education, experiences that continue to influence my life. For me, being a co-op student was the single most influential aspect of any career education I received. It was most valuable not because it showed me what I wanted to do with my life, but rather what I did *not* want to do—at a time when I was not forced to make irrevocable decisions on majors, careers, and locations. It provided me with the opportunity to navigate the transition from adolescence to adulthood gradually, and it is an experience I will never forget.

References

Aamodt, M. G. (2000). *Applied industrial/organizational psychology* (3rd ed.). Pacific Grove, CA: Brooks/Cole * Wadsworth.

Aburdene, P., & Naisbitt, J. (1993). *Megatrends for women: From liberation to leadership.* New York: Fawcett.

Adams, C. L. & Kimmel, D. C. (1997). Exploring the lives of older African American gay men. In B. Greene (Ed.). Ethnic and cultural diversity among lesbians and gay men (pp. 132–152). Thousand Oaks, CA: Sage.

Adkins, D. C. (1947). *Construction and analysis of achievement tests.* Washington, DC: U.S. Government Printing Office.

Alexander, L. C. (1985). *Women in nontraditional careers: A training program manual.* Washington, DC: Women's Bureau, U.S. Government Printing Office.

Allen, A. M., Allen, D. N., & Sigler, G. (1993). Changes in sex-role stereotyping in Caldecott Medal Award picture books 1938–1988. *Journal of Research in Childhood Education, 7,* 67–72.

Amatea, E. S., & Cross, E. G. (1980). Going places: A career guidance program for high school students and their parents. *Vocational Guidance Quarterly, 28* (3), 274–282.

American College Testing Program. (1984). *DISCOVER: A computer-based career development and counselor support system.* Iowa City, IA: Author.

American College Testing Program. (1987). *DISCOVER.* Iowa City, IA: Author.

American College Testing Program. (1996a, Winter). *Activity, 34* (1). Iowa City, IA: Author.

American College Testing Program. (1996b). *The high school profile report, normative data. ACT high school profile report: H.S. graduating class 1995.* Iowa City, IA: Author.

American Council on Education. (1997). Many college graduates participate in training courses to improve their job skills. *Higher Education and National Affairs, 46*(19), 3.

American Psychiatric Association. (1994). *Diagnostic and statistical manual of mental disorders* (4th ed., rev.). Washington, DC: Author.

American Psychological Association. (1985). *Standards for educational and psychological testing.* Washington, DC: Author.

American Psychological Association. (1990). Ethical principles of psychologists (amended June 2, 1989). *American Psychology,* pp. 453–484. New York: Wiley.

American Psychological Association. (1991). Avoiding heterosexual bias in language. *American Psychologist, 46,* 973–974.

American Psychological Association. (1992). *Ethical guidelines of the American Psychological Association.* Washington, DC: Author.

Anastasi, A. (1954). *Psychological testing.* New York: Macmillan.

Anastasi, A. (1988). *Psychological testing* (6th ed.). New York: Macmillan.

Anderson, D. A. (1994). Lesbian and gay adolescents: Social and developmental considerations. *High School Journal, 77*(1/2), 13–19.

Anderson, J. R. (1985). *Cognitive psychology and its implication* (2nd ed.). San Francisco: Freeman.

Anderson, T. B., & Olsen, L. C. (1965). Congruence of self and ideal self and occupational choices. *Personnel and Guidance Journal, 44,* 171–176.

Arbona, C. (1989). Hispanic employment and the Holland typology of work. *Career Development Quarterly, 37,* 257–268.

Arbona, C. (1995). Theory and research on racial and ethnic minorities: Hispanic Americans. In Frederick T. L. Leong (Ed.), *Career development and vocational behavior of racial and ethnic minorities* (pp. 37–61). Mahwah, NJ: Erlbaum.

Arbona, C. (1996). Career theory and practice in a multicultural context. In M. L. Savickas & W. B. Walsh (Eds.), *Handbook of career counseling theory and practice* (pp. 45–55). Palo Alto, CA: Davies-Black.

Argeropoulous, J. (1981). *Burnout, stress management, and wellness.* Moravia, NY: Chronicle Guidance.

Arredondo, P. (1996). MCT theory and Latina(O)-American populations. In D. W. Sue, A. E. Ivey, & P. B. Pedersen, *A Theory of Multicultural Counseling and Therapy* (pp. 217–233). Pacific Grove, CA: Brooks/Cole.

Ashkenas, R., Ulrich, D., Jick, T., & Kerr, St. (1995). *The boundaryless organization: Breaking the chains of organizational structure.* San Francisco: Jossey-Bass.

Astin, A. W. (1984). Student values: Knowing more about where we are today. *Bulletin of the American Association of Higher Education, 36*(9), 10–13.

Atkinson, D. R., Morten, G., & Sue, D. W. (1993). *Counseling American minorities: A cross-cultural perspective* (4th ed.). Dubuque, IA: William C. Brown.

Axelson, J. A. (1993). *Counseling and development in a multicultural society* (2nd ed.). Pacific Grove, CA: Brooks/Cole.

Axelson, J. A. (1999). *Counseling and development in a multicultural society* (4th ed.). Pacific Grove, CA: Brooks/Cole.

Bailey, L. J., & Stadt, R. W. (1973). *Career education: New approaches to human development.* Bloomington, IL: McKnight.

Baker, D. B., Strub, S. O., & Henning, W. (1995). *Cracking the corporate closet.* New York: HarperCollins.

Baker, L. J., Dearborn, M., Hastings, J. E., & Hamberger, K. (1988). Type A behavior in women: A review. *Health Psychology, 3,* 477–497.

Ballard, D. (1997). *Doing it ourselves: Success stories of African-American women in business.* New York: Berkley.

Bandura, A. (1977). *Social learning theory.* Englewood Cliffs, NJ: Prentice-Hall.

Bandura, A. (1986). *Social foundations of thought and action: A social cognitive theory.* Englewood Cliffs, NJ: Prentice-Hall.

Bandura, A. (1989). Regulation of cognitive processes through perceived self-efficacy. *Developmental Psychology, 25,* 729–735.

Barnet, R. J., & Cavanagh, J. (1994). *Global dreams: Imperial corporations and the new world order.* New York: Simon & Schuster.

Barnett, R. C., & Rivers, C. (1996). *She works, he works: How two-income families are happier, healthier, and better off.* San Francisco: Harper

Basow, S. A. (1992). *Gender: Stereotypes and roles* (3rd ed.). Pacific Grove, CA: Brooks/ Cole.

Beck, A. T. (1976). *Cognitive therapy and the emotional disorders.* New York: International Universities Press.

Beck, A. T. (1985). Cognitive therapy. In H. J. Kaplan & B. J. Sadock (Eds.), *Comprehensive textbook of psychiatry* (pp. 1432–1438). Baltimore: Williams & Wilkins.

Bell, A. & Weinberg, M. (1978). *Homsexualities: A study of diversity among men and women.* New York: Simon & Schuster.

Benin, M. H., & Agostinelli, J. (1988). Husbands' and wives' satisfaction with the division of labor. *Journal of Marriage and the Family, 50,* 349–361.

Bennett, C. E. & DeBarros, K. A. (1995). *The Black population.* In U.S. Bureau of the Census, Current Population Reports, Series P23-189, Population Profile of the United States: 1995 (pp. 44–45). Washington, DC: U.S. Government Printing Office.

Bennett, G. K., Seashore, H. G., & Wesman, A. G. (1974). *Differential aptitude test.* San Antonio, TX: Psychological Corporation.

Bernardo, D. H., Shehan, C. L., & Leslie, G. R. (1987). A residue of tradition: Jobs, careers, and spouses' time in housework. *Journal of Marriage and the Family, 49,* 381–390.

Berry, R. E., & Williams, F. L. (1987). Assessing the relationship between quality of life and marital and income satisfaction: A path analytical approach. *Journal of Marriage and the Family, 49,* 107–116.

Betz, N. E. (1992a). Career assessment: A review of critical issues. In S. D. Brown & R. W. Lent (Eds.), *Handbook of counseling psychology* (pp. 453–484). New York: Wiley.

Betz, N. E. (1992b). Counseling uses of career self-efficacy theory. *Career Development Quarterly, 41,* 22–26.

Betz, N. E. (1993). Issues of the use of ability and interest measures with women. *Journal of Career Assessment, 1,* 217–232.

Betz, N. E. (1994a). Basic issues and concepts in career counseling for women. In W. B. Walsh & S. H. Osipow (Eds.), *Career counseling for women: Contemporary topics in vocational psychology* (pp. 1–41). Hillsdale, NJ: Erlbaum.

Betz, N. E. (1994b). Self-concept theory in career development and counseling. *Career Development Quarterly, 43,* 32–42.

Betz, N. E., & Fitzgerald, L. F. (1987). *The career psychology of women.* Orlando, FL: Academic.

Betz, N. E., & Fitzgerald, L. F. (1995). Career assessment and intervention with racial and ethnic minorities. In Frederick T. L. Leong (Ed.), *Career development and vocational behavior of racial and ethnic minorities* (pp. 263–277). Mahwah, NJ: Erlbaum.

Betz, N. E., & Hackett, G. (1986). Applications of self-efficacy theory to understanding career choice behavior. *Journal of Social and Clinical Psychology, 4,* 279–289.

Beymer, L. (1995). *Meeting the guidance and counseling needs of boys.* Alexandria, VA: American Counseling Association.

Biehler, R. F., & Hudson, L. M. (1986). *Developmental psychology.* Boston: Allyn & Bacon.

Biernat, M., & Wortman, C. (1991). Sharing of home responsibilities between professionally employed women and their husbands. *Journal of Personality and Social Psychology, 60,* 844–860.

Bingham, R. P., & Ward, C. M. (1996). Practical applications of career counseling with ethnic minority women. In M. L. Savickas & W. B. Walsh (Eds.), *Handbook of career counseling theory and practice* (pp. 291–315). Palo Alto, CA: Davies-Black.

Blau, P. M., Gustad, J. W., Jessor, R., Parnes, H. S., & Wilcox, R. S. (1956). Occupational choices: A conceptual framework. *Industrial Labor Relations Review, 9,* 531–543.

Bloland, P. A., & Edwards, P. B. (1981). Work and leisure: A counseling synthesis. *Vocational Guidance Quarterly, 30*(2), 101–108.

Blotzer, M. A., & Ruth, R. (1995). *Sometimes you just want to feel like a human being: Case studies of empowering psychotherapy with people with disabilities.* Baltimore: Paul H. Brookes.

Blustein, D. L. (1990). An eclectic definition of psychotherapy: A developmental contextual view. In J. K. Zeig & W. M. Munion (Eds.), *What is psychotherapy? Contemporary perspectives* (pp. 244–248). San Francisco: Jossey-Bass.

Bolles, R. N. (1991). *Job-hunting tips for the so-called handicapped or people who have disabilities.* Berkeley, CA: Ten Speed.

Bolles, R. N. (1993). *A practical manual for job-hunters and career changers: What color is your parachute?* (9th ed.). Berkeley, CA: Ten Speed.

Bolles, R. N. (2000). *A practical manual for job-hunters and career changers: What color is your parachute?* (16th ed.). Berkeley, CA: Ten Speed.

Borow, H. (Ed.). (1964). *Man in the world at work.* Boston: Houghton Mifflin.

Bottoms, J. E., Evans, R. N., Hoyt, K. B., & Willer, J. C. (Eds.). (1972). *Career education resource guide.* Morristown, NJ: General Learning Corporation.

Bowman, S. L. (1995). Career intervention strategies and assessment issues for African Americans. In Frederick T. L. Leong (Ed.), *Career development and vocational behavior of racial and ethnic minorities* (pp. 137–161). Mahwah, NJ: Erlbaum.

Brammer, L. M., & Abrego, P. J. (1981). Intervention strategies for coping with transitions. *Counseling Psychologist, 9,* 27.

Brammer, L. M., Abrego, P. L., & Shostrom, E. L. (1993). *Therapeutic counseling and psychotherapy* (2nd ed.). Englewood Cliffs, NJ: Prentice-Hall.

Bretz, R. D., Jr., & Judge, T. A. (1994). Person-organization fit and the theory of work adjustment: Implications for satisfaction, tenure, and career success. *Journal of Vocational Behavior, 44,* 32–54.

Brewer, J. M. (1918). *The vocational guidance movement.* New York: Macmillan.

Brislin, R. (1993). *Understanding culture's influence on behavior.* Fort Worth, TX: Harcourt Brace Jovanovich.

Brolin, D. E., & Gysbers, N. C. (1989). Career education for students with disabilities. *Journal of Counseling and Development, 68,* 155–159.

Brooks, S. (1991). Resources. In J. J. Evans & V. A. Walls (Eds.), *Beyond tolerance: Gays, lesbians, and bisexuals on campus* (pp. 213–232). Alexandria, VA: American College Personnel Association.

Brown, B. B., Mounts, N., Lamborn, S. D., & Steinberg, L. (1993). Parenting practices and peer group affiliation in adolescence. *Child Development, 65,* 467–482.

Brown, D. (1996). Brown's values-based, holistic model of career and life-role choices and satisfaction. In D. Brown, L. Brooks, & Associates (Eds.), *Career choice and development* (3rd ed.) (pp. 337–338). San Francisco: Jossey-Bass.

Brown, D., & Brooks, L. (1991). *Career counseling techniques.* Boston: Allyn & Bacon.

Brown, D., Brooks, L., & Associates. (1990). *Career choice and development* (2nd ed.). San Francisco: Jossey-Bass.

Brown, D., Brooks, L., & Associates. (1996). *Career choice and development* (3rd ed.). San Francisco: Jossey-Bass.

Brown, D., & Crace, R. K. (1995). A values-based model of career choice and satisfaction. *Career Development Quarterly, 44.*

Brown, D., & Minor, C. W. (1989). *Working in America: A status report on planning and problems.* Alexandria, VA: National Career Development Association.

Brown, L. S. (1995). Lesbian identities: Concepts and issues. In A. R. D'Augelli &
C. J. Patterson (Eds.), *Lesbian, gay, and bisexual identities over the lifespan*
(pp. 3–24). New York: Oxford University Press.

Brown, M. T. (1995). The career development of African Americans: Theoretical and
empirical issues. In F. T. L. Leong (Ed.), *Career development of and vocational
behavior of racial and ethnic behaviors* (pp. 7–36). Mahwah, NJ: Erlbaum.

Bryan, W. V. (1996). *In search of freedom: How people with disabilities have been
disenfranchised from the mainstream of American Society.* Springfield, IL: Charles
C. Thomas.

Bureau of Indian Affairs. (1993). *Federally recognized tribes.* Washington, DC: U.S.
Department of Interior, Bureau of Indian Affairs.

Burgos-Ocasio, H. (2000). Hispanic women. In M. Julia (Ed.), *Constructing gender:
Multicultural perspectives in working with women* (pp. 109–139). Pacific Grove,
CA: Brooks/Cole.

Burlew, Larry D. (1996). Career counseling is not mental health counseling: More myth
than fact. In R. Feller & G. Walz (Eds.), *Career transitions in turbulent times*
(pp. 371–379). Greensboro, NC: ERIC Counseling and Student Services
Clearinghouse, University of North Carolina.

Buros, O. K. (Ed.) (1938). *The first mental measurements yearbook.* Highland Park, NJ:
Gryphon.

Burton, M., & Wedemeyer, R. (1991). *In transition.* New York: Harper Business
Publications.

California Advisory Council on Vocational Education. (1977). *Barriers and bridges.*
Sacramento: California State Department of General Services.

Campbell, R. E. & Cellini, J. V. (1981). A diagnostic taxonomy of adult career problems,
Journal of Vocational Behavior, 19, 175–190.

Campbell, R. E., & Heffernan, J. M. (1983). Adult vocational behavior. In W. B. Walsh &
S. H. Osipow (Eds.), *Handbook of vocational psychology: Vol. 1* (pp. 223–262).
Hillsdale, NJ: Erlbaum.

Carson, A. D., & Mowesian, R. (1993). Moderators of the prediction of job satisfaction
from congruence: A test of Holland's theory. *Journal of Career Assessment, 1,*
130–144.

Carter, J. K. (1995, Winter). Applying customer service strategies to career services.
Journal of Career Development, 22 (2).

Carter, R. T. (1995). *The influence of race and racial identity in psychotherapy: Toward
a racially inclusive model.* New York: Wiley.

Cass, V. C. (1979). Homosexuality identity formation: A theoretical model. *Journal of
Homosexuality, 4*(3), 219–235.

Cass, V. C. (1984). Homosexual identity formation: Testing a theoretical model. *Journal
of Sex Research, 20*(2), 143–167.

Cattell, R. B., Eber, H. W., & Tatsuoka, M. M. (1970). *Handbook for the sixteen
personality factor questionnaire (16PF).* Champaign, IL: Institute for Personality
and Ability Testing.

Cautela, J., & Wisock, P. (1977). The thought-stopping procedure: Description, application
and learning theory interpretations. *Psychological Record, 2,* 264–266.

Cejka, M. A., & Eagly, A. H. (1999). Gender-stereotypic images of occupations
correspond to the sex segregation of employment. *Personality and Social
Psychology Bulletin, 25,* 413–423.

Centers for Disease Control (1999). *HIV/AIDS Surveillance Report, 1999, 11* (No.1)
pp. 2–43. Washington, DC: U.S. Department of Health and Human Services.

Cetron, M., & Gayle, M. (1991). *Educational renaissance.* New York: St. Martin's.

Chadwick, B. A., & Heaton, T. B. (1992). *Statistical handbook on the American family.* Phoenix: Oryx.

Chan, C. S. (1997). Don't ask, don't tell, don't know: The formation of homosexual identity and sexual expression among Asian American lesbians. In B. Greene (Ed.), *Ethnic and cultural diversity among lesbians and gay men* (pp. 240–249). Thousand Oaks, CA: Sage.

Chan, C. S. (1989). Issues of identity formation among Asian-American lesbians and gay men. *Journal of Counseling Development, 68,* 16–20.

Charting the projections: 1994–2005. (1995, Fall). *Occupational Outlook Quarterly, 39*(2), 2–3.

Chartrand, J. M. (1991). The evolution of trait-and-factor career counseling: A person-environment fit approach. *Journal of Counseling & Development, 69,* 518–524.

Cherniss, C. (1980). *Staff burnout: Job stress in the human services.* Newbury Park, CA: Sage.

Cherniss, C. (1995). *Beyond burnout: Helping teachers, nurses, therapists, and lawyers recover from stress and disillusion.* New York: Routledge.

Chipping away at the glass ceiling. (1991, May). *Nations Business,* pp. 20–21.

Chodorow, N. J. (1989). *Feminism and psychoanalytic theory.* New Haven, CT: Yale University Press.

Chu, L. (1981, April). *Asian-American women in educational research.* Paper presented at annual conference of the American Educational Research Association, Los Angeles.

Chu, P. H. (1975). Cross-culture study of vocational interests measured by the Srong Campbell Interest Inventory. *ACTa Psychlogical Taiwanica, 17,* 69–84.

Chung, Y. B. & Katayama, M. (1999). Ethnic and sexual identity development of Asian American lesbian and gay adolescents. In K. S. Ng (Ed.), *Counseling Asian families from a systems perspective* (pp. 159–171). Alexandria, VA: American Counseling Association.

Chusmir, L. H. (1983). Characteristics and predictive dimensions of women who make nontraditional vocational choices. *Personnel and Guidance Journal, 62*(1), 43–48.

Chusmir, L. H. (1990). Men who make nontraditional career choices. *Journal of Counseling and Development, 69,* 11–16.

Chusmir, L. H., & Parker, B. (1991). Gender and situational differences in managers' lives: A look at work and home lives. *Journal of Business Research, 23,* 325–335.

Clark-Stewart, A. (1993). *Daycare* (rev. ed.). Cambridge, MA: Harvard University Press.

Clausen, J. S. (1991). Adolescent competence and the shaping of the life course. *American Journal of Sociology, 96,* 805–842.

Cochran, L. (1994). What is a career problem? *Career Development Quarterly, 42,* 204–215.

Coleman, E. & Remafedi, G. (1989). Gay, lesbian, and bisexual adolescents: a critical challenge to counselors. *Journal of Counseling & Development, 68,* 36–40.

Coleman, M. T. (1988). The division of household labor. *Journal of Family Issues, 9*(1), 132–148.

Collin, A. (1994). Fracture lines for career. *NICEC Bulletin, 42,* 6–11.

Comas-Diaz, L. (1996). Cultural considerations in diagnosis. In F. W. Kaslow (Ed.), *Handbook on relational diagnosis and dysfunctional family patterns* (pp. 159–160). New York: Wiley.

Comas-Diaz, L., & Grenier, J. R. (1998). Migration and acculturation. In J. Sandoval, C. L. Frisby, K. F. Geisinger, J. D. Scheuneman, & J. R. Grenier, *Test interpretation and diversity* (pp. 213–241). Washington, DC: American Psychological Association.

Comstock, G. A., with Haejung Paik. (1991). *Television and the American child.* San Diego: Academic.

Cook, D. W. (1981). Impact of disability on the individual. In R. M. Parker & C. E. Hansen (Eds.), *Rehabilitation counseling*. Boston: Allyn & Bacon.

Coon-Carty, H. M. (1995). *The relation of work-related abilities, vocational interests, and self-efficacy beliefs: A meta-analytic investigation*. Unpublished master's thesis, Loyola University, Chicago.

Copeland, L., & Griggs, L. (1985). *Going international*. New York: Random House.

Cordes, C. L., & Dougherty, T. W. (1993). A review and integration of research on job burnout. *Academy of Management Review, 18*, 621–656.

Corey, G. (1991). *Theory and practice of counseling and psychotherapy*. Pacific Grove, CA: Brooks/Cole.

Cormier, L. S., & Hackney, H. (1987). *The professional counselor: A process guide to help*. Englewood Cliffs, NJ: Prentice-Hall.

Cormier, W., & Cormier, L. S. (1991). *Interviewing strategies for helpers: Fundamental skills and cognitive behavioral interventions* (3rd ed.). Pacific Grove, CA: Brooks/Cole.

Courtenay, B. C. (1994). Are psychological models of adult development still important for the practice of adult education? *Adult Education Quarterly, 44*(3), 145–153.

Cox, M. J., Owen, M. T., Henderson, V. K., & Margand, N. A. (1992). Prediction of infant-father and infant-mother attachment. *Developmental Psychology, 28*, 474–483.

Cozby, P. C. (1973). Self-disclosure: A literature review. *Psychological Bulletin, 79*, 73–91.

Crace, R. K., & Brown, D. (1996). *Life values inventory*. Minneapolis: National Computer Systems.

Craig, R. J. (1989). *Clinical and diagnostic interviewing*. Northvale, NJ: Aronson.

Crites, J. O. (1973). *Theory and research handbook: Career maturity inventory*. Monterey, CA: CTB-MacMillan-McGraw-Hill.

Crites, J.O. (1981). *Career models: Models, methods, and materials*. New York: McGraw-Hill.

Crites, J. O., & Savickas, M. L. (1995). *The career maturity inventory—Revised form*. Clayton, NY: Careerware: ISM.

Crites, J. O., & Savickas, M. L. (1996). Revision of the career maturity inventory. *Journal of Career Assessment, 4*(2), 131–138.

Cronbach, L. J. (1949). *Essentials of psychological testing*. New York: Harper & Brothers.

Cronbach, L. J. (1984). *Essentials of psychological testing* (4th ed.). New York: Harper & Row.

Cronbach, L. J. (1990). *Essentials of psychological testing* (5th ed.). New York: Harper & Row.

Cross, T. L., Bazron, B. J., Dennis, K. W., & Isaacs, M. R. (1989). *Towards a culturally competent system of care*. Washington, DC: Georgetown University Child Development Center.

Cunningham, J. L. (1998). Learning disabilities. In J. Sandoval, C. L. Frisby, K. F. Geisinger, J. D. Scheuneman (Eds.), *Test interpretation and diversity* (pp. 317–349). Washington, DC: American Psychological Association.

Curnow, T. C. (1989). Vocational development of persons with disability. *Career Development Quarterly, 37*, 269–277.

Dancer, L. S., & Gilbert, L. A. (1993). Spouses' family work participation and its relation to wives' occupational level. *Sex Roles, 28*, 127–145.

Daniels, J. L. (1981). World of work in disabling conditions. In R. M. Parker & C. E. Hansen (Eds.), *Rehabilitation counseling* (pp. 169–199). Boston: Allyn & Bacon.

Danish, S. J., & D'Augelli, A. R. (1983). *Helping skills II: Life-development intervention*. New York: Human Sciences Press.

D'Augelli, A. R. (1991). Gay men in college: Identity processes and adaptations. *Journal of College Student Development, 32*, 140–146.

Davidson, P. E., & Anderson, H. D. (1937). *Occupational mobility in an American community.* Palo Alto, CA: Stanford University Press.

Davis, D. A., Hagan, N., & Strouf, J. (1962). Occupational choice of twelve-year-olds. *Personnel and Guidance Journal, 40,* 628–629.

Davis, D. M. (1990). Portrayals of women in prime-time network television: Some demographic characteristics. *Sex Roles, 23,* 325–332.

Davis, F. B. (1947). *Utilizing human talent.* Washington, DC: American Council on Education.

Dawis, R. V. (1991). Vocational interests, values, and preferences. In M. D. Dunnette & L. M. Hough (Eds.), *Handbook of industrial and organizational psychology: Vol. 2* (2nd ed.) (pp. 833–871). Palo Alto, CA: Consulting Psychologists Press.

Dawis, R. V. (1996). The theory of work adjustment and person-environment-correspondence counseling. In D. Brown, L. Brooks, & Associates (Eds.), *Career choice and development* (3rd ed.) (pp. 75–115). San Francisco: Jossey-Bass.

Dawis, R. V., Dohm, T. E., Lofquist, L. H., Chartrand, J. M., & Due, A. M. (1987). *Minnesota occupational classification system III.* Minneapolis: Vocational Psychology Research, Department of Psychology, University of Minnesota.

Dawis, R. V., & Lofquist, L. H. (1984). *A psychological theory of work adjustment: An individual differences model and its application.* Minneapolis: University of Minnesota.

De Becker, G. (1997). *The gift of fear: Survival signals that protect us from violence.* Boston: Little, Brown.

Defrank, R., & Ivancevich, J. M. (1986). Job loss: An individual-level review and model. *Journal of Vocational Behavior, 19,* 1–20.

Dent, H. S., Jr. (1998). *The roaring 2000's.* New York: Simon & Schuster.

de Vaus, D., & McCallister, I. (1991). Gender and work orientation. *Work and Occupations, 18,* 72–93.

Diamond, E. E. (1975). Overview. In E. E. Diamond (Ed.), *Issues of sex bias and sex fairness in career interest movement.* Washington, DC: U.S. Government Printing Office.

Dickson, G. L., & Parmerlee, J. R. (1980). The occupational family tree: A career counseling technique. *School Counselor, 28*(2), 27–31.

Diller, J. V. (1999). *Cultural diversity: A primer for the human services.* Pacific Grove, CA: Wadsworth.

Dosser, D. A. (1982). Male inexpressiveness: Behavioral interventions. In K. Solomon & N. B. Levy (Eds.), *Men in transition* (pp. 343–432). New York: Plenum.

Doyle, J. A. (1983). *The male experience.* Dubuque, IA: Wm. C. Brown.

Doyle, R. E. (1992). *Essential skills and strategies in the helping process.* Pacific Grove, CA: Brooks/Cole.

Drucker, P. F. (1992). *Managing for the future.* New York: Truman Talley Brooks/Dutton.

Drummond, R. (1992). *Appraisal procedures for counselors and helping professionals* (2nd ed.). New York: Macmillan.

Drummond, R. J. & Ryan, C. W. (1995). *Career counseling: A developmental approach.* Columbus, OH: Merrill.

Dudley, G. A., & Tiedeman, D. V. (1977). *Career development: Exploration and commitment.* Muncie, IN: Accelerated Development.

Duran, E. & Duran, B. (1995). *Native American postcolonial psychology.* Albany: State University of New York Press.

Dworkin, S. H. & Gutierrez, F. J. (Eds.). (1992). *Counseling gay men and lesbians: Journey to the end of the rainbow.* Alexandria, VA: American Association for Counseling and Development.

Eccles, J. S. (1987). Gender roles and women's achievement-related decisions. *Psychology of Women Quarterly, 11,* 135–172.

Eccles, J. S. (1993). School and family effects on the ontogeny of children's interests, self-perceptions, and activity choices. In J. E. Jacobs (Eds.), *Nebraska Symposium on Motivation: 1992, Vol. 40* (pp. 145–208). Lincoln: University of Nebraska Press.

Eccles, J. S., Barber, B., & Jozefowicz, D. (1999). Linking gender to educational, occupational, and recreational choices: Applying the Eccles et al. Model of achievement-related choices. In W. B. Swann, J. H. Langlois, & L. A. Gilbert (Eds.), *Sexism and stereotypes in modern society* (pp. 153–192). Washington, DC: American Psychological Association.

Edelwich, J., & Brodsky, A. (1980). *Burnout: Stages of disillusionment in the helping professionals.* New York: Human Sciences Press.

Eldridge, N. S. (1987). Gender issues in counseling same-sex couples. *Professional Psychology: Research and Practice, 18*(6), 567–572.

Eldridge, N. S., & Barnett, D. C. (1991). Counseling gay and lesbian students. In N. J. Evans & V. A. Wall (Eds.), *Beyond tolerance: Gays, lesbians and bisexuals on campus* (pp. 147–178). Alexandria, VA: American College Personnel Association.

Elkind, D. (1968). Cognitive development in adolescence. In J. F. Adams (Ed.), *Understanding adolescence.* Boston: Allyn & Bacon.

Elkind, D. (1981). *A sympathetic understanding of the child from six to sixteen.* Boston: Allyn & Bacon.

Elliot, J. E. (1993). Career development with lesbian and gay clients. *Career Development Quarterly, 41*(3), 210–226.

Ellis, A. (1962). *Reason and emotion in psychotherapy.* Secaucus, NJ: Lyle Stuart.

Ellis, A. (1971). *Growth through reason.* Hollywood, CA: Wilshire.

Ellis, A., & Grieger, R. (1977). *Handbook of rational-emotive therapy.* New York: Springer.

Emener, W. G., & Rubin, S. E. (1980). Rehabilitation counselor roles and functions and sources of role strain. *Journal of Applied Rehabilitation Counseling, 11*(2), 57–69.

Engels, D. W. (Ed.). (1994). *The professional practice of career counseling and consultation: A resource document* (2nd ed.). Alexandria, VA: American Counseling Association.

Englander, M. E. (1960). A psychological analysis of a vocational choice: Teaching. *Journal of Counseling Psychology, 7,* 257–264.

Epstein, C. F. (1980). Institutional barriers: What keeps women out of the executive suite? In M. O. Morgan (Ed.), *Managing career development.* New York: Van Nostrand.

Erikson, E. H. (1950). *Childhood and society.* New York: Norton.

Erikson, E. H. (1963). *Childhood and society* (2nd ed.). New York: Norton.

Espin, O. M. (1987). Issues of identity in psychology of Latina lesbians. In Boston Lesbian Psychologies Collective (Eds.), *Lesbian psychologies: Exploration and challenges* (pp. 35–55). Urbana: University of Illinois Press.

Etaugh, C., & Liss, M. B. (1992). Home, school, and playroom. Training grounds for adult gender roles. *Sex Roles, 26,* 129–147.

Etringer, B. D., Hillerbrand, E., & Hetherington, C. (1990). The influence of sexual orientation on career decision making: A research note. *Journal of Homosexuality, 19*(4), 103–111.

Ettinger, J. M. (Ed.). (1991). *Improved career decision making in a changing world.* Garrett Park, MD: Garrett Park.

Evanoski, P. O., & Tse, F. W. (1989). Career awareness program for Chinese and Korean American parents. *Journal of Counseling and Development, 67,* 472–474.

Fagot, B. I., & Leinbach, M. D. (1989). The young child's gender schema: Environmental input, internal organization. *Child Development, 60,* 663–672.

Farber, B. A., & Heifetz, L. J. (1981). The satisfaction and stresses of psychotherapeutic work: A factor analytic study. *Professional Psychology, 12* (5), 621–630.

Fassinger, R. E., & Schlossberg, N. K. (1992). Understanding the adult years: Perspectives and implications. In S. D. Brown & R. W. Lent (Eds.), *Handbook of counseling psychology* (2nd ed., pp. 217–249). New York: Wiley.

Feldman, D. C. (1988). *Managing careers in organizations.* Glenview, IL: Scott, Foresman.

Feller, R. (1994). *650 Career videos: Ratings, reviews and descriptions.* Ft. Collins: Colorado State University.

Feller, R., & Walz, G. (1996). *Career transitions in turbulent times: Exploring work, learning and careers.* Greensboro: ERIC Counseling and Student Services Clearing House, University of North Carolina.

Fernandez, J. P. (1986). *Child care and corporate productivity.* Lexington, MA: Lexington.

Fernandez, J. P. (1999). *Race, gender, & rhetoric.* New York: McGraw-Hill.

Fernandez, M. S. (1988). Issues in counseling southeast Asian students. *Journal of Multicultural Counseling and Development, 16,* 157–166.

Ferree, M. M. (1984). Class, housework, and happiness: Women's work and life satisfaction. *Sex Roles, 11,* 1057–1074.

Figler, H. (1988). *The complete job-search handbook.* New York: Henry Holt.

Fine, M., & Asch, A. (1988). Disability beyond stigma: Social interactions, discrimination, and activism. *Journal of Social Issues, 44*(1), 3–21.

Fitzgerald, L. F., & Betz, N. E. (1994). Career development in cultural context: The role of gender, race, class and sexual orientation. In M. Savickas & R. Lent (Eds.), *Convergence in career development theories: Implications for science and practice* (pp. 103–115). Palo Alto, CA: Consulting Psychologists Press.

Fitzgerald, L. F., & Ormerod, A. J. (1991). Perceptions of sexual harassment: The influence of gender and academic context. *Psychology of Women Quarterly, 15,* 281–294.

Flanders, R. B. (1980). NOICC: A coordinator for occupational information. *Occupational Outlook Quarterly, 24*(4), 22–28.

Flannelly, S. (1995). *A study of values shifts across life roles.* Unpublished dissertation, University of North Carolina, Chapel Hill.

Ford, D. H. (1987). *Humans as self constructing living systems: A developmental perspective personality disorder.* Hillsdale, NJ: Erlbaum.

Ford, M. E., & Ford, D. H. (Eds.). (1987). *Humans as self-constructing living systems: Putting the framework to work.* Hillsdale, NJ: Erlbaum.

Forney, D. S., Wallace-Schultzman, F., & Wiggens, T. T. (1982). Burnout among career development professionals: Preliminary findings and implications. *Personnel and Guidance Journal, 60,* 435–439.

Fouad, N. A. (1995). Career behavior of Hispanics: Assessment and career intervention. In F. T. L. Leong (Ed.), *Career development and vocational behavior of racial and ethnic minorities* (pp. 165–187). Mahwah, NJ: Erlbaum.

Fouad, N. A. & Bingham, R. P. (1995). Career counseling with racial/ethnic minorities. In W. B. Walsh & S. H. Osipow (Eds.), *Handbook of vocational psychology* (2nd ed.). Hillsdale, NJ: Erlbaum.

Fouad, N. A., & Spreda, S. L. (1995). Use of interest inventories with special populations. *Journal of Career Assessment, 3,* 453–468.

Fox, A. (1991). Development of a bisexual identity: Understanding the process In L. Hutchins & L. Kaahumanu (Eds.), *Bi any other name: Bisexual people speak out* (pp. 29–36). Boston: Alyson.

French, M. (1992). *The war against women.* New York: Summit.

French, S. (1996). The attitudes of health professionals towards disabled people. In G. Hales (Ed.), *Beyond disability: Towards an enabling society* (pp. 151–162). London: Sage.

Frenza, M. (1982). *Counseling women for life decisions.* Ann Arbor: ERIC Counseling and Personnel Services Clearinghouse, University of Michigan.

Freudenberger, H. J. (1974). Staff burnout. *Journal of Social Issues, 30*(1), 159–165.

Freudenberger, H. J., & Richelson, G. (1980). *Burnout: The high cost of high achievement.* Garden City, NY: Anchor.

Friedman, M., & Rosenman, R. (1974). *Type A behavior and your heart.* Greenwich, CT: Fawcett.

Friskopp, A., & Silverstein, S. (1995). *Straight jobs gay lives.* New York: Scribner.

Furnham, A., & Bitar, N. (1993). The stereotyped portrayal of men and women in British television advertisements. *Sex Roles, 29,* 297–310.

Garbarino, J. (1992). The meaning of poverty in the world of children. *American Behavioral Scientist, 35,* 220–237.

Garcia, E. E. (Ed.) (1995). *Meeting the challenge of linguistic and cultural diversity in early childhood education.* New York: Teachers College Press.

Garland, S. B. (1991, Aug. 19). Throwing stones at the glass ceiling. *Business Week,* p. 29.

Geary, J. (1972). Forty newspapers forty. In J. E. Bottoms, R. N. Evans, K. B. Hoyt, & J. C. Willer (Eds.), *Career education resource guide.* Morristown, NJ: General Learning Corporation.

Gebhardt, D. L., & Crump, C. E. (1990). Employee fitness and wellness programs in the workplace. *American Psychologist, 45,* 262–272.

Geisinger, K. F. (1998). Psychometric issues in test interpretation. In J. Sandoval, C. L. Frisby, K. F. Geisinger, J. D. Scheuneman, & J. R. Grenier (Eds.), *Test interpretation and diversity* (pp. 17–31). Washington, DC: American Psychological Association.

Gelatt, H. B. (1989). Positive uncertainty: A new decision-making framework for counseling. *Journal of Counseling Psychology, 36*(2), 252–256.

Gelatt, H. B. (1996). Developing a future sense. In R. Feller & G. Walz (Eds.), *Career transitions in turbulent times* (pp. 387–393). Greensboro, NC: ERIC Counseling and Student Services Clearinghouse, University of North Carolina.

Gelberg, S., & Chojnacki, J. T. (1996). *Career and life planning with gay, lesbian, & bisexual persons.* Alexandria, VA: American Counseling Association.

Gianakos, I., & Subick, L. M. (1986). The relationship of gender and sex-role orientation to vocational undecidedness. *Journal of Vocational Behavior, 29,* 42–51.

Gibson, R. L., Mitchell, M. H., & Basile, S. K. (1993). *Counseling in the elementary school: A comprehensive approach.* Boston: Allyn & Bacon.

Gilbert, L. A. (1993). *Two careers/one family.* Newbury Park, CA: Sage.

Gillies, P. (1989). A longitudinal study of the hopes and worries of adolescents. *Journal of Adolescence, 12,* 69–81.

Ginzberg, E. (1966). *Lifestyles of educated American women.* New York: Columbia University Press.

Ginzberg, E. (1972). Toward a theory of occupational choice: A restatement. *Vocational Guidance Quarterly, 20,* 169–176.

Ginzberg, E. (1984). Career development. In D. Brown & L. Brooks (Eds.), *Career choice and development.* San Francisco: Jossey-Bass.

Ginzberg, E., Ginsburg, S. W., Axelrad, S., & Herma, J. L. (1951). *Occupational choice: An approach to general theory.* New York: Columbia University Press.

Goldberg, H. (1983). *The new male-female relationship.* New York: Morrow.

Goldfried, M. R., & Friedman, J. M. (1982). Clinical behavior therapy and the male sex role. In K. Solomon & N. B. Levy (Eds.), *Men in transition.* New York: Plenum.

Golding, J. M. (1989). Role occupancy and role-specific stress and social support as predictors of depression. *Basic and Applied Social Psychology, 10,* 173–195.

Gonsiorek, J. C. (Ed.). (1985). *A guide to psychotherapy with gay and lesbian clients.* New York: Harrington Park.

Goodenough, F. L. (1949). *Mental testing.* New York: Rinehart.

Goodman, J. (1993, April 29). *Using nonstandardized appraisals tools and techniques.* Presentation to Michigan Career Development Association Annual Conference. Kalamazoo, MI.

Gordon, L. V. (1967). *Survey of personal values.* Chicago: Science Research Associates.

Gottfredson, G. D., & Holland, J. L. (1989). *Dictionary of Holland occupational codes.* Odessa, FL: Psychological Assessment Resources.

Gottfredson, G. D., & Holland, J. L. (1991). *The position classification inventory: Professional manual.* Odessa, FL: Psychological Assessment Resources.

Gottfredson, G. D., & Holland, J. L. (1994). *The career attitudes and strategies inventory.* Odessa, FL: Psychological Assessment Resources.

Gottfredson, G. D., Jones, E. M., & Holland, J. L. (1993). Personality and vocational interests: The relation of Holland's six interest dimensions to five robust dimensions of personality. *Journal of Counseling Psychology, 40,* 518–524.

Gottfredson, L. S. (1981). Circumscription and compromise: A developmental theory of occupational aspirations. *Journal of Counseling Psychology, 28* (6), 545–579.

Gottfredson, L. S. (1996). Gottfredson's theory of circumscription and compromise. In D. Brown, L. Brooks, & Associates (Eds.), *Career choice and development* (3rd ed.) (pp. 179–228). San Francisco: Jossey-Bass.

Gould, S., & Parzen, J. (Eds.). (1990). *Enterprising women.* Organization for Economic Cooperation and Development. Columbus: ERIC Clearinghouse on Adult, Career, and Vocational Education. (ERIC Report No. ED 335 463)

Green, F. (1994). *GAYELLOW PAGES.* New York: Renaissance House.

Green, L. B., & Parker, H. J. (1965). Parental influence upon adolescents' occupational choice: A test of an aspect of Roe's theory. *Journal of Counseling Psychology, 12,* 379–383.

Greenberger, E., & Steinberg, L. (1986). *When teenagers work: The psychological and social costs of adolescent employment.* New York: Basic.

Greenglass, E. R. (1991). Type A behavior, career aspirations, and role conflict in professional women. In M. J. Strube (Ed.), *Type A behavior* (pp. 277–292). Newbury Park, CA: Sage.

Grossman, G. M., & Drier, H. N. (1988). *Apprenticeship 2000: The status of and recommendations for improved counseling, guidance, and information processes.* Columbus: National Center for Research in Vocational Education, Ohio State University (ERIC Report No. ED 298 356).

Grubb, W. N., Davis, G., Lum, J., Plihal, J., & Mograine, C. (1991). *The cunning hand, the cultured mind: Models for integrating vocational and academic education.* Berkeley, CA: National Center for Research in Vocational Education (ERIC Report No. ED 334 421).

Gulliksen, H. (1950). *Theory of mental tests.* New York: Wiley.

Gysbers, N. C. (1996). Beyond career development—life career development revisited. In R. Feller & G. Walz (Eds.), *Career transitions in turbulent times* (pp. 11–20). Greensboro: ERIC Counseling and Student Services Clearinghouse, University of North Carolina.

Gysbers, N. C., & Henderson, P. (1988). *Developing and managing your school guidance program.* Alexandria, VA: American Association for Counseling and Development.

Gysbers, N. C., & Moore, E. J. (1987). *Career counseling, skills and techniques for practitioners.* Englewood Cliffs, NJ: Prentice-Hall.

Hackett, G. (1995). Self-efficacy in career choice and development. In A. Bandura (Ed.), *Self-efficacy in changing societies* (pp. 232–258). Cambridge: Cambridge University Press.

Hackett, G., & Lent, R. W. (1992). Theoretical advances and current inquiry in career psychology. In S. D. Brown & R. W. Lent (Eds.), *Handbook of counseling psychology* (2nd ed.) (pp. 419–451). New York: Wiley.

Hackett, G., Lent, R. W., & Greenhaus, J. H. (1991). Advances in vocational theory and research: A 20-year retrospective. *Journal of Vocational Behavior, 38,* 3–38.

Hackett, J. C., & Lonborg, S. D. (1994). Career assessment and counseling for women. In W. B. Walsh & S. H. Osipow (Eds.), *Career counseling for women: Contemporary topics in vocational psychology* (pp. 43–85). Hillsdale, NJ: Erlbaum.

Hackett, R. D., & Betz, N. E. (1981). A self-efficacy approach to the career development of women. *Journal of Vocational Behavior, 18,* 326–329.

Halaby, C. N., & Weakliem, D. L. (1989). Worker control and attachment to the firm. *American Journal of Sociology, 95,* 549–591.

Hall, A., & Fradkin, R. (1992). Affirming gay men's mental health: Counseling with a new attitude. *Journal of Mental Health, 14,* 362–374.

Hall, D. T. (Ed.). (1986). *Career development in organizations.* San Francisco: Jossey-Bass.

Hall, D. T. (1990). Career development theory in organizations. In D. Brown & L. Brooks (Eds.), *Career choice and development* (2nd ed.) (pp. 422–455). San Francisco: Jossey-Bass.

Hall, D. T. (1996). *The career is dead: Long live the career.* San Francisco: Jossey-Bass.

Hall, E. T. (1971). *Beyond culture.* New York: Anchor/Doubleday.

Hall, E. T. (1982). *The hidden dimension.* New York: Anchor/Doubleday.

Halle, E. (1982). The abandoned husband: When wives leave. In K. Solomon & N. B. Levy (Eds.), *Men in transition.* New York: Plenum.

Halpern, A., Raffeld, P., Irvin, L. D., & Link, R. (1975). *Social and prevocational information battery.* Monterey, CA: CTB-Macmillan-McGraw-Hill.

Halpern, T. P. O. (1977). Degree of client disclosure as a function of past disclosure, counselor disclosure, and counselor facilitativeness. *Journal of Counseling Psychology, 24,* 42–47.

Hammer, M., & Champy, J. (1993). *Reengineering the corporation: A manifesto for business revolution.* New York: HarperCollins.

Hansen, J. C., Collins, R. C., Swanson, J. L., & Fouad, N. A. (1993). Gender differences in the structure of interests. *Journal of Vocational Behavior, 42,* 200–211.

Hansen, L. S. (1970). *Career guidance practices in school and community.* Washington, DC: National Vocational Guidance Association.

Hansen, L. S. (1978). *BORN FREE. Training packets to reduce stereotyping in career options.* Minneapolis: University of Minnesota Press.

Hansen, L. S. (1990). *Integrative life planning: Work, family and community.* Paper presented at International Round Table for the Advancement of Counseling, July 1990. Helsinki, Finland.

Hansen, L. S. (1991). Integrative life planning: Work, family, community. [Special Issue from World Future Society Conference on "Creating the Future: Individual Responsibility," Minneapolis: July 25]. *Futurics, 14*(3 & 4), 80–86.

Hansen, L. S. (1996). ILP: Integrating our lives, shaping our society. In R. Feller & G. Walz (Eds.), *Career transitions in turbulent times* (pp. 21–30). Greensboro: ERIC Counseling and Student Services Clearinghouse, University of North Carolina.

Hansen, L. S. (1997). *Integrative life planning: Critical tasks for career development and changing life patterns.* San Francisco: Jossey-Bass.

Hansson, R. O., DeKoekkoek, P. D., Neece, W. M., & Patterson, D. W. (1997). Successful aging at work: Annual review, 1992–1996: The older worker and transitions to retirement. *Journal of Vocational Behavior, 51*, 202–233.

Harley, S. (1995). When your work is not who you are: The development of a working-class consciousness among Afro-American women. In D. Clark-Hine, W. King, & L. Reed (Eds.), *We specialize in the wholly impossible: A reader in Black women's history* (pp. 25–38). Brooklyn, NY: Carlson.

Harmon, L. W. (1996). A moving target: The widening gap between theory and practice. In M. L. Savickas & W. B. Walsh (Eds.), *Handbook of career counseling theory and practice* (pp. 37–45). Palo Alto, CA: Davies-Black.

Harmon, L. W., & Meara, N. M. (1994). Contemporary developments in women's career counseling: Themes of the past, puzzles for the future. In W. B. Walsh & S. H. Osipow (Eds.), *Career counseling for women: Contemporary topics in vocational psychology* (pp. 355–367). Hillsdale, NJ: Erlbaum.

Harrington, T. F., & O'Shea, A. J. (1980). Applicability of the Holland model of vocational development with Spanish-speaking clients. *Journal of Counseling Psychology, 27*, 246–251.

Harrington, T. F., & O'Shea, A. J. (1992). *The Harrington/O'Shea System for Career Decision Making Manual.* Circle Pines, MN: American Guidance Service.

Harris-Bowlsbey, J., Dikel, M. R., & Sampson, J. P. (1998). *The Internet: A tool for career planning.* Columbus, OH: National Career Development Association.

Harris, P. R., & Moran, R. T. (1991). *Managing cultural differences* (3rd ed.). Houston: Gulf.

Harway, M. (1980). Sex bias in educational-vocational counseling. *Psychology of Women Quarterly, 4*, 212–214.

Havighurst, R. (1953). *Human development and education.* New York: Longman.

Havighurst, R. (1972). *Developmental tasks and education* (3rd ed.). New York: Longman.

Healy, C. C. (1982). *Career development: Counseling through life stages.* Boston: Allyn & Bacon.

Healy, C. C. (1990). Reforming career appraisals to meet the needs of clients in the 1990s. *Counseling Psychologist, 18*, 214–226.

Healy, C. C., & Quinn, O. H. (1977). *Project Cadre: A cadre approach to career education infusion.* Unpublished manuscript.

Heaton, J. A., & Wilson, N. L. (1995). *Tuning in trouble: Talk TV's destructive impact on mental health.* San Francisco: Jossey-Bass.

Hein, K. (1988). *AIDS in adolescence: Exploring the challenge.* Presented at the National Invitational Conference on AIDS and adolescents. New York.

Helms, J. E. (1990a). *Black and white racial identity: Theory, research, and practice.* Westport, CT: Greenwood.

Helms, J. E. (1990b). An overview of Black racial identity theory. In J. E. Helms (Ed.), *Black and White racial identity: Theory, research and practice* (pp. 9–32). Westport, CT: Greenwood.

Helwig, A. A. (1992). Book review of career development and services. *Journal of Employment Counseling, 29*, 77–78.

Henderson, A. (1984). Homosexuality in the college years: Developmental differences between men and women. *Journal of American College Health, 32*, 216–219.

Heppner, P. P., & Krauskopf, C. J. (1987). An information processing approach to problem solving. *Counseling Psychologist, 15*, 371–447.

Hermans, H. J. M. (1992). Telling and retelling one's self-narrative: A contextual approach to life-span development. *Human Development, 35*, 361–375.

Herr, E. L. (1989). Career development and mental health. *Journal of Career Development, 16* (1), 5–18.

Herr, E. L. (1996). Toward convergence of career theory and practice: Mythology, issues, and possibilities. In M. L. Savickas & W. B. Walsh (Eds.), *Handbook of career counseling theory and practice* (pp. 70-85). Palo Alto, CA: Davies-Black.

Herr, E. L., & Cramer, S. H. (1996). *Career guidance and counseling through the life span: Systematic approaches* (5th ed.). New York: HarperCollins.

Herring, R. D. (1990). Attacking career myths among Native Americans: Implications for counseling. *School Counselor, 38,* 13–18.

Herring, R. D. (1998). *Career counseling in schools.* Alexandria, VA: American Counseling Association.

Hersen, M., & Turner, S. M. (1985). *Diagnostic interviewing.* New York: Plenum.

Higginbotham, E. (1994). Black professional women: Job ceilings and employment sectors. In M. Zinn & B. Dill (Eds.), *Women of color in the U.S. society* (pp. 113–131). Philadelphia: Temple University Press.

Highwater, J. (1990). *Sex and myth.* Boston: Harper & Row.

Hirschorn, M. W. (1988). Students over 25 found to make up 45 pct. of campus enrollments. *Chronicle of Higher Education, 34,* p. A35.

Hoffman, L. W. (1983). Increased fathering: Effects on the mother. In M. E. Lamb & A. Sagi (Eds.), *Fatherhood and family policy.* Hillsdale, NJ: Erlbaum.

Hoffreth, S. L., & Phillips, D. A. (1987). Child care in the United States: 1970 to 1985. *Journal of Marriage and the Family, 49,* 559–571.

Hofstede, G. (1984). *Culture's consequences: International differences in work-related values.* Newbury Park, CA: Sage.

Holland, J. L. (1966). *The psychology of vocational choice.* Waltham, MA: Blaisdell.

Holland, J. L. (1985a). *Making vocational choices: A theory of careers* (2nd ed.). Englewood Cliffs, NJ: Prentice-Hall.

Holland, J. L. (1985b). *Manual for the vocational preference inventory.* Odessa, FL: Psychological Assessment Resources.

Holland, J. L. (1987a). Current status of Holland's theory of careers: Another perspective. *Career Development Quarterly, 36,* 31–34.

Holland, J. L. (1987b). *The self-directed search professional manual.* Odessa, FL: Psychological Assessment Resources.

Holland, J. L. (1987c). *The occupations finder.* Odessa, FL: Psychological Assessment Resources.

Holland, J. L. (1992). *Making vocational choices* (2nd ed.). Odessa, FL: Psychological Assessment Resources.

Holland, J. L. (1994a). *Self-directed search (SDS), Form R.* Odessa, FL: Psychological Assessment Resources.

Holland, J. L. (1994b). *You and your career booklet.* Odessa, FL: Psychological Assessment Resources.

Holland, J. L. (1996). Exploring careers with a typology: What we have learned and some new directions. *American Psychologist, 51,* 397–406.

Holland, J. L., Daiger, D., & Power, P. G. (1980). *My vocational situation.* Odessa, FL: Psychological Assessment Resources.

Holland, J. L., Fritzsche, B. A., & Powell, A. B. (1994). *The SDS technical manual.* Odessa, FL: Psychological Assessment Resources.

Holland, J. L., Johnston, J. H., & Asama, N. (1993). The vocational identity scale: A diagnostic and treatment tool. *Journal of Career Assessment, 1,* 1–12.

Holland, J. L., Powell, A. B., & Fritzsche, B. A. (1994). *The SDS: Professional user's guide.* Odessa, FL: Psychological Assessment Resources.

Hollender, J. (1967). Development of a realistic vocational choice. *Journal of Counseling Psychology, 14,* 314–318.

Holmberg, K., Rosen, D., & Holland, J. L. (1990). *Leisure activities finder.* Odessa, FL: Psychological Assessment Resources.

Hopkinson, K., Cox, A., & Rutter, M. (1981). Psychiatric interviewing techniques III: Naturalistic study: Eliciting feelings. *British Journal of Psychiatry, 138,* 406–415.

Hotchkiss, L., & Borow, H. (1996). Sociological perspective on work and career development. In D. Brown, L. Brooks, & Associates (Eds.), *Career choice and development* (3rd ed.) (pp. 281–326). San Francisco: Jossey-Bass.

Houston, B. K., & Kelly, K. E. (1987). Type A behavior in housewives: Relation to work, marital adjustment, stress, tension, health, fear-of-failure and self esteem. *Journal of Psychosomatic Research, 31,* 55–61.

Hoyt, K. B., & Lester, J. N. (1995). *Learning to work: The NCDA Gallup survey.* Alexandria, VA: National Career Development Association.

Hsia, J. (1981, April). *Testing and Asian and Pacific Americans.* Paper presented at the National Association for Asian and Pacific American Education, Honolulu.

Hudson, J. S. (1992). *Vocational counseling with dual-career same-sex couples.* Unpublished manuscript, Southwest Texas State University.

Huffine, C. L., & Clausen, J. A. (1979). Madness and work: Short- and long-term effects of mental illness on occupational careers. *Social Forces, 57*(4), 1049–1062.

Humes, C. W., Szymanski, E. M., & Hohenshil, T. H. (1989, Nov./Dec.). Roles of counseling in enabling persons with disabilities. *Journal of Counseling & Development, 68,* 145–149.

Hunter, J. E., & Hunter, R. F. (1984). Validity and utility of alternative predictors of job performance. *Psychological Bulletin, 96,* 72–98.

Hunter, J. K. (1996). African American homeless women. In C. F. Collins (Ed.), *African American women's health and social issues* (pp. 135–148). Westport, CT: Auburn House.

Icard, L. (1986). Black gay men and conflicting social identities: Sexual orientation versus racial identity. In J. Gripton & M. Valentich (Eds.), *Special issue of the Journal of Social Work & Human Sexuality, Social work practice in sexual problems, 4*(1/2), 83–93.

ISO 9000: Providing the basis for quality. (1992, April 29). *CHEMICALWEEK,* pp. 30–41.

Issacson, L. E. (1985). *Basics of career counseling.* Boston: Allyn & Bacon.

Ivancevich, J. J., & Matteson, M. T. (1980). *Stress and work, a managerial perspective.* Dallas: Scott Foresman.

Ivey, A. E. (1986). *Development therapy.* San Francisco: Jossey-Bass.

Ivey, A. E. & Ivey, M. B. (1999). *Intentional interviewing & counseling* (4th ed.). Pacific Grove, CA: Brooks/Cole.

Jackson, E. L. (1988). Leisure constraints: A survey of past research. *Leisure Sciences, 10,* 203–215.

Jacobson, E. (1938). *Progressive relaxation.* Chicago: University of Chicago Press.

Jay, K. & Young, A. (Eds.). (1979). *The gay report: Lesbians and gay men speak out about their sexual experiences and lifestyles.* New York: Simon & Schuster.

Jepsen, D. A. (1986). Getting down to cases: Editor's introduction. *Career Development Quarterly, 35*(2), 67–68.

Jepsen, D. A. (1996). Relationships between development career counseling theory and practice. In M. L. Savickas & W. B. Walsh (Eds.), *Handbook of career counseling theory and practice* (pp. 135–155). Palo Alto, CA: Davies-Black.

Jiang, W., Babyak, M., Krantz, D. S., Waugh, R. A., Coleman, R. E., Hanson, M. M., Frid, D. J., McNulty, S., Morris, J. J., O'Connor, C. M., & Blumenthal, J. A.

(1996). Mental stress-induced myocardial ischemia and cardiac events. *Journal of the American Medical Association, 275,* 1651–1656.

JIST. (1993). *Enhanced guide for occupational exploration.* Indianapolis: Author.

Job market for UCLA 1987 graduates. (1988). Los Angeles: University of California at Los Angeles.

Job stress at work around the world. (1993, Spring). *San Antonio Express-News,* p. 1B.

Johnson, G. J. (1990). Underemployment, underpayment, and self-esteem among black men. *Journal of Black Psychology, 16*(2), 23–44.

Johnson, M. J., Swartz, J. L., & Martin, W. E., Jr. (1995). Applications of psychological theories for career development with Native Americans. In F. T. L. Leong (Ed.), *Career development and vocational behavior of racial and ethnic minorities* (pp. 103–129). Mahwah, NJ: Erlbaum.

Johnson, P. R., & Indvik, J. (1994). Workplace violence: An issue of the nineties. *Public Personnel Management, 23,* 515–523.

Jones, M. (1991). Gender stereotyping in advertisements. *Teaching of Psychology, 18,* 231–233.

Jourard, S. M. (1964). *The transparent self.* Princeton, NJ: Van Nostrand.

Judge, T. A., & Bretz, R. D., Jr. (1992). Effects of work values on job choice decisions. *Journal of Applied Psychology, 77,* 261–271.

Kail, R. V., & Cavanaugh, J. C. (1996). *Human development.* Pacific Grove, CA: Brooks/Cole.

Kail, R. V., & Cavanaugh, J. C. (2000). *Human development,* 2nd ed. Belmont, CA: Wadsworth.

Kando, T. M., & Summers, W. C. (1971). The impact of work on leisure: Toward a paradigm and research strategy. *Pacific Sociological Review, 14,* 310–327.

Kaneshige, E. (1979). Cultural factors in group counseling and interaction. In G. Henderson (Ed.), *Understanding and counseling ethnic minorities* (pp. 457–467). Springfield, IL: Charles C. Thomas.

Kanfer, G. H. (1980). Self-management methods: In F. H. Kanfer & A. P. Goldstein (Eds.), *Helping people change* (pp. 309–355). New York: Pergamon.

Kanter, M. (1989). *When giants learn to dance.* New York: Simon & Schuster.

Kapes, J. T., Borman, C. A., Garcia, G., Jr., & Compton, J. W. (1985, April). *Evaluation of microcomputer based career guidance systems with college students: SIGI and DISCOVER.* Paper presented at the annual meeting of the American Educational Research Association, Chicago.

Kapes, J. T., Mastie, M. M., & Whitfield, E. A. (1994). *A counselor's guide to career assessment instruments* (3rd ed.). Alexandria, VA: National Career Development Association.

Karasek, R., & Theorell, T. (1990). *Healthy work: Stress, productivity, and the reconstruction of working life.* New York: Basic Books.

Kasl, S. V. (1978). Epidemiological contributions to the study of work stress. In C. L. Cooper & R. Payne (Eds.), *Stress at work.* New York: Wiley.

Katz, M. R. (1975). *SIGI: A computer-based system of interactive guidance and information.* Princeton, NJ: Educational Testing Service.

Katz, M. R. (1993). *Computer-assisted career decision-making: The guide in the machine.* Hillsdale, NJ: Erlbaum.

Kavruck, S. (1956). Thirty-three years of test research: A short history of test development in the U.S. Civil Service Commission. *American Psychologist, 11,* 329–333.

Keating, D. P. (1980). Thinking processes in adolescence. In J. Adelson (Ed.), *Handbook of adolescent psychology.* New York: Wiley.

Keller, L. M., Bouchard, T. J., Jr., Arvey, R. D., Segal, N., & Dawis, R. V. (1992). Work values: Genetic and environmental influences. *Journal of Applied Psychology, 77,* 79–88.

Kibrick, A. K., & Tiedeman, D. V. (1961). Conception of self and perception of role in schools of nursing. *Journal of Counseling Psychology, 8,* 26–29.

Kinnier, R. T., & Krumboltz, J. D. (1984). Procedures for successful career counseling. In N. C. Gysbers (Ed.), *Designing careers: Counseling to enhance education, work, and leisure* (pp. 307–335). San Francisco: Jossey-Bass.

Kinsey, A. C., Pomeroy, W. B., & Martin, C. E. (1948). *Sexual behavior in the human male.* Philadelphia: Saunders.

Kivlighan, D. J., Jr., Johnston, J. A., Hogan, R. S., & Mauer, E. (1994). Who benefits from computerized career counseling? *Journal of Counseling and Development, 72,* 289–292.

Kjos, D. (1996). Linking career counseling to personality disorders. In R. Feller & G. Walz (Eds.), *Career transitions in turbulent times* (pp. 267–273). Greensboro: ERIC Counseling and Student Services Clearinghouse, University of North Carolina.

Kleinfield, N. R. (1996). A new and unnerving workplace. In *New York Times* (et al.), *The downsizing of America* (pp. 37–76). New York: Time Books.

Klinger, G. (1988). *Dual-role model.* Unpublished manuscript, Southwest Texas State University, San Marcos.

Knapp, R. R., & Knapp, L. (1977). *Interest changes and the classification of occupations.* Unpublished manuscript, EDITS, San Diego, CA.

Knapp, R. R., & Knapp, L. (1984). *COPS interest inventory technical manual.* San Diego: EDITS.

Knapp, R. R., & Knapp, L. (1985). *California occupational preference system: Self-interpretation profile and guide.* San Diego: EDITS.

Knowdell, R. L., McDaniels, C., & Walz, G. R. (1983). *Outplacement counseling.* Ann Arbor: ERIC Counseling and Personnel Service Clearinghouse, University of Michigan.

Kohlberg, L. (1973). Continuities in childhood and adult moral development revisited. In P. B. Baltes & K. W. Schase (Eds.), *Lifespan development psychology: Personality and socialization.* New York: Academic.

Kotter, J. P. (1984). The psychological contract: Managing the joining-up process. In J. A. Sonnenfeld (Ed.), *Managing career systems* (pp. 499–509). Homewood, IL: Irwin.

Kram, K. E. (1985). Improving the mentoring process. *Training and Development Journal, 39*(4), 40–43.

Kram, K. E. (1988). *Mentoring at work: Developmental relationships in organizational life.* Lanham, MD: University Press of America.

Kriegel, L. (1982). Claiming the self: The cripple as American male. In M. G. Eisenberg, D. Kriggins, & R. J. Duvall (Eds.), *Disabled people as second-class citizens.* New York: Springer.

Kronenberger, G. K. (1991, June). Out of the closet. *Personnel Journal,* 40–44.

Krumboltz, J. D. (1983). *Private rules in career decision making.* Columbus, OH: National Center for Research in Vocational Education.

Krumboltz, J. D. (1988). *Career Beliefs Inventory.* Palo Alto, CA: Consulting Psychologists Press.

Krumboltz, J. D. (1991). *Career beliefs inventory.* Palo Alto, CA: Consulting Psychologists Press.

Krumboltz, J. D. (1992). Thinking about careers. *Contemporary Psychology, 37,* 113.

Krumboltz, J. D. (1993). Integrating career and personal counseling. *Career Development Quarterly, 42,* 143–148.

Krumboltz, J. D. (1996). A learning theory of career counseling. In M. L. Savickas & W. B. Walsh (Eds.), *Handbook of career counseling theory and practice* (pp. 55–81). Palo Alto, CA: Davies-Black.

Krumboltz, J. D., & Hamel, D. A. (1977). *Guide to career decision-making skills.* New York: Educational Testing Service.

Krumboltz, J. D., Mitchell, A., & Gelatt, H. G. (1975). Applications of social learning theory of career selection. *Focus on Guidance, 8,* 1–16.

Krumboltz, J., & Nichols, C. (1990). Integrating the social learning theory of career decision making. In W. B. Walsh & S. H. Osipow (Eds.), *Career counseling: Contemporary topics in vocational psychology* (pp. 159–192). Hillsdale, NJ: Erlbaum.

Krumboltz, J. D., & Sorenson, D. L. (1974). *Career decision making.* Madison, WI: Counseling Films.

Kuder, G. F. (1963). A rationale for evaluating interests. *Educational and Psychological Measurement, 23,* 3–10.

Kuder, G. F. (1964). *Kuder general interest survey: Manual.* Chicago: Science Research Associates.

Kuder, G. F. (1966). *Kuder occupational interest survey: General manual.* Chicago: Science Research Associates.

Kumata, R., & Murata, A. (1980, March). *Employment of Asian/Pacific American women in Chicago.* Report of conference sponsored by the Women's Bureau, U.S. Department of Labor, Chicago.

Kurpius, D., Burello, L., & Rozecki, T. (1990). Strategic planning in human service organizations. *Counseling and Human Development, 22*(9), 1–12.

LaFromboise, T. D. & Jackson, M. (1996). MCT theory and Native-American populations. In D. W. Sue, A. E. Ivey, & P. B. Pedersen, *A Theory of Multicultural Counseling & Therapy* (pp. 192–202). Pacific Grove, CA: Brooks/Cole.

LaFromboise, T. D., Trimble, J. E., & Mohatt, G. V. (1990). Counseling intervention and American Indian tradition: An integrative approach. *Counseling Psychologist, 18*(4), 628–654.

Lamb, M. E., Frodi, A. M., Hwang, C., & Frodi, M. (1982). Varying degrees of paternal involvement in infant care: Attitudinal and behavioral correlates. In M. E. Lamb (Ed.), *Nontraditional families: Parenting and child development.* Hillsdale, NJ: Erlbaum.

Lapan, R. T., & Jingeleski, J. (1992). Circumscribing vocational aspirations in junior high school. *Journal of Counseling Psychology, 39,* 81–90.

Lauer, R. H., & Lauer, J. C. (1986). Factors in long-term marriages. *Journal of Family Issues, 7,* 382–390.

Lazarus, A. A. (1989). *The practice of multimodal therapy.* Baltimore: Johns Hopkins University Press.

Lazarus, R. S. (1980). The stress and coping paradigm. In L. A. Bond & J. C. Rosen (Eds.), *Primary prevention of psychopathology: Vol. 4.* Hanover, NH: University Press of New England.

Leahy, R. L., & Shirk, S. R. (1984). The development of classificatory skills; and sex-trait stereotypes in children. *Sex Roles, 10,* 281–292.

Leana, C. R., & Feldman, D. C. (1991). Gender differences in responses to unemployment. *Journal of Vocational Behavior, 38,* 65–77.

Leclair, S. W. (1982). The dignity of leisure. *School Counselor, 29*(4), 289–296.

Lent, R. W., Brown, S. D., & Hackett, G. (1996). Career development from a social cognitive perspective. In D. Brown, L. Brooks, & Associates (Eds.), *Career choice and development* (3rd ed.) (pp. 373–416). San Francisco: Jossey-Bass.

Leong, F. T. L. (1991). Career development attributes and occupational values of Asian American and white high school students. *Career Development Quarterly, 39,* 221–230.

Leong, F. T. L. (1993). The career counseling process with racial/ethnic minorities: The case of Asian Americans. *Career Development Quarterly, 42,* 26–40.

Leong, F.T.L. (1996a). Challenges to career counseling: Boundaries, cultures, and complexity. In M. L. Savickas & W. B. Walsh, *Handbook of career counseling theory and practice* (pp. 333–347). Palo Alto, CA: Davies-Black.

Leong, F. T. L. (1996b). MCT theory and Asian-American populations. In D.W. Sue, A. E. Ivey, & P. B. Pedersen, *A theory of multicultural counseling and therapy* (pp. 204–214). Pacific Grove, CA: Brooks/Cole.

Leong, F. T. L., & Serafica, F. C. (1995). Career development of Asian Americans: A research area in need of a good theory. In F. T. L. Leong (Ed.), *Career development and vocational behavior of racial and ethnic minorities* (pp. 78–99). Mahwah, NJ: Erlbaum.

Leung, S. A., Conoley, C. W., & Scheel, M. J. (1994). The career and educational aspirations of gifted high school students: A retrospective study. *Journal of Counseling & Development, 72,* 298–303.

Levi, L. (1984). *Preventing work stress.* Reading, MA: Addison-Wesley.

Levine, H., & Evans, N. J. (1991). The development of gay, lesbian, and bisexual identities. In N. J. Evans & V. A. Walls (Eds.), *Beyond tolerance: Gays, lesbians, and bisexuals on campus* (pp. 1–24). Alexandria, VA: American College Personnel Association.

Levinson, D. J. (1980). The mentor relationship. In M. A. Morgan (Ed.), *Managing career development.* New York: Van Nostrand.

Levinson, D. J. (1996). *The seasons of a woman's life.* New York: Knopf.

Levinson, D. J., Darrow, C. N., Klein, E. B., Levinson, M. H., & McKee, B. (1978). *The seasons of a man's life.* New York: Knopf.

Lindsey, L. L. (1990). *Gender roles: A sociological perspective.* Englewood Cliffs, NJ: Prentice-Hall.

Livson, N., & Peskin, H. (1980). Perspectives on adolescence from longitudinal research. In J. Adelson (Ed.), *Handbook of adolescent psychology.* New York: Wiley.

Locke, E. A., & Latham, G. P. (1990). *A theory of goal setting and task performance.* Englewood Cliffs, NJ: Prentice-Hall.

Lofquist, L. H., & Dawis, R. V. (1984). Research on work adjustment and satisfaction: Implications for career counseling. In S. Brown & R. Lent (Eds.), *Handbook of counseling psychology* (pp. 216–237). New York: Wiley.

Lofquist, L. H., & Dawis, R. V. (1991). *Essentials of person-environment-correspondence counseling.* Minneapolis: University of Minnesota Press.

Loiacano, D. K. (1989). Gay identity issues among black Americans: Racism, homophobia, and the need for validation. *Journal of Counseling & Development, 68,* 21–25.

Loiacano, D. K. (1993). Gay identity issues among black Americans: Racism, homophobia, and the need for validation. In L. D. Garnets & D. C. Kimmel (Eds.), *Psychological perspectives on lesbian and gay male experiences* (pp. 364–376). New York: Columbia University Press.

Lorde, A. (1984). *Sister outsider.* Trumansburg, NY: Crossing.

Lott, B. E. (1994). *Women's lives: Themes and variations in gender* (2nd ed.). Pacific Grove, CA: Brooks/Cole.

Lowman, R. L. (1993). *Counseling and psychotherapy of work dysfunctions.* Washington, DC: American Psychological Association.

Lucas, M. S. (1996). Building cohesiveness between practitioners and researchers: A practitioner-scientist model. In M. L. Savickas & W. B. Walsh (Eds.), *Handbook of career counseling theory and practice* (pp. 81–89). Palo Alto, CA: Davies-Black.

Lunneborg, P. W. (1981). *The vocational interest inventory (VII) manual.* Los Angeles: Western Psychological Services.

Lunneborg, P. W. (1984). Practical application of Roe's theory of career development. In D. Brown & L. Brooks (Eds.), *Career choice and development* (pp. 54–61). San Francisco: Jossey-Bass.

Lytton, H., & Romney, D. M. (1991). Parents' differential socialization of boys and girls: A meta-analysis. *Psychological Bulletin, 109,* 267–296.

Mackelprang, R., & Salsgiver, R. (1999). *Disability: A diversity model approach in human service practice.* Pacific Grove, CA: Brooks/Cole.

Magnuson, J. (1990). Stress management. *Journal of Property Management, 55,* 24–28.

Malcolm, S. M. (1990). Reclaiming our past. *Journal of Negro Education, 59*(3), 246–259.

Mankiller, W. & Wallis, M. (1993). *Mankiller.* New York: St. Martin's.

Manson, N. M. (Ed.). (1982). *Topics in American Indian mental health prevention.* Portland: Oregon Health Sciences University Press.

Mantell, M. (1994). *Ticking bombs: Defusing violence in the workplace.* Burr Ridge, IL: Irwin.

Marcia, J. E. (1967). Ego identity status: Relationship to change in self-esteem, "general adjustment," and authoritarianism. *Journal of Personality, 35*(1), 119–133.

Marcia, J. E. (1980). Identity in adolescence. In J. Adelson (Ed.), *Handbook of adolescent psychology.* New York: Garland.

Marcia, J. E. (1991). Identity and self-development. In R. M. Lerner, A. C. Petersen, & J. Brooks-Gunn (Eds.), *Encyclopedia of adolescence: Vol. 1.* New York: Garland.

Mariani, M. (1994, Fall). The young and the entrepreneurial. *Occupational Outlook Quarterly, 38,* 2–10.

Mariani, M. (1995–96, Winter). Computers and career guidance: Ride the rising ride. *Occupational Outlook Quarterly, 39,* 16–27.

Mariani, M. (1998, Summer). Job shadowing for college students. *Occupational Outlook Quarterly, 40,* 46–49.

Marsh, H. W. (1991). Employment during high school: Character building or a subversion of academic goals? *Sociology of Education, 64,* 172–189.

Martin, W. E., Jr. (1995). Career development assessment and intervention strategies with American Indians. In F. T. L. Leong (Ed.), *Career development and vocational behavior of racial and ethnic minorities* (pp. 227–246). Mahwah, NJ: Erlbaum.

Maslach, C. (1976). Burned out. *Human Behavior, 5*(9), 16–22.

Maslach, C. (1981). Burnout: A social psychological analysis. In J. W. Jones (Ed.), *The burnout syndrome: Current research, theory, interventions.* Park Ridge, IL: London House.

Maslach, C., & Jackson, J. E. (1981). The measurement of experienced burnout. *Journal of Occupational Behavior, 2,* 99–113.

Matsumoto, David. (1994). *People: Psychology from a cultural perspective.* Pacific Grove, CA: Brooks/Cole.

Matsumoto, David. (1996). *Culture and psychology.* Pacific Grove, CA: Brooks/Cole.

Matsumoto, David. (2000). *Culture and psychology,* 2nd ed. Belmont, CA: Wadsworth.

Mauer, E. B., & Gysbers, N. C. (1990). Identifying career concerns of entering university freshmen using *My Vocational Situation. Career Development Quarterly, 39,* 155–165.

Maze, M., & Cummings, R. (1982). Analysis of DISCOVER. In M. Maze & R. Cummings, *How to select a computer-assisted guidance system* (pp. 97–107). Madison: University of Wisconsin, Wisconsin Vocational Studies Center.

McBay, S. M. (1992). The condition of African American education: Changes and challenges. In B. J. Tidwell (Ed.), *The state of black America 1992* (pp. 141–156). New York: National Urban League.

McBride, A. B. (1990). Mental health effects of women's multiple roles. *American Psychologist, 45,* 381–384.

McCormac, M. E. (1988). Information sources and resources. *Journal of Career Development, 16,* 129–138.

McDaniels, C. (1984). Work and leisure in the career span. In N. C. Gysbers & Associates (Eds.), *Designing careers, counseling to enhance education, work and leisure* (Chap. 21). San Francisco: Jossey-Bass.

McDaniels, C. (1990). *The changing workplace: Career counseling strategies for the 1990s and beyond.* San Francisco: Jossey-Bass.

McDonald, G. J. (1982). Individual differences in the coming out process for gay men: Implications for theoretical models. *Journal of Homosexuality, 8*(1), 47–60.

McGinn, D., & Naughton, K. (2001). How safe is your job? *Newsweek,* Feb. 5 (pp. 37–43). New York: Newsweek, Inc.

McGowan, B. G. (1984). *Trends in employee counseling programs.* New York: Pergamon.

McKinlay, B. (1990). *Developing a career information system.* Eugene, OR: Career Information System.

McNeil, J. (1995). Disability: In U.S. Bureau of the Census, Current population reports, Series P23–189, *Population Profile of the United States,* 1995 (pp. 32–33). Washington, DC: U.S. Government Printing Office.

Meara, N. M. (1996). Prudence and career assessment: Making our implicit assumptions explicit. In M. L. Savickas, & W. B. Walsh (Eds.), *Handbook of career counseling theory and practice* (pp. 315–331). Palo Alto, CA: Davies-Black.

Meichenbaum, D. (1977). *Cognitive behavior modification: An integrative approach.* New York: Plenum.

Meir, E. I., Esformes, Y., & Friedland, N. (1994). Congruence and differentiation as predictors of workers' occupational stability and job performance. *Journal of Career Assessment, 2,* 40–54.

Meister, J. C. (1994). *Corporate quality universities: Lessons in building a world-class work force.* New York: Irwin.

Michael, R. T., Gagnon, J. H., Lauman, E. O., & Kolata, G. (1994). *Sex in America: A definitive survey.* Boston: Little Brown.

Mickens, E. (1994). *The 100 best companies for gay men and lesbians.* New York: Pocket.

Micro-tower: The group vocational and research center. (1977). New York: ICD Rehabilitation and Research Center.

Military Career Guide (1989). North Chicago, IL: U.S. Military Processing Command.

Miller, D. C., & Form, W. H. (1951). *Industrial sociology.* New York: Harper & Row.

Miller, J. M., & Springer, T. P. (1986). Perceived satisfaction of a computerized vocational counseling system as a function of monetary investment. *Journal of College Student Personnel, 27,* 142–146.

Miller, M. J. (1986). Usefulness of Gati's hierarchical model of vocational interests for career counselors. *Journal of Employment Counseling, 23,* 57–65.

Miller, N. B. (1982). Social work services to urban Indians. In J. W. Green (Ed.), *Cultural awareness in the human services.* Englewood Cliffs, NJ: Prentice-Hall.

Miller-Tiedeman, A. (1988). *Lifecareer: The quantum leap into a process theory of career.* Vista, CA: LIFECAREER Foundation.

Miller-Tiedeman, A. L., & Tiedeman, D. V. (1990). Career decision making: An individualistic perspective. In D. Brown, L. Brooks, & Associates (Eds.), *Career choice and development: Applying contemporary theories to practice* (2nd ed.) (pp. 308–337). San Francisco: Jossey-Bass.

Mitchell, L. K., & Krumboltz, J. D. (1984). Social learning approach to career decision making: Krumboltz's theory. In D. Brown & L. Brooks (Eds.), *Career choice and development.* San Francisco: Jossey-Bass.

Mitchell, L. K., & Krumboltz, J. D. (1987). Cognitive restructuring and decision making training on career indecision. *Journal of Counseling and Development, 66,* 171–174.

Mitchell, L. K., & Krumboltz, J. D. (1990). Social learning approach to career decision making: Krumboltz's theory. In D. Brown & L. Brooks (Eds.), *Career choice and development: Applying contemporary theories to practice* (2nd ed.) (pp. 145–196). San Francisco: Jossey-Bass.

Mitchell, L. K., & Krumboltz, J. D. (1996). Krumboltz's learning theory of career choice and counseling. In D. Brown, L. Brooks, & Associates (Eds.), *Career choice and development* (3rd ed.) (pp. 233–276). San Francisco: Jossey-Bass.

Mondimore, F. M. (1996). *Homosexuality.* Baltimore: Johns Hopkins University Press.

Money, J. (1982). Introduction. In K. Solomon & N. B. Levy (Eds.), *Men in transition.* New York: Plenum.

Morales, E. S. (1992). Counseling Latino gays and Latina lesbians. In S. H. Dworkin and F. J. Gutierrea (Eds.), *Counseling gay men and lesbians: Journey to the end of the rainbow* (pp. 125–141). Alexendra , VA: American Counseling Association.

Morrow, P. C. (1985). Retirement planning: Rounding out the career process. In D. W. Myers (Ed.), *Employee problem prevention and counseling.* Westport, CT: Quorum.

Muchinsky, P. M. (1997). *Psychology applied to work* (5th ed.) Pacific Grove, CA: Brooks/Cole.

Multon, K. D., Brown, S. D., & Lent, R. W. (1991). Relation of self-efficacy beliefs to academic outcomes: A meta-analytic investigation. *Journal of Counseling Psychology, 38,* 30–38.

Munsterberg, H. (1913). *Psychology and industrial efficiency.* Boston: Houghton Mifflin.

Myers, D. W. (1984). *Establishing and building employee assistance programs.* Westport, CT: Quorum.

Myers, L. J., Speight, S. L., Highlen, P. S., Cox, C. I. Reynolds, A. L., Adams, E. M., & Hanley, C. P. (1991). Identity development and worldviews toward an optimal conceptualization. *Journal of Counseling and Development, 70,* 55–63.

Nadelson, T., & Nadelson, C. (1982). Dual careers and changing role models. In K. Solomon & N. B. Levy (Eds.), *Men in transition.* New York: Plenum.

National Commission on Children. (1993). *Just the facts: A summary of recent information on America's children and their families.* Washington, DC: Author.

National Consortium of State Career Guidance Supervisors. (1996). *Planning for life: 1995 compendium of recognized career planning programs.* Columbus, OH: Center on Education and Training for Employment, Ohio State University.

National Occupational Information Coordinating Committee (NOICC), U.S. Department of Labor. (1989). *National career development guidelines.* Washington, DC: U.S. Department of Labor.

National Occupational Information Coordinating Committee (NOICC), U.S. Department of Labor. (1992). *The national career development guidelines project.* Washington, DC: U.S. Department of Labor.

National Science Foundation. (1989). *Science and engineering indicators—1989.* Washington, DC: National Science Foundation.

Neal, B. E. (2000). Native American women. In M. Julia (Ed.), *Constructing gender: Multicultural perspectives in working women* (pp. 157–174). Pacific Grove, CA: Brooks/Cole.

Neff, N., & Levine, A. (1997). *Where women stand: An international report on the status of women in 140 countries, 1997–1998.* New York: Random House.

Neff, W. S. (1985). *Work and human behavior* (2nd ed.). Chicago: Aldine.

Nelson, C. (1990, March). The beast within Winnie the Pooh reassessed. *Children's Literature in Education, 21,* 17–22.

Neukrug, E. (1999). *The world of the counselor.* Pacific Grove, CA: Brooks/Cole.

Nevill, D. D., & Super, D. E. (1986). *The Salience Inventory manual: Theory, application, and research.* Palo Alto, CA: Consulting Psychologists Press.

Nevo, O. (1987). Irrational expectations in career counseling and their confronting arguments. *Career Development Quarterly, 35,* 239–250.

Newman, B. M., & Newman, P. R. (1995). *Development through life: A psychosocial approach.* Pacific Grove, CA: Brooks/Cole.

Newman, B. M., & Newman, P. R. (1999). *Development through life: A psychosocial approach* (7th ed.). Belmont, CA: Wadsworth.

Newman, B. S., & Muzzonigro, P. G. (1993). The effects of traditional family values on the coming out process of gay male adolescents. *Adolescence, 28,* 213–226.

Nielsen Media Research. (1989). *'89 Nielsen report on television.* Northbrook, IL: Author.

Nihira, K., Foster, R., Shellhaas, M., & Leland, H. (1975). *AAMD adaptive behavior scale.* Washington, DC: American Association on Mental Deficiency.

Noble, M. (1992). *Down is up for Aaron Eagle: A mother's spiritual journey with Down Syndrome.* San Francisco: Harper.

Norrell, G., & Grater, H. (1960). Interest awareness as an aspect of self-awareness. *Journal of Counseling Psychology, 7,* 289–292.

Obear, K. (1991). Homophobia. In N. J. Evans & V. A. Wall (Eds.), *Beyond tolerance: Gays, lesbians, and bisexuals on campus* (pp. 39–66). Alexandria, VA: American College Personnel Association.

O'Driscoll, M. P., Ilgen, D. R., & Hildreth, K. (1992). Time devoted to job and off-job activities, interrole conflict, and affective experiences. *Journal of Applied Psychology, 77,* 272–279.

Ogbu, J. (1990). Cultural model, identity and literacy. In J. Stigler, R. Shweder, & G. Herdt (Eds.), *Cultural psychology* (pp. 520–541). New York: Cambridge University Press.

O'Hara, R. P., & Tiedeman, D. V. (1959). Vocational self-concept in adolescence. *Journal of Counseling Psychology, 6,* 292–301.

Okun, B. F. , Fried, J., & Okun, M. L. (1999). *Understanding diversity: A learning practice primer.* Pacific Grove, CA: Brooks/Cole.

O'Neil, J. M. (1982). Gender role conflict and strain in men's lives: Implications for psychiatrists, psychologists, and other human-services providers. In K. Solomon & N. B. Levy (Eds.), *Men in transition.* New York: Plenum.

O'Neil, J. M. (1990). Assessing men's gender role conflict. In D. Moore & F. Leafgren (Eds.), *Men in conflict* (pp. 23–38). Alexandria, VA: American Association of Counseling and Development.

Ortiz, V. (1996). Migration and marriage among Puerto Rican women. *International Migration Review, 30*(2), 460–484.

Osipow, S. H. (1983). *Theories of career development* (3rd ed.). New York: Appleton-Century-Crofts.

Osipow, S. H., & Fitzgerald, L. (1996). *Theories of career development* (4th ed.). Needham Heights, MA: Allyn & Bacon.

Osipow, S. H. & Littlejohn, E. M. (1995). Toward a multicultural theory of career development: Prospects and dilemmas. In F. T. L. Leong (Ed.), *Career development and vocational behavior of racial and ethnic minorities* (pp. 251–261). Mahwah, NJ: Erlbaum.

Othmer, E., & Othmer, S. (1989). *The clinical interview.* Washington, DC: American Psychiatric Press.

O'Toole, J. (1981). *Making America work.* New York: Continuum.

Out! Resource Guide. (1994). Chicago: Lambda.

Paisley, P. O., & Hubbard, G. T. (1994). *Developmental school counseling programs: From theory to practice.* Alexandria, VA: American Counseling Association.

Palkovitz, R. (1984). Parental attitudes and fathers' interactions with their 5-month-old infants. *Developmental Psychology, 20,* 1054–1060.

Parcel, T. L., & Menaghan, E. G. (1994). Early parental work, family, social capital, and early childhood outcomes. *American Journal of Sociology, 9,* 972–1009.

Pardine, P., Higgins, R., Szeglin, A., Beres, J., Kravitz, R., & Fotis, J. (1981). Job stress, worker-strain relationship moderated by off-the-job experience. *Psychological Reports, 48,* 963–970.

Pareles, J. (1990, October 21). The women who talk back in rap. *New York Times,* pp. H33, H36.

Parham, T. (1996). MCT theory and African-American populations. In D. W. Sue, A. E. Ivey, & P. B. Pedersen, *A theory of multicultural counseling & therapy* (pp. 177–190). Pacific Grove, CA: Brooks/Cole.

Parker, R. M., & Hansen, C. E. (1981). *Rehabilitation counseling.* Boston: Allyn & Bacon.

Parsons, F. (1909). *Choosing a vocation.* Boston: Houghton Mifflin.

Pascarella, E. T., & Terenzini, P. T. (1991). *How college affects students: Findings and insights from twenty years of research.* San Francisco: Jossey-Bass.

Patterson, M. (1996). Women's employment patterns, pension coverage, and retirement planning. In C. Costello & B. Krimgold (Eds.), *The American Women 1996–97. Women and work* (pp. 148–165). New York: Norton.

Peatling, J. H., & Tiedeman, D. V. (1977). *Career development: Designing self.* Muncie, IN: Accelerated Development.

Peplau, L. A., Cochran, S. D., & Mays, V. M. (1997). A national survey of intimate relationships of African American lesbians and gay men: A look at commitment, satisfaction, sexual behavior, and HIV disease. In B. Greene, *Ethnic and cultural diversity among lesbians and gay men* (pp. 11–39). Thousand Oaks, CA: Sage.

Pernanen, K. (1991). *Alcohol in human violence.* London: Guilford.

Peterson, G. W., Ryan-Jones, R. E., Sampson, J. P., Jr., Reardon, R. C., & Shahnasarian, M. (1987). *A comparison of the effectiveness of three computer-assisted career guidance systems on college students' career decision making processes* (Technical Report No. 6). Tallahassee: Florida State University, Center for the Study of Technology in Counseling and Career Development.

Peterson, G. W., Ryan-Jones, R. E., Sampson, J. P., Reardon, R. C., & Shahnasarian, M. (1994). A comparison of the effectiveness of three computer-generated career guidance systems: DISCOVER, SIGI, and SIGI PLUS. *Computers in Human Behavior, 10,* 189–198.

Peterson, G. W., Sampson, J. P., & Reardon, R. C. (1991). *Career development and services: A cognitive approach.* Pacific Grove, CA: Brooks/Cole.

Peterson, G. W., Sampson, J. P., Jr., Reardon, R. C., & Lenz, J. G. (1996). A cognitive information processing approach to career problem solving and decision making. In D. Brown, L. Brooks, & Associates (Eds.), *Career choice and development* (3rd ed.) (pp. 423–467). San Francisco: Jossey-Bass.

Peterson, M. (1982). VALPAR component work sample system. In J. T. Kapes & M. M. Mastie (Eds.), *A counselor's guide to vocational guidance instruments.* Falls Church, VA: National Vocational Guidance Association.

Peterson, N., & Gonzalez, R. C. (2000). *The role of work in people's lives: Applied career counseling and vocational psychology.* Pacific Grove, CA: Brooks/Cole–Wadsworth.

Piaget, J. (1929). *The child's conception of the world.* New York: Harcourt Brace.

Piaget, J., & Inhelder, B. (1969). *The psychology of the child.* New York: Basic.

Picchioni, A. P., & Bonk, E. C. (1983). *A comprehensive history of guidance in the United States.* Austin: Texas Personnel and Guidance Association.

Pietrofesa, J. J., & Splete, H. (1975). *Career development: Theory and research.* New York: Grune & Stratton.

Pine, G. J., & Innis, G. (1987). Cultural and individual work values. *Career Development Quarterly, 35*(4), 279–287.

Pines, A., & Aronson, E. (1988). *Career burnout causes and cures.* New York: Free Press.

Pines, A., & Maslach, C. (1979). Characteristics of staff burnout. *Psychiatry, 29,* 233–237.

Pleck, J. H. (1985). *Working wives/working husbands.* Newbury Park, CA: Sage.

Polkinghorne, D. E. (1990). Action theory approaches to career research. In R. A. Young & W. A. Borgen (Eds.), *Methodological approaches to the study of career* (pp. 87–105). New York: Praeger.

Ponterotto, J. G. (1987). Counseling Mexican Americans: A multimodal approach. *Journal of Counseling and Development, 65,* 308–311.

Poole, M. E., & Clooney, G. H. (1985). Careers: Adolescent awareness and exploration of possibilities for self. *Journal of Vocational Behavior, 26,* 251–263.

Pope, R. L., & Reynolds, A. L. (1991). Including bisexuality: It's more than just a label. In N. J. Evans & V. A. Wall (Eds.), *Beyond tolerance: Gays, lesbians, and bisexuals on campus* (pp. 205–212). Alexandria, VA: American College Personnel Association.

Porter, T. L. (1981). Extent of disabling conditions. In R. M. Parker & C. E. Hansen (Eds.), *Rehabilitation counseling.* Boston: Allyn & Bacon.

Posner, B. Z. (1992). Person-organization values congruence: No support for individual differences as a moderating influence. *Human Relations, 45,* 351–361.

Powell, D. H. (1957). Careers and family atmosphere: An empirical test of Roe's theory. *Journal of Counseling Psychology, 4,* 212–217.

Prediger, D. J. (1994). Multicultural assessment standards: A compilation for counselors. *Measurement and Evaluation in Counseling and Development, 27,* 68–73.

Prediger, D. J. (1995). *Assessment in career counseling.* Greensboro: ERIC Counseling and Student Services Clearinghouse, University of North Carolina.

Prediger, D. J., & Swaney, K. B. (1995). Using the UNIACT in a comprehensive approach to assessment for career planning. *Journal of Career Assessment, 3,* 429–452.

Purcell, P., & Stewart, L. (1990). Dick and Jane in 1989. *Sex Roles, 22,* 177–185.

Rabinowitz, F. E., & Cochran, S. V. (1994). *Man alive: A primer of men's issues.* Pacific Grove, CA: Brooks/Cole.

Radin, N. (1982). Primary caregiving and role-sharing fathers. In M. E. Lamb (Ed.), *Nontraditional families: Parenting and child development.* Hillsdale, NJ: Erlbaum.

Ragheb, M. B., & Griffith, C. A. (1982). The contribution of leisure participation and leisure satisfaction to life satisfaction of older persons. *Journal of Leisure Research, 14,* 295–306.

Rapoport, R., & Rapoport, R. (1978). The dual career family. In L. S. Hansen & R. S. Rapoza (Eds.), *Career development and the counseling of women.* Springfield, IL: Charles C Thomas.

Reardon, R. C. (1981). *Developing career education at the college level.* Columbus, OH: ERIC Clearinghouse on Adult, Career, and Vocational Education. (ERIC Document Reproduction Service No. ED 205 775).

Reardon, R. C. (1996a). *Curricular career information service.* Unpublished manuscript, Florida State University, Tallahassee.

Reardon, R. C. (1996b). A program and cost analysis of self-directed career advising services in a university career center. *Journal of Counseling and Development, 74,* 280–285.

Reardon, R. C., & Domkowski, D. (1977). Building instruction into a career information center. *Vocational Guidance Quarterly, 25,* 274–278.

Reardon, R. C., Lenz, J. G., Sampson, J. P., & Peterson, G. W. (2000). Career development and planning: A comprehensive approach. Pacific Grove, CA: Brooks/Cole.

Reardon, R. C., Petersen, G. W., Sampson, J. P., Ryan-Jones, R. E., & Shahnasarian, M. (1992). A comparative analysis of the impact of SIGI and SIGI PLUS. *Journal of Career Development, 18,* 315–322.

Reich, R. B. (1991). *The work of nations.* New York: Knopf.

Reschke, W., & Knierim, K. H. (1987, Spring). How parents influence career choice. *Journal of Career Planning and Employment,* 54–60.

Reskin, B. F. (1993). Sex segregation in the workplace. *Annual Review of Sociology, 19,* 241–270.

Reskin, B. F., & Pakavic, I. (1994). *Women and men at work.* London: Pine Forge.

Reynolds, A. L. & Pope, R. (1991). The complexity of diversity: Exploring multiple oppressions. *Journal of Counseling and Development, 70,* 174–180.

Rice, P. L. (1999). *Stress and health* (3rd ed.). Pacific Grove, CA: Brooks/Cole.

Rich, A. R., & Schroeder, H. E. (1976). Research issues in assertiveness training. *Psychological Bulletin, 83,* 1081–1096.

Richards, M. H., & Larson, R. (1993). Pubertal development and the daily subjective states of young adolescents. *Journal of Research on Adolescence, 3,* 145–169.

Richardson, B. (1991). Utilizing the resources of the African American church: Strategies for counseling professionals. In C. Lee & B. Richardson (Eds.), *Multicultural issues in counseling: New approaches to diversity* (pp. 65–75). Alexandria, VA: American Association for Counseling and Development.

Richardson, E. H. (1981). Cultural and historical perspectives in counseling American Indians. In D. W. Sue (Ed.), *Counseling the culturally different* (pp. 216–292). New York: Wiley.

Richardson, M. S. (1993). Working people's lives. *Journal of Counseling and Development, 40,* 425–433.

Rider, E. A. (2000). *Our voices: Psychology of women.* Pacific Grove, CA: Wadsworth.

Rifkin, J. (1995). *The end of work: The decline of the global labor force and the dawn of the post-market era.* New York: Putnam's.

Rimer, S. (1996). The fraying of community. In *New York Times* (et al.), *The downsizing of America* (pp. 111–138). New York: Time Books.

Robinson, R. K., Allen, B. M., & Abraham, Y. T. (1992). Affirmative action plans in the 1990's: A double edged sword? *Public Personnel Management, 21*(2), 261–272.

Rodriguez, M., & Blocher, D. (1988). A comparison of two approaches to enhancing career maturity in Puerto Rican college women. *Journal of Counseling Psychology, 35,* 275–280.

Roe, A. (1956). *The psychology of occupations.* New York: Wiley.

Roe, A. (1972). Perspectives on vocational development. In J. M. Whiteley & A. Resnikoff (Eds.), *Perspectives on vocational development.* Washington, DC: American Personnel and Guidance Association.

Roe, A., & Lunneborg, P. W. (1990). Personality development and career choice. In D. Brown & L. Brooks (Eds.), *Career choice and development. Applying contemporary theories to practice* (pp. 68–101). San Francisco: Jossey-Bass.

Roessler, R., & Rubin, E. (1982). *Case management and rehabilitation counseling: Procedures and techniques.* Baltimore: University Park Press.

Roessler, R. T., & Rumrill, P. D. (1995). Promoting reasonable accomodations: An essential postemployment service. *Journal of Applied Rehabilitation Counseling, 26*(4), 3–7.

Rogers, C. R. (1942). *Counseling and psychotherapy.* Boston: Houghton Mifflin.

Rogler, L. H. (1994). International migrations: A framework for directing research. *American Psychologist, 49,* 701–708.

Rokeach, M. (1973). *The nature of human values.* New York: Free Press.

Roos, P. A., & Jones, K. W. (1993). Women's inroads into academic sociology. *Work and Occupations, 20,* 395–428.

Roselle, B., & Hummel, T. (1988). Intellectual development and interaction effectiveness with DISCOVER. *The Career Development Journal, 35–36,* 241–251.

Rosen, D., Holmberg, K., & Holland, J. L. (1994a). *Dictionary of educational opportunities.* Odessa, FL: Psychology Assessment Resources.

Rosen, D., Holmberg, K., & Holland, J. L. (1994b). *Educational opportunities finder.* Odessa, FL: Psychological Assessment Resources.

Rosenberg, M. (1957). *Occupations and values.* Glencoe, IL: Free Press.

Rosenthal, R. H., & Akiskal, H. S. (1985). Mental status examination. In M. Hersen & S. M. Turner (Eds.), *Diagnostic interviewing.* New York: Plenum.

Rosenwasser, S. M. (1982, April). *Differential socialization processes of males and females.* Paper presented to the Texas Personnel and Guidance Association, Houston.

Rosenwasser, S. M., & Patterson, W. (1984, April). *Nontraditional males: Men with primary childcare/household responsibilities.* Paper presented to the Southwestern Psychological Association, New Orleans.

Roskies, E., & Louis-Guerin, C. (1990). Job insecurity in managers: Antecedents and consequences. *Journal of Organizational Behavior, 11,* 345–359.

Ross, C. C., & Stanley, J. C. (1954). *Measurement in today's schools* (2nd ed.). New York: Prentice-Hall.

Rotter, J. B. (1966). Generalized expectancies for internal versus external control of reinforcement. *Psychological Monographs, 80* (Whole No. 609).

Rounds, J. B. (1990). The comparative and combined utility of work value and interest data in career counseling with adults. *Journal of Vocational Behavior, 37,* 32–45.

Rounds, J. B., Henly, G. A., Dawis, R. V., Lofquist, L. H., & Weiss, D. J. (1981). *Manual for the Minnesota Importance Questionnaire.* Minneapolis: University of Minnesota, Psychology Department Work Adjustment Project.

Rounds, J. B., & Tinsley, H. E. A. (1984). Diagnosis and treatment of vocational problems. In S. D. Brown & R. W. Lent (Eds.), *Handbook of counseling psychology* (pp. 137–177). New York: Wiley.

Rounds, J. B., & Tracey, T. J. (1990). From trait-and-factor to person-environment-fit counseling: Theory and process. In W. B. Walsh & S. J. Osipow (Eds.), *Career counseling: Contemporary topics in vocational psychology* (pp. 1–44). Hillsdale, NJ: Erlbaum.

Rounds, J. B., & Tracy, T. J. (1993). Prediger's dimensional representation of Holland's RIASEC circumplex. *Journal of Applied Psychology, 78,* 875–890.

Rowland, D. T. (1991). Family diversity and the life cycle. *Journal of Comparative Family Studies, 22,* 1–14.

Russell, G. (1982). Shared-caregiving families: An Australian study. In M. E. Lamb (Ed.), *Nontraditional families: Parenting and child development.* Hillsdale, NJ: Erlbaum.

Russo, N. F., Kelly, R. M., & Deacon, M. (1991). Gender and success-related attributions: Beyond individualistic conceptions of achievement. *Sex Roles, 25,* 331–350.

Rust, P. C. (1996). Managing multiple identities: Diversity among bisexual women and men. In B. A. Firestein (Ed.), *Bisexuality (*pp. 53–84). Thousand Oaks, CA: Sage.

Ryan, L., & Ryan, R. (1982). *Mental health and the urban Indian.* Unpublished manuscript.

Rychlak, J. F. (1993). A suggested principle of complementarity for psychology. *American Psychologist, 48,* 933–942.

Sadker, M., & Sadker, D. (1986, March). Sexism in the classroom: From grade school to graduate school. *Phi Delta Kappan,* pp. 512–515.

Sadker, M. & Sadker, D. (1994). *Failing at fairness: How America's schools cheat girls.* New York: Scribners.

Sadri, G., & Robertson, L. T. (1993). Self-efficacy and work-related behavior: A review and meta-analysis. *Applied Psychology: An Internal Review, 42,* 139–152.

Saghir, M. T. & Robins, E. (1973). *Male and female homosexuality: A comprehensive investigation.* Baltimore: Williams and Wilkins.

Sagi, A. (1982). Antecedents and consequences of various degrees of paternal involvement in child rearing: The Israeli project. In M. E. Lamb (Ed.), *Nontraditional families: Parenting and child development.* Hillsdale, NJ: Erlbaum.

Salomone, P. R. (1996, Spring). Tracing Super's theory of vocational development: A 40-year restrospective. *Journal of Career Development, 22* (3).

Salomone, P. R., & Slaney, R. B. (1978). The applicability of Holland's theory to professional workers. *Journal of Vocational Behavior, 13,* 63–74.

Salsgiver, R. O. (1995). *Persons with disabilities and empowerment: Building a future of independent living.* Unpublished invitational speech to the Council on Social Work Education Annual Program Meeting. March 4, San Diego, CA.

Sampson, J. P. (1983). Computer-assisted testing and assessment: Current status and implications for the future. *Measurement and Evaluation in Guidance, 15*(3), 293–299.

Sampson, J. P. (1994). *Effective computer-assisted career guidance: Occasional paper number 2.* Center for the Study of Technology in Counseling and Career Development, Florida State University.

Sampson, J. P., Peterson, G. W., Lenz, J. G., & Reardon, R. C. (1992). *Career Development Quarterly, 41,* 67–73.

Sampson, J. P., Jr., Peterson, G. W., Lenz, J. G., Reardon, R. C., & Saunders, D. E. (1996a). *Career thoughts inventory: Professional manual.* Odessa, FL: Psychological Assessment Resources.

Sampson, J. P., Jr., Peterson, G. W., Lenz, J. G., Reardon, R. C., & Saunders, D. E. (1996b). *Improving your career thoughts: A workbook for the career thoughts inventory.* Odessa, FL: Psychological Assessment Resources.

Sampson, J. P., & Pyle, K. R. (1983). Ethical issues involved with the use of computer-assisted counseling, testing and guidance systems. *Personnel and Guidance Journal, 61* (3), 283–287.

Samuelson, R. J. (1995). *The good life and its discontents: The American dream in the age of entitlement, 1945–1995.* New York: Time Books.

Sandoval, J. (1998a). Testing in a changing world: An introduction. In J. Sandoval, C. L. Frisby, K. F. Geisinger, J. D. Scheuneman, & J. R. Grenier, *Test interpretation and diversity* (pp. 3–17). Washington, DC: American Psychological Association.

Sandoval, J. (1998b). Test interpretation in a diverse future. In J. Sandoval, C. L. Frisby, K. F. Geisinger, J. D. Scheuneman, & J. R. Grenier, *Test interpretation and diversity* (pp. 387–403). Washington, DC: American Psychological Association.

Sanguiliano, I. (1978). *In her time.* New York: Morrow.

Sastre, M. T. M., & Mullet, E. (1992). Occupational preferences of Spanish adolescents in relation to Gottfredson's theory. *Journal of Vocational Behavior, 40,* 306–317.

Saunders, L. (1995). Relative earnings of black and white men by region, industry. *Monthly Labor Review, 118* (4), 68–73.

Savickas, M. L. (1990). The use of career choice measures in counseling practice. In E. Watkins & V. Campbell (Eds.), *Testing in counseling practice* (pp. 373–417). Hillsdale, NJ: Erlbaum.

Savickas, M. L. (1995). Current theoretical issues in vocational psychology: Convergence, divergence, and schism. In W. B. Walsh & S. H. Osipow (Eds.), *Handbook of vocational psychology* (2nd ed.) (pp. 1–34). Hillsdale, NJ: Erlbaum.

Savickas, M. L., & Walsh, W. B. (Eds.). (1996). *Handbook of career counseling theory and practice.* Palo Alto, CA: Davies-Black.

Scarr, S., Phillips, D., & McCartney, K. (1989). Working mothers and their families. *American Psychologist, 44,* 1402–1409.

Schlossberg, N. K. (1981). A model for analyzing human adaptation to transition. *Counseling Psychologist, 9*(2), 2–18.

Schlossberg, N. K. (1984). *Counseling adults in transition, linking practice with theory.* New York: Springer.

Schnall, M. (1981). *Limits: A search for new values.* New York: Clarkson N. Potter.

Schunk, D. H. (1995). Education and instruction. In J. E. Maddux (Ed.), *Self-efficacy, adaptation, and adjustment: Theory, research, and application.* New York: Plenum.

Schutz, R. A., & Blocher, D. H. (1961). Self-satisfaction and level of occupational choice. *Personnel and Guidance Journal, 39,* 595–598.

Schwab, R. L. (1981). The relationship of role conflict, role ambiguity, teacher background variables and perceived burnout among teachers. (Doctoral dissertation, University of Connecticut, 1980.) *Dissertation Abstracts International, 41*(9), 3823-A.

Schwartz, E. (1989). The mental status examination. In R. J. Craig (Ed.), *Clinical and diagnostic interviewing.* Northvale, NJ: Aronson.

Schwartz, R. D. & Harstein, N. B. (1986). Group psychotherapy with gay men: Theoretical and clinical considerations. In T. Stein & C. J. Cohen (Eds.), *Perspectives on psychotherapy with lesbian and gay men* (pp. 157–177). New York: Plenum.

Scott, K. P. (1981, April). Whatever happened to Jane and Dick? Sexism in texts reexamined. *Peabody Journal of Education,* 135–140.

Sewell, T. E. & Martin, R. P. (1976). Racial differences in patterns of occupational choice in adolescents. *Psychology in Schools, 13,* 326–333.

Shaffer, D. R. (1999). *Developmental Psychology: Childhood and adolescence* (5th ed.). Pacific Grove, CA: Brooks/Cole.

Sharf, R. S. (1984). Vocational information-seeking behavior: Another view. *Vocational Guidance Quarterly, 33*(2), 120–129.

Sharf, R. S. (1992). *Applying career development theory to counseling.* Pacific Grove, CA: Brooks/Cole.

Sharf, R. S. (1996). *Theories of psychotherapy and counseling: Concepts and cases.* Pacific Grove, CA: Brooks/Cole.

Shelton, B. A., & John, D. (1993). Ethnicity, race, and difference: A comparison of white, black, and Hispanic men's household labor time. In J. C. Hood (Ed.), *Men, work and family* (pp. 131–150). Newbury Park, CA: Sage.

Sheppard, H. L., & Rix, S. E. (1977). *The graying of working America.* New York: Free Press.

Shostak, A. B. (1980). *Blue-collar stress.* Reading, MA: Addison-Wesley.

Shotter, J. (1993). *Conversational realities: Constructing life through language.* Newbury Park, CA: Sage.

Sigelman, C. K. (1999). *Life-span human development* (3rd ed.). Pacific Grove, CA: Brooks/Cole.

Sigelman, C. K., & Shaffer, D. R. (1995). *Life-span human development* (2nd ed.). Pacific Grove, CA: Brooks/Cole.

Signorelli, N., & Lears, M. (1992). Children, television, and conceptions about chores: Attitudes and behaviors. *Sex Roles, 27,* 157–170.

Signorile, M. (1993). *Queer in America: Sex, media, and the closets of power.* New York: Random House.

Silberstein, L. R. (1992). *Dual-career marriage: A system in transition.* Hillsdale, NJ: Erlbaum.

Siltanen, J. (1994). *Locating gender: Occupational segregation, wages, and domestic responsibility.* Greensboro: ERIC Counseling and Student Services Clearinghouse, University of North Carolina. (ERIC Report No. ED 377 373)

Simmons, R. G., & Blyth, D. A. (1987). *Moving into adolescence: The impact of pubertal change and school context.* New York: Aldine De Gruyter.

Simon, S. B., Howe, L. W., & Kirschenbaum, H. (1972). *Value clarification.* New York: Hart.

Skill, T. (1994). Family images and family actions as presented in the media: Where we've been and what we've found. In D. Zillman, J. Byrant, & A. C. Huston (Eds.), *Media, children, and the family: Social scientific, psychodynamic, and clinical perspectives* (pp. 37–50). Hillsdale, NJ: Erlbaum.

Skovalt, T. M., Morgan, J. I., & Negron-Cunningham, H. (1989). Mental imagery in career counseling and life planning: A review of research and intervention methods. *Journal of Counseling and Development 67,* 287–292.

Skovholt, T. M. (1978). Feminism and men's lives. *Counseling Psychologist, 7*(4), 3–10.

Skovholt, T. M. (1990). Career themes in counseling and psychotherapy with men. In D. Moore & F. Leafgren (Eds.), *Men in conflict* (pp. 39–56). Alexandria, VA: American Association for Counseling and Development.

Smith, A., & Chemers, M. (1981). Perception of motivation of economically disadvantaged employees in a work setting. *Journal of Employment Counseling, 18,* 24–33.

Smith, A. B., & Inder, P. M. (1993). Social interaction in same and cross gender preschool peer groups: A participant observation study. *Educational Psychology, 13,* 29–42.

Smith, C. K., Smith, W. S., Stroup, K. M., & Ballard, B. W. (1982). *Broadening career options for women.* Ann Arbor: ERIC Counseling and Personnel Services Clearing House, University of Michigan.

Smith, E. J. (1983). Issues in racial minorities' career behavior. In W. B. Walsh & J. H. Osipow (Eds.), *Handbook of vocational psychology: Vol. 1* (pp. 161–222). Hillsdale, NJ: Erlbaum.

Snodgrass, G., & Wheeler, R. W. (1983). A research-based sequential job interview training model. *Journal of College Student Personnel, 24*(5), 449–454.

Solomon, K. (1982). The masculine gender role: Description. In K. Solomon & N. B. Levy (Eds.), *Men in transition*. New York: Plenum.

Sophie, J. (1986). A critical examination of stage theories of lesbian identity development. *Journal of Homosexuality, 12*(2), 39–51.

Sorapuru, J., Theodore, R., & Young, W. (1972a). Financial facts of life. In J. E. Bottoms, R. N. Evans, K. B. Hoyt, & J. C. Willer (Eds.), *Career education resource guide*. Morristown, NJ: General Learning Corporation.

Sorapuru, J., Theodore, R., & Young, W. (1972b). Job hunting. In J. E. Bottoms, R. N. Evans, K. B. Hoyt, & J. C. Willer (Eds.), *Career education resource guide*. Morristown, NJ: General Learning Corporation.

Speight, S. L., Myers, L. J., Cox, C. I., & Highlen, P. S. (1991). A redefinition of multicultural counseling. *Journal of Counseling and Development, 70,* 29–35.

Spence, J. T. (1999). Thirty years of gender research: A personal chronicle. In W. B. Swann, J. H. Langlois, & L. A. Gilbert (Eds.), *Sexism and stereotypes in modern society* (pp. 255–290). Washington, DC: American Psychological Association.

Spencer, A. L. (1982). *Seasons*. New York: Paulist.

Spicher, C. H. & Hudak, M. A. (1997, August 18). *Gender role portrayal on Saturday morning cartoons: An update*. Presented at the American Psychological Association annual meeting. Chicago.

Spindler, G. (Ed.). (1955). *Education and culture*. Stanford, CA: Stanford University Press.

Splete, H. (1996). Adult career counseling centers train career counselors. In R. Feller and G. Walz (Eds.), *Career transitions in turbulent times* (pp. 405–414). Greensboro: ERIC Counseling and Student Services Clearinghouse, University of North Carolina.

Splete, H., Elliott, B. J., & Borders, L. D. (1985). *Computer-assisted career guidance systems and career counseling services*. Unpublished manuscript, Oakland University, Adult Career Counseling Center, Rochester, MI.

Splete, H., & Stewart, A. (1990). *Competency-based career development strategies and the national career development guidelines*. (Information Series No. 345). Columbus, OH: ERIC Clearinghouse on Adult, Career, and Vocational Education (ERIC Report No. ED 327 739).

Spokane, A. R. (1985). A review of research on person-environment congruence in Holland's theory of careers [Monograph]. *Journal of Vocational Behavior, 26,* 306–343.

Spokane, A. R. (1991). *Career intervention*. Englewood Cliffs, NJ: Prentice-Hall.

Spokane, A. R. (1996). Holland's theory. In D. Brown, L. Brooks, & Associates (Eds.), *Career choice and development* (3rd ed.) (pp. 33–69). San Francisco: Jossey-Bass.

Spokane, A. R., & Holland, J. L. (1995). The self-directed search: A family of self-guided career interventions. *Journal of Career Assessment, 3,* 373–390.

St. Peter, S. (1979). Jack went up the hill . . . but where was Jill? *Psychology of Women Quarterly, 4,* 256–260.

Staats, A. W. (1981). Paradigmatic behaviorism, unified theory, unified theory construction methods, and the zeitgeist of separatism. *American Psychologist, 36,* 239–256.

Steidl, R. (1972). Financial facts of life. In J. E. Bottoms, R. N. Evans, K. B. Hout, & J. C. Willer (Eds.), *Career education resource guide*. Morristown, NJ: General Learning Corporation.

Stein, T. S. (1982). Men's groups. In K. Solomon & N. B. Levy (Eds.), *Men in transition* (pp. 275–307). New York: Plenum.

Stephenson, W. (1949). *Testing school children*. New York: Longmans, Green.

Stimpson, D., Jensen, L., & Neff, W. (1992). Cross-cultural gender differences in preferences for a caring morality. *Journal of Social Psychology, 132,* 317–322.

Stoltz-Loike, M. (1992). *Dual-career couples: New perspectives in counseling*. Alexandria, VA: American Association for Counseling and Development.

Stone, J., & Gregg, C. (1981). Juvenile diabetes and rehabilitation counseling. *Rehabilitation Counseling Bulletin, 24*, 283–291.

Strong, E. K. (1927). *The Strong vocational interest blank*. Stanford, CA: Stanford University Press.

Strong, E. K. (1983). *Vocational interest blank for men*. Stanford, CA: Stanford University Press.

Strube, M. J. (Ed.). (1991). *Type A behavior*. Newbury Park, CA: Sage.

Subich, L. M. (1996). Addressing diversity in the process of career assessment. In M. L. Savickas & W. B. Walsh (Eds.), *Handbook of career counseling theory and practice* (pp. 277–291). Palo Alto, CA: Davies-Black.

Suchet, M., & Barling, J. (1985). Employed mothers: Interrole conflict, spouse support, and marital functioning. *Journal of Occupational Behavior, 7*, 167–178.

Sue, D. W. (1978). Counseling across cultures. *Personnel and Guidance Journal, 56*, 451.

Sue, D. W. (1981). *Counseling the culturally different*. New York: Wiley.

Sue, D. W. (1992). The challenge of multiculturalism: The road less traveled. *American Counselor, 1*, 7–14.

Sue, D. W. (1994). Asian American mental health and help-seeking behavior: Comment on Solberg, et al. (1994), Tata & Leong (1994), and Lin (1994). *Journal of Counseling Psychology, 41*, 292–295.

Sue, D. W., Arredondo, A., & McDavis, R. J. (1992). Multicultural counseling competencies and standards: A call to the profession. *Journal of Counseling and Development, 70*, 477–486.

Sue, D. W., Ivey, A. E., & Pedersen, P. B. (1996). *A theory of multicultural counseling and therapy*. Pacific Grove, CA: Brooks/Cole.

Sue, D. W., & Sue, D. (1990). *Counseling the culturally different: Theory and practice* (2nd ed.). New York: Wiley.

Sue, S., & Okazaki, S. (1990). Asian American educational achievements: A phenomenon in search of an explanation. *American Psychologist, 45*, (8), 913–920.

Super, D. E. (1949). *Appraising vocational fitness*. New York: Harper & Brothers.

Super, D. E. (1957). *The psychology of careers*. New York: Harper & Row.

Super, D. E. (1970). *The work values inventory*. Boston: Houghton Mifflin.

Super, D. E. (1972). Vocational development theory: Persons, positions, and processes. In J. M. Whiteley & A. Resnikoff (Eds.), *Perspectives on vocational development*. Washington, DC: American Personnel and Guidance Association.

Super, D. E. (1974). *Measuring vocational maturity for counseling and evaluation*. Washington, DC: National Vocational Guidance Association.

Super, D. E. (1977). Vocational maturity in mid-career. *Vocational Guidance Quarterly, 25*, 297.

Super, D. E. (1980). A life-span, life-space approach to career development. *Journal of Vocational Behavior, 16*, 282–298.

Super, D. E. (1984). Career and life development. In D. Brown & L. Brooks (Eds.), *Career choice and development*. San Francisco: Jossey-Bass.

Super, D. E. (1990). A life-span, life-space approach to career development. In D. Brown, L. Brooks, & Associates (Eds.), *Career choice and development: Applying contemporary theories to practice* (2nd ed.) (pp. 197–261). San Francisco: Jossey-Bass.

Super, D. E., & Overstreet, P. L. (1960). *The vocational maturity of ninth grade boys*. New York: Teachers College, Columbia University.

Super, D. E., Savickas, M. L., & Super, C. M. (1996). The life-span, life-space approach to careers. In D. Brown, L. Brooks, & Associates (Eds.), *Career choice and development* (3rd ed.) (pp. 121–170). San Francisco: Jossey-Bass.

Super, D. E., Starishesky, R., Matlin, N., & Jordaan, J. P. (1963). *Career development: Self-concept theory.* New York: College Entrance Examination Board.

Super, D. E., Thompson, A. S., & Lindeman, R. H. (1988). *Adult career concerns inventory: Manual for research and exploratory use in counseling.* Palo Alto, CA: Consulting Psychologists Press.

Suro, R. (1998). *Strangers among us: How Latino immigration is transforming America.* New York: Knopf.

Swanson, J. L. (1992). Vocational behavior, 1989–1991: Life-span career development and reciprocal interaction of work and nonwork. *Journal of Vocational Behavior, 41,* 101–161.

Swanson, J. L. (1996). The theory is the practice: trait-and-factor/person-environment. In M. L. Savickas & W. B. Walsh (Eds.), *Handbook of career counseling theory and practice* (pp. 93–109). Palo Alto, CA: Davies-Black.

Szymanski, E. M., Hershenson, D. B., Enright, M. S., & Ettinger, J. M. (1996). Career development interventions for people with disabilities. In E. M. Szymanski & R. M. Parker (Eds.), *Work and disability: Issues and strategies in career development and job placement* (pp. 255–276). Austin, TX: PRO-ED.

Tafoya, T. (1997). Native gay and lesbian issues: The two-spirited. In B. Greene (Ed.), *Ethnic and cultural diversity among lesbians and gay men* (pp. 1–10). Thousand Oaks, CA: Sage.

Tannen, D. (1990). *You just don't understand.* New York: Ballantine.

Tanner, J. M. (1972). Sequence, tempo, and individual variation in growth and development of boys and girls aged twelve to sixteen. In J. Kagan & R. Coles (Eds.), *Twelve to sixteen: Early adolescence.* New York: Norton.

Taylor, R. L. (1990). Black youth: The endangered generation. *Youth and Society, 22*(1), 4–11.

Telljohann, S. K., & Price, J. H. (1993). A qualitative examination of adolescents homosexuals' life experiences: Ramifications for secondary school personnel. *Journal of Homosexuality, 26*(1), 41–56.

Texas Rehabilitation Commission. (1985). *Career orientation manual.* Austin: Author.

Texas Rehabilitation Commission. (1994). *Eligibility requirements of rehabilitation.* Austin: Author.

Thase, M., & Page, R. A. (1977). Modeling of self-disclosure in laboratory and nonlaboratory settings. *Journal of Consulting Psychology, 24,* 35–40.

Thomas, J. K. (1973). Adolescent endocrinology for counselors of adolescents. *Adolescence, 8,* 395–406.

Thomas, K. R., & Butler, A. J. (1981). Counseling for personal adjustment. In R. M. Parker & C. E. Hansen (Eds.), *Rehabilitation Counseling.* Boston: Allyn & Bacon.

Thomason, T. C. (1991). Counseling Native Americans: An introduction for non-Native American counselors. *Journal of Counseling & Development, 69,* 321–327.

Thompson, A. S., Lindeman, R. H., Super, D. E., Jordaan, J. P., & Myers, R. A. (1984). *Career development inventory: Technical manual.* Palo Alto, CA: Consulting Psychologists Press.

Thompson, C. L., & Rudolph, L. B. (2000). *Counseling children,* 5th ed. Belmont, CA: Wadsworth.

Thompson, E. H., Grisanti, C., & Pleck, J. H. (1987). Attitudes toward the male role and their correlates. *Sex Roles, 13,* 413–427.

Thompson, T., & Zerbinos, E. (1997). Television cartoons: Do children notice it's a boy's world? *Sex Roles, 37,* 415–432.

Thorndike, R. L. (1949). *Personnel selection tests, and measurement techniques.* New York: Wiley.

Thorndike, R. L. (1997). *Measurement and evaluation in psychology and education* (6th ed.). Upper Saddle River, NJ: Simon & Schuster.

Thurer, S. (1980). Vocational rehabilitation following coronary bypass surgery: The need of counseling the newly well. *Journal of Applied Rehabilitation Counseling, 11,* 98–99.

Tiedeman, D. V., & O'Hara, R. P. (1963). *Career development: Choice and adjustment.* Princeton, NJ: College Entrance Examination Board.

Tomasko, R. T. (1987). *Downsizing.* New York: American Management Association.

Tower, K. D. (1994). Consumer-centered social work practice: Restoring client self-determination. *Social Work, 41*(1), 191–196.

Tracy, D. M. (1990). Toy-playing behavior, sex role orientation, spatial ability, and science achievement. *Journal of Research in Science Teaching, 27,* 637–649.

Triandis, H. C. (1992, February). *Individualism and collectivism as a cultural syndrome.* Paper presented at the Annual Convention of the Society for Cross-Cultural Researchers, Santa Fe, NM.

Triandis, H. C. (1994). *Culture and social behavior.* New York: McGraw-Hill.

Trimble, J. E., & LaFromboise, T. (1985). American Indians and the counseling process: Culture, adaptation, and style. In P. Pedersen, *Handbook of cross-cultural counseling and therapy* (pp. 125–134). Westport, CT: Greenwood.

Troll, L., Israel, J., & Israel, K. (1977). *Looking ahead.* Englewood Cliffs, NJ: Prentice-Hall.

Trower, P., Casey, A., & Dryden, W. (1988). *Cognitive-behavioral counseling in action.* Newbury Park, CA: Sage.

Uchitelle, L., & Kleinfield, N. R. (1996). The price of jobs lost. In *New York Times* (et al.), *The downsizing of America* (pp. 3–36). New York: Time Books.

Unger, R. (1979). Toward a redefinition of sex and gender. *American Psychologist, 34,* 1085–1094.

Unger, R., & Crawford, M. (1992). *Women and gender: A feminist psychology.* Philadelphia: Temple University Press.

University of Minnesota. (1984). *Minnesota Importance Questionnaire.* Minneapolis: Author.

U.S. Bureau of the Census. (1990). *Characteristics of American Indians by tribe and selected areas.* Washington, DC: U.S. Government Printing Office.

U.S. Bureau of the Census. (1993). *We the Americans: Pacific Islanders in the United States.* Washington, DC: U.S. Government Printing Office.

U.S. Department of Commerce, Bureau of Census (1996). *Percent of population by race: 1990, 2000, 2025, 2050.* Washington, DC: U.S. Government Printing Office.

U.S. Department of Education. (1990). *Individuals with Disabilities Education Act of 1990.* Washington, DC: U.S. Government Printing Office.

U.S. Department of Education and U.S. Department of Labor. (1996). *School-to-work opportunities.* Washington, DC: National School-to-Work Office.

U.S. Department of Justice. (1991). *Americans with disabilities handbook.* Washington, U.S. Government Printing Office.

U.S. Department of Labor (1939). *Dictionary of occupational titles.* Washington, DC: U.S. Employment Services.

U.S. Department of Labor. (1970a). *Career thresholds.* Washington, DC: U.S. Government Printing Office.

U.S. Department of Labor. (1970b). *Manual for the general aptitude test battery.* Washington, DC: U.S. Government Printing Office.

U.S. Department of Labor. (1977). *Dictionary of occupational titles* (4th ed.). Washington, DC: U.S. Government Printing Office.

U.S. Department of Labor. (1992–1993). *Occupational Outlook handbook.* Washington, DC: U.S. Government Printing Office.

U.S. Department of Labor, Bureau of Labor Statistics. (1991). *Employment and earnings, February 1991.* Washington, DC: U.S. Government Printing Office.

Uribe, V. & Harbeck, K. M. (1992). Addressing the needs of lesbian, gay, and bisexual youth: The origins of Project 10 and school-based intervention. *Journal of Homosexuality, 22*(3/4), 9–28.

Valach, L. (1990). A theory of goal-directed action in career analysis. In R. A. Young & W. A. Borgen (Eds.), *Methodological approaches to the study of career* (pp. 107–126). New York: Praeger.

Vargo, M. E. (1998). *Acts of disclosure: The coming-out process of contemporary gay men.* New York: Haworth.

Velasquez, J. S., & Lynch, M. M. (1981). Computerized information systems: A practice orientation. *Administration in Social Work, 5*(3/4), 113–127.

Veneri, C. M. (Fall, 1997). The 1995 employment projections: How accurate were they? *Occupational Outlook Quarterly,* pp. 34–52.

Vetter, B. M. (1989). *Professional women and minorities: A manpower data resource service* (8th ed.). Washington, DC: Commission on Professionals in Science and Technology.

Vocational biographies (1985). Sauk Centre, MN: Author.

von Cranach, M., & Harre, R. (Eds.). (1982). *The analysis of action: Recent theoretical and empirical advances.* Cambridge, England: Cambridge University Press.

Vondracek, F. W., Lerner, R. M., & Schulenberg, J. E. (1986). *Career development: A life-span developmental approach.* Hillsdale, NJ: Erlbaum.

Vontress, C. E. (1979). Cross-cultural counseling: An existential approach. *Personnel and Guidance Journal, 58,* 117–121.

Wall, W. (1984, May). Student values in the workplace. *Bulletin of the American Association of Higher Education,* 2–6.

Walsh, W. B. (1990). A summary and integration of career counseling approaches. In W. B. Walsh & S. H. Osipow (Eds.), *Career Counseling: Contemporary topics in vocational psychology* (pp. 263–283). Hillsdale, NJ: Erlbaum.

Walsh, W. B. (1996). Career counseling theory: Problems and prospects. In M. L. Savickas & W. B. Walsh (Eds.), *Handbook of career counseling theory and practice* (pp. 267–277). Palo Alto, CA: Davies-Black.

Walsh, W. B., & Chartrand, J. M. (1994). Person-environment fit: Emerging directions. In M. L. Savickas & R. W. Lent (Eds.), *Convergence in career development theories: Implications for science and practice* (pp. 185–194). Palo Alto, CA: Consulting Psychologists Press.

Walsh, W. B., Craik, K. H., & Price, R. H. (1992). Person-environment psychology: A summary and commentary. In W. B. Walsh, K. H. Craik, & R. H. Price (Eds.), *Person-environment psychology: Models and perspectives* (pp. 243–268). Hillsdale, NJ: Erlbaum.

Walsh, W. B., & Osipow, S. H. (1988). *Career decision making.* Mahwah, NJ: Erlbaum.

Walz, A. (1972). Required courses. In J. E. Bottoms, R. N. Evans, K. B. Hoyt, & J. C. Willer (Eds.), *Career education resource guide.* Morristown, NJ: General Learning Corporation.

Wanous, J. P. (1980). *Organizational entry.* Reading, MA: Addison-Wesley.

Ward, C. M., & Bingham, R. P. (1993). Career assessment of ethnic minority women. *Journal of Career Assessment, 1,* 246–257.

Ward, C. M. & Tate, G. (1990). *Career counseling checklist.* Atlanta: Georgia State University: Counseling Center.

Warr, P. (1992). Age and occupational well-being. *Psychology and Aging, 7,* 37–45.

Watson, M. A., & Ager, C. L. (1991). The impact of role valuation and life satisfaction in old age. *Physical and Occupational Therapy in Geriatrics, 10,* 27–62.

Wehrly, B. (1995). *Pathways to multicultural counseling competence.* Pacific Grove, CA: Brooks/Cole.

Weinrach, S. G. (1984). Determinants of vocational choice: Holland's theory. In D. Brown & L. Brooks (Eds.), *Career choice and development.* San Francisco: Jossey-Bass.

Weinrach, S. G., & Srebalus, D. J. (1990). Holland's theory of careers. In D. Brown & L. Brooks (Eds.), *Career choice and development: Applying contemporary theories to practice* (2nd ed.) (pp. 37–67). San Francisco: Jossey-Bass.

Wentling, R. M. (1992, Jan./Feb.). Women in middle management: Their career development and aspirations. *Business Horizons,* 48–54.

Westermeyer, J. J. (1993). Cross-cultural psychiatric assessment. In A. Gaw (Ed.), *Culture, ethnicity, and mental illness* (pp. 125–144). Washington, DC: American Psychiatric Press.

White, R. W. (1959). Motivation reconsidered: The concept of competence. *Psychological Review, 66,* 297.

Wigglesworth, D. C. (1992). Meeting the needs of the multicultural work force. In J. Kummerow (Ed.), *New directions in career planning and the workplace* (pp. 155–167). Palo Alto, CA: Consulting Psychological Press.

Wiinamaki, M. K. (1988). *My vocational experience.* Unpublished manuscript, Southwest Texas State University, San Marcos, TX.

Wilcox-Matthew, L., & Minor, C. W. (1989). The dual career couple: Concerns, benefits, and counseling implications. *Journal of Counseling and Development, 68,* 194–198.

Williams, W. L. (1993). Persistence and change in the berdache tradition among contemporary Lakota Indians. In L. D. Garnets & D. C. Kimmel (Eds.), *Psychological perspectives on lesbian and gay male experiences* (pp. 339–348). New York: Columbia University Press.

Williamson, E. G. (1939). *How to counsel students: A manual of techniques for clinical counselors.* New York: McGraw-Hill.

Williamson, E. G. (1949). *Counseling adolescents.* New York: McGraw-Hill.

Williamson, E. G. (1965). *Vocational counseling: Some historical, philosophical, and theoretical perspectives.* New York: McGraw-Hill.

Winbush, G. B. (2000). African American women. In M. Julia (Ed.), *Constructing gender: Multicultural perspectives in working with women* (pp. 11–35). Pacific Grove, CA: Brooks/Cole.

Winfeld, L., & Spielman, S. (1995). *Straight talk about gays in workplace.* New York: AMACOM.

Wolfson, K. T. P. (1972). *Career development of college women.* Unpublished doctoral dissertation. University of Minnesota, Minneapolis.

Wolpe, J. (1958). *Psychotherapy by reciprocal inhibition.* Palo Alto, CA: Stanford University Press.

Wolpe, J. (1973). *The practice of behavior therapy.* New York: Pergamon.

Wood, J. T. (1994). *Gendered lives: Communication, gender, and culture.* Belmont, CA: Wadsworth.

Wooden, W. S., Kawasaki, H., & Mayeda, R. (1983). Lifestyles and identity maintenance among gay Japanese-American males. *Alternative Lifestyles, 5*(4), 236–243.

Woodman, S. (1991, May). How super are heroes? *Health,* pp. 40, 49, 82.

Woods, J. F., & Ollis, H. (1996). *Labor market & job information on the Internet.* Submitted for publication in the Winter (March 1996) issue of *Workforce Journal.*

Woody, B. (1992). *Black women in the workplace.* Westport, CT: Greenwood.

Wrenn, C. G. (1988). The person in career counseling. *Career Development Quarterly, 36*(4), 337–343.

Wright, B. A. (1983). *Physical disability—a psychological approach* (2nd ed.). New York: Harper & Row.

Wright, G. N. (1980). *Total rehabilitation.* Boston: Little, Brown.

Yankelovich, D. (1979). Work, values and the new breed. In C. Kerr & J. M. Rosow (Eds.), *Work in America: The decade ahead* (pp. 3–26). New York: Van Nostrand Reinhold.

Yankelovich, D. (1981a). *New rules.* New York: Random House.

Yankelovich, D. (1981b). The meaning of work. In J. O'Toole, J. L. Scheiber, & L. C. Wood (Eds.), *Working: Changes and choices* (pp. 33–34). New York: Human Sciences.

Yost, E. B., & Corbishley, M. A. (1987). *Career counseling: A psychological approach.* San Francisco, Jossey-Bass.

Young, R. A., & Valach, L. (1996). Interpretation and action in career counseling. In M. L. Savickas & W. B. Walsh (Eds.), *Handbook of career counseling theory and practice.* Palo Alto, CA: Davies-Black.

Young, R. A., Valach, L., & Collin, A. (1996). A contextual explanation of career. In D. Brown, L. Brooks, & Associates (Eds.), *Career choice and development* (3rd ed.) (pp. 477–508). San Francisco: Jossey-Bass.

Zaccaria, J. (1970). *Theories of occupational choice and vocational development.* Boston: Houghton Mifflin.

Zaharlick, A. (2000). South Asian-American women. In M. Julia (Ed.), *Constructing gender: Multicultural perspectives in working with women* (pp. 177–205). Pacific Grove, CA: Brooks/Cole.

Zajonc, E. (1980). Feeling and thinking: Preferences need no influence. *American Psychologist, 35,* 151–175.

Zimmerman, B. J. (1995). Self-efficacy and educational development. In A. Bandura (Ed.), *Self-efficacy in changing societies.* Cambridge: Cambridge University Press.

Zmud, R. W., Sampson, J. P., Reardon, R. C., Lenz, J. G., & Byrd, T. A. (1994). Confounding effects of construct overlap. An example from IS user satisfaction theory. *Information Technology and People, 7,* 29–45.

Zunker, V. G. (1987). The life-style and career development standard. *Counselor Education and Supervision, 27,* 110–118.

Zunker, V. G. (1990). *Using assessment results in career counseling.* Pacific Grove, CA: Brooks/Cole.

Zunker, V. G. (1994). *Using assessment results for career development* (4th ed.). Pacific Grove, CA: Brooks/Cole.

Zunker, V. G. (1998). *Career counseling: Applied concepts of life planning* (5th ed.). Pacific Grove, CA: Brooks/Cole.

Zunker, V. G., & Norris, D. (1998). *Using assessment results for career development* (5th ed.) Pacific Grove, CA: Brooks/Cole.

Zunker, V. G., & Osborn, D. (2002). *Using assessment results for career development* (6th ed.). Pacific Grove, CA: Brooks/Cole.

Zytowski, D. G. (1969). Toward a theory of career development for women. *Personnel and Guidance Journal, 47,* 660–664.

Zytowski, D. G. (1994). Tests and counseling: We are still married, and living in discriminant analysis. *Measurement and Evaluation in Counseling and Development, 26,* 219–223.

Name Index

Subject Index

TO THE OWNER OF THIS BOOK:

We hope that you have found *Career Counseling: Applied Concepts of Life Planning*, Sixth Edition, useful. So that this book can be improved in a future edition, would you take the time to complete this sheet and return it? Thank you.

School and address:_____

Department:_____

Instructor's name:_____

1. What I like most about this book is:_____

_____

_____

2. What I like least about this book is:_____

_____

_____

3. My general reaction to this book is:_____

_____

4. The name of the course in which I used this book is:_____

_____

5. Were all of the chapters of the book assigned for you to read?_____

   If not, which ones weren't?_____

6. In the space below, or on a separate sheet of paper, please write specific suggestions for improving this book and anything else you'd care to share about your experience in using the book.

_____

_____

_____

_____

Optional:

Your name: _____ Date: _____

May Brooks/Cole quote you, either in promotion for *Career Counseling: Applied Concepts of Life Planning*, Sixth Edition, or in future publishing ventures?

Yes: _____ No: _____

Sincerely,

Vernon G. Zunker

Attention Professors:

Brooks/Cole is dedicated to publishing quality publications for education in the social work, counseling, and human services fields. If you are interested in learning more about our publications, please fill in your name and address and request our latest catalogue, using this prepaid mailer. Please choose one of the following:

☐ social work   ☐ counseling   ☐ human services

Name: _____

Street Address: _____

City, State, and Zip: _____